THE GREEN GUIDE

Languedoc Roussillon Tarn Gorges

Cathédrale St-Nazaire, Bézier, A. Thuillier/MICHELIN

General Manager Cynthia Clayton Ochterbeck

THE GREEN GUIDE **LANGUEDOC ROUSSILLON TARN GORGES**

Editor Jonathan P. Gilbert
Principal Writer Terry Marsh
Production Manager Natasha G. George
Cartography Stephane Anton, Andrew Thompson
Photo Editor Yoshimi Kanazawa
Proofreader Jenni Hairsine
Interior Design Chris Bell
Layout Michelin Apa Publications Ltd., Anna Gatt
Cover Design Chris Bell, Christelle Le Déan
Cover Layout Michelin Apa Publications Ltd.

Contact Us
The Green Guide
Michelin Maps and Guides
One Parkway South
Greenville, SC 29615
USA
www.michelintravel.com

Michelin Maps and Guides
Hannay House
39 Clarendon Road
Watford, Herts WD17 1JA
UK
✆01923 205240
www.ViaMichelin.com
travelpubsales@uk.michelin.com

Special Sales
For information regarding bulk sales, customized editions and premium sales, please contact our Customer Service Departments:
USA 1-800-432-6277
UK 01923 205240
Canada 1-800-361-8236

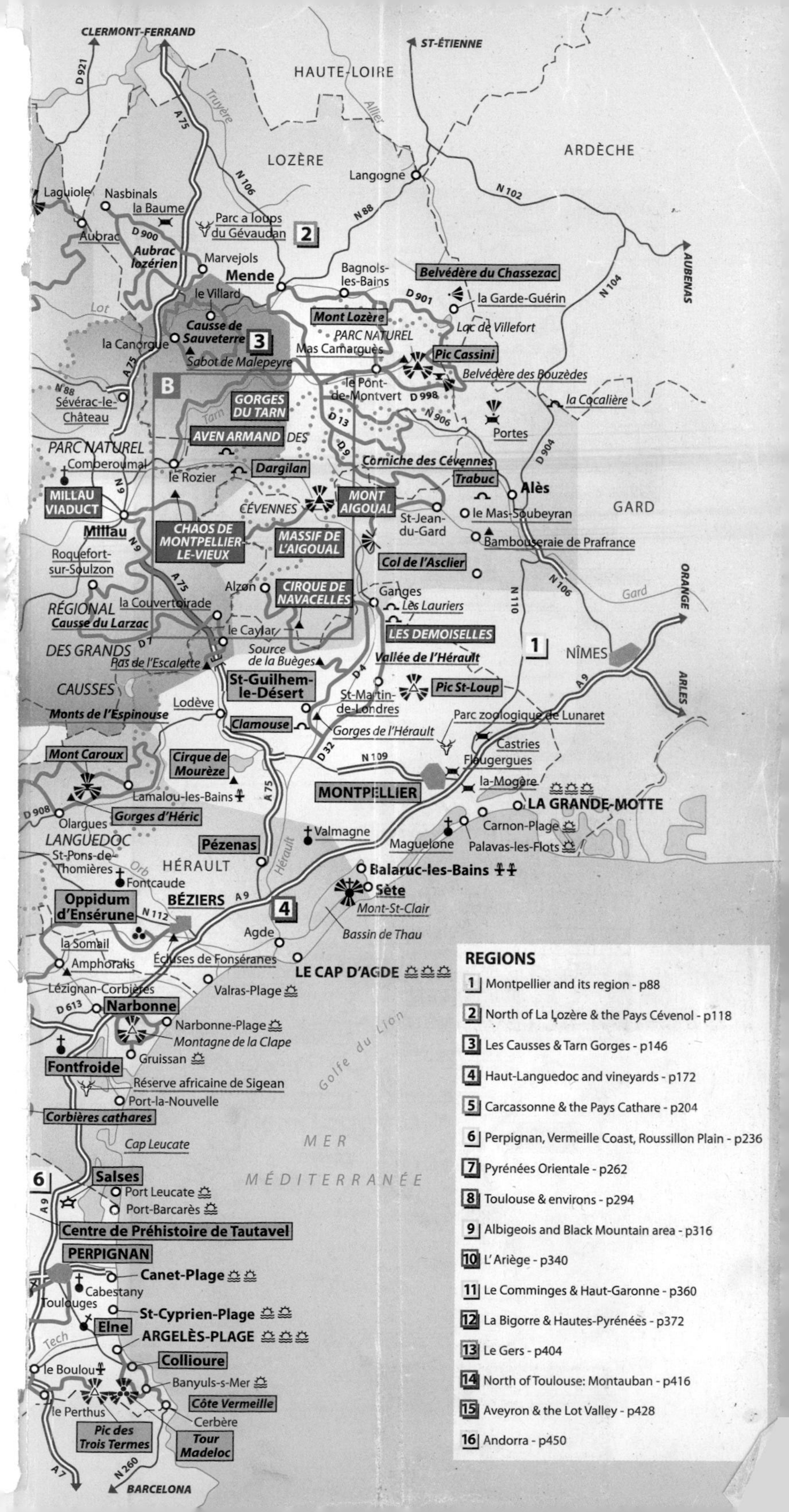
CLERMONT-FERRAND
ST-ÉTIENNE
HAUTE-LOIRE
ARDÈCHE
LOZÈRE
Langogne
Laguiole
Nasbinals
la Baume
Aubrac
Aubrac lozérien
Parc a loups du Gévaudan
2
Marvejols
Mende
Bagnols-les-Bains
Belvédère du Chassezac
la Garde-Guérin
Lac de Villefort
AUBENAS
le Villard
Causse de Sauveterre
3
la Canorgue
Sabot de Malepeyre
Mont Lozère
PARC NATUREL
Mas Camarguès
Pic Cassini
Belvédère des Bouzèdes
le Pont-de-Montvert
la Cocalière
Portes
B
Sévérac-le-Château
GORGES DU TARN
AVEN ARMAND
DES
PARC NATUREL
Comberoumal
le Rozier
Dargilan
Corniche des Cévennes
Trabuc
Alès
GARD
MILLAU VIADUCT
Millau
CÉVENNES
MONT AIGOUAL
St-Jean-du-Gard
le Mas-Soubeyran
Bambouseraie de Prafrance
CHAOS DE MONTPELLIER-LE-VIEUX
MASSIF DE L'AIGOUAL
Col de l'Asclier
Roquefort-sur-Soulzon
Alzon
CIRQUE DE NAVACELLES
Ganges
Les Lauriers
ORANGE
RÉGIONAL
la Couvertoirade
Causse du Larzac
le Caylar
LES DEMOISELLES
DES GRANDS
Source de la Buèges
Vallée de l'Hérault
1
NÎMES
ARLES
Pas de l'Escalette
CAUSSES
St-Guilhem-le-Désert
St-Martin-de-Londres
Pic St-Loup
Monts de l'Espinouse
Lodève
Clamouse
Gorges de l'Hérault
Parc zoologique de Lunaret
Castries
Fougergues
Mont Caroux
Cirque de Mourèze
MONTPELLIER
la Mogère
LA GRANDE-MOTTE
Lamalou-les-Bains
Olargues
Gorges d'Héric
Valmagne
Carnon-Plage
LANGUEDOC
Pézenas
Maguelone
Palavas-les-Flots
St-Pons-de-Thomières
HÉRAULT
Balaruc-les-Bains
Fontcaude
Sète
Oppidum d'Ensérune
BÉZIERS
4
Mont-St-Clair
Bassin de Thau
Agde
la Somail
Amphoralis
Écluses de Fonséranes
LE CAP D'AGDE
Lézignan-Corbières
Valras-Plage
Narbonne
Narbonne-Plage
Montagne de la Clape
Gruissan
Golfe du Lion
Fontfroide
Réserve africaine de Sigean
Port-la-Nouvelle
Corbières cathares
Cap Leucate
MER
MÉDITERRANÉE
6
Salses
Port Leucate
Port-Barcarès
Centre de Préhistoire de Tautavel
PERPIGNAN
Canet-Plage
Cabestany
Toulouges
St-Cyprien-Plage
Elne
ARGELÈS-PLAGE
Collioure
le Boulou
Banyuls-s-Mer
Côte Vermeille
le Perthus
Cerbère
Pic des Trois Termes
Tour Madeloc
BARCELONA
REGIONS
1 Montpellier and its region - p88
2 North of La Lozère & the Pays Cévenol - p118
3 Les Causses & Tarn Gorges - p146
4 Haut-Languedoc and vineyards - p172
5 Carcassonne & the Pays Cathare - p204
6 Perpignan, Vermeille Coast, Roussillon Plain - p236
7 Pyrénées Orientale - p262
8 Toulouse & environs - p294
9 Albigeois and Black Mountain area - p316
10 L'Ariège - p340
11 Le Comminges & Haut-Garonne - p360
12 La Bigorre & Hautes-Pyrénées - p372
13 Le Gers - p404
14 North of Toulouse: Montauban - p416
15 Aveyron & the Lot Valley - p428
16 Andorra - p450

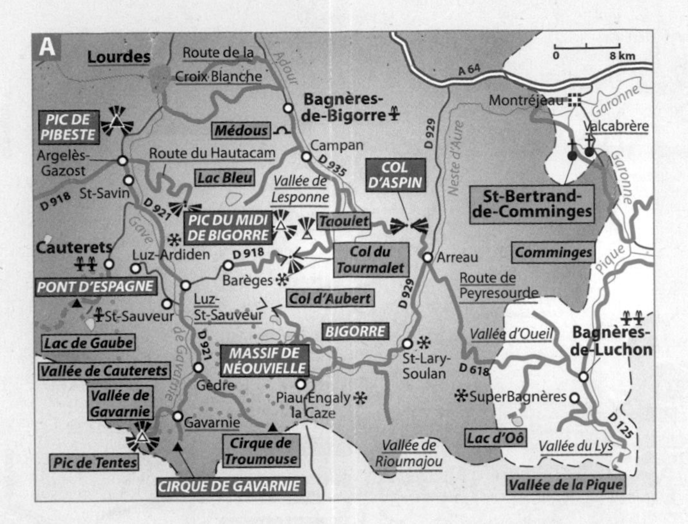
A
Lourdes
Route de la Croix Blanche
Adour
Bagnères-de-Bigorre
Médous
PIC DE PIBESTE
Argelès-Gazost
Route du Hautacam
Campan
D 935
COL D'ASPIN
D 929
Neste d'Aure
A 64
0 8 km
Montréjeau
Garonne
Valcabrère
St-Bertrand-de-Comminges
St-Savin
D 918
Lac Bleu
Vallée de Lesponne
D 921
Gave
PIC DU MIDI DE BIGORRE
Taoulet
Cauterets
Luz-Ardiden
D 918
Col du Tourmalet
Arreau
Comminges
Pique
Barèges
PONT D'ESPAGNE
Luz-St-Sauveur
St-Sauveur
Col d'Aubert
D 929
Route de Peyresourde
Lac de Gaube
Gave de Gavarnie
D 921
BIGORRE
Vallée d'Oueil
Bagnères-de-Luchon
Vallée de Cauterets
MASSIF DE NÉOUVIELLE
St-Lary-Soulan
D 618
Gèdre
Vallée de Gavarnie
Piau-Engaly
la Caze
SuperBagnères
Gavarnie
Pic de Tentes
Cirque de Troumouse
Vallée de Rioumajou
Lac d'Oô
Vallée du Lys
D 125
CIRQUE DE GAVARNIE
Vallée de la Pique

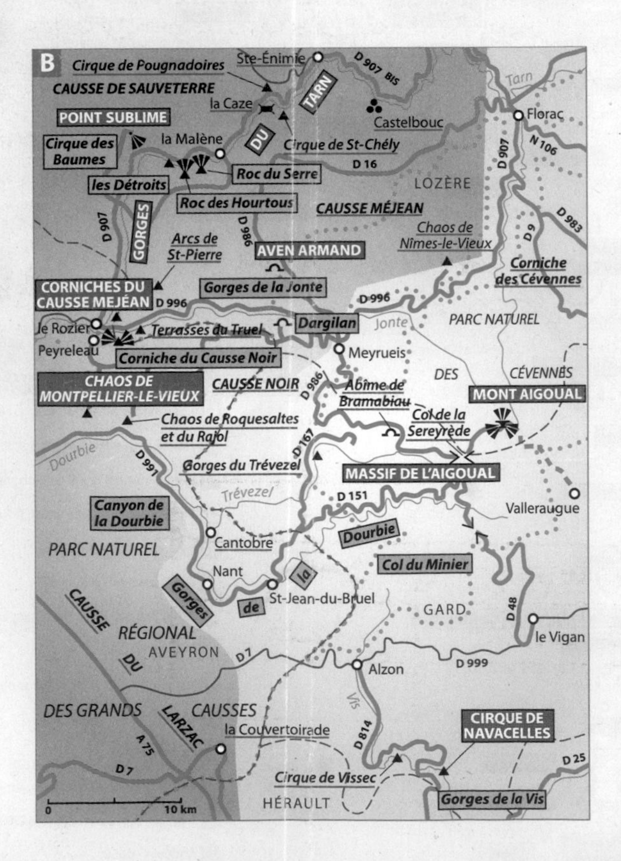
B
Cirque de Pougnadoires
Ste-Énimie
D 907 BIS
CAUSSE DE SAUVETERRE
la Caze
TARN
Tarn
Castelbouc
Florac
POINT SUBLIME
DU
Cirque de St-Chély
Cirque des Baumes
la Malène
D 16
N 106
D 907
Roc du Serre
les Détroits
LOZÈRE
Roc des Hourtous
GORGES
CAUSSE MÉJEAN
D 983
D 907
D 986
Chaos de Nîmes-le-Vieux
D 9
Arcs de St-Pierre
AVEN ARMAND
Corniche des Cévennes
CORNICHES DU CAUSSE MEJÉAN
Gorges de la Jonte
D 996
D 996
Jonte
PARC NATUREL
Le Rozier
Terrasses du Truel
Dargilan
Peyreleau
Meyrueis
Corniche du Causse Noir
DES
CÉVENNES
CHAOS DE MONTPELLIER-LE-VIEUX
CAUSSE NOIR
D 986
Abîme de Bramabiau
MONT AIGOUAL
Col de la Sereyrède
Chaos de Roquesaltes et du Rajol
Dourbie
D 991
D 157
Gorges du Trévezel
MASSIF DE L'AIGOUAL
Trévezel
D 151
Valleraugue
Canyon de la Dourbie
Cantobre
Dourbie
PARC NATUREL
Col du Minier
la
Nant
Gorges
St-Jean-du-Bruel
de
CAUSSE
GARD
D 48
RÉGIONAL
le Vigan
AVEYRON
DU
D 7
Alzon
D 999
Vis
DES GRANDS
CAUSSES
LARZAC
la Couvertoirade
D 814
CIRQUE DE NAVACELLES
A 75
D 7
D 25
Cirque de Vissec
HÉRAULT
Gorges de la Vis
0 10 km

HOW TO USE THIS GUIDE

PLANNING YOUR TRIP

The blue-tabbed PLANNING YOUR TRIP section at the front of the guide gives you **ideas for your trip** and **practical information** to help you organize it. You'll find tours, practical information, a host of outdoor activities, a calendar of events, information on shopping, sightseeing, kids' activities and more.

INTRODUCTION

The orange-tabbed INTRODUCTION section explores the Languedoc and Roussillon's **Nature** and geology. The **History** section spans from the Paleolithic to the Cathars. The **Art and Culture** section covers architecture, art, literature and music, while the **Region Today** delves into modern Languedoc and Roussillon.

DISCOVERING

The green-tabbed DISCOVERING section features Principal Sights by region, featuring the most interesting local **Sights, Walking Tours**, nearby **Excursions**, and detailed **Driving Tours**. Admission prices shown are normally for a single adult.

ADDRESSES

We've selected the best hotels, restaurants, cafes shops, nightlife and entertainment to fit all budgets. See the Legend on the cover flap for an explanation of the price categories. See the back of the guide for an index of hotels and restaurants.

Sidebars

Throughout the guide you will find blue, orange and green-coloured text boxes with lively anecdotes, detailed history and background information.

A Bit of Advice

Green advice boxes found in this guide contain practical tips and handy information relevant to the sight in the Discovering section.

STAR RATINGS★★★

Michelin has given star ratings for more than 100 years. If you're pressed for time, we recommend you visit the ★★★, or ★★ sights first:

- ★★★ **Highly recommended**
- ★★ **Recommended**
- ★ **Interesting**

MAPS

- Regional Driving Tours map, Places to Stay map and Principal Sights map.
- Region maps.
- Maps for major cities and villages.
- Local tour maps.

All maps in this guide are oriented north, unless otherwise indicated by a directional arrow. The term "Local Map" refers to a map within the chapter or Tourism Region. A complete list of the maps found in the guide appears at the back of this book.

PLANNING YOUR TRIP

INTRODUCTION TO LANGUEDOC

DISCOVERING LANGUEDOC

Languedoc Roussillon Tarn Gorges

High, wide and handsome, the Languedoc-Roussillon's mountains, valleys, vineyards and towns and villages are a perfect companion to an identical landscapeof neighbouring Tarn and Aveyron. There is great history here, landscapes to make the heart ache with joy and stories to make you weep.

LANGUEDOC ROUSSILLON

Montpellier region *(p88)*

There is great intimacy about the Montpellier region, a vibrant, buzzing, bustling friendliness and captivating atmosphere, fanned by the warm breezes of the Mediterranean that raise the soft thyme, rosemary, broom and rock rose scents of the scrubland, the *garrigue*.

North of La Lozère, Pays Cévenol *(p118)*

The Cévennes will be forever linked with the story of Robert Louis Stevenson and his journeys with a donkey called Modestine. This vast upland plateau is a place of singular beauty, riven by valleys and decorated by attractive villages of ancient charm.

Les Causses, Tarn Gorges *(p146)*

Between the Causse Méjean and the Cause de Sauveterre, the Gorges du Tarn form a canyon fashioned by the River Tarn. The so-called *causses* are part of a vast, wild and beautiful limestone plateau, les Grandes Causses.

Haute Languedoc and vineyards *(p172)*

Wine production in Haut Languedoc is marked by the choice of grape varieties – Cabernet Franc and Chardonnay are almost completely absent. Instead you have Carignan, Grenache, Mourvèdre, Syrah, Cabernet-Sauvignon, Picpoul, Bourboulenc, Clairette and Sauvignon. Add in a significant diversity of soils, and the result is the production of varied wines.

Ramparts of Carcassonne

A. Thuillier/MICHELIN

Carcassone, Pays Cathare *(p204)*

The history of the Cathar believers permeates many parts of France, but is nowhere more focused than in Languedoc-Roussillon and the great citadels among the mountains to the south. The story continues, too, in the city of Carcassonne, both in the *bastide* lower town south of the Canal du Midi, and in the ancient walled citadel beyond the river.

Perpignan, Vermeille Coast, Roussillon Plain *(p236)*

The eastern end of the Pyrenees, where the mountains tumble down to the sea is neither France nor Spain. This is Catalonia, a region and culture as old as the hills themselves; passionate, vibrant and with a luminous light that attracts artists, and those in search of less crowded places.

Pyrénées Orientales *(p262)*

With the Roussillon Plain to the north and the mountain of Canigou to the south, the Pyrénées-Orientales are a region of great contrast, favoured by cellist Pablo Casals. Attractive villages dot a verdant and peaceful landscape of great natural beauty.

MIDI-PYRÉNÉES

Toulouse and environs *(p294)*

Nicknamed the 'Pink City' for its red-brick buildings, Toulouse is a mildly frenetic, hugely entertaining and vibrant place. This capital of France's largest region (Midi-Pyrénées) very much has its own glorious identity.

Albigeois and the Black Mountain *(p316)*

Albi may lend its name to an horrific episode in the history of France, but its villages are delightful, decorating the Tarn river, Montagne Noire, and south-western tip of the Massif Central, and a broad ridge of densely forested upland separating Tarn from Aude.

L'Ariège *(p340)*

The Ariège is particularly renowned as a frontier, between Gascony and Languedoc, France and Spain.
But it is also a region of a considerable prehistoric interest that manifests itself in numerous caves, decorated with fine cave paintings, and artefacts.

Le Comminges and Haut-Garonne *(p360)*

The region of Comminges, historically a province of the ancient kingdom of Gascony, lies at the centre of the Pyrenees, midway between the Atlantic and Mediterranean. It was once attached to the Couserans area and Val d'Aran. Le Comminges extends from the heights of the Upper Garonne basin to the mild alluvial plains.

La Bigorre and Hautes Pyrénées *(p372)*

Far from being the preserve of the *alpinistes*, the Hautes-Pyrénées offer exploration for all levels, not least in the white waters and narrow gorges of the Gavarnie and Cauterets valleys.

"Pink City" of Toulouse by the Garonne

M.-H. Carcanague/MICHELIN

Le Gers *(p404)*

Characterised by charming villages and with the Pyrenees to the south, Le Gers is renowned for its gastronomic specialities, including Armagnac brandy, Côtes de Gascogne wines, Floc de Gascogne and foie gras.

North of Toulouse *(p416)*

The area north of the city of Toulouse is a peaceful haven of contrasting scenery, teeming with wildlife and dotted with attractive medieval villages. There is a strong historical heritage here, but at the same time the area's profile with tourists is low. The principal town is Montauban, on the boundary between Bas Quercy and the alluvial plains of the Garonne.

Aveyron, Lot Valley *(p428)*

In the west of Aveyron lie a group of fortified medieval bastides. In the south-east there are strong links with the Knights Templar. In the centre, lies the city of Rodez from which roads splay out like the spokes of a wheel. The Lot valley is lush and green and sparsely populated.

Andorra *(p450)*

High among encircling hills, Andorra relies almost entirely on tourism, popular in winter as a ski destination, and in summer for walking. Tax-free shopping adds to its appeal.

Transhmance in Cévennes

PLANNING YOUR TRIP

Michelin Driving Tours

The following is a brief description of each of the driving tours shown on the inside back cover.

1 BASTIDES AND STRONGHOLDS OF ARMAGNAC COUNTRY

225km/140mi starting from Auch

This tour also offers opportunities to taste foie gras between visits to bastides and strongholds. From Auch visit **Mirande**, **Montesquieu** and **Bassoues** with its medieval keep. On the way to the castle at **Termes-d'Armagnac**, don't miss the Jazz Museum in **Marciac**. The picturesque village of **Sabazan** is close to **Aignan** where Armagnac tasting is a must. Beyond **Eauze** and its treasure is the Gallo-Roman villa of **Séviac**, near Montréal-du-Gers. Two more *bastides* await you further north, a round one at **Fourcès** and the smallest fortified town in France at **Larressingle**. **Condom** offers boat trips on the Baïse and La Romieu has its collegiate church. Stop by **Lectoure's** Gallo-Roman museum and the **Abbaye de Flaran** before returning to Auch.

2 PYRENEAN MINERAL SPRINGS

250km/155mi starting from Tarbes

Leave **Tarbes** south-east towards **Lourdes**, a world-famous place of pilgrimage. The Pyrenean summits and resorts are quite close: **Pic de Pibeste**, **Argelès-Gazost**, **Luz-St-Sauveur** and **Gavarnie;** they are the ideal starting points of walks to the impressive **Cirque de Gavarnie** and **Pic du Midi de Bigorre**. Beyond **Col d'Aspin** is **Arreau**, a quiet little town at the confluence of two rivers. Take time to admire the churches of the Louron valley with frescoes decorating their wooden vaulting. Continue to **Bagnères-de-Luchon** and turn north towards **Valcabrère** Basilica and **St-Bertrand-de-Comminges**. Further north is the prehistoric **Grotte de Gargas** near Montréjeau and the last part of the itinerary includes **Bagnères-de-Bigorre** and its hot springs.

3 TALES AND LEGENDS OF FOIX COUNTRY

280km/174mi starting from Foix

Follow in the footsteps of the Cathars from **Foix** to **Roquefixade** and **Montségur**. Close by, nature joins in with the intermittent **Fontestorbes** spring. On your way you come to the splendid **Mirepoix** *bastide*; in **Vals** you will see an amazing rock church, in **Pamiers** a lovely Gothic bell-tower and, in **Mas-d'Azil**, a prehistoric cave. Then when you cross the Ariège mountains, you will be won over by the beauty of the landscapes as you drive along valleys such as **Bethmale**, where legend thrives. Further on, past the Romanesque churches of **Vic** and **Massat** and the breathtaking panorama of **Port de Lers**, you reach one of the main prehistoric areas in the Pyrenees: the **Grotte de Niaux**, **Tarascon** and its **Parc pyrénéen d'Art préhistorique** and the **Grotte de Lombrives**. Having admired the Romanesque church in **Unac**, you reach the French-chalk quarry at **Trimouns**.

4 PEAKS AND VALLEYS OF THE PYRENEES

270km/168mi starting from Font-Romeu

This drive takes you to the heart of the Pyrenees. From **Font-Romeu**, whose Hermitage is a place of pilgrimage, head for **Mont-Louis**, a stronghold built by Vauban, which now boasts a solar furnace seen from afar. The **Lac des Bouillouses** is nearby. At **Les Angles** you can ski or meet bear and izard in the zoological park. The **Grotte de Fontrabiouse** is the ideal refuge when it gets too hot outside. As for **Ax-les-Thermes**, you will love it for its skiing, walking and mineral springs. Andorra can be reached via **Pas de la Casa**. Drive down to **Andorra la Vella**, the capital. Back in France, go through the **Puymorens tunnel** to reach the **Chaos de Targasonne** and make a detour to Llo before returning to Font-Romeu.

5 CATALAN ROMANESQUE AND BAROQUE ARCHITECTURE

290km/180mi starting from Perpignan
The discovery of Catalan art begins appropriately in **Perpignan**. Nearby, **Cabestany** gave its name to the fine artist who carved the tympanum of its Romanesque church. The cathedral cloisters in **Elne** are a jewel of Romanesque and Gothic sculpture. Farther south, **Collioure** boasts the monumental altarpiece of the Église Notre-Dame-des-Anges. The churches of **St-André** and **St-Génis-des-Fontaines** to the west have splendid carved Romanesque lintels, whereas the doorway of the Romanesque church in **Le Boulou** was carved by the Master of Cabestany. Nearby you can see the Romanesque frescoes decorating the chapel of **St-Martin-de-Fénollar**, including superb representations of the Three Wise Men. Continue westwards to **Arles-sur-Tech** to see the holy sepulchre, then on to **Coustouges**. Between the Tech and Têt valleys stand the **Chapelle de la Trinité** and the **Prieuré de Serrabone**, both worth a visit for their Romanesque treasures, whereas the churches in **Vinca** and **Espira-de-Conflent** contain fine Baroque altarpieces. Near **Prades**, the abbeys of **St-Michel-de-Cuxa** and **St-Martin-du-Canigou** are a must. Drive on eastwards to **Ille-sur-Têt** and its wealth of Baroque ornamentation. As you leave Ille, do not miss the **Orgues**, where nature competes favourably with the splendours of human art. The tour ends in **Baixas** and the monumental Baroque altarpiece of its church.

6 THE VIA DOMITIA

300km/186mi from Lunel to Le Perthus or Port-Vendres
Ancient Rome was linked to Spain by the Via Domitia, sections of which are still visible. This journey starts from the **Oppidum d'Ambrussum**, near Lunel. Driving south-east, you first reach **Lattes**, which has an interesting archaeological museum. Admire the fine mosaics of the Gallo-Roman villa of **Loupian**, standing on the shores of the Étang de Thau, then take an hour's walk between Montbazin and **Pinet** to go on to the Via Domitia. **Cap d'Agde** Museum contains the magnificent Éphèbe d'Agde, a bronze statue of a young Greek man found in the Hérault. Take a short break in **Béziers** and visit the Musée du Biterrois. Return to the Via Domitia and the **Oppidum d'Ensérune**. Farther west, in Sallèdes-d'Aude, archaeological excavations have revealed a huge pottery workshop with numerous amphorae (Musée **Amphoralis**). The road then reaches **Narbonne**, which boasts an excellent archaeological museum (fine Roman painting collection) and a section of Roman road. Head south along N 9 to the **Lapalme** crossroads to see the Via Domitia exhibition. From **Perpignan**, you can either follow the Roman road along the coast or through the Pyrenees, the very route followed by Hannibal and his elephants. The coastal route goes through **Elne** (archaeological museum) to reach **Port-Vendres**. The mountain route leads to **Les Cluses** (beautiful panorama) then on to the **Fort de Bellegarde** and the **Site archéologique de Panissars**.

7 CATHAR COUNTRY

300km/186mi starting from Carcassonne
From medieval Carcassonne, drive south-west to **Limoux** where you can taste the famous sparkling *Blanquette* before going on to visit several Cathar castles. Heading south through **Alet** and its Romanesque abbey, you soon reach the **Donjon d'Arques** then **Rennes-le-Château** and its legendary treasure. **Puivert** was one of the castles besieged during the Albigensian Crusade. To the south-east (via the **Défilé de Pierre-Lys**) stands

another Cathar castle, **Puilaurens**. Farther east are the castles of **Peyrepertuse** and **Queribus** towering above the surrounding landscape. From the nearby **Grau de Maury** pass, there is a view of the Canigou in the distance. The itinerary then takes in the ruins of **Padern**, **Aguillar** and **Durban-Corbières** castles. On your way back to Carcassonne, take time to visit the **Château de Villerouge-Termenès**, where you can enjoy medieval cooking in the former stables, then on to the **Château des Termes** and **Lagrasse Abbey** to complete the tour.

8 THE MONTAGNE NOIRE

170km/106mi starting from Caunes-Minervois

After admiring the handsome 16C mansions of **Caunes-Minervois**, head for the heights of the Montagne Noire, stopping on the way to visit the **Gouffre de Cabrespine** and **Grotte de Limousis**. Halfway up the slopes, the four **Lastours** castles bear witness to the fighting that took place during the Albigensian Crusade. Other half-ruined castles overlook **Saissac** and **Mas-Cabardès**, adding to the charm of these villages. The Montagne Noire is also where a vast complex of lakes and reservoirs were dug from **St- Ferréol** to the **Seuil de Naurouze** in order to supply the Canal du Midi with water. Having reached the plain through which the canal meanders, take a break in **Castelnaudary** to indulge in a cassoulet. Drive south-east to **Fanjeaux** then turn east to **Carcassonne**, still surrounded by its ramparts, before returning to **Caunes-Minervois**.

9 LAND OF MILK AND HONEY

230km/143mi starting from Toulouse

Prosperous **Toulouse** is the starting point of this drive. Before leaving, don't miss the Airbus industrial complex and the Cité de l'Espace on the outskirts of town. Drive south-east to **Port-Lauragais** along the **Canal du Midi** and visit the Ovalie, a museum devoted to rugby. Turn north-east through the Lauragais hills via **St-Félix** and **Revel** to the **Bassin de Saint-Ferréol**, ideal for water sports. The road wends its way through **Arfons** to **Mazamet**, with its long-standing tawing tradition, and **Castres**, where you can take a trip on the River Agout, then on to **Lautrec** and its pink garlic, **Graulhet** and its leather, **Lavaur** and its old town. On the way back to Toulouse, D 130 between **Magrin** and **Loubens-Lauragais** will take you through dyer's woad country.

10 RUGGED LIMESTONE PLATEAUX

290km/180mi starting from Millau

Millau is at the heart of the four main limestone plateaux which this tour explores. Driving eastwards, you soon come across the impressive rock formation known as the **Chaos de Montpellier-le-Vieux**. The **Grotte de Dargilan** with its pink concretions is located a few miles farther on. On the border of the Causse Noir and Causse Méjean stands the picturesque village of **Meyrueis** with its weathered stone houses. The road runs through the barren Causse Méjean before reaching the **Aven Armand**, one of the most attractive underground caves in France. **Ste-Énimie**, towering above the Tarn is another picturesque village. The road then crosses the Causse de Sauveterre towards **La Canourgue**, a peaceful village criss-crossed by a network of charming canals. Visit the medieval castle of **Séverac-le-Château** then continue on your journey along D 995 towards the **Tarn Gorges** and turn south to **Le Rozier;** from there, head south to **Roquefort-sur-Soulzon** and its extensive galleries hewn out of the rock, where the famous cheese is left to mature. Flocks of sheep are a familiar sight on the Causse de Larzac, which has retained medieval fortifications built by the Knights Templars and Knights Hospitallers; some of the most remarkable can be seen in **La Couvertoirade** before returning to Millau.

1 1 CAVES, CIRQUES AND ROCK FORMATIONS

425km/264mi starting from Ganges

This tour leads in turn to all the natural wonders which the area has to offer. The impressive **Grotte des Demoiselles** is located a few miles from **Ganges**. Farther east, near Anduze, is the **Grotte de Trabuc**, lined with tiny soldiers! You next enter the **Cévennes** mountain area and follow the famous **Corniche** north to Florac. The road then skirts the southern border of the Causse Méjean to reach the stunning **Chaos de Nîmes-le-Vieux**. Across the River Jonte towers **Mont Aigoual**, offering a breathtaking panorama from its summit. To the west is the **Abîme de Bramabiau**, where you can see the resurgence of the River Bonheur. Nearby there are three more natural wonders, the **Aven Armand**, the **Grotte de Dargilan** and the **Chaos de Montpellier-le-Vieux**. Turning south along the **canyon of the River Dourbie**, the road leads to the vast and barren **Cirque de Navacelles**. Continuing south past the **Lac du Salagou**, you reach the rock-strewn **Cirque de Mourèze** and visit one last cave, the **Grotte de Clamouse** before returning to Ganges.

When and Where to Go

WHEN TO GO

CLIMATE

Although much of this region is predominantly Mediterranean in climate, it is open to oceanic influences from the Atlantic and, in its northern part, to the harsher climatic conditions of the Massif Central. As for the Pyrenees mountain range, its valleys are under the influence of several weather systems determined by the altitude and the direction the slopes are facing.
Late **winter** and **early spring** offer plenty of snow for cross-country skiing in the Aubrac, and Alpine skiing in the Pyrenees.
Spring is the ideal season for hiking and riding tours and for discovering the region in general.
Summer is dry and hot with luminous skies, particularly along the Mediterranean. Sudden, violent storms bring relief from the scorching heat from time to time but the sun rarely admits defeat for more than a few hours.
In **autumn**, rainfall is often abundant particularly in the Toulouse and Albi areas, while warm south-west winds blowing over the whole region bring alternating periods of dry and wet weather.

WEATHER FORECAST

Météo-France offers recorded information at national, departmental and local levels. This information is updated three times a day and is valid for up to seven days.

- **National and departmental forecast:**
  ℘3250 followed by
  1 – for all the information about the département for the next 7 days, or
  2 – for information about towns.
- **Local forecast:** ℘08 92 68 02 followed by the number of the *département – see below.*

Weather forecasting is also available on www.meteo.fr.

THEMED TOURS

Travel itineraries on specific themes have been mapped out to help you discover the regional architectural heritage and the traditions which make up the cultural heritage of the region. You will find brochures in tourist offices, and the routes are generally well marked and easy to follow *(signs posted along the roads)*.

HISTORY

Some of these itineraries are managed by the **Fédération Nationale des Routes Historiques** *(www.routes-historiques.com)*. Apply to local tourist offices for leaflets with mapped itineraries. The list below includes a local contact when appropriate:

- **Route historique du pastel en pays de cocagne** (dyer's woad country between Toulouse and Albi; contact M. Rufino, Château-Musée du Pastel, 81220 Magrin, 05 63 70 63 82).
- **Route historique en Languedoc-Roussillon** (Château de Flaugergues, 1744 avenue Albert-Einstein, 34000 Montpellier, 04 99 52 66 44).
- **Route historique en Terre Catalane: de l'Homme de Tautavel à Picasso** (Réseau culturel Terre catalane, 16 avenue des Palmiers, BP 60244, 66002 Perpignan Cedex, 04 68 51 52 90).

Other thematic itineraries (*information available from local tourist offices*) include:

Route des Cadets de Gascogne
Maison Départementale du Tourisme, 3 boulevard Roquelaure, 32002 Auch. 05 62 05 95 95. www.gers-gascogne.com.

Via Domitia
along the old Roman road running from Beaucaire to Spain. Association Via Domitia, 20 rue de la République, 34000 Montpellier. 04 67 22 81 00. www.viadomitia.org.

Route de la Catalogne Romane
Romanesque art in Catalonia and Roussillon; tourist office, Perpignan. 04 68 66 30 30.

TRADITIONS AND NATURE

- **Sur les pas de St-Jacques-de-Compostelle** 137km/85mi from Toulouse to St-Bertrand-de-Comminges.
- **Sur la route des vins** Wine tour of the area between the River Garonne and River Tarn.
- **Route des grottes en Ariège** (tour of natural and prehistoric caves of the Ariège region).
- **Chemin de la soie** (focusing on traditional silk production in the region: museums, silk worm breeding establishments, spinning mills) 95 Grand'Rue, 30270 St-Jean-du-Gard. 04 66 85 10 48).

What to See and Do

OUTDOOR FUN

WATER SPORTS

Swimming, water-skiing, sailing

Beaches – The Languedoc coast has vast sandy beaches which stretch invitingly for miles, often sandwiched between the sea and lagoons. The best are to be found between La Grande-Motte and Palavas-les-Flots, from Sète to Cap-d'Agde, and around Cap-d'Agde and Valras. Bathing conditions are indicated by flags on beaches which are surveyed by lifeguards (no flags means no lifeguards): green indicates it is safe to bathe and lifeguards are on duty; yellow warns that conditions are not that good, but lifeguards are still in attendance; red means bathing is forbidden as conditions are too dangerous.

Lakes and reservoirs – The main lakes and reservoirs with facilities for swimming and various water sports, including sailing and windsurfing, and where it is possible to go for walks

Beach at Frontignan

L. Campion/MICHELIN

or picnic on the lake shore, include: Bages, Sigean, Leucate, Ganguise, Jouarre (**Aude**); Pareloup, Pont-de-Salars, Villefranche-de-Panat (**Aveyron**); Les Camboux (**Gard**); La Raviège, Thau, Salagou (**Hérault**); Naussac, Villefort (**Lozère**), Matemale (**Pyrénées-Orientales**).

Useful addresses

- **Fédération française de Voile** 17 Rue Henri-Bocquillon, 75015 Paris Cedex 16. ✆01 40 60 37 00; www.ffvoile.org.
- **Ligue de voile du Languedoc-Roussillon** Espace Voile, Bât. C, Le Patio Santa Monica, 1815 Ave Marcel Pagnol, 34470 Perols. ✆04 67 50 48 30. www.ffvoilelr.net.
- **France Station Voile – Nautisme et Tourisme** 17 Rue Henri-Bocquillon, 75015 Paris. ✆01 44 05 96 55; www.france-nautisme.com.
- **Fédération française de ski nautique** 27 rue d'Athènes, 75009 Paris. ✆01 53 20 19 19.

Marinas – The numerous marinas dotted along the coast offer pleasure craft over 100 000 moorings. They are shown on the map of *Places to Stay* at the beginning of the guide. Information is available from the various harbour master's offices or from the

- **Association des ports de plaisance du Languedoc-Roussillon**, Hôtel de Ville, 34250 Palavas-les-Flots. ✆04 67 07 73 50.

CANOEING, KAYAKING AND RAFTING

Canoeing is a popular family pastime on the peaceful waters of the region. **Kayaking** is practised on the lakes and, for more experienced paddlers, rapid sections of the rivers. The upper and middle valley of the Tarn, and the valleys of the Dourbie, the Orb, the Hérault and the Garonne among others are wonderful places to explore by canoe, with their beautiful scenery, stretches of rapids and tiny beaches ideal as picnic spots. Centres for canoeing have been set up in the Parc régional du Haut-Languedoc. Various canoeing guides and a map, *France canoe-kayak et sports d'eau,* are on sale from the **Fédération française de canoë-kayak**, 87 quai de la Marne, BP 58, 94344 Joinville-le-Pont, ✆01 45 11 08 50; www.ffck.org.

OTHER USEFUL ADDRESSES

- **Comité départemental de canoe-kayak de l'Ariège** Complexe sportif de l'Ayroule, 09000 Foix. ✆05 61 65 20 65.
- **L'Échappée Verte** 21 rue de la Cavalerie, 34090 Montpellier. ✆04 67 41 20 24. www.echappeeverte.com. (trips throughout the region).

Canoeing in the Gorges de l'Ardèche at Pont d'Arc

J. Damase/MICHELIN

Rafting is the easiest of these fresh-water sports, since it involves going down rivers in inflatable craft steered by an instructor; special equipment is provided.

CANYONING, HYDROSPEED AND DIVING

Canyoning is a technique for body-surfing down narrow gorges and over falls, as though on a giant water slide, whereas **hydrospeed** involves swimming down rapids with a kickboard and flippers. These sports require protection: wear a wet suit and a helmet.
Information: **Fédération Française de la Montagne et de l'Escalade**, 8-10 Quai de la Marne, 75019 Paris. ✆01 40 18 75 50. www.ffme.fr
The list of **diving** clubs in the region is available from the **Fédération Française d'Études et de Sports Sous-marins**, 24 quai de Rive-Neuve, 13284 Marseille Cedex 07, ✆04 91 33 99 31; www.ffessm.fr.

FRESHWATER FISHING

A brochure called *Pêche en France* is available from the **Conseil Supérieur de la Pêche**, 16 avenue Louison-Bobet 94132 Fontenay-sous-Bois, ✆01 45 14 36 00. This can also be obtained from local branches of the **Fédérations Départementales de Pêche et de Pisciculture** (at Albi, Carcassonne, Mende, Montpellier, Nîmes, Perpignan, Rodez, Tarbes and Toulouse). Mountain lakes and streams of the Pyrenees region are ideal for trout fishing. Two-week holiday fishing permits are available in some areas – contact the local federation for details (or try local fishing tackle shops or tourist offices). For information on fishing regulations in the 20 or so lakes in the Bouillouses area, contact the tourist office in Font-Romeu.

SEA FISHING

Salt-water fishing can be practised on foot, from a boat or underwater with diving gear along the coast and in the lagoons where fish abound. Half and full-day sea fishing trips are organised at locations like the rocky coast around Grau d'Agde and offshore from Banyuls-sur-Mer: www.agde-croisiere-peche.com.

- **Fédération Française des Pêcheurs en Mer**
  résidence Alliance, centre Jorlis, 64600 Anglet,
  ✆05 59 31 00 73.
  www.ffpm-national.com.
- **Fédération Française Pêche Mer Languedoc-Roussillon**
  12 rue Font-Martin, 34470 Pérols,
  ✆04 67 17 04 93.
  www.koifaire.com.

WALKING

There is an extensive network of well-marked footpaths in France which make walking *(la randonnée)* easy. Several **Grande Randonnée** (**GR**) trails – recognisable by the red and white horizontal marks on trees, rocks and in town on walls, signposts etc – go through the region, the most famous being, no doubt, the Santiago de Compostela trail from Moissac to St-Jean-Pied-de-Port (GR 65). Along with the GR trails are the **Petite Randonnée (PR)** paths, which are usually blazed with blue (2hr walk), yellow (2hr 15min–3hr 45min) or green (4–6hr) marks. Of course, with appropriate maps, you can combine walks to suit your desires.

To use these trails, obtain the "*Topo-Guide*" for the area published by the **Fédération Française de la Randonnée Pédestre**, 14 rue Riquet, 75019 Paris, ℘01 44 89 93 93; www.ffrp.asso.fr. Some English-language editions are available as well as an annual guide ("*Rando Guide*") which includes ideas for overnight itineraries and places to stay, together with information on the difficulty and accessibility of trails.

Another source of maps and guides for excursions on foot is the **Institut Géographique National (IGN)**, which has a boutique in Paris at 107 rue de la Boétie (off the Champs-Elysées); to order from abroad, visit www.ign.fr, for addresses of wholesalers in your country. Among their publications, France 1M903 is a map showing all of the GR and PR in France (5€); the "*Série Bleue*" and "Top 25" maps, at a scale of 1:25 000 (1cm=250m), show all paths, whether waymarked or not, as well as refuges, campsites, beaches etc (from7.50€). In the region, you can find many of the publications cited above in bookstores, at sports centres or equipment shops, and in some of the country inns and hotels which cater to the sporting crowd.

Stanfords (12–14 Long Acre, London WC2E 9LP. ℘020 7836 1321 (Monday-Friday). www.stanfords.co.uk) has a wide selection of books and maps for travellers.

Hiking on Mont Lozère
A. Thuillier/MICHELIN

Suggestions and useful addresses

The **Parc National des Pyrénées** is a perfect for walkers, whether your expedition is planned for half a day or includes overnight stops.

From July to the end of September mountain refuges under park surveillance are open to accommodate 30-40 people a night; there are also smaller, year-round refuges which are not guarded. In the summer, it is imperative to reserve in advance. One- or two-night stays are generally the rule; some refuges may provide meals prepared by the guardian (*see PARC NATIONAL DES PYRÉNÉES*).

- **La Balaguère**
  route du Val d'Azun,
  65403 Arrens-Marsous
  ℘05 62 97 20 21.
  www.balaguere.com.
  Organises walking trips in the Pyrenees, sometimes round a theme (history, flora, fauna…).
- **Chamina Voyages**
  Naussac, BP 5, 48300 Langogne.
  ℘04 66 69 00 44.
  www.chamina-voyages.com.
  Organises walks with or without guide in the southern part of the Massif Central and in the Pyrenees.

Leave only footprints; take only memories

Choosing the right equipment for a walking expedition is essential: flexible walking shoes with non-slip soles, a waterproof jacket or poncho, an extra sweater, sun protection (hat, glasses, lotion), drinking water (1-2l per person), high energy snacks (chocolate, cereal bars, bananas), and a first aid kit. Of course, you'll need a good map (and a compass if you plan to leave the main trails). Plan your itinerary well, keeping in mind that while the average walking speed for an adult is 4kph/2.5mph, you will need time to eat and rest, and children will not keep up the same pace. Leave details of your itinerary with someone before setting out (innkeeper or fellow camper).

Respect for nature is a cardinal rule and includes the following precautions: don't smoke or light fires in forests, which are particularly susceptible in the dry summer months; always carry your rubbish out; leave wild flowers as they are; walk around, not through, farmers' fields; close gates behind you.

In the dry, rocky scrubland of the *garrigues* and the *causses*, walkers may come across snakes, so it is important to wear stout footwear, preferably with some protection around the ankle. Most of the time the snakes will make themselves scarce as soon as they hear someone coming, so make plenty of noise, and avoid lifting up rocks so as not to disturb any snakes resting beneath them.

It is also possible to follow **herds** on their way to summer pastures in the Aubrac region (apply to the tourist office in St-Chély-d'Aubrac, ✆05 65 44 21 15) or to take a **donkey** with you contact the **Fédération nationale ânes et randonnées**, Le Pré du Meinge, 26560 Eourres, ✆04 92 65 09 07; www.ane-et-rando.com, for a list of organisers).
The **Association "Sur le chemin de R.L. Stevenson"**, 48220 Le Pont-de-Montvert, ✆04 66 45 86 31; www.chemin-stevenson.org, provides a list of B&B, hotels, restaurants, places where donkeys can be hired and tourist offices along the itinerary followed by Stevenson in 1878 and described in his *Travels With a Donkey in the Cévennes.*

CYCLING AND MOUNTAIN BIKING

Many GR and GRP footpaths are accessible to mountain bikers. However, in areas particularly suitable for cycling, there are special trails waymarked by the **Fédération Française de Cyclisme** (5 rue de Rome, 93561 Rosny-sous-Bois Cedex, ✆01 49 35 69 00; www.ffc.fr); these are graded in difficulty *(green is easy; blue is fairly easy; red is difficult; black is very difficult)*; ask for the *"Guide des centres VTT"*, which supply itineraries and brochures as well as information on where to stay and where to call for urgent repairs.
The **Office National des Forêts** publishes some 20 mountain-biking guides under the general heading *VTT Évasion,* focusing on the discovery of the Languedoc-Roussillon forests. These guides are available from the Comité régional du tourisme Languedoc-Roussillon *(see PLANNING YOUR TRIP, Local tourist offices).*
For additional information about cycling clubs, rental etc, contact the **Fédération Française de Cyclotourisme** (12 rue Louis-Bertrand, 94200 Ivry-sur-Seine, ✆01 56 20 88 88; www.ffct.org), the **Ligue Régionale de Cyclotourisme du Languedoc-Roussillon** (M. Morand Guy, 4 rue Ernest-Vieu, 11000 Narbonne, ✆04 68 32 52 62) as well as local tourist offices.

RIDING TOURS

The **Comité National du Tourisme Équestre** (9 boulevard MacDonald, 75019 Paris, ✆01 53 26 15 50, publishes a brochure updated yearly, *Cheval Nature, l'Officiel du Tourisme Équestre en France,* listing horse-riding leisure activities throughout France. In addition, this organisation will give you the address of the nearest Comité Départmental du Tourisme Équestre (CDTE) who can provide maps and brochures and lists of riding centres in your area. It is also possible to contact regional associations directly:

- **Association Régionale pour le Tourisme Équestre et l'Équitation de Loisirs en Languedoc-Roussillon** (ATECREL) 14 rue des Logis, 34140 Loupian, ℘04 67 43 82 50.
- **Ligue Midi-Pyrénées Tourisme Équestre** (ARTEMIP) 31 chemin des Canalets, 31400 Toulouse, ℘05 61 14 04 58; www.tourisme-equestre.fr.

EXPLORING CAVES

Some of the numerous caves and chasms in the region, such as the avens (swallow-holes) of the limestone plateaux, are among the most famous in France. Exploring caves can be a dangerous pastime; it is therefore essential to have the right equipment and be accompanied by a qualified guide – many local clubs can provide both. For more information contact:

- **Fédération Française de Spéléologie** 28 rue Delandine, 69002 Lyon ℘04 72 56 09 63. www.ffspeleo.fr
- **École Française de Spéléologie** As above.
- **Comité Régional de Spéléologie Midi-Pyrénées** 7 rue André-Citroën, 31130 Balma, ℘05 61 11 71 60.

GOLF

The Michelin map Golf, les parcours français (French golf courses) will help you locate golf courses in the region covered by this guide.
For further information, contact the **Fédération Française de Golf**, 68 rue Anatole-France, 92309 Levallois-Perret Cedex, ℘01 41 49 77 00; www.ffg.org.

The **Comité Régional de Tourisme Languedoc-Roussillon** (see *PLANNING YOUR TRIP, Local tourist offices*) proposes a golf pass (150€) for five days' green fees.

MOUNTAIN SPORTS

Safety first is the rule for beginners and old hands alike. The risk associated with avalanches, mud slides, falling rocks, bad weather, fog, glacially cold waters, the dangers of becoming lost or miscalculating distances, should not be underestimated.
Avalanches occur naturally when the upper layer of snow is unstable, in particular after heavy snowfalls, and may be set off by the passage of numerous skiers or walkers over a precise spot. A scale of risk, from 1 to 5, has been developed and is posted daily at resorts and bases for walking trails. It is important to consult this *Bulletin Neige et Avalanche* (BNA) before setting off on any expeditions cross-country or off-piste. You can also call toll free ℘08 92 68 10 20 *(in French)*.
Lightning storms are often preceded by sudden gusts of wind, and put climbers and walkers in danger. In the event, avoid high ground, and do not move along a ridge top; do not seek shelter under overhanging rocks, isolated trees in otherwise open areas, at the entrance to caves or other openings in the rocks, or in the proximity of metal fences or gates.
For general information on mountain sports in the Pyrenees, apply to: **Centre d'Information Montagne et Sentiers** (CIMES-Pyrénées), 1 rue Maye-Lane, 65420 Ibos, ℘05 62 90 09 92; www.cimes-pyrenees.net.

Mountain guides suggest a choice of guided activities.

- **Bureau des guides de Luchon** 18 allée d'Étigny, 31110 Luchon, ℘05 61 79 69 38.
- **Bureau des guides de St-Savin** 1 place du Trey, 65400 St-Savin. ℘05 62 97 91 09.

Useful Contacts for Skiers

Comprehensive information about skiing localities in Languedoc-Rousslllon is listed on **www.sunfrance.com**, in great detail. The principal organisation in the UK for skiing is the **Ski Club of Great Britain** (The White House, 57–63 Church Road, Wimbledon, London SW19 5SB. ☏0845 45 807 80. www.skiclub.co.uk).
But a number of other website-based organisations maintain accurate, up-to-date information, e.g. www.snowheads.com, and the **Eagle Ski Club**, the UK's largest and most active ski-touring and ski-mountaineering club (www.eagleskiclub.org.uk).

- **Bureau des guides de la vallée de Cauterets**
  2 place Georges-Clemenceau, 65110 Cauterets.
  ☏05 62 92 62 02.
- **Bureau des guides de la vallée de Luz**
  1 pl du 8-Mai, 65120 Luz-St-Sauveur.
  ☏05 62 92 87 28.
- **Bureau des guides de la vallée d'Aure** 65170 St-Lary-Soulan.
  ☏05 62 40 02 58.
- **Bureau des guides des vallées d'Ax**
  11 rue du Gén.-de-Gaulle, 09110 Ax-les-Thermes.
  ☏05 61 64 31 51.

Useful tips

Always bear ski-slope etiquette in mind when out on the piste: never set off without checking that the way uphill and downhill is clear; never ignore signposts; beware of the danger of avalanches on loosely packed snow (especially skiing off-piste). If in any doubt, check the rules at the ski resort before setting off.

ROCK CLIMBING

The Pyrenees, the Cévennes, and even the deep Tarn Gorges provide excellent conditions for rock climbing with the assistance of local guides (*see above*). Beginners should take advantage of the numerous courses available to learn a few basic techniques. For additional information, contact:

- **Fédération Française de la Montagne et de l'Escalade**,
  8-10 quai de la Marne, 75019 Paris,
  ☏01 40 18 75 50; www.ffme.fr.

The *Guide des sites naturels d'escalade en France* by D Taupin (published by Cosiroc/FFME) provides the location of all the rock-climbing sites in France.

SKIING

When it comes to snow adventure, the resorts in the south of France have long been regarded as the poor relation to the Alps. Yet there is excellent downhill and cross-country skiing, snowboarding and snow-shoeing to be enjoyed here, not least among the **Pyrenees**, which remain largely under-valued by winter sports enthusiasts, and are a prized location, offering fresh, varied pistes – as well as some highly regarded off-piste runs – enjoyed mainly by locals. Indeed, the whole range of the Pyrenees and the mountain uplands of the **Aubrac**, **Lozère** and the **Cévennes** to the north, lend themselves perfectly to all forms of winter snow activities.
The **Cévennes** are not as high or as developed as the Pyrenean resorts, but still offer excellent cross-country skiing and down-hill runs.
The most convenient **Lozère** ski station is Prat Peyrot on Mount Aigoual, which, at 1 500m/4 921ft above sea level, enjoys claims that from the summit you can see the Mediterranean on one side and the Atlantic on the other. The **Aubrac** is mainly a domain for cross-country skiing, with 200km/124mi of signposted trails linking Brameloup, Nasbinals, Aubrac, Saint-Urcize and Laguiole.

Skiing in the Languedoc Roussillon is remarkably cheap compared with the Alps, but they are just as well equipped, and offer downhill skiing, cross-country skiing, tobogganing and sledging, country snow hiking, and even treks with dog sleighs for the very fit. The station at Mas de la Barque specialises in cross-country. Among the Pyrenees in particular, there is remarkably little evidence of the overcrowding experienced in the Alps (except at weekends), and so these dramatic mountains offer a care-free skiing experience amid scenery every bit as dramatic and inspiring as the Alps. Because development to accommodate skiers has been gradual, most Pyrenean resorts have avoided descending into unsightly, charmless places, and many retain an atmosphere of village identity and beauty. Significant investment in lift systems and the improved quality of the accommodation means the gap between the Alps and the Pyrenees is closing all the time.

In the **Pyrenees** there are over 50 skiing resorts to choose from, most notably Tourmalet and La Mongie, the biggest linked resort with more than 100km/62mi of slopes and a 1000m/3281ft off-piste descent from the Pic du Midi observatory. Font Romeu is one of the oldest ski resorts not only in the Pyrenees but in Europe, dating back to the 1920s, and it remains a justly popular destination today. For après ski try the lively towns of Cauterets, Saint Lary-Soulan, Luz-Ardiden, Luchon or Les Angles. Gentler slopes are also being used above Gavarnie, making the most of the 'alpine' pastures that are lush with flowers in the summer months.

The principality of **Andorra** has long been a popular goal for skiers originally drawn by the duty-free status looking for cheap après ski and budget holiday destinations. Andorran ski schools have an excellent reputation for good English-speaking instructors, and the result of continuing investment in the facilities and infrastructure has been to provide Andorra with some of the most modern, efficient lift systems in Europe. Grand Valira is the linked ski area of Pas de la Casa and Soldeu el Tarter, and has just started expanding into France. The other linked area is Vallnord, which includes Pal-Arinsal, Ordino-Arcalis and La Massana. You can also try cross-country skiing at La Rabassa.

Snowboarding in the Pyrénées

HANG-GLIDING, PARAGLIDING AND KITE-FLYING

On **hang-gliders** *(deltaplanes)*, fliers skillfully suspend themselves from what is little more than a rudimentary, kite-like wing.

Almost anyone with the willpower to jump off a cliff can give **paragliding** *(parapente)* a try (with the assistance of trained professionals, of course).

A number of centres offer instruction and rent equipment, particularly around Millau, in the Grands Causses, around Marvejols and Mende and in the Pyrenees (Barèges, Campan, Peyragudes, Superbagnères, Moulis near St-Girons, Prat d'Albi near Foix).

Kite-flying is a popular activity in the region, particularly on the beaches.

General information (hang-gliding, paragliding and kite-flying) is available from: **Fédération Française de Vol Libre**, 4 rue de Suisse, 06000 Nice. ✆04 97 03 82 82; www.ffvl.fr.

SPECTATOR SPORT – RUGBY

Rugby is big in the South-West. Every town and village has its team, and passions run high as enthusiastic supporters follow their team's progress in the weekly Sunday matches which take place from October to May. More information is available from the **Fédération Française de Rugby**, 9 rue de Liège, 75431 Paris Cedex 09, ✆01 53 21 15 15; www.ffr.fr.

SPAS

The spa resorts in this region are shown on the map of Places to Stay.

France has long been renowned for its health spas, a popular retreat for many, who could often be granted spa treatment on the French national health service.

The Pyrenees are home to numerous mineral and thermal springs, which have brought fame to the area for their health, restoring qualities since Antiquity. Pyrenean spas fall into two categories: sulphurated or salt water springs.

Sulphurated springs – Waters can reach temperatures up to 80°C/176°F. The main spa resorts in this category are *Cauterets, Bagnères-de-Luchon, Saint-Sauveur, Ax-les-Thermes, Amélie-les-Bains, Bagnols-les-Bains and Balaruc-les-Bains.*

Salt water springs – The main spa resorts in this category are *Ussat-les-Bains, Alet-les-Bains, Le Boulou, Lamalou-les-Bains* and the water in *Avène-les-Bains* makes it particularly suitable for treatment of skin diseases.

USEFUL ADDRESSES

- **Chaîne Thermale du Soleil/ Maison du Thermalisme** 32 avenue de l'Opéra, 75002 Paris, ✆01 44 71 37 00. www.chainethermale.fr.
- **Union Nationale des Établissements Thermaux** 1 rue Cels, 75014 Paris, ✆01 53 91 05 75. www.france-thermale.org.

SEA-WATER THERAPY

Known as *thalassothérapie* in French, this kind of cure has increased in popularity in recent years. The main centres in Languedoc-Roussillon are at **La Grande-Motte**, **Cap-d'Agde**, **Port-Barcarès** and **Banyuls-sur-Mer**.

Useful addresses

- **Fédération Mer et Santé**, 57 rue d'Amsterdam,75008 Paris, ✆01 44 70 07 57; www.mer-et-sante.asso.fr.

ACTIVITIES FOR CHILDREN

In this guide, sights of particular interest to children are indicated with a FAMILY symbol (👪). This region of France has a lot to offer children from swimming and playing in the sand along the sunny Mediterranean coast to having fun in amusement parks or visiting zoos, safari parks, aquariums, museums and sights of special interest.

Aqualand at Cap d'Agde (*p179*) will fascinate children with a liking for all things that swim in the sea, while underground adventure can be had in the **Grotte de Clamouse** (*p107*), and the **Grotte des Demoiselles** (*p108*), where they can also enjoy a simple train ride. Staying on the underground theme, the **Labouiche underground river** (*pp341, 348*) near Foix is quite an experience revealing superb examples of stalagmites and stalactites.

In Carcassonne, children will enjoy an evening stroll or dinner in the medieval city, especially later in the day as the sun goes down and the lights of the modern city below cast an eerie glow into the sky. During the day, take a ride on the **Canal du Midi**, if only to amaze at its ingenuity. In Mont-Louis the **solar furnace** (*p281*) is always popular with children, while a chance to see the **wolves** at Gévaudan (*p140*) should not be missed; arrive before feeding time. The **Réserve Africaine de Sigean** (*p203*), south of Narbonne, is a perfect place to get up close with the wild animals of Africa. Animals of a less fiercesome nature can be hired in Gavarnie, for a simple **pony trek** (*p397*) up to see the magnificent waterfall. On the Parc de la Plaine, just outside Toulouse the **Cité de l'Espace** will entertain children all day.

SHOPPING

BUSINESS HOURS

Most of the larger shops are open Mondays to Saturdays from 9am to 6.30 or 7.30pm. Smaller, individual shops may close during the lunch hour. Hypermarkets usually stay open non-stop from 9am until 9pm or later.

MARKETS

Traditional markets known as *marchés au gras* were previously held in winter months only for the sale of ducks and geese, prepared and raw livers. The most picturesque of these markets are now held in Samatan *(Gers)* on Mondays year-round and in Mirande *(Gers)* on Mondays from November through to March.

LOCAL SPECIALITIES

Gastronomy – Apart from foie gras and confit, the region is rich in gastronomic products: cassoulet from the Toulouse region (tinned), honey from the Cévennes, nougat from Limoux, cured ham and varied charcuterie from the mountainous areas, not forgetting cheeses such as Roquefort and Fourme de Laguiole. The region also offers a choice of red, rosé and white wines, natural sweet wines and stronger tipple such as Armagnac.

Handicraft – Glazed pottery adds a touch of colour to most local markets in the Cévennes and Languedoc regions, whereas the Cerdagne specialises in rope-soled shoes. The Pyrenees are famous for the softness of their woollen blankets and pullovers.

Shopping – Major shopping malls are few and far between, Montpellier and Toulouse being the exceptions. Elsewhere there are numerous shopping opportunities in the narrow streets of Narbonne, Perpignan and Carcassone. But the best shopping experience comes from the countless local and regional markets held every week in virtually every town and village, and which range from small stalls offering produce grown by the man selling it to you, to some of the finest, freshest food and drink produce available. Just walking round the markets, especially that in La Capitole in Toulouse is a memorable and aromatic experience.

J. Malburet/MICHELIN

Handcrafted espadrilles

SIGHTSEEING

TOURIST TRAINS

These are a pleasant and original way of exploring the region. In the Cévennes, a little steam train runs between Anduze and St-Jean-du-Gard, via Prafrance bamboo plantation and following the Gardon rivers.

The **Autorail touristique du Minervois** takes passengers from Narbonne to Bize-Minervois; the train stops in Sallèdes-d'Aude allowing passengers to visit Amphoralis *(see NARBONNE)*.

The **Petit train des Lagunes** links Narbonne and Perpignan via Île Ste-Lucie.

The **Petit train jaune** offers a picturesque journey through the Cerdagne and Conflent regions; it runs between Latour-de-Carol and Villefranche-de-Conflent, once a day each way.

FROM ABOVE

For an aerial view of the region either as passenger or pilot, apply to flying clubs usually located within the perimeter of airports:

- **Fédération Française de Planeur Ultra-léger Motorisé,** 96 bis rue Marc-Sangnier, 94709 Maisons-Alfort. ☎01 49 81 74 43. www.ffplum.com.

COOKING COURSES

A number of farmhouse-inns offer sessions which include lessons on preparing *foie gras, confits, cou farci* and other delights, as well as lodging and board. For information, contact:

- **Loisirs-Accueil du Gers**, Maison de l'agriculture, route de Tarbes, BP 178, 32003 Auch Cedex, ✆05 62 61 79 00.

WINE-TASTING

The Languedoc-Roussillon AOC appellation covers 50,000ha/120,000 acres of vines on the slopes of the garrigue from Narbonne to Nimes, an area that covers 156 communes, of which 5 are in Aude, 14 in Gard and the rest in Hérault. All sizeable vineyards offer the chance of a *dégustation*, or tasting, and while there is no obligation to buy, it's proper to do so.

Information on visiting wine-growing establishments and wine cooperatives.can be obtained from the following addresses:

- **Vins de pays d'Oc**
  Addresses of wine-growers and co-operatives are available from the Syndicat des Producteurs de Vin de Pays d'Oc, Domaine de Manse, avenue Paysagère, Maurin, 34970 Lattes. ✆04 67 13 84 20.

Reserve of vintage wines at Banyuls

L. Campion/MICHELIN

Wine tasting and **guided tours** of vineyards are organised by the:

- **Maison des Vins**, 1 avenue de la Promenade, 34360 St-Chinian. ✆04 67 38 11 69; www.saint-chinian.com. *(tasting of St-Chinian wine daily 9am–noon and 2–6.30pm; S Wine festival on 3rd Sunday in July).*
- **Minervois**, Syndicat du cru Minervois, Château de Siran, ave du Château, 34210 Siran. ✆04 68 27 80 00.
- **Syndicat des vins VDQS Estaing**, 3 rue Flandres Dunkerque, l'Escalière, 12190 Estaing. ✆05 65 44 75 38.
- **Blanquette de Limoux**
  Contact the Syndicat des vins AOC de Limoux, 20 avenue du Pont-de-France. ✆04 68 31 12 83, or the tourist office at Limoux.
- **Cru Fitou**, Maison des vignerons du Fitou, RN 9, aire de la Via Domitia, 11480 La Palme. ✆04 68 40 42 77. www.cru-fitou.com.
  Gaillac, Comission Interprofessionnelle des Vins de Gaillac, Maison des Vins, Abbaye St-Michel, 81600 Gaillac, ✆05 63 57 15 40. www.vins-gaillac.com.
- **Madiran and Pacherenc du Vic-Bilh**
  Maison des vins de Madiran et Pacherenc du Vic-Bilh, Le Prieuré, place de l'Église, 65700 Madiran, ✆05 62 31 90 67.
- **Armagnac and Floc de Gascogne**
  Bureau national interprofessionnel de l'Armagnac AOC, 11 pl de la Liberté, BP 3, 32800 Eauze, www.armagnac.fr. ✆05 62 08 11 00. Maison du Floc de Gascogne, rue des Vignerons, 32800 Eauze, ✆05 62 09 85 41. www.floc-de-gascogne.fr.

RIVER AND CANAL CRUISING

Take a boat trip of a few hours or more on the lakes of the Narbonne region, down the River Tarn, along the Canal du Midi or along the coast from Sète. Rivers, canals and lakes offer numerous possibilities to enjoy pleasant boat trips, thus slowing down the pace and alleviating the stress of a busy touring holiday.

- **Trips aboard a passenger barge**, see *CASTRES and ALBI*.
- **Trips on the Garonne and Canal du Midi**, Péniche Baladine and Le Capitole, see *TOULOUSE*.
- **Trips on the Canal du Midi**, **Bateau Lucie**, see *Canal du MIDI*.
- **Trips on the River Baïse**, **Gascogne-Navigation**, see *CONDOM*.
- **Trips down the River Tarn**, see *Gorges du TARN*. **Sea trips**, see *SÈTE*.

House-boats

House-boats with a capacity for six to eight people enable visitors to get a different perspective on the canals of the region. Nautical maps and plan-guides are available from:

- **Éditions Grafocarte-Navicarte**
  125 rue Jean-Jacques Rousseau, BP 40, 92132 Issy-les-Moulineaux Cedex, 01 41 09 19 00. Order the guide "Canaux du Midi" in English: www.guide-fluvial.com).
- **Éditions du Plaisancier**
  43 porte du Grand-Lyon, Neyron 01707 Miribel Cedex, 04 72 01 58 68.

Companies from which houseboats can be **hired** (or contact local tourist offices for information):

- **Adnavis**, La Maison du Canal, 80 Grand'rue, 34290 Servian. 04 67 90 95 51. www.adnavis.com.
- **Camargue Plaisance**, Base fluviale de Carnon, 34280 Carnon. 04 67 50 77 00.
- **Crown Blue Line**
  Port Cassafières, 34420 Portiragnes. 04 67 90 91 70, or Le grand bassin, BP 1201, 11492 Castelnaudry. 04 68 94 52 72. www.crownblueline.com.

House-boat on Canal du Midi

L. Cazenave/MICHELIN

- **Locaboat Plaisance**
  Port Occitanie, 11120 Argens-Minervois. 04 68 27 03 33; reservations 03 86 91 72 72. www.locaboat.com.
- **Nicols:** Route du Puy St Bonnet - 49300 CHOLET (reservations 02 41 56 46 56). www.nicols.com.
- **Rives de France**, Port de plaisance, 34440 Colombiers, 04 67 37 14 60. www.rivedefrance.com.

NATIONAL AND REGIONAL NATURE PARKS

The reception and information centre for the **Parc national des Cévennes**, Château de Florac, 6 bis place du Palais, 48400 Florac, 04 66 49 53 01. Go to *www.bsi.fr* and click on the Parc national des Cévennes link. Useful information on the park includes the Institut Géographique National (IGN) maps at a scale of 1:100 000 or 1:25 000, "Topo-guides" of the long-distance footpaths which cross the region and the tourist guide "Parc national des Cévennes" *(description and map,* *see Le PONT-DE-MONTVERT in the Sights section)*.
For information on the **Parc national des Pyrénées**, apply to 59 route de Pau, 65000 Tarbes, 05 62 44 36 60; www.parc-pyrenees.com. Several *Maisons du Parc* throughout the park provide information on the park's flora

and fauna and on rambling opportunities in this mountainous area (*description and map, see Parc national des PYRÉNÉES in the Sights section).*

The information centre of the **Parc Naturel Régional du Haut-Languedoc**, Maison du tourisme du Parc, place fu Foirail, 34220 St-Pons-de-Thomières, 04 67 97 06 65 *(description and map, see SAINT-PONS-DE-THOMIÈRES in the Discovering section).*

The **Parc Naturel Régional des Grands Causses**, 1, pl du Beffroi, BP 331, 12101 Millau Cedex, 05 65 60 02 42 *(description and map, see MILLAU in the Sights section).*

BOOKS

Travels with a Donkey in the Cévennes. Robert Louis Stevenson, 1879. One of the classic travel books. Penned by Stevenson while still in his 20s, it tells of his epic 12-day 120-mile hike with a donkey through the mountains of the Cévennes.

Notes from the Languedoc. Rupert Wright, 2003. A beautifully crafted collection of anecdotes about Languedoc, originally written as letters for the author's grandmother. A gem!

Virgile's Vineyard. Patrick Moon, 2003. The story of a year in the Languedoc wine country; enthusiastic, informative, and above all throughly entertaining.

Rick Stein's French Odyssey. Rick Stein, 2005. The TV chef's account of his sedate journey at 4mph on a canal barge called 'The Anjodi' through the Languedoc-Roussillon along the Canal du Midi. Stein focuses on country food prepared from ingredients found in local markets.

French Leaves: Letters from the Languedoc. Christopher Campbell-Howes, 2002. Retired headmaster from Scotland evokes the scents, sights and sounds, the vibrant colours and earthy vitality of the area with British detachment.

In the High Pyrenees: A new life in a mountain village. Bernard Loughlin, 2003. A loving and hilarious account of the sensations and intrigues of a mountain village.

FILMS

Bernadette 1988. Actress Sydney Penny gives a poignant performance as the teenager Bernadette Soubirous, who has visions of the 'Lady in White' – the Virgin Mary – in a cave at Lourdes. Shot in and around the pilgrimage site and the local Pyrenean villages in winter.

Calendar of Events

Many Regional Tourist Offices publish brochures listing local fêtes, fairs and festivals. Most places hold festivities for France's National Day (14 July) and 15 August, a public holiday, but almost all towns and villages enjoy a plethora of reasons for dropping everything and having a party. Enquire locally.

FEBRUARY

Toulouse

"Fête de la Violette" (violet festival). 05 62 16 31 31.

Limoux

Traditional carnival every weekend (and Shrove Tuesday). All-night *"Blanquette"* party follows. 04 68 31 11 82. www.limoux.fr.

Prats-de-Mollo, St-Laurent-de-Cerdans, Arles-sur-Tech

Traditional carnival. 04 68 39 70 83. www.pratsdemollolapreste.com.

MARCH-APRIL

Toulouse

Laughter in springtime. 05 62 21.23 24. www.printempsdurire.com.

APRIL (TO OCTOBER)

Parc national des Cévennes

Nature festival: themed walks, exhibitions, shows, markets. ✆04 66 49 53 01. www.cevennes-parcnational.fr.

MAY

Aubrac

"Fête de la transhumance": Seasonal shepherd's festival held on the weekend nearest to the 25th May. ✆ 05 65 44 21 15. www.traditionsenaubrac.com.

JUNE

Perpignan

Saint-Jean Festa Major (with mid-summer bonfires around 21 June). ✆04 68 66 30 30. www.perpignantourisme.com.

Toulouse

Festival Rio Loco: rock, jazz, pop, tango dancing. ✆05 61 32 77 28. www.rio-loco.org.

Montpellier

International Festival of Dance. ✆0 800 600 740. www.montpellierdanse.com.

Maguelone

Festival of ancient and baroque music (1st two weeks). ✆04 67 60 69 92.

JULY

Carcassonne

Festival of the City: Medieval Cité is "set alight" by an evening firework display; classical music concerts, theatre, opera, dance, jazz (14 July). ✆04 68 11 59 15. www.festivaldecarcassonne.com.

Céret

International Sardana festival (400 dancers in costume; 2nd fortnight). ✆04 68 87 00 53.

Cordes-sur-Ciel

"Fête médiévale du Grand Fauconnnier" (historical pageant and entertainments (mid July). ✆05 63 56 34 63. www.grandfauconnier.com.

Fête de la transhumance, Aubrac

M.-H. Carcanague/MICHELIN

Cap d'Agde

"Fête de la Mer" (sea festival; last weekend). ✆ 04 67 01 04 04. www.capdagde.com.

Frontignan

"Festival du Muscat" (mid month). ✆04 67 18 31 60. www.tourisme-frontignan.com.

Luz-St-Sauveur

"Jazz à Luz" (early July) ✆05 62 92 38 30. www.jazzaluz.com.

Montauban

Jazz festival. (2nd fortnight) ✆05 63 63 56 56. www.jazzmontauban.com.

Montpellier

"Festival de Radio-France et de Montpellier Languedoc-Roussillon" opera, symphonies, chamber music, jazz (2nd fortnight). ✆04 67 61 66 81. www.festivalradiofrancemont pellier.com.

Perpignan

"Estivales" (theatre festival). ✆04 68 66 30 30. www.estivales.com.

St-Guilhem-le-Désert

Musical season at the abbey (1st fortnight). ✆04 67 96 86 19. www.st-guilhem-le-Desert.com.

Poster of the Féria in Béziers

S. Quillon/MICHELIN

JULY – AUGUST

Agde
"*Joutes nautiques*" (water jousting). 04 67 94 44 73.

Lastours
Son et lumière show. 04 68 77 56 01.

Moissac
Musical evenings. 05 63 04 63 85.

Sète
Festival of St Louis – jousting, fireworks. 0 4 67 74 48 44. www.fiestasete.com.

Prades: St-Michel-de-Cuxa
Pablo Casals festival (concerts in the abbey, mid-July to mid-August). 04 68 96 33 07. www.prades-festival-casals.com.

St-Bertrand-de-Comminges, St-Just-de-Valcabrère, St-Gaudens, Martres-Tolosane.
"*Festival du Comminges*", classical music, chamber music. 05 61 88 32 00. www.festival-du-comminges.com.

AUGUST

Bagnères-de-Luchon
Flower festival (last Sunday). 05 61 94 68 86.

Banyuls-sur-Mer
Sardana festival (2nd weekend). 06 12 36 94 57. www.banyuls-sur-mer.com.

Béziers
"*Féria*" (around 15 August). 04 67 36 76 76. www.ville-beziers.fr.

Bouzigues
Oyster fair (1st or 2nd weekend in the month). 04 67 78 3 2 93.

Mirepoix
Puppet festival (1st weekend). 05 61 68 83 76. www.mirepoix.fr.

Palavas-les-Flots
Jousting by night on canal (15 Aug)

Pont de Salers and other villages
International folklore festival (5th–12th). 05 65 46 80 67. www.festival-rouergue.com.

Vic-Fezensac
Feria (1st week).
Medieval festival (3rd weekend). 05 61 68 83 76.

SEPTEMBER

Méritxell
National festival of Andorra. (8 Sept)

Toulouse
Piano recitals at Les Jacobins. 05 61 22 40 05. www.pianojacobins.com.

OCTOBER

Montpellier
International fair. 04 67 17 67 17. www.enjoy-montpellier.com..

Perpignan
Jazz festival; 04 68 86 08 51. www.jazzebre.com.

Sauveterre-de-Rouergue
Chestnut and cider festival 05 65 72 02 52.

Know Before You Go

USEFUL WEBSITES

www.sunfrance.com
A dedicated, multi-language website for Languedoc-Roussillon. All the practical information you might need for a stay in the region.

www.franceguide.com
The **French Government Tourist Office/Maison de la France** site is packed with practical information and tips for those travelling to France. The home page has a number of links to more specific guidance, for American or Canadian travellers for example, or to the FGTO's London pages.

www.fr-holidaystore.co.uk
The **Travel Centre in London** has gone on-line with this service, providing information on all of the regions of France, including updated special travel offers and details on available accommodation.

www.FranceKeys.com
This site has plenty of practical information for visiting France. It covers all the regions, with links to tourist offices and related sites. Very useful for planning the details of your tour in France!

www.franceway.com
This is an online magazine which focuses on culture and heritage. For each region, there are also suggestions for activities and practical information on where to stay and how to get there.

www.ambafrance-uk.org
The **French Embassy**'s website provides basic information (geography, demographics, history), a news digest and business-related information. It offers special pages for children, and pages devoted to culture, language study and travel, and you can reach other selected French sites (regions, cities, ministries) with a hypertext link.

www.F-T-S.co.uk
The French Travel Service specialises in organising holidays in France using the rail network. Let FTS organise your travel and hotels anywhere in France.

www.pyrenees-online.fr
This regional site has a mine of information about accommodation, ski resorts and activities in the Pyrenees mountains.

www.randonnees-ariege.com
This site focuses on walking and hiking in the Ariège, offering some 50 different itineraries in the area.

TOURIST OFFICES ABROAD

Australia – New Zealand
Sydney – Level 13, 25 Bligh Street, Sydney, New South Wales 2000
✆(02) 9231 5244
Fax: (02) 9221 8682.

Canada
Montreal –
1800 Avenue McGill College
Suite 1010, Montreal,
Quebec H3A 3J6
✆(514) 288-2026
Fax: (514) 845 4868.

Ireland
No office ✆+15 60 235 235
(Irish information line);
http://ie.franceguide.com.

South Africa
3rd floor, Village Walk, Office Tower, cnr Maude and Rivonia, Sandton ✆(0) 11 523 82 92;
http://za.franceguide.com.

United Kingdom
London Maison de France –
Lincoln House, 300 High Holborn,
London WC1V 7JH
✆(09068) 244 123;
Fax: 020 7061 6646;
http://uk.franceguide.com.

United States
http://us.franceguide.com
New York – 825 Third Avenue, 29th floor (entrance on 50th Street), New York NY 10022
France-on-Call Hotline (514) 288 1904
Los Angeles – 9454 Wilshire Blvd, Suite 210, 90212 Beverly Hills, CA 310-271-6665
Chicago – Consulate General of France, 205 N Michigan Ave., Suite 3770, 60601 Chicago, Illinois 312 327 0290

TOURIST OFFICES

Visitors may also contact local tourist offices for more precise information, and to receive brochures and maps. The addresses and telephone numbers of tourist offices in the larger towns are listed after the symbol ℹ. Below, the addresses are given for local tourist offices of the *départements* and *régions* covered in this guide.

For each département within the region, address inquiries to the Comité départemental de tourisme (CDT):

- **Ariège**
  31 bis av. du Gén.-de-Gaulle, BP 143 09000, Foix
  05 61 02 30 70
  www.ariegepyrenees.com
- **Aude**
  Allée Raymond Courrière
  Carcassonne Cedex 9
  04 68 11 66 00
  www.audetourisme.com
- **Aveyron**
  17 rue Aristide-Briand, BP 831
  12008 Rodez, 05 65 75 55 70
  www.tourisme-aveyron.com
- **Gard**
  3 rue Cité Foule, BP 122
  30010 Nîmes Cedex 04
  04 66 36 96 30
  www.tourismegard.com
- **Gers**
  3 boulevard Roquelaure, BP 106
  32002 Auch Cedex
  05 62 05 95 95
  www.tourisme-gers.com
- **Haute-Garonne**
  14 rue Bayard, BP 71509
  31015 Toulouse Cedex 6
  05 61 99 44 00.
  www.tourisme-haute-garonne.com
- **Hautes-Pyrénées**
  Htes-Pyrénées Tourisme Environnement, 11 rue Gaston-Manent, BP 9502
  65950 Tarbes Cedex 9
  05 62 56 70 65, www.tourisme-hautes-pyrenees.com
- **Hérault**
  avenue des Moulins
  34034 Montpellier Cedex 4
  04 67 67 71 71
  www.herault-tourisme.com
- **Lozère**
  14 boulevard Henri-Bourillon, BP 4 48001 Mende Cedex
  04 66 65 60 00
  www.lozere-tourisme.com
- **Pyrénées-Orientales**
  16 avenue des Palmiers, BP 80540
  66005 Perpignan Cedex
  04 68 51 52 53
  www.cdt-66.com
- **Tarn**
  41 rue Porta, BP 225.
  81006 Albi Cedex
  05 63 77 32 10
  www.tourisme-tarn.com
- **Tarn-et-Garonne**
  15 boulevard Midi-Pyrénées
  82005 Montauban Cedex
  05 63 21 79 65
  www.tourisme82.com

Regional tourist offices

- **Midi-Pyrénées:**
  54 boulevard de l'Embouchure, BP 52166, 31022 Toulouse 2,
  05 61 13 55 48
  www.tourisme-midi-pyrenees.co.uk

- **Languedoc-Roussillon:** 954, Avenue Jean Mermoz 34960 Montpellier, 04 67 20 02 20 www.sunfrance.com

See the Principal Sights in the *Discovering the Region* section for the addresses and telephone numbers of the local tourist offices *(Syndicats d'Initiative)*. Eight towns and areas, labelled **Villes et Pays d'Art et d'Histoire** by the Ministry of Culture, are mentioned in this guide (Lectoure, Mende, Montauban, Narbonne, Perpignan, Pézenas, Toulouse and the Têt Valley). More information is available from local tourist offices and from *www.vpah.culture.fr.*

INTERNATIONAL VISITORS

EMBASSIES AND CONSULATES

Australia Embassy
4 rue Jean-Rey, 75724 Paris Cedex.
01 40 59 33 00
france.embassy.gov.au.

Canada Embassy
35 avenue Montaigne, 75008 Paris
01 44 43 29 00
Fax: 01 44 43 29 99

Ireland Embassy
4 rue Rude, 75116 Paris
01 44 17 67 00
paris@dfa.ie.

New Zealand Embassy
7 ter rue Léonard-de-Vinci,
75116 Paris
01 45 00 24 11.
nzembassy.paris@wanadoo.fr

UK Embassy
35 rue du Faubourg St-Honoré,
75383 Paris Cedex 08.
01 44 51 31 00.
www.britishembassy.gov.uk.

UK Consulate
1b bis, rue d'Anjou,
75008 Paris
01 44 51 31 02. (visas)
www.amb-grandebretagne.fr.

USA Embassy
2 avenue Gabriel,
75382 Paris Cedex.
01 43 12 22 22. www.amb-usa.fr.

USA Consulate
2 rue St-Florentin,
75382 Paris
01 43 12 22 22. www.amb-usa.fr.

ENTRY REQUIREMENTS

Passport

Nationals of countries within the European Union entering France need only a national identity card. Nationals of other countries must be in possession of a valid national **passport**. In case of loss or theft, report to your embassy or consulate and the local police.

Visa

No **entry visa** is required for Canadian, US or Australian citizens travelling as tourists and staying fewer than 90 days, except for students planning to study in France. If you think you may need a visa, apply to your local French Consulate.

US citizens should obtain the booklet *Safe Trip Abroad*, which provides useful information on visa requirements, customs regulations, medical care etc for international travellers. Published by the **Government Printing Office**, it can be ordered by phone ((202) 512-1800) or consulted online (www.access.gpo.gov). General passport information is available by phone toll-free from the **Federal Information Center** (item 5 on the automated menu), *800-688-9889*. US passport application forms can be downloaded from *http://travel.state.gov.*

CUSTOMS REGULATIONS

Apply to the Customs Office (UK) for a leaflet on customs regulations and the full range of duty-free allowances; available from **HM Customs and Excise**, *Thomas Paine House, Angel Square, Torrens Street, London EC1V 1TA, 08450 109 000.* The **US Customs Service** offers a publication *Know Before You Go* for US citizens: for your

DUTY-FREE ALLOWANCES	
Spirits (whisky, gin, vodka etc)	10 litres
Fortified wines (vermouth, port etc)	20 litres
Wine (not more than 60 bottles sparkling)	90 litres
Beer	110 litres
Cigarettes	800
Cigarillos	400
Cigars	200
Smoking Tobacco	1 kg

nearest office, consult the phone book, Federal Government, US Treasury *(www.customs.ustreas.gov)*.
There are no customs formalities for holidaymakers bringing their caravans or pleasure boats into France for a stay of less than six months but the registration certificate should be available.
Americans can take home, tax-free, up to US$ 400 worth of goods (limited quantities of alcohol and tobacco products); Canadians up to CND$ 300; Australians up to AUS$ 400 and New Zealanders up to NZ$ 700.
Residents from a member state of the European Union are not restricted with regard to purchasing goods for private use, but the recommended allowances for alcoholic beverages and tobacco are as follows:

HEALTH

First aid, medical advice and chemists' night service rota are available from chemists/drugstores *(pharmacie)* identified by the green cross sign.
You should take out comprehensive insurance coverage as the recipient of medical treatment in French hospitals or clinics must pay. **Nationals of non-EU countries** should check with their insurance companies about policy limitations. All prescription drugs should be clearly labelled; it is essential that you carry a copy of prescriptions.
British and **Irish citizens** (and all EU citizens) should apply for a European Health Insurance Card (EHIC), which entitles the holder to treatment for accident or unexpected illness in EU countries. **British citizens** apply online at www.dh.gov.uk/travellers, or telephone 0845 606 2030. **Irish citizens** should consult www.ehic.ie.
Americans and **Canadians** can contact the **International Association for Medical Assistance to Travelers**, which can also provide details of English-speaking doctors in different parts of France: ✆ for the US (716) 754-4883; for Canada (416) 652 0137. www.iamat.org.
The American Hospital of Paris is open 24hr for emergencies as well as consultations, with English-speaking staff, at 63 boulevard Victor-Hugo, 92200 Neuilly-sur-Seine, ✆01 46 41 25 25. Accredited by major insurance companies. www.american-hospital.org.
The British Hospital is just outside Paris in Levallois-Perret, 3 rue Barbès, ✆01 46 39 22 22. www.british-hospital.org.

ACCESSIBILITY

The sights described in this guide which are easily accessible to people of reduced mobility are indicated in the *Admission times and charges* by this symbol: ♿.
Since 2001, the designation **Tourisme at Handicap** has applied to a thousand sites accessible to the disabled: go to www.franceguide.com.
The principal French source for information on facilities is the **Association des Paralysés de France**, www.apf.asso.fr.
On **TGV and Corail trains**, operated by the national railway (SNCF), there are special wheelchair slots in 1st class carriages available to holders of 2nd-class tickets. On **Eurostar** and Thalys special rates are available for accompanying adults. All **airports** are equipped to receive less abled passengers.
Web-surfers can find information for slow walkers, mature travellers and others with special needs at www.access-able.com.

For information on museum access for the disabled contact La Direction, Les Musées de France, Service Accueil des Publics Spécifiques, 6 rue des Pyramides, 75041 Paris Cedex 1, ℘01 40 15 35 88.

The **Michelin Guide France** and the **Michelin Camping Caravaning France** indicate hotels and campsites with facilities suitable for physically handicapped people.

Getting There and Getting Around

BY PLANE

The various international and other independent airlines operate services to **Paris** (Roissy-Charles de Gaulle and Orly airports), **Montpellier** and **Toulouse**. Check with your travel agent, however, before booking direct flights, as it may be cheaper to travel via Paris. Air France *(℘0820 820 820; www.airfrance.fr)*, links Paris to Montpellier, Béziers-Agde and Toulouse several times a day. Other airlines offering flights to several towns in the region include British Airways, Flybe, EasyJet and Ryanair.

Contact airline companies and travel agents for details of package tour flights with a rail or coach link-up as well as fly-drive schemes.

BY SHIP

There are numerous **cross-Channel services** (passenger and car ferries) from the United Kingdom and Ireland, as well as the rail Shuttle through the Channel Tunnel **(Le Shuttle-Eurotunnel**, ℘08705 35 35 35, www.eurotunnel.com).

To choose the most suitable route between your port of arrival and your destination use the Michelin Tourist and Motoring Atlas France, Michelin map 726 (which gives travel times and mileages) or Michelin maps from the 1:200 000 series (with the yellow cover).

For details apply to travel agencies or to:

- **P&O Ferries** ℘08716 645 645 (UK dialling), or 0825 120 156 (in France), www.poferries.com. Service, between Dover and Calais.
- **Norfolk Line** ℘0844 847 5042 www.norfolkline-ferries.co.uk. Service, between Dover and Dunkerque.
- **Brittany Ferries** ℘0871 244 0744 (in UK); 0825 828 828 (in France). www.brittany-ferries.com. Services from Portsmouth, Poole and Plymouth.
- **LD Lines**, ℘0844 576 8836, www.ldlines.co.uk. Services from Portsmouth, Dover and Rosslare.
- **Condor Ferries**, ℘01202 207216, www.condorferries.co.uk. Services from Weymouth, Poole and Portsmouth.
- **Seafrance** ℘0871 22 22 500. www.seafrance.com. Services between Dover and Calais.

BY TRAIN

All rail services throughout France can be arranged through **Rail Europe** in the UK, online (www.raileurope.co.uk), by telephone ℘0844 848 4070, or call into the Rail Europe Travel Centre at 1 Regent Street, London SW1. Rail Europe can also book Eurostar travel. **Eurostar** runs from **London** (St Pancras) to **Paris** (Gare du Nord) in under 3hr (up to 20 times daily). In Paris it links to the high-speed rail network (TGV) which covers most of France. There is fast inter-city service from **Paris** (Gare Montparnasse) to **Vendôme** *(45min)*, **Le Mans** *(50min)*, **Tours** *(1hr)* and **Angers** *(1hr 30min)* on the TGV.

Bookings and information ✆08705 186 186 (£5 booking fee applies) in the UK, www.eurostar.com.

Citizens of non-European Economic Area countries will need to complete a landing card before arriving at Eurostar check-in. These landing cards can be found at dedicated desks in front of the check-in area and from Eurostar staff. Once you have filled in the card please hand it to UK immigration staff.

Eurailpass, **Flexipass**, **Eurailpass Youth**, **EurailDrive Pass** and **Saverpass** are travel passes which may be purchased by residents of countries outside the European Union. In the US, contact your travel agent or **Rail Europe** 2100 Central Ave. Boulder, CO, 80301, ✆1-800-4-EURAIL or **Europrail International** ✆1 888 667 9731. If you are a European resident, you can buy an individual country pass, if you are not a resident of the country where you plan to use it.

Information on schedules can be obtained on websites for these agencies and the **SNCF**, respectively: www.raileurop.com.us, www.eurail.on.ca, www.sncf.fr. At the SNCF site, you can book ahead, pay with a credit card, and receive your ticket in the mail.

There are numerous **discounts** available when you purchase your tickets in France, from 25–50% below the regular rate. These include discounts for using senior cards and youth cards, and seasonal promotions. There are a limited number of discount seats available during peak travel times, and the best discounts are available for travel during off-peak periods.

Tickets for rail travel in France must be validated (*composter*) by using the (usually) automatic date-stamping machines at the platform entrance (failure to do so may result in a fine).

The French railway company **SNCF** operates a telephone information, reservation and prepayment service in English from 7am to 10pm (French time). In France call ✆08 36 35 35 39 (when calling from outside France, drop the initial 0).

BY COACH/BUS

- **Eurolines (National Express)**
  Ensign Court, 4 Vicarage Road, Edgbaston, Birmingham, B15 3ES. ✆08705 808080. www.nationalexpress.com/eurolines.
  A **Disabled Persons Travel Helpline** is available on ✆08717 818170. A textphone is provided for customers who are deaf or hard of hearing on ✆0121 455 0086.
- **Eurolines (Paris)**
  Ave du General de Gaulle 93177 Bagnolet.
  ✆892 89 90 91.
  www.eurolines.fr
- **www.eurolines.com** is an international web site with information about travelling all over Europe by coach (bus).

BY CAR

ROUTE PLANNING

The area covered in this guide is easily reached by main motorways and national routes. **Michelin map 726** indicates the main itineraries as well as alternate routes for avoiding heavy traffic during busy holiday periods, and gives estimated travel times. **Michelin map 723** is a detailed atlas of French motorways, indicating tolls, rest areas and services along the route; it includes a table for calculating distances and times. The Michelin route-planning service is available at **www.ViaMichelin.com**. Travellers can calculate a precise route using such options as shortest route, route avoiding toll roads, Michelin-recommended route and gain access to tourist information (hotels, restaurants, attractions).

The roads are very busy during the holiday period (particularly weekends in July and August) and, to avoid traffic congestion it is advisable to follow the recommended secondary routes (signposted as *Bison Futé – itinéraires bis)*. The motorway network includes rest areas *(aires de repos)* and petrol stations *(stations-service)*, with restaurant and shopping complexes attached, about every 40km/25mi.

DOCUMENTS

Travellers from other European Union countries and North America can drive in France with a valid national or home-state **driving licence**.
An **international driving licence** is useful because the information on it appears in nine languages (keep in mind that traffic officers are empowered to fine motorists). A permit is available (US$10) from the **National Automobile Club**, 1151 East Hillsdale Blvd., Foster City, CA 94404, ✆650-294-7000 or http://nationalautoclub.com/; or contact your local branch of the **American Automobile Association**. For the vehicle, it is necessary to have the registration papers and a nationality plate of the approved size.

INSURANCE

Certain motoring organisations (AAA, AA, RAC and The Caravan Club) offer accident **insurance** and breakdown service schemes for members. Check with your current insurance company in regard to coverage while abroad. If you plan to hire a car using your credit card, check with the company, which may provide liability insurance automatically (and thus save you having to pay the cost for optimum coverage).

ROAD REGULATIONS

The minimum driving age is 18.
Traffic drives on the right.
All passengers must wear **seat belts**. Children under the age of 10 must ride in the back seat. Headlights must be switched on in poor visibility and at night; dipped headlights should be used at all times outside built up areas. Use side-lights only when the vehicle is stationary. In the case of a **breakdown**, a red warning triangle or hazard warning lights are obligatory as are reflective safety jackets. In the absence of stop signs at intersections, cars must **give way to the right**. Traffic on main roads outside built-up areas (priority indicated by a yellow diamond sign) and on roundabouts has right of way. Vehicles must stop when the lights turn red at road junctions and may filter to the right only when indicated by an amber arrow. The regulations on **drinking and driving** (limited to 0.50g/l) and **speeding** are strictly enforced – usually by an on-the-spot fine and/or confiscation of the vehicle.

Speed limits

Although liable to modification, these are as follows:

- **toll motorways** (autoroutes) 130kph/80mph (110kph/68mph when raining);
- **dual carriageways and motorways without tolls** 110kph/68mph (100kph/62mph when raining);
- **other roads 90kph/56mph** (80kph/50mph when raining) and in towns 50kph/31mph;
- **outside lane on motorways** during daylight, on level ground and with good visibility – minimum speed limit of 80kph/50mph.

CAR RENTAL

There are car rental agencies at airports, railway stations and in all large towns throughout France.
European cars have manual transmission; automatic cars are available in larger cities only if an advance reservation is made. Drivers must be over 21; between ages 21–25, drivers are required to pay an extra daily fee; some companies allow drivers under 23 only if the reservation has been made through a travel agent. Take advantage of **fly-drive offers when you buy your ticket**, or seek advice from a travel agent, specifying

RENTAL CARS – CENTRAL RESERVATION IN FRANCE	
Avis:	✆08 20 05 05 05
Europcar:	✆08 25 35 83 58
Budget France:	✆08 25 00 35 64
Hertz France:	✆01 39 38 38 38
SIXT-Eurorent	✆08 20 00 74 98
National-CITER	✆0825 16 12 20

requirements. There are many online services that will look for the best prices on car rental around the globe. **Nova** can be contacted at *www.rentacar-worldwide.com* or *℘0800 018 6682 (freephone UK)* or *℘44 28 4272 8189 (from outside the UK)*.

PETROL/GASOLINE

French service stations dispense:

- *sans plomb 98* (super unleaded 98)
- *sans plomb 95* (super unleaded 95)
- *diesel/gazole* (diesel)
- *GPL* (LPG).

Prices are listed on signboards on the motorways; fill up off the motorway for better prices; check hypermarkets on the outskirts of towns.

Where to Stay and Eat

Hotel & Restaurant listings fall within the Address Books within the Discovering the Region section of the guide.

WHERE TO STAY

The Green Guide is pleased to offer descriptions of selected lodgings for this region. The Address Books in the *Discovering the Region* section of the guide give descriptions and prices *(based on double ocupancy)* of typical places to stay with local flair. The Legend on the cover flap explains the symbols and prices used in the Address Books. Use the **map of Places to Stay** on the inside cover to identify recommended places for overnight stops. For an even greater selection, use the **Michelin Guide France**, with its famously reliable star-rating system and hundreds of establishments all over France. Book ahead to ensure that you get the accommodation you want. Some places require an advance deposit or a reconfirmation. Reconfirming is especially important if you plan to arrive after 6pm.

For further assistance, **Loisirs Accueil**, (www.loisirsaccueilfrance.com), is a booking service that has offices in some French *départements* – contact the tourist offices listed above for further information.

A guide to good-value, family-run hotels, **Logis et Auberges de France**, (www.logisdefrance.fr), is available from the French Tourist Office, as are lists of other kinds of accommodation such as hotel-châteaux, bed-and-breakfasts, etc.

Relais et châteaux (www.relais chateaux.com), provides information on booking in luxury hotels with character: 15 rue Galvani, 75017 Paris, ℘08 23 32 32 32 (within France).

Economy Chain Hotels

If you need a place to stop en route, these can be useful, as they are inexpensive and generally located near the main road. While breakfast is available, there may not be a restaurant; rooms are small, with a television and bathroom.

Central reservation numbers:

- **Akena** ℘01 69 84 85 17
- **B&B**℘0 892 78 29 29 (inside France); +33 2 98 33 75 00 (from outside France)
- **Etap** ℘0 892 68 89 00
- **Mister Bed** ℘01 46 14 38 00
- **Villages Hôtel** ℘03 80 60 92 70

The hotels listed below are slightly more expensive, and offer a few more amenities and services.

Central reservation number:

- **Campanile** ℘01 64 62 46 46
- **Kyriad** ℘0 825 003 003
- **Ibis** ℘0 825 882 222

Many chains have on-line reservations:
www.etaphotel.com
www.ibishotel.com

RENTING A COTTAGE, BED AND BREAKFAST

The **Maison des Gîtes de France** is an information service on self-catering accommodation in France. Gîtes usually take the form of a cottage or apartment, or bed and breakfast accommodation *(chambres d'hôtes)*. Contact the **Gîtes de France** office in Paris: 59 rue St-Lazare, 75439 Paris Cedex 09, ✆01 49 70 75 75, www.gites-de-france.fr, or their representative in the UK, **Brittany Ferries** *(address above)*. From the site, you can order catalogues for different regions illustrated with photographs of the properties, as well as specialised catalogues (bed and breakfasts, farm stays etc). You can also contact the local tourist offices.

The **Fédération nationale Clévacances**, 54 boulevard de l'Embouchure, BP 52166, 31022 Toulouse Cedex 2, ✆05 61 13 55 66, www.clevacances.com, offers a wide choice of accommodation throughout France. It publishes a brochure for each *département*.

The **Fédération des Stations vertes de vacances** (6 rue Ranfer-de-Bretenières, BP 71698, 21016 Dijon Cedex, ✆03 80 54 10 50; www.stationsvertes.com) is an association which promotes 865 rural localities throughout France, selected for their natural appeal as well as for the quality of their environment, of their accommodation and of the leisure activities available.

FARM HOLIDAYS

The guide *Bienvenue à la ferme*, lists the addresses of farms providing guest facilities, which have been vetted for quality and for meeting official standards. For more information, apply to local tourist offices *(addresses above)* or to Service Agriculture et tourisme, 9 avenue George-V, 75008 Paris, ✆01 53 57 11 44; www.bienvenue-a-la-ferme.com.

HOSTELS, CAMPING

To obtain an **International Youth Hostel Federation** card (there is no age requirement) you should contact the IYHF in your own country for information and membership applications (US ✆202 783 6161; England ✆01707 324170; Scotland ✆01786 891400; Canada ✆613-273 7884; Australia ✆61-2-9565-1669). There is a booking service, www.hihostels.com, which you may use to reserve rooms as far as six months in advance.

The main youth hostel association *(auberges de jeunesse)* in France is the **Ligue Française pour les Auberges de la Jeunesse**, 67 rue Vergniaud, 75013 Paris, ✆01 44 16 78 78; www.auberges-de-jeunesse.com.

There are numerous officially graded **campsites** with varying standards of facilities throughout the Languedoc-Roussillon region. The **Michelin Camping France** guide lists a selection of campsites. The area is very popular with campers in the summer months, so it is wise to reserve in advance.

WALKERS

Walkers can consult the guide, *Gîtes d'Étapes et Refuges* by A and S Mouraret, which can be ordered from: www.gites-refuges.com.

This guide, which lists 4000 places to stay, also contains much information to help with planning itineraries and is intended for those who enjoy walking, cycling, climbing, skiing and canoeing-kayaking holidays.

WHERE TO EAT

The Green Guide is pleased to offer a selection of restaurants for this region. The Address Books in the *Discovering the Region* section of the guide give descriptions and prices of typical places to eat with local flair. The Legend on the cover flap explains the symbols and prices used in the Address Books. Use the red-cover **Michelin Guide France**, with its famously reliable star-rating system and descriptions of hundreds of esta-

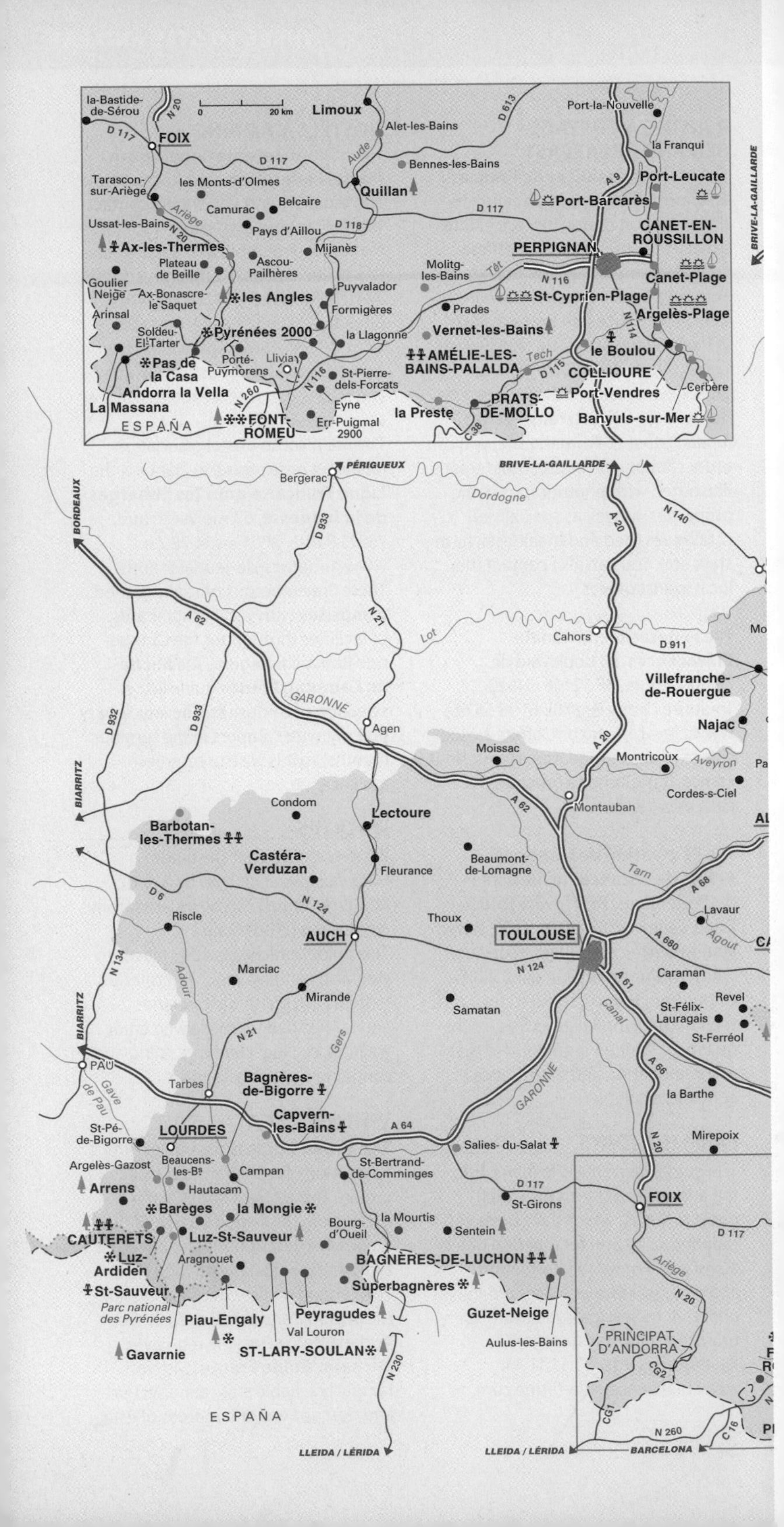

la-Bastide-de-Sérou
FOIX
Limoux
Alet-les-Bains
Bennes-les-Bains
Port-la-Nouvelle
la Franqui
Port-Leucate
Tarascon-sur-Ariège
les Monts-d'Olmes
Camurac
Belcaire
Quillan
Port-Barcarès
Ussat-les-Bains
Pays d'Aillou
Ax-les-Thermes
Mijanès
PERPIGNAN
CANET-EN-ROUSSILLON
Plateau de Beille
Ascou-Pailhères
Molitg-les-Bains
Canet-Plage
Goulier Neige
Ax-Bonascre-le Saquet
les Angles
Puyvalador
St-Cyprien-Plage
Formigères
Prades
Argelès-Plage
Arinsal
Soldeu-El-Tarter
Pyrénées 2000
la Llagonne
Vernet-les-Bains
le Boulou
Pas de la Casa
Porté-Puymorens
Llivia
AMÉLIE-LES-BAINS-PALALDA
COLLIOURE
St-Pierre-dels-Forcats
Andorra la Vella
Eyne
Port-Vendres
Cerbère
La Massana
FONT-ROMEU
Err-Puigmal 2900
la Preste
PRATS-DE-MOLLO
Banyuls-sur-Mer
ESPAÑA
0
20 km
PÉRIGUEUX
BRIVE-LA-GAILLARDE
Bergerac
Dordogne
BORDEAUX
Lot
Cahors
Villefranche-de-Rouergue
GARONNE
Agen
Najac
Moissac
Montricoux
Aveyron
Cordes-s-Ciel
Montauban
BIARRITZ
Condom
Lectoure
Barbotan-les-Thermes
Castéra-Verduzan
Fleurance
Beaumont-de-Lomagne
Tarn
Lavaur
Riscle
Thoux
AUCH
TOULOUSE
Agout
Marciac
Caraman
Mirande
Samatan
Revel
St-Félix-Lauragais
St-Ferréol
Canal
PAU
Gave de Pau
Adour
Gers
Tarbes
Bagnères-de-Bigorre
la Barthe
Capvern-les-Bains
LOURDES
Mirepoix
St-Pé-de-Bigorre
Salies-du-Salat
Beaucens-les-Bns
St-Bertrand-de-Comminges
Argelès-Gazost
Campan
Hautacam
Arrens
St-Girons
FOIX
Barèges
la Mongie
la Mourtis
CAUTERETS
Bourg-d'Oueil
Sentein
Luz-St-Sauveur
Luz-Ardiden
Aragnouet
BAGNÈRES-DE-LUCHON
Ariège
St-Sauveur
Superbagnères
Parc national des Pyrénées
Piau-Engaly
Peyragudes
Guzet-Neige
Val Louron
Aulus-les-Bains
PRINCIPAT D'ANDORRA
Gavarnie
ST-LARY-SOULAN
ESPAÑA
LLEIDA / LÉRIDA
LLEIDA / LÉRIDA
BARCELONA
N 20
D 117
D 613
Aude
D 118
A 9
Têt
N 116
N 114
N 260
Tech
D 115
C 38
A 62
D 933
N 21
A 20
N 140
D 911
D 932
D 6
N 124
A 68
A 680
A 61
N 134
A 66
A 64
N 230
CG2
CG1
C 16

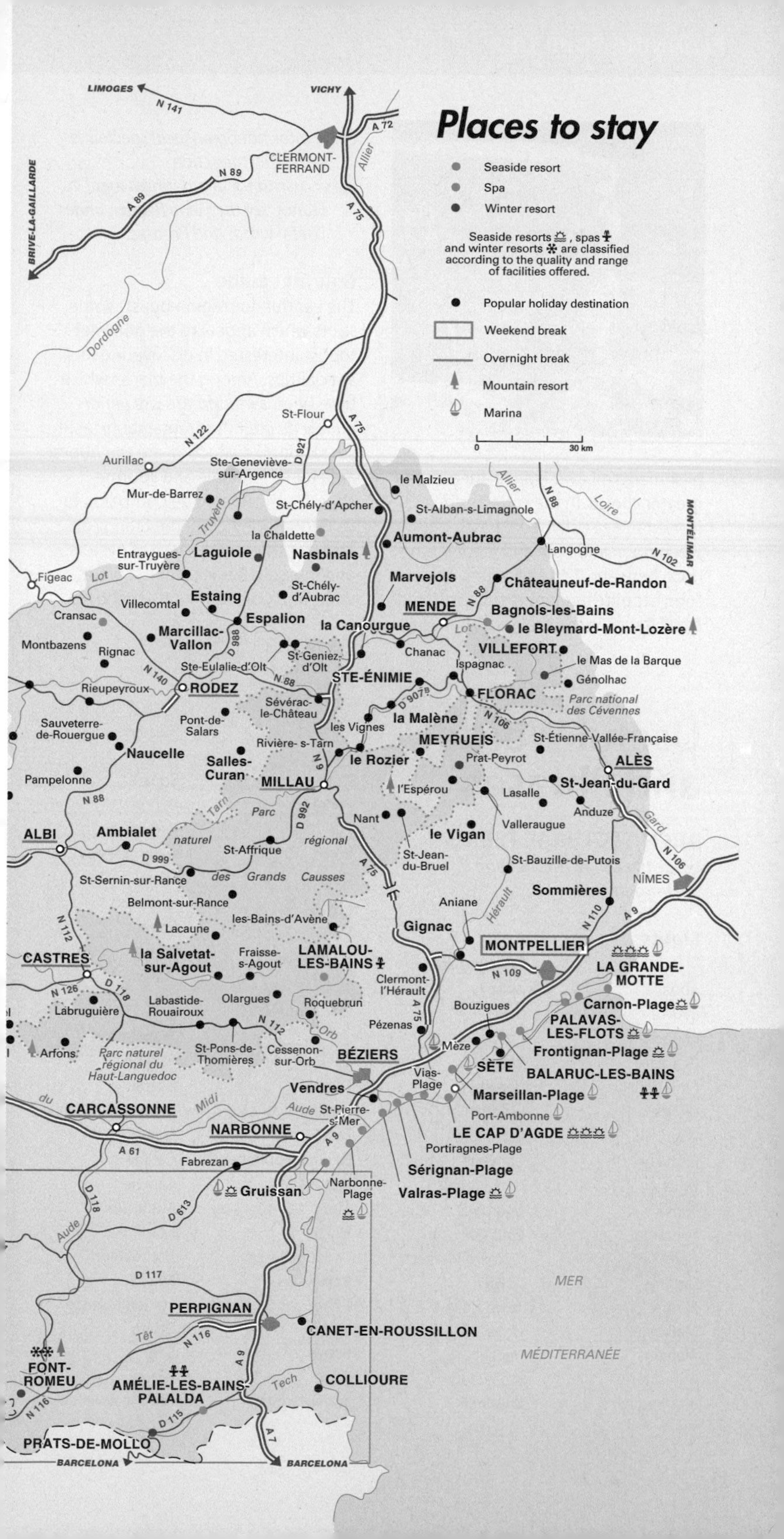
Places to stay
Seaside resort
Spa
Winter resort
Seaside resorts, spas and winter resorts are classified according to the quality and range of facilities offered.
Popular holiday destination
Weekend break
Overnight break
Mountain resort
Marina
0
30 km
LIMOGES
VICHY
N 141
CLERMONT-FERRAND
A 72
Allier
N 89
A 89
BRIVE-LA-GAILLARDE
A 75
Dordogne
St-Flour
N 122
D 921
Aurillac
Ste-Geneviève-sur-Argence
Mur-de-Barrez
Truyère
St-Chély-d'Apcher
le Malzieu
St-Alban-s-Limagnole
N 88
Loire
MONTÉLIMAR
la Chaldette
Aumont-Aubrac
Langogne
N 102
Entraygues-sur-Truyère
Laguiole
Nasbinals
Marvejols
Châteauneuf-de-Randon
Figeac
Lot
St-Chély-d'Aubrac
Villecomtal
Estaing
MENDE
Bagnols-les-Bains
Cransac
Espalion
la Canourgue
le Bleymard-Mont-Lozère
Montbazens
Marcillac-Vallon
D 988
St-Geniez-d'Olt
Chanac
VILLEFORT
Rignac
Ste-Eulalie-d'Olt
Ispagnac
le Mas de la Barque
N 140
N 88
STE-ÉNIMIE
Génolhac
Rieupeyroux
RODEZ
D 907B
FLORAC
Parc national des Cévennes
Sauveterre-de-Rouergue
Sévérac-le-Château
la Malène
N 106
Pont-de-Salars
les Vignes
MEYRUEIS
St-Étienne-Vallée-Française
Naucelle
Rivière-s-Tarn
le Rozier
Prat-Peyrot
ALÈS
Salles-Curan
N 9
Pampelonne
MILLAU
l'Espérou
St-Jean-du-Gard
N 88
Lasalle
Tarn
Parc
D 992
Anduze
Nant
Gard
ALBI
Ambialet
le Vigan
Valleraugue
naturel
St-Affrique
régional
D 999
St-Jean-du-Bruel
N 106
St-Sernin-sur-Rance
des Grands Causses
A 75
St-Bauzille-de-Putois
NÎMES
Belmont-sur-Rance
Sommières
Aniane
Hérault
N 112
les-Bains-d'Avène
A 9
Lacaune
Gignac
N 110
MONTPELLIER
CASTRES
la Salvetat-sur-Agout
Fraisse-s-Agout
LAMALOU-LES-BAINS
Clermont-l'Hérault
N 109
LA GRANDE-MOTTE
N 126
D 118
Labastide-Rouairoux
Olargues
Roquebrun
Carnon-Plage
Labruguière
A 75
Bouzigues
PALAVAS-LES-FLOTS
N 112
Pézenas
Orb
Arfons
Parc naturel régional du Haut-Languedoc
St-Pons-de-Thomières
Cessenon-sur-Orb
Mèze
Frontignan-Plage
BÉZIERS
SÈTE
BALARUC-LES-BAINS
Vendres
Vias-Plage
Marseillan-Plage
du
Midi
CARCASSONNE
Aude
St-Pierre-s-Mer
Port-Ambonne
NARBONNE
LE CAP D'AGDE
A 9
A 61
Portiragnes-Plage
Fabrezan
Sérignan-Plage
Gruissan
Narbonne-Plage
Valras-Plage
D 118
D 613
Aude
D 117
MER
PERPIGNAN
CANET-EN-ROUSSILLON
Têt
N 116
MÉDITERRANÉE
FONT-ROMEU
A 9
AMÉLIE-LES-BAINS-PALALDA
Tech
COLLIOURE
N 116
D 115
PRATS-DE-MOLLO
A 7
BARCELONA
BARCELONA

S. Sauvignier/MICHELIN

blishments all over France, for an even greater choice. In the countryside, restaurants usually serve lunch between noon and 2pm and the evening meal between 7.30 and 10pm. The "non-stop" restaurant is still a rarity in small towns in the provinces.

For information on local specialities, see the Introduction.

For assistance in ordering a meal in France, see the Menu Reader, under Useful words and Phrases.

Gourmet guide

The Languedoc region boasts some spots which appeal to the gourmet tourist interested in discovering local specialities. Among the places which have been awarded the *Site remarquable du goût* (for "remarkable taste sensations") distinction are the Aubrac area for its Laguiole and Fourme cheeses, the Rocher de Combalou for its Roquefort cheese, the Étangs de Thau for their production of oysters, and mussels, Banyuls for its sweet wine, and Collioure for its anchovies.

Useful Words and Phrases

ARCHITECTURAL TERMS

See the ABC of Architecture in the Introduction

Sights

	Translation
Abbaye	Abbey
Beffroi	Belfry
Chapelle	Chapel
Château	Castle
Cimetière	Cemetery
Cloître	Cloisters
Cour	Courtyard
Couvent	Convent
Écluse	Lock (Canal)
Église	Church
Fontaine	Fountain
Halle	Covered Market
Jardin	Garden
Mairie	Town Hall
Maison	House
Marché	Market
Monastère	Monastery
Moulin	Windmill
Musée	Museum
Parc	Park
Place	Square
Pont	Bridge
Port	Port/harbour
Porte	Gate/gateway
Quai	Quay
Remparts	Ramparts
Rue	Street
Statue	Statue
Tour	Tower

On The Road

	Translation
Car Park	Parking
Diesel	Gazole
Driving Licence	Permis De Conduire
East	Est
Garage (For Repairs)	Garage
Left	Gauche
Motorway/highway	Autoroute
North	Nord
Parking Meter	Horodateur
Petrol/gas	Essence
Petrol/gas Station	Station Essence
Right	Droite
South	Sud
Toll	Péage
Traffic Lights	Feu Tricolore

Tyre	Pneu
Unleaded fuel	Sans Plomb
West	Ouest
Wheel Clamp	Sabot
Zebra Crossing	Passage Clouté

Time

	Translation
Today	Aujourd’hui
Tomorrow	Demain
Yesterday	Hier
Winter	Hiver
Spring	Printemps
Summer	Été
Autumn/fall	Automne
Week	Semaine
Monday	Lundi
Tuesday	Mardi
Wednesday	Mercredi
Thursday	Jeudi
Friday	Vendredi
Saturday	Samedi
Sunday	Dimanche

Numbers

	Translation
0	zéro
1	un
2	deux
3	trois
4	quatre
5	cinq
6	six
7	sept
8	huit
9	neuf
10	dix
11	onze
12	douze
13	treize
14	quatorze
15	quinze
16	seize
17	dix-sept
18	dix-huit
19	dix-neuf
20	vingt
30	trente
40	quarante
50	cinquante
60	soixante
70	soixante-dix
80	quatre-vingt
90	quatre-vingt-dix
100	cent
1000	mille

Food and Drink

	Translation
Beef	Bœuf
Beer	Bière
Bread	Pain
Breakfast	Petit-déjeuner
Butter	Beurre
Cheese	Fromage
Chicken	Poulet
Dessert	Dessert
Dinner	Dîner
Fish	Poisson
Fork	Fourchette
Fruit	Fruits
Glass	Verre
Ham	Jambon
Ice Cream	Glace
Ice Cubes	Glaçons
Knife	Couteau
Lamb	Agneau
Lettuce Salad	Salade
Lunch	Déjeuner
Meat	Viande
Mineral Water	Eau Minérale
Mixed Salad	Salade Composée
Orange Juice	Jus D’orange
Plate	Assiette
Pork	Porc
Red Wine	Vin Rouge
Restaurant	Restaurant
Salt	Sel
Spoon	Cuillère
Sugar	Sucre
Vegetables	Légumes
Water	De L’eau
White Wine	Vin Blanc
Yoghurt	Yaourt

Useful Phrases

	Translation
The bill, please	[illegible]ddition s’il vous plaît
Goodbye	[illegible]voir
Hello/good Morn[illegible]	[illegible]
How	[illegible]
Excuse Me	[illegible]
Thank you	[illegible]
Yes/No	[illegible]
I’m sorry	[illegible]
Why?	[illegible]
When?	[illegible]
Pleas[illegible]	[illegible]

MENU READER

La Càrte	The Menu
ENTRÉES	**STARTERS**
Crudités	Raw vegetable salad
Terrine de lapin	Rabbit terrine (pâté)
Frisée aux lardons	Curly lettuce with bacon bits
Escargots	Snails
Cuisses de grenouille	Frog's legs
Salade au crottin	Goat cheese on a bed of lettuce
PLATS (VIANDES)	**MAIN COURSES (MEAT)**
Bavette à l'échalote	Flank steak with shallots
Faux filet au poivre	Sirloin with pepper sauce
Côtes d'agneau	Lamb chops
Filet mignon de porc	Pork fillet
Blanquette de veau	Veal in cream sauce
Nos viandes sont garnies	Our meat dishes are served with vegetables
PLATS (POISSONS, VOILAILLE)	**MAIN COURSES (FISH, FOWL)**
Filets de sole	Sole fillets
Dorade aux herbes	Sea bream with herbs
Saumon grillé	Grilled salmon
Coq au vin	Chicken in red wine sauce
Poulet de Bresse rôti	Free-range roast chicken from the Bresse
Omelette aux morilles	Wild-mushroom omelette
PLATEAU DE FROMAGES	**SELECTION OF CHEESES**
DESSERTS	**DESSERTS**
Tarte aux pommes	Sticky apple tart
Crème caramel	Cooled baked custard with caramel sauce
Sorbet: trois parfums	Sorbet: choice of three flavours
BOISSONS	**BEVERAGES**
Bière	Beer
Eau minérale (gazeuse)	(Sparkling) mineral water
Une carafe d'eau	Tap water (no charge)
Vin rouge, vin blanc, rosé	Red wine, white wine, rosé
Jus de fruit	Fruit juice
MENU ENFANT	**CHILDREN'S MENU**
Jambon	Ham
Steak haché	Ground beef
Frites	French fried potatoes

Well-done, medium, rare, raw = *bien cuit, à point, saignant, cru*

Basic Information

BUSINESS HOURS

In the Provinces the banks open from 10am–1pm and 3–4.30 Tue–Sat. (They often close early the day before a Public Holiday).

COMMUNICATIONS

Most public phones in France use pre-paid phone cards *(télécartes)*, rather than coins. Some telephone booths accept credit cards (Visa, Master-card/Eurocard). *Télécartes* (50 or 120 units) can be bought in post offices, branches of France Télécom, *bureaux de tabac* (cafés that sell cigarettes) and newsagents and can be used to make calls in France and abroad. Calls can be received at phone boxes where the blue bell sign is shown; the phone will not ring, so keep your eye on the little message screen.

NATIONAL CALLS

French telephone numbers have 10 digits. Paris and Paris region numbers begin with 01; 02 in north-west France; 03 in north-east France; 04 in south-east France and Corsica; 05 in south-west France.

INTERNATIONAL CALLS

To call France from abroad, dial the country code (33) + 9-digit number (omit the initial 0). When calling abroad from France dial 00, then dial the country code followed by the area code and number of your correspondent.

INTERNATIONAL DIALLING CODES *(00 + code)*			
Australia	61	**New Zealand**	64
Canada	1	**United Kingdom**	44
Eire	353	**United States**	1

International information:
US and Canada: 00 33 12 11
International operator:
00 33 12 + country code
Local directory assistance: 12

MOBILE PHONES

In France these have numbers which begin with 06. Two-watt (lighter, shorter reach) and eight-watt models are on the market, using the Orange (France Télécom) or SFR networks. *Mobicartes* are prepaid phone cards that fit into mobile units. Mobile phone rentals (delivery or airport pick-up provided):

Rent a Cell Express
01 53 93 78 00
Fax: 01 53 93 78 09
Ellinas Phone Rental
01 47 20 70 00

TO USE YOUR PERSONAL CALLING CARD	
AT&T	0-800 99 00 11
Sprint	0-800 99 00 87
MCI	0-800 99 00 19
Canada Direct	0-800 99 00 16

DISCOUNTS

Significant discounts are available for senior citizens, students, young people under the age of 25, teachers, and groups for public transportation, museums and monuments and for some leisure activities such as the cinema (at certain times of day). Bring student or senior cards with you, and bring along some extra passport-size photos for discount travel cards.
The **International Student Travel Confederation** (www.isic.org), global administrator of the International Student and Teacher Identity Cards, is an association of student travel organisations. ISTC members collectively negotiate benefits with airlines, governments, and providers of other goods and services for the student and teacher community. The corporate headquarters address is

Herengracht 479, 1017 BS Amsterdam, The Netherlands +31 20 421 28 00.
Carte Intersites Terre Catalane – This "passport" is available at many sites in the area where the Catalonia culture and traditions are still strongly felt. Visitors pay the full price at the first site they tour, and thereafter the passport entitles them to reductions of up to 60% at the other sites. Each site is associated with a walking tour or hike (1 to 3hr, not climbing more than 400m/1 300yd from the starting point). *www.paisos-catalans.com.*
Carte Intersites Pays Cathare – This is a similar offer covering 16 sites of Cathar heritage: the châteaux of Lastours, Arques, Quéribus, Puilaurens, Termes, Villerouge-Termenès, Saissac, Peyrepertuse, Usson, the château Comtal de Carcassonne, the abbeys of Caunes-Minervois, Saint-Papoul, Saint-Hilaire, Lagrasse, Fontfroide and the Musée du Quercorb in Puivert. It also gives free admission for one child. It is on sale at all the sites at a price of 4€.

ELECTRICITY

The electric current is 220 volts. Circular two-pin plugs are the rule. Adapters and converters should be bought before you leave home. If you have a rechargeable device read the instructions carefully or contact the manufacturer or shop. You may need a voltage converter.

EMERGENCIES

EMERGENCY NUMBERS	
Police:	**17**
SAMU (Paramedics):	**15**
Fire (Pompiers):	**18**

MAIL/POST

Post Offices are open from 9am–4.30pm with 2 hours for lunch. Note that if a Public Holiday falls on a Tuesday or Thursday then the nearest Monday or Friday will be taken also. Stamps are also available from newsagents and tobacconists.

POSTAGE VIA AIR MAIL TO:		
UK	Letter	(20g) 0.75 €
North America	Letter	(20g) 1.00 €
Australia	Letter	(20g) 1.00 €
New Zealand	Letter	(20g) 1.00 €

MONEY

CURRENCY

There are no restrictions on the amount of currency visitors can take into France. Visitors carrying a lot of cash are advised to complete a currency declaration form on arrival, because there are restrictions on currency export.

NOTES AND COINS

The **euro** is the only currency accepted as a means of payment in France. It is divided into 100 cents or centimes.

BANKS

For opening hours see section on business hours above. A passport is necessary as identification when cashing travellers cheques in banks. Commission charges vary and hotels usually charge more than banks for cashing cheques.
One of the most economical ways to use your money in France is by using **ATM machines** to get cash directly from your bank account either with a debit or credit card. Code pads are numeric; use a telephone pad to translate a letter code into numbers. Pin numbers have 4 digits in France; inquire with the issuing company or bank if the code you usually use is longer. Visa is the most widely accepted credit card. .
Before you leave home, **check with the bank that issued your card for emergency replacement procedures**. Carry your card number and emergency phone numbers separately. You must report any loss or theft of credit cards or traveller's cheques to the French police, who

will issue you with a certificate (useful proof to show the issuing company). **24-hour hotline numbers** are posted at most ATM machines.

TAXES

In France a sales tax (TVA or Value Added Tax ranging from 5.5% to 19.6%) is added to almost all retail goods – it can be worth your while to recover it. VAT refunds are available to visitors from outside the EU only if purchases exceed US$235 per store.

PUBLIC HOLIDAYS

Public services, museums and other monuments may be closed or may vary their hours of admission on public holidays:
National museums and art galleries are closed on Tuesdays; municipal museums are generally closed on Mondays. In addition to school holidays at Christmas and in spring and summer, there are long mid-term breaks in February and early November.

1 January	New Year's Day *(Jour de l'An)*
	Easter Day and Easter Monday *(Pâques)*
1 May	May Day *(Fête du Travail)*
8 May	VE Day *(Fête de la Libération)*
Thurs 40 days after Easter	Ascension Day *(Ascension)*
7th Sun-Mon after Easter	Whit Sunday and Monday *(Pentecôte)*
14 July	France's National Day *(Fête de la Bastille)*
15 August	Assumption *(Assomption)*
1 November	All Saint's Day *(Toussaint)*
11 November	Armistice Day *(Fête de la Victoire)*
25 December	Christmas Day *(Noël)*

SMOKING

Smoking is now banned in shopping malls, schools, offices and other public places, including restaurants, bars and cafés, if not on the terrace.

TIME

France is 1hr ahead of Greenwich Mean Time (GMT). France goes on daylight-saving time from the last Sunday in March to the last Sunday in October.

WHEN IT IS NOON IN FRANCE, **IT IS**	
3am	in Los Angeles
6am	in New York
11am	in Dublin
11am	in London
7pm	in Perth
9pm	in Sydney
11pm	in Auckland

In France "am" and "pm" are not used but the 24-hour clock is widely applied.

TIPPING

Since a service charge is automatically included in the prices of meals and accommodation in France, it is not necessary to tip in restaurants and hotels. Restaurants usually charge for meals in two ways: a *menu* that is a fixed-price menu with 2 or 3 courses all for a stated price, or à la carte with each course ordered separately.
Cafés have very different prices, depending on where they are located. The price of a drink or a coffee is cheaper if you stand at the counter.

SCHOOL HOLIDAYS

French schools close for vacations five times a year. In these periods, all tourist site and attractions, hotels, restaurants and roads are busier than usual. These school holidays are one week at the end of October, two weeks at Christmas, two weeks in February, two weeks in Spring and the whole of July and August

Abbaye-St-Martin-du-Canigou
M. Buffard/MICHELIN

INTRODUCTION TO LANGUEDOC ROUSSILLON TARN GORGES

Region Today

ECONOMY

The economic diversity of Languedoc-Rousillon and the Midi-Pyrenees is as vast and varied as its geography, ranging from artisanal crafting of fine leather goods, and the wondrous church bells cast at the Hérault foundry at Hérépian, to tourist-pampering spas and resorts, high-tech wonders like the Airbus A380 produced in Toulouse, bio and nano technologies, and sustainable energy endeavors. The population growth of Languedoc-Rousillon is twice the French national average, with 20,000 new inhabitants per year, 90% of these from other cities and regions in France. Immigration and changing demographics have recharged the region's populace, which seems to be always on the move between big cities and rural havens, energised by the lifestyle and economic advantages of both. Balancing the long, slow exodus of inhabitants from isolated rural villages migrating to the cities, are young "neo-rurals," new settlers who are reviving these phantom villages with organic farming schemes, theatres and radio stations, cultural projects and schools.

Languedoc-Rousillon is the fourth most visited tourist area in France. With some 15 million visitors a year, one-third from outside France, tourism is a huge economic player in the region. Summer beach-going on Languedoc's "sunshine coast," cultural tourism, sybaritic spas like d'Amélie-les Bains at Vallespir and ski resorts like Cerdagne et le Capcir.

And as for recycling... These days, the only miners working the open-pit mine at Carmaux, are statues of miners stationed at the heritage interpretation centre. The coal mine which has been a centre of coal extraction since the 13th century is now a tourist attraction.

Three commercial ports Sète, Port-la-Nouvelle et Port-Vendres transport 6.5 million tons of merchandise per year, and Sète is a gateway for Mediterranean cruises to Morocco.

The region's booming demographics pose a challenge to the protection and management of the environment, ecosystem and natural resources, and have stimulated a concerned consciousness and the growth of sustainable wind and solar energy development and technology. Air Languedoc-Roussillon is the first regional association in France created to control the quality of the air, and the Cerbère-Banyuls natural marine reserve is another regional environmental protection initiative.

FOOD AND DRINK ON THE MOUNTAIN PLATEAUX

The region stretching from the Aveyron *département* to the Cévennes has a delectable local cuisine, based on livestock bred on the *causses*. Local cheeses include: Fourme de Laguiole, a type of Cantal used to make the local dish *aligot*; Bleu de Causses, a blue cheese made from cow's milk; Pérail and the well-known Roquefort, both from ewe's milk; and Cabécou or Cévennes *pélardons* from goat's milk. Lamb from the causses is a delicious, but pricey, main course. Many local recipes feature mutton or pork, common in traditional cooking. Offal such as tripe also features widely on local menus: *tripoux de Naucelles* (tripe stewed in white wine with ham and garlic); charcuterie from Entraygues; sausages from St-Affrique and Langogne; *trénels de Millau* (sheep's tripe stuffed with ham, garlic, parsley and egg); *alicuit* from Villefranche-en-Rouergue (stewed chicken livers). Visitors to the Tarn should not miss charcuterie from the Montagne Noire, *bougnettes* from Castres (small, flat pork sausages) and cured hams and sausages from Lacaune. Fresh fish is hard to come by, apart from river trout, but recipes featuring salted or dried fish are common, such as *estofinado* (stockfish stew). Chestnuts are traditionally used in soups and stews, or roasted and eaten whole with a glass of cider.

For those with a sweet tooth, there are *soleils* from Rodez (round yellow cookies flavoured with almonds and orange blossom), fouaces from Najac (*brioches* flavoured with angelica), Cévennes *croquants* (hard almond cookies) and nènes (small aniseed biscuits) from St-Affrique.

LANGUEDOC

Languedoc cuisine is typical Mediterranean cuisine, featuring herbs from the *garrigues* (rosemary, thyme, juniper, sage, fennel), garlic and olive oil, and fresh aubergines, tomatoes, courgettes and peppers. A local garlic soup called *aigo boulido* is made with garlic, olive oil and thyme. Some dishes include snails, delicious wild mushrooms (*cèpes, morilles*) or even – as a special treat – truffles, found growing at the foot of the holm-oaks on the slopes of the Hérault and the Gard.

Common meat dishes feature mutton or pork, and occasionally veal. Local game raised on fragrant wild herbs, juniper berries and thyme, has a remarkable flavour, as do the lambs and sheep raised on the causses. They are used in pies or stews. Regional cheeses are mainly from goat's milk, very tasty when heated and served on a bed of lettuce. Menus near the coast are based on a variety of seafood: oysters and mussels from Bouzigues, *bourride sétoise* (fish stew from Sète), gigot de mer de Palavas (fish baked with garlic and vegetables) and seafood pasties. In Montpellier, fish dishes are accompanied by beurre de Montpellier, a sauce of mixed herbs, watercress, spinach, anchovies, yolks of hard-boiled eggs, butter and spices. Sweets include *oreillettes* (orange biscuits fried in olive oil), eaten in Montpellier at Epiphany and on Shrove Tuesday, or grisettes (candy made from honey, wild herbs and liquorice).

TOULOUSE TO THE PYRENEES

The rich local cuisine of the Périgord or South-West France features goose and duck, either preserved as *confits* or as foie gras, or in stews. Assorted charcuterie includes the delicious *saucisson sec* (a sort of local salami). Meat dishes are usually stews which have simmered gently for hours. The most famous dish from this region is **cassoulet**, a thick stew of haricot beans, sausage, pork, mutton and preserved goose. Vegetables include sweetcorn, olives, asparagus from the Tarn Valley and the fragrant purple garlic from Lautrec. The Pyrenees produce a tasty ewe's milk cheese called brebis. Those with a sweet tooth should sample nougat from Limoux, *marrons glacés* (candied chestnuts) from Carcassonne or rosemary-scented honey from the Corbières.

Catalan cuisine

This is a typically Mediterranean cuisine, using olive oil, garlic mayonnaise (*ail y oli* in Catalan, *aïoli* in French) and a paste made of anchovies, olive oil and garlic (el pa y all, or anchoïade). **Bouillinade**, the Catalan version of bouillabaisse (fish soup), and civet de langouste au Banyuls – spiny lobster stewed in dry Banyuls wine, make a delicious follow-up to a starter of Collioure anchovies. In Les Aspres, **escalade** is a fragrant soup made with thyme, garlic, oil and egg. Mushrooms fried in oil with an olive sauce are eaten with game (partridge and hare). Catalan charcuterie includes such delicacies as black pudding (boutifare or boudin), pig's liver sausage, and cured hams and salami from the Cerdagne mountain. **Cargolade**, snails from the garrigue grilled over burning vine cuttings, frequently feature in the open-air meals which follow prayer retreats at the hermitages. Sweets include crème catalane (crème brûlée with caramel), bunyettes (orange-flavoured doughnuts), rousquilles from Amélie-les-Bains (small almond biscuits) and fresh fruit from Roussillon's many orchards (peaches, pears, and melons).

WINE

Coteaux du Languedoc

The wine growing region of Languedoc is blessed with a Mediterranean climate and a variety of soil types (layers of schist, pebble terraces and red clay). It is the main producer of French table wine *(vins de table and vins de pays),* but today wine-growers here are concentrating on improving local grape varieties and the way they are blended. Their efforts have been rewarded with an increase in the number of designated AOCs (Appellations d'Origine Contrôlée) in the region. Promoted to AOC in 1985, the **Coteaux**

du Languedoc appellation includes red, rosé and white wines produced in the Hérault, Gard and Aveyron *départements*. Besides Faugères and St-Chinian, whose heady, powerful wines have won these areas their own AOC designations, the AOC has been awarded to particular vintages. For red and rosé wines, these are: Cabrières, La Clape, La Méjanelle, Montpeyroux, Pic-St-Loup, St-Christol, St-Drézéry, St-Georges-d'Orques, St-Saturnin and Vérargues, and for white wines: Picpoul-de-Pinet, aged in oak casks. The Carignan grape is the main grape variety cultivated in the region. The Cabrières region also produces **Clairette du Languedoc**, a dry white wine made from the Clairette grape, an AOC winner. Local table wine is sold under the label "Vins de pays d'Oc" or "Vin de Pays" followed by its département of origin. Notable vins doux naturels from the Coteaux du Languedoc include Muscat de Frontignan, Muscat de Mireval and Muscat de Lunel.

Minervois

The Minervois region is reputed for its fine, fruity robust red wines which are well balanced and have a deep, rich red colour. The St-Jean-du-Minervois vineyard, covering the limestone *garrigues* on the uplands in the north-west, produces a fragrant muscat dessert wine.

The vineyards of the Aveyron

The Aveyron vineyards were once a source of great wealth to the region, thanks to the work of the monks from Conques. Covring steep slopes, these vineyards stand out from the surrounding mountain landscape. The well balanced red wines of **Marcillac** (AOC), with a hint of raspberry, go well with the tripe dishes of the Rouergue region. The red wines from **Entraygues** and **Fel**, classified as VDQS (*Vin Délimité de Qualité Supérieure* – one step down from AOC), have substance and a nice fruity flavour. The whites from these designations are lighter with more finesse. In the Lot Valley, the **Estaing** VDQS vineyards are cultivated on the valley sides up to an altitude of 450m/1 476ft and produce pleasant dry whites and subtle, fragrant reds. The sheltered sides of the Tarn valley between Peyreleau and Broquiès are home to the **Côtes de Millau** VDQS vineyards, which produce mainly red and rosé wine. **Cerno** is a local aperitif made from Côtes de Millau wine and herbal extracts.

Gaillac

The wines of the Gaillac vineyards, to the west of Albi, are classified as *Appellation d'Origine Contrôlée*. Dry white wines with a fragrant bouquet are made using local grape varieties Mauzac, Len de Lel and Ondec. There are three types of Gaillac white: sweet (moelleux), very slightly sparkling *(perlé)* and sparkling *(mousseux)*. Gaillac red is made from traditional grapes such as Gamay, Syrah, Merlot and Cabernet, mixed with local varieties like Braucol or Duras for a robust wine, or Négrette.
Slightly farther west, just north of Toulouse, **Côtes du Frontonnais** wines are produced from a very old grape variety, the Négrette, mixed with Cabernet, Syrah, Fer Servadou and Cot, to give supple fruity wines which are best drunk young. There are two AOCs around Carcassonne: Cabardès, well balanced with plenty of body, and Malepère, a fruity red wine. Both of these wines are perfect complements to game and red meat.

Corbières and Roussillon wines

The **Fitou** *Appellation d'Origine Contrôlée* is reserved for a red wine from a specific area in the Corbières. Its alcohol content must be at least 12%, output is limited to 30hl per hectare/330gal per acre, and the wine must have been aged in a cellar for at least nine months. Fitou wines, produced from high quality grapes, are strong and full-bodied.
The **Corbières** *Appellation d'Origine Contrôlée* covers an area with a mixture of soil types, producing a variety of wines. Besides red wines with a fine bouquet, production includes fruity rosés and some dry white wines.
The Roussillon vineyards are noted for their high quality vins doux naturels (dessert wines), the **Côtes du Roussillon** and **Côtes du Roussillon Village** wines classified as Appellation d'Origine

Contrôlée, and their robust, earthy local wines. Just north of Agde, the tiny village of Pinet produces a dry white wine called Picpoul de Pinet (from the Picpoul grape). It makes the perfect accompaniment to oysters from the nearby Bassin de Thau. This region's *vins doux naturels* represent the majority of French production of wines of this type. The grape varieties – Grenache, Maccabeu, Carignan, Malvoisie, among others – add warmth and bouquet to these wines. The warm local climate and the sunny vineyards make these wines mature perfectly with a high natural sugar content. The most famous examples are **Banyuls, Maury, Muscat de Rivesaltes and Rivesaltes.**

Blanquette de Limoux

This sparkling white wine, much in demand for its fine quality, is made from the Mauzac and Clairette grapes ripened on the slopes around Limoux.

History

PREHISTORY

During the Quaternary Era some two million years ago, glaciers spread over the highest mountains (Günz, Mindel, Riss and Würm Ice Ages) and humans began to populate Europe, particularly the Pyrenees. Phases of human evolution are divided into periods and classified according to archaeological and scientific methods of dating. Earliest is the Paleolithic (Old Stone Age), followed by the Mesolithic (Middle Stone Age) and finally the Neolithic (New Stone Age).

LOWER PALEOLITHIC

In the Pyrenees the Lower Paleolithic is represented by **Tautavel man**, whose skull was discovered in a layer of ancient sediment in the **Caune de l'Arago** by Professor H de Lumley and his team in 1971 and 1979. Tautavel man belongs to the "Homo erectus" genus, which inhabited Roussillon 450 000 years ago. He was 20-25 years old, 1.65m/5ft 6in tall and stood upright. He had a flat receding forehead, prominent cheekbones and rectangular eye sockets beneath a thick projecting brow. No trace of any hearth has been found, so it is assumed that this intrepid hunter probably ate his meat raw. He used caves as look-outs to track animal movements, as temporary places to camp and to dismember prey, and as workshops for manufacturing tools.

Palynology, the analysis of fossilised pollen grains, helps scientists determine the characteristics of flora and fauna from different prehistoric periods. We know that Mediterranean plant species like pines, oaks, walnut trees, plane trees and wild vines have been indigenous since prehistory. Large prehistoric herbivores included deer and mountain goats, prairie rhinoceros, bison, musk ox and an ancient species of wild sheep. Carnivores (bears, wolves, dogs, polar foxes, cave lions and wild cats) were hunted for their fur. Small game comprised rodents (hares, voles, beavers, field mice) and birds still found today: golden eagles, lammergeyer vultures, pigeons, rock partridges, and red-billed choughs. Prehistoric tools consisted of quite small scrapers and notched tools (with the largest stones averaging 6-10cm/2-4in) made into choppers, or flat two- or more-sided implements of varying degrees of sharpness.

MIDDLE PALEOLITHIC

The presence of numerous Mousterian deposits is evidence that Neanderthal man lived in the Pyrenees. Taller than "homo erectus," he had a well-developed skull (1 700cm3/103in3), constructed vast dwelling and burial places, and produced more sophisticated, specialised tools such as double-sided implements, stone knives with curved edges, chisels, scrapers, pointed tools and various notched implements.

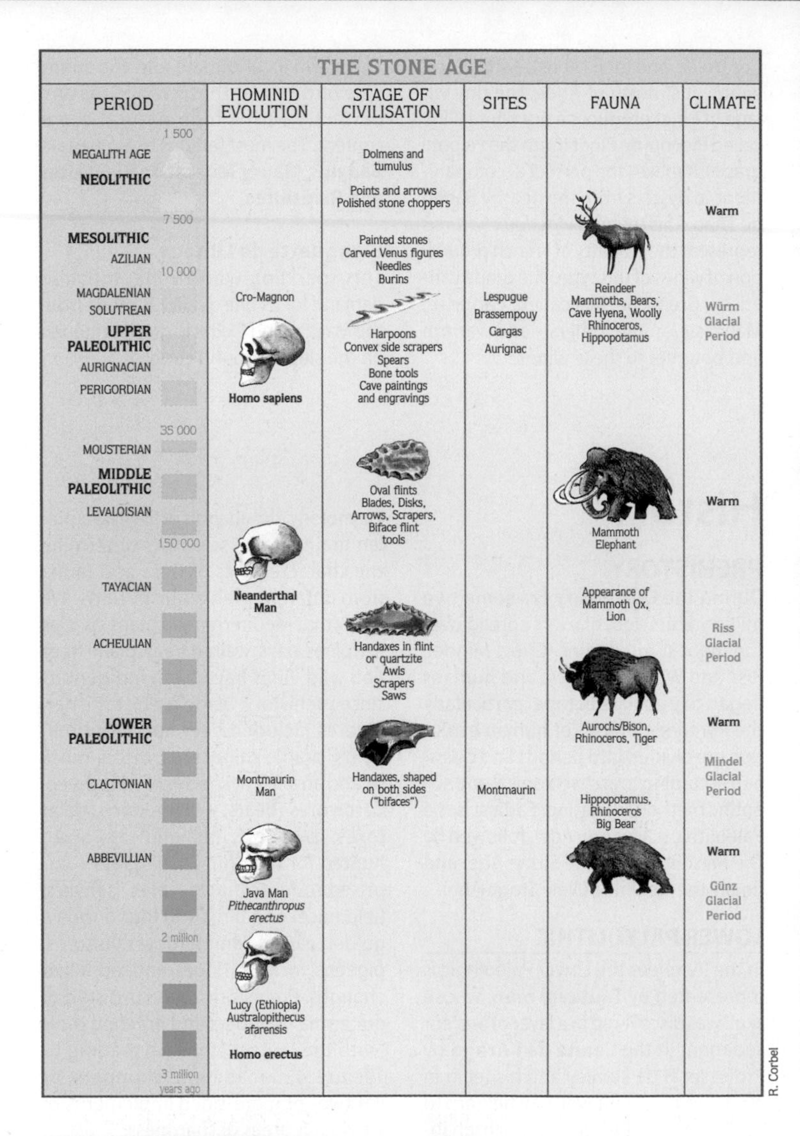

THE STONE AGE

PERIOD	HOMINID EVOLUTION	STAGE OF CIVILISATION	SITES	FAUNA	CLIMATE
1 500 MEGALITH AGE **NEOLITHIC**		Dolmens and tumulus Points and arrows Polished stone choppers			
7 500 **MESOLITHIC** AZILIAN		Painted stones Carved Venus figures Needles Burins			Warm
10 000 MAGDALENIAN SOLUTREAN **UPPER PALEOLITHIC** AURIGNACIAN PERIGORDIAN	Cro-Magnon **Homo sapiens**	Harpoons Convex side scrapers Spears Bone tools Cave paintings and engravings	Lespugue Brassempouy Gargas Aurignac	Reindeer Mammoths, Bears, Cave Hyena, Woolly Rhinoceros, Hippopotamus	Würm Glacial Period
35 000 MOUSTERIAN **MIDDLE PALEOLITHIC** LEVALOISIAN		Oval flints Blades, Disks, Arrows, Scrapers, Biface flint tools		Mammoth Elephant	Warm
150 000 TAYACIAN	**Neanderthal Man**			Appearance of Mammoth Ox, Lion	
ACHEULIAN		Handaxes in flint or quartzite Awls Scrapers Saws			Riss Glacial Period
LOWER PALEOLITHIC				Aurochs/Bison, Rhinoceros, Tiger	Warm
CLACTONIAN	Montmaurin Man	Handaxes, shaped on both sides ("bifaces")	Montmaurin	Hippopotamus, Rhinoceros Big Bear	Mindel Glacial Period
ABBEVILLIAN	Java Man *Pithecanthropus erectus*				Warm Günz Glacial Period
2 million	Lucy (Ethiopia) Australopithecus afarensis **Homo erectus**				
3 million years ago					

R. Corbel

UPPER PALEOLITHIC

With "homo sapiens" a significant human presence developed in the Pyrenees. During the Aurignacian period, stone implements were supplemented with tools made of bone and horn, and during the Solutrean and Magdalenian periods, technical evolution progressed even further. Towards the end of the last Würm Glacial Period (Würm IV), boar and deer inhabited the changing landscape. Humans hunted and fished, yet their greatest innovation was the birth of art--remarkable cave paintings and sculpted human figures like the Aurignacian "Venuses."

MESOLITHIC AGE

The historical landscape of the Pyrenees stabilised at the end of the Ice Age. During the intermediary Mesolithic Age, a multitude of civilisations appeared. In the late Upper Paleolithic, the Azilian culture employed the harpoon as an important weapon, but their art consisted only of enigmatic pebbles with symbolic markings.

NEOLITHIC AGE

The Neolithic Age brought polished stone tools and earthenware, but the cave swelling population in the eastern Pyrenees and the Ariège adopted earthenware sometime later. Valuable ethnological information was discovered in the Font-Juvénal shelter, between the River Aude and the Montagne Noire. Here cattle-rearing and wheat and barley cultivation had become a means of subsistence by the fourth millennium, and dwellings became more elaborate, with supporting structures, flat hearths for cooking and silos for storage.
In the Narbonne region communities developed specialised activities and began bartering and trading with one other. During the third millennium, Megalithic constructions like dolmens and tumuli were introduced to the Pyrenees from the western zone. Inhabitants of the densely populated middle mountain slopes raised stock and developed weapons (arrows, axes and knives), jewelry and earthenware. In the Catalan region, the Megalithic culture lasted until the Bronze Age.

THE PYRENEAN DOLMENS (2500-1500 BC)

Dolmens are prehistoric grave sites usually found at altitudes of 600-1 000m/ 1 968-3 280ft. These massive stone structures were originally covered by a tumulus of earth or a heap of stones as high as 20m/65ft, and could be enclosed by a stone circle. The largest dolmens, erected in areas with a stable population, contain the remains of hundreds of people. Dolmens on the higher pastures were much smaller and were eventually replaced by cists, individual burial chests made of stone slabs.

TIME LINE

ANTIQUITY

BC

1800-50 – Metal Age.

1800-700 – Bronze Age. End of Pyrenean Megalithic culture.

1000-600 – End of Bronze Age and first Iron Age. Arrival of continental, then Mediterranean influences.

600-50 – Foundation of **Massalia** (Marseille) by the Phoceans. Development of metallurgy in ancient Catalonia (Catalan forges). The eastern Pyrenees are populated by numerous small clans.

6C – The Celts invade Gaul.

214 – **Hannibal** crosses the Pyrenees into Roussillon.

2C – Roman Conquest. The **Romans** occupy the region later known as Bas Languedoc.

118 – Foundation of Narbonne, capital of **Gallia Narbonensis**, at the crossing of the Via Domitia and the road to Aquitaine.

58-52 – **Caesar** conquers Gaul.

27 – Bas Languedoc becomes part of Gallia Narbonensis, marking the beginning of a long period of prosperity.

AD3C and 4C – Christianity arrives in the region. Decline of Narbonne and Toulouse.

313 – **Edict of Milan**. Emperor Constantine grants Christians freedom of worship.

356 – **Council of Béziers**, Arian heresy.

INVASIONS, THE MIDDLE AGES

3C-5C – **Invasions** by the Alemanni, the Vandals, then the Visigoths. Toulouse becomes the capital of the Visigothic kingdom.

507 – Battle of Vouillé: **Clovis** defeats the Visigoths, and restricts their kingdom to seven cities (Carcassonne, Narbonne, Béziers, Agde, Nîmes, Elne and Maguelone).

719 – The **Saracens** capture Narbonne.

732 – **Charles Martel** defeats the Saracens at Poitiers.

737 – Charles Martel recaptures the seven cities from the Visigoths.

759 – Pépin the Short recaptures Narbonne.

801 – **Charlemagne** marches into Spain and integrates Catalonia into his Empire, allowing it to remain autonomous.

843 – The **Treaty of Verdun** divides Charlemagne's Empire: territories west of the Rhône to the Atlantic Ocean are given to Charles the Bald.

877 – **Charles the Bald** dies and most of the great princely houses that will rule the south of France until the 13C are established. The counts of Toulouse own the old kingdom of seven cities and the Rouergue; the Gévaudan belongs to the Auvergne family.

10C – Religious revival and **pilgrimages to St James's** shrine in Santiago de Compostela, Spain.

987 – Hugues Capet is crowned king of France.

11C – Renewed economic and demographic growth in the West. The counts of Toulouse assert their power. Wave of construction of ecclesiastical buildings. Tour of Languedoc by Pope Urban II.

1095 – **First Crusade.**

1112 – The count of Barcelona becomes viscount of Béziers, Agde, Gévaudan and Millau.

UNION WITH THE FRENCH CROWN

12C-13C – Flowering of the art and culture of the troubadours. **First bastides** (fortified towns) are constructed.

1140-1200 – The **Cathar** doctrine spreads.

1152 – Henry II Plantagenet marries Eleanor of Aquitaine.

1204 – The king of Aragon gains sovereignty of Montpellier, Gévaudan and Millau.

1207 – Raymond VI, count of Toulouse is excommunicated.

1208 – Pierre de Castelnau, legate to Pope Innocent III, is assassinated.

1209 – **Albigensian Crusade** *(details below in the section on The Cathars).* Simon de Montfort captures Béziers and Carcassonne.

1213 – Battle of Muret.

1226 – A new crusade: **Louis VIII** seizes Languedoc.

1229 – The **Treaty of Paris** ends the war against the Albigensians. St Louis annexes the whole of Bas Languedoc. Toulouse University is founded.

1250-1320 – The **Inquisition** quells the last strongholds of the Cathars.

1270 – St Louis dies.

1276-1344 – Perpignan is capital of the **kingdom of Majorca** and the Balearic Islands, which was founded by Jaime I of Aragon and includes the Cerdagne, Roussillon and Montpellier.

1290 – The counts of Foix inherit the Béarn.

1292 – Annexation of Pézenas, the Rouergue and the Gévaudan.

1312 – **Philip the Fair** dissolves the Order of the Templars, and their considerable estates in the Causses are given to the Knights Hospitallers of St John of Jerusalem (or of Malta).

1331-91 – Life of Gaston Fébus.

1337 – Beginning of the **Hundred Years War** lasting until 1453.

1348 – The **Black Death** decimates one third of the population of Languedoc.

1349 – The king of Majorca sells the seigneury of Montpellier to Philip of Valois.

1350-1450 – The Pyrenees and Languedoc suffer a long period of war, unrest, epidemics and famine.

1360 – **Treaty of Bretigny**: end of the first part of the Hundred Years War. Saintonge, Poitou, Agenais, Quercy, Rouergue and Périgord are ceded to the king of England. Languedoc is then divided into three seneschalsies: Toulouse, Carcassonne and Beaucaire.

1361 – Outlaws plunder the countryside.

1420 – Charles VII enters Toulouse.

1462 – Intervention of Louis XI in Roussillon.

WARS OF RELIGION AND UNION WITH FRANCE

1484 – The **princes of Albret**, "kings of Navarre," gain ascendancy in the Gascon Pyrenees (Foix, Béarn, Bigorre).

1512 – Ferdinand, the Catholic monarch, divests the Albrets of their territory.

1539 – The edict of **Villers-Cotteret** decrees French the legal language of France.

1560-98 – Protestants and Roman Catholics engage in **Wars of Religion**.

1598 – The **Edict of Nantes** gives Protestants freedom of worship and guaranteed strongholds (Puylaurens, Montauban).

1607 – Henri IV unites his own royal estate (Basse-Navarre and the fiefs of Foix and Béarn) to the French Crown.

1610 – **Henri IV is assassinated** and religious strife is renewed.

1629 – Under the **Treaty of Alès**, Protestants keep their religious freedoms but lose their strongholds.

1643-1715 – Reign of Louis XIV.

1659 – The **Treaty of the Pyrenees** unites Roussillon and the Cerdagne with the French Crown.

1666-80 – Riquet constructs the **Canal du Midi**.

1685 – **Revocation** of the Edict of Nantes. Numerous Protestants flee the country.

1702-04 – **War of the Camisards**.

FROM FIRST SPA RESORT TO MODERN TIMES

1746 – De Bordeu's thesis on Aquitaine's mineral springs promotes the creation of **spa resorts** and the popularity of "taking cures."

1787 – Ramond de Carbonnières, first enthusiast of the Pyrenees, stays in Barèges.

1790 – The Languedoc is divided into new administrative districts *(départements)*.

1804-15 – First **Empire**. New thermal springs are discovered in the Pyrenees.

1852-1914 – Second Empire and Third Republic. Development of spa resorts, rock climbing and scientific studies of the Pyrenees.

1875 – **Phylloxera** destroys Languedoc's vineyards.

1901 – First **hydroelectric** schemes implemented.

1907 – Wine-growers in Bas Languedoc join a protest *("Mouvement des gueux")* against overproduction, competition from imported Algerian wines and falling prices.

1920 – The Pyrenees convert to hydroelectric power.

1940-44 – The Pyrenees prove to be of vital importance to the **French Résistance**. The Massif de l'Aigoual is a major headquarters for the maquis.

1955 – Inauguration of the Compagnie Nationale d'Aménagement du Bas-Rhône-Languedoc, to develop an **irrigation** system in the region.

1963 – Plans are made to develop the Languedoc-Roussillon coastline.

1969 – Maiden flight of "**Concorde** 001."

1970 – Designation of the **Parc National des Cévennes**. Founding of Airbus Industrie.

1973 – Designation of the **Parc naturel régional du Haut Languedoc**.

1992-97 – The new motorway (A 75) linking Clermont-Ferrand with Béziers opens in progressive sections.

1993 – Toulouse underground railway *(**métro**)* begins operation.

1994 – **Puymorens tunnel** opens in the Pyrenees.

1995 – Designation of the **Parc naturel régional des Grands Causses**.

1996 – The **TGV** high-speed rail link opens between Paris and Perpignan *(journey time: 6hr)*. The Canal du Midi joins the UNESCO World Heritage List.

1997 – The medieval city of Carcassonne and the Cirque de Gavarnie join the **UNESCO World Heritage** List.

1999 – Massive December storms slam the southwest coast of France.

1999 – The **euro** was introduced in France to replace the franc.

THE NEW MILLENNIUM

2001 – Explosion rocks the AZF chemical plant near Toulouse, killing 29 and wounding 2,400.

March 2005 – The maiden flight of **Airbus 380**, a 555-seat superjumbo jet assembled in Toulouse.

2007 – **Nicolas Sarkozy** is elected President of France.

2008 – France ratifies the **Lisbon Treaty** on EU reform.
– EU governments **pledge up to 1.8 trillion euros** to shore up their financial sectors following economic crisis.

2009 – Govermment unveils **$33.1bn economy stimulus** package.

WAY OF ST JAMES

According to legend, St James travelled from Palestine to Spain to Christianise the country, but was beheaded. Two of his disciples carrying his body were stranded on the coast of Galicia and buried St. James remains there. The site of the grave was unknown until around 813 when a shower of stars falling over an earth mound drew a hermit's attention to the grave. The spot became known as *Campus stellae* (Compostela) and a chapel was erected here. St James became the patron saint of all Christians as well as the symbol of the Spaniards' struggle to regain their land from the Moors. After the first French pilgrimage in 951, Compostela grew as famous as Rome and Jerusalem, attracting pilgrims from all over Europe.

In 1130, the French monk Aymeri Picaud wrote a tourist guide for pilgrims, the Codex Calixtinus, which included a layout of the routes leading to Santiago de Compostela. Included in this guide are St-Jean-Pied-de-Port in the foothills of the Pyrenees, part of the *camino frances* (the French way): the **via Podiensis** which links the Aubrac mountains and Condom, the **via Tolosane** (coming from Arles and traversing Toulouse and Auch) and the **Caussade** (via Conques, Rodez, Foix and Lourdes).

Over the last millennium, the pilgrimage tradition has enhanced the region's cultural heritage, particularly in Conques, Rocamadour, Saint-Sernin de Toulouse and St-Bertrand-de-Comminges.

THE CATHARS

The 13C repression of the Cathar sect profoundly affected the history of the Languedoc, which then became linked with that of the French kingdom.

THE CATHAR DOCTRINE

The Cathar doctrine originated in a labyrinth of Eastern influences prevalent in Europe during the 11C and 12C, and focused on the opposition of "Good" and "Evil." Obsessed with a fear of evil, the Cathars (from the Greek *kathari* or "pure ones") sought to free man from the material world, restoring him to divine purity. Their interpretation of biblical texts collided head-on with Christian orthodoxy. They strove to emulate Christ but denied Christ's divinity.

THE CATHAR CHURCH

Four bishops from Albi, Toulouse, Carcassonne and Agen headed this breakaway Church which came to be called "Albigensian." The Cathar Church comprised a hierarchy of vocations which distinguished between **Parfaits** ("Perfect ones") and **Croyants** ("Believers"). Reacting against the decadent laxity of the Roman Catholic clergy, the austere Parfaits embraced poverty, chastity, patience and humility. The Cathar Church administered only one sacrament, the **Consolamentum**, used at the ordination of a Parfait, or to bless a dying Croyant. The Cathars rejected the traditional sacraments of baptism and marriage, and tolerated different customs and attitudes. Their beliefs, way of life and religious rituals challenged Roman Catholic thought, causing violent disputes.

A FAVOURABLE ENVIRONMENT

The Cathar heresy spread to the towns, centres of culture and trade, and then into the Languedoc lowlands. It was probably no coincidence that the Cathar Church flourished between Carcassonne and Toulouse, Foix and Limoux, areas dominated by the Languedoc cloth industry. The **"Bonhommes"** (Parfaits) were often textile manufacturers or merchants. Powerful lords such as Roger Trencavel, viscount of Béziers and Carcassonne, and Raymond, count of Foix, supported the heresy.

THE WAR AGAINST THE CATHARS

In 1150 St Bernard arrived in the Albigeois region to convert the Cathar heretics, but met with minimal success. In 1179 the Third Lateran Council drew up plans to counter the spread the heretical sect. In 1204, Pope Innocent III sent three legates to preach against the Cathars and persuade the Count of Toulouse, **Raymond VI**, to withdraw his protection of them. The count refused and was excommunicated in 1207. In January 1208, the papal legate Pierre de Castlenau was assassinated and Raymond VI was immediately accused of his murder. This sparked the **First Albigensian Crusade** in March 1208, preached by Pope Innocent III. Knights from the Paris region, Normandy, Picardy, Flanders, Champagne and Burgundy, and noblemen from the Rhineland, Friesland, Bavaria and even Austria rallied forces under the command of Abbot Arnaud-Amaury of Cîteaux, and then under **Simon de Montfort**. The "Holy War" was to lasted over 20 years. In 1209, 30 000 residents of Béziers were massacred. Carcassonne was besieged and fell in 1209. Viscount Raymond-Roger de Trencavel was taken prisoner and was replaced by Simon de Montfort, who captured one Cathar fortress after another: Lastours, Minerve, Termes and Puivert (1210). By 1215, the whole of the Count of Toulouse's territory was in the hands of Montfort. Raymond VII avenged his father by waging a war of liberation for eight years. Simon de Montfort died in 1218 and was succeeded by his son, Amaury.

Strongholds might fall, but the Cathar doctrine was not easily quashed. In 1226, a **Second Albigensian Crusade** was preached, lead by the King of France himself, Louis VIII. The Holy War evolved into a political struggle. In the Treaty of Meaux-Paris in 1229, Blanche of Castille annexed a vast territory to the French Royal estate. A century later, it became the Languedoc. The battle against heresy was not over; it was continued by the **Inquisition**. Pope Gregory IX entrusted the **Inquisition** to the Dominican Order in 1231. In 1240 the Crusaders captured Peyrepertuse. Pierre-Roger de Mirepoix, the governor of the main Cathar stronghold at Montségur, undertook an expedition to Avignonet in 1242, killing members of an Inquisition tribunal. Six thousand Crusaders installed themselves at the foot of his castle, and their siege lasted ten months.

In March 1244 the fortress capitulated to the besieging Crusaders, and they built an enormous pyre on which they burned alive 220 unrepentant Cathars. Other Cathars took refuge in the fortress at Puilaurens, where they were butchered after the fall of Montségur. The war against the Cathars reached its bloody conclusion in 1255 with the siege and fall of Quéribus, the last remaining Cathar stronghold.

Architecture

PREHISTORY & ANTIQUITY

The Causses and the Cévennes are rich in vestiges of Neolithic art.

MEGALITHS

These large (Greek: *mega*) stone (Greek: *lithas*) monuments comprise dolmens, menhirs, covered alleyways, alignments of menhirs and "cromlechs" (groups of menhirs serving as boundary markers). The Aveyron *département* has the greatest concentration of dolmens in France. Rare menhirs are found in the Gard and the Aveyron. Scientists believe the earliest megaliths are from just before the Bronze Age.

MENHIRS

These colossal standing stones sunk into the earth surely had great significance to these early peoples. In the south of the Aveyron *département,* numerous statue-menhirs depict a human figure, perhaps a protective goddess. The figure has arms, hands, short lower limbs, a face tattooed in patterns, neck adorned with jewelry, eyes, nose, but strangely, no mouth.

DOLMENS

These horizontal slabs supported by vertical stones are believed to be tombs. Some were originally buried beneath a tumulus, a mound of earth or stones. Erecting dolmens required teamwork and an inclined ramp, plumb line, rollers capable of transporting stones weighing up to 350t, and the construction of roads. And to think that the installation of the 220t Luxor obelisk on Place de la Concorde in Paris was regarded a phenomenal feat in the year 1836!

BRONZE AND IRON AGES

The elegantly shaped bowls and jewellery displayed in the Musée Ignon-Fabre in Mende date from these periods.

GALLO-ROMAN PERIOD

Ceramic ware from the Graufesenque pottery near Millau, was renowned throughout the entire Roman Empire. Banassac was highly reputed for its fine earthenware.

MILITARY ARCHITECTURE IN THE MIDDLE AGES

The intense military activity of the Middle Ages left many traces throughout the Languedoc. The Albigensian Crusade, the pillaging bands of outlaws during the Hundred Years War, and the proximity of Guyenne, under English rule until 1453, all prompted feudal lords to build strong defences. Castles were erected at the mouths of canyons and on rocky pinnacles. Now reduced to ruins, the numerous fortresses on the Montagne Noire lend a austere grandeur to the landscape.

In the 10C and 11C, the collapse of public power and the crumbling authority of the princes and counts led to a increased number of fortified strongholds. During the 12C and 13C, the castles were once again in the hands of the king and great feudal lords, and were a source of frequent rivalry in Languedoc, constantly seething with border disputes.

CASTLES

Cities could be defended by the Gallo-Roman city walls like those of Carcassonne. But outside the city limits, fortresses were always built on high ground. In the 10C, crude **mounds, either** natural or man-made hillocks large enough for a simple shelter, multiplied rapidly on flat land. Over the centuries they evolved into impregnable citadels, like Cathar castles.

The end of the 11C marked the advent of stone **keeps** or donjons, either rectangular (Peyrepertuse) or rounded (Catalonia) with thick walls and narrow window slits. The only means of access was on the first floor, via a ladder or a retractable gangway. The interior was divided into several storeys. The dark and vaulted ground floor was a store room; the upper floors could be used as reception or living rooms. As residences, most keeps had limited facilities. Many were merely defensive towers housing a garrison. The lords preferred to live in larger building in the **lower courtyard**, either

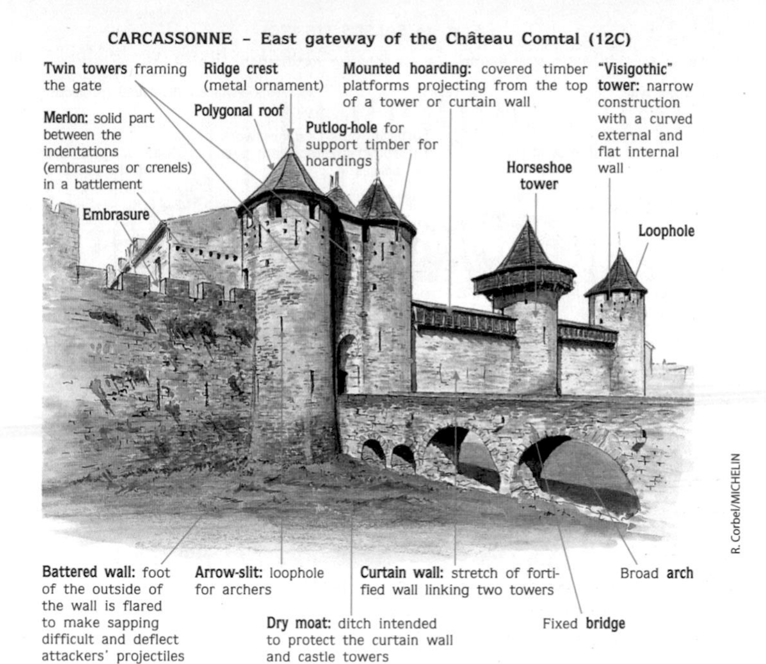

adjacent to or detached from the keep. During the 13C and 14C, the main castle building was extended and made more comfortable as a residence. The keep then became incorporated with the other buildings and acquired one or several enclosing walls, interrupted at intervals by towers. **Puilaurens Castle**, with its fortified wall and four corner towers, is a fine example of this new trend, whereas the keep at **Arques** is a remarkable specimen of 13C military construction.

WATCHTOWERS

These are a common feature in the Corbières, Fenouillèdes, Vallespir and Albères. They transmitted signals using fire by night and smoke by day, and a specific code to convey the nature or gravity of the danger. These visual communications links in the Catalan mountains sent information from the far reaches to **Castelnou Castle** in Les Aspres during the Catalan earldoms of the early Middle Ages, and to Perpignan during the reign of the kings of Aragon.

FORTIFIED CHURCHES

Towards the end of the 10C, churches in southern France became fortified. The church's robust architecture and bell-tower suited for keeping watch, gave the local inhabitants a refuge in times of warfare. The church was traditionally a place of asylum: the Truce of God defined the areas of immunity as extending as far as 30 paces all around the building.

Machicolations, either mounted on corbels or supported on arches between buttresses, as in Beaumont-de-Lomagne (*see The Green Guide Atlantic Coast*), appeared in France at the end of the 12C on Languedoc churches. Also known as murder-holes, they allowed stones and lethally hot liquids to be dropped on attackers at the base of a defensive wall.

Strict regulations on the fortification of churches were prescribed at the time of the Albigensian Crusade. The count of Toulouse and his vassals were accused of abusing their privilege in this regard, so the bishops regained a monopoly which had long eluded them.

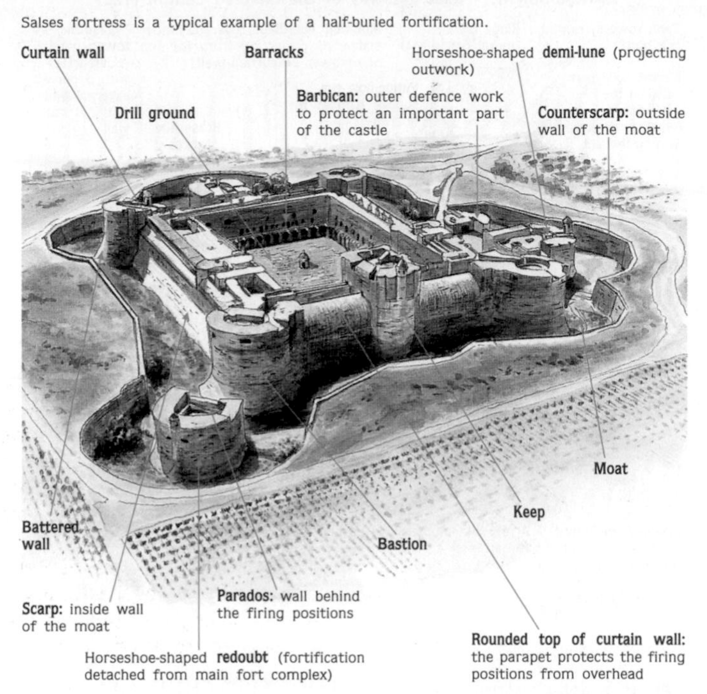

For Languedoc the 13C marked the union with the French crown and the triumph of orthodoxy over heresy. Large brick churches in the Gothic style of Toulouse were constructed, with a layout and height appropriate for fortifications.

The cathedral of Ste-Cécile, with its severe 40m/131ft high walls, looks like a massive fortress at the heart of the subjugated Cathar country. Bernard de Castanet, Bishop of Albi, laid its first stone in 1282. Fortified churches and villages still scatter the upper valleys of the Pyrenees. In Prats-de-Mollo, the church of Stes-Juste-et-Ruffine is a curious blend of roofs and fortifications. One of the finest sights is Villefranche-de-Conflent with its ramparts refurbished by Vauban. Languedoc abounds with fine examples of fortified churches – the cathedral at Maguelone, the church of St-Étienne in Agde, the cathedral of Notre-Dame in Rodez and the cathedral of St-Nazaire in Béziers, to name but a few.

BASTIDES

In 1152, Eleanor of Aquitaine took as her second husband Henry Plantagenet, count of Anjou and lord of Maine, Touraine and Normandy. Their joint estates equalled those of the King of France. Two years later, Henry Plantagenet inherited the throne of England, ruling as Henry II. The Franco-English wars that followed lasted for over 300 years. In the 13C the kings of France and England built *Bastides*, or fortified "new" towns, to secure their territorial claims. The *bastides* had grid layouts with straight streets intersecting at right angles. At the town's centre was a square surrounded by covered arcades, called *couverts* (Mirepoix). Carcassonne's "Ville Basse," Montauban and Villefranche-de-Rouergue are particularly fine examples of these "new towns" (13C and 14C).

Siege warfare

When a castle couldn't be taken by surprise attack, long sieges often ensued. Perched on rocky outcrops and surrounded by steep rock faces, Cathar fortresses confounded conventional techniques of siege warfare. In 1210, thirst and disease forced the fortress of **Termes** to succumb, and in 1255 the fall of **Quéribus**, last bastion of the Cathars, was achieved by treacherous means.

When laying a siege, the attackers surrounded the stronghold and built trenches, stockades, towers, block-houses etc. to counter attacks by relief armies and to prevent those under seige from making a possible sortie. Lengthy sieges could go on for months if not years, so an entire fortified town would be built round the besieged fortress.

To break through the stronghold's curtain wall, sappers dug tunnels into the foot of it, shoring up the cavity with wooden props. They set these props alight so the tunnel and part of the curtain wall above collapsed. They employed slings, mobile siege towers and battering rams. Military engineers supervised the construction of the various siege devices, about which they had learned much during the Crusades.

The age of the cannon

Methods of bombardment evolved over the centuries. Towards the mid-15C the inventions of two talented gunners, the Bureau brothers, placed the French royal artillery on top of the world. No feudal fortress could withstand French attacks and in one year, Charles VII recaptured 60 positions from the English. Military architecture was transformed. Low thick bastions replaced towers and curtain walls were built lower and up to 12m/40ft thick. In the 17C, these new defence systems were perfected by **Vauban**, resulting in defences like the **Fort de Salses**. It is half-buried and protected with curtain walls with rounded tops to shield it from bullets and attackers scaling the walls.

RELIGIOUS ARCHITECTURE

ROMANESQUE ARCHITECTURE

Languedoc, crossroads of many civilisations, has enjoyed various architectural influences: from Auvergne, the church of Ste-Foy in Conques; from Provence, the abbey of St-Victor in Marseille, from Aquitaine, the basilica of St-Sernin in Toulouse and the church of St-Pierre in Moissac. Red or grey sandstone was used in the Rouergue region and farther south, brick and stone were combined harmoniously .

Early Romanesque churches

At the beginning of the 11C, Church prosperity promoted an ecclesiastical construction boom. Austere rustic buildings were erected of rough-hewn stones mixed with mortar, having only a few narrow deeply splayed windows. The walls around the outside of the

Detail on the tympanum of the Ste-Foy church doorway in Conques

S. Sauvignier/MICHELIN

ELNE - Cloisters of the cathedral of Ste-Eulalie-et-Ste-Julie (12-14C)

The cloisters are a set of four roofed galleries around a central quadrangle, enabling monks to walk under cover from the conventual buildings to the church.

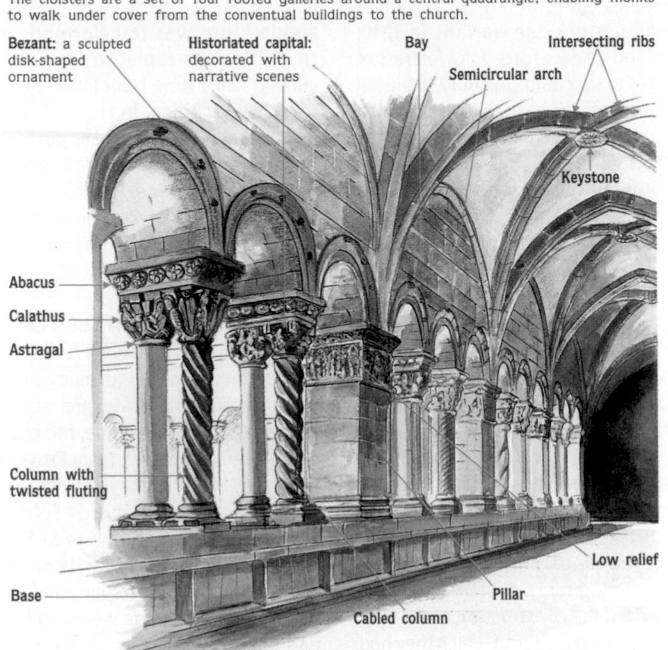

R. Corbel/MICHELIN

apse were often adorned with Lombard bands, vertical pilasters projecting only slightly from the apse wall and linked at the top by small arcades. Inside, naves were roofed with barrel vaulting and ended in an oven-vaulted apse (quarter sphere).

The heavy stone vaulting put a heavy a load on the supporting walls, so windows were reduced to a minimum, and side aisles were built to buttress the nave. The abbey church at St-Guilhem-le-Désert dates from this period.

The Romanesque churches of Gévaudan in Haut Languedoc

The churches in this area encompass a wide range of layouts, with the single nave predominating. At the end of the 11C, it became a feature of larger churches like Maguelone Cathedral, St-Étienne in Agde.

Massive exterior walls reinforced by arcades, and a sober architectural style reflect the Provençal influence. Inside, ambulatories and radiating chapels like those of great pilgrimage churches like Ste-Foy in Conques or **St-Sernin** in Toulouse, are unusual in the simple countryside. In Conques, **Ste-Foy** is a jewel of 12C Romanesque sculpture.

Catalan architecture

Towards the mid-10C an original architectural style combining Mozarabic and Carolingian influences appeared in the Catalan Pyrenees. The abbey church of **St-Michel-de-Cuxa** in Conflent is a good example, with its low, narrow transept, elongated chancel with an apse, side aisles, and barrel vaulting throughout, lending it an Early Romanesque complexity. The simpler style of **St-Martin-du-Canigou, with** vaulted nave supported by pillars, was widely copied during the 11C.

Following this, church construction evolved with barrel vaulting supported by transverse arches (Arles-sur-Tech, **Elne**) and the use of richer decorative motifs. The introduction of domes on pendentives was one of the most remarkable achievements of Catalan architecture.

ST-MICHEL-DE-CUXA – Bell-tower of the abbey church (11C)

The Romanesque churches in Roussillon and Catalonia nearly all feature one or two Lombard bell-towers. This style was probably imported from Italy in the 11C, making its earliest appearance at St-Michel-de-Cuxa, and later became typical of the architecture of this region. The bell-tower at Cuxa stands at the far south end of the transept (originally, there was a matching tower at the far north end).

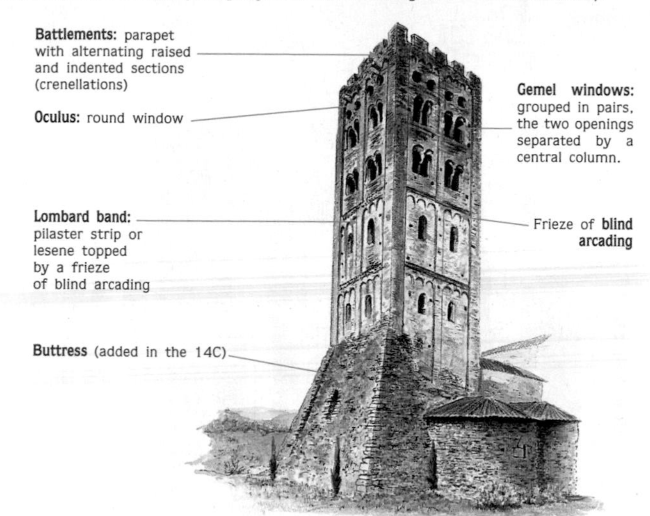

TOULOUSE – Cross section of the basilica of St-Sernin (11-14C)

Barrel-vaulted roof (semicircular section)

Transverse arch: reinforcing strip of masonry in the form of an arch running beneath the vault

Pointed arch

Arcade

Upper gallery, running above the side aisle and overlooking the nave

Upper window

Half-barrel vault beneath the eaves

Great arch

First **side aisle** with a rib vault (four-part)

Window

Nave

Second **side aisle**

Buttress supporting the base of the wall

Beneath the chancel lies the **crypt,** an underground chapel designed to house holy relics

CONQUES – Dome of the abbey church of Ste-Foy (12-14C)

The dome supported on squinches above the transept crossing was built in the 12C. Eight supporting ribs were added in the 14C.

R. Corbel/MICHELIN

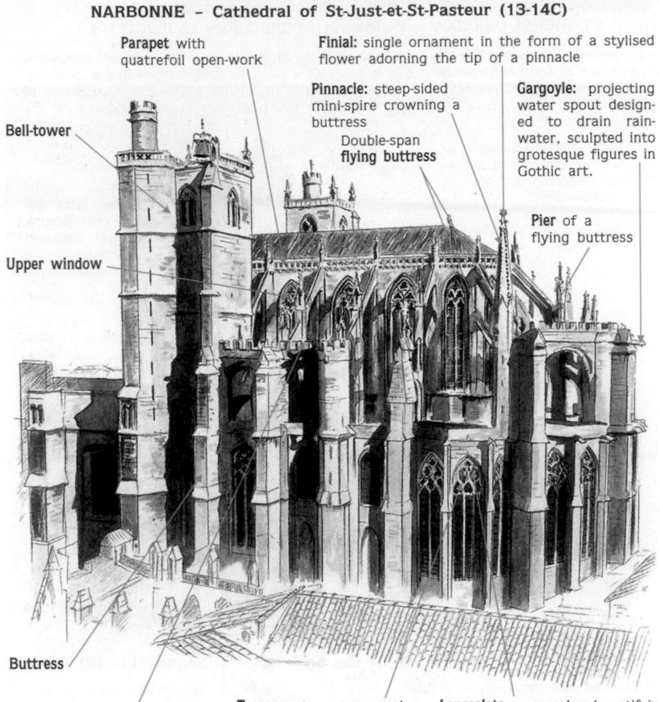

Crudely made from roughly hewn rock, remote mountain sanctuaries are notable for their fine square towers decorated with small arcades and their Lombard bands, constructed down to the 13C. The beautiful grey or pink marble from the Conflent and Roussillon quarries was used for sculptural elements, and Pyrenean craftsmen produced more and more altar tables. **Serrabone** priory's 12C decoration of is one of Roussillon's finest examples of Romanesque art. Painted murals are an important feature of the architecture of this period; apses were painted with the image of Christ in Majesty, or of the Apocalypse or the Last Judgement.

Moissac

Moissac Abbey on the road to Santiago de Compostela, was important throughout Languedoc in the 11C and the 12C. Its doorway and cloisters are masterpieces of Romanesque art. The **tympanum**, a stone rendering of a book illumination, represents Christ in Majesty surrounded by the symbols of the four Evangelists. It suggests a latent Eastern influence via Spain. The trefoil and polylobed arcades are reminiscent of Mozarabic art. The decorative style at Moissac bears some relation to that of Toulouse, another cradle of medieval Romanesque sculpture.

Toulouse

Toulouse flourished as the centre of the Languedoc Romanesque School in the peak of its glory. The largest Romanesque basilica in western Europe, and a major pilgrimage church, the basilica of **St-Sernin** is grandiose.

This subtle blend of stone and brick is vaulted throughout, and features several typical Romanesque techniques: semicircular barrel vaulting on transverse arches in the main nave; half-barrel vaulting in the galleries; ribbed vaulting in the side aisles; and a dome over the transept crossing. Bernard Gilduin's workshop completed the sculpted decoration in less than 40 years (1080-1118).

TOULOUSE - Interior of the church of Les Jacobins (13-14C)

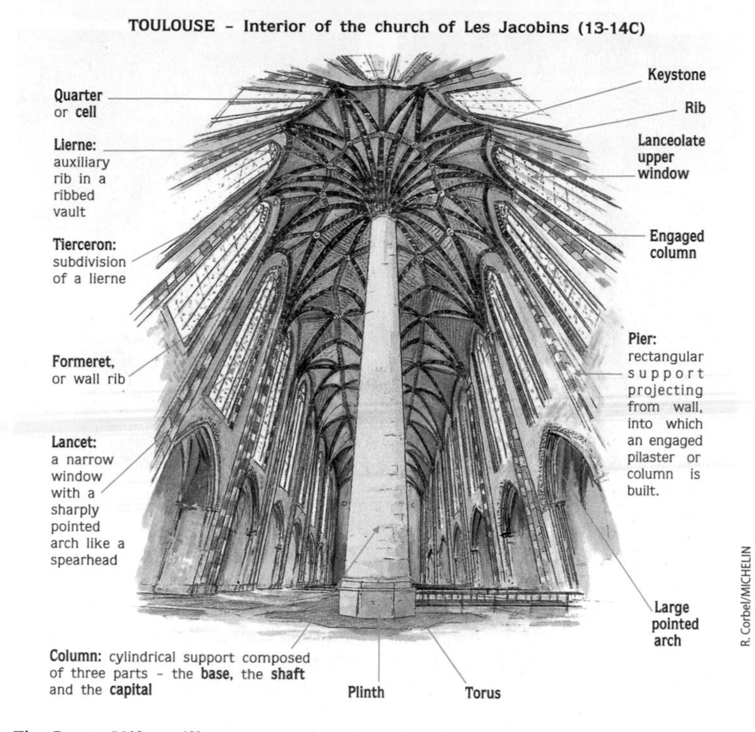

The **Porte Miègeville** was completed in 1100 and reflects Spanish influences from the workshops of Jaca and Compostela. The shape of the capitals is influenced by the classical Corinthian order, to which decorative motifs of animals or narrative scenes have been added. The cloisters of St-Sernin Abbey, La Daurade Monastery and St-Étienne Cathedral were destroyed in the 19C, but architectural fragments are exhibited in the Musée des Augustins).

SOUTHERN FRENCH GOTHIC

The south of France did not adopt the principles of Gothic architecture used in the north, but developed its own style inspired by Romanesque. The chancel of Narbonne Cathedral is virtually the only French Gothic style construction.

Languedoc Gothic

In the 13C, a specifically southern Languedoc Gothic style developed, characterised by the use of brick, interior painted walls, and a belfry wall or a bell-tower decorated with mitre-shaped arched openings, (as in the church of Notre-Dame-du-Taur or the upper storeys of the bell-tower of the basilica of St-Sernin, both in Toulouse). Massive buttresses interspersed with chapels supported the roof vault.The light weight of brick made it possible to build vaulted roofs instead of the earlier timber roofing. Its vast size accommodated the large congregations desired by preachers in the wake of the Albigensian Crusade.

Albi Cathedral

Albi's Ste-Cécile Cathedral, begun in 1282 and completed two centuries later, demonstrates southern French Gothic at its best. The cathedral's single nave, lit through very narrow window openings, is 100m/328ft long and 30m/98ft high and has 12 bays supported by massive buttresses. The absence of side aisles, transept or ambulatory results in a better structural balance. In 1500, the Flamboyant Gothic style expressed itself in the shape of the choir screen and **rood screen**, and in the last three storeys of the bell-tower. The ornate canopy porch was added in 1533.

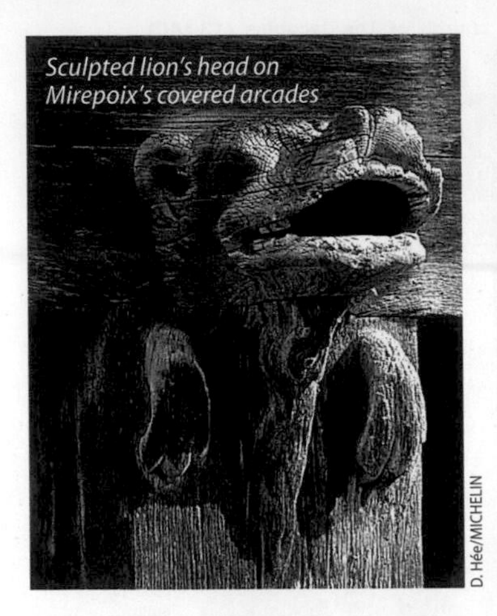

Sculpted lion's head on Mirepoix's covered arcades

D. Hée/MICHELIN

Sculpted face on Mirepoix's covered arcades

D. Hée/MICHELIN

The mendicant orders

The Dominican friars, known as "Jacobins" in France, built their first monastery in Toulouse in 1216, but sadly, it was destroyed by fire in 1871. In 1222, during the lifetime of their founder St Francis of Assisi, it was occupied by the Franciscan Order. The vaulting of the church of **Les Jacobins**, with its "palm-tree" ribbing and twin colonnettes of the cloisters, contribute to the grace of the structure.

The bastide churches

The *bastides*, or "new towns", inspired the construction of churches accessible to the central market place. The southern French Gothic style was particularly suitable to the building of small churches in confined spaces, Although it has been modified over the centuries, Montauban's church of St-Jacques is a good example of the Languedoc School, with its single nave and octagonal brick bell-tower.

CATALAN BAROQUE

Spanish in origin and inspiration, Catalan Baroque art developed when Catalonia was embroiled in a territorial dispute (1640-60) splitting it between Spain and France (Cerdanya, part of Catalonia, was annexed to Roussillon under the Treaty of the Pyrenees in 1659). Catalan Baroque art, primarily religious, came to represent the unity of a people.

Altarpieces

The Catalan Baroque style altarpiece was so appreciated that from 1640, even the smallest parishes were commissioning their own with marble from Caune (Aude) and Villefranche-de-Conflent, pine from the forests of the Canigou, and Spanish gold from America. Built to increasingly huge dimensions, the Catalan Baroque altarpiece incorporated architectural elements such as the column, entablature, cornice, baldaquin or niche. In the early 17C, altarpieces were a sensible size with fairly restrained ornamentation. Between 1640 and 1675, gilded altarpieces covered in sculpture came into vogue, with two or three tiers embellished with pinnacle turrets, broken pediments and canopies, and geometric motifs, winged cherubs and fluted columns. From 1670 to 1730, the style became unabashedly Baroque. Decorative elements swamped the architectural order: pediments were invaded by crowds of angels; every inch was covered with floral motifs (bouquets, garlands, foliage); and the fluted column was replaced by the twisted one. A Catalan Baroque altarpiece at the height of the style's excesses is that at Notre-Dame-des-Anges (1699) in Collioure.

Masters of Catalan Baroque

With the advent of Catalan Baroque, numerous workshops flourished

CORNEILLA-DE-CONFLENT - Ground plan of the church of Ste-Marie (11-12C)

This church originally had a basilical ground plan with three aisles, a very common layout in Roussillon in the 11C. The transept was added in the 12C.

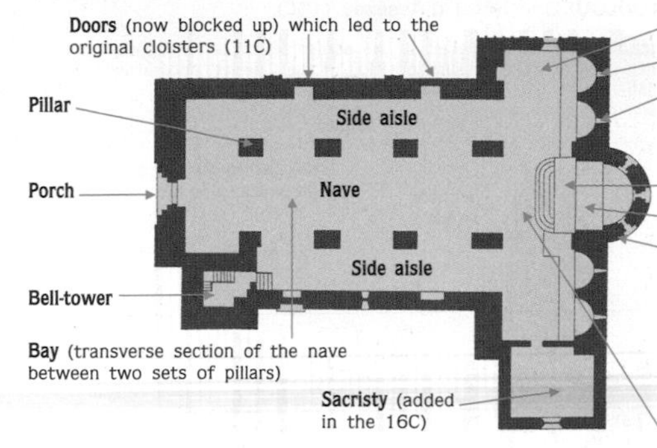

throughout Roussillon. After 1640, schools sprang up around **Lazare Tremullas**, a Catalan sculptor who introduced the carved altarpiece to France. He carved the altarpiece in Notre-Dame-du-Rosaire, now displayed in the church of St-Jacques in Perpignan. **Lluis Generès** created the 17C high altar at Espira-de-Conflent *(18km/11mi E of Prades)* and altarpieces at Prats-de-Mollo and Baixas *(13km/8mi NW of Perpignan)*.

Jean-Pierre Geralt, known for more everyday figures, sculpted the high altars at Pallalda and Trouillas and Notre-Dame-du-Rosaire. But the master of late-17C and early-18C Catalan Baroque extravagance was **Joseph Sunyer**, who confected the high altar of St-Pierre in Prades (1695), that of Notre-Dame-de-l'Assomption in Collioure, an altarpiece in Vinça,and decorations in the hermitage in Font-Romeu.

Sculpture

Catalan Baroque altarpieces rely heavily on sculpture. Lazare Tremullas's sculptural innovations evolved until the 18C. The Rosary altarpiece in the church in **Espira-de-Conflent** is the 1702 masterpiece of the anonymous "Master of Espira." Its low-relief sculptures show a profusion of animated figures, attention to detail, rounded forms and smooth-featured faces. This church also contains a theatrically Baroque, painted and gilded sculpture of the Entombment by Sunyer.

SECULAR ARCHITECTURE

The "triangle" between Albi, Toulouse and Carcassonne is the centre of dyer's woad production. During the textiles and dye economic boom of the mid-15C to the mid-16C, wealthy merchants built beautiful Renaissance mansions here. The 17C and 18C saw the building of private mansions – or *hôtels particuliers* – inspired by the Italian Renaissance. particularly in Montpellier and Pézenas. Their façades feature loggias and colonnades crowned with balusters or pediments. Interior decoration is lavish, and monumental staircases abound.

At the end of the 17C, the architect **D'Aviler** created a revolution by decorating the exteriors of such mansions. D'Aviler replaced lintels with heavily depressed "davilerte arches" over which was an triangular pediment. Magnificent staircases with balusters evoked the grandeur of the preceding period. As the century came to a close, façades were adorned with sculptures and wrought-iron balconies, but pilasters and orders of columns fell out of use. Montpellier's architectural school is represented by D'Aviler, the Girals and Jacques Donnat, with master craftsmen working in wrought iron and carved wood. The school of painting includes such artists as: Antoine Ranc, Hyacinthe Rigaud, Jean de Troy (17C), Jean Raoux and Joseph-Marie Vien (18C). The Peyrou water tower (château d'eau) and aqueduct demonstrate the artistry of this period.

Secular architecture

TOULOUSE – Hôtel d'Assézat (16C)

The Hôtel d'Assézat, designed by Nicolas Bachelier, is the earliest example of Palladian style architecture in Toulouse, with its characteristic superposition of the Classical decorative orders – Doric, Ionic and Corinthian.

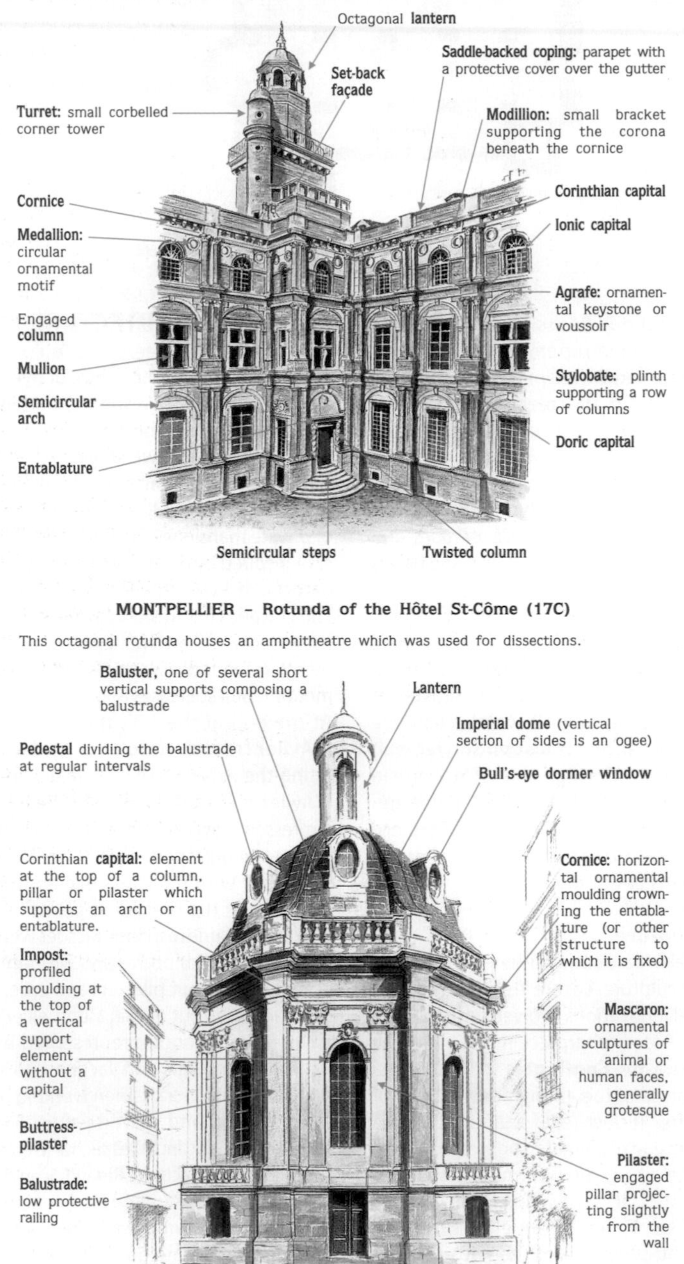

MONTPELLIER – Rotunda of the Hôtel St-Côme (17C)

This octagonal rotunda houses an amphitheatre which was used for dissections.

TRADITIONAL RURAL ARCHITECTURE

The design and construction of rural houses reveal much about the industry of the locality. In the stock raising regions of Causses, the Cévennes and the Aubrac,sheepfolds are a common architectural feature; in the plains of Bas Languedoc, it is the wine cellar (chai) .
Construction materials typically derive from local sources. In the Cévennes, roofs may be of volcanic lava, slate and schist slabs, and in the Causses, made of limestone slabs.
Today's rural houses employ new construction methods, often because craftsmen skilled in traditional techniques are hard to find. Evolving agricultural practices have also changed the style of traditional rural cottages. Now that grain is stored in silos, houses do not require large lofts.

AUBRAC

The **buron** is typical of this region. This solid one-room hut of lava and granite, used by cowherds as living quarters from May to October, is usually built in pastureland on sloping ground near a spring. The single room serves for accommodation and for cheesemaking, and the cellar for maturing the cheese.

CAUSSES

On the *causses*, robust thick-walled houses covered in dry white limestone are built in hamlets on riverbanks or close to land suitable for cultivation. The ground floor comprises a cellar and tool room, and the first floor provides living quarters. An outside staircase leads to the upper floor, and a cistern near the kitchen collects rain water. In such regions where timber is scarce, roofs are replaced by a stone vault.
The sheepfold, usually a vast low-lying rectangular building of rough-hewn stone, may be quite distant from the house.

CÉVENNES

Solid mountain houses designed to withstand the rigorous climate are typical of this region. Walls and roofs are built of schist, and windows are small. Lintels, window frames and corner stones may be built of sand or limestone, and chestnut trees provide timber. If the house is built on sloping ground, the stone steps leading to the first floor living quarters sometimes look like a bridge. Stable and barn are on the ground floor. The second floor could be used for silkworm breeding. On the roofs covered with rough schist slabs *(lauzes)*, the only decorative features are the chimneys.
East of the Cévennes, towards the Vivarais mountains, houses are more Mediterranean in style, with pantile roofs and wavy edged cornices. On the Lozère and Sidobre slopes, granite is featured in walls and around window openings.

ESPINOUSE RANGE

The Monts de l'Espinouse are cloaked in forests of beech, oak and chestnut, interspersed patches of pastureland and broom-covered heath. Farmhouses here feature large slate tiles on sides exposed to the rainladen north-westerly winds. The large two-storey barn of the Prat d'Alaric farmstead in Fraisse-sur-Agout has walls of granite and gneiss, and a roof thatched with broom. Local barns feature gable walls with stepped edges.

LANGUEDOC

The gently sloping roofs of Languedoc houses are covered by curved brick pantiles. The houses of wine-growers in Bas Languedoc, usually plastered with a pink or ochre sand-based material, have tiny windows to keep out the strong Mediterranean sun. Houses in the cereal crop farming region of Haut Languedoc are usually made of brick.

BAS LANGUEDOC

The main façades of houses in this region often feature a triangular pediment. Living quarters are separated from the stable and barn. The rectangular wine cellar (chai) occupies the ground floor. There are two doors in the façade: a large round-arched doorway leading into the wine cellar, and a smaller entrance leading to the first-floor living quarters.

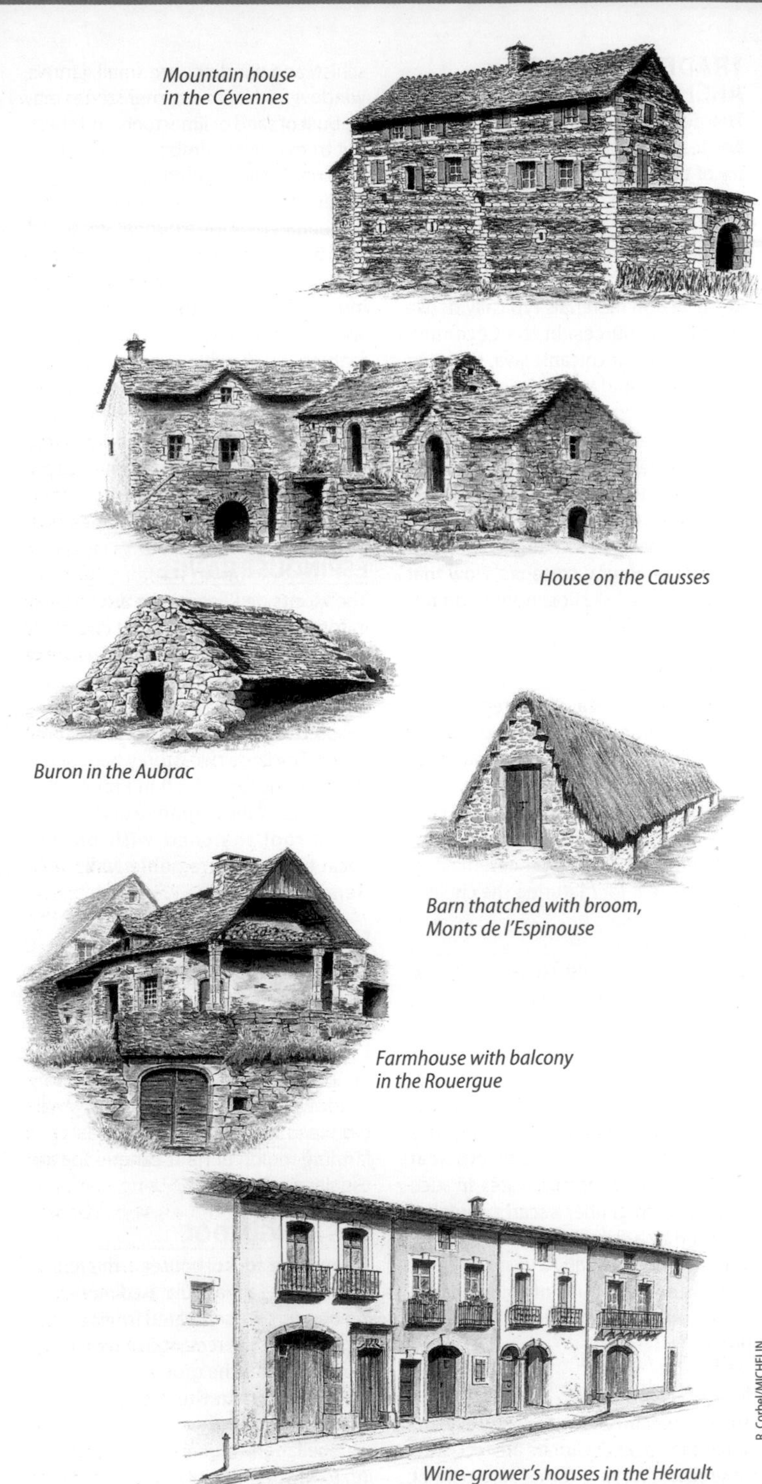

Mountain house in the Cévennes

House on the Causses

Buron in the Aubrac

Barn thatched with broom, Monts de l'Espinouse

Farmhouse with balcony in the Rouergue

Wine-grower's houses in the Hérault

R. Corbel/MICHELIN

HAUT LANGUEDOC

In the Castres region, as in the region around Albi, walls are built entirely of brick, whereas in the eastern parts of Haut Languedoc brick is used only for framing doors and windows, sometimes decoratively. Many farms in Haut Languedoc boast a **dovecot**, either attached to the main farmhouse, or close by.
In centuries past, pigeons were used to fertilise poor soils, and twere therefore a sign of wealth or privilege.

MEDITERRANEAN LANGUEDOC

Small drystone huts, known as **capitelles** or **cazelles**, dot this region's garrigue and vineyards. These served as shelters for shepherds or to store farming implements. The generally circular walls are built of schist or limestone, and the corbelled roof vault is formed by overlapping layers of *lauzes* like the scales of a fish. Small, square, drystone constructions known as **mazets**, dot wine-growing areas in the Hérault *département*. Those tending the vineyards use them for meal breaks and as shelters.

ROUERGUE

Walls are of schist or granite rubble masonry. On the roof, covered with schist or slate *lauzes*, are dormer windows which make the main façade look as if it has pediments. On the ground floor, are the wine cellar and tool room; on the first floor, the living quarters and the attic serves for drying chestnuts. The houses of well-to-do farmers comprise several buildings (living quarters, stable, barn and a turret serving as a dovecot) and a courtyard. In the fields, small, round conical-roofed drystone huts which resemble the *bories* of Haute Provence serve as shelters, barns or tool-sheds. Known by a wide variety of local names, drystone huts like these are a common architectural feature of Jurassic limestone regions.
In the Lot valley, some barn roofs are shaped like the keel of an upturned boat for extra storage space.

Traditions

THE "LANGUE D'OC"

The fusion of Vulgar Latin with the old Gallic language gave rise to a group of "Romance" languages, with the "Langue d'Oïl" in the north of France and the "Langue d'Oc" in the south. The languages were distinguised by the way the word *oui* was pronounced in each region, and the border between the two lay north of the Massif Central. Today the term **Occitan** has replaced the term Langue d'Oc and comprises several major dialects spoken in Languedoc, Gascony, Limousin, Auvergne and Provence.

LANGUAGE OF THE TROUBADOURS

The language of Oc is the language of the troubadours, wandering poets who composed plaintive songs of unrequited love and travelled around southern France, entertaining the court nobility during the 11C to 13C. Their poetry of "courtly love" replaced the earthy, vaguely erotic sensibilities of the 12C with a purely spiritual celebration of love, often embellished with references to the Virgin Mary. Famous troubadours include Bernard de Ventadour from the Limousin, who sang at the court of Raymond V of Toulouse; Peire Vidal, whose reputation stretched from Provence to the Holy Land; Jaufré Rudel and Guiraut Riquier. Political satire against Rome and the clergy held a special place in Occitan literature.
The troubadours' influence spread to Germany and Italy, where it was said that Dante in writing his *Divine Comedy*, hesitated between Provençal and Tuscan.
In the destructive wake of the Albigensian Crusade, the Occitan tongue declined. A group of Toulouse poets tried to revive it in the early 14C, by initiating

Street sign in Occitan, St-Côme-d'Olt

S. Sauvignier/MICHELIN

the Jeux Floraux medieval poetry competition. But Occitan was dealt a heavy blow with the 1539 Edict of Villers-Cotterêts, which made Parisian French the official national language, Reforms introduced for Provençal by Frédéric Mistral and the Félibrige gave renewed impetus to the revival of Occitan. The Escola Occitana was founded in 1919 and the Institut d'Études Occitanes in Toulouse in 1945, with the aim of disseminating and standardising Occitan. A 1951 law allowed Occitan to be taught in schools, and in 1969 it became a language for examination at *baccalauréat* level.

CATALAN

The Catalan language is very close to Occitan, spoken from Salses in Roussillon to Valencia in Spain, and Andorra and Capcir to the west. Catalan is the national language of Andorra.
Catalan reached its height during the 13C, through the writings of poet and philosopher Ramon Llull. Like the language of Oc, it declined in the 16C when Philip II imposed Castilian Spanish over other regional dialects. Catalan is still spoken in everyday life, and the literary renaissance begun in the 19C is enhancing Roussillon's cultural identity.
English words derived from Catalan include 'aubergine' (*albergínia*) and barracks (*barraca* - meaning hut).

FOLKLORE AND RELIGIOUS FESTIVALS

LOCAL LEGENDS

The Languedoc countryside is scattered with megalithic monuments, and their names reflect local superstitions: Planted Stone, Giant's Tomb, Fairies' Dwellings etc. The fantastic shapes of these rock formations have also inspired folk tales of their origins. Common are tales of animals that have been bewitched – cows which no longer give milk, dogs which lose their sense of smell. Local people have traditions to guard against malevolent spirits, like wearing clothes back to front or throwing salt on the fire. Myths like the Bête du Gévaudan abound in regions where wild beasts have preyed upon livestock and even people. Wild animals like the Pyrenean bears have had festivals dedicated to them, the Fête de l'Ours held in the Vallespir region (Arles-sur-Tech, Prats-de-Mollo and St-Laurent-de-Cerdans) in late February-early March, and again during the summer tourist season.

CARNIVAL TIME

Carnival time in the Aude traditionally begins with the winter slaughtering of the pig. Children with masked or blackened faces go from house to house asking for food, and adults join the fun by dressing back-to-front, cross-dressing, or dressing up as babies or old people. A straw dummy is paraded round the village and made the scapegoat for all the misfortunes which have befallen the villagers. The dummy is sentenced before a mock court held in the local *patois* slang, before it is hanged or burnt and children dance around the fire.
At the famous carnival in Limoux (Sundays from January to March, as well as Shrove Tuesday and Ash Wednesday) people dressed as Pierrot figures dance around place de la République, beating time with sticks decorated with ribbons. They are pursued by revellers in various disguises all acting the clown. The festivities last until nightfall, when resin torches light the square. The carnival ends with the Nuit de la Blanquette.

Black Penitents Procession, Perpignan

M.-H. Carcanague/MICHELIN

SARDANA

This Catalan dance is accompanied by a **cobla**, an orchestra with a dozen or so brass, wind and percussion instruments which evoke a range of emotions from gentle to passionate. The sight of the whirling dancers flourishing garlands at festivals and local competitions is exciting, and the sardana festival at Céret is the most famous.

RELIGIOUS FESTIVALS

The most common religious festivals are in honour of local patron saints. St Peter, patron saint of fishermen, is honoured in Gruissan on 29 June. Mass is celebrated for local fishermen at the parish church, then a procession winds to the harbour where a wreath is cast into the water to commemorate those lost at sea.

On Good Friday in Perpignan, a procession is held by the Pénitents de la Sanch, a religious brotherhood founded in the 15C and dedicated to the Holy Blood, Penitents dress in long black or red robes with pointed hoods and walk through Perpignan's streets to the cathedral, carrying *misteris* – painted or sculpted images of Scenes of the Passion of Christ.

RUGBY

The game of rugby was born in 1823 in Rugby, England when William Webb Ellis broke the rules during a football game at Rugby College by grabbing the football with both hands. Rugby came to France in the early 20C and caught on in the South-West, where it suits the robust Occitan temperament. It is now played and followed with huge enthusiasm in every town and village throughout the Pyrenees. Despite the rough physical nature of the game, played in true Occitan *"jusqu'au bout"* spirit, teams lay rivalry aside after the game, and players share a lavish meal to round off the event. Around Carcassonne, **rugby league**, a variation of rugby with teams of 13 players (jeu à XIII), is played, earning itself the nicknames "heretic rugby" or "the Cathar sport."

Star teams

Competition is fierce for the French national rugby championships. Since they were first held in 1892, the **Championnats de France** have been won:

- 16 times by Toulouse (star player Jean-Pierre Rives)
- 11 times by Béziers
- 6 times by Perpignan
- 3 times by Castres
- twice by Narbonne (star players the Spanghero brothers)
- once each by Montauban, Carmaux and Quillan

The fact that rugby is more popular in the South-West than elsewhere in France is evident in the fact that the French international rugby team (victor 10 times of the Five Nations Tournament

Rugby match of Agen vs Toulouse

E. Larribère/MICHELIN

and 4 times of the Grand Slam) is comprised almost entirely of players from South-West France. The most famous include Spanghero (Narbonne), Rives (Toulouse), Castaignède and Christian Califano (both from Toulouse).

Team colours:

- Toulouse: red and black strip
- Béziers: red and blue strip
- Perpignan: red and gold strip
- Narbonne: orange and black strip

TRADITIONAL CRAFTS

The enchanting settings and traditional ways of small isolated villages in the Cévennes, Rouergue, Causses and Languedoc, have long been an attraction for crafts workers setting up workshops here. **Revel** has been famous for its fine furniture and marquetry ever since the cabinet-maker Alexandre Monoury arrived from Versailles in 1889. It is also home to weavers, gilders, lacquerers, wood sculptors, bronze-smiths and blacksmiths. Wool-making and its related crafts have centred around **Mazamet** since the mid-19C. From the late Middle Ages, **Durfort** specialised in beaten copper traditionally used to make pots and cauldrons. **Laguiole** is renowned for its elegant pocket knives with curved handles made of horn. Fine kid gloves are made in and around **Millau**, and since the revival of silk farming in the region, the **Cévennes** has evolved as a silk making centre. The wood of the nettle tree is used in making pitchforks at **Sauve** (Gard). The glazed vases of **Anduze**, which adorn many a garden, have been renowned since the 17C. Sheep bells are produced in village workshops at Castanet-le-Bas or Hérépian, in the Hérault valley. Brickworks abound on the Garonne river plain and on the Roussillon coast where red clay is plentiful.

In the Albi region are several tanning workshops and others related to shoemaking. **Graulhet** produces leather for lining shoes, Dyer's woad *(Isatis tinctoria)* is still cultivated around **Magrin** and the blue dye is used to colour clothes and textiles. Stone has been cut and polished in the Ariège region since the end of the 19C and **Saurat** has the last sandstone quarry in operation, and the last millstone producer in France.

The **Bethmale valley** is a production centre for traditional wooden sabots. They are made from locally grown beech or birch and marked with a heart shape, recalling the local legend of a shepherd betrayed by his fiancée. High-quality, luxurious horn combs are made in **Lavelanet**, near Foix, In French **Catalonia**, typical crafts include whips made from nettle tree wood of Sorède in the Lower Tech valley, corks from Roussillon cork oak, espadrilles at St-Laurent-de-Cerdans, the red and yellow Catalan textiles in geometric designs, and garnets cut and set at Perpignan.

Nature

LANDSCAPES

The regions described in this guide encompass a wealth of spectacular landscapes. To the north-east lie the rounded hills of the Auvergne and the rolling green pastures of the Aubrac. The cattle fairs of Laissac and Nasbinals really enliven the region. Winter snows intensify the peacefulness of the landscape, a haven for cross-country skiers seeking silence and pure air. Farther east the undulating plateaux of the Margeride are chequered with pastureland and forests, vital resources for the local economy.

To the south the countryside around the River Lot changes dramatically, with limestone plateaux, sheer cliffs and deep river gorges. These arid rocky limestone plateaux are known as the **Causses**. Cutting between them are spectacular river gorges or canyons carved by eons of water erosion. Although today this river may seem like an innocent trickle, during a flash flood it becomes a raging torrent.

To the east of this breathtaking landscape of causses and river gorges rise the rugged **Cévennes** mountains with their complex network of ridges and gullies crowned by impressive fortifications. The **Cévennes** was impenetrable for centuries, and today its mystery and utter remoteness gives modern travellers the thrilling sense of treading where no-one has gone before.

To the west the harsh landscape of the Grands Causses gives way to the **ségalas** - "rye fields"- where gentle hills shelter fertile valleys. The sun-scorched limestone hills of the **garrigues** form the geographical transition between the Causses and the Cévennes, and the fertile wine-growing plains of the Bas Languedoc. The *garrigues* bristle with white rocks and clumps of holm-oak, broom and aromatic wild thyme and rosemary, and with the olive trees, mulberry bushes and vines cultivated here, create a truly Mediterranean landscape.

Between the garrigues and the long straight Languedoc coast glittering with lagoons, vineyards seem to stretch forever over the plains and hillsides. Summer enlivens this landscape with colourful crowds of holidaymakers, and autumn brings the cheerful bustle of the grape harvest.

Moving farther south, the Pyrenees make a formidable natural frontier between France and Spain. The steep slopes on the French side drop sharply down into France. They are scored by valleys separated by high ridges, which link the Pyrenees to the inland plains and the coast. From the Montcalm summit (3 078m/10 098ft) to the Albères massif (1 256m/4 120ft at the Neulos peak), the Pyrenean range gradually descends into the Mediterranean.

The Pyrenees' formation began at the end of the Secondary Era and continued through the Tertiary Era, when massive folding in the earth's crust disturbed the old Hercynian layers. Erosion leveled the mountain range, exposing primary sedimentary rock formations and along the axial crests, the granite core itself.

THE CAUSSES, THE CÉVENNES AND THE TARN GORGES

The Aubrac and the Margeride

The **Aubrac** mountains run north-west to south-east between the Truyère and Lot valleys. Produced by volcanic activity in the Tertiary Era, these formidable streams of solidified basalt several hundred metres thick cover a granite core. The asymmetric mountain range slopes gently down to the Truyère in the north-east, where it remains about 1 000m/3 280ft above sea level. Ravines score the steeper south-western slopes.

Above 850m/2 788ft, the Aubrac is a vast pasture with daffodils and narcissi blooming in the spring, and beech woods, moorland and lakes in the west. Crops do not thrive in this sparsely populated region of only 14 inhabitants per km2, compared to the national average of 96 per km2. Long arduous winters bury the plateau under tons of snow. The region's inhabitants live principally by stock rearing. One or two

Landscape in the Aubrac region

S. Sauvignier/MICHELIN

local cheesemakers still produce *fourme de Laguiole* in their drystone huts. The spring and autumn livestock fairs of Laissac and Nasbinals are major events rich in local colour. The **Margeride**, a granite massif running parallel to the volcanic mountains of the Velay to the north, stretches between the Allier, to the east, and the high volcanic plateaux of the Aubrac, to the west. Its highest point at the Randon beacon (signal) is 1 551m/5 088ft above sea level.

The high-lying ground of the **Montagne** averages 1 400m/4 593ft in altitude. Vast stretches of pastureland and occasional forests of pine, fir and birch cover its undulating plateaux. North of Mende, the plateaux (Palais du Roi, La Boulaine) are littered with granite rocks eroded into fascinating columns, obelisks or rounded blocks, sometimes piled precariously on top of one another.

Below the Montagne lie rolling plains (the **Plaines**) scattered with numerous rocky outcrops, where people live in large farmhouses either isolated or grouped into small hamlets. The Margeride's local economy is based on timber, livestock and uranium.

West of the mountain range lies the **Gévaudan**, a lower-lying plateau (alt 1 000-1 200m/3 280-3 937ft) in the shadow of the Aubrac.

For more details on the northern part of the Margeride, consult the *The Green Guide Auvergne Rhône Valley.*

The Causses

South of the Massif Central, the vast limestone plateaux of the Causses constitute one of France's most unusual natural regions. The Causses are bordered by the Cévennes to the east, by the Lot Valley to the north and by the plains of the Hérault and Bas Languedoc to the south. To the west they stretch as far as the Lévézou and Ségala plateaux, and beyond to the *causses* of Quercy which form the eastern limit of the Aquitaine basin.

The limestone rock creates a landscape rich in contrasts: the arid tablelands of the causses, the colossally deep river gorges, and the curious natural wells formed by swallow-holes. The white drystone dwellings in villages and hamlets accentuate the rugged surroundings. In 1995 the causses became part of the Parc naturel régional des Grands Causses, conserving the unique natural, architectural and cultural heritage of this region.

Contrasting with the deep green ravines, the *causses* seem an endless expanse of grey, rocky semi-desert. The dry ground formed of limestone rock soaks up rainwater like a sponge, yet beneath this arid surface is a hive of aquatic activity. The plateaux, some 1 000m/3 280ft above sea level, have dry scorching summers and long cold winters, with deep snows and violent sweeping gales.

To the west, at the edge of the cliffs beside new plantations of black Austrian pine, the groves of beech, oak and Scots pine show all that remain of the ancient forest destroyed by grazing flocks during the Middle Ages. To the east, thistles and tufts of lavender splash the moorland with radiant blues, and clumps of juniper grow on rocky outcrops as stunted bushes or small trees up to 10m/33ft high. Their leaves are sharp and spiny, and their small blueish-black berries enhance local game dishes.

The causses have traditionally been the preserve of sheep, which thrive easily on the sparse local vegetation. Traditionally, sheep supplied wool for the local textile industries in the towns (serge and caddis). Today sheep are reared for their ewe's milk (*lait des brebis*) for the famous cheese matured underground in caves. The Roquefort area has about 500 000 head. Lambskin is processed in Millau, and *Bleu des Causses*, a blue cheese from cows' milk, is produced nearby.

Eroded rock formations

Here and there spectral landscapes of bizarrely shaped rocks haunt the skyline. The protruding ledges and sheer sides of the huge rock strata resemble abandoned cities with streets, monumental doorways, ramparts and strongholds all falling into ruin. They are created by **dolomite**, composed of soluble carbonate of lime, and rather insoluble carbonate of magnesium. Water streaming down the rocks erodes them into rounded crests up to 10m/33ft high, which then morph into pillars, arcades, towers, and unworldly beasts inspiring the imagination. The eroded rock forms clay residues which nourish vegetation that enhances the scenic beauty of Montpellier-le-Vieux, Nîmes-le-Vieux, Mourèze, Les Arcs de St-Pierre, Roquesaltes and Le Rajol.

The river gorges

Known also as *canyons*, from the Spanish *cañon*, the Tarn gorges between Les Vignes and Le Rozier, and the Jonte and Dourbie gorges are magnificent examples. Here the sweeping horizons give way to a vertiginous vertical landscape of cliff faces which may drop 500m/1 640ft or more.The cliff walls are pocked with caves called baumes, from the local word "balma" in use before the Romans arrived. Many local villages and hamlets are named after baumes, including Cirque des Baumes and Les Baumes-Hautes in the Tarn gorges, Baume-Oriol on the Causse du Larzac and St-Jean-de-Balmes on the Causse Noir.

Caves and chasms

The caves *(grottes)* and chasms *(avens)* on the surface of the causses or in the hollow of a valley shelter strange watery subterranean worlds contrasting with the aridity of the plateaux. Rainwater does not flow over the limestone plateaux of the Causses here, but percolates down into fissures, dissolving the limestone to produce natural chasms called **avens** or **igues**, which gradually increase in size and widen into caves.

Underground rivers and resurgent springs

A water course that disappears into a chasm in the causses may create a network of underground rivers spanning several hundred miles. These water courses join up with larger rivers, widen their course and gush along as cascades. Slow flowing underground rivers form small lakes above natural dams known as **gours**. The Grotte de Dargilan contains many examples of gours. Although underground rivers are not easy to access, speleologists believe they are quite numerous. On the Causse du Larzac, the underground river Sorgues was discovered through the **Aven du Mas Raynal**. On the Causse du Comtal north of Rodez, the Salles-la-Source stream is accessed via the **Gouffre du Tindoul de la Vayssière**. The Bonheur, gushing into the open air at the Bramabiau "Alcôve," is another underground river.

Speleology

The first Paleolithic cave explorers were probably just looking for safe places to live. During the age of flint knapping some 50 000 years ago, these peoples searched for caves for inhabitation. In the later Neolithic Age, humans used caves as burial places. Over the passing millenia, daring cave explorers braved the damp and dark to search for precious metals. By the Middle Ages, people believed that caves were inhabited by demons. Systematic cave explorations began in the 18C, but it wasn't until 1890 that Édouard-Alfred Martel made speleology a respected science.

Édouard-Alfred Martel (1859-1938)

The father of modern speleology was an attorney at the Paris law courts of the Tribunal de Commerce. Martel took up geology and travelling as a recreational escape from his legal career. Although this intrepid mountaineer explored well-known caves and discovered new ones in Italy, Germany, Austria, the United Kingdom and Spain, he concentrated his explorations in France. In 1883 he undertook a methodical study of the Causses, about which nothing was known at the time. Martel was fascinated by the Pyrenees, the Vercors and the Dévoluy. His daring expedition along the River Verdon's Grand Canyon enabled the public to explore one of France's most breathtaking natural features. *(see The Green Guide Alpes du Sud in French)*. A scientist at heart, Martel founded a new branch of scientific study - underground geography or **speleology**. His numerous publications made him world-famous and his lively inspired writings were an invaluable resource for explorers who followed him. Martel's studies of the region's network of underground rivers lead to the creation of a safer, more hygienic public water supply. His exciting discoveries inspired a tourist boom that boosted the local economy of the Causses. Caves are home to a huge variety of invertebrates like beetles and millipedes, and the underground laboratory of Moulis in Ariège *(⊶ not open to the public)* studies these cave dwelling creatures.

The Cévennes

Lying to the south-east of the Massif Central and stretching from the Tarnague to the Aigoual, the schist and granite peaks of the Cévennes appear as a succession of almost flat plateaux clad in peat bogs – the *Aigoual Pelouse* (or "lawn") and the Mont Lozère Plat ("dish"). The Mediterranean side is very steep and the Atlantic side slopes more gently on either side of a watershed at the eastern end of Mont Lozère, at the Col de Jacreste *(pass on N 106, east of Florac)* and the Col du Minier.

The crests

The Cévennes are not very high; Mont Lozère, with its long granite ridges, has an altitude of 1 699m/5 574ft. Mont Aigoual, which offers a fine panorama, does not exceed 1 567m/5 141ft. The crests are covered by meagre pastureland and grazing sheep. Pastoral hamlets dot the landscape, with houses made from granite blocks built low to

Cévennes landscape seen from Mont Aigoual

A. Cassaigne/MICHELIN

resist the wind. Lower slopes shelter small villages and holm-oaks, heather and *châtaigneraies* (chestnut groves).

The upper valleys

Numerous streams flow along deep, steep-sided ravines created by erosion of granite and schist relief. Some streams, surging with trout and scented by grassy slopes covered with apple trees, are reminiscent of the Alps.

The lower valleys

These all face south and mark the transition between the Cévennes and Mediterranean country. The sun is intense here, where green meadows adjoin terraced slopes cultivated with vines, olive trees and mulberry bushes. Lavender is distilled throughout the region. You can still find traces of the silkworm breeding which once flourished in the region: large three-storey buildings with narrow windows and spinning mills of old silkworm farms *(magnaneries)*.

The Cévennes landscape

The upper valleys of the Cévennes have dwindling populations, and crops are sparse and meagre. Alongside small streams, meadows planted with apple trees intersperse with fields. The sweet chestnut tree covers most of the slopes, leaving little room for the vines trained to grow on trees, vegetable gardens and fruit trees growing near water sources at the base of the valleys. In certain villages on the periphery of Mont Lozère and in the Margeride, sheep owners gather their sheep into a communal flock led by a single shepherd to graze by day on the mountain, and to return at night to their enclosures to fertilize the soil.

> And still it was perhaps the wildest view of all my journey. Peak upon peak, chain upon chain of hills ran surging southward, channelled and sculptured by the winter streams, feathered from head to foot with chestnuts, and here and there breaking out into a coronal of cliffs. The sun, which was still far from setting, sent a drift of misty gold across the hilltops, but the valleys were already plunged into a profound and quiet shadow.
>
> **Robert Louis Stevenson:** *Travels With a Donkey in the Cévennes*

The Ségalas and the Lévézou

The Grands Causses are separated from the Quercy Causses by the Lévézou massif and a group of plateaux named the Ségalas, after the rye *(seigle)* cultivated here.

The Lévézou

This large rugged massif of crystalline rock between Millau and Rodez rises to 1 155m/3 789ft at the Puech del Pal, its peak. The uplands around Vezins, with clumps of undergrowth and moorland populated by sheep, are bleak compared to the lowlands, with their woodlands, meadows and large lakes. The Lévézou has stimulated its economic activity by developing its rivers for hydroelectric power, and its lakes of Pont-de-Salars, Bage, Pareloup and Villefranche-de-Panat for tourism. During the 19C the Ségalas began to prosper by producing lime from the Carmaux coal basin and the Aquitaine's limestone rocks.

The Carmaux-Rodez, Capdenac-Rodez railway lines facilitated the transport of this precious soil conditioner, which enabled moorland and rye fields to grow clover, wheat, maize and barley. Stock rearing also developed: cattle and pigs in the west, and sheep in the east and south-east, particularly around Roquefort. Today the gently undulating landscape of the Ségalas is covered with green pastures, copses and meadows hedged with hawthorn, topped by chapels on the hilltops *(puechs)*.

The rich red soil colored by iron oxide sediments, particularly in the Camarès or Marcillac regions. This extremely fertile soil is ideal for growing fruit. Rodez is the principle town in the Ségalas, followed by Villefranche-de-Rouergue on the boundary of the Ségalas and the Quercy Causses.

M. Janvier/MICHELIN
Chestnut tree

Forests

The Causses and the Cévennes once boasted thick forests roaming with wild beasts. In the 18C, the "*Bête du Gévaudan*" terrorised the region for three years, devouring over 50 people, mostly young girls and children. Superstitions abounded that the "beast" was some kind of Divine scourge.

After a huntsman shot what was probably a wolf, the "beast" was adopted by folklore as a means of subduing unruly children.

The dangers of deforestation

The consequences of deforestation have been particularly severe in the Cévennes, a region prone to violent storms. In September 1900, 98cm/38in of rain fell in Valleraugue in 48 hours--about 40cm/15in more than the average rainfall in Paris in a whole year.

The sparse plant cover cannot contain the rain, so it gushes downhill into the valleys, becoming 18-20m/59-65ft high flood waves which destroy everything in their path.

Sheep: an enemy of the forest

Sheep diminish the forest by grazing on young leaves and shoots, on the ridges and plateaux, and along the **drailles** used to move them to and from mountain pastures. Towards the mid-19C, when only tiny vestiges of the immense forests of antiquity remained, Georges Fabre, the forest's benefactor, undertook to reafforest the massif with pine, firs and spruce.

Reafforestation

About 14 000ha/34 594 acres have been reafforested by Fabre and his successors, an achievement for which the French National Forestry Commission is justly proud. Yet much remains to be done: other denuded areas must be replanted, and forests consisting largely of pine trees must be replanted with hardier fire-resistant species better suited to the local environment.

The chestnut

Although chestnuts are no longer part of the staple diet of the Cévennes inhabitants, chestnut trees still adorn the region, growing at altitudes of 600m/1 968ft, to 950m/3 116ft on well-exposed slopes. Nevertheless, chestnuts are a threatened species, threatened by grazing animals and Cryptogamic diseases.

"Bête du Gévaudan"
S. Sauvignier/MICHELIN

Lagoon near Maguelone

F. Gégot/MICHELIN

LANGUEDOC

Bas Languedoc

The Languedoc region stretches from the Rhône to the Garonne. Toulouse is the capital of Haut Languedoc and Montpellier is the capital of Bas (Mediterranean) Languedoc. Bas Languedoc covers a 40km/25mi wide strip along the Mediterranean coast. South of the Cévennes, the Garrigues rise 200-400m/600-1 400ft above sea level. Below the Garrigues stretches a sandy plain covered with vineyards, and a necklace of lagoons which ornament the coast. The flat of the plain is broken by limestone outcrops like La Gardiole mountain at Montpellier, Mont St-Clair at Sète, La Clape mountain at Narbonne, and the mountains of Agde (Pic St-Loup). Bas Languedoc lies between mountains of the Massif Central, from the Cévennes, the Espinouse, Minervois and Lacaune mountain ranges, as far as the Montagne Noire, and the first limestone foothills of the Pyrenees, the Corbières.

The Garrigues

The name Garrigues derives from the Occitan garric: kermes oak. This region of mountain and limestone plateaux is watered by the Hérault, the Vidourle and the Gard rivers. The mountains of St-Loup and Hortus loom over the flat landscape. Like the causses, the Garrigues were formed by marine deposits from the Secondary Era. Pastures scorched by the sun, and stunted vegetation like dwarf kermes oaks, rockroses and tufts of thyme and lavender cover the region. In spring this arid countryside is a carpet of brilliant wildflowers.

The coast

Languedoc's Mediterranean coast is lined with lagoons separated from the sea by sand bars created by waves and currents. These salt water lagoons teem with eels, grey mullet, sea perch, sea bream and clams. The Aude and the Orb did not form such lagoons, nor did they create deltas, because coastal currents constantly swept away their alluvial deposits.

The invasive sand left the old ports of Maguelone and Agde stranded inland. The Thau lagoon, virtually an inland sea, is the only navigable lagoon. The Thau is noted for its oyster and mussel farms, and the small fishing ports of Marseillan and Mèze which have developed marinas. Sète, built in the 17C,is now the second largest French port on the Mediterranean.

The Garonne corridor

The Garonne river and its tributaries cut a vast aquatic corridor linking Aquitaine and Languedoc. At the edges of this corridor, the relief becomes undulating: to the south, tiny beaches at the foot of the Pyrenees are shored up by gravel; to the north, the ancient plateau merges with the sedimentary hills of the Tarn region.

Haut Languedoc, between the Aude and the Garonne

Agricultural regions

Modern pressures are forcing small farms to expand their production beyond the traditional mixed cultivation of wheat, maize and vines.

The prospering agricultural Toulouse and Lauragais regions are the "granary" of the south of France. The alluvial plains of the Garonne and the Tarn brim with strawberry beds, and apple, pear and peach orchards. Market gardening and poultry farming are big here. Vineyards grow around Carcassonne and Limoux and also on the Gaillac slopes to the west.

The designs of rural houses change according to the landscapes. In the Lauragais and Toulouse regions, you'll see low brick houses with living quarters, stable, barn and cart shed covered by the same gently sloping roof. Dwellings in Bas Languedoc are taller. The stable and cellar (cave) are on the ground floor, the living quarters, originally a single room, occupy the first floor, with the hay loft above.

Industrial modernity

Toulouse's aerospace industries have spawned chemical, electrometallurgical, textile, leather, farm-produce and granite industries all contributing to the area's economic growth. In the Carmausin, coal-mining at the Découverte Ste-Marie pit is open-cast only. The **Canal du Midi** is a popular tourist attraction. The Toulouse conurbation, with some 600 000 inhabitants, is the hub of the Midi-Pyrénées region. Its considerable research resources, state-of-the-art industries and public facilities extend its influence far and wide.

THE PYRENEES AND ROUSSILLON

The Central Pyrenees

The Pyrenean mountain range is characterised by massive longitudinal geological formations.

The Pre-Pyrenees

Eons ago, Jurassic folding movements shaped a landscape marked by rows of limestone ridges intersected by transverse valleys: the "Petites Pyrénées" and the Plantaurel ridge. Rivers flow to the plain through the ravines of Boussens on the Garonne and of Labarre on the Ariège.

The foothills

During the Secondary Era (Cretaceous or Jurassic), the Pyrenean foothills were formed by strata which folded more violently. Around Foix, the deeply grooved limestone or sandstone ridges give way to crystalline massifs of dark rock such as the St-Barthélemy massif.

Toulouse "granary"

Jacass/MICHELIN

Canal du Midi

D. Pazery/MICHELIN

The axial zone

This zone is the very backbone of the Pyrenees. From the primary sediments rise towering crags of granite whose jagged crests were carved by glacial erosion. These granite massifs have the greatest number of mountain lakes in the Pyrenees.

Peaks and valleys

The Pyrenees mountain chain has no lateral valley to connect its transverse valleys, and so communication and transportation within the chain has always difficult, especially when mountain passes are impassable in winter.

This enforced isolation has preserved local traditions and ways of life, making each valley a tiny kingdom of its own. The fortress-like mountains of **Andorra** and the **upper Ariège valley** guard a bleak and rugged landscape of rocks and scree. These isolated regions link the Central and Mediterranean Pyrenees.

Mediterranean Pyrenees

The Mediterranean Pyrenees, more open to the outside world, connect with the Corbières massif to the north. This stretches as far as the Montagne Noire, the furthest southern outpost of the Massif Central, and separates the Aquitaine basin from the plains of Mediterranean Languedoc.

The mountains

The limestone foothills between the Corbières and the axial ridge of the Pyrenees differ from the northern sedimentary surface of the Central Pyrenees. **The Plateau de Sault** gives way to rows of jagged crests towering over the **Fenouillèdes'** deep furrow. The River Aude cuts through this crust in a burst of breathtaking gorges. The eastern Pyrenees were first peaks to emerge from the earth's crust, pushed upwards to staggering heights by the earth's ancient folding movements. Over the geologic eons, they have been worn down to a lower altitude than the Central Pyrenees. The valleys of the **Cerdagne** and the **Capcir** (1 200m/3 937ft and 1 600m/5 249ft above sea level) shelter villages and cultivated land. These valleys were formed by erosion in the flanks of the Pyrenees, and filled up with clay, marl and gravel accumulated towards the end of the Tertiary Era. East of Canigou (alt 2 784m/9 133ft), the Pyrenean range drops into the trench occupied by the Mediterranean. The **Albères**, the chain's final set of peaks cut between the Roussillon, to the north, and the Ampurdan, to the south (in Spain).

The Roussillon

The parallel valleys of the Têt and the Tech allow Mediterranean influences to penetrate to the heart of the mountain range. Renowned for their brilliant

Corbières vineyards

D.Pazery/MICHELIN

sunlight, dry climate, orange trees and pink oleander, these valleys have very attractive resorts.

The Roussillon plain, stretching for 40km/24mi, was originally a gulf which was filled in with debris from the mountain range at the end of the Tertiary/beginning of the Quaternary Era. Arid rocky terraces (**Les Aspres**) are cultivated with fruit trees and vines. An offshore sand bar separates the sea from the **salanques** marshes, where alluvial deposits from the Têt and the Agly are several hundred metres deep.

TRADITION AND MODERNITY

Straddling two regions (Midi-Pyrénées and Languedoc-Roussillon), the Pyrénées-Roussillon-Albigeois area is a palette of contrasts blending old traditions with modern ways.

The mountains

Traditional rural life

Mountain countryside consists of three zones: the lower slopes with villages and cultivated fields; an intermediate zone of forests alternating with hay meadows; and high mountain pastures. Wheat, rye and maize still grow in Haut Vallespir, Cerdagne and Conflent, but the vines and olive trees which once festooned the Mediterranean valleys have all but disappeared. Outside villages, a scrubland of broom or garrigues replaces the groves of holm-oak, Scots pine and beech diminished by felling. In remote valleys and villages, depopulation leads to a fading of old ways and traditions, and cultivated land becomes fallow or reverts to heathland.

Renewed growth

The Pyrenees' industrial potential depends on exploiting its energy sources. Hydroelectric schemes introduced in the mountains in 1901 are still evolving. Other industrial ventures which boost the local economy include chalk mines at Luzenac, cement works, textile manufacturing, aluminium works, various metallurgy and timber concerns. Busy roads crisscross the region's liveliest valleys, where densely populated, well developed towns cater to tourism with spas, winter sports resorts and new accomodations. As local inhabitants move off the land, newcomers from other parts of France or abroad settle here, creating a new population mix.

The Roussillon coast

The garden of Roussillon

Orchards, market gardens and vineyards make the Roussillon plain a true cornucopia. Produce includes tomatoes, new potatoes, winter lettuce and endive, and peaches, nectarines and apricots, also cultivated on the mountain slopes.

Vineyards

Vineyards cover the banks of the Agly, the rocky terrace of Les Aspres and the sweep of land along the Côte Vermeille,

Mountain rains meet Mediterranean sun

The Languedoc **climate** is basically Mediterranean, with summer temperatures soaring towards 30°C (over 80°F) in Perpignan – one of the hottest places in France in season. The region has its own version of the Provençal mistral, the **tramontane**, which periodically whistles through the Languedoc corridor from the north-west. July and August are hot and, as elsewhere in France, may be crowded, especially towards the coast. (Although the Languedoc coast is never as busy as the Côte d'Azur at this time of year.) Those seeking respite from the coastal plain's blistering heat should head up to the mountains...or down into some of the region's numerous caves. June and September are generally good months to visit, as the weather is fine and warm, apart from the odd shower of rain.

Autumn on the Mediterranean coast remains relatively mild, making it a good season for a tour of the Corbières vineyards and neighbouring ruined Cathar strongholds. Rainfall in the Pyrenees and over Mont Aigoual is heavy, particularly in the autumn. But this is the harvest season, which adds a splash of colour to the Cévennes and the Montagne Noire.

The first snow falls from late October, and by Christmas the resorts are alive with keen skiers, both downhill and cross-country in the Pyrenees, Andorra, and the Capcir and Cerdagne mountain plateaux, and predominantly cross-country in the Aubrac, Mont Lozère and Aigoual massif.

The coming of milder spring weather brings a burst of colour to the Pyrenees, with mountain wildflowers in bloom, and a show of petals in Roussillon's many orchards. Spring and summer are the best seasons to visit the Causses, as temperatures are rarely oppressively hot. It is the ideal time of year for exploring the gorges by canoe, or for pot-holing, rock-climbing and hiking.

the most typical of Roussillon coastal regions. These vineyards produce a vast range of vins de coteaux, including young white wines, rosés and robust, and heady reds. The **Côtes du Roussillon** covers the southern slope of the Corbières, and the arid terraces of Les Aspres to the Albères range. Most local wine is the vin doux naturel (dessert wine), such as Rivesaltes, Banyuls and Maury. Roussillon is focusing more on quality vintage wines and new sidelines like apéritifs (Thuir), vermouth (Noilly Prat at Marseillan) and liqueurs.

Sea fishing

Fishing fleets in the harbours along the Côte Vermeille and coast of the Aude delta have diversified into four types of fishing. Lamparo or lamplight fishing, mainly for sardines or anchovies, requires an accompanying vessel installed with powerful lamps. Red tunny fishing requires powerful deep-sea fishing vessels equipped with huge mechanically-wound nets. Trawling, mainly from Port-Vendres, Port-la-Nouvelle and St-Cyprien, uses huge pocket-shaped nets dragged along the sea bed. Small-scale fishing with mesh nets, trammel nets or floating lines is used at sea and in coastal lagoons. Oyster-farming on the Leucate lagoon, and sea mussel-farming near Gruissan and Fleury-d'Aude are on the increase.

Beaches

The Golfe du Lion coast offers enticing contrasts: on the sandy Languedoc-Roussillon coast, modern resorts beckon the holidaymaker, whereas on the rocky coast shadowed by rocky cliffs of the Côte Vermeille near the Spanish border, narrow bays shelter old fishing ports which harbour the traditions of these tiny cities.

La Grande Motte

DISCOVERING LANGUEDOC ROUSSILLON

MONTPELLIER *and its region*

The city of Montpellier has improved dramatically in the last 20 years, a worthy 'capital' of a region that contrasts the lush countrysides of the Vallée de l'Hérault, wherein lie delightful retreats like St Guilhem-le-Désert and the limestone cave system at Clamouse, with coastal resorts like La Grande Motte, with its pyramid buildings, the ancient fishing port of Sète, and picturesque old villages **like Mourèze, with narrow streets and small houses, so characteristic of the** ***garrigue*** **hinterland.**

Highlights

1. The main starting point for any tour is the **Place de la Comédie** (pp91, 92)
2. The oldest botanical garden in France: the **Jardin des plantes** (p98)
3. Enjoy the view from the **promenade du Peyrou** (p96)
4. The architecture of the **Antigone** district is quite outstanding (p97)

Introducing Hérault

In this luxurious sun-soaked region you find long, golden sand beaches, oyster-growing lagoons, monasteries, castles and wild inland spaces, the *garrigue*, where olives are grown, and the vineyards yield some of the finest wines in France. The rugged landscape ripples south-eastwards from the craggy fringes of the Central Massif to form a more restrained amphitheatre bordering the Mediterranean. The region has seen it all, from Romans to builder monks, from crusades to an Age of Enlightenment.

The envy of France

No European city can match the growth of Montpellier. In the last 40 years, its population, 25% of which is student, has risen tenfold. Montpellier is today France's seventh city; it used to be the twenty-fifth. It was founded in AD 985 at an advantageous position at the crossroads of the Roman 'Via Domitia', the salt road a little to the south, and the 'Cami Roumieu' taken by the pilgrims bound for Compostella. Cultures from far and wide have contributed to the city's growth.

Montpellier is envied throughout France as a centre for intellectual excellence, and at the Faculty of Medicine, Rabelais is said to have found the inspiration for the scenes of drunkenness that fill the lives of the students in his Pantagruel... hard to imagine, of course.

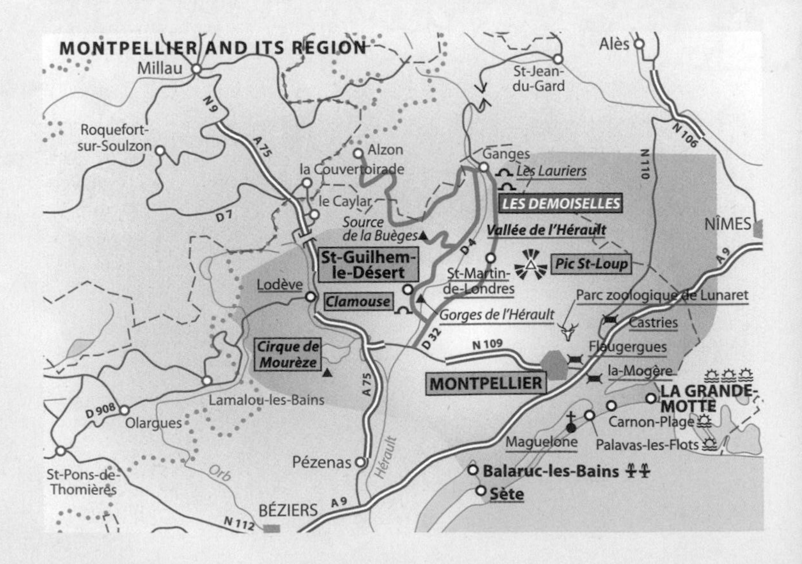

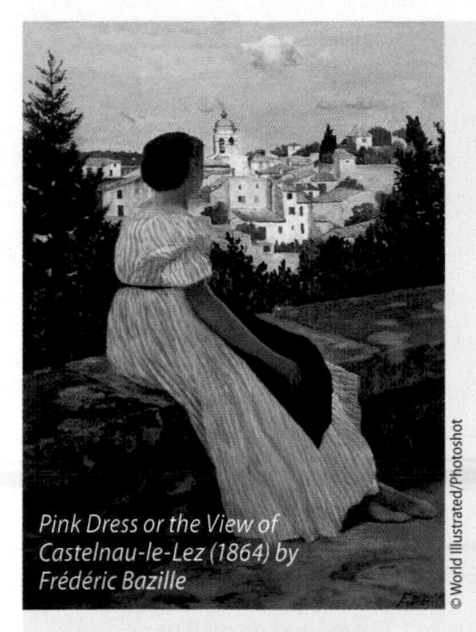
Pink Dress or the View of Castelnau-le-Lez (1864) by Frédéric Bazille

© World Illustrated/Photoshot

Egg shaped

Twenty years ago with traffic tearing round it, the place de la Comédie was oval shaped and known as the place de l'Oeuf. Today, the oval is still there, but as a pattern of embedded marble lost in the middle of a huge plateau flanked on one side by elegant 19th-century buildings and on the other by the sleek new blue trams that criss-cross the city and are set for considerable expansion. Bistros, brassséries and cafés spill out into the square, which at night is often a stage setting for impromptu student dance sessions. More professional displays take place in the 19th-century theatre, which serves as a backdrop to a statue of the Three Graces. In the Grand Rue Jean Moulin is the Hotel Perier – not so much a hotel as a *maison particulière*, or mansion house. It was the birthplace of **Frédéric Bazille** (1841–1870), an impressionist painter of some distinction. The image of Bazille crops up in a few places throughout Montpellier, notably his head, which appears on a number of the statues of other distinguished people, in particular Saint Roch. The sculptor of these statues was **Auguste Baussan**, a good friend of Bazille, who saw nothing extraordinary in using his friend's head, not literally of course, in place of the real thing.

The private mansions are rather more numerous in the centre of Montpellier than is generally evident. They lie tucked away behind huge doorways, beyond which intimate courtyards give into opulent houses of some evident wealth. The 15th-century **Hotel des Trésoriers de la Bourse** is one, and the house at the top of the rue des Soeurs Noires built by the celebrated Marquis de Montcalm, another. Many are not open to the public, but guided tours from the tourism office can often get you in for a glimpse into an altogether different world.

Place de la Comédie

A. de Valroger/MICHELIN

Montpellier★★

The capital of Languedoc-Roussillon, Montpellier is an administrative centre and university city with beautiful historical districts and superb gardens.

- **Population:** 248 000.
- **Michelin Map:** 339: I-7.
- **Info:** 30 allée De-Lattre-de-Tassigny (esplanade Comédie), 34000 Montpellier, ℘04 67 60 60 60. www.ot-montpellier.fr.
- **Location:** 170km/106mi west of Marseille. The tourist office organises guided tours which include access to many areas usually closed to the public. *Reservation required.*
- **Don't Miss:** Place de la Comédie; a walk in the Old Town; the view from the promenade du Peyrou; the neo-classical architecture of Quartier Antigone.
- **Kids:** The Lunaret Zoo; Agropolis Museum.

A BIT OF HISTORY

Origins – Montpellier had its beginnings with two villages: Montpellieret and Montpellier. In 1204 Montpellier became a Spanish enclave and remained so until 1349 when John III of Majorca sold it to the king of France for 120 000 *écus*. After that, the town developed quickly by trading with the Levant. In the 16C, the Reformation arrived in Montpellier, and Protestants and Catholics in turn became masters of the town. In 1622 royal armies of Louis XIII laid siege to Montpellier's fortifications and Richelieu built a citadel to keep watch over the rebel city.

Modern Montpellier – After the Revolution the town became the simple *préfecture* of the Hérault *département*. When the French returned from North Africa after 1962, the city regained its dynamism. The high speed (TGV) rail makes Paris only 4hr away. The city's dynamism is reflected in the **Corum** conference and concert centre, the **Antigone** district, linked to old Montpellier by the Triangle and Polygone shopping centres and the new **Odysseum** district.

HISTORIC MONTPELLIER★★

3hr. Most hôtel courtyards are closed to the public but you can take guided tours organised by the tourist office. Avoid driving into this town centre of one-way streets, by hiring a bicycle or taking a **cycling tour** *(bicycle rental, half-day (3€) or full day (6€). Contact TaM Vélo, ℘04 67 22 87 82).*

TRANSPORTATION

TRAMWAY

Transports de l'Agglomération de Montpellier. ℘04 67 22 87 87. www.tam-way.com A new Montpellier tram allows passengers to go just about anywhere within the city and beyond in minutes.

Between place de la Comédie and the Peyrou Arc de Triomphe are Montpellier's historic districts, last vestiges of its original medieval town. Superb 17C and 18C private mansions, *hôtels*, line the streets, with their remarkable staircases hidden in inner courtyards.

Place de la Comédie

Guided tours (45min) by written request. Tours of the Corum and Berlioz Opera House are subject to bookings and schedule modifications. No charge. ℘04 67 61 67 61.

This lively square links the city's old districts with the new. Place de la Comédie continues north to the **Esplanade** promenade with plane trees, outdoor cafés and musical bandstands.

The **Corum** complex designed by Claude Vasconi includes the 2 000 seat Berlioz opera house. The Corum terrace overlooks the town's rooftops, St-Pierre Cathedral and white spire of Ste-Anne's Church. To the east lie the **Triangle** and the **Polygone** complex (shopping cen-

Hôtel de Varennes
D. Chapuis/MICHELIN

tre, administrative buildings, including the town hall).

Take rue de la Loge.

The name of this street is a reminder of the all powerful merchants' lodge in the 15C.

Turn right onto rue Jacques-Cœur.

Hôtel des Trésoriers de France

No 7. This private mansion housing the Musée Languedocien was the Hôtel Jacques-Cœur when the king's treasurer lived here in the 15C. In the 17C it became the Hôtel des Trésoriers de France, occupied by senior magistrates administering the royal estates in Languedoc.
Finally it was named "Lunaret" in memory of Henri de Lunaret who bequeathed it to the Société Archéologique de Montpellier. To the right of the hôtel stands the **Chapelle des Pénitents Blancs**, rebuilt in the 17C.

Turn left onto rue Valedeau and right onto rue Embouque-d'Or.

On the left is the Hôtel de Manse (*4 rue Embouque-d'Or*). The count of Manse, treasurer to the king of France, had Italian artists design this interior façade with its double colonnade and beautiful staircase called the "Manse's Steps." Opposite is the **Hôtel Baschy du Cayla**, with its Louis XV façade.

Hôtel de Varennes★

2 place Pétrarque. Information at the tourist office. ℘04 67 60 60 60.
Gothic rooms contain Romanesque columns and capitals from the original church of Notre-Dame-des-Tables. Gemel windows and castle doors have been incorporated into the walls. The city of Montpellier uses the 14C Salle Pétrarque for receptions. The mansion houses two museums (*see Museums, below*).

Turn right onto rue de l'Aiguillerie.

As this street's name ("needle factory") suggests, it was the town's street for arts and crafts in the Middle Ages. Some shops still retain their beautiful 14C and 15C vaulted roofs.

Take rue Glaize on the right and continue along rue Montpellieret.

Hôtel de Cabrières-Sabatier d'Espeyran

An excellent example of a Second Empire mansion. Visit by applying to the Musée Fabre (*see Museums below*).

Return to rue de l'Aiguillerie going N around the Musée Fabre, then turn left onto rue de la Carbonnerie.

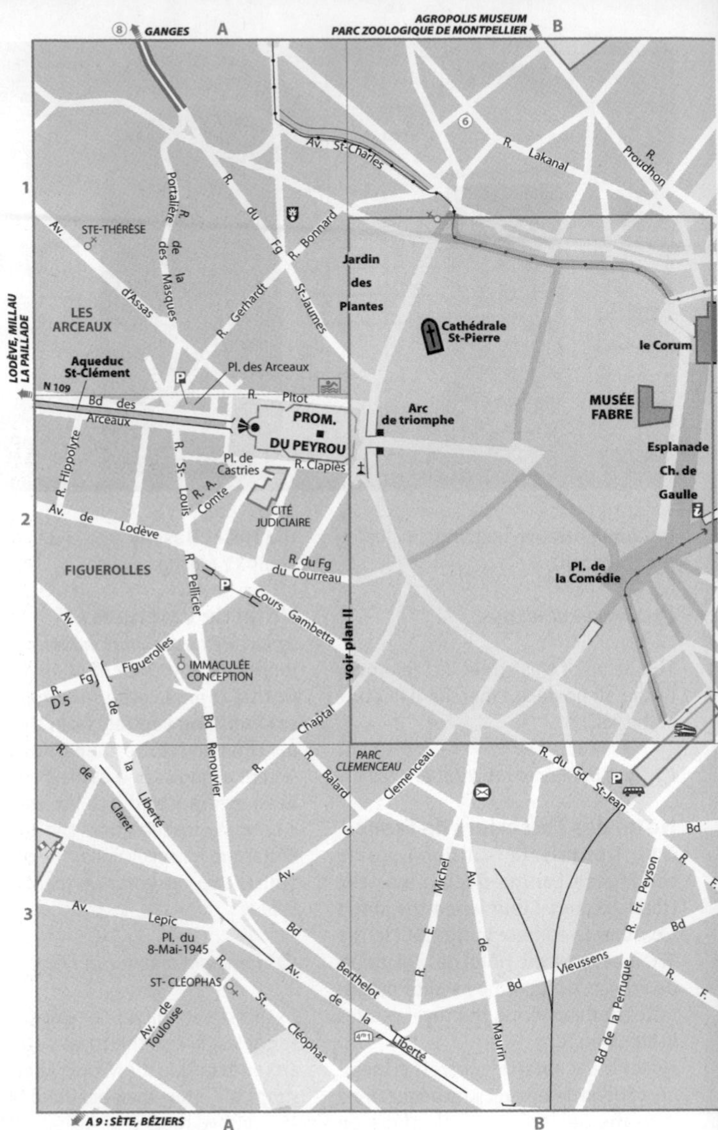

Hôtel Baudon de Mauny

1 rue de la Carbonnerie.

This house features an elegant Louis XVI façade decorated with flower garlands.

Rue du Cannau

This street is lined with classical town houses: at no 1, **Hôtel de Roquemaure**; at no 3, **Hôtel d'Avèze**; at no 6, **Hôtel de Beaulac**; at no 8, **Hôtel Deydé**.

Turn back and take rue de Girone on the right, then rue Fournarié.

Hôtel de Solas

1 rue Fournarié. This 17C town house features a Louis XIII door. Note the plasterwork on the porch ceiling.

Hôtel d'Uston

3 rue Fournarié.

This house dates from the first half of the 18C.

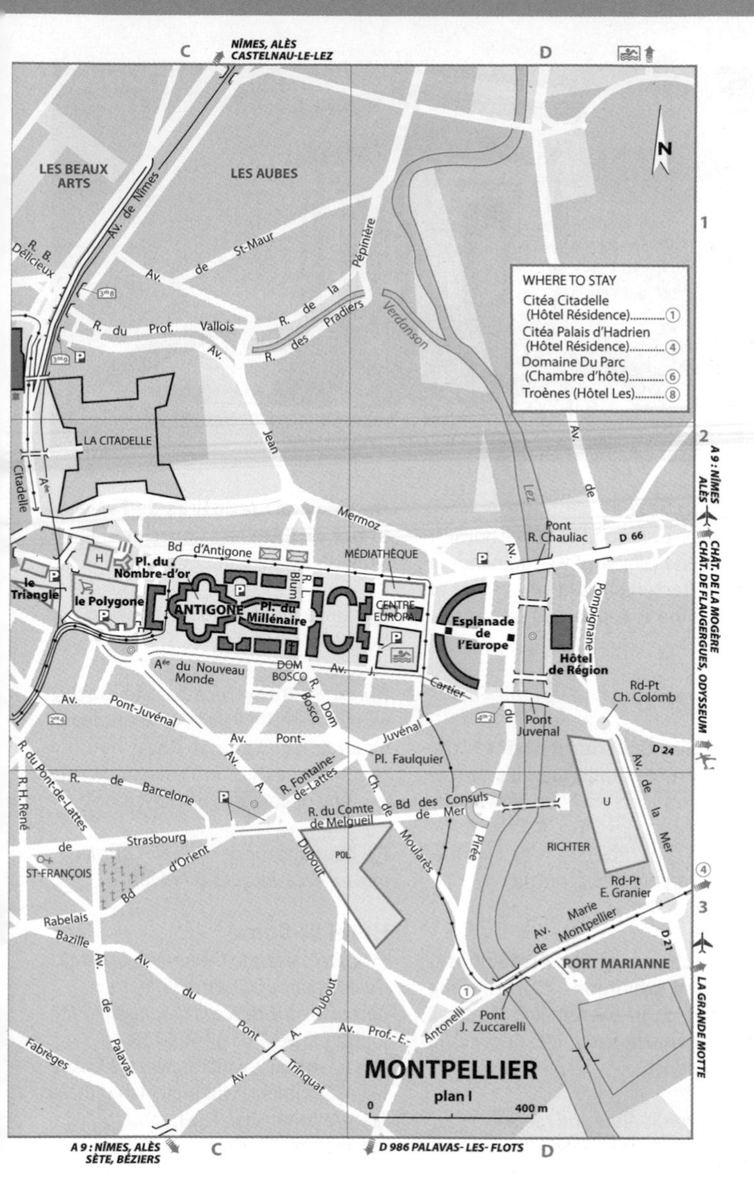

Follow rue de la Vieille-Intendance.

At no 9 is the **Hôtel de la Vieille Intendance**, whose former residents include philosopher Auguste Comte and writer Paul Valéry.

Place de la Canourgue

In the 17C this square was the centre of Montpellier, and numerous *hôtels* remain around the garden with its Unicorn fountain. From here enjoy a view onto the cathedral of St-Pierre.

Hôtel Richer de Belleval (*annexe of the law courts)* once housed the town hall. The square courtyard is decorated with busts and balustrades typical of the late 18C. The façade of **Hôtel de Cambacérès**, by Giral, demonstrates elegant 18C ornamentation and wrought-iron work.

Château d'eau in the Peyrou

A. Thuillier/MICHELIN

Hôtel du Sarret

The Maison de la Coquille ("shell house") is so called because of its squinches, a real architectural feat in which part of the building is supported on part of the vault.

Take rue Astruc and cross rue Foch.

The **Ancien Courrier district** is the oldest part of Montpellier, its narrow pedestrian streets are lined with luxury boutiques.

From rue Foch, take rue du Petit-Scel.

The 19C **church of Ste-Anne** houses temporary exhibitions. Opposite the church porch are the remains of a small building whose early 17C decor is in Antique style.

Take rue St-Anne and rue St-Guilhem to rue de la Friperie, then turn left onto rue du Bras-de-Fer and right onto rue des Trésoriers-de-la-Bourse.

Hôtel des Trésoriers de la Bourse★

4 rue des Trésoriers-de-la-Bourse. Also called Hôtel Rodez-Benavent, this town house by architect Jean Giral features an impressive open staircase and courtyard whose rear wall is decorated with flame ornaments.

Retrace your steps.

The medieval **rue du Bras-de-Fer** leads to **rue de l'Ancien-Courrier**★, lined with art galleries and boutiques.

Turn left onto rue Joubert which leads to place St-Ravy.

Place St-Ravy retains the Gothic windows of the Palace of the Kings of Majorca. The **Salle St-Ravy**, housing temporary exhibitions, has beautiful vaulting decorated with keystones.

Return to rue de l'Ancien-Courrier and take rue Jacques-d'Aragon.

Hôtel St-Côme

Free access to the inner courtyard. Guided tours of the amphitheatre as part of the theme tours organised by the tourist office. ℘04 67 60 60 60.

This town house which is now the Chamber of Commerce was built in the 18C by Jean-Antoine Giral. The famous polygonal anatomical theatre, under a superb dome with oculi and lanterns, lets in a flood of light.

Return to place de la Comédie via the busy grand-rue Jean-Moulin.

PROMENADE DU PEYROU★★ *1hr*

The upper terrace of the promenade affords a sweeping **view**★ of the Garrigues, Cévennes, Mediterranean and Mont Canigou. The key feature of the

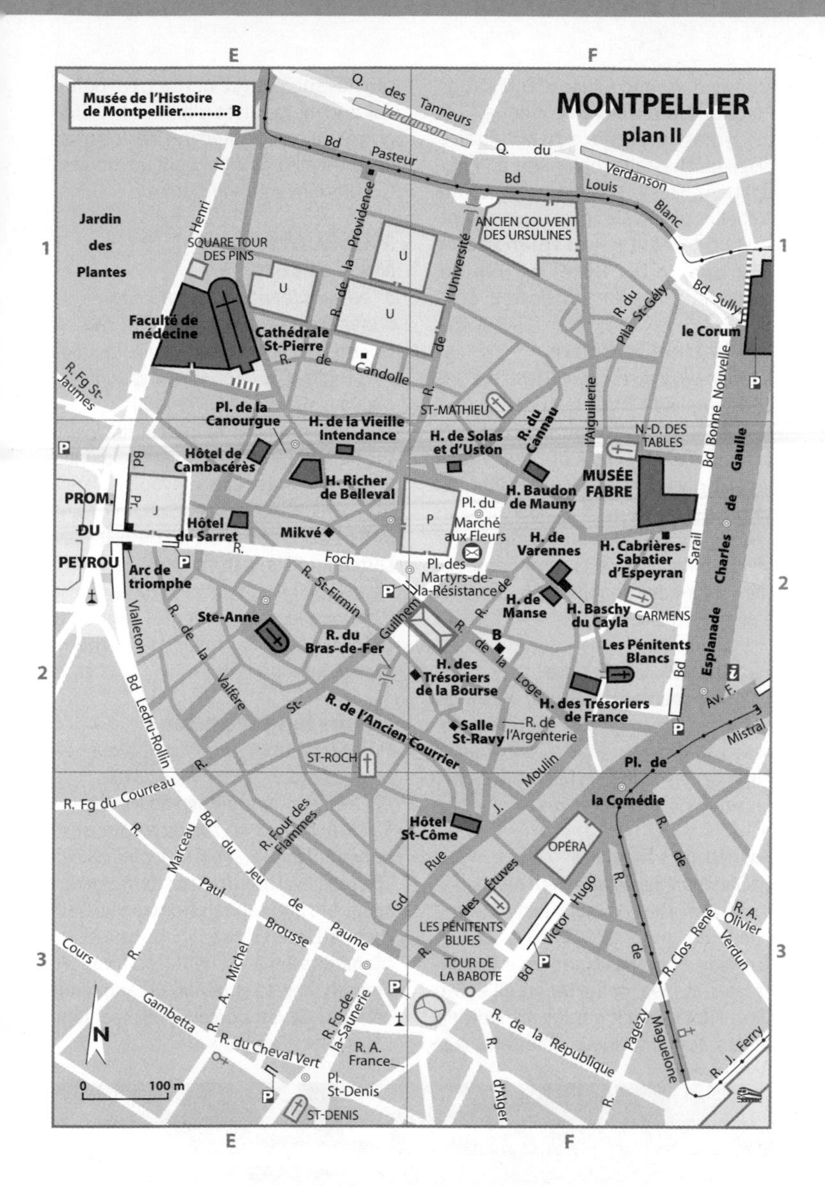

Promenade du Peyrou is the ensemble of the *château d'eau* and St-Clément aqueduct, 880m/2 890ft long and 22m/72ft high. On Saturday, Promenade des Arceaux becomes a flea market.

The late 17C **Arc de Triomphe** depicts the victories of Louis XIV and major events from his reign: the Canal du Midi, revocation of the Edict of Nantes, the capture of Namur in 1692 and the United Provinces of the Netherlands kneeling before Louis XIV.

ANTIGONE DISTRICT★

45min. Starting from place de la Comédie (east side), walk to the Antigone district via the Polygone shopping centre.

Catalan architect **Ricardo Bofill** designed the bold new Antigone district. This vast neo-Classical housing project combines prefab technology with harmonious design. Behind a profusion of entablatures, pediments, pilasters and columns are low-income housing, public facilities and local shops, arranged around squares and patios. **Place du Nombre-d'Or** continues with the cypress-lined **place du Millénaire**, place de Thessalie then place du Péloponnèse. The vista stretches from the "Échelles de la Ville" past the crescent-shaped buildings of **esplanade de l'Europe**, to the **Hôtel de Région**, converted into a dock for Port Juvénal.

Cathédrale St-Pierre

Open daily except Sun afternoon.
Towering like a fortress, the cathedral seems more massive with the adjacent façade of the Faculty of Medicine. It is the only church in Montpellier not completely destroyed during the Wars of Religion. Although built in the Gothic style, the cathedral is reminiscent of the single-nave Romanesque churches along the coast.

Faculté de Médecine

The Montpellier Faculty of Medicine occupies a former Benedictine monastery founded in the 14C by order of Pope Urban V. The Faculty houses two museums (*see Museums below*).

Jardin des Plantes

Open Jun-Sep daily except Mon noon-8pm; Oct-May daily except Mon noon-6pm. 4€ 04 67 63 43 22.
The oldest botanical gardens in France, created in 1593 for the Montpellier Faculty of Botany for the study of medicinal plants, contain various Mediterranean species such as the nettle tree, holm-oak and mock privet (phillyrea). A large ginkgo biloba planted in 1795 is a graft from the first ginkgo plant introduced to France by Antoine Gouan.

MUSEUMS

Musée Fabre★★

37 bd Sarrail; enter through 39 bd Bonne-Nouvelle. Open Tue, Thu, Fri and Sun 10am-6pm; Wed 1-9pm; Sat 11am-6pm. Closed Mon and public holidays. 6€. 04 67 14 83 00.
The museum was founded in 1825 with the generosity of the Montpellier painter **François-Xavier Fabre** (1766-1837) displays Greek and European ceramic ware, and paintings from the Spanish, Italian, Dutch and Flemish schools. Early-19C French painting features works by the *luminophiles* (light-lovers), Languedoc painters who captured the region's superb light on canvas.

Musée languedocien★

Hôtel des Trésoriers de France, 7 rue Jacques-Cœur – 04 67 52 93 03. Open mid Jun-mid Sep daily except Sun 3-6pm. Rest of year except Sun and public holidays 2.30pm-5.30pm. 6€.
The medieval room houses Romanesque sculpture and capitals from the St-Guilhem-le-Désert cloisters. Other museum highlights are a 13C Vias lead font, 17C Flemish tapestries, beautiful Languedoc cabinets, Sèvres porcelain, archaeological artefacts and folk art.

Jardin des Plantes

F. Gégot/MICHELIN

Musée du Vieux Montpellier

Hotel de Varennes, 2 place Pétrarque, first floor. ℘04 67 66 02 94. Open daily except Sun and Mon 9.30am-noon, 1.30-5pm. No charge.
This local history museum contains old maps, religious objects and documents from the Revolution.

Musée Fougau

Hôtel de Varennes, 2 place Pétrarque, second floor. Open Wed and Thu 3-6pm. Closed mid-Jul to mid-Aug. No charge.
The museum derives its name from the Languedoc expression *lou fougau* (the hearth). Objects, furniture and decors represent popular 19C local arts and traditions.

Musée de l'histoire de Montpellier

Place Jean-Jaurès (via rue de la Loge). Open daily except Sun 10.30am-12.30pm, 1.30-6pm. Closed public holidays. 1.50€. ℘04 67 54 33 16.
The crypt of the original Église Notre-Dame-des-Tables hosts a multimedia presentation on Montpellier's history and destiny.

Musée Atger★

Faculté de Médecine, 2 rue de l'École-de-Médecine, first floor, access (signposted) via the Houdan staircase. Open Mon, Wed, Fri 1.30-5.45pm. Closed Aug. No charge. ℘04 67 41 76 30.
This museum contains drawings bequeathed by Xavier Atger (1758-1833) and works by artists of the 17C and 18C French School, the 16C, 17C and 18C Italian School, and the 17C and 18C Flemish School.

EXCURSIONS

Parc zoologique de Lunaret★

6km/4mi N of the Hôpitaux-Facultés district. Leave town on rue Proudhon and take the road to Mende. Open mid May-mid Sep 9am-7pm; rest of year 9am-5pm (6pm in autumn). Closed Mon morning from mid Sep-mid May. Zoo, no charge: conservatory 5€ (children under 6, free).

Musée Fabre
D. Chapuis/MICHELIN

℘04 67 63 45 50. www.zoo.montpellier.fr.
In this vast park bequeathed to the town by Henri de Lunaret, animals seem at liberty in a setting of garrigues and undergrowth. Stroll and observe zebras, bison, alpacas, moufflons, wolves and exotic birds.

Agropolis Museum

951 av. Agropolis, 500m from the Parc de Lunaret. Parking on the right-hand side of the road. Open daily except weekends 2-6pm. 7€. ℘04 67 04 75 00. www.museum.agropolis.fr
This fascinating museum devoted to agriculture and food has thematic exhibitions, a Cybermuseum and children's activities. The comparison between a Moroccan shepherd from the Atlas mountains and a corn grower from Illinois is particularly striking.

Pic St-Loup

23km/14mi N along D 986 then D 113 to Cazevieille. Park the car to the E of the village and follow the directions to Pic St-Loup. The wide stone path leads up to a Calvary. From there, take a little winding footpath which climbs up to the chapel and observatory. Allow 3hr there and back.
St-Loup peak is the highest point of a long ridge above the Montpellier Garrigues. The summit offers a

panorama★★ of Hortus mountain, the Cévennes, the Nîmes plain and Mont Ventoux, the Alpilles and the Luberon, the Camargue, the Montpellier plain and the Mediterranean string of coastal lagoons.

Lattes

6km/4mi S of Montpellier.
Leave by ④ on the town plan.
In 1963, the Lattes rediscovered the archaeological site of Lattara, which from 6C BC to AD 3C was a thriving port supplying the hinterland, particularly Sextantio, as Castelnau-le-Lez was known in Antiquity. Lattara imported wine, oil, luxury ceramic ware and exported freshwater fish, wool and pelts, resin and mineral ore. Lattara's marshy site led to gradual subsidence. After having served as a river port during Gallo-Roman times, Lattara was abandoned when increased rainfall silted up the port. Lattara comes to life at the **Musée archéologique Henri-Prades** (*leave Lattes SE on D 132 towards Pérols open daily except Tue 10am-noon, 2-5.30pm; closed 1 Jan, 1 May, 14 Jul, 25 Dec; 3.50€, no charge 1st Sunday in the month. 04 67 99 77 20; www.musee.lattes.fr*), sited in the old farmhouse of the painter Bazille. An exhibition shows the creation of the town during the second Iron Age and the creation of the port, and daily life in Lattara, featuring house, furniture, kitchen, ceramic and glass ware, funerary steles and funerary furniture. Another exhibit presents the 3C and 4C necropolis of St-Michel in which 76 tombs were discovered.

Château de Castries★

12km/7mi NE of Montpellier.
(*not open to the public*).
The 16C Renaissance château built by Pierre de Castries is still owned by the Castries family. Sadly, one of the wings was destroyed during the Wars of Religion and its stones were used for terraces designed by Le Nôtre. After visiting the château, take D 26 to Guzargues, off N 110, for an interesting **view** of the **aqueduct** built by Riquet to supply water to the château.

Palavas-les-Flots

12km/7mi S of Montpellier.
Leave on ④ on the town plan.
After the railway line opened in 1872, Palavas became a seaside resort popular with Montpellier families. Palavas was the only beach on this stretch of coast until the Languedoc-Roussillon shoreline was developed for tourism.
Palavas is home to the **Musée Albert-Dubout** (*access on foot from the east bank along quai des Arènes or by boat open Jul-Aug 10am-noon, 4-9pm; Mar-Jun, Sep-Nov daily except Mon 2-6pm; Dec-Feb Sat, Sun and school holidays 2-6pm. 5€. 04 67 68 56 41*). This museum occupies the Ballestras redoubt, a reconstruction of an 18C fortified tower built in the middle of Levant lagoon. It commemorates cartoonist Albert Dubout, who drew amusing renderings of Montpellier holidaymakers and numerous scenes of bull-fighting. Enjoy terrace views from Mont St-Clair to the gulf of Aigues-Mortes.

DRIVING TOURS

Montpellier "Follies" – On Montpellier's outskirts are some thirty 18C aristocratic summer residences with acres of vineyards and pretty gardens with lakes and fountains.

East of Montpellier

9km/6mi. From the city centre, follow the signs to the "Montpellier-Méditerranée" airport. After the bridge over the Lez, take the road to Mauguio (D 24). The Château de Flaugergues is about 2km/1mi down the road, in the Millénaire district.

Château de Flaugergues★

Jun, Jul and Sep guided tours of the château (1hr30min) daily except Mon 2.30-6.30pm; rest of the year, tours of the château by request. Park and gardens all year round daily except Sun 9am-12.30pm, 2.30-7pm (Jul-Aug and Sep only Sun and public holidays 2.30-7pm) 7.50€ (5€ park and gardens). 04 99 52 66 37. www.flaugergues.com.

This château purchased by Étienne de Flaugergues, Montpellier financier and advisor to the Parlement de Toulouse in 1696, is the oldest of the Montpellier "follies." The tour of Flaugergues ends with a tasting of wine produced on the estate.

Return to the road to Mauguio, heading right, and drive past the Château de Flaugergues and under the motorway to get to the Château de la Mogère.

Château de la Mogère★

Gardens open to visitors, guided tours of the château (45min) 2.30-6.30pm. 5€ (gardens only: 3€). By appointment for tours of the chateau. 04 67 65 72 01. www.lamogere.fr.

This elegant early 18C château designed by Jean Giral has a harmonious façade surmounted by a pediment. Inside are 18C paintings by Brueghel, Hyacinthe Rigaud, Louis David, Jouvenet.

Return to the city centre on D 172E.

West of Montpellier

Round tour of 22km/14mi. From the city centre take the road to Ganges (D 986) for 6km/4mi, then turn left towards Celleneuve, and then right onto D 127. A little further on, two lion-topped pillars indicate the turn-off to Château d'O.

Château d'O

Open for exhibitions and events.

The 18C château has a beautiful park with statues from Château de La Mosson. Owned by the Conseil Général de l'Hérault, it is used as a theatre during the Printemps des Comédiens festival held every summer.

Carry onto Celleneuve. Follow signs to Juvignac, then turn left onto the road leading to the Château de La Mosson.

Château de La Mosson

This most sumptuous residence in the Montpellier area was built from 1723 to 1729 by rich banker, Joseph Bonnier, Baron de La Mosson. The Baroque fountain is a reminder of the originally lavish decoration of Bonnier's estate, now a public park.

Return to N 109 and take the first road on the left towards Lavérune.

Before long, the road passes through vineyard country.

Château de l'Engarran

Beyond the superb wrought-iron entrance gate from the Château de La Mosson is a Louis XV style building.

Carry on towards Lavérune. The Château de Lavérune is on the far west side of the village.

Château de Lavérune

Open Sat-Sun 3-6pm. 2€ (children under 12 1€). 04 99 51 20 00 (town hall) or 04 99 51 20 25 (museum).

This imposing 17C-18C residence once belonged to the bishops of Montpellier. The first floor **Musée Hofer-Bury** displays paintings and sculptures by contemporary artists, including Henri de Jordan, Gérard and Bernard Calvet, Roger Bonafé, Vincent Bioulès and Wang Wei-Xin.

Take D 5 back to the city centre.

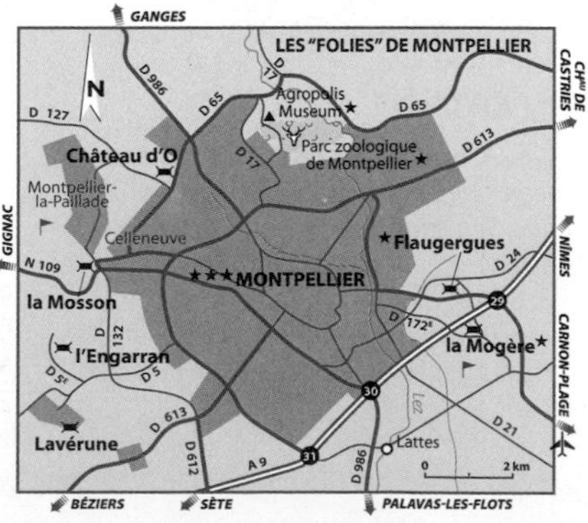

ADDRESSES

STAY

Hôtel de la Comédie – *1 bis r. Baudin. ℘04 67 58 43 64 – hoteldelacomedie@cegetel.net – 20 rms.* Located just off of La Place de la Comédie, this renovated hotel with 19C facade offers pleasingly modern bedrooms. Its lively Montpellier neighbourhood makes an excellent base for discovering the city. Relaxed ambience.

Hôtel du Palais – *3 r. du Palais. ℘04 67 60 47 38 – www.hoteldupalais-montpellier.fr – 26 rms.* This family hotel near the Peyrou gardens and the Place de la Canourgue has small stylish and well kept rooms.

Hotel les Troènes – *17 av. Emile-Bertin-Sans – ℘04 67 04 07 76 – www.hotel-les-troenes.fr – closed Dec-Feb – 14 rms.* Linked to the town centre by the tramway, this 1960s hotel has been completely renovated.

Chambre d'hôte Domaine du Parc – *8 r. Achille-Bège – ℘04 67 41 16 49 – www.hotelduparc-montpellier.com – P – closed Dec-Feb – 19 rms.* A former stately residence, close to the historic centre.

Hotel Résidence Citéa Citadelle – *357 r. du Professuer Antonelli – ℘04 99 51 36 00 – www.citea.com – P – 52 rms, 16 apartments.* Close to the Antigone quarter, and accessible by tram, this hotel has all modern conveniences.

Hotel Résidence Citéa Palais d'Hadrien – *1035 av. Léonard de Vinci - 34970 Lattes - 8km/5mi S of Montpellier on D 132 – ℘04 99 51 35 00 – www.citea.com – P – 42 apartements.* Between Montpellier and the coast, offering 2-5 rooms apartments, ideal for families.

EAT

C'an Jose – *8 bis r. du Petit-Saint-Jean. ℘04 67 60 70 71 – closed 14 Jul-15 Aug, Sun and Mon.* This Old Montpellier establishment serving Tapas and Catalan, Spanish and Balearic cuisine has a dining room covered with photographs of Minorca. *Buen provecho*!

Le Petit Jardin – *20 r. Jean-Jacques-Rousseau. ℘04 67 60 78 78 – www.petit-jardin.com – closed Jan and Mon.* This charming house in the renovated Écusson quarter welcomes diners to its terrace-garden to enjoy tasty regional fare and splendid views of the cathedral.

Les Bains de Montpellier – *6 r. Richelieu. ℘04 67 60 70 87 – closed in Feb, Toussaint and Christmas holidays, Mon lunchtime and Sun – reservation recommended.* Dine in the shade of the courtyard palm trees or in one of the drawing rooms in these wonderfully restored old "Parisian baths." Cuisine using fresh market produce.

L'Image – *6 r. du Puits-des-Esquilles ℘04 67 60 47 79 – closed lunch Sun and public holidays.* Close by the Arc de Triomphe and the Promenade du Peyrou, hidden in a narrow street, this lovely restaurant offers carefully prepared regional cuisine.

TAKING A BREAK

Dorian's Kawa – *12 r. Four-des-Flammes. ℘04 67 66 18 71 – Mon-Sat 8am-7pm – closed Aug and public holidays.* A tearoom to make a note of – the coffee is excellent and the owner very friendly. The shop sells coffeepots, tea services and English china. Ideal for a break or a tête-à-tête.

L'Heure Bleue – *1 r. de la Carbonnerie. ℘04 67 66 41 05 – Tues-Sat noon-7pm.* This literary tearoom in an 18C mansion is also an art gallery and second-hand shop with a lavish collection of sculptures and curios. Home-baked pastries and some 30 varieties of tea.

STOPPING FOR A DRINK

Café de la Mer – *5 pl. du Marché-aux-Fleurs. ℘04 67 60 79 65 – end Jun-end Aug: Mon-Sat 8am-2am, Sun and holidays 3pm-2am; rest of the year: 8am-1am, Sun and holidays: 3pm-1am.* A large, popular café in the town centre, with coloured mosaics and sunny terrace. A fashionable meeting point for Montpellier residents.

Grand Café Riche – 8 *Pl. de la Comédie – ☎04 67 54 71 44 – daily 6.30am-2am; summer: 6am-2am.* This century-old café is a Montpellier institution. Its large terrace is a front row seat for observing street entertainment on the Place de la Comédie. Art exhibitions are frequently held here.

La Pleine Lune – *28 r. du Fg-Figuerolles – ☎04 67 58 03 40 – daily 10.30am-1am.* This bar in the Plan Cabannes district has an inimitable clientele of artists and local characters. Happenings, exhibitions and concerts are organized here regularly.

ON THE TOWN

As a student city, Montpellier's cultural landscape is quite diverse, with jazz enthusiasts, accordion fans and lovers of salsa or classical music. Bars and music cafés cater to new trends so you might find a rap concert being performed round the corner from a bourgeois manor.

Rockstore – *20 r. de Verdun – ☎04 67 06 80 00 – www.rockstore.fr – bars: Mon-Sat 6pm-4am; disco: 11pm-4am.* This nightlife hotspot hosts rock groups and organizes techno, rap and sound system evenings in the techno and rock bars and the disco.

Centre dramatique national – *Domaine de Grammont, Avenue Albert-Einstein – ☎04 67 99 25 25 : reserv. by phone: 04 67 60 05 45.*

Opéra Comédie – *11 bd Victor-Hugo – ☎04 67 60 19 99 – tickets: Mon 2pm-6pm, Tue-Sat noon-6pm, Sundays of performances – closed Aug.*

Zénith – *Av. Albert-Einstein – ☎04 67 64 50 00 – www.zenith-montpellier.com – performance schedule variable – closed Aug.* Variety and rock shows.

SHOPPING

Aux Croquants de Montpellier – *7 r. du Faubourg-du-Courreau – ☎04 67 58 67 38 – Tue-Sun 7am-7pm, Mon 7am-1pm and 4-7pm ; closed Aug.* For over a century this tiny shop with an extensive array of confections has been a mecca for biscuit lovers.

Aux Gourmets – *2 r. Clos-René – ☎04 67 58 57 04.* Run by the Fournier family for over 45 years, this shop close to Place de la Comedie offers a wide variety of sweets and cakes.

Librairie Sauramps – Pl de la *Comédie, Allée Jules-Milhau (Le Triangle) – Tramway Comédie – ☎04 67 06 78 78 – www.sauramps.com – Mon-Sat 10am-7pm – closed public holidays.* This huge bookstore carries a good choice of literature about the area.

Markets – Food markets open every morning in the centre city halles (covered markets): Castellane and Arceaux, on the Esplanade Charles-de-Gaulle, the halles Laissac, the new halles Jacques-Cœur in the Antigone district and on the Plan Cabannes. Organic produce is sold Tuesdays and Saturdays on Place des Arceaux. On the 3rd Saturday of each month, used-book sellers gather on Rue des Étuves. Avenue Samuel-Champlain in the Antigone district holds a farmers' market Sunday mornings. A flower market Tuesdays and a flea market Sundays are held at La Paillade, Esplanade de la Mosson.

Maison régionale des vins et produits du terroir – *34 R. St-Guilhem – ☎04 67 60 40 41 – daily (except Sun in Dec) 9.30am-8pm.* All the finest produce of the region is represented here.

CALENDAR OF EVENTS

Montpellier and the surrounding area are rich in all manner of festivals

Festival international Montpellier danse – *☎0 800 600 740 (free call) – www.montpellierdanse.com – late Jun-early Jul.* Traditional music and dance.

Festival de Radio France et Montpellier Languedoc-Roussillon – *☎04 67 02 02 01– www.festivalradiofrancemontpellier.com – first 3wks of Jul.* Concerts, chamber music, jazz, world music.

Festival international cinéma méditerranéen – *☎04 99 13 73 73 – www.cinemed.tm.fr – late Oct-early Nov.* Film festival.

La Grande-Motte ☼☼☼

La Grande-Motte is a Mediterranean seaside resort enjoying 6km/4mi of fine sandy beach and a proximity to Nîmes and Montpellier. Its tall eye-catching pyramids create an original skyline and its Palais des Congrès (conference centre) overlooks a marina accommodating 1 410 yachts.

- **Population:** 8 202.
- **Michelin Map:** 339: J-7.
- **Info:** Office du tourisme de la Grande-Motte; Ave Jean-Bene and All de Pins, 34280 La Grande-Motte, 04 67 56 42 00. www.ot-lagrandemotte.fr.
- **Location:** Only 23km/14.3mi southeast of Montpellier.
- **Don't Miss:** The huge fine sandy beach and architecture by Jean Balladur
- **Kids:** L'Espace Grand Bleu leisure park and nautical activities.

THE RESORT

The resort's resolutely modern design employs honeycomb **pyramids, buildings shaped like seashells** and Provençal style **villas.** La Grande-Motte is known as a "kid" resort and was awarded the Pavillon bleu d'Europe for the quality of its sea water. Visitors enjoy water sports on Ponant Lake and angling in Or Lake.

Aquarium panoramique

Open Jul and Aug: 10am-11.30pm; mid to late Jun and mid to late Sep: daily 10am-12.30pm, 2-7.30pm, 8.45-10.30pm; mid-Sep-late Dec and Feb: daily except Sun morning 10am-noon, 2-6pm; Jan: Sat-Sun and public holidays 2-6pm. 5€ (14 and under: 3.50€). 04 67 56 85 23.

Sea-horses, sea eagles, groupers, sharks, octopus and 300 other species of fish and invertebrates from the French coast and Camargue lagoons swim around the different pools.

EXCURSION

Carnon-Plage

8km/5mi.

This lido-style beach on the Gulf du Lion, situated along a thin strip of land between La Grande-Motte and Palavas-les-Flots is popular with people from Montpellier. The marina links to the Rhône-to-Sète canal. The actual beach is separated from the nearby road by sand dunes, which offer some protection from the occasional breeze.

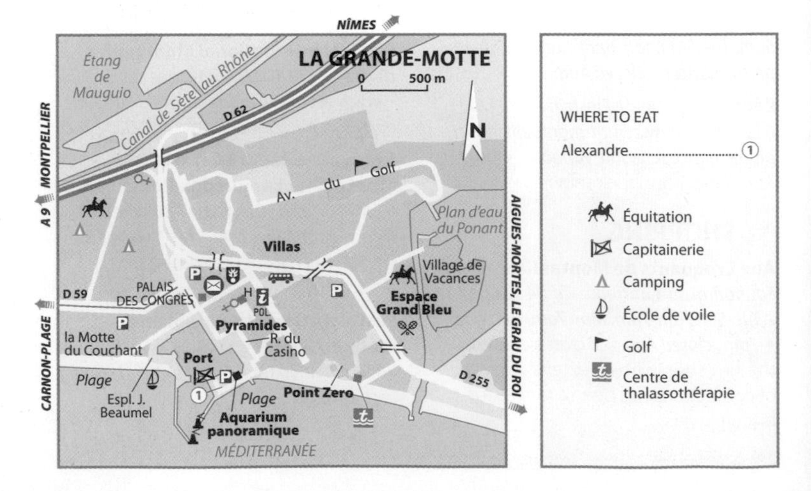

ADDRESSES

STAY

Golf – *1920 Ave. du Golf – 04 67 29 72 00 – golfhotel34@wanadoo.fr –* P *– 45 rms –* *14€.* Rooms with balconies that overlook the golf course or Ponant lake.

SPORT

This seaside resort offers sport and leisure activities from relaxing seaside walks to the thrill of hurtling down giant **Grand Bleu** water chutes.

Blue Dolphin – *71 Quai Eric-Tabarly, Le Miramar shopping centre – 04 67 56 03 69 – www.bluedolphin.fr – daily 9am-noon, 2pm-7pm – closed Jan and Tue.* Diving club: All levels of diving are taught, from initiation to level 4.

Étrave croisière – *Quai d'Honneur – 04 67 29 10 87 – www.etrave-crosieres.com – daily 7am-8pm – closed Nov-Feb –* Étrave Croisières offers discovery voyages around the coast, sea-fishing excursions and boats for hire.

EAT

La Cuisine du Marché – *89 R. du Casino – 04 67 29 90 11 – closed Mon and Tue from Sep-Jun – reservation recommended.* This little restaurant employs high quality produce, fine service and fixed price menus.

SHOPPING

Marché provencal – *Pl. de la Mairie – 04 67 29 03 01 – www.lagrandemotte.fr – Sun 7.30am-2pm (Jun-Sep Thu 7am-2pm.* Provençal market, with wide range of regional produce and crafts.

Vallée de l'Hérault★

With such delights as the village of St Guilhem-le-Désert, and the limestone cave at Clamouse, the Vallée de l'Hérault is quite special, and also ideal for adventure activities like canoeing and rafting.

- **Michelin Map:** 339: H-5.
- **Info:** 34190 Ganges, 04 67 73 00 59.
- **Location:** Ganges is 47km(29.3mi) north of Montpellier via D986 and 52km(32.5mi) east of Lodève via D25.
- **Don't Miss:** The gorges of the Hérault Valley, and the imposing columns of the Grotte des Demoiselles.
- **Kids:** Village of Cambous and Grotte de Clamouse.

DRIVING TOURS

94km/58mi round-trip – allow one day.

Ganges

This small industrial town at the confluence of the Hérault and Rieutord rivers makes a good base for exploring.

Leave Ganges SW along D 4.

Brissac

The town's oldest district lies in the shadow of a castle dating from the 12C and 16C.

Gorges de l'Herault

The river gorge narrows to the Pont du Diable. The Hérault cuts through sheer rock faces adorned with scrubby trees. There are intermittent signs of cultivation: vines and olive trees clinging to hillsides.

St-Guilhem-le-Désert★★

Parking at the entrance to the village. In high season, mornings are quieter. Allow 1 hour. Population: 245.

2 R. de la Font-du-Portal, 34150 St-Guilhem-le-Désert, 04 67 57 44 33. www.saintguilhem-valleeherault.fr.

This pretty little village is built around an old abbey, in a delightful site, at the

St-Guilhem-le-Désert

L. Campion/MICHELIN

mouth of untamed river gorges, where the Verdus flows into the Hérault. It owes much of the story of its origins to legend, related in a 12C chanson de geste.

Childhood friends – Guilhem, the grandson of Charles Martel, was born in about 755. He was brought up with Pépin the Short's sons and was soon noted for his skilful handling of weapons, his intelligence and his piety. The young princes were very attached to him; his friendship with one of them, Charles, the future Charlemagne, was to last until his death.

Guilhem was one of Charlemagne's most valiant officers. Military victories against the Saracens at Nîmes, Orange and Narbonne earned him the title of Prince of Orange. He retuned home but on finding that his wife had died while he had been away, he decided on a life of solitude and delegated the government of Orange to his son. During a visit to the Lodève region he discovered the Gellone Valley and had a monastery built there. Despite being recalled by Charlemagne, Guilhem finally took leave of his king who gave him the relic of the Cross. Guilhem returned to his monastery and a year later he retreated to his cell until he died in 812.

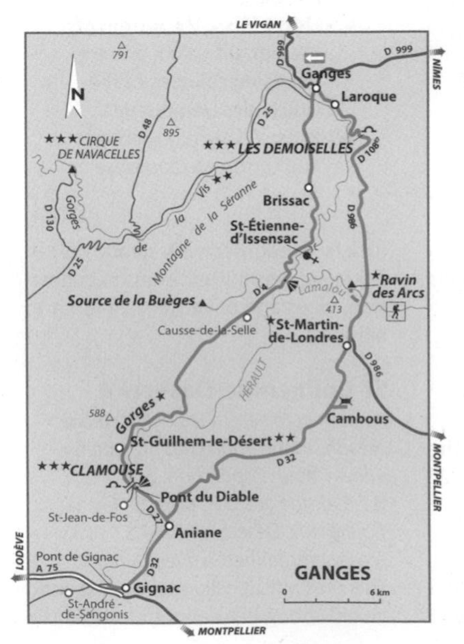

The abbey of St-Guilhem – After Guilhem's death, the monastery of Gellone became an important place of pilgrimage. By the 12C and 13C, the monastery was home to more than 100 monks and the village of Gellone was renamed St-Guilhem-le-Désert.

Abbey Church★

Narrow winding streets lead through St-Guilhem to place de la Liberté, the square onto which the abbey's west doorway opens. All that remains of the abbey founded in 804 by Guilhem is the abbey church, which was built in the 11C and deconsecrated during the Revolution, when the monastic buildings were demolished.

Chevet★ – *To see this, walk round the church to the left.* From the alley lined with old houses, the rich decoration of the chevet can really be appreciated. Flanked by two apsidal chapels, it features three windows and a series of tiny arched openings.

Interior – The 11C nave is austere in design. The oven-vaulted apse is decorated with seven great arches. On either side are niches in the walls, displaying on the left the reliquary of St Guilhem, complete with his bones, and on the right the fragment of the True Cross given by Charlemagne.

Cloisters– *Entrance through the door in the south arm of the transept.* Only the north and west galleries on the ground floor remain of the two-storey cloisters.

Delicate Crystallisations

The Grotte de Clamouse is renowned for its great number and variety of delicate crystalline formations. The calcite formations at Clamouse are made of aragonite, calcite or a mixture of these two different forms of calcium carbonate crystallisation. Their clear white colour indicates that they contain hardly any impurities or mineral deposits.

Clamouse's underground network provides ideal conditions for the formations of such crystallisations: dolomitic rocks, porous rock walls, a plentiful water supply, above average temperatures and a permanent slight draught.

Museum

Open Jul to Aug: daily, 11am–noon except Sun, every day 2.30–6pm exc. Wed, 3.30–6pm. Rest of year, every day from 2–5pm exc. Tue. 2€. 04 67 57 75 80. This contains sculpture work from the abbey and a sarcophagus in white marble (4C) said to be that of St Guilhem.

Grotte de Clamouse★★★

Jul and Aug: guided tours (1hr). Temperature: 17°C/62.5°F. Jul–Aug 10am–7pm; Jun and Sep 10am–6pm; Mar-May and Oct 10am-5pm. 8.50€ (children 4-14 years, 5€). 04 67 57 71 05. www.clamouse.com.

The Clamouse dolomitic limestone cave in the Causse du Sud Larzac was explored in 1945 and opened to tourists in 1964. It is called Clamouse "the howler" because it cascades quite noisily into the Hérault after heavy rain. The Clamouse cave is hollowed out of the Causse du Sud Larzac, near where the gorge of the River Hérault opens onto the Aniane plain.

The cave takes its name from the resurgent spring which bubbles out below the road, cascading noisily into the Hérault after heavy rain, justifying its dialect name of Clamouse ("howler").

Crystallisations, Grotte de Clamouse

D. Pazery/MICHELIN

The guided tour goes through various natural galleries to the Gabriel Vila chamber, called the sand chamber for the layers of sand deposited by the Hérault river when it floods. The route follows the old river bed through fossilised galleries with chiselled, jagged rock forming a ghostly backdrop. Here are classic calcite stalagmites, stalactites, columns, discs and draperies coloured by mineral deposits; sparkling white **crystallisations** and rarer aragonite **"flowers;" crystalline dams** transforming subterranean lakes into jewellery caskets filled with **"cave pearls"** (pisolites). The Grande Finale is a huge translucent concretion known as the "Méduse" (jellyfish).

Cross the river over a modern bridge near **Pont du Diable***, an early-11C bridge built by Benedictine monks. See view of the Hérault gorge and aqueduct supplying vineyards in the St-Jean-de-Fos area. Drive down D 27 to the small town of Aniane.*

Aniane

Aniane is a quiet wine-growing town where St Benedict founded a prosperous abbey in the 8C. Stroll its narrow streets to see the church of St-Jean-Baptiste-des-Pénitents (housing temporary exhibitions), the 17C French Classical church of St-Sauveur and the 18C town hall.

Gignac

The 17C towering **Chapelle Notre-Dame-de-Grâce** has an unusual Italian-style west front. The N 109 crosses the Hérault over **Pont de Gignac**, considered the finest 18C bridge in France.

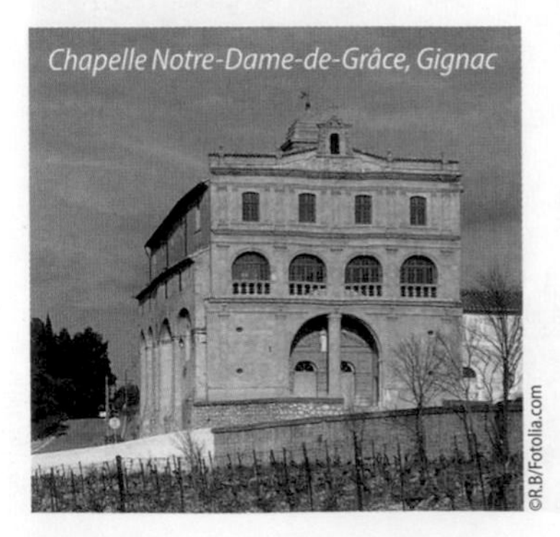
Chapelle Notre-Dame-de-Grâce, Gignac

©R.B/Fotolia.com

Return to Aniane and follow D 32 to St-Martin-de-Londres.

Village préhistorique de Cambous

Leave the car in the Cambous car park and walk to the prehistoric village. 1hr guided visit year round on demand. 2.50€ Open Jul-Aug daily except Mon 2-7pm; Apr-Jun, Sep-Oct Sat-Sun and public holidays 2pm-6pm. 5€. 04 67 86 34 37. www.archeologue.org.

Discovered here in 1967 were remains of 2800–2300 BC stone dwellings with 2.5m/8ft-thick drystone walls and corridors. An original house has been reconstructed.

St-Martin-de-Londres

This charming village retains traces of its 14C defensive wall and parish close fortified in the 12C. The 11C early Romanesque **church★** has an oven-vaulted semicircular east end and Lombard-band decoration.

Follow D 986 N towards Ganges.

Ravin des Arcs

Stop the car by the bridge spanning the Lamalou. Take a path on the left leading to the Ravin des Arcs. It rises as far as a wall then veers to the left. From that point the path is clearly waymarked in red and white (GR 60). Allow 2hr round-trip.

The path goes through scrubland dotted with holm-oaks then descends to the Ravin des Arcs, a narrow canyon 200m/656ft deep in places.

Grotte des Demoiselles★★★

At St-Bauzille-de-Putois, take the hairpin road (one-way) up to two terraces (parking facilities) near the entrance to the cave. From the terraces there is an attractive view of Séranne mountain and Hérault Valley. *Allow 1hr; temperature: 14°C/57°F. guided tours (1hr, last departure 30min before*

closing) Jul-Aug daily 10am-6pm; Apr-Jun and Sep 10am-5.30pm; Oct and Mar 10am, 11am, 2pm, 2.45, 3.30, 4.30 Nov-Feb daily except Sat 2pm, 3pm and 4pm. Closed 25 Dec. 1 Jan and 3rd week in Jan 8.50€ (children: 1€–5€). 04 67 73 70 02. www.demoiselles.fr.
This cave was discovered in 1770, and according to locals, was home to fairies. Martel explored it in 1884, 1889 and 1897, revealing it to be an old swallow-hole opening onto the **Plateau de Thaurac**.
The most striking thing about the cave is the number and size of the concretions thickly covering its walls. Narrow corridors lead to a platform overlooking an immense chamber, 120m/394ft long, 80m/262ft wide and 50m/164ft high. The awesome silence and hanging mist give the impression of being in a gigantic cathedral.
Walkways lead all round this spectacular chamber to the stalagmite resembling a Virgin and Child. Admire the fantastic set of "organ pipes" adorning the north wall of the cave.

The road traverses a sheer-sided gorge gouged by the River Hérault.

Laroque

Worth a stroll to discover the belfry topped by a campanile, the castle and the old silkworm-breeding establishment overlooking the river.

Grotte des Lauriers★

Discovered by Martel in 1930, this cave's rock carvings date from the Magdalenian period. The Salle de l'Éboulis and Salle du Lac feature fossils, and other areas an amazing variety of limestone concretions.

Lodève★

Surrounded by graceful hills, Lodève is close to the mountainous areas of Causse du Larzac and Monts de l'Orb as well as to the Hérault Valley and Lac du Salagou.The look-out on the N 9 diversion from Millau offers a sweeping view of the site.

- **Population:** 7 400.
- **Michelin Map:** 339: E-6.
- **Info:** 7 Pl. de la République, 34700 Lodève, 04 67 88 86 44. www.lodeve.com.
- **Location:** 60km/37.5mi south of Millau and 58km/36.25mi northwest of Montpellier via A75.
- **Don't Miss:** Musée Fleury's contemporary art.
- **Kids:** Grotte de Labeil.

A BIT OF HISTORY

At Lodève, Nero minted the coins needed to pay the Roman legions. Bishops ruled the fortified town and diocese during the Middle Ages The 10C Bishop Fulcran was noted for giving food to the poor, caring for the sick and defending the town against brigands. In the 12C, one of his successors founded one of the first mills to make paper from rags. The cloth trade developed in the 13C, and in the 18C Lodève had a monopoly on producing soldiers' uniforms for the king's armies.

SIGHT

The Gothic **Pont de Montifort** spans the Soulondres river and has a very pronounced arch. It was built in the 14C to provide access to the Tines Quarter, where the workshops of the leather workers were located.

Ancienne Cathédrale St-Fulcran★

Place de l'Hotel de Ville.
The original cathedral is now the crypt. The church was rebuilt in the 10C by St Fulcran, and again in the 13C and 14C. The buttressing and the two watchtowers framing the façade show its defensive function. Eighty four bishops of Lodève are buried in the first chapel. The

third chapel leading to the cloisters (14C-17C) has latticed vaulting characteristic of Late Gothic.

Musée Fleury★

Sq. Georges-Auric. Open daily except Mon 9.30am-noon, 2-6pm. Closed public holidays (except Jul-Aug) 3.50€. 04 67 88 86 10. www.lodeve.com.

The geology and paleontology section of the museum in the 17C-18C cardinal's palace contains rare fossilised flora and reptile (or batrachian) tracks from the late Primary Era and those of huge dinosaurs from the Secondary Era. Other exhibits show Paleolithic and Neolithic remains from the Lodève area, local history from Gallo-Roman times and engravings by Barthélemy Roger (18C-19C) and sculptures by Paul Dardé (20C).

Manufacture Nationale de Tapis

Ave. du Gén.-de-Gaulle (Montpellier road). Guided tour Tue, Wed, Thu 1.30-3.30pm. 3.20€. 04 67 96 40 40.

This tapestry-weaving mill is the only annexe of the Gobelins in Paris. Visit workshops dedicated to weaving copies of ancient works for use in national monuments.

EXCURSION

Prieuré St-Michel de-Grandmont★

8km/5mi E. Leave on N 9 towards Millau and turn right onto D 153 towards Privat. Daily Jun-Sep 10am-7pm; Oct-May 10am-6pm. 5.60€. 04 67 44 09 31. www.prieure-grandmont.fr.

This priory was founded in the 12C by monks of the Grandmont order and is one of the remaining examples of the 150 Grandmont monasteries. The grounds contain fascinating dolmens.

Grotte de Labeil

12km/8mi N. Leave on N 9 towards Millau. Turn off W at the junction for Lauroux and take D 151 to Labeil. Open Jul-Aug 10am-7pm; mid Mar-Jun, Sep-Oct 11am, 2pm, 3pm and 4pm. 7.50€ (children 4€). 04 67 96 49 47.

The **Cirque de Labeil** comprises the southern foothills of Larzac plateau. The cave entrance offers a good view of Lauroux valley. The main features of this damp cave once used for producing Roquefort cheese, are stalactites, stalagmites and frozen falls.

Maguelone★

Peaceful and charming Maguelone is linked by a narrow road to the seaside resort of Palavas-les-Flots. The Rhône-Sète canal cuts across the road which linked Maguelone to dry land until 1708.

- **Michelin Map:** 339: I-7.
- **Location:** 15km/9.3mi S of Montpellier via D 986.
- **Don't Miss:** The cathedral stained glass windows by Robert Morris.
- **Kids:** The tourist train.

A BIT OF HISTORY

Maguelone is believed to have begun as either a Phoenician trading post or as a colony of Greek navigators. In the 8C it fell to the Saracens. In 1030 Bishop Arnaud I rebuilt its cathedral and added extensive fortifications. In the 12C, the church was enlarged and its fortifications were strengthened, and during the 13C to 14C expansion, 60 canons reputed for their generosity and hospitality lived here. On the orders of Richelieu, Maguelone was demolished in 1622. From the original town, only the cathedral and bishops' palace remain.

ANCIENT CATHEDRAL★

30min Open 9am-7pm (early Jun-mid Sep: visitors must park on the car park and continue their journey by tourist train – see below). No charge. 04

67 50 63 63. www.espace-maguelone.com. Out of season, via a road (cul-de-sac), 4km/2.5mi long, which begins at Palavas-les-Flots, at the end of rue Maguelone. In summer, park 2km/1.2mi away in the car park and take the tourist train to the cathedral, or take the ferry, and then the **petit train** *from Villeneuve. (Pilou car park: open Jun-Aug 8am-8.30pm; June 9am-8pm; May, Sep, 10am-7pm; Oct-Apr 1-5pm. 04 67 69 75 87).*

Exterior – All that is left of the crenellated parapet that once surmounted the building are a few machicolations. A remarkable sculpted doorway leads into the church. The lintel is an antique Roman military column sculpted with fine foliage and inscribed with the date 1178.

Interior – Fragments of tombstones are set into the wall. Some date from the Roman era and others from 11C, when Pope Urban II absolved the sins of all those who asked to be buried in Maguelone.

Cirque de Mourèze★★

The Cirque de Mourèze hides between the Orb and Hérault valleys, on the south side of Liausson mountain. This vast jumble of dolomitic rocks crisscrossed by footpaths forms a magnificent natural amphitheatre covering over 340ha/840 acres.

- **Michelin Map:** 339: F-7
- **Info:** Office du tourisme de Clermont-l'Hérault, 9 r Doyen-René-Gosse 34800 04 67 96 23 86. www.ot-clermont-salagou.com.
- **Location:** 31km/19.3 south of Lodève via the A 75, and 53km/33.1 west of Montpellier via the N 109.
- **Don't Miss:** The picturesque village streets and view over the cirque from Courtinals park overlook.
- **Kids:** Reconstructed cabin in the Parc des Courtinals.

VISIT

The picturesque old **village** of Mourèze, with its narrow streets, little houses with outside staircases and its red-marble fountain, lies at the foot of a sheer rock face, the top of which is home to a castle.

The cirque★★ is surrounded by enormous boulders, and a number of waymarked footpaths lead through fresh, green nooks and crannies in between rocks eroded into strange shapes. From the viewpoint enjoy a panorama of the dolomitic cirque.

Parc des Courtinals

Open Jul-Aug 9.30-7pm; Apr-Jun and Sep-Oct 10am-6pm; Closed Nov-Mar. 4€ (children 2€). 04 67 96 08 42. www.courtinals.com.

Courtinals park is an ancient Gallic settlement, inhabited from the Middle Neolithic Age until about 450 BC. It is almost surrounded by a high barrier of rocks; at their foot there are natural cavities which once contained flints and pottery.

View of the Cirque de Mourèze
A. Thuillier/MICHELIN

Sète

Hérault

Sète was built on the slopes and at the foot of Mont St-Clair, a limestone outcrop 175m/541ft high, on the edge of the Thau lagoon. Once an island, it is linked to the mainland by two narrow sand spits. The new town, east and north-east of Mont St-Clair, runs right up to the sea itself and is divided up by several canals. Sète is the scene of the famous ***joutes nautiques*****, jousting tournaments, particularly well attended on the day of St-Louis in August.**

- **Population:** 43 300.
- **Michelin Map:** 339: H-8.
- **Info:** 60 Grand'Rue Mario-Roustan, 34200 Sète. 04 67 74 71 71. www.ot-sete.fr. Guided tours of the town organised by the Sète tourist office cover the themes of "Façades and canals," "Old Sète" and "The fish market auction."
- **Location:** 36km/22.5mi SW of Montpellier. The main strolling and shopping streets are found on the east side of the "island;" beaches to the west.
- **Parking:** You'll find lots near the canal fringing Séte on the east.
- **Don't Miss:** The trip up Mont St-Clair, for memorable views of the surrounding area.
- **Timing:** Stroll about the town before heading up to Mont St-Clair. If your time allows, head for the beach or take a cruise on the lagoon or the harbour area.
- **Also See:** Sète is one of the principal bases for excursions to the Thau lagoon.

A BIT OF HISTORY

Birthplace of poets – **Paul Valéry** (1871–1945) wrote to Sète town council, which had congratulated him on his election to the Académie Française, "It seems to me that all my work reflects my roots." In *Charmes*, published in 1922, the poet celebrated the marine cemetery where he was to be buried in July 1945. At the foot of this peaceful setting, the sea can be seen spreading away to the horizon like a vast flat roof.

Another famous native of Sète, the singer-songwriter **Georges Brassens** (1921–81) sang about his place of birth in his *Supplique pour être enterré à la plage de Sète (Request to be buried on Sète beach).*

Vieux port - Quai de l'Aspirant Herber

D. Pazery/MICHELIN

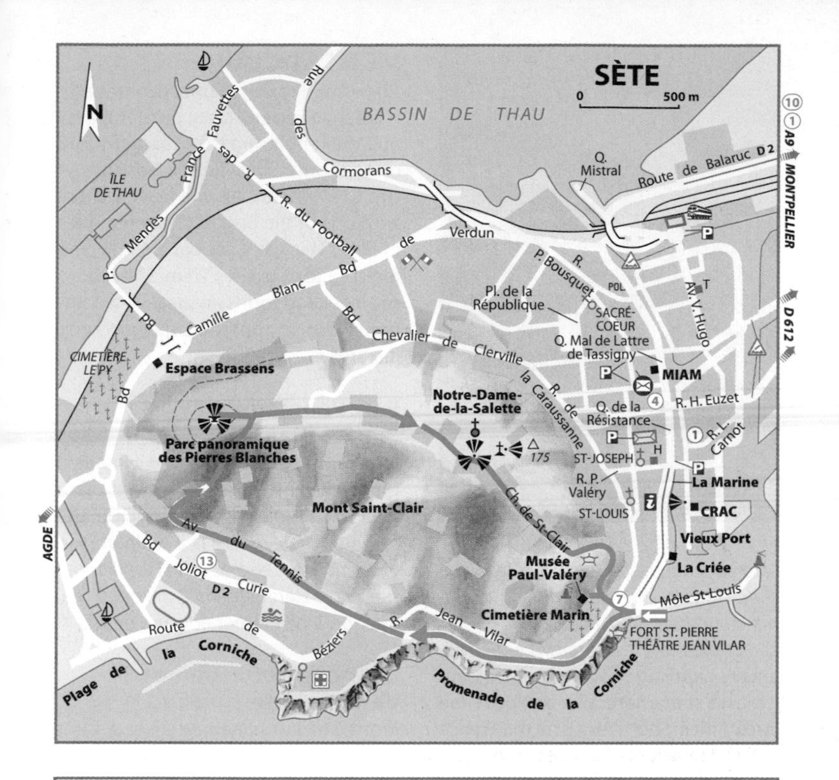

WHERE TO STAY	
Balajan (Hôtellerie de)	①
Grand Hôtel	④
Port Marine (Hôtel)	⑦
Tamaris (Camping Les)	⑩
ritons (Hôtel Les)	⑬

WHERE TO EAT	
The Marcel	①

The town developed in the 17C when Colbert decided to have a port constructed, making Sète the outlet on the Mediterranean for the Canal des Deux-Mers. The foundation stone was laid in 1666 by **Pierre-Paul Riquet**, architect of the Canal du Midi. To stimulate expansion, in 1673 Louis XIV gave permission for "everyone to build houses, sell and produce any goods with exemption from tax duty." Before very long the town had become a thriving commercial and industrial centre.

Nevertheless, it was not until the 19C that Sète embarked upon its golden age. The harbour and the maritime canal were developed, while the railway companies linked Sète to the PLM network and to the Midi network. By about 1840 Sète was the fifth most important French port.

TOURS

Guided tours of the city:

Organised by the Service Tourisme de Sète. Three themes: 'Façades et canaux', 'le Vieux Sète' or 'La Criée' (fisherman's wharf). Sète Croisières – Quai de la Marine. *℘04 67 46 00 46. www.sete-croisieres.com*.

Closed Dec 1–28. A 1 hr cruise aboard the Aquarius, a glass-bottomed boat. Discover the shellfish parks at the Etang de Thau (Mon–Fri, leaves from the Quai de la Pointe-Courte) or the rocky coast (weekends, leaves from the Quai de la Marine). Also: sea cruise and visit of the harbour aboard the Atlantide.

Tour boats
A. Thuillier/MICHELIN

After the conquest of Algeria, Sète, which specialised in the wine trade, found its main outlets in North Africa.
Today, the three main areas of its activity are the handling of bulk goods, passenger and container traffic to North and West Africa, South America, the French Caribbean and Australia, and storage.

SEA FRONT

Vieux port★

The old harbour, with its picturesque fishing boats and yachts, is the most interesting part of Sète port.
Quai de la Marine is lined with fish and seafood restaurants, with terraces overlooking the Sète canal. It is the departure point for various **boat trips** (see *Address Book)* around the coastline and harbour.
A little farther down, fishermen and bystanders are summoned by the **"criée électronique"** (electronic auction) when the boats come in at around 3.30pm. It is worth taking a stroll round the other basins and the canals as well. Sailing is practised at high level near the St-Louis pier. **Promenade de la Corniche** – This busy road, leading to the Plage de la Corniche, situated 2km/1mi from the centre of town, cuts around the foot of Mont St-Clair with its slopes covered by villas. **Plage de la Corniche** – This 12km/7.5mi-long sandy beach stretches across a conservation area.

MONT ST-CLAIR★

Allow half a day. From promenade Maréchal-Leclerc, carry on along avenue du Tennis and take the right fork on to montée des Pierres Blanches. A trip to Mont St-Clair will leave visitors with one of the best of their memories of Sète. This hill, once covered by pine forests and oaks, rises 175m/574ft above sea level and forms an ideal viewpoint from which to appreciate the surrounding area.

Parc Panoramique des Pierres Blanches

This park is well covered by waymarked footpaths and makes a pleasant place for a stroll exploring the area. From the viewing table, there is a wide **view**★ over the west end of the Thau lagoon, the lower Hérault plains, the open sea, the Corniche Promenade and beach.

Chapelle Notre-Dame-de-la-Salette

Mont St-Clair is named after a saint who was venerated here as early as the Middle Ages. In the 17C, a hermitage still existed near the small fort of "La Montmorencette" built by the Duke of Montmorency. But when the duke rebelled, the king had the fort dismantled and a former blockhouse transformed into an expiatory chapel. In 1864, it was dedicated to Notre-Dame-de-la-Salette.

Viewpoints

From the esplanade opposite the chapel, where a large cross is lit up every night, there is a splendid **view**★ of Sète, the east end of the Thau lagoon, the Garrigues, the Cévennes, St-Loup peak, the Gardiole mountain and the coast itself with its necklace of lagoons and small towns. A viewing tower on the presbytery terrace gives a marvellous **panorama**★★.
Whereas the foreground reflects light and colour, shapes in the distance blend into hazy tints. On a clear day, the view extends over the lagoons and the sea as far as the Pyrenees, to the south-west, and the Alpilles, to the east.

Carry on along chemin de St-Clair, which drops steeply downhill.

On the right lies the cliff-top **cemetery**★ celebrated by Paul Valéry and the museum dedicated to him.

Return to Sète along Grande-Rue-Haute.

MUSEUMS AND EXHIBITIONS

Espace Brassens

67 boulevard Camille-Blanc. Open Jul-Aug 10am-noon, 2-6pm; Jun and Sep 10am-noon, 2-6pm; Oct-May daily except Mon 10am-noon, 2-6pm. Closed 1 Jan, Easter, 1 and 8 May, 11 Nov, 25 Dec. 5€. 04 67 53 32 77. www.ville-sete.fr/brassens.

This museum traces the life and work of the singer-songwriter from Sète, Georges Brassens (1921-81) in an interesting and original exhibition combining audio-visual input with visual displays. Georges Brassens is buried in the Le Py cemetery, which is to be found opposite the museum.

Musée Paul-Valéry

Open Jul-Aug 10am-noon, 2-6pm; Sep-Jun daily except Tue and public holidays 10am-noon, 2-6pm. 4€, no charge 1st Sunday in the month. 04 67 46 20 98.

Facing the sea and very close to the **cimetière marin** where Paul Valéry and Jean Vilar are buried, the museum contains many documents on the history of Sète.

Musée international des Arts modestes (MIAM)

Quai Mar.-de-Lattre-de-Tassigny, along the Grand Canal. Open daily except Mon and public holidays (except Jul and Aug) 10am-noon, 2-6pm. 5€, no charge 1st Sunday in the month. 04 67 18 64 00. www.miam.org.

This entertaining museum is devoted to daily-life objects and publicity (hence the name *"modestes"*) going back to the mid-20C.

EXCURSION

Bassin de Thau

The Bassin de Thau covers a massive area of 8 000ha/19 768 acres, the largest lagoon on the Languedoc coast. It is separated from the sea by the isthmus of Onglous (Sète beach). Its shores are home to a whole range of activities: to the east is a busy industrial complex; to the south, the offshore sand bar is a beach; whereas on the north shore several villages, such as Bouzigues and Mèze, specialise in oyster and mussel farming. Boat trips enable visitors to take a closer look at the oyster and mussel farming concerns in the lagoon.

Built on flat land on the shores of the Bassin de Thau, **Balaruc-les-Bains** *(5km/3mi N of Sète)*, the third most popular spa resort in France, has many amenities to offer.

Oyster beds in Bassan de Thau

M.-H. Carcanague/MICHELIN

ADDRESSES

STAY

Hôtel Port Marine – *Môle St-Louis. ℘04 67 74 92 34. www.hotel-port-marine.com. 46 rms. 9€ Restaurant.* A modern hotel located near the marina and pier. The functional rooms are reminiscent of a boat's cabin; six suites overlook the sea. Regional food is served in the Bleu Marine restaurant.

Grand Hôtel – *17 quai du Mar.-de-Lattre-de-Tassigny. ℘04 67 74 71 77. www.legrandhotelsete.com. Closed 18 Dec–2 Jan. 43 rms. 9€.* This fine 1882 edifice on the quays is a local institution. Visitors will be charmed by the vast patio topped by a Belle Époque-style glass roof, cosy bedrooms, period furniture and chic bar.

EAT

La Huchette – *82 Grand'Rue Mario-Roustan. ℘04 67 74 40 24.Closed lunchtime and Sun except Jul–Aug.* Night-owls and theatregoers are partial to this little bistro open from 9pm to 1am where you can nibble on a few tapas or try the bourride, a house speciality.

The Marcel – *5 R. Lazare-Carnot. ℘04 67 74 20 89. Closed Jun 26–Jul 9 and Dec 23–Jan 5.* Much appreciated by local residents, this restaurant in a quiet street in the old part of Sète is a pleasant place to meet. The eclectic decor happily blends Art Deco with velvet armchairs, bistro furniture etc; it is also used as an art gallery by local painters. Regional dishes, among others.

Le Jas d'Or – *2 Bd. Victor-Hugo, 34110 Frontignan. ℘04 67 43 07 57. Closed Tue evening and Wed off-season, Monday lunchtime Jul–Aug.* Exagerration is the order of the day here: colorfully-designed plates, high-sounding names and elaborate cuisine. This former *chai* welcomes a devoted slate of regular clients to its intimate dining room decorated with rustic stonework.

Palangrotte – *Rampe Paul-Valéry, quai Marine. ℘04 67 74 80 35. kiefferbern@wanadoo.fr. Closed Sun evening and Mon, Jul–Aug.* This Marine restaurant offers seafood specialties in its softly-colored dining room.

SHOPPING

Marché aux Puces – *Pl. de la République – Sun 6am–1pm. Flea market.*

Chez David – *67 R. Paul-Bousquet ℘04 67 53 14 30. Daily except Tues 7am–12.30pm, 4pm–8pm. Closed Feb.* If you fancy ***tielles sétoises***, a sort of small pasty filled with fresh octopus, it is worth going out of your way to find this shop beyond the town centre.

Biscuits Catagnia – *35 Grand'Rue Mario-Roustan. ℘04 67 74 49 11. Mon–Fri, 6am–7pm. Closed 3 weeks in Jan.* A wonderful aroma of baking sweets pervades this tiny factory in the centre of town. Twenty six different types of biscuits are sold here.

Cave coopérative du Muscat de Frontignan – *14 Ave. du Muscat – 34110 Frontignan. ℘04 67 48 12 26/04 67 48 93 20. www.frontignan-coopérative.fr. Jun–Sep:* ***guided tour*** *(20min): 10am, 11am, 3.30pm, 4.30pm;* ***shop****: Jun–Sep: 9.30am–12.30pm, 3–7.30pm; Oct–May: 9.30am–12.30pm, 2.30–6.30pm. Closed Christmas day and New Years day.*

Bar du Passage – *1 quai Mistral. ℘04 67 74 21 25. Jul–Aug: daily 7am–2am; Sep and Jun: daily 7am–8pm.* Located in the Pointe Courte fishing district, where Varda's film Bar du Passage was shot, its namesake is a magical place. Come and savour the beauty and poetry of this place or simply savour a kebab.

CinéGarage – *29 Grande Rue Haute. ℘04 67 46 12 18.Sept–Jun: Mon–Fri 9am–noon, 2–5pm; Jul-Aug: Mon–Fri 2–6pm.* A new, multi-purpose cultural locale proposes exhibitions of paintings, film production, creative workshops, and short films festival (July).

Théâtre de la Mer – *Rte. de la Corniche. ℘04 67 74 70 55. culture@ville-sete.fr. Open mid-Jun–mid-Aug. Closed Sep-May.* Also called the 'Théâtre Jean-Vilar', this 2,000-seat outdoors theatre at the foot of the maritime cemetery is set in a fort built by Vauban. Several festivals take place here in summer, including a theatre, music and dance festival and a jazz festival.

© Viel/photocuisine/Corbis

Something fishy

Perched on a limestone hill – Mont St Clair, once covered with oak and pine and rising to 175m (575ft) between the Mediterranean and the Étang de Thau – **Sète** is the largest fishing port on the French Mediterranean, and catches of sole, sea bass, gilt-head bream, mackerel and rascasse come in daily to be auctioned off.

Nearby, the old trading port, known as La Marine, has been used for centuries, from a time when its quays were dotted with Catalan and Moorish ships, feluccas, cattle boats and schooners. It has numerous 18th-century façades and art deco buildings to go with its reputation for fish soup, bourride, squid, stuffed mussels and octopus, which find their way into La Tielle, a local delicacy, a pie made with a bread dough and filled with baby octopus in a spicy tomato sauce.

Sète was founded in the 17th century, when it was decided to build a port, making this the outlet on the Mediterranean for the Canal des Deux-Mers, linking the Mediterranean and the Atlantic. This is no place to hurry. Arrive quite early, park by the station and saunter along the quays on the east side of the Canal de Sète (the west side buildings are favoured by the morning sun), cross the Pont de la Savonnerie and maybe take a coffee and croissant before ambling through the town centre and down towards the lighthouse for no good reason other than you have to come back, which makes it doubly pleasurable.

Go down the rue des Marins or the rue des Pecheurs onto the quai Maximin Licciardi, and there you'll find the quayside restaurants and ample excuse to brush up on your culinary French. By the time you set off back the sun will be illuminating the buildings on the opposite side of the canal.

Fishing boat in the harbour

M.-H. Carcanague/MICHELIN

The Cévennes, renowned in English literature for the exploits of Robert Louis Stevenson, form a huge range of mountains covering the *départements* of Gard, Lozère, Ardèche and Haute-Loire. The mountains are part of the Central Massif of France, and run from Montagne Noir in the southwest to Monts du Vivarais in the northeast. The highest point is Mont Lozère (1702m/5584ft), and the area is embraced in the Cévennes National Park.

Highlights

1. **Alès**, a bustling town (p123)
2. **Florac**, centrepiece of the Cévennes National Park (p129)
3. **Gorges de la Dourbie**, a good way to study the landscape (p132)
4. **Mont Lozère**, highest point of the Cévennes (p134)
5. **Marvejols**, a royal city (p138)

Travels with a donkey

In 1878, the Scottish author of *Treasure Island*, Robert Louis Stevenson, crossed the Cévennes accompanied by his donkey, Modestine, following a route that has today become the GR 70. His book *Travels with a Donkey in the Cévennes* recounts this journey which took him from Monastier-sur-Gazeilles to St Jean-du-Gard, and in the process brought the beauties of the Cévennes to the notice of a wider and willingly appreciative audience.

Land of limestone and rivers

The Cévennes rise above the plains of the Languedoc and the Mediterranean, a labyrinth of deep, steep-sided and winding valleys and hill slopes cloaked in forests of chestnut along with the ubiquitous mulberry planted to provide food for silkworms bred in mills called *magnaneries*.

Not so much a mountain chain as a multitude of many-sided open spaces, the highest ground is made up of slightly undulating plateaux, sometimes green like Mont Aigoual, or flat as on the Mont Lozère. This is the heart of the Cévennes National Park.

The landscape opens out into vast limestone spaces called "Causses". Below these bare surfaces, the Mediterranean side is hollowed by deep and narrow valleys dominated by crests and swept by the torrents of the Cévennes.

In the past, the Causses and the Cévennes were the domain of the forest and wild animals. The so-called "Beast of Gevaudan, spread fear across the land for several years in the 18C. Today the region is mainly the domain of wild boar and walkers.

S. Sauvignier/MICHELIN

Aubrac: a hardy breed

The Aubrac cattle that populate much of this region are especially hardy, able to survive on poor food and in living condtions that would see off less resilient beasts. The cattle were originally used for three purposes: for meat, dairy production – particularly cheese making – and as draft cattle.

The cattle are most evident in the area north of Lozère, and have soft brown-to-deep brown coats on well-muscled bodies, their heads topped by long, lyre-type horns. Just how muscled will become evident if you visit the cutlery capital of France, **Laguiole**, for in the town square, the Place du Forail, stands a huge bronze bull, not much larger than life, if at all. A very old beef cattle breed, the Aubrac has over 150 years of breeding history. After centuries of breeding selection by Benedictine monks, it was decided to open a herd book in the late 19C, a golden age of the breed.

Aubrac cattle have strong black hooves and can produce an average of over 2 000kg/4 409lb of milk every 240 days. Their milk has a fat percentage of around 4 per cent. Once they reach maturity, they stand at about 130cm/51in high, and weigh an average of 850kg/1 874lb. The cows are smaller and stand at about 125cm/50in, and weighing only 600kg/1 323lb.

Cows spend the winter within the farm confines and give birth to calves that come easily and without trouble, often a concern for farmers. The calves grow quickly and muscle up within a few weeks of calving. Then at the end of spring, the cows and calves head up into the Aubrac mountains where feeding on lush grass and flowers will give the best milk to make a cheese named after the nearby Laguiole.

©emmanuelle bonzami/Bigstockphoto.com

Massif de l'Aigoual

A region of the Aigoual mountain massif falls within the Parc National des Cévennes. Breathtaking river gorges like the Dourbie, the Jonte and the Trévezel carve through the massif, and scenic roads wind through forests and skirt spell-binding ridges, all the way to the panoramic summit.

- **Michelin Map:** 339: G-4.
- **Location:** 70km/45mi E of Millau. The route covers the whole Aigoual massif and leads to the summit. Follow it from Meyrueis to Le Vigan to see the particularly spectacular stretch of road across the Minier Pass and down to the Arre valley.
- **Timing:** Allow 5hr for the driving tour: 3hr Meyrueis – Mont Aigoual, 1hr 30min for the stretch to Le Vigan.

A BIT OF HISTORY

From July 1944 onwards, the Aigoual massif was the centre of the important "Aigoual-Cévennes" resistance movement, headquartered at L'Espérou.

GEOLOGICAL NOTES

A gigantic water tower – The Aigoual is one of the major water catchment areas in the Massif Central, as clouds rolling in from the chilly Atlantic converge with warm Mediterranean air over the summit. Called "Aiqualis" or "the watery one," the mountain's average annual rainfall can be 2.25m (over 7ft).

DRIVING TOURS

Driving: between November and May roads may be blocked by snow.

Walking: the GR 6 (Alps-Atlantic) and GR 7 (Vosges-Pyrenees) footpaths meet in the Aigoual massif, with subsidiary walks like GR 66, described in the topoguide Tour du mont Aigoual. In summer the Parc national des Cévennes organises 1hr guided walks around the Aigoual summit.

1 MEYRUEIS TO MONT AIGOUAL

32km/20mi – allow 3hr.

Take D 986.

The road up to the Col de Montjardin traverses forest before climbing the edge of the Causse Noir. The pass affords marvellous views of the Larzac plateau and Aigoual and Espérou peaks. After passing through a larch forest, the road follows a dizzying course past old silver mines in Villemagne and the curious rocky cirque "l'Alcôve."

Abîme de Bramabiau★

Temperature: 8°C/46°F 2km there and back. Jul and Aug guided tour 9am-6.30pm; Apr-Jun and Sep 10am-6pm; Oct-mid Nov 11am-5.00pm. 7.50€. 04 67 82 60 78.

The River Bonheur bursts into a rocky cirque called the "Alcôve" as a glorious waterfall. When the river is in spate, the deafening waterfall is like the bellowing of a bull – hence the river's name "Bramabiau" (*Brame-Biâou*: singing bull).

You enter the underground world at the point where the Bramabiau river reemerges. After crossing the Bramabiau between the first waterfall and the second (underground), the path leads to the "Salle du Havre" (harbour chamber). At the **"Grand Aven"** swallow-hole, you can admire the cave paintings of Jean Truel. A path along a ledge 20m/65ft above the river leads back up the Martel gallery overlooking the "Pas de Diable" (devil's footprint). Here some 200m/220yd of the cavern's length are dug out of a whitish barite seam, which opens into the "Petit Labyrinthe," leading to the **"Salle de l'Étoile"** (star chamber).

A few hundred yards beyond the Abîme de Bramabiau is the junction with D 157, which leads to the ***Gorges du Trévezel***★

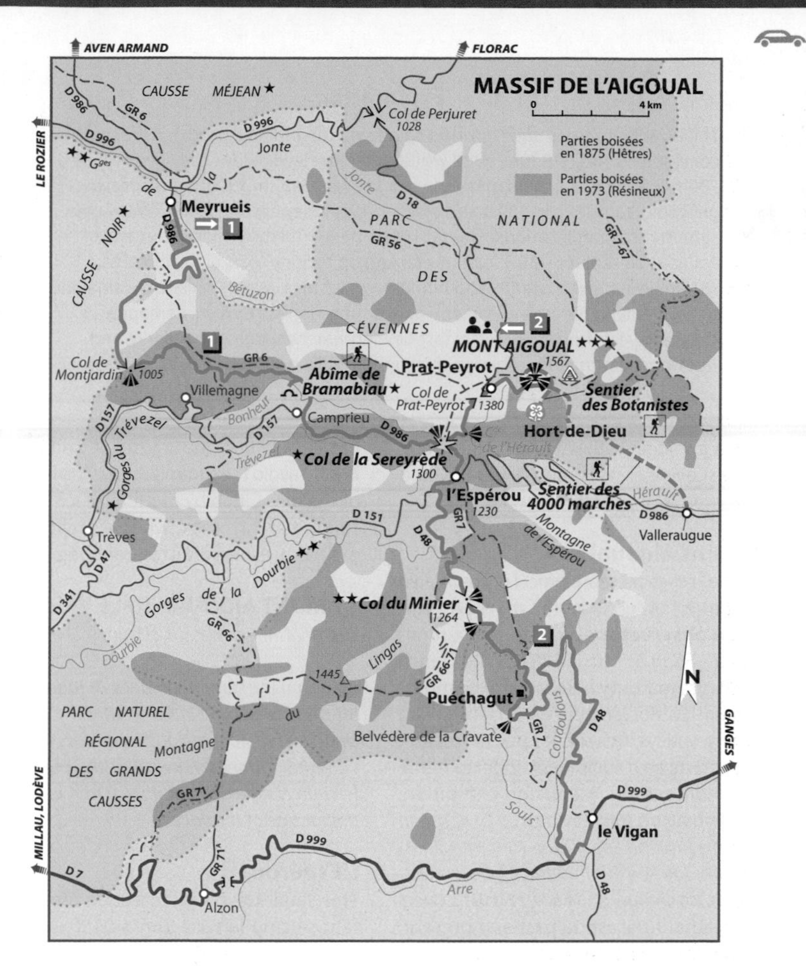

Col de la Sereyrède★

This pass 1 300m/4 265ft above sea level straddles the Atlantic-Mediterranean watershed. The road from the Col de la Sereyrède to the Aigoual summit offers spectacular **views** over the Hérault Valley.

Sentier des Botanistes

1.5km/1mi below the summit, a signpost indicates the trail. 20min walk.

It loops round the Trépaloup Peak for 1km/0.6mi and overlooks the arboretum **Hort-de-Dieu**, "God's garden." The footpath affords marvelous views of the

Reforestation on the Aigoual

A century ago, **Aigoual**'s mountain massif was devoid of trees and vegetation. A reforestation scheme was launched in 1875 by **Georges Fabre**, head warden of the French Rivers Authority and Forestry Commission. He obtained the rights to purchase communal and privately owned land, and planted large stands of trees along the river banks to prevent soil erosion. Some towns and villages were hostile and refused to part with their pastureland, but over time Fabre restored the Aigoual to its forested glory. He also developed the network of roads and footpaths which covers the Aigoual, restored foresters' lodges, set up arboretums and built an observatory for meteorological research.

Exploration

The River Brambiau's underground course was first followed by Martel and his companions on 27-28 June 1888 while water levels were low. They discovered 700m/2 300ft of the main river course and over 1 000m/3 300ft of secondary galleries. From 1890 to 1892, and again in 1924, they explored 7km/4mi of new subterranean ramifications. This labyrinth, nearly 10km/6mi long, consists of galleries 20-40m/65-130ft in diameter and up to 50m/165ft high, linked by extremely narrow passages and numerous cascades. Martel declared Bramabiau to be a remarkable example of still-active subterranean erosion. Perhaps a thousand years from now, as the fast-flowing water enlarges the galleries and transforms caverns into canyons, the Bonheur will once again flow in the open air.

craggy ridges of the Aigoual's south face, the Cévennes peaks and forest-covered eastern slopes of the Aigoual.

Mont Aigoual★★★

The French meteorological office *(Météo France)* now occupies this **meteorological observatory** built on the summit *(alt 1 567m/5 141ft)* in 1887 by the French Rivers Authority and Forestry Commission. Overlooking the Gard, Hérault and Tarn valleys, this site is ideal for testing sophisticated equipment under extreme conditions. An interesting exhibition, **Exposition Météo-France** *(♿, open May-Jun and Sep 10am-1pm and 2pm-6pm; Jul-Aug 10am-7pm. closed Oct-Apr. No charge. 04 67 82 60 01)*, covers weather forecasting past and present, and the French Météotel system.

From the observatory tower, the **panorama** encompasses the Causses and the Cévennes, the Cantal range, Mont Ventoux, the Alps, the Languedoc plain, the Mediterranean and the Pyrenees. In January you can see both Mont Blanc (Alps) and Maladetta (Pyrenees). In July and August, a heat haze often blurs the landscape and it's best to avoid the summit during the heat of the day. Climb by night to reach the summit at daybreak, when visibility is excellent, especially in September.

2 MONT AIGOUAL TO LE VIGAN

39km/24mi – allow 1hr 30min.

From the summit of Mont Aigoual, return to the Col de la Sereyrède.
On the left before the pass, look for the waterfall formed by the sprightly young Hérault tumbling through in a ravine on the far side of the valley.

L'Espérou

This small town's picturesque mountain setting (alt 1 230m/4 035ft) and the ski slopes at **Prat-Peyrot** make it a popular summer and winter holiday destination.

Col du Minier★★

This pass 1 264m/4 147ft above sea level offers views of the Mediterranean in fine weather. A memorial stone commemorates Général Huntziger (Commander

The Great "Draille du Languedoc"

The Col de la Sereyrède was once part of the great "draille du Languedoc," or wide sheep trail used for transferring flocks from summer to winter pastures. *(Follow the path of the old "draille" north along D 18, and south along the GR 7 to the town of L'Espérou, where the track turns off towards Valleraugue.)* Sheep tracks are recognisable by the deep channels they cut into the Cévennes ridges.
Herds are still driven up to L'Espérou on foot during the Fête de la Transhumance in mid-June.

of the French II Armée in Sedan) and his colleagues killed in an air crash in November 1941.

As the vertiginous cliff road begins its long descent down the south face of the Aigoual, it overlooks the deep Souls ravine, with magnificent views of the Montdardier plateau and the Séranne range. The road passes the Puéchagut forester's lodge and another arboretum for studying tropical species.

As the road curves sharply left around the Belvédère de la Cravate, enjoy the panorama of the Arre Valley, Larzac plateau, Séranne range and the St-Loup Peak with the Med beyond. Farther on, the road overlooks the Coudoulous Valley, its sides thick with chestnut trees, before crossing a Mediterranean landscape of vines, mulberry bushes, olive and cypress trees to reach Le Vigan.

Le Vigan

This little town in the Cévennes lies on the southern slope of Mont Aigoual in the fertile Arre Valley. An old bridge dating from before the 13C spans the Arre. There is a good view of it from a platform on the riverbank, upstream of the bridge.

Musée Cévenol★

Open Apr-Oct daily except Tue 10am-noon, 2-6pm; Nov-Mar Wed 10am-noon, 2-6pm. Closed 1 May. 4.50€. 04 67 81 06 86.

This Cévennes folk museum in an 18C silk spinning mill features reconstructions of craftsmen's workshops, a typical Cévennes interior, a collection of silk costumes and exhibits on basket weaving, wickerwork, gold panning and tinsmithing. A room is devoted to André Chamson (1900-83), a Cévennes writer of novels set in the Aigoual foothills.

WALK

Sentier des 4 000 marches (four-thousand-step path)

21km/13mi. Allow one day.

This is for experienced walkers, and starts from the Hort-de-Dieu arboretum. Follow signposts showing a walking shoe or two footprints.

This stony footpath winds through the Hort-de-Dieu arboretum and across wilder heathland dotted with broom. Winding down the chestnut-covered slopes, the trail offers fine views of Valleraugue and the upper Hérault Valley. From Valleraugue, return along the same path or follow a more varied but longer itinerary via Aire-de-Côte *(leave Valleraugue along D 10 to Berthézène).*

Alès

Alès is a typical town of the Cévennes plain, with broad bustling streets and esplanades, and loads of summer festivals.

- **Location:** 96km/60mi N of Montpellier. The town named after an obscure Roman citizen, Allectus, was called "Alais" until 1926. An oppidum once stood on the Colline de l'Ermitage. Enjoy a panorama of Alès from the chapel.
- **Walking:** Alès is the starting point of the long-distance footpaths, GR 44C and GR 44D, in the network covering the Cévennes from Mont Lozère to Mont Aigoual.

A BIT OF HISTORY

Peace Treaty of Alès

In the 16C, Alès was an important Huguenot centre. The Edict of Grace between Louis XIII and the Protestants was signed here in 1629. Under the **treaty** terms, Protestants lost their political rights and their *places de Sureté* (garrison towns), and other priviliges, but retained their freedom of worship. A bishopric was established here in 1694 but was suppressed a hundred years later.

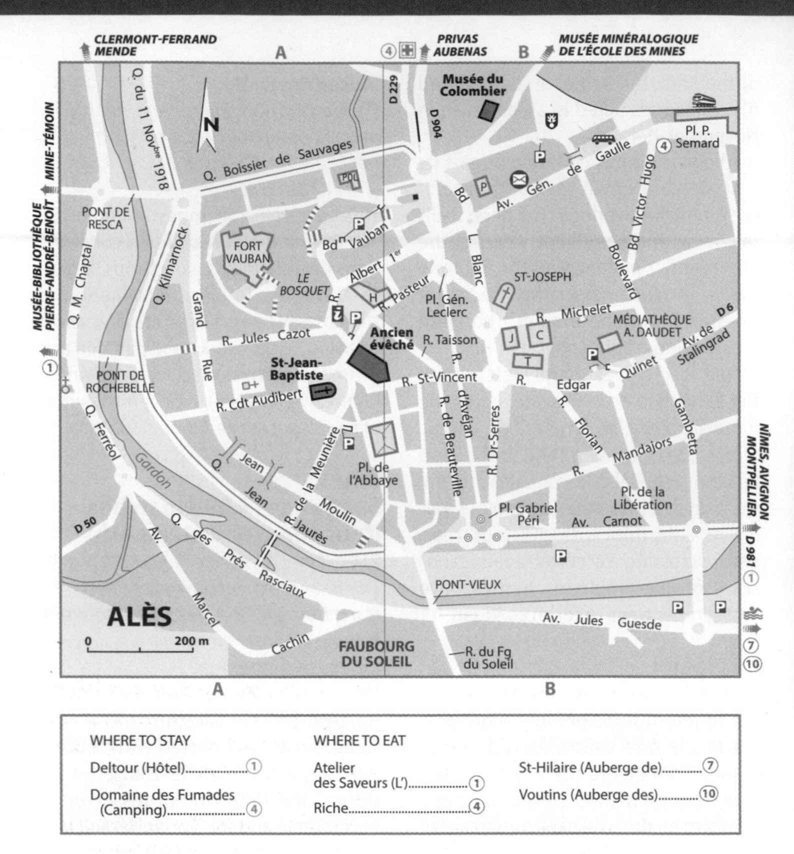

Louis Pasteur at Alès

In 1847, an epidemic attacked the region's traditional source of income – silkworms. By 1865, 3 500 silkworm breeders were in despair and Louis Pasteur was recruited to find a remedy. By 1868 Pasteur found a method of prevention and a **statue** to honour him was erected in the Bosquet gardens.

Industrial development

From the 12C, Alès prospered from textile manufacturing and the cloth trade. In the 19C, the town became a major industrial centre with mining for coal, iron, lead, zinc and asphalt. Today Alès specialises in metallurgy, chemistry and mechanical engineering.

MINING IN ALÈS

Musée minéralogique de l'École des Mines★

6 avenue de Clavières, in the Chantilly district. Leave the town centre via avenue de Lattre-de-Tassigny and avenue Pierre-Coiras. Open mid Jun-mid Sep daily except Sat-Sun and public holidays 2-5pm; mid Sep-mid Jun by request. 4€. 04 66 78 51 69. www.ema.fr.

This museum showcases over 1 000 minerals from around the world, including Australian opal, Moroccan chalcedony, morion quartz and black cairngorm from Aveyron. A 3-D audio-visual show highlights the stones' diversity of shapes and colours.

Mine-témoin★

3km/2mi W. Take the Rochebelle bridge over the Gardon and continue north on rue du Faubourg-de-Rochebelle. Turn left onto chemin de St-Raby, then right onto chemin de la Cité-Ste-Marie. Temperature: 13-15°C/55-59°F. 20min audio-visual presentation on coal formation and mining technology. guided tours (1hr, last departure

1hr30min before closing) ♿ ⓘ*Open Jul-Aug 10am-7pm; Mar-Jun and Sep-mid Nov 9.30am-12.30pm, 2-6pm. 6.70€. ☎04 66 30 45 15. www.mine-temoin.fr.*
The museum presents the history of mining in the Cévennes from the Industrial Revolution to the present, and comprises 650m/710yd of shafts which Benedictine monks used to extracted coal in the 13C.

SIGHTS

Cathédrale St-Jean-Baptiste

The cathedral's Romanesque west front has a Gothic porch dating from the 15C. The vaulted neo-Gothic nave dates from the 17C and the great choir from the 18C. Next to the cathedral, in rue Lafare-Alès, is the 18C bishops' palace, **Ancien Évêché**.

Musée du Colombier

Open Jul-Aug 2-7pm (last admission 30min before closing); Sep-Jun daily except Mon 2-6pm. Closed 1 Jan, 1 May, 1 Nov, 25 Dec. No charge. ☎04 66 86 30 40.
This museum in the 18C Château du Colombier contains art spanning the 16C-20C, with an early 16C triptych of the Holy Trinity by Jean Bellegambe, and paintings by Van Loo, Mieris, Bassano, Velvet Brueghel, Masereel, Mayodon, Marinot, Benn and others.

Musée-Bibliothèque Pierre-André Benoît★

Take the Rochebelle bridge over the Gardon and follow the signposted route. Montée des Lauriers, Rochebelle. Open Jul-Aug 2-7pm (last admission 30min before closing); Sep-Jun: daily except Mon 2-6pm. Closed Feb, 1 Jan, 1 May, 1 Nov, 25 Dec. No charge. ☎04 66 86 98 69.
The 18C Château de Rochebelle was once the residence of the bishops of Alès. Now restored, it contains the bequeathed collections of Pierre-André Benoît (1921-93) printer, publisher, writer, painter and draughtsman. Benoît collected works of art and books by his friends, who included Char, Claudel, Tzara, Seuphor, Braque, Picasso, Miró, Jean Hugo, Villon, Camille Bryen, Picabia, Braque, and L Survage.

EXCURSIONS

Château de Portes★

20km/12.5mi NW. Leave Alès on D 904 towards Aubenas, then turn left onto D 906. Park the car at the pass to explore the castle ruins on foot. Open Jul-Aug daily except Mon 10am-7pm; rest of year call for information. 4.50€. ☎04 66 54 92 05. www.chateau-portes.org.
The now ruined castle of Portes, which provides a **panorama** the Chamborigaud valley, Mont Lozère and the Tanargue foothills, once offered protection for pilgrims travelling to St-Gilles. The castle belonged to the lords of Budos from 1320 to the 17C. The Renaissance building is now used for exhibitions and concerts.

Parc Ornithologique des Isles

21km/13mi NE. Leave Alès on D 904 towards Aubenas then turn right to Les Mages. Go through the village and take D 132 to the right. The bird sanctuary is 800m/870yd beyond the turn-off to St-Julien-de-Cassagnas. Currently closed for renovations. ☎04 66 25 76 70.
The sanctuary shelters wild fowl, waders, birds of prey, parrots and budgerigars, web-footed and many other species.

Château de Rousson

9km/5.6mi N. Leave Alès on D 904 towards Aubenas then take the third road on the right after Les Rosiers (D 131). Jul-Aug guided tour (45min) 2pm-7pm. 5€. ☎04 66 85 60 31.
This robust castle overlooking the Aigoual and Ventoux ranges has barely been modified since its construction between 1600-15. Its main façade features mullioned windows and an impressive Louis XIII door with bosses.

Préhistorama★

11km/6.8mi N. Leave Alès along D 904, towards Aubenas. Turn left onto a path signposted "Prehistorama." ♿ *Open Jul-Aug 10am-7pm; Feb-May and Sep-*

Bambouseraie de Prafrance

Nov daily except Sat 2-6pm. Closed Dec and Jan. 5€. 04 66 85 86 96.
This centre retraces the origins of life on earth and the evolution of the human species.

Bambouseraie de Prafrance★★

17km/10.5mi SW. Leave Alès on N 110, turn right on D 910A then right again on D 129. Open Easter-mid-Nov 9.30am-6pm (Apr-Jun 7pm; Jul-Aug 7.30pm). 7.50€. 04 66 61 70 47. www.bambouseraie.fr.
This 10ha/25-acre bamboo plantation was founded in 1855 by Cévennes native Eugène Mazel. Mazel became fascinated with bamboo while studying silkworm breeding in Asia, where bamboo is used for making everything from baskets, umbrella handles, ladders, irrigation pipes, scaffolding, and building houses to making musical instruments. Mazel imported bamboo cuttings, and in this soil enriched by alluvial deposits of the Gardon, the bamboo grew into a spectacular 20m/65ft jungle. The plantation also contains Californian sequoias, palm trees, a Virginian tulip tree, and a Laotian bamboo village with trees from Japan, China and America.

Le Mas Soubeyran, Musée du Désert★

15km/9mi SW along D 50 via Générargues to Luziers then right. Open Jul-Aug 9.30am-7pm; Mar-Jun and Sep-Nov 9.30am-noon, 2-6pm. Closed Dec to Feb. 4€. 04 66 85 02 72. www.museedudesert.com 4.50€.
Le Mas Soubeyran overlooks the rugged countryside around River Gardon, where a few huddled houses stand out on a small plateau surrounded by mountains. This historic hamlet is a Protestant Mecca, and its annual "general assembly" in early September attracts 10 000 to 20 000 Protestants.
The **Maison de Roland** remains as it was in the 17C and 18C. Note the *"jeu de l'Oye"* (game of snakes and ladders) to teach Roman Catholic principles to young Huguenots imprisoned in convents. Documents, maps and paintings retrace the history of the Protestant struggle from the revocation of the Edict of Nantes (1685) to the Edict of Tolerance (1787).

Grotte de Trabuc★★

16km/9.9mi SW along D 50 to Luziers via Générargues then right to Trabuc. Jul-Aug guided tours (1hr) 10am-6.30pm; Mar-Jun and Sep-Oct 2-5.30pm; Feb and Nov call for opening hours. Closed Dec-Jan. 8€. 04 66 85 03 28. Underground safari upon reservation 35€ 04 67 66 11 11.
Trabuc cave, the largest in the Cévennes, was inhabited in the Neolithic period and later used by the Romans. During the Wars of Religion, Camisards hid in its labyrinthine galleries. The cave is named after a band of brigands known as the Trabucaires, who used it as their den. Cave highlights include the Gong chamber, which resonates like a gong, the *gours*, or underground lakes formed by weirs of calcite, the "red cascades," petrified calcite torrents coloured with oxides,

and the aragonite crystallisations, tinted black by manganese. Most impressive is the underground landscape formed by the **"Hundred thousand soldiers"★★**, extraordinary concretions formed in *gours* resembling the Great Wall of China. Other wonders are the butterfly shapes in the Lake Chamber. jellyfish-shaped concretions, and the emerald waters of "Midnight Lake."

St-Christol-lès-Alès, Musée du Scribe

2km/1.2mi S towards Anduze and Montpellier; follow the signposting on the right before reaching the "pyramid" where the two roads separate. 42 rue du Clocher. Jul-Aug guided tours (1hr15min) 10am-7pm; Jun and early to mid Sep daily 2-6pm; Feb and end May and mid Sep-Dec Sat-Sun 2.30-7pm. 4.50€. 04 66 60 88 10. www.museeduscribe.com.

This tastefully restored village house with a reconstruction of a 19C classroom celebrates the history of writing materials through the ages – from papyrus and parchment to paper. Exhibits of writing instruments include quills, nibs, pen-holders and unusual inkwells.

Vézénobres

11km/7mi S. Leave Alès on N 106.

Old medieval Vézénobres perches on a hillside overlooking the Gardon d'Alès and the Gardon d'Anduze. Several houses date from the 12C, 14C or 15C and further evidence of the medieval town is the Sabran gateway, old ramparts and fortress ruins. Stroll through picturesque alleyways and enjoy the view from the top of the village.

ADDRESSES

STAY

Camping Domaine des Fumades – *30500 Allègre-les-Fumades – 17km/10.5mi NE of Alès on D 16 then D 241 – 04 66 24 80 78 – domaine.des.fumades.com – open 17 May-7 Sep – reservations required – 230 sites.* On the outskirts of Alauzène, this campsite's natural surroundings are well preserved and a magnificent patio, restaurants, shops, three swimming pools and a Children's club add to the enjoyment.

Hotel Deltour – *Chemin des Trespeaux. 04 66 54 98 10 – www.deltourhotel.com – – 30 rms – 6€.* With rooms at reasonable prices, this hotel offers all modern conveniences, including internet connections.

EAT

Le Guévent – *12 bd Gambetta – 04 66 30 31 98 – closed 18 Jul-23 Aug, Sun evening, Tue evening and Mon.* This small local restaurant has a welcoming bright yellow decor. Traditional Cévennes cuisine prepared by a passionate chef.

Riche – *42 pl. Semard – 04 66 86 00 33 – www.leriche.fr – closed 1-25 Aug.* This hotel-restaurant opposite the station has an art noveau dining room and a high quality classic menu. Rooms are modern and functional.

Atelier des Savuers – *16 fg de Rochebelle – 04 66 86 27 77 – closed Sat lunch, Sun evening and Mon.* This small restaurant offers a taste of the countryside as well as of regional produce.

Auberge de St-Hilaire – *30560 St-Hilaire-de-Brethmas – 3km/2mi SE of Alès on N 106 – 04 66 30 11 42 – aubergedesainthilaire@hotmail.com- closed Sun evening and Mon.* This inn has a pleasant garden courtyard, warm Mediterranean colours and attractive modern cuisine.

Auberge des Voutins – 409 Route des Écoles, *30340 Méjannes-les-Alès – 04 66 61 38 03 – closed 1-15 Sep, 21-28 Feb; Sun evening and Mon except public holidays.* This country dwelling offers traditional cuisine by the fireside or on a shady terrace.

SHOPPING

Jean-Luc Billard – *21 r. de la Montagnade – 11km/6.6mi S of Alès – 30720 Ribaute-les-Tavernes – 04 66 83 67 35 – gard@orpailleur.com.* This "gold-digger" promises to find gold by panning in the River Gard. Afternoon tours are organised Mon-Fri in Jul-Aug.

Grotte de la Cocalière★

This cave northwest of St-Ambroix on the Gard plateau contains a network of galleries running for over 46km/29mi underground. The site of La Cocalière was a densely populated prehistoric settlement between the Paleolithic period (40 000 BC) and the Iron Age (400 BC).

- **Michelin Map:** 339: J-k 3.
- **Info:** "Cevennes Active" Tourism Office 30 r de la République – 30160 Besseges 04 66 25 08 60. www.cevennes-actives.org
- **Location:** From St-Ambroix, follow D 904 towards Aubenas then turn right onto a minor road beyond the intersection with the Courry road.
- **Kids:** The return by miniature train from the underground tour.

CAVE

Guided tour 1hr; temperature 14°C/57.2°F. guided tours (1hr) Jul-Aug 10am-7pm; mid Mar-Jun and Sep-Nov 10am-noon, 2-5pm. 7.50€ (children: 5€). 04 66 24 34 74. www.grotte-cocaliere.com.

At the end of the entrance tunnel, a path leads for about 1 200m/1 310yd along the bottom of a horizontal gallery linking the various chambers. The cave contains a remarkable number and variety of deposits and formations. These are reflected in pools of water fed by tiny waterfalls on either side of the path. Numerous discs are suspended from or attached to the overhanging rockface and often grow upwards in an irregular way. The formation of these huge concretions continues to mystify experts. Some rocky roofs feature a geometric coffering of fragile stalactites of pure white calcite or coloured with metal oxides. A small underground lake enclosed by a natural dam contains cave pearls still being formed.

After the speleologists' camp, walk through the Chaos chamber beneath roofs covered with evidence of erosion, to a gallery of frozen falls overlooking an imposing, sparkling waterfall and wells linked to the lower levels where underground rivers flow. Pass a prehistoric deposit before taking a small train back to the entrance.

In the immediate surroundings outside the cave, note a dolmen, some tumuli (piles of earth or stones built above graves), small drystone constructions like the *bories* of Provence, prehistoric shelters and a variety of karst phenomena (caves, sinkholes, faults).

Grotte de la Cocalière

©Andre/Grotte de la Cocalière

ADDRESSES

STAY

"THE FRAGRANT BASTIDE"

La Bastide des Senteurs – *30500 St-Victor-de-Malcap – 8km/5mi from the Grotte de la Cocalière on D 904 and D 51C – 04 66 60 24 45 – www.bastide-senteurs.com Closed Nov-Mar; noon in Jul-Aug, except Sun.* The young owners have transformed this old country house into a charming inn reflecting Mediterranean flavours and colours. The food is good and the welcome friendly, with pretty rooms, swimming pool and pleasant terrace.

Florac

and Parc National de Cévennes

On the edge of the Causse Méjean, the Cévennes and Mont Lozère, Florac contains the head office of the Parc national des Cévennes. Florac survived a turbulent history, subjected to a tough feudal regime in the *pays du Gévaudan, pays de tyrans* (Gévaudan, land of tyrants) and then the Wars of Religion. Today this peaceful town is famous for its good food and outdoor leisure activities. Every summer the town hosts the *24 heures de Florac*, with riders completing a 160km/99mi circuit on horseback around Mont Lozère, Mont Aigoual and Causse Méjean.

Info: 33 Ave. Jean-Monestier, 48400 Florac, ☎04 66 45 01 14. www.mescevennes.com

Location: In the Tarnon valley at Tarn gorges entrance.

Don't Miss: The 150 menhirs along the Sentier des menhirs de la cham des Bondons.

Kids: The dinosaurs of St-Laurent-de-Trèves

TOWN

The town is quite small, but has a couple of large open squares with restaurants and a few shops – the 'esplanade' is the larger of the two.

Château

Open Jul-Aug 9am-6pm; Easter-Jun and Sep 9.30am-12.15pm, 1.30-5.30pm; Oct-Easter daily except weekends 9.30am-12.15pm, 1.30-5.30pm. Closed 1 Jan, 25 Dec. ☎04 66 49 53 01.

This 17C building displays exhibits on the landscape, flora, fauna and activities in the Parc National des Cévennes. The **Information Centre** has information on park hikes, guided tours, open-air museums (*écomusées*) and overnight accommodation. The nearby "Spring Trail" (*Sentier de la Source*) is signposted with information on the natural environment of the River Pêcher.

Couvent de la Présentation

This convent was a commandery of the Knights Templar. The façade and monumental doorway date from 1583.

Source du Pêcher

Situated at the foot of the Rochefort rock, this is one of the main resurgent springs on the Causse Méjean. The river bubbles and froths up from the spring during heavy rain or melting snows.

EXCURSION

Le Pont-de-Montvert

21 km (13m) west of Florac on the D998. ☎04 66 45 81 94

The tall grey houses of Le Pont-de-Montvert stand on either bank of the Tarn, which is spanned by a 17C humpback bridge surmounted by a toll tower. The **Abbot of Chayla**, in charge of Roman Catholic operations in the Cévennes, was staying in Le Pont-de-Montvert and holding some Protestants prisoner there.

On 24 July 1702, two members of the Protestant movement rescued their colleagues and caused the death of the abbot, thus sparking off the Camisard uprising.

LE PARC NATIONAL DES CÉVENNES

The Cévennes National Park covers an area of 91 500ha/226 101 acres, surrounded by a peripheral zone of 237 000ha/585 639 acres. It was founded in September 1970 and is the largest of the seven French national parks.

Maison du Mont Lozère

Open Jun-Sep 10.30am–12.30pm, 2.30–6.30pm; Apr-May and Oct 2-6pm; rest of year Sat 3-6pm. 3.50€. ☎04 66 45 80 73.

This centre is the headquarters of the Écomusée du Mont Lozère, an open-air museum set up by the Parc National des Cévennes. A large polygonal building houses an exhibition on the natural and human history of Mont Lozère, and an overnight shelter (*gîte*) for walkers.

Sentier de l'Hermet

6km/4mi from the Tour de l'Horloge, the clock tower in the centre of Le Pont-de-Montvert; allow 3hr there and back.

This footpath, which includes 12 observation points, reveals the landscapes, flora and fauna of the Tarn gorge, the traditional architecture of L'Hermet hamlet, various types of shepherds' huts and a panorama of the south face of Mont Lozère.

DRIVING TOURS

1 CORNICHE DES CÉVENNES★

58km/36mi from Florac to St-Jean-du-Gard – allow 2hr.

This scenic trip is best in late afternoon, when the low-lying sun's rays throw the jagged outline of the ridges and the depth of the valleys into vivid relief.

Leave Florac heading S on D 907. The road hugs the Tarnon Valley and Causse Méjean escarpments, before climbing to St-Laurent-de-Trèves.

St-Laurent-de-Trèves

On a limestone promontory overlooking this village, 190 million-year-old remains indicate the area was covered by a lagoon inhabited by two-legged, 4m/13ft tall **dinosaurs**. The church contains a display on dinosaurs and local excavations (*open Jul and Aug: 10am-1.30pm, 2.30-6pm; 3.50€. 04 66 49 53 00; www.cevennes-parc-national.fr).*

The Corniche des Cévennes starts from the Col du Rey and continues through the windswept limestone plateau of the **Can de l'Hospitalet**, a Camisard assembly point in the 18C. The road then follows the edge of the plateau overlooking the Vallée Française watered by the Gardon de Ste-Croix.

From **Col des Faïsses** (*faïsse*: a bank of cultivated land) the mountain drops away steeply on either side, providing a good view of the Cévennes. The road crosses the bare and rocky Can de l'Hospitalet plateau with stunning views of Mont Lozère, Barre-des-Cévennes, the Vallée Française and the Aigoual massif. At Le Pompidou, the road winds through chestnut groves and sparse daffodil meadows.

Before St-Roman-de-Tousque, turn left onto D 140 then right onto D 983.

The road enters the **Vallée Française** travelled by Robert Louis Stevenson and his donkey Modestine (*p118*). The name Vallée Française dates from pre-medieval times when it was a Frankish enclave within Visigoth territory.

Notre-Dame de Valfrancesque

This charming 11C Romanesque sanctuary is now a Protestant church. The road runs down to St-Jean-du-Gard along the Gardon de Mialet riverbed, past the Marouls farm, a handy stopover for walkers.

2 CÉVENNES ROUND TRIP

75km/47mi – allow 3hrs.

This trip explores the Cévennes, criss-crossed by deep valleys containing houses roofed with schist slabs, roads lined with chestnut trees, and villages steeped in memories of the Camisard uprising.

THE PRACTICAL PARK

RECEPTION AND INFORMATION

The map shows the whereabouts of the Cévennes National Park's information centres, which are also the point of departure, in season, for day-long guided tours. The largest of these is in the Château at Florac, which houses the administrative headquarters and an exhibition on the park *(BP 15, 48400 Florac, 04 66 49 53 01).*

Gentiâne – *Castagnols-Vialas – 04 66 41 04 16 – anegenti@free.fr – closed 15 Nov-15 Mar.* Donkey hire for family walks (a donkey can carry luggage and a child).

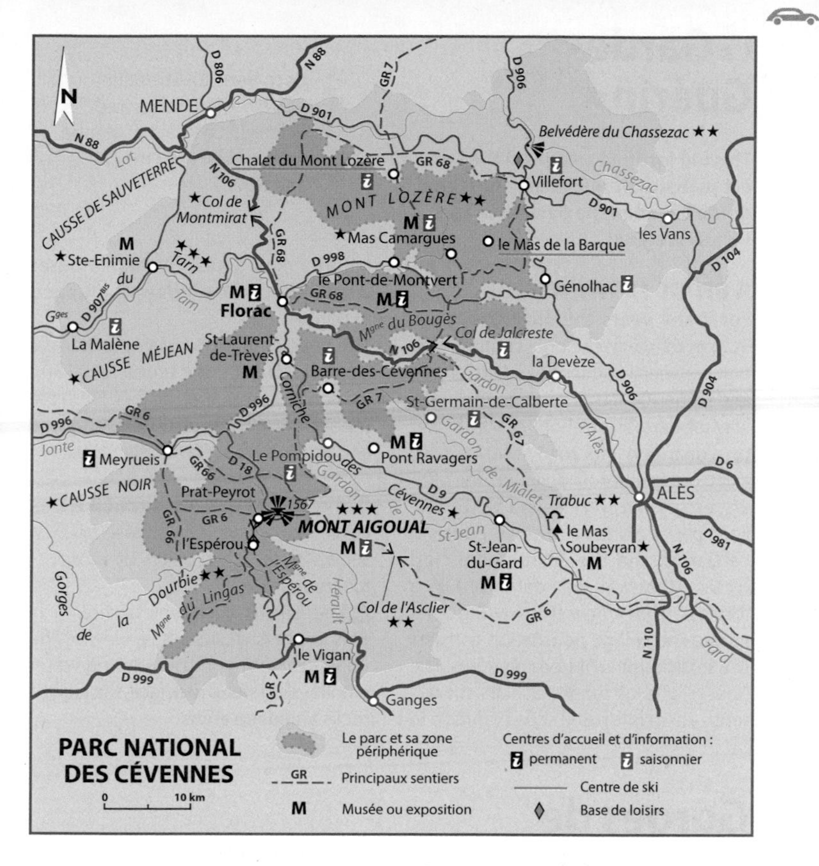

Head S from Florac on D 907 and N 106 towards Alès. The road follows the Mimente Valley flanked by schist cliffs. Beyond the ruins of the Château de St-Julien-d'Arpaon is a view of Le Bougès, rising to an altitude of 1 421m/4 618ft. At the Col de Jalcreste, turn right onto D 984 to St-Germain-de-Calberte.

Enjoy views of the Gardon de St-Germain Valley. Beyond the pass, the road to **St-Germain-de-Calberte** is graced by chestnut trees, holm-oaks and broom, and then Cévennes-style houses with stone-slab roofs and decorative chimneys. The Château de Calberte, perched on a spur of rock, comes into view in a bend of the road.

Beyond St-Germain-de-Calberte, turn right onto D 13.

Plan de Fontmort

Alt 896m/2 912ft. In the Fontmort forest an 1887 obelisk celebrates the Edict of Tolerance signed by Louis XVI, and commemorates battles between Camisard rebels and the Maréchal de Villars.

Barre-des-Cévennes

This small village with its tall bare house fronts was a major defensive position during the Camisard uprising. See remains of entrenchments on the Colline du Castelas. Walk along the Barre-des-Cévennes footpath to discover the village's history and natural environment.

Join the Corniche des Cévennes at the Col du Rey and turn right onto D 983. There are views of the Mont Aigoual range to the left and the Mont Lozère ridge to the right. Return to Florac via St-Laurent-de-Trèves and the Tarnon valley.

La Garde-Guérin★

This old fortified village on the Lozère plateau overlooks the Chassezac gorge between the Gévaudan and Vivarais regions.

- **Location:** 109km/68mi northwest of Nimes and 57km/35.6mi east of Mende via the N88, then the D6 and D906.

A BIT OF HISTORY

For many years the old Régordane Roman road was the only communication between Languedoc and Auvergne, and in the 10C it was fraught with highway robbers. The bishops of Mende set up a guard post for road security here, and a community of noblemen, the pariers, escorted travellers who paid a toll. Each parier owned a fortified house in La Garde, and the village encircled by a curtain wall was defended by a fortress. That's how this town got its name. The village population consists of a small number of stock breeders. The houses of large granite ashlars characterise an architectural style common in mountainous areas. The taller houses with mullioned windows belonged to pariers.

The keep (*entrance under a porch to the left of the church*) is the largest remaining section of the original fortress. From the top see the village and Chassezac gorge and **panorama**★ of Mont Ventoux.

Belvédère du Chassezac★★

Leave the car near the signpost "belvédère" to the left of D 906. 15min on foot round-trip.

A path leads to a narrow terrace.

This impressive site sets a view of the Chassezac gorge to thundering water amplified by steep rock face, the jagged rocks and deep abyss.

Gorges de la Dourbie

The old market town of Nant lies on the banks of the Dourbie at the mouth of the river gorge. A 7C monastic community transformed this swamp into a fertile valley with vineyards and meadows.

- **Population:** 846.
- **Michelin Map:** 338: L-6.
- **Info:** Nant, Chapelle des Pénitents, 12230 ✆05 65 62 24 21.
- **Location:** 34km/21mi SW of Millau.

NANT

The original monastery destroyed by Saracens in the 8C was rebuilt two centuries later. The Benedictine monastery prospered and in 1135 was promoted to the status of abbey. The fortified town that grew up around it became a Roman Catholic bastion during the Wars of Religion. The college founded at Nant in 1662 specialised in literature and philosophy.

The austere abbey church (**Église abbatiale St-Pierre**) has a central arch with a Gothic doorway and trefoil arch moulding. Inside, note the decoration on the **capitals**★.

The old covered market (**Vieille halle**), once part of the monastery, has a squat, sturdy gallery with five arcades (14C).

From the Chapelle du Claux (Wars of Religion memorial) there is a good view of the 14C bridge (**Pont de la Prade**).

DRIVING TOURS

1 GORGES DE LA DOURBIE★★

Leave Nant SE on D 999. From Nant to L'Espérou 35km/22mi – about 1hr.

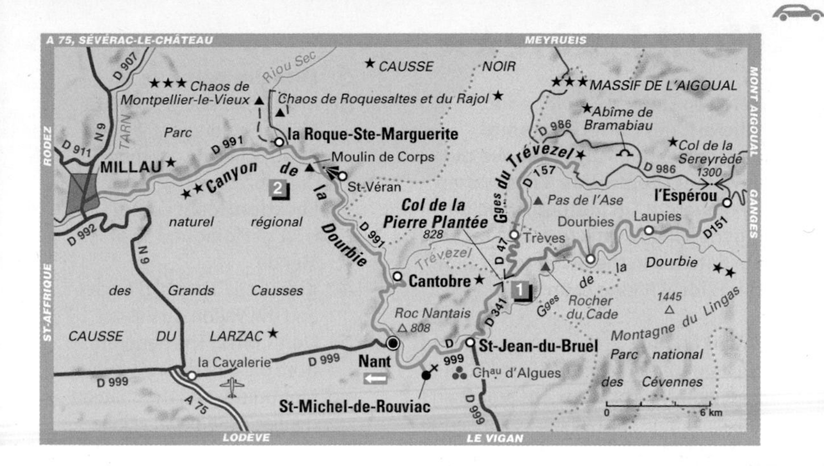

There are numerous sharp bends and difficult road junctions.

Between St-Jean and Nant, the Dourbie Valley is wide and cultivated. On the left are the four towers of Castelnau Castle, now a farm. Leave the car at the "St-Michel" signpost to the left of the road and climb the narrow path to the chapel.

St-Michel-de-Rouviac

In the 12C this Romanesque chapel was a priory and a daughter-house of Nant Abbey. Both buildings have similar capitals with knotwork and palmettes.

St-Jean-du-Bruel

This summer holiday resort opening onto the Dourbie gorge, makes a base for various hikes. A 15C **humpback bridge** spans the Dourbie, and near the new bridge is an attractive 18C covered market.

Col de la Pierre Plantée

Alt 828m/2 691ft. A view from the pass overlooks the Dourbie Valley, Lingas mountain range and Causse du Larzac.

Turn left onto D 47.

Gorges du Trévezel★

The Trévezel River flows between the Aigoual range and the Dourbie Valley, over a bed strewn with boulders. The valley gradually narrows to become a ravine and the narrowest part is known as the *Pas de l'Ase* ("Donkey's Step").

Return to Col de la Pierre Plantée and turn right onto D 151.

The narrow winding road runs high above the **Gorges de la Dourbie**★★ all the way to Dourbies.

L'Espérou

See Massif de l'AIGOUAL.

2 CANYON DE LA DOURBIE★★

From Nant to Millau 32km/20mi. Allow 1hr. Downstream from Nant, the valley narrows again between the limestone rocks of the Grands Causses.

Cantobre★

This picturesque village at the confluence of the Trévezel and Dourbie Rivers deserves its name: *quant obra*, meaning "what a masterpiece."

Canyon de la Dourbie★★

The road offers a superb **view**★ of the village and remains of the old castle of the **Marquis de Montcalm** (1712-59) who died on the Plains of Abraham in Quebec City, Canada, defending the town against the English. The road continues past **Moulin de Corps**, a watermill powered by a resurgent spring.

La Roque-Ste-Marguerite

This village lies in the shadow of the ruin-shaped rocks of Le Rajol and Montpellier-le-Vieux and a 17C castle tower.

Mont Lozère★★

Between Florac, Génolhac and Villefort, this powerful granite massif rises majestically above the Cévennes countryside. Crisscrossed by numerous GR footpaths, including the six-day walk round Mont Lozère detailed in the GR 68 topoguide, this is ideal hiking country.

- **Michelin Map:** 330: J-8
- **Info:** Génolhac ✆04 66 61 18 32. Gagnières ✆04 66 25 40 65. www.cevennes-montlozere.com
- **Location:** Mont Lozère is NE of Florac and SE of Mende.
- **Kids:** The Château d'Aujac and the Vallon du Villaret.
- **Don't Miss:** The panoramas from pic Cassini and Montmirat, and the château d'Aujac's medieval village.

"Mont Chauve" – Mont Lozère is called "Bald Mountain" for its 35km/22mi of bare, high-lying plateaux. The mountain's Finiels summit (alt 1 699m/5 573ft) is the highest non-volcanic peak in the Massif Central. Its eroded granite has weathered into curious boulders amidst heathland and remnants of ancient beech forest. Architecture is robust: some houses have granite boulders in their walls. Life is harsh on these exposed plateaux and most villages are deserted, yet storm bells once used to guide travellers during blizzards are still found here. In the 19C, 100 000 head of sheep grazed the hillside pastures during the summer. Today herds of cattle replace them and the old sheep trails (drailles) are being overgrown.

SKI AREAS

Mont-Lozère-Le Bleymard ski area

Alt 1 350-1 560m/ 4 429–5 118ft.
✆04 66 48 66 48. Cross-country skiing and snowshoeing over 22km/14mi of tracks, and five ski lifts and 8km/5mi of Alpine ski runs for all levels.

Mas de la Barque ski area

Alt 1 340–1 650m/ 4 396–5 413ft.
✆04 66 46 92 72. Here are 38km/24mi of cross-country skiing and snowshoeing tracks.

ÉCOMUSÉE DU MONT-LOZÈRE

This open-air museum of local crafts and traditions consists of the **Maison du Mont Lozère at Pont-de-Montvert** and sites of architectural and natural interest throughout the massif. Most museum sights are mentioned in the itineraries described below.

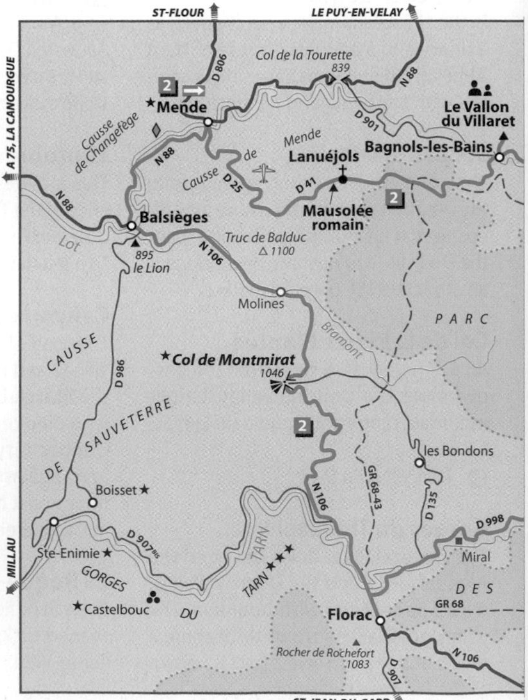

DRIVING TOURS

1 EASTERN MONT LOZÈRE★

Round tour from Le Pont-de-Montvert. 130km/80mi – allow one day.

Follow D 20 N and turn right immediately after leaving Le Pont-de-Montvert.

The narrow road *(heavy summer traffic)* crosses barren pastures and heathland dotted with rocks.

L'Hôpital

Summer visitors have bought and restored some old granite buildings in this hamlet and the Écomusée has re-thatched the roofs of the watermill and old grange.

The GR 7 footpath which crosses L'Hôpital leads to Pont-du-Tarn.

Pont-du-Tarn

1hr on foot there and back from L'Hôpital.

The GR 7 follows the old Margeride sheep trail. A pretty bridge spans the river as it threads its way through polished rocks at the foot of the Commandeur woods.

Mas Camargues★

Open Jul-Aug daily except Sat 10.30am-12.30pm, 2.30-6.30pm (Sun 2.30-6.30pm). Closed 14 Jul, 15 Aug (morning). 3.50€ 04 66 45 80 73. This family mansion has been restored by the Parc national des Cévennes. An **observation trail** winds through a sheepfold, mill, small canal, reservoir and countryside.

Continue the walk to **Bellecoste** *(1km/0.6mi)* to see a communal oven and thatched shepherd's house.

Return to D 20 and turn right.

The road climbs towards Finiels Pass and crosses deserted countryside marked with granite boulders. See Bougès mountain to the south and the hilly outline of the Causse Méjean.

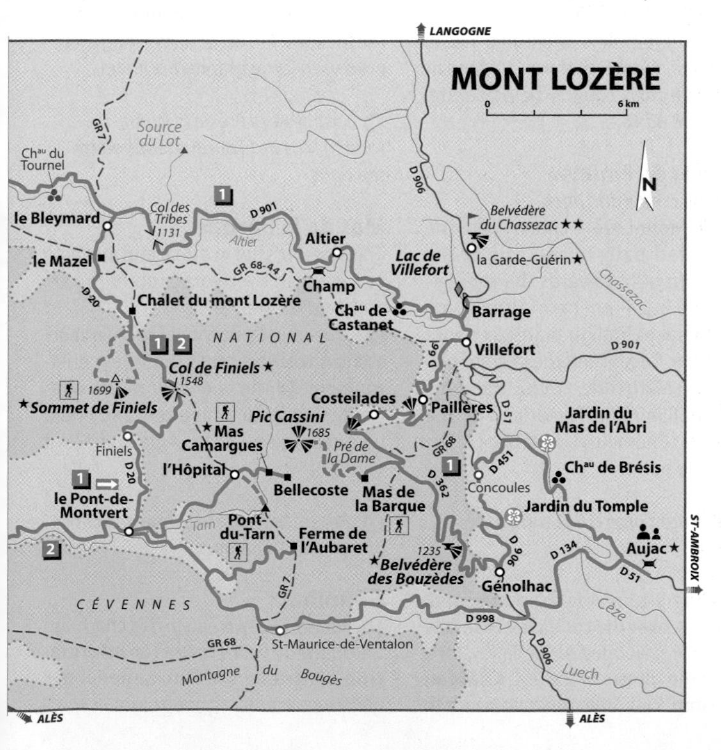

Villefort dam

A. Thuillier/MICHELIN

Col de Finiels★

Alt 1 548m/5 077ft.

From the pass the **view**★ encompasses Mont Aigoual and the Causses. Starting the descent, see the Tanargue massif ahead and to the right.

Chalet du Mont Lozère

Here are a refuge chalet, hotel, **information centre** for the Cévennes park and a large UCPA building (for the French open-air sports centres association) welcoming ramblers and horse-riders in summer. From December to April, it becomes a cross-country skiing centre. *℘04 66 48 66 48.*

Sommet de Finiels★

3hr on foot there and back.

From Mont Lozère chalet, take the waymarked path to the top of the ridge. Turn right towards the remains of a stone hut. From here, a sweeping **view**★★ takes in high plateaux peaks as far as Pic Cassini and the granite plateau of La Margeride. Follow the ridge to the 1 685m/5 527ft marker and the "Route des Chômeurs" leads back to the departure point.

Turn right onto D 901 towards Villefort.

The scenery turns bleak and rugged. The road leaves the Lot Valley to follow the winding, wooded Altier Valley, for a view of the towers of the 15C **Château de Champ**. Past Altier the road winds to Lake Villefort and the ruins of the Renaissance **Château de Castanet**.

Villefort reservoir and dam

The 190m/623ft long dam rises to a height of 70m/230ft above the river bed. The reservoir supplies the Pied-de-Borne plant downstream. On the road to Langogne are a water sports centre and beach. **Villefort** attracts water sports enthusiasts and makes an ideal base for trips into the Cévennes, Bas Vivarais and Mont Lozère. The Villefort Syndicat d'Initiative runs a seasonal **information centre** on the Parc national des Cévennes (*open Jul-Aug 9.30am-12.30pm, 3-7pm (Sun 10am-1pm); Sep-Jun daily except weekends 10am-noon, 3-6 pm. Closed 1 May. ℘04 66 46 87 30).*

On leaving Villefort, take D 66.

The road winds through Paillères and Costeilades and the plateaux formed by the Borne and Chassezac gorges come into view. Then a stretch of granite outcrops offer views of the Tanargue and Mézenc massifs and Alps. The road reaches the Pré de la Dame ledge, covered with large granite boulders.

Just beyond Pré de la Dame, the road to Mas de la Barque leads off to the right.

Mas de la Barque

This forester's hut in a peaceful meadow serves as an overnight stop for hikers and a ski centre.

An Écomusée du Mont Lozère **observation trail** presents the forest environment. The two-hour return path to the Cassini summit offers a splendid **panorama**★★ of the Alps and Mont Ventoux.

Return to Pré de la Dame and carry on towards Génolhac.

Génolhac

The Maison de l'Arceau in this charming Gardonnette Valley town is an **information centre** on the Parc national des Cévennes and offers overnight accommodation. (open 9am-noon, 1.30-5.30pm. 04 66 61 19 97. www.pnc.fr).

Drive N along D 906 to La Banlève and turn right onto D 155.

The road leads to Brésis, and its handsome medieval castle.

Turn right onto D 51 which runs down towards Bessèges.

Château d'Aujac

In Aujac, turn left onto a minor road up to the castle. Park the car and walk to the entrance (10min). Open Jul-Aug guided tours (1hr) daily except Mon 11am-7pm; Easter-Oct Sun and public holidays 2-6pm. 5€. 04 66 61 19 94. www.chateau-aujac.com

The 11C castle watching over the Cèze Valley is one of the best-preserved in the area and is gradually being restored by a team of volunteers.

Follow D 134 W towards Génolhac, turn left onto the road to Alès, then right onto D 998 towards Florac.

The road along the Luech Valley is particularly scenic as far as St-Maurice-de-Ventalon.

Continue 2km/1mi after Les Bastides, a road on the right leads to Troubat farm-house.

Ferme de Troubat

Open Jul-Aug guided tours (45min) 10.30am, 2.30 and 6.30pm; May-Jun daily except Tue 3-6pm. 3.50€. 04 66 45 80 73.

This old farmstead restored by the Parc national des Cévennes has a stable barn, bread oven, mill and threshing area.

Ferme-fortifiée de l'Aubaret

This pink-granite walls of this fortified farm on the Margeride sheep trail have mullioned windows.

Rejoin D 998 and turn right to return to Le Pont-de-Montvert.

2 WESTERN MONT LOZÈRE★★

Round trip from Mende. 100km/62mi – allow half a day. Leave Mende on D 25 heading SE towards the airport. In Langlade, turn left onto D 41.

Lanuéjols

The **Roman mausoleum** was erected by wealthy Roman citizens to the memory of their two young sons. The Romanesque **Église St-Pierre** has a barrel-vaulted nave.

Continue along D 41 to Bagnols-les-Bains.

Bagnols-les-Bains

The mineral waters of this spa resort were first exploited by the Romans. Bagnols' altitude (913m/2 995ft) and nearby forests contribute to its healthy mountain air.

From Bagnols drive N along a road leading to Le Villaret.

Le Vallon du Villaret

Open Jul-Aug 10am-6.45pm; Apr-Jun 10.30am-6.45pm; mid Sep-Oct weekends 11am-6pm. 9-11€ according to season. 04 66 47 63 76.

This leisure park has a nature theme and village with artist studios, exhibitions and concert venues.

Return to Bagnols and turn left to Le Bleymard.

Rambling on Mont Lozère

A. Thuillier/MICHELIN

The valley sides become steep rocky gorges and in the distance Tournel Castle ruins perch on a rocky spur.

Le Bleymard

See 1 above.

Right onto D 20 to Le Pont-de-Montvert. This tour is described in 1 above in the other direction.

Le Pont-de-Montvert

See Le PONT-DE-MONTVERT.

Turn right onto D 998 to Florac.

The upper Tarn Valley narrows into rugged gorges, and the ruined 14C Miral Castle perches on a promontory.

Florac

See FLORAC.

Drive N along N 106 towards Mende.

Beyond the intersection with the road to Ispagnac along the **Tarn gorge**★★★ is a spectacular cliff-edge passage overlooks Florac.

Col de Montmirat★

Alt 1 046m/3 432ft. The pass slices between the granite of Mont Lozère and the limestone of the Causse de Sauveterre. Enjoy the **panorama**★: looming Causse Méjean cliffs, Cévennes ridges and Mont Aigoual. The road descends into the Bramon Valley with views of the "Truc de Balduc" and Mont Lozère foothills.

Balsièges

To the south of this village tower the cliffs of the Causse de Sauveterre. N 88 follows the Lot between the Causses de Mende and de Changefège.

Marvejols

The Aubrac and Gévaudan

Marvejols benefits from a favourable climate and setting which has inspired the founding of several medical and pedagogical centres. This "Royal City" which played an important role in 14C wars eventually became a Protestant fortress town, and was destroyed in 1586 by Admiral Joyeuse. Its fortified gatehouses are reminiscent of its war-torn past.

- **Population:** 5 501
- **Michelin Map:** 330: H-7.
- **Info:** Pl. du Soubeyran, 48100, 04 66 32 02 14.
- **Location:** 180km/112.50mi NW of Montpellier and 69km/43mi N of Millau via the A75.
- **Don't Miss:** château de la Baume.
- **Kids:** Wolves of Gévaudan.

MARVEJOLS

Fortified gatehouses command the three entrances to the old town. The **Porte du Soubeyran**★ records how the town was rebuilt by Henri IV and the other two gatehouses, the **Porte du Théron** and **Porte de Chanelles**, also bear inscriptions recounting the good deeds of Henri IV.

Once within the gateways, narrow streets ripple away past shops, cafés and restaurants, with little to betray its bloody history.

DRIVING TOURS

1 EASTERN AUBRAC

Round tour north-west of Marvejols. 97km/60mi – allow 4hrs. Leave Marvejols NW along D 900. Bonnecombe Pass is snowbound from Dec–Apr.

As it climbs, D 900 offers a broad view of Marvejols, La Margeride, Mont Lozère, the Causses and the Cévennes before passing through forests, fields, meadows and pastureland before reaching Nasbinals.

Nasbinals

Nasbinals, which has several lively agricultural **fairs** throughout the year, is also a resort for alpine and cross-country ski and snowshoeing.

Turn back along D 900 to Montgrousset then take D 52 to the right.

Grotte et Cascade de Déroc

30min there and back on foot. Park the car by D 52 and take a rough path lined with drystone walls to the left, towards a farm. The path follows the bank of a stream, to a magical waterfall and a cave with a ceiling vault made of rock prisms.

The D 52 skirts the shores of Lake Salhiens before cutting across pastureland to the **Col de Bonnecombe**. Beyond the pass, the road drops down through Les Hermaux to St-Pierre-de-Nogaret, then follows a scenic route through the Doulou Valley to St-Germain-du-Teil.

Take D 52 to the left to the Col du Trébatut. Turn right at the crossroads onto D 56, which leads to the Colagne Valley. In Le Monastier, take N 9 back to Marvejols.

2 The Gévaudan

Round tour north of Marvejols. 52km/32mi – about 3hr 30min. From Marvejols drive to the A 75 motorway and follow it towards Clermont-Ferrand. Leave at Exit 37, take the bridge across the motorway and follow signs to Château de la Baume.

Château de la Baume★

Jul and Aug: guided tours (45min) daily 10am-noon, 2-6pm; Sep-Jun: by request. 6€. 04 66 32 51 59. www.chateaudelabaume.org.

This 17C granite residence boasts a main staircase with Louis XIV balusters and large fireplaces made of chestnut wood soaked in Aubrac peatbogs to impart a dark brown luster and make them rot-proof. The great hall's parquet floor forms a geometric pattern around coats of arms.

Return to the motorway and take the bridge across it. At the second roundabout, take the third road to the right, then turn right onto D 53 towards St-Sauveur-de-Peyre. Follow signs to Roc de Peyre.

Roc de Peyre

15min on foot there and back.

The top of the rock affords a remarkable panorama of the Aubrac, the Plomb du Cantal, the Margeride, Mont Lozère, Mont Aigoual and the Causses. (1 179m/3 867ft, *viewing table*)

It is hard to imagine that a fortress once occupied this rocky pinnacle, yet Admiral Joyeuse used 2 500 cannonballs to destroy the keep of this Protestant fief in 1586. Time destroyed the rest.

Turn back and take N 9 to the left then a little road on the left towards Ste-Lucie, then turn right immediately onto a road going uphill (past a chapel).

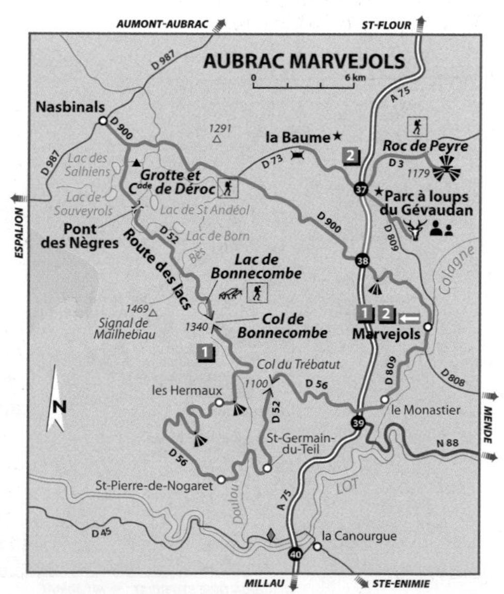

Parc des loups du Gévaudan★

Wolf feedings three times per week (Mon, Wed, Fri) are open to the public. Jul-Aug 10am-7pm; Apr-Jun, Sep-Oct: 10am-6pm; Feb-Mar, Nov-Dec 10am-5pm. Closed Jan. 6.50€ (reduced Nov-Mar; children: 3.50€). 04 66 32 09 22. www.loupsdu gevaudan.com.

This 4ha/10-acre **wild animal reserve** shelters some 100 wolves from Europe, Canada and Mongolia. A documentary shot in the park can be viewed on request. A viewing table along the 30min walk provides an attractive vista. Take a guided tour in summer, as wolves are less visible than in autumn/winter.

N 9 leads back to Marvejols.

Mende★

The capital of the Lozère, the least populated French *département*, is a market town with an imposing cathedral. Its narrow winding streets are lined with lovely old houses with timber doors, portals and oratories.

- **Population:** 12 600
- **Michelin Map:** Map 330: J-7.
- **Info:** Pl. du Forail, 48000 Mende, 04 66 94 00 23. www.ot-mende.fr.
- **Location:** 95km/59.3mi NE of Millau via the A 75.
- **Don't Miss:** The Aubusson tapestries at the cathédral; the panorama from the Mont-Mimat cross
- **Also See:** Mont Lozère

A BIT OF HISTORY

Beautiful mansions graced the north bank of the Lot as early as Roman times. In the 3C, St Privat sought refuge from the Barbarians in a cave on Mont Mimat and the town developed as a place of Roman Catholic pilgrimage. Mende suffered atrocities and bloodshed during the Wars of Religion, at the hands of Captain **Merle**, a fanatical Protestant eventually appointed Mende governor by Henri IV.

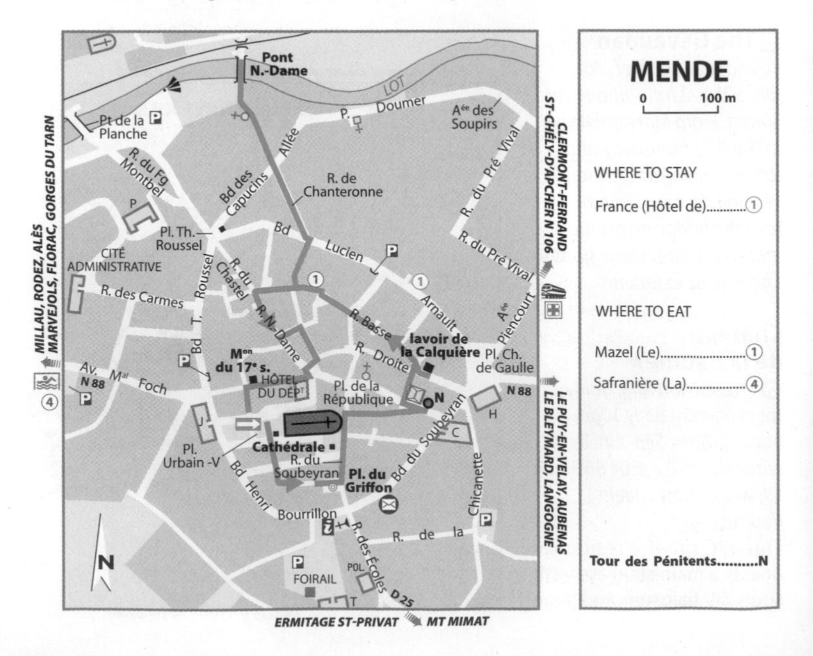

CATHEDRAL★

Most of this cathedral (restored in the early 17C) was built in the 14C under Pope Urban V. The belfries date from the 16C. When Captain Merle seized Mende in 1579, he blew up the cathedral pillars and left only the belfries, north side walls and apsidal chapels. Mende Cathedral once had the largest bell in Christendom, the "Non Pareille" ("Unequalled"), weighing 20t. Broken by Merle's men in 1579, all that remains is the enormous clapper, 2.15m/7ft long. Under the nave are the tomb and crypt of St Privat.

Take rue de l'Arjal, to the right of the cathedral.

The street leads to **place Griffon** and the fountain once used to clean the streets.

Turn left onto rue du Soubeyran then right onto rue de la Jarretière leading to place au Blé.

ADDRESSES

STAY

Hôtel de France – *9 Bd. L.-Arnault – 04 66 65 00 04 – www.hoteldefrance-mende.com – closed Jan – 27 rooms – 7€ – restaurant* . This former coaching inn in the heart of town has newly renovated rooms.

EAT

La Safranière – *In Chabrits, 5km/3mi north of Mende on the D42 – 04 66 49 31 54 – closed Mar, Sun and Mon – reservations required.* The energetic young chef, returned from abroad to open up a restaurant in the house in which he grew up, now plays host to the region's well informed foodies.

Le Mazel *25 r. du Collège – 04 66 65 05 33 – closed 8 Nov-29 Mar.* A fresco in soft clay by Loul Combes decorates the wall in the dining room, its theme celebrating the cuisine du terroir; good, local produce, imaginatively served.

GUIDED TOURS

Half day and 1.30h guided tours of Mende, "City of Art and Culture," are available in July and August.
For information contact the tourist office or www.ot-mende.fr. ***4.50€***

Meyrueis

Clear mountain air and varied attractions make Meyrueis a popular destination. Ancient plane trees decorate place Sully, generating a relaxing ambiance. Meyrueis was the birthplace of Guilhem Ademar (1190), a troubadour of some renown.

- **Michelin Map:** 330: I-9.
- **Info:** Tour de l'Horloge, 48150 Meyrueis, 04 66 45 60 33. www.meyrueis-office-tourism.com.
- **Location:** 43km/28.8mi E of Millau and 58km/36.25mi N of Vigan.
- **Don't Miss:** Mont Aigoual, Jonte Gorge, and the chaos de Montpellier-le-Vieux.
- **Kids:** Aven Armand; Dargilan cave.

TOWN WALK

While strolling along quai Sully, look out for the elegant Renaissance windows of Maison Belon, and the **Tour de l'Horloge** a clock tower left from the town's fortification.

DRIVING TOURS

Leave town on D 986 and take a small road on the left to a car park. A 15min forest walk brings you to the castle.

Château de Roquedols

The massive 15C-16C square castle stands out against the green Bétuzon Valley. Inside is a Renaissance staircase, fine antique furniture and horse-drawn carriages. Property of the Parc National des Cévennes, the château has an **information centre** overlooking the main courtyard.

Aven Armand★★★

11km/6.8mi then 45min tour. Leave Meyrueis N along D 986; the road leading to the underground chasm branches off 9.5km/6mi farther on. *See AVEN ARMAND.*

Grotte de Dargilan★★

8.5km/5.3mi then 1hr tour. Drive 7km/4.3mi W along D 39 and turn onto D 139. *See Grotte de DARGILAN.*

Massif de l'Aigoual★★★

See Massif de l'AIGOUAL.

Gorges de la Jonte★★

21km/13mi from Meyrueis to Le Rozier – allow 1hr. We recommend driving down along D 996 from Meyrueis to Le Rozier, rather than up the gorge, since the canyon becomes increasingly impressive nearing the confluence of the Jonte and the Tarn. The Jonte gorge can also be visited on foot along the clifftop footpaths over the Causse Méjean (see Causse MÉJEAN) and the Causse Noir (see Causse NOIR).

Downstream from Meyrueis the road along the Jonte gorge follows the river's north bank. Some 5km/3mi from Meyrueis, the mouths of two Causse Méjean caves open into the cliff, the **Grotte de la Vigne** and the **Grotte de la Chèvre**. Beyond these caves the gorge becomes narrower and in summer the Jonte disappears. Outside Les Douzes, the river enters a second gorge so deep that you can scarcely see its huge poplars.

Arcs de St-Pierre★

4.5km/3mi then 1hr 30min on foot there and back. Leave from Le Truel. *See Causse MÉJEAN.*

Le Belvédère des vautours

Open Jul-Aug 10am-7pm; Apr-mid Jun and Sep-early Nov 10am-5pm. Last entry 1hr before closing. 6.50€ (children 3€). 05 65 62 69 69. www.vautours-lozere.com.

Vultures were reintroduced into the area in 1970 and this exhibition explains their way of life and feeding habits. You can observe them at close range with a camera and giant screen. An observation platform overlooks the Jonte gorge. The road comes into sight of the Capluc rock, then the village of Peyreleau, and finally Le Rozier.

Le Rozier

See Gorges du TARN.

ADDRESSES

STAY / EAT

Family Hôtel – *04 66 45 60 02 www.hotel-family.com– closed 4 Nov-31 Mar – – 48 rooms – 7.50€ – restaurant* . The white façade of this hotel in Meyrueis faces the Jonte river. Functional rooms. Swimming pool and riverbank garden, Generous portions of typical Lozère fare will satisfy most appetites.

Mont Aigoual – *R. de la Barrière – 04 66 45 65 61 – www.hotel-mont-aigoual.com – closed 3 Nov-31Mar – – 30 rooms – 7€ – restaurant* . This hotel offers a pretty garden, fine Cévennes cuisine based on local produce, faultless rooms and a swimming pool.

Cirque de Navacelles★★★

The Cirque de Navacelles is the most impressive natural feature of the Vis valley, which cuts between the causses of Blandas to the north and Larzac to the south. The cirque is formed by an immense, magnificent meander, deeply embedded in almost vertical walls of rock.
The meander, which once encircled a little promontory, was abandoned by the River Vis, which broke through the neck of a loop, just where the village of Navacelles had established itself.

- **Info:** Point Info belvédère de la Baume-Auriol. ✆04 67 44 63 10.
- **Location:** 72 km/45mi NW of Montpellier, 34 km/21m NE of Lodève and SE of Ganges by the D25 & D130.
- **Don't Miss:** The Belvédère Nord, the Cirque de Vissec and the Gorges of the Vis.
- **Timing:** Allow two hours.

DRIVING TOUR

Alzon to Ganges

57km/35mi – allow 2hr. Downstream from Alzon, the road (D 814) drops to the floor of the valley, then crosses the river which makes wider and wider meanders on the flat valley floor. D 113 runs along the floor of the valley to Vissec and crosses a bridge over the river, which is frequently dried up at this point.

Vissec

The village, squatting deep down inside the canyon, consists of two districts, each on an outcrop, one of which is almost completely encircled by the Vis.

Cirque de Vissec★

During the climb up to Blandas (*gradient 9 per cent),* there is a view of the gorge with its bare cliff walls.

The road reaches Blandas across the bleak limestone plateau. D 713 branching off D 158 reaches the edge of the Causse de Blandas.

Cirque de Navacelles

H. Champollion/MICHELIN

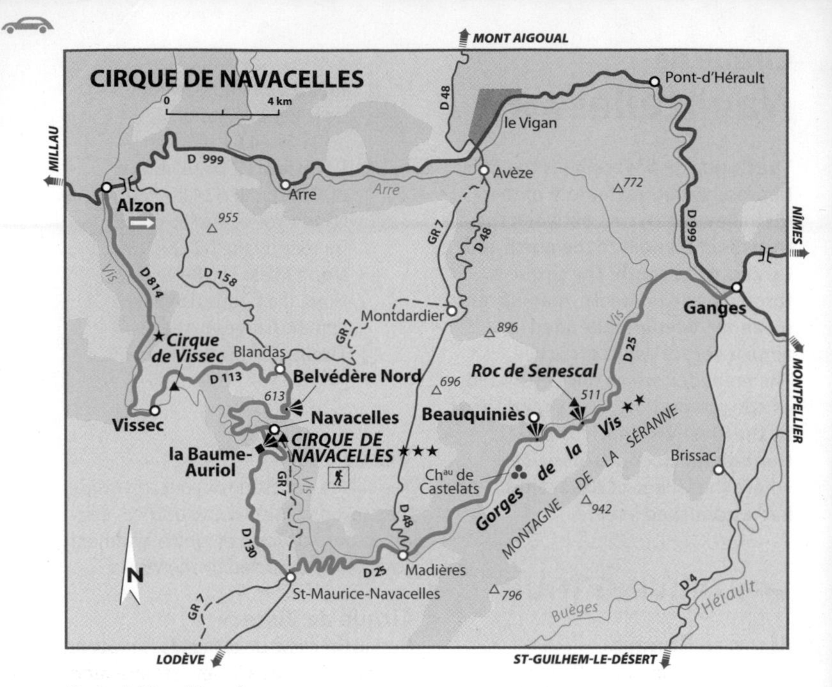

Belvédère Nord

Alt 613m/2 011ft. From this viewpoint on the north edge of the plateau there is an interesting view over the **Cirque de Navacelles**★★★ and the Vis canyon. The clearly marked road winds down one or two hairpin bends at the top of the cliff, then forms a large loop round the Combe du Four, before dropping steeply down to the floor of the cirque and onto the village of Navacelles perched on and around a rocky outcrop.

Navacelles

This little village 325m/1 066ft above sea level has a pretty single-arched bridge over the Vis. A path starting from Navacelles leads to the resurgence of the River Vis and the River Virenque near three watermills. From Navacelles D 130 climbs up the south face of the canyon.

Cliff Hanger

Roads in this region tend to be poorly maintained and can often be wide enough for a single vehicle only. The road down into the valley is sheer, clinging to the cliff face; a dangerous but dramatic drive.

La Baume-Auriol

Alt 618m/2 037ft.

From north of the farm, there is a magnificent view of the cirque.

Beyond La Baume-Auriol, the road continues to St-Maurice-Navacelles, where you should turn left towards Ganges. Farther along, the road plunges downhill in a series of hairpin bends. At the start of the downhill stretch to Madières, there is a good view of the gorge.

Gorges de la Vis★★

Beyond Madières, the road sticks closely to the bank of the Vis, which cuts a pretty course between the tall dolomitic cliffs of the Causse de Blandas, on the left, and the slopes of Séranne mountain, on the right. After Gorniès, a bridge spans the Vis. Look out for a lovely view of **Beauquiniès**, a pretty terraced village, and then of the **Roc de Senescal**, which juts out like a ship's prow from the slope on the left. The valley becomes narrow and rugged, before running into the Hérault gorge. Carry on along the banks of the Hérault to Le Pont and Ganges.

St-Jean-du-Gard

The narrow high street of this ancient town, lying on the banks of the Gardon, is lined with austere houses. An old humpback cutwater bridge spanning the river, which was partially destroyed by flooding in 1958, adds a picturesque note to the scenery.

- **Population:** 2 563
- **Michelin Map:** 339: I-4.
- **Info:** Pl. Rabaut-St-Étienne, 30270 St-Jean-du-Gard, 04 66 85 31 11.
- **Location:** 30 km/19m W of Alès by the N110, then the D910A and 88 km/55m from Montpellier by the A9 and the N110. Follow the D907 to St Jean du Gard.
- **Parking:** Difficult especially on Tuesday (Market). Park out of town.
- **Don't Miss:** The view from the Col d'Asclier.
- **Timing:** Allow one hour for the town – more if you visit the market.

ATTRACTIONS

Musee des Vallées Cévenoles★

Open Jul-Aug 10am–7pm; Apr-Jun, Sep-Oct 10am–12.30pm, 2–7pm; Nov-Mar, Tue and Thur 9am–noon and 2–6pm, Sun 2-6pm. 4.50€. 04 66 85 10 48. www.museedescevennes.com. Housed in a former 17C inn, this museum illustrates daily life and traditions.

Atlantide Parc

Avenue de la Résistance, on the right bank of the Gardon. Open Jun-Aug 11am-7pm; Apr-May and Sep-Oct daily except Mon 11am-6pm; Mar Sun only 11am–6pm. Guided tours by request (1hr). Nov-Feb. 8€ (children 4€). 04 66 85 40 53. www.aquarium-cevennes.com. Several aquariums present a variety of colourful tropical fauna. A foaming waterfall feeding the artificial river enhances the exotic atmosphere.

DRIVING TOURS

Route du col de l'Asclier★★

44km/27mi from St-Jean-du-Gard to Pont-d'Hérault – allow 1hr 30min. Take extra care along the twisting narrow road, particularly between l'Estréchure and Col de l'Asclier; the pass is usually blocked by snow from December to March.

This itinerary leads from the Gardon Valley to the Hérault Valley across a typical Cévennes ridge. D 907 meanders up the Gardon Valley from St-Jean, following the river closely. Just before l'Estréchure, turn left onto D 152 towards Col de l'Asclier. Beyond Milliérines, the landscape becomes wild; the road overlooks the valleys of several tributaries of St-Jean-Gardon, then runs round the Hierle ravine.

Turn left towards Col de l'Asclier.

Col de l'Asclier★★

Alt 905m/2 969ft. The road runs beneath a bridge, part of the Margeride track (*draille*) used by flocks of sheep on their way to high pastures. From the pass there is a magnificent panoramic view to the west.

Col de la Triballe

Alt 612m/2008ft. From the pass there is an extensive view of the Cévennes range; the village of St-Martial can be seen in the valley below. The picturesque D 420 leads down into the Hérault Valley, with a few hamlets hanging onto the slopes on both sides.

Cross the River Hérault in Peyregrosse then turn left onto D 986 to Pont-d'Hérault.

Corniche des Cévennes★

See FLORAC.

Located between the Causse Méjean and the Cause de Sauveterre, the stunning Gorges du Tarn are essentially a canyon fashioned by the River Tarn. Most of the gorge is in the département of Lozère, with a little in Aveyron. The so-called *causses* are part of a vast, wild and beautiful limestone plateau, les Grandes Causses, at an altitude of between 800m and 1250m.

Highlights

1. The **Millau viaduct** is outstanding (p147)
2. Stunning in its simplicity and appeal, **La Couvertoirade** (p149)
3. In spite of the temptation to whizz on by, **Millau**, is an engaging halt on the way south (p156)
4. The chaos of **Montpellier-le-Vieux** (p161)

All in a great causse

The curious thing about the *causses*, is that few, not even the French, can pinpoint them on a map; it's a huge, amorphous, limestone plateau sprawled across three *départements*, embraced within their own regional park. What is certain is that once you've found them, you face many happy days, weeks and months exploring them. This is a wilderness in the true sense of the word; a place that leaves you bewildered, a splendid, rugged and endearing *lieu*.

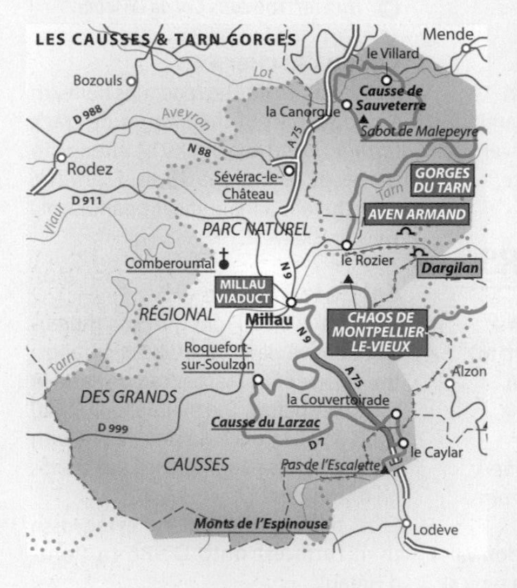

Millau the town

Lying at the centre of the Grands Causses Regional Nature Park, at the confluence of the Tarn and the Dourbie, Millau's industrial tradition dates to Roman times when the town used to make pottery. Later, the manufacture of leather products and glove-making became the town's principal economy, but during the 1930s the glove-making business suffered a decline, largely due to the import of cheap imitations. Recently, however, Parisian fashion houses have realised that the old ways are the best, and Millau's glove makers have seen a revival of their fortunes.

Millau, which has an atmosphere that hints at the Mediterranean, is a fascinating and lively provincial town, a maze of narrow streets that lead to secluded squares, fountains, markets, shops and churches. It is the second town after Rodez in the old province of Rouergue, and its setting, between the Causse Noir and the Causse du Larzav, is quite spectacular. Along the place Foch, in the shade of plane trees, lie numerous cafés and restaurants, and ancient houses supported on stone pillars.

M.-H. Carcanague/MICHELIN

Millau Viaduct★★★

It is impossible not to be excited when first you see the Millau viaduct, spanning the Tarn gorge (*see region map opposite*). This immense span of architectural ingenuity, designed by the British architect, Norman Foster, in collaboration with the celebrated French engineer, Michel Virlogeux, carries the A75 autoroute through the clouds on its way from Clermont Ferrand to Béziers.

The structure, built at a cost of 394 million euros, and consuming two million working hours, is so impressive that there is a specially constructed pedestrian viewing point close by, just so that you can come and look at it. But, to fully appreciate the viaduct you need to find your way out of Millau and along the road to Peyre – one of France's 'Most Beautiful Villages' – which will take you directly under the bridge, and on to the village. The bridge is awesome; the village quite simply beautiful.

The 2.5km/1.5mi bridge stands on seven huge but slender concrete pillars, and with a total height 343m/1 125ft higher than the Eiffel Tower, it is the tallest bridge in the world. More than 150 steel stays hold it all in place, and the effect of late afternoon sunlight catching this metal network is quite magical, the whole edifice shimmering in a most captivating way. Nominally, the life-span of the bridge is 120 years. How will it age? Will it survive as well as the Pont du Gard near Nimes? Will it become a regional icon, a symbol of Anglo-French technical achievement? Or simply a high-speed link that takes people away from the town of Millau? Only time will tell. Unlike the Millau viaduct, however, the Pont du Gard never had to cope with thousands of high-speeding vehicles carrying goods and holiday-makers south to the summer sun and sea of Languedoc.

View of Millau Viaduct from Peyre

©Sunset/Tips Image

Stalagmites

A. Cassaigne/MICHELIN

Aven Armand ★★★

Hidden beneath the Causse Méjean, the Aven Armand is one of the wonders of the underground world, opened to the public in 1927.

Location: 48km/30mi S of Mende; 43km/27mi NE of MIllau.

Visit: Jul-Aug 9.30am-6pm; mid-Mar-mid-Jun and Sep-Oct 10am-noon, 1.30pm-5pm. 8.50€. 04 66 45 61 31. www.aven-armand.com. Allow one hour. Temperature: 10°C/50°F.

A BIT OF HISTORY

Discovery of the Aven Armand

The famous speleologist E-A Martel began exploring the *causses* in 1883, accompanied by **Louis Armand**, a locksmith from Le Rozier. On 18 September 1897 Armand returned from an outing to the Causse Méjean greatly excited. The next day an expedition investigated the enormous crevice, known by local farmers as *l'aven* ("the swallow-hole"). Armand was enraptured at this wonderland of rock formations.

CAVE

The tour explores the vast subterranean gallery, 60×100m/195×325ft long by 45m/146ft high.

Spectacular concretions form a luxuriant jungle of fantastically shaped trees up to 15-25m/50-80ft in height. Glistening with calcite crystals, they have trunks resembling palm trees or cypresses, and large jagged "leaves" measuring three feet across. Stalagmites explode into a riot of arabesques, needles, palm branches and elegant pyramids. The variety of concretions is amazing: gigantic candles, monstrous figures with club-shaped heads and curly cabbages and delicately engraved fruit.

La Couvertoirade★

This tiny fortified town in the Causse du Larzac on the Larzac plateau, once belonged to the Knights Templars. By 1880 La Couvertoirade had only 362 inhabitants, but today it is popular with weavers and artisans working in enamel and pottery.

- **Population:** 153.
- **Michelin Map:** 338: L-7 .
- **Info:** Point info turisme de La Couvertoirade ✆05 65 58 55 59.
- **Location:** 81km/50.6mi northwest of Montpelier.
- **Don't Miss:** The view of the village from the ramparts

TOWN WALK

Park the car near the north gate, outside the ramparts.

Ramparts

Jul-Aug 10am-7pm; Apr-Jun and Sep 10am-noon, 2-6pm; Mar and Oct-mid-Nov 10am-noon, 2-5pm Closed mid-Nov-early Mar 3€. Guided tours possible by request. 3€. ✆05 65 58 55 59. www.lacouvertoirade.com.

Go through the north gateway and climb the steps at the foot of a Renaissance house. Following the watch-path round to the left to the round tower for a view over the town and its main street, rue Droite.

Return to the foot of the north tower and go into the village, bearing left.

Fortified Church

Jul-Aug 10am-7pm; Apr-Jun and Sep 10am-noon, 2-6pm; Mar and Oct-mid-Nov 10am-noon, 2-5pm Closed mid-Nov-early Mar 3€. Guided tours possible by request. 3€. ✆05 65 58 55 59. www.lacouvertoirade.com.

This fortified 14C church, an integral part of the town's defences, has two disc-shaped steles showing different representations of the cross and a graveyard with unusual disc-shaped gravestones.

Château

This fortress was built by the Templars in the 12C and 13C; the two upper floors have since disappeared.

Keep left until you reach a large square, once a village pond, where you walk round a block of houses to the right to reach rue Droite.

La Couvertoirade

P. Bolt/MICHELIN

The "Cardabelle"

Many doors in La Couvertoirade and other nearby villages are adorned with a dried plant resembling a sunflower surrounded by ragged spiny leaves – the *Carlina acanthifolia* thistle known locally as the **cardabelle**. It opens and closes according to the humidity, making it the local equivalent of seaweed hung outside to forecast the weather.

Rue Droite

This main street has very attractive houses with outside stone steps leading to a balcony and door into the living area. Sheep were kept on the ground floor below. Just past the corner of the town wall is a fine example of a *lavogne*, or village sheep pond, common in the *causses*.

Walk along the outside of the ramparts, round to the right, to get back to the car.

Grotte de Dargilan★★

In 1880 a shepherd called Sahuquet chased a fox into a huge dark underground chamber which he thought looked like the antechamber to Hell. He fled, and so it was not until 1888 that Dargilan cave was explored, by E A Martel and six companions. Eventually Dargilan became the property of the Société des Gorges du Tarn which fitted it with iron steps, ramps and railings to accommodate visitors. In 1910 electric lighting was installed in all the galleries.

- **Michelin Map:** 330: I-9.
- **Info:** 04 66 45 60 20.
- **Location:** 36km/22.5mi E of Millau via the D907 then the D996.
- **Don't Miss:** La Grande Salle du Chaos and the stalagmites in Salle de la Mosquée

Clocher' of Grotte de Dargilan

A. Cassaigne/MICHELIN

CAVE

Allow 1hr; temperature: 10°C/50°F. guided tours (1hr). Jul-Aug 10am-6.30pm; Apr-Jun and Sep 10am-5.30pm; Oct 10am-4.30pm. 8.50€ (children 6-18 years 6€). 04 66 45 60 20.

You first enter the **Grande Salle du Chaos**, a gallery 142m/465ft long by 44m/114ft wide and 35m/115ft high. that looks like a chaotic underground heap of rocks. The smaller Salle de la Mosquée contains many beautiful stalagmites.

The "Mosque" formation of stalagmites with glints of mother-of-pearl is flanked by the "Minaret," a lovely column 20m/66ft high. Other cave wonders include the "corridor of petrified cascades" – magnificent calcite drapery 100m/330ft long and 40m/130ft high, a labyrinth, underground lakes and stalagmitic frozen falls. The "clocher", a slender pyramid, is quite unexpected and beautiful.

Causse du Larzac★

The Causse du Larzac, dotted with villages and Templar estates, is famous for Roquefort cheese.

A BIT OF HISTORY

The Causse du Larzac, with its arid limestone plateaux and green valleys, is the largest of the *causses*. Like other causses, Larzac is full of limestone rock "chimneys" like **Mas Raynal**, explored in 1889 by E A Martel, L Armand, G Gaupillat and E Foulquier.

In the 12C, the Order of the Knights Templar built a local headquarters at Ste-Eulalie-de-Cernon. After the Order was dissolved in 1312, the Hospitallers of St John of Jerusalem (or Malta) took over the Templars' estates, including fortress towns on the Causse du Larzac. In the turbulent 15C the Hospitallers erected the many walls, towers and fortified gates which give the Causse du Larzac its rugged appearance.

- **Info:** Milau, 1 Pl. du Beffroi ℘05 65 60 02 42. www.ot-millau.fr
- **Location:** This is the closest causse to Montpellier
- **Don't Miss:** Roquefort cheese-making caves
- **Kids:** Ste-Eulalie-de-Cernon's Reptilarium, ℘05 65 61 32 08 www.reptilarium-larzac.com

DRIVING TOURS

Templars and Hospitallers

166km/103mi round tour from Millau (See MILLAU) – allow one day. Leave Millau along N 9 towards Béziers.

The road crosses the Tarn *département* and climbs up the northern flank of the Causse du Larzac, offering superb panoramas of Millau, the Causse Noir and the River Dourbie gorge.

Maison du Larzac

Open Apr-May weekends 10am-7pm; Jun-Sep 10am-7.30pm. No charge. ℘05 65 60 43 58 (or 06 77 38 13 01, off season)

To the right of N 9 is an enormous sheepfold roofed with limestone slabs (*lauzes*) called La Jasse. Here the outdoor **Écomusée du Larzac** provides an excellent introduction to the Causse du Larzac, with a traditional farm, an ultra-modern sheepfold and exhibitions on local architecture, archaeology and history.

Carry on to La Cavalerie. The road runs alongside Larzac Military Camp.

La Cavalerie

This large fortified village with ancient ramparts evokes the age of chivalry. The Larzac Military Camp installations can be seen from the road to Nant.

From N 9, take D 999 on the right towards St-Affrique. After 3.4km/2mi, take the road to Lapanouse-de-Cernon on the left.

Ste-Eulalie-de-Cernon

In the cool valley of the Cernon, Ste-Eulalie was the seat of the Templars' commandery and this medieval fortress has kept most of its ramparts, towers and gates.

Follow D 561 S; right onto D 23.

The road goes through another Knights Templars village, **Le Viala-du-Pas-de-Jaux** (*Guided tours ℘05 65 58 91 89*).

Roquefort-sur-Soulzon★

See ROQUEFORT-SUR-SOULZON.

Drive S from Roquefort along D 93 towards Fondamente then turn right at the signpost "St-Jean-d'Alcas".

St-Jean-d'Alcas

Opening times, call ℘05 65 97 61 07.

The fortified Romanesque church is enclosed within the ramparts of this picturesque village. Some restored houses feature round doorways and mullioned windows.

Follow D 516 and D 7, cross the A 75, continue on D 185 to La Couvertoirade.

La Couvertoirade★

See La COUVERTOIRADE.

Follow D 55 S towards Le Caylar.

As it climbs, the road offers a good view of Le Caylar and the distant Aigoual massif.

Le Caylar

The name of this village crowned by jagged rock formations means "rock." From afar these eroded rocks look like impressive ramparts and fortified towers. The small Romanesque chapel of **Notre-Dame-de-Roc-Castel** contains a 12C stone altar. The old town's **Tour de l'Horloge** (clock tower) is all that remains of the ramparts. Some medieval houses retain their 14C and 15C doors and windows.

Leave Le Caylar S on the road past the cemetery and turn left onto a slip road under the A 75. Take D 155E to St-Félix-de-l'Héras, then turn left onto D 155. Where the road crosses the motorway (the old N 9), continue on foot.

Pas de l'Escalette★

Alt 616m/2 021ft.

This rocky cleft between towering cliffs offers good **views** of the Lergue waterfall. Steps cut into the rockface lead down from the Larzac plateau.

Return to A 75 and Millau.

Causse Méjean★

The Causse Méjean has a harsh climate with freezing winters, scorching summers, and temperature extremes between day and night.

- **Michelin Map:** Map 330: H-9 to I-9.
- **Info:** Office du tourisme du Rozier, Route de Meyrueis, 48150; 05 65 62 60 89 – www.officedetourisme-gorgesdutarn.com.
- **Location:** 30km/18.75mi NE of Millau via the D 907.
- **Don't Miss:** The Przewalski horses at Villaret; the chaos de Nîmes-le-Vieux and a walk on the corniches.
- **Kids:** The Caussenarde farm at Hyelzas.

NATURE

The plateau of dolomite limestone outcrops is scattered with megaliths, indicating the habitation by Stone Age people. The Causse Méjean is sheep (*brebis*) country and has a low population density. The griffon vulture was re-introduced in 1970, and Przewalski horses (the last surviving wild horse subspecies) have recently been seen in the region.

DRIVING TOUR

Round trip 87km/54mi starting from Florac – allow 3hrs. Leave Florac W along D 16 and turn left onto D 63.

The D 63 passes through Le Villaret where a stud farm breeds small wild Przewalski horses originally from Mongolia. See them galloping across nearby fields.

Aven Armand★★★

See AVEN ARMAND.

Causse Méjean

A. Cassaigne/MICHELIN

Hyelzas

Open Jul-Aug 10am-7pm; Apr-Jun, Sep-Oct 10am-noon, 2-6pm. Closed public holidays and from Nov to Easter. 5.50€. 04 66 45 65 25. www.ferme-caussenarde.com

The **Hyelzas** farmstead of drystone roofed with limestone slabs represents traditional Causses architecture. Tour the farmhouse and exhibit of models of Meyrueis clock tower, Millau viaduct, Causses farmsteads and Lozère houses.

Return to the D 986 intersection and turn right.

Meyrueis

See MEYRUEIS.

Follow D 996 towards Florac

Note the striking contrast between the barren Causse Méjean and the forested Aigoual massif.

Turn left at Col de Perjuret.

Chaos de Nîmes-le-Vieux★

From the pass, head towards Veygalier or l'Hom or Gally; park the car. This walk is not good in rainy and foggy weather or when winter winds drop the temperature to -15°C.

The Chaos de Nîmes-le-vieux rises like a ruined city from the bare expanse of the Causse Méjean. During the Wars of Religion, royal armies pursuing Protestants were shocked at their surroundings because they thought they'd reached their intended destination, Nîmes.

From Veygalier

Apr-Sep unaccompanied tours from Hom or Gally.

This typical Veygalier house has an exhibit on local geology. From here a trail leads off through "streets" of stone overlooked by rock formations 10-50m/30-160ft high. From high above Veygalier, enjoy views over the cirque, where stone houses blend in with their dolomitic surroundings.

From l'Hom or Gally

1hr 30min on foot from Gally to Veygalier.

This Parc National des Cévennes discovery trail is a window onto the Causses natural environment.

Drive back to Florac along D 907.

WALKING TOURS

Corniches Causse Méjean★★★

Walking tour from Le Rozier – allow 7hrs. This well-maintained footpath has spectacular clifftop passages requiring great care; the path can be slippery and is crowded in July and August. Wear stout walking shoes and carry a day's worth of food and water.

Corniches du Causse Méjean
A. Thuillier/MICHELIN

Behind the church in Le Rozier, the footpath leads off from the junction of two roads (GR 6A waymarked in red and white).

Half an hour's climb brings you to the pretty little hamlet of **Capluc**, now deserted.

Rocher de Capluc

Not recommended for anyone suffering from vertigo. Bear left towards Capluc rock at the far end of a promontory on the south-west edge of the Causse Méjean. At the top of a flight of stone steps is a house leaning against the rock face. The terrace around the rock leads to a dizzying climb to the summit, with exhilarating views of Peyreleau and the Jonte and Tarn rivers and villages of Liaucous and Mostuéjouls.

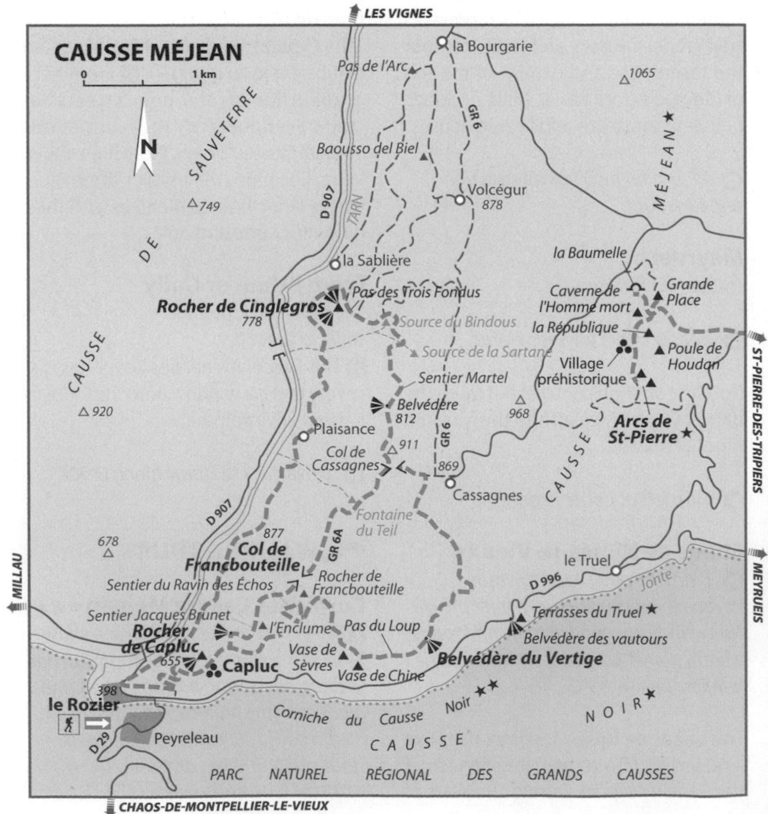

Return to Capluc.

Climb to the Col de Francbouteille

Beyond Capluc are two ways of reaching the Francbouteille Pass: The "Ravin des Echos" along a section of the GR 6A footpath, winds gently uphill, with fine views of the causse. The *steep, vertiginous* Jacques-Brunet path climbs through juniper, boxwood and pine then threads between little chimneys to a crest offering magnificent views of the Tarn and Jonte canyons. After a stretch through cool undergrowth with views of the Tarn valley, the path reaches the pass.

Col de Francbouteille

At this "pass of the two canyons" the Francbouteille rock looms like the prow of a colossal ship.

Follow the arrows to the GR 6A footpath.

Soon, Teil spring comes into view, much appreciated by walkers.

At the Col de Cassagnes, leave the Martel footpath leading to Cinglegros rock (see below) to the left, and bear right towards the isolated village of Cassagnes.

The footpath crosses the causse. Leave a pine plantation and follow the footpath over the Jonte gorge.

Belvédère du Vertige

An hour's walk leads to an impressive view over the Jonte canyon. Later on the footpath runs in front of a cave once used as a sheep pen, then between two natural bridges. The steep descent is called **Pas du Loup** ("Wolf's step"). Immediately after, the **Vase de Chine** and **Vase de Sèvres monoliths** come into sight and then distant Peyreleau and Le Rozier, Capluc rock and Causse Noir cliffs.

Return to the footpath which drops downhill amid jagged dolomitic rocks. Leave the footpath to the Col de Francbouteille to the right, and return to Capluc and Le Rozier along the Ravin des Echos and Brèche Magnifique paths.

Rocher de Cinglegros

One day walking tour from Le Rozier.
This walk is for the fit and nimble who do not suffer from vertigo.

Follow the route of the Corniches du Causse Méjean as far as the Col de Cassagnes, then turn left to Cinglegros rock.

This well laid out path offers exhilarating views of cliffs overhanging the Tarn, the Cinglegros gap and the Cinglegros rock itself.

Return to base by a footpath leading down to the hamlet of Plaisance, then to Le Rozier on the path to La Sablière.

Arcs de St-Pierre

1hr 30min on foot there and back.
There are two ways to get to the Arcs de St-Pierre:

Either *via D 63 which branches off D 986 at Hures-la-Parade; after 3km/2mi, take the little road on the right to St-Pierre-des-Tripiers; 1km/0.6mi past this village, take the small unsurfaced road, again to the right, opposite the junction for La Viale.*

Or *up the steep, narrow hairpin road branching off D 996 from Le Truel towards St-Pierre-des-Tripiers, in the Jonte Valley. Level with the junction for La Viale, take the small unsurfaced road to the left.*

The "Arcs de St-Pierre" is a mass of eroded rock formations resembling ruins.
Take the footpath downhill (*waymarked in red*) to the **Grande Place**. In this rocky amphitheatre stands a 10m/32ft-high monolith. The footpath climbs up to the cave of **La Baumelle**. After returning to the Grande Place, follow the waymarked path leading from it to the Caverne de l'Homme mort

Arcs de St-Pierre

A. Thuillier/MICHELIN

("Dead Man's Cave"); 50 skeletons similar to that of Cro-Magnon man were discovered here; most of them had had their skulls operated on with flint. Past the huge boulders **Poule de Houdan** ("Houdan's hen") and **La République**, the path leads to the site of a **prehistoric village** and finally arrives at the **Arcs de St-Pierre**, three natural arches, some of the finest in the Causses.

ADDRESSES

STAY / EAT

COUNTING SHEEP

Auberge du Chanet – *Hameau de Nivoliers – 48150 Hures-la-Parade – ℘04 66 45 65 12 – www.aubergeduchanet.com – closed 20 Nov-25 Mar.*
This old sheep farm at the heart of the Causse is an oasis of peace and quiet. Being on the GR 60, it is convenient for a number of walking route. Traditional cuisine is served in the vaulted dining room or on the sunny terrace. Several accommodation options, from rooms to dormitories.

Millau★

This bustling valley town at the confluence of the Tarn and Dourbie makes a great base for excursions to the Causses and the Tarn gorges. The nearby slopes of Borie Blanque and Brunas and Andan peaks are popular for paragliding and hang-gliding.

- **Population:** 21 900.
- **Michelin Map:** 338: K-6.
- **Info:** Office du tourisme de Millau 1 pl. du Beffroi, 12100 Millau, ℘05 65 60 02 42. www.ot-millau.fr.
- **Location:** 116km/72.5mi N of Montpellier. A lookout on the N 9 over the causse du Larzac offers a spectacular view★ of Millau and its 15th-century mill and 12th century arched bridge.
- **Parking:** There is ample covered parking in place Emma-Calvé.
- **Don't Miss:** The paleontology section of the musée de Millau; watching the stages of leather glove production at the musée de la Peau et du Gant.
- **Kids:** The city has many "Station Kid" activities.

A BIT OF HISTORY

A glove-making town– In this ewe's milk cheese-making part of the Causses, a leather industry naturally developed, and Millau became known for lambskin gloves. Today Millau annually produces some 250 000 pairs of gloves exported around the world, and has also expanded into *haute couture*, shoe-making, diverse leather goods and furnishings.

The Graufesenque potteries – During the 1C AD this town called Condatomagus – "the market where the rivers meet"– was a Roman centre for earthenware production, with its fine local clay, plentiful water supply and wood from the forests. Condatomagus produced *terra*

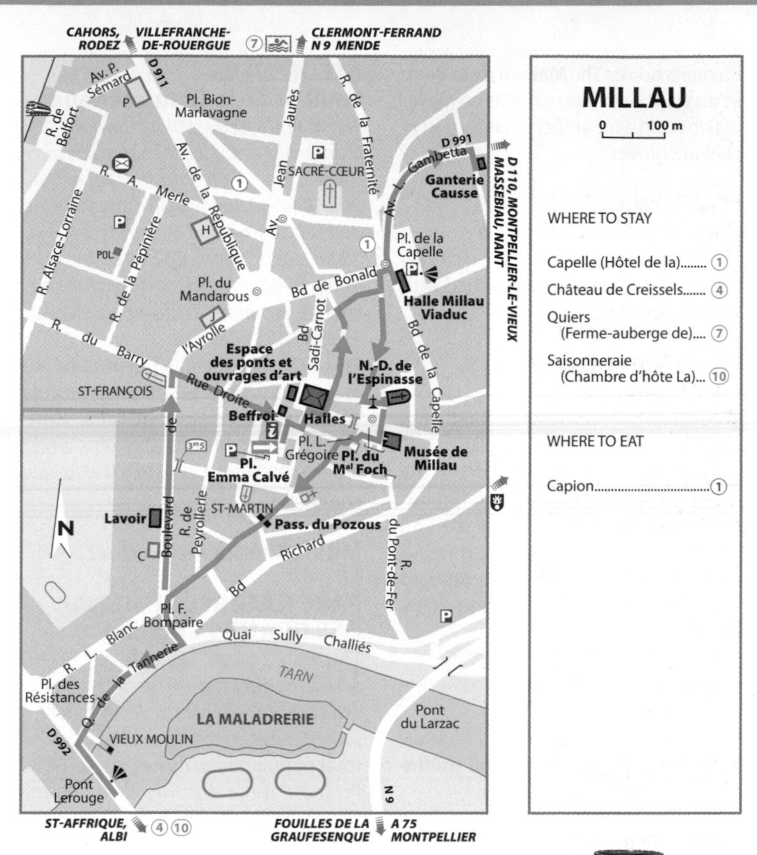

sigillata ware, bright-red glazed pottery decorated with floral, geometric or historiated patterns of Hellenistic influence. Over 500 potters created millions of pieces for export throughout Europe, the Middle East and even India. Visit the Graufesenque archaeological site and see the Musée de Millau's large collection of earthenware.

MUSEUM

Musée de Millau★

Pl du Mar-Foch.

Open Jul-Aug 10am-6pm; rest of year 10am-noon, 2-6pm daily except Sun and public holidays. 5€; no charge 1st Saturday in the month.

05 65 59 01 08.

The museum is housed in the 18C Hôtel de Pégayrolles. Its **paleontology** section includes fossils from secondary marine sediments and the 4m/13ft-long 180-million-year-old skeleton of a plesiosaurus marine reptile from Tournemire. There is a remarkable collection of Gallo-Roman **earthenware**★, found at Graufesenque, including moulds and potter's chisels and

J.P. Séguret/Musée du Millau

Terra sigillata ware from Graufesenque

accounts books. The **Maison de la Peau et du Gant**★ includes exhibits on glove-making and a magnificent collection of evening gloves.

TOWN WALK

Place du Maréchal-Foch

This most attractive part of the old town has a covered square embellished with 12C-16C arcades.

Église Notre-Dame-de-l'Espinasse

This church once possessed a thorn from the Crown of Thorns, hence its name. An important pilgrimage centre in the Middle Ages, the Romanesque building was partly destroyed in 1582 and rebuilt in 17C. The frescoes decorating the chancel (1939) are by Jean Bernard and the stained-glass windows by Claude Baillon.

Follow rue des Jacobins.

Continue through **passage du Pozous**, a 13C fortified gateway. Rue du Voultre leads to boulevard de l'Ayrolle.

Turn right onto this boulevard.

Lavoir

The semicircular shape of this unusual 18C wash-house is emphasised by a neo-Classical colonnade.

Continue along the boulevard to Église St-François then take rue Droite opposite the church.

Beffroi (Belfry)

Jul-Aug 10am-noon, 2.30-6pm; mid Jun-end Jun and Sep 2.30-6pm. unaccompanied visits 2.70€; guided tour 3.50€. 05 65 60 02 42.

Standing in rue Droite, this Gothic tower is all that remains of the old town hall. The 12C square tower used as a prison in the 17C is topped by an octagonal 17C one. Good view from **place Emma-Calvé**.

Return to rue Droite and continue straight on to place du Maréchal-Foch.

EXCURSIONS

Fouilles de la Graufesenque

1km/0.6mi S. Leave Millau towards Montpellier and Albi, then turn left after the bridge over the Tarn. Open Jul-Aug 10am-12.30pm, 2.30-7pm; May-Jun and Sep 10am-noon, 2-6pm; Oct-Apr 10am-noon, 2-5pm. Closed Mon and public holidays 4€ (children free) no charge 1st Sunday in the month Oct-Apr. 05 65 60 11 37.

This archaeological site contains the foundations of a Gallo-Roman potters' village with central street, canal, workshops, slaves' houses and kilns which fired 30 000 vases at a time (*video presentation*).

Millau Viaduct★★★ (*see p147*)

PARC NATUREL RÉGIONAL DES GRANDS CAUSSES

This park covers 315 640ha/779 963 acres, roughly the whole of the southern part of the Aveyron *département*. It incorporates 94 towns or villages with a total population of more than 64 000. Projects are under way to save traditional landscape features like village ovens, drystone shepherds' huts, village ponds, dovecots, wash-houses and fountains.

Prieuré de Comberoumal

18km/11mi NW along D 911 then D 30 left to St-Beauzély. Park the car at the end of the path leading to the priory. Open 10am-6pm. No charge. 05 65 62 02 28.

The Prieuré founded in the 11C is one of the best-preserved Grandmont Order priories.

Sévérac-le-Château★

32km/20mi N along N 9.

Imposing castle ruins overlook this once fortified village. The Sévérac barony, one of the oldest and most powerful in France, included famous personages like **Amaury de Séverac** (1365-1427), a Maréchal de France who undertook daring feats of arms, and the composer **Déodat de Séverac** (1873-1921), born

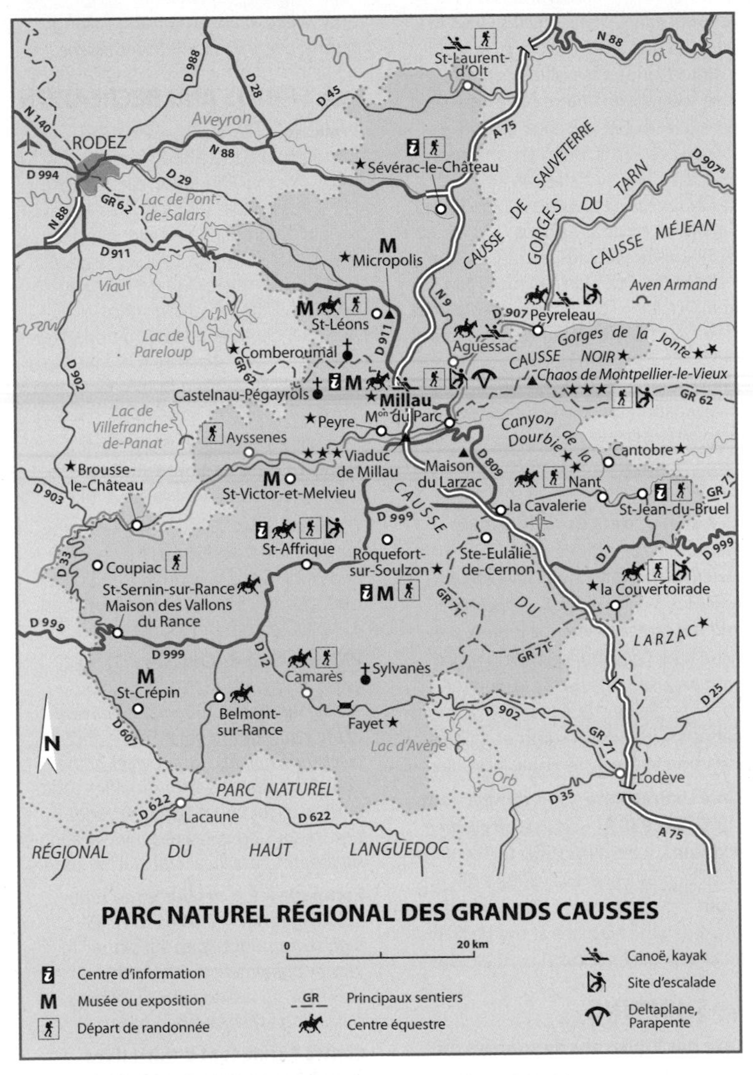

in St-Félix-Lauragais (see ST-FÉLIX-LAURAGAIS).

Streets leading to the **Château** contain **picturesque old houses** (15C-16C) with corbelled turrets and upper storeys overhanging the street.

A 17C entrance gate leads into the main courtyard of the **château**. (*open Jul-Aug 9.30am-9pm; Apr-Jun and Sep 10am-12.30pm 2-6pm; 6.50€ (children 3.50€). 05 65 47 67 31. www.severac-le-chateau.com).*

ADDRESSES

STAY

Hotel de la Capelle – *7 pl. de la Capelle – 05 65 60 14 72 – www.hotel-millau-capelle.com – 45 rms – 9€ – meals* . This hotel has two distinct advantages: reasonable prices and an air of tranquillity.

Ferme-auberge de Quiers – *In Quiers – 12520 Compeyre – 12km/7.4mi N of Millau by N 9 and D 907 – 05 65 59 85 10 www.quiers.net - open early*

Apr-Toussaint – 5 rms – meals ⊖⊜. In a quiet hamlet amid the crags, this old restored farmhouse offers comfortable rooms with charm of yesteryear, several with exposed beams and stonework. Rustic dining room, and a superb view over the valley.

⊖⊜ *Château de Creissels – 2 km/1.25mi S of Millau, rte de St-Affrique ℘05 65 60 16 59 – www.chateau-de-creissels.com – closed Jan-Feb, Mon lunch and Sun from Oct-Apr – P – 9 € – meals* ⊖⊜. This 12C château dominates the town of Millau. The main building houses a salon bourgeois and two dining rooms; lovely panoramic terrace and rooms with old furniture.

EAT

⊖ **Auberge de la Borie Blanque** – *Rte. de Cahors – ℘05 65 60 85 88 – closed Feb holidays, weekday evenings Nov-Mar, Mon evening, Sat lunchtime and Sun except Jul-Aug.* Stunning natural setting. Vaulted dining room with exposed stonework for winter cosiness; pleasantly shaded terrace with panoramic views for summer. Cuisine incorporates fresh, regional ingredients.'

⊖⊜ **La Braconne** – *7 Pl. du Mar.-Foch – ℘05 65 60 30 93 – closed Sun evening and Mon.* This old house in the centre of Millau has a fine 13C vaulted dining room. We recommend the grilled dishes cooked in the fireplace at the back and local specialities cooked by the owner.

SHOPPING

Cave des Vignerons des gorges du Tarn – *Ave. Causses – 5km/3mi from Millau – 12520 Aguessac – ℘05 65 59 84 11.* This co-op produces wines with the Vin délémité de qualité supérieure (VDQS) label côtes de Millau (red and rose). You will also find Cerno here, an apéritif made from Gamay flavoured with herbal essences.

J. Bonami – *4 R. Peyssière – ℘05 65 60 07 40 – Mon-Sat 6am-1.30pm, 3.30-8pm – closed a fortnight in Feb, 3 weeks after 15 Aug and holidays.* The Bonamis attitude to good ingredients translates to the highest quality cakes, pastries and sweets made according to long tradition at this excellent *pastisserie*.

SPORTS AND RECREATION

Walking – The main waymarked footpaths are the GR 62 ("Causse Noir-Lévezou-Rouergue") and several PR, "Causse Noir" (13 itineraries around Millau for rambling and mountain biking), "Millau et les causses majeurs," "St-Affrique-Vallée du Tarn-Pays de Roquefort" (footpaths around St-Affrique, Camarès and Roquefort). These paths are marked on the IGN maps to a scale of 1: 25 000 and on the PR "Aveyron Midi-Pyrénées" topoguide (ref 082).

Millau is an international centre for **Hang-gliding and paragliding**, offering courses from April to November.

Children – Millau organises many activities and workshops for children and publishes a brochure listing organisers catering for children. Information is available from the tourist office.

PNR des Grands Causses – *71 boulevard de l'Ayrolle – ℘05 65 61 35 50 – – May-Sep: 9am-12.30pm, 2-6pm; rest of the year: 9am-noon, 2-5pm – closed weekends, holidays, and 1 week at the end of the year.* The Parc provides useful addresses for finding accommodation, practising unusual activities and discovering the local cultural heritage.

Escapade – *Rte. des Gorges du Tarn, 12520 Aguessac – ℘05 65 59 72 03 – high season: 8am-8pm; rest of the year by appointment.* Canoeing, kayaking, canyoning, rock climbing, potholing and mountain biking.

Centre Permanent d'Initiatives pour l'Environnement (CPIE) du Rouergue – *La Maladrerie – ℘05 65 61 06 57.* The centre organises walks aimed at the discovery of nature and the local cultural heritage.

Roc and Canyon – *55 Ave. Jean-Jaurès – ℘05 65 61 17 77 – www.roc-et-canyon.com – Jul-Aug: daily 8am-8pm; reception: daily 9am-noon, 2pm-5pm.* Rock-climbing, pot-holing, cross-country cycling, rafting, hiking, canyoning, riding, canoeing, free flight, via ferrata, tandem paragliding, adventure circuit. All these activities are offered under the supervision of state-qualified instructors.

Chaos de Montpellier-Le-Vieux ★★★

The chaos of Montpellier-le-Vieux is an extraordinary collection of eroded dolomite formations covering 120ha/300 acres of the Causse Noir. Shepherds thought this gigantic rock jumble resembled a vast ruined city, and locals thought this chaos of rocks was a haunt of the devil himself.
Stray sheep or goats that entered vanished into the night, devoured by wolves. In 1883 Montpellier-le-Vieux was discovered by J. and L. de Malafosse and De Barbeyrac-Saint-Maurice, who were amazed at the intricate maze of alleyways, arches and corbelled ledges. In 1885, E A Martel mapped the site.

- **Michelin Map:** 338: L-6.
- **Info:** Millau 1 pl du Beffroi ℘05 65 60 02 42 – www.ot-millau.fr.
- **Location:** 18km/11mi NE of Millau. Access to the park is from the hamlet of Maubert.
- **Kids:** Take the Petit Train Vert to the most fascinating rock formations.
- **Timing:** At least 3 hours, or whole day trip if you can. Keep to waymarked paths.
- **Don't Miss:** The natural dunjeon of Douminal; the Porte de Mycènes.

VISIT

To get to Maubert: From Millau, take D 110 (16km/10mi); from Rozier or from Peyreleau, take D 29 and then D 110 off to the right (10km/6mi); from Nant, take D 991 to La Roque-Ste-Marguerite, from which you take a very narrow road up past the church heading north of the village and then turn left onto D 110 (26km/16mi). Open Jul-Aug 9.30am-6.30pm; mid Mar-Jun and Sep-mid Nov 10am-5pm; Closed rest of year. 5.30€ (children 5-15 years 3.80€). ℘05 65 60 66 30. www.montpellierlevieux.com.

The **Petit Train Vert** goes to the most picturesque rock formations: **Porte de Mycènes** and **Circuit Jaune**, trips of 1.5h, including a short walk. *8.70€. ℘05 65 60 66 30.*

Pick up a map of a variety of **walks** along marked footpaths at the site entrance.

Montpellier-le-Vieux's captivating rock formations have names like Skittle, Crocodile, Mycenae Gate, Sphinx, and Bear's Head, after their shapes. **Douminal** offers fabulous views of "Rocher de la Croix," the Cirque du Lac, Tarn gorge cliffs, the Dourbie Valley, the Cirque des Rouquettes and the Chaos de Roquesaltes.

"Porte de Mycènes"

Martel thought Montpellier-le-Vieux's Mycenae Gate resembled the Lion Gate of ancient Greece for its sheer size and grandiose natural arch (12m/39ft). This path crosses a culvert before leading to the **"Baume Obscure"** cave where Martel discovered the bones of cave-bears. Look out for the **"Nez de Cyrano"** Cyrano de Bergerac's huge rocky nose.

Porte de Mycènes
B. Kaufmann/MICHELIN

Causse Noir★

The smallest of the Grands Causses (200km2/77sq mi), is called "Noir" ("black" or "dark") because of the dense pine forests which once covered most of the plateau. It is bordered to the north by the Jonte river gorge and to the south by the Dourbie Valley. Dolomitic limestone predominates, with the result that the *causse* includes some of the finest "ruined cities" of rocks in the area.

Location: SW of Le Rozier and W of Millau.
Don't Miss: The Chaos de Montpellier-le-Vieux

DRIVING TOUR

Round trip 75km/47mi – allow 4hr.

Peyreleau

Situated at the confluence of the rivers Jonte and Tarn and built on the steep slopes of a hill, Peyreleau is an interesting place to stay. A modern church and an old crenellated square keep tower above the village.
From D 29 which climbs onto the Causse Noir, there are views of the 15C **Château de Triadou** where a treasure stolen by its owner from the Protestant army in the 17C was eventually found by peasants during the 1789 Revolution.

Reach the Causse Noir via D 29 S of Peyreleau. After 7km/4.3mi, turn right onto D 110.

Chaos de Montpellier-le-Vieux★★★

See Chaos de Montpellier-le-Vieux.

Return to D 29 and turn right. Beyond La Roujarie, turn right onto D 124 to St-André-de-Vézines. At the entrance of the village, take the street on the right and follow signposts to Roquesaltes. Leave the car at the intersection of the road with an unsurfaced path and walk along this path, signposted "Roquesaltes," to the right.

Chaos de Roquesaltes et du Rajol★

See Walking Tours below. *2hr.*

Return to St-André-de-Vézines and turn right towards Veyreau. After 7km/4.3mi, turn left onto D 139.

Peyreleau
©Gérard Labriet/Photononstop/Tips Images

Grotte de Dargilan★★

See Grotte de DARGILAN.

Meyrueis

See PAYS CEVENOL, Meyrueis.

Gorges de la Jonte★★

See PAYS CEVENOL, Meyrueis.

WALKING TOURS

Corniche du Causse Noir★★

Starting from Peyreleau - 6hr - beware of cliff passages.

Leave the car in the hamlet of Les Rouquets (east of Peyreleau – first road to the left coming from Le Rozier) and continue on foot along a road branching off to the left towards the River Jonte. Keep to the red markings.

The wide path runs along the Jonte then climbs to the right through woods before reaching St-Michel Hermitage.

It is possible to get close to the hermitage via three metal ladders (extreme caution is advisable). Rejoin the path waymarked in red.

The path leads to "Point Sublime," a rocky promontory jutting out into the Jonte canyon. Exceptional **view**★★.

Keep following the red markings which lead you through woodland.

Terraces make it possible to walk to the edge of the cliff and take in the view of the austere Jonte canyon and the peaceful village of Le Rozier.

Continue along the GR de Pays.

The path leads to the television mast from which there is a great **view**★ of Peyreleau in its site at the confluence of the River Jonte and River Tarn.

Continue along the path to a clearing and turn right.

The path runs down among box trees and rocks then skirts the Costalade ravine. It continues through forest pines and eventually joins up with a path running alongside vineyards near Les Rouquets.

Chaos de Roquesaltes et du Rajol★

2hr on foot. Medium difficulty.

In St-André-de-Vézines, turn right to Roquesaltes. Leave the car at the intersection of the road with an unsurfaced path and walk along this path, signposted "Roquesaltes," to the right.

The path runs down through forest pines and junipers.

When you reach Roquesaltes farm, take GR 62 towards Montméjean.

Roquesaltes, meaning "tall rocks," looks for all the world like a natural fortress overlooking the hamlet of Roquesaltes. From these rocky ramparts, the view extends over Montpellier-le-Vieux.

From a natural look-out platform, the view plunges down into the extraordinary Dourbie valley.

From the television mast, turn left onto a track leading to the surfaced road which you had previously followed from St-André; turn left to return.

ADDRESSES

EAT

Auberge du Maubert – *12720 Peyreleau. 05 65 61 25 28. Closed 10 Nov–1 Apr.* Simple home cooking with a local zest. Wood furniture, panelling and a cheerful open fire. View of the Larzac plateau from the terrace. Snacks served any time.

Roquefort-sur-Soulzon★

Aveyron

The name of this market town, situated in the heart of the Parc Naturel Regional des Grands Causses, has become synonymous with one of the most famous and widely appreciated of French cheeses, succulent Roquefort.

- **Population:** 679.
- **Michelin Map:** 338: J-K7.
- **Info:** Ave. de Lauras, 12250. ☎05 65 58 56 00. www.roquefort.com.
- **Location:** 26km/16mi SW of Millau on the D992 and 62km/39mi NW of Lodève by the A75. Follow the D999 before turning left onto the D23 and enter Roquefort.
- **Parking:** In front of the Tourist Office.
- **Timing:** Allow one hour.
- **Advice:** Wear warm clothes.

A BIT OF HISTORY

A romantic legend – Legend has it that, one day, a shepherd and his sweetheart met in one of the Combalou caves; when they left, the shepherd forgot his bag containing a piece of rye bread and some ewe's cheese. A few days later he met his sweetheart in the same cave and found his bag with the bread and cheese still inside; however, the cheese was covered with greenish blue mould, its smell and taste were different, but the two lovers found it delicious!

Roquefort cheese – Strict boundaries define the area of production of ewe's milk and the region of caves in which Roquefort cheese is matured. French law decrees that only ewe's milk cheese produced within these boundaries may be labelled "Roquefort." As an official label of origin (*appellation d'origine*), "Roquefort" is probably one of the oldest in France. Roquefort is known to have been appreciated in Rome by Pliny and by Charlemagne. The cheese's official status was confirmed by decree on 22 October 1979.

In the dairies, the milk is first made into a cheese in which the curd has been mixed with a natural mould, *Penicillium roqueforti*, which comes from the caves at Combalou. The cheese is transported to Roquefort for maturation.

ROQUEFORT CAVES

Roquefort Société

Open mid Jul-Aug 9.30am-6pm; mid Mar-Jun and Sep-Nov 9.30am-noon, 1.30-5pm (May-Jun and Sep 5.30pm); rest of year 10am-noon, 1.30-4.30pm. Closed 1 Jan and 25 Dec. 3€.

Roquefort-sur-Soulzon

P. Blot/MICHELIN

05 65 58 54 38. www.roquefort-societe.com

Roquefort Papillon

Open Jul-Aug 9.30am-6.30pm; Sep-Jun 9.30-11.30am and 1.30-5.30pm; Oct-Mar: 9.30-11.30pm and 1.30-5.30pm (Oct-Mar 4.30pm). Closed 1 Jan, 25 Dec. No charge. 05 65 58 50 08. www.roquefort-papillon.com.

Above the town of Roquefort, which lies at the foot of the cliff, is a little limestone plateau known as "Combalou," the north-east side of which collapsed when it slipped on its clay substratum. These special conditions gave rise to natural caves between the displaced rocks, in which temperature and humidity are constant and ideal for curing cheese.

WALKS AND VIEWS

Rocher St-Pierre

Access via some steps from the Caves Société car park.

This rock (alt 650m/2 132ft) against the Combalou cliff offers a **view**★ (*viewing table*) as far as the Lévézou mountains to the left, over the Soulzon Valley and Tournemire cirque to the right; opposite to the tabular cliffs of the Causse du Larzac, and to the town of Roquefort at the foot of the cliff.

Sentier des Echelles

Allow 2hr 30min; some difficult sections (narrow passages, slippery ladders in rainy weather).

On the way out of the village (alt 630m/2 067ft), this path leads to the Combalou plateau (alt 791m/2 595ft), from which there is a **panoramic view**.

There are two more walking trails around Roquefort: Sentier du Menhir *(3.5km/2.2mi)* and Sentier de Trompette (4km/2.5mi).

FARM VISITS

See how ewes are milked, how and where the cheese is made before being taken to mature in the Roquefort cellars. Five sheep farmers offer farm visits followed by tastings, *(by reservation, Jun to mid-Sep, daily from 4pm).* **Martine Fabrèges**, *05 65 62 76 19*; **Alice Ricard**, *05 65 99 06 46*; **Anne-Marie Gineste**, *05 65 62 53 22*; **Isabelle Anglars**, *05 65 47 69 40*; **Annie Bernat**, *05 65 99 51 53.*

Causse de Sauveterre

Location: N of Gorges du Tarn; W of Sévérac.
Timing: Allow half a day.

Bordered to the north by the River Lot, this is the most northerly and least arid of the Grands Causses. Its western section (SW of D 998) has vast stretches of woodland and fairly steep hills.

DRIVING TOURS

Round trip of 66km/41mi – allow 5hr.

La Canourgue

Leave the car in the parking area located on the other side of D 998.

Narrow canals carry water from the River Urugne through this ancient city overlooked by an imposing clock tower. The former collegiate church built in Provençal style between the 12C and the 14C is surrounded by old corbelled houses straddling canals.

Leave La Canourgue along D 998 towards Ste-Énimie and, after 2km/1.2mi, turn right onto D 46; 1.8km/1.1mi further on, leave the car on the left near the Sabot de Malepeyre.

Sabot de Malepeyre★

This enormous clog-shaped (*sabot*) rock, 30m/98ft tall, also known as the *pont naturel* (natural bridge) *de Malepeyre* was formed by the erosive action of the water which once flowed on the surface of the *causse*.

Continue and turn left onto D 43 which joins up with D 32; turn left again, drive on to D 998 and turn right. 6km/3.7mi further on, turn left towards Roussac and Sauveterre.

Champerboux

Picturesque hamlet with typical causses houses.

Follow D 44 left.

The road to Chanac is lined with drystone shepherds' huts.

Chanac

The old keep is proudly camped at the top of the village (*from the tourist office, follow the signpost to "La Tour")*. Note the clock tower in place du Plö (*market on Thursdays*).

Cross the River Lot and turn left onto N 88.

Le Villard

This charming village overlooking the Lot valley was once guarded by a fortress built in the 14C to protect the inhabitants from roaming bands of robbers.

Domaine médieval des Champs

This group of fine traditional buildings has been brought back to life by volunteers dressed in period costumes.

The road follows the River Lot southwards. Cross over to reach Banassac.

Banassac

Housed in the town hall, the **Musée archéologique** *(open daily except Sat-Sun and public holidays 8am-noon, 2-6pm. No charge. 04 66 32 82 10)* displays sigillated pottery, sought after all over Europe between the 1C and 3C AD.

Tarn Gorges ★★★

Aveyron

The Tarn gorges are one of the most spectacular sights in the Causses region. Stretching over more than 50km/30mi, the gorges offer a seemingly endless succession of admirable landscapes and sites.

- **Location:** North of Millau. Drive along the scenic road; take boat trips along the most spectacular stretch of the valley (*see Boat Trips);* or stride out along the many footpaths.
- **Don't Miss:** Glorious views of the gorges, perhaps the finest is from Point Sublime.
- **Kids:** The gorges are a wonderland for kids, with hiking paths, rocky outcrops, lone castles and cliffside villages.

GEOGRAPHICAL NOTES

The course of the Tarn – The Tarn rises in the uplands of Mont Lozère, at an altitude of 1 575m/5 167ft, and gushes turbulently down the Cévennes slopes. On its way, it picks up many tributaries, notably the Tarnon near Florac.

The Tarn then reaches the Causses region. Its course is now determined by a series of rifts which it has deepened into canyons. In this limestone region, it is fed solely by 40 resurgent springs from the Causse Méjean or Causse de Sauveterre, of which only three form small rivers over a distance of a few hundred yards. Most of them flow into the Tarn as waterfalls.

Tarn Gorges

M.-H. Carcanague/MICHELIN

DRIVING TOURS

D 907bis, which runs along the entire stretch of the gorges, offers a magnificent landscape of castles, look-out points and picturesque villages.
Travelling by boat or canoe gives a close-up view of the cliffs and beautiful scenery views otherwise invisible from the road.

TARN GORGES ROAD

The scenic road D 907bis runs along the floor of the gorges, on the right bank of the Tarn. The journey is never monotonous owing to the constantly changing appearance of the gorges, tinted with different hues depending on the time of day.

1 FLORAC TO STE-ÉNIMIE

30km/18mi – about 1hr 30min.
All along this road, there are one or two houses that are still roofed with the heavy schist slabs known as *lauzes*; the roof ridge is made of slabs laid out like the sails of a windmill, which is evidence of the proximity of the Cévennes.

Florac

See PAYS CEVENOL, Florac.
N 106 heads N along the Tarn valley bordered to the east by the Cévennes and to the west by the cliffs of the Causse Méjean which tower above the river-bed by 500m/1 640ft.

Within sight of the village of Biesset, on the opposite bank of the Tarn, leave the road to Mende via Montmirat Pass to the right and take D 907bis to the left, which runs along the north bank of the river.

Level with Ispagnac, the Tarn makes a sharp meander; this is where the canyon really begins, as a gigantic defile 400-600m/1 300-2 000ft deep separating the Causse Méjean and the Causse de Sauveterre.

Ispagnac

At the mouth of the Tarn canyon, the little dip in which Ispagnac lies, sheltered from the north and north-west winds and basking in a mild climate which has always been renowned, is planted with orchards and vineyards.

Continue 1km/0.6mi after Ispagnac then bear left.

Quézac

At Quézac a Gothic **bridge** spans the Tarn enabling pilgrims to reach the sanctuary founded by Pope Urban V in Quézac.
A narrow street, lined with old houses, leads to **Quézac Church**, built on the same site where a statue of the Virgin Mary, was discovered in 1050. A major pilgrimage takes place in September.

Return to D 907bis.

Between Molines and Blajoux stand two castles. First, on the north bank, is the **Château de Rocheblave** (16C) – with its distinctive machicolations – overlooked by the ruins of a 12C manor and by a curious limestone needle. Farther down, on the south bank, stands the **Château de Charbonnières** (16C), situated downstream of Montbrun village.

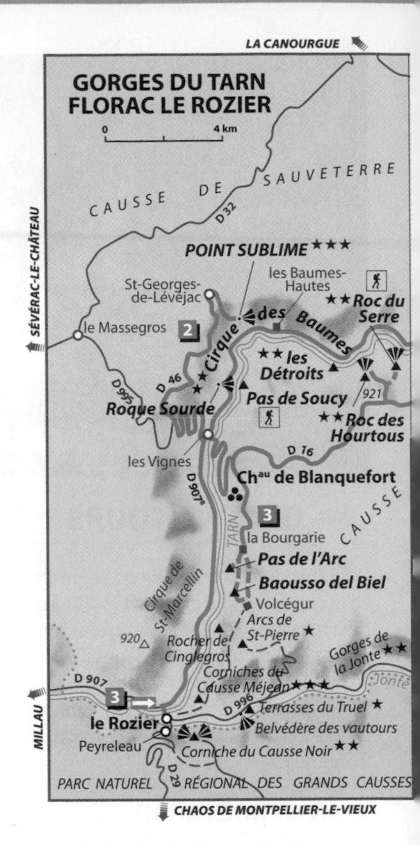

Castelbouc★

On the south bank of the Tarn. The strange site of Castelbouc ("Goat's Castle") can be seen from the road. The name is said to date from the Crusades. A lord, who stayed at home with the womenfolk, died of his complacency. The story goes that when his soul left his body, an enormous billy-goat was seen in the sky above the castle, which after that became known as Castelbouc.

A very powerful resurgent spring gushes out of three apertures, two in a cave, and one in the village.

Shortly after, to the left of the road, Prades Castle comes into view.

Château de Prades

Perched on a rocky spur overhanging the Tarn, this castle was built in the early 13C to protect Ste-Énimie Abbey and to defend access to the gorges. At the outset, it belonged to the bishops of Mende then, from 1280 to the Revolution, to the priors of Ste-Énimie Abbey.

Ste-Énimie★

Ste-Énimie lies in terraced rows below the steep cliffs bordering a loop of the Tarn, where the canyon is at its narrowest. The village is named after a Merovingian princess who chose to live in a grotto in order to dedicate her life to God, and founded a convent.

A leisurely stroll through the pretty little streets of Ste-Énimie is a good way to discover the village's charm.

2 STE-ÉNIMIE TO LE ROZIER

60km/37mi – allow 2hr 30min. Leave Ste-Énimie on D 907bis to the S.

Cirque de St-Chély★

The pretty village of St-Chély stands on the south bank of the Tarn at the threshold of the huge desolate cirque of St-Chély with its superb cliffs, at the foot of the Causse Méjean. D 986 on the opposite bank of the Tarn also affords fine **views**★★ of the cirques of St-Chély and Pougnadoires.

Cirque de Pougnadoires★

The houses in Pougnadoires village are embedded in the rock. The village is built against the colossal cliffs of the Pougnadoires cirque, pocked with caves. The reddish hue of the rocks indicates the presence of dolomite.

Château de la Caze★

This 15C château *(hôtel-restaurant)* stands in a romantic setting on the banks of the Tarn.

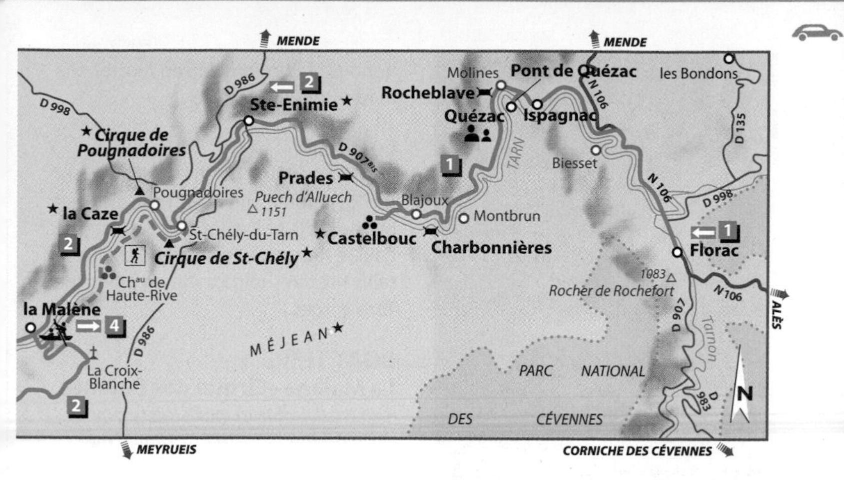

La Malène

Located at the junction of the roads which wind through the Causse de Sauveterre and Causse Méjean, La Malène has always been a thoroughfare.
Tourists should visit the 12C Romanesque **church**, the little street lined with historical houses beneath Barre rock, and the 16C castle which is now a hotel.

Cross the bridge over the Tarn out of La Malène and take D 43.

Just off the road to the right stand a cave chapel and a statue of the Virgin Mary from where there is a fine view of the village and its surroundings. The climb up the south bank of the Tarn is spectacular – 10 hairpin bends offer a splendid view of La Malène tucked in its hollow.

At Croix-Blanche, take D 16 to the right; 5km/3mi farther on, turn right again. After passing through the village of Rieisse, take the road signposted "Roc des Hourtous-Roc du Serre" near a café.

Roc des Hourtous★★

Follow the signs along the surfaced track off to the left. Car park. This cliff overlooks La Momie cave, just upstream from the Détroits gully, which is the narrowest section of the Tarn canyon. From here there is a superb **view**★★ of the Tarn gorges, from the hamlet of L'Angle to the Cirque des Baumes and the Point Sublime.

Go back to the fork in the road; leave the car and take the track on the right to the Roc du Serre.

Roc du Serre★★

30min on foot there and back. This is the only place that gives this marvellous **view**★★ of the narrow river gorge as it squeezes between the Causse de Sauveterre and Causse Méjean, with, farther off, Mont Lozère, the Aigoual range, the village of La Malène and the hairpin bends of D 16 as it wends its way up the causse.
Take D 16 on the right across the causse and down to Les Vignes via an impressive cliff-face road that runs past the ruins of the **Château de Blanquefort**. *Return to La Malène.*

On leaving La Malène, the road runs through some narrow straits known as the **Détroits**★★ (*see boat trips below*).
A **viewpoint**, on the left, offers a good view over this, the narrowest part of the gorges.
Farther along, the road passes round the foot of the **Cirque des Baumes**★★ (*see Boat Trips below*).

Pas de Soucy

At this point, the Tarn disappears beneath a chaotic heap of enormous boulders – the result of two rock slides (*soussitch* in dialect), the more recent being due to an earthquake in 580.

Canoe trips over the fast-flowing rivers

A. Thuillier/MICHELIN

A climb *(steps; 15min there and back)* to the **viewpoint** *(open Apr–Nov 8am–7.30pm. 0.50€. 04 66 48 81 40)* on **Roque Sourde** will give an aerial view of the Pas de Soucy.

At Les Vignes turn right onto D 995, a cliff road with tight hairpin bends. After 5km/3mi, take D 46 to the right which runs across the Causse de Sauveterre and, at St-Georges-de-Lévéjac, turn right once more.

Point Sublime★★★

From the Point Sublime, there is a splendid view over the Tarn gorges, from the Détroits to the Pas de Soucy and the Roche Aiguille.

Return to Les Vignes and the Tarn gorges road.

Soon, flanking the Causse Méjean, the last remaining ruins of **Château de Blanquefort** can be seen clinging tenaciously to a large rock.

Farther along, the huge Cinglegros (*see Causse MÉJEAN*) rock looms into sight, jutting up starkly detached from the Causse Méjean. On the right bank, cliffs at the edge of the Causse de Sauveterre slope away from the Tarn, forming the cirque of St-Marcellin.

Finally, having crossed a bridge over the river adorned with a monument in honour of Édouard-Alfred Martel, the road comes to Le Rozier.

Le Rozier

This little village on the confluence of the River Jonte and River Tarn, dwarfed by the cliffs of the Causse Sauveterre, Causse Noir and Causse Méjean, is inevitably the threshold for those visiting the Tarn gorges.

BOAT TRIPS

La Malène–Cirque des Baumes

It is advisable to make this trip in the morning, since this section of the canyon is at its best in the morning light.

Apr-Oct guided tours with commentary (1hr) by a local boatman. In Jul and Aug, departure before 9.30am and after 5pm. 80€ per boat of 4 people or 20€ for an individual. Bateliers des Gorges du Tarn, 48210 La Malène, 04 66 48 51 10. www.gorgesdutarn.com.

Les Détroits★★

This is the most spectacular, and the narrowest, section of the Tarn gorges.

Cirque des Baumes★★

Downriver from Les Détroits, the gorge widens, flowing into the splendid Cirque des Baumes (*baume* means cave).

CANOE TRIPS

These can be undertaken by any canoeist with some experience of fast-flowing rivers. Apart from a few passages of rapids, the journey from Ste-Énimie to the Pas de Soucy is easy. The short stretch of river from here to the Pont des Vignes is very dangerous, so canoes will have to be carried overland. The stretch from Pont des Vignes to Le Rozier is quite turbulent; care should be taken negotiating some of the rapids.

WALKING TOURS

3 Corniche du Tarn

Round tour from Le Rozier – 21km/13mi by car, then 3hr 30min on foot.

From Le Rozier, take the road along the Tarn gorges (D 907) as far as Les Vignes. Turn right towards Florac. The steep road climbs in a series of hairpin bends above the gorges. Turn towards La Bourgarie and park the car there.

At the end of the hamlet, follow the path waymarked in red. It passes in front of the Bout du Monde ("End of the World") spring. Soon after, at a fork, the right-hand path leads down to the Pas de l'Arc.

Pas de l'Arc

This is a natural pointed arch, formed by erosion of the rock.

Turn back to the fork and then continue to Baousso del Biel.

Baousso del Biel

This opening, measuring 40m/131ft up to the arch roof, is the largest natural arch in the region.

The path reaches the point where the arch merges with the plateau. Several hundred yards after this bridge, follow the path up to the left to reach the abandoned farm of Volcégure.

From here, a forest footpath (GR 6A) leads back to La Bourgarie.

4 Tarn valley footpath

From La Malène to St-Chély-du-Tarn – 3hr one way. In La Malène, cross the bridge and follow a footpath on the left, waymarked in yellow and green, which leads to another path running along the river bank towards Hauterives (crowded in summer).

This footpath which follows the River Tarn offers hikers the freedom of discovering the gorges and the cliffs at their own pace.

The path first runs through a wooded area where weeping-willows lean over the river dipping their branches into the water. On the opposite bank stand the Causse de Sauveterre limestone cliffs eroded by the river.

The path then climbs some steps hewn out of the rock, affording a totally different landscape: the luxuriant vegetation growing close to the river has given way to Mediterranean-type scrubland with stunted oaks and sparse wild grasses. Follow the path across a scree *(take particular care here)* to the ghost hamlet of Hauterives (abandoned ruins) then through a forest of pines and oaks; further on, the Château de la Caze and the Cirque de Pougnadoires come into view just before St-Chély.

ADDRESSES

STAY

Chambre d'hôte Jean Meljac – *Quartier des Salles, 12640 Rivière-sur-Tarn. At Millau, drive toward les Gorges-du-Tarn; at the Rivière-sur-Tarn exit, take a left toward «Chambres d'hôtes Vin-de-Côtes de Millau» 05 65 59 85 78. Closed Jan - 5 rms. Meals* . This guesthouse run by winegrowers, is located in the village just minutes from the gorges. Rooms are simple but very well maintained, and the garden offers great views. Wine tastings available.

Manoir de Montesquiou – *48210 La Malène. 04 66 48 51 12 montesquiou@demeures-de-lozere.com. Closed end Oct–end Mar. 10 rms 14€ Meals* . Immerse yourself in the history of La Malène by staying in this enticing 15C residence. You can admire the wild beauty of the natural surroundings before savouring their flavoursome local cuisine and making the most of the inviting, comfortable rooms.

EAT

La Calquière – *12720 Mostuéjouls. 05 65 62 64 17. www.lacalquiere.fr. Closed Oct–Mar. Reservations required.* This inn has a terrace with a pretty view overlooking a small 10C church and graveyard on the banks of the Tarn. The simple family-style cuisine prepared from fresh farm produce is served in an enjoyable vaulted dining room.

Renowned for its fine wines, Haute-Languedoc also enjoys a cluster of fabled cities, towns and villages all with ancient pedigrees, fine buildings and monuments. Any tour through the countryside, the *garrigue*, will take you past private and co-operative vineyards, where the chance to sample wine – and for that matter, olive oil – should be taken seriously.

Highlights

1 Visit lively **Narbonne** (p184)
2 **Canal du Midi** boat trip (p180)
3 **Dégustation** at a vineyard
4 Follow in Molière's footsteps through lovely **Pézenas** (p195)
5 **Sigean African Reserve** (p203)

Something to grape about

The odd thing about French wines is that (generally) we think of Bordeaux, Burgundy, Loire and Rhone wines long before we start thinking about those with the Languedoc-Roussillon AOC. Yet this now-prized appellation covers 50 000ha/120 000 acres of vines on the slopes of the *garrigue* from Narbonne to Nimes, an area including 156 communes, of which five are in Aude, fourteen in Gard and all the rest in Hérault. The annual production is around 70 000 gallons of red or rosé, and 150 000 gallons of white – that's quite some party! There are three main vineyards in Hérault: Saint Chinian, west of Béziers, Faugères to the north of the town, and Clairette du Languedoc, to the north of Pézenas, plus twelve others: Pic Saint Loup, Montpeyroux, Cabrières, Pinet, Saint Saturnin, Saint Georges d'Orques, la Méjanelle, Saint Christol, Saint Drézéry, Vérargues, Quatorze and la Clappe – staggering business for what is, in reality, a rather small place. What makes wine production here all the more fascinating is the marked absence of familiar grape varieties (*cépage*) – Cabernet Franc and Chardonnay are almost completely absent. Instead you get Carignan, Grenache, Mourvèdre, Syrah, Cabernet-Sauvignon (reds), Picpoul, Bourboulenc, Clairette and Sauvignon (whites).

Add in a significant diversity of soils, and the result is the production of unique and jealously guarded wines. For many years the wines of this region were poorly regarded. But all that has changed: quantity is no longer important, now it is quality that counts.

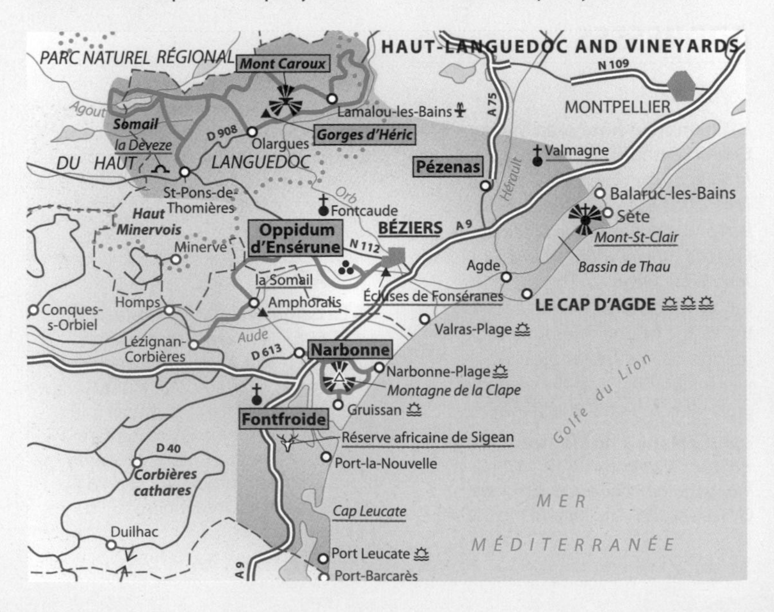

Well oiled

Lucques olives

©Frédéric Daniau/Fotolia.com

Since antiquity, the olive producer has played a very important role in the life of the Mediterranean populations, who think of them as sacred trees. The oil produced from the olives has long been put to many uses: cooking, of course, but also for lighting, washing and heating. The Greeks used the olive as a form of currency, and claim to have had the first olive tree saying that it was given to the Goddess Athena and grown on the Acropolis. To destroy a man's olive trees, they said, was an act of war.

Many of the olive producers in Languedoc were wiped out by a severe frost in 1956, after which they switched to producing wine. This was a major turning point in French *oléiculture*. But in recent times, the production of olives and olive oil is back in vogue. The twenty-fifth of November, the Feast of Sainte Catherine Labouré, is officially the first day on which olives can be harvested, though in practice the seasons and the ripeness of the drupes (olives still on the tree) have rather more of a say in the matter. And gathering olives (la cueillette des olives) may well go on well into the following year.

No-one seems quite sure how many varieties of olive tree there are. They flourish all along the Med coast from Menton in the east all the way round to Perpignan in the Pyrénées-Orientales. In the Drome it's the tanche, in Hérault and Aude, the picholine or the much-prized lucques (the so-called Rolls Royce of olives), a rare variety of olive grown in the region around Carcassonne. As well as being unusual, the lucques is also difficult to harvest by machine, making it extremely labour intensive. This unique olive has a light, nutty taste, crescent shape and bright green colour. So numerous are the varieties of olive tree that there are 15 species growing on the Riviera alone that cannot be identified, and which have survived since before 1956.

Olive groves in Haute-Languedoc

©George Munday/Pictures Colour Library

Béziers★

As capital of the Languedoc vineyards region, Béziers takes festivals and merrymaking very seriously. The Feria d'Été summer wine festival, the region's oldest, has a definite Spanish flavour and the achievements of the local rugby team (ASB) have spread the city's name abroad.

Info: 29 av. St-Saëns, 34500 Béziers. ☎04 67 76 47 00. www.beziers-tourisme.fr.

Location: For a city overview, take a guided tour (Jul-Aug, 1hr 30min; 5.60€); enquire at the tourist office.

Parking: ample underground parking places.

Don't Miss: Cathédrale St-Nazaire, European ceramics in the Chateau de Raissac.

A BIT OF HISTORY

A Roman Presence – Béziers was a thriving city when the Romans colonised it in 36 or 35 BC. It was renamed Julia Baeterrae and fell within the Naronensis province. Modern Béziers occupies the same pre-Roman site of its origins, on a plateau on the east bank of the Or. The old Roman forum, surrounded by temples and a market, probably stood in front of the site of the present town hall. Between rue St-Jacques and place du Cirque, the old houses, with their neat urban gardens and garages, are laid out in an elliptical pattern, reflecting the presence of Béziers' buried Roman amphitheatre. The site is currently being excavated. During the 3C Barbarian threat, the amphitheatre's stones were used to build a wall around the city.

The Cost of Backing the Cathars – During the Aligensian Crusade, the Crusaders besieged Béziers in 1209. The resident Roman Catholics fought alongside Cathars to defend Béziers, but all were butchered in the ensuing massacre, even those hiding in the churches. Béziers was pillaged and torched and not a creature there remained living. Béziers miraculously rose from these ashes, but was a sleepy backward community until the 19C, when the development of its vineyards revived its old wealth and vigour. Béziers was the home town of **Pierre-Paul Riquet**, designer of the Canal du Midi, and of **Jean Moulin**, hero of the World War II Resistance movement commemorated in Béziers' "Plateau des Poètes."

WALKING TOUR

Leave the car in the Jean-Jaurès car park. This walk starts from the statue of Pierre-Paul Riquet (see Canal du MIDI) in the centre of Pierre-Paul Riquet avenue. Walk NW towards the theatre.

Cathedral of St-Nazaire and the Pont Vieux

A. Thuillier/MICHELIN

Allées Paul-Riquet

This road avenue shaded by plane trees bustles with life. David d'Angers' statue of Riquet stands at the centre of the avenue, and the mid-19C theatre, also by d'Angers, has a façade decorated with allegorical sculptures.

At the end of the avenue, turn left onto oulevard de la République, then right onto rue Casimir-Péret, and left again onto rue Vannières.

Basilique St-Aphrodise

The church dedicated to the town's patron saint contains a handsome 4C-5C **sarcophagus** carved with the scene of a lion hunt. Opposite the pulpit is a 16C polychrome wood Crucifix.

Turn back along rue Casimir-Péret then, just before reaching boulevard de la République, take rue Trencavel (right).

Église de la Madeleine

Peaceful now, this Romanesque church remodelled during the Gothic period and again in the 18C was one of the sites of the 1209 massacre. *(see A Bit of History).*

From place de la Madeleine, follow rue Paul-Riquet; cross place Semard to the right and take rue Tourventouse.

A vaulted passageway leads to rue du Capus and the **Hôtel Fayet**, an annexe of the Fine Arts Museum.

Turn right onto rue du Gén.-Pailhès then left onto rue du Gén.-Crouzat leading to place des Bons-Amis (note the charming small fountain), then to place de la Révolution.

Ancienne cathédrale St-Nazaire★

On a terrace above the River Or, the cathedral symbolised the power of Béziers bishops between 760 and 1789. The Romanesque building was badly damaged in 1209, and repairs on it continued from 1215 until the 15C. The west front, flanked by late 14C fortified towers, contains a magnificent rose window. The Jardin de l'Évêché affords a pretty view of the church of St-Jude and the River Or spanned by the 13C Pont Vieux (the newer Pont Neuf dates from the 19C).

Enter through the doorway in the north transept.

The bay directly in front of the chancel contains some 11C sculpted capitals. The colonnettes decorated with crocketed capitals and the cross-ribbed vaulting were added in the 13C. Note the lovely 13C chancel apse, modified in the 18C. The terrace near the cathedral affords a view of the Or flowing through vineyards, the Canal du Midi and the hill fort of Ensérune. Beyond are Mont Caroux, the Pic de Nore and Canigou.
From place de la Révolution, follow rue de Bonsi: the **Hôtel Farégat** houses the Fine Arts Museum. Take rue Massot to your right then continue along rue des Dr-Bourguet.

From place St-Cyr, follow rue St-Jacques.

You are now in the district known as *"quartier des arènes romaines,"* a reminder that the town was once a Roman colony in the Naronensis province (c 35 BC).

Église St-Jacques

This church has a remarkable 12C five-sided apse and its gardens afford a special **view**★ of the cathedral.

Walk past the Musée du Biterrois and follow avenue de la Marne to place Garialdi then turn right onto avenue du Mar.-Joffre.

Plateau des Poètes

Busts of poets line the path in this hilly landscaped park which runs on from allées Paul-Rique. Designed by the Bühler brothers in the 19C, it features a Caucasian elm, Californian sequoia, magnolias and the Cedar of Lebanon.

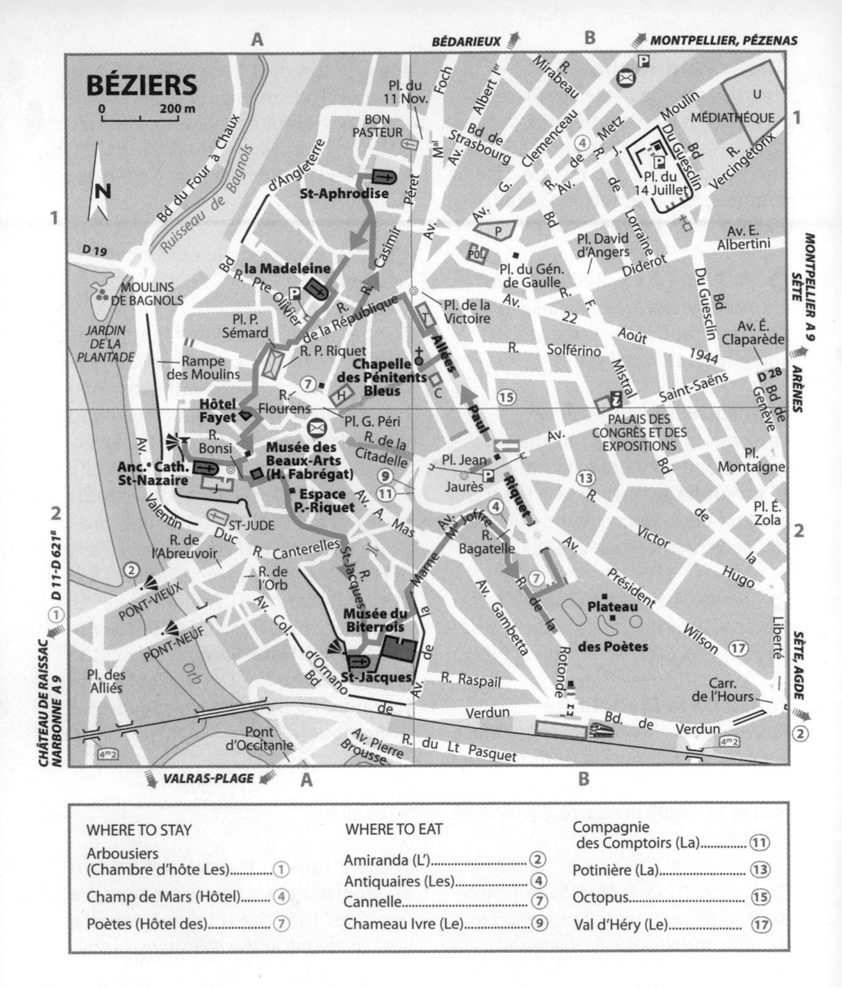

The Fontaine du Titan (fountain) was designed by Injalert.

Return to place Jean-Jaurès along allées Paul-Riquet.

ADDITIONAL SIGHTS

Musée du Biterroisa

Same hours as the the Musée des Beaux-Arts below). 04 67 36 71 01.

Contained in the 1702 St-Jacques barracks designed by Charles d'Aviler, this museum features local archaeology, ethnology and natural history. Here are dioramas on regional fauna; displays of Greek, Iberian and Roman amphorae discovered on the seabed nearby at Cap d'Agde; galleries on geology and volcanic activity in the Languedoc region, and Bronze and Iron Age life. Gallo-Roman treasures excavated in the city include sigillated pottery from La Graufesenque (*see MILLAU*), the milestones which once lined the Via Domitia, and the "Trésor de Béziers"– three large chased silver platters found in 1983 in a vineyard on the city's outskirts.

Musée des Beaux-Arts

Open Jul-Aug daily except Mon 10am-6pm; Apr-Jun, Sep-Oct daily except Mon 9am-noon, 2-6pm; Nov-Mar daily except Mon 9am-noon, 2-5pm. 2.60€ (children under 12 free); 5.60€ (combined ticket includes Musée du Biterrois). 04 67 28 38 78.

The museum of fine art occupies two old private mansions near the cathedral. The

Hôtel Farégat contains works by Martin Schaffner, Dominiquin, Guido Reni, Pillement, Languedoc painter J Gamelin, Géricault, Devéria, Delacroix, Corot, Dauigny, Othon Friesz, Soutine, Chirico, Kisling, Dufy and Utrillo, among others. The **Hôtel Fayet** houses 19C paintings, a bequest y J G Goulinat (1883-1972) and the contents of the workshop of Béziers sculptor **J A Injalert** (1845-1933).

EXCURSIONS

Sérignan

11km/7mi S on D 19 towards Valras.
The old **collegiate church**, dating from the 12C–14C, graces the south-west bank of the Or. Its exterior evidences traces of fortifications such as loopholes, machicolations and remnants of watch turrets. Inside, admire the nave's ceiling and elegant heptagonal apse.

Valras-Plage

15km/9.5mi S on D 19.
This fishing port and yachting harbour at the mouth of the Or has a fine sandy beach. The Théâtre de la Mer hosts various summer shows.

Abbaye de Fontcaude

18km/11mi NW via D 14. Open daily except Sun morning: Jun-Sep 10am-noon, 2.30-7pm (Jul-Aug Mon-Fri 10am-7pm); Oct-May 10am-noon, 2.30-5.30pm. Closed Jan (except Sun afternoon), 25 Dec. 4.50€. 04 67 38 23 85. www.abbaye-de-fontcaude.com.
This Romanesque Premonstratensian abbey was destroyed during the Wars of Religion. The transept and the east end are all that remains of the **abbey church**. The large scriptorium, where monks once copied and illuminated manuscripts, is now a **museum** displaying fragments of the **capitals** from the cloisters.

ADDRESSES

STAY

Chamre d'hôte Les Arbousiers – *34370 Maureilhan – 9km/6mi NW of Béziers towards Castres on D 112 – 04 67 90 52 49 – www.gites.de.france34.com/les-arousiers – 6 rms.* This large establishment with Mediterranean style rooms offers a friendly ambience, a menu featuring home-made cold cuts, home-grown vegetables, and local wine.

Hotel Champ de Mars – *17 r. de Metz – 04 67 28 35 53 – www.hotelchampdemars.com – 10 rms.* Quiet family hotel in a quiet street (except market day, Friday) in the heart of Béziers.

Hôtel des Poètes – *80 Allées Paul-Riquet – 04 67 76 38 66 – www.hoteldespoetes.net – P – 14 rms.* Ideally situated opposite the park des Poètes, a small hotel with simple rooms.

EAT

Cannelle – *11 Pl. de la Mairie – 04 67 28 06 01 – closed Sun.* This *salon de thé* also has a lunchtime menu or a choice of salads. Contemporary decor.

Le Chameau Ivre – *15 pl Jean Jaurès – 04 67 80 20 20 – closed Sun, Mon lunch, Tue and Wed evening; reservations advised.* Exceptional wine list to be enjoyed with charcuterie and cheese in the shade of ancient plane trees and palms.

Le Val d'Héry – *67 av. du Prés.-Wilson – 04 67 76 56 73 www.valdhery.com – closed 15-30 Jun, Sun and Mon.* After a stroll in the plateau des Poètes, enjoy the artistic creativity of this restaurant's chef which decorate the walls and enhances the fine cuisine.

La Potinière – *15 r. Alfred-de-Musset – 04 67 11 95 25 – closed 19 Jun-19 Jul and Sun evening.* Popular with the locals, this restaurant has a cosy ambience and appealing sophisticated menu.

L'Amiranda – *Av de la Méditerranée, 34420 Villeneuve-les-Béziers, 7km/4.5mi S of Béziers – 04 67 93 83 97 – closed Mon evening, and Tue.* On the way to the beach, this modern building houses a fine restaurant serving regional and traditional cuisine in a relaxed atmosphere.

Octopus – *12 r. Boïeldieu – ℘04 67 49 90 00 – www.restaurant-octopus.com – closed Sun and Mon.* Well prepared daily menus of local produce.

Les Antiquaires – *4 r. Bagatelle, bas des Allées Paul-Riquet – ℘04 67 49 31 10 – closed lunch and Mon – reservations required.* Popular restaurant decorated with ancient porcelain, black and white photographs, and musical instruments. Seasonal market produce forms the heart of every meal.

La Compagnie des Comptoirs – *15 pl. Jean Jaurès - ℘ 04 99 58 39 29 – www.lacompagniedescomptoirs.com – closed Sun – reservations required.* A well-stocked wine list of local and regional wines accompanies and inventive cuisine that will delight your taste buds. Terrace dining also.

SHOPPING

Markets – The central covered market is open Tue-Sun. Other food markets: Tue morning pl. Émile-Zola, Wed morning in the Iranget neighbourhood, Fri morning pl. David-d'Angers.

Antolin Glacier – *21 r. Martin-Luther-King – ℘04 67 62 03 10 – glaces.antolin@wanadoo.fr – Mon-Fri 8am-6pm – closed pulic holidays.* Antolin has been part of the local landscape since 1916, with over 120 different ice creams and sorets.

Les caves de Béziers – *3 rte de Pézenas – ℘04 67 31 27 23 – lescaves.deeziers@wanadoo.fr – Mon-Sat 9am-noon, 2-6.30pm (7pm in summer).* Co-op selling local wines, spirits and olive oils. Béziers

Le Cap d'Agde ☼☼☼

Created in 1970, Le Cap d'Agde is one of Languedoc-Roussillon's most popular coastal resorts and a favourite haunt of kite-flying enthusiasts.

- **Population:** 19 988.
- **Michelin Map:** 339: G-9.
- **Info:** Bulle d'accueil, 34305 Le Cap-d'Agde. ℘04 67 01 04 04. www.capdagde.com.
- **Location:** 27km/17mi W of Béziers. This holiday town of pastel walls, tiled roofs, shady winding streets and piazzas boasts eight marinas.
- **Kids:** The Aquarium, Aqualand and Île des Loisirs. Cap d'Agde has been nominated a "kid" resort for its activities and facilities.

Marina, Le Cap d'Agde

D. Pazery/MICHELIN

BEACHES

The resort's beaches – Footpaths known as "ramblas" access 14km/8.7mi of golden sandy beaches offering pedalos, wind-surfing, volley ball and children's clubs.

Plage **Richelieu** is the largest and Plage du **Môle** the most popular. The sands of Grande Conque are black and Plage de la **Roquille** is beached with seashells.

Nearby beaches – **Le Grau-d'Agde** is *5km/3mi W beyond the harbour* and Plage de la **Tamarissière** is on the other side of the Grau-d'Agde canal.

SIGHTS

Île des Loisirs
This leisure island offers mini golf, amusement park, discotheques, casino, cinema, bars and restaurants.

Aquarium
Open Jun-Sep 10am-7pm (Jul-Aug, 11pm); Oct-May 2-6pm (Sun and public holidays 11am-7pm). 7€ (children 5€). 04 67 26 14 21. www.aquarium-agde.com.
Squids, sharks, sea breams and colourful corals occupy some 30 pools.

Musée de l'Éphèbe, Le Cap d'Agde

Éphèbe d'Agde

Aqualand
Open mid Jun-mid Sep 10am-6pm (Jul-Aug 7pm). 24€ (children 17.50€). 04 67 26 85 94. www.aqualand.fr.
This 4ha/10-acre aquatic leisure park features wave pools, giant water chutes, shops and restaurants.

Musée de l'Éphèbe
Open 9am-noon, 2-5pm (Jun-Oct 6pm). Closed Tue and Sun morning (except Jun-Oct); 4.50€ (children 2€) 04 67 94 69 60.
This underwater archaeology museum contains 25 years of excavated treasures from the Mediterranean and coastal lagoons – including Ancient Greek and Roman boats and amphorae, the magnificent **Éphèbe d'Agde**★★, and a statue of a young Greek man, unearthed in 1964.

EXCURSION

Agde
5km/3mi N along D 32E.
Many buildings in Agde are made from the dark grey lava from nearby Mont St-Loup, an extinct volcano. The town enjoys with neighbouring Sète the tradition of *joutes nautiques*, or jousting in boats.
The fortified **Ancienne cathédrale St-Étienne**★ was rebuilt in the 12C, probably to replace a 9C Carolingian building. Note the small round window in the vault through which food and ammunition were passed in times of siege.
The **Musée agathois** *(5 rue de la Fraternité open 9am-noon, 2-5pm (Jun-Oct 6pm); closed Tue and Sun morning (except Jun-Oct); 4€. 04 67 94 82 51)* focuses on local folk art and traditions. It occupies a Renaissance mansion converted to a hospital in the 17C. In addition to reconstructions of the interiors of local houses, model boats, memorabilia of local seafarers, liturgical exhibits and collected amphorae from the ancient Greek port, the museum includes artefacts, paintings, glazed earthenware and local costumes and exhibits on traditional seafaring, fishing, viticulture, crafts and other aspects of daily life in Agde.

ADDRESSES

STAY

Camping Neptune – *34300 Agde – 2km/1mi S of Agde near the Hérault – 04 67 94 23 94 – www.campingleneptune.com – open Apr-Sep – reservation recommended – 165 sites.* This landscaped campsite has a swimming pool surrounded by a pleasant beach, games for young and old, mobile homes for hire and boat moorings.

Camping Californie-Plage – *34450 Vias – 3km/2mi SW of Vias on D 137E and road to left, along the each – 04 67 21 64 69 – open 5 Apr-10 Oct – reservation recommended – 371 sites* – food service. Pleasant shady spot by the sea, with swimming pool and free entry to the water sports area at Cap Soleil. Chalets, bungalows and studios for hire.

Hotel Les Grenadines – *6 imp. Marie-Céleste – 34300 Agde – 04 67 26 27 40 – www.hotelgrenadines.com – closed 16 Nov-28 Feb – P – 20 rms –*

10€. This hotel in a quiet residential area has tidy rooms with whitewashed walls and tiles, swimming pool and simple meals.

ON THE TOWN

La Guinguette – *Rte de Mareillan – 34300 Agde – 04 67 21 24 11 – Jun-Sep daily 8am-midnight. Closed Oct-Mar.* This delightful open-air café-bar near the Canal du Midi bewitches with its magical spell of accordeon tangos and waltzes.

Mamita Café – *41 quai Jean-Miquel – 34300 Agde – 04 67 26 92 84 – May-Dec: daily 11am-2am; Jan, Mar-Apr: weekends 11am-2am; Apr-Sep. 11am-2am – closed Dec-Jan except weekends.* The Latino-salsa music, terrace and friendly welcome makes this a great venue for a few tapas and a rum cocktail.

Restaurant-ar Casa Pepe – *29 r. Jean-Roger – 34300 Agde – 04 67 21 17 67 – daily 8am-midnight (except Wed Sep-Jun) – closed Nov.* This small popular bar and seafood restaurant has a clientele of regulars, fishermen, rugby players and jousters, and the proprietor, Aimé Catanzano, a fisherman by trade, is a well known figure about town.

RECREATION

Canal du Midi boat trips – *04 67 94 08 79 – www.bateaux-du-soleil.com. 2hr trips from Beziers 9€ (children under 10 : 6€) – Les Bateaux du Soleil.* 2hr trips on horse-drawn canal boats, the traditional method used until around 1960.

SARL Trans.Cap.Croisière – *Quai Jean-Miquel-Cap d'agde BP 631 – 34300 Agde – 06 08 47 22 32 / 06 08 31 45 20 – from early Apr-early Nov:* All aboard the catamaran Cap'Nemo for a cruise around old Fort Brescou, with fascinating commentary about the fort's use as a prison.

Joutes nautiques d'Agde – From Jun to Sep, Agde, like Sète, has water tournaments involving jousting from boats, that provide great entertainment.

Oppidum d'Enserune★★

The Enserune hill fort above the Béziers plain has a Mediterranean location, extraordinary pine wood and a fascinating archaeological story: in 1915, traces of an Iberian-Greek settlement and a crematorium dating from the 4C and 3C BC were uncovered.

Michelin Map: 339: D-9.
Info: Office du tourisme de Béziers, 29 Av St-Saens, 34500 04 67 76 47 00. www.ville-eziers.fr
Location: 15km/9.3mi SW of Beziers via D11.
Don't Miss: The silos, cistern and 5-3C B.C. funerary ojects in the Museum

Oppidum d'Enserune
L. Campion/MICHELIN

OPPIDUM

Excavated food stores show that Ensérune began as a 6C BC settlement of mud huts clustered around a hillfort. The Romans arrived in 118 BC and installed a sewage system, laid paving stones, plastered and painted walls and after 1C AD *Pax Romana* people abandoned the hillfort to settle on the plains.

The **Museum★** (*visit with audioguide May-Aug 10am-7pm (last admission*

1hr before closing); Apr and Sep daily except Mon 10am-12.30pm, 2pm-4pm; Oct-Mar daily except Mon 9.30am-12.30am, 2pm-5.30pm. closed 1 Jan, 1 May, 1 & 11 Nov, 25 Dec; 6.50€; under age 18: no charge. 04 67 37 01 23) built on the ancient city's site contains artefacts of daily life from the 6C to the 1C BC: *dolia* (jars) buried beneath houses, ceramics, vases, amphorae, and pottery of Phocaean, Iberian, Greek, Etruscan, Roman and local origins. Funerary objects (5C-3C BC) include Greek vases and urns used for cremation or offerings. The Mouret room displays an egg found inside a grave, symbolising the renewal of life. The hillfort encompasses a panorama of the Cévennes to Canigou and across the coastal plain. The **view★** to the north takes in the **old Montady Lake**, drained in 1247.

ADDRESSES

EAT

Restaurant du Château de Colomiers – *R. du Château – 34440 Colomiers – 2.5km/1.5mi E of the oppidum of Ensérune on B-road – 04 67 37 06 93 – closed Jan and Mon – reservations required off-season.* This castle built on top of 12C vaulted cellars in the 16C and 17C has a restaurant with a lordly atmosphere and a pleasant terrace under the chestnut trees.

Abbaye de Fontfroide★★

Fontfroide's spectacular Cistercian abbey enjoys a tranquil setting amidst cypress trees, and sunset lights up its flame-coloured ochre and pink Corbières sandstones.

- **Info:** 04 68 45 11 08 www.fontfroide.com
- **Location:** 14km/8.75mi SW of Narbonne.
- **Don't Miss:** The cloister and exquisite early 20th century windows.

ABBEY

The welcome centre contains the ticket office, bookstore, winery and restaurant. mid Jul-Aug guided tours (1hr) 10am-6pm (every 30mn); Apr-mid Jul and Sep-Oct 10am, 10.15am, 11.30am, 12.15pm, 1.45pm, 2.30pm, 3.15pm, 4pm, 4.45pm and 5.30pm; Nov-Mar 10am, 11am, noon, 2pm, 3pm and 4pm. 9€.(10-18 yrs 2€) 04 68 45 11 08. www.fontfroide.com. In 1093 a Benedictine abbey was founded on land belonging to Aymeric I, Viscount of Narbonne, and the 12C and 13C saw great prosperity. Pope Pierre de Castelnau's legate, whose assassination sparked off the Aligensian Crusade,

Abbaye de Fontfroide

B. Kaufmann/MICHELIN

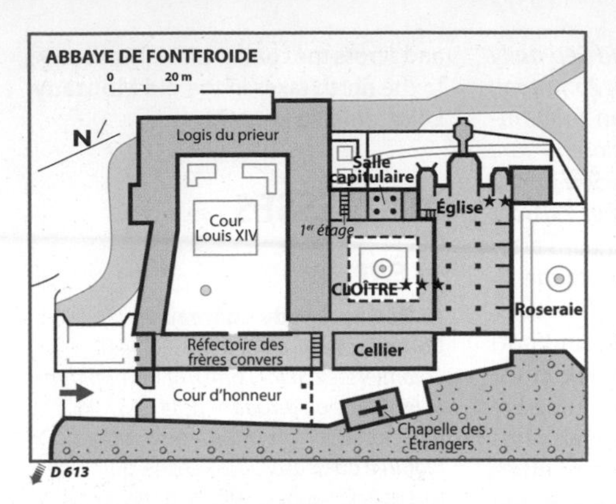

buildings. The cloisters are an example of architectural elegance. The oldest gallery (mid-13C) adjoins the church. Building began on the **Abbey church** in the mid-12C and south chapels were added in the 14C-15C.

The Chapter-house is roofed with nine Romanesque vaults supported on decorative ribs that spring from slender marble colonnettes.

The Monks' dormitory above the storeroom is roofed with 12C fine ribbed barrel-vaulting. The **Rose garden** contains about 3 000 rose bushes (11 varieties). Follow footpaths around the abbey to appreciate the charms of its setting.

stayed here after his trip to Maguelone. Jacques Fournier, who reigned under the name of Benedict XII, was abbot here from 1311 to 1317.

Most abbey buildings were erected in the 12C and 13C. The tour begins in the 17C Cour d'honneur, moves through the 13C guard-room and on to the medieval

Gruissan

Gruissan once served as a point of defence for the port of Narbonne. The new resort adjoins the old village on the shores of the Grazel lagoon, and coastal houses are set on high stilts. Gruissan makes an ideal centre for exploring Languedoc beauty spots like the Massif de la Clape (*see NARBONNE*).

- **Info:** Bd. du Pech-Meynaud, 11430 Gruissan, 04 68 49 09 00. www.ville-gruissan.fr.
- **Location:** 20km/12.5mi SW of Narbonne on the D32
- **Don't Miss:** Ruins of the Barbarossa Tower, Cite de la vigne et du vin.
- **Kids:** This town is nicknamed "Station Kid" – see why!

RESORT

The demands of tourism have thrown up hundreds of pastel-coloured apartments stacked like freight containers on a ship, plus all the trappings of a marina and popular beach-side holiday resort.

Salins de l'Île St-Martin

Rte. de l'Ayrolle. guided visits Jul-Aug 9.30am, 11am, 2.30pm, 4pm and 5.30pm; May-Jun and Sep 10.30am and 2.30pm; Mar and Oct by request. 7.60€. 04 68 49 59 97.

Sea water invades this salt marsh along 35km/22mi of channels, and salt is harvested in September.

Gruissan-Plage

This seaside resort has chalets built upon piles to protect them from equinox floods.

Old Village

The old village was home to fishermen and salt-pan workers, and their houses form concentric circles around the ruins of the Barbarossa tower.

Gruissan

P. Blot/MICHELIN

Lamalou-les-Bains

Lamalou springs were discovered in the 13C and their soothing powers were quickly appreciated. This spa treats people with poliomyelitis and other mobility problems. Mounet-Sully, Alphonse Daudet, André Gide have all taken the waters here. Lamalou-les-Bains makes a base for excursions around the Caroux region.

- **Info:** 1 Ave. Capus, 34240 Lamalou-les-Bains, 04 67 95 70 91.
- **Location:** 38km/23.75mi N of Béziers on D909.
- **Don't Miss:** the Hérépian bell making Foundry.
- **Kids:** La Maison des arts at Bédarieux.

ST-PIERRE-DE-RHÈDES★

200m/220yd W of town, towards St-Pons. Open year-round: self-guided visit during the week; Feb-Nov: guided tours Wed 2.30pm. No charge. 04 67 95 70 91.

This 12C Romanesque rural parish church has an elegant apse decorated with Lombard arcades. The south façade's doorway lintel has a Chi Rho monogram in Arabic script, blossoming into a crucifix. The church interior features Mozarabic capitals and two 12C low-relief sculptures by the Toulouse School.

EXCURSIONS

Gorges d'Héric★★

In Mons-la-Trivalle, take D 14E to the NE. Leave the car at the mouth of the river gorge. A track runs along the gorge to the hamlet of Héric. 3hr on foot there and back.

Follow the stream to the **Gouffre du Cerisier**. Farther on is a majestic amphitheatre, the **Cirque de Farrières**. The path leads past Mont Caroux before arriving in **Héric**, a hamlet of stone sla-roofed houses.

The gorge attracts swimmer, walkers, picnickers and rock climbers.

Sanctuaire de Notre-Dame-de-Capimont

5km/3mi NE. Leave the car in the parking area and walk up to the sanctuary.

This pilgrimage Chapel offers a fine view of the Or valley. From St-Anne's chapel behind Notre-Dame-de-Capimont, you can see Monts de l'Espinouse with Lamalou and the Bitoulet valley in the foreground, and Pic de la Coquillade and the ruins of St-Michel to the south.

Monts de l'Espinouse★

80km/50mi round tour from Olargues. *See OLARGUES.*

Narbonne★★

Narbonne, which has been in its time the ancient capital of Gallia Narbonensis, the residence of the Visigoth monarchy and an archiepiscopal seat, is now a lively Mediterranean city playing an important role as a wine-producing centre and a road and rail junction.

- **Info:** 31 r. Jean Jaurès, 11100 Narbonne, ℘04 68 65 15 60. www.mairie-narbonne.fr.
- **Location:** 30 km/19mi SW of Béziers by the N 9, and 60 km/37.5mi E of Carcassonne by the A 61. The N 9 surrounds Narbonne, offering direct access to the historic centre.
- **Parking:** Seek out the parking areas along the canal, near the Quai Valière.
- **Don't Miss:** The Archaeological Museum, with its Roman paintings.
- **Timing:** Allow a full day.

A BIT OF HISTORY

A sea port – Narbonne may well have served as a harbour and market for a 7C BC Gallic settlement on the Montlaurès hill to the north of the modern city. The town of "Colonia Naro Martius," established in 118 BC by decree of the Roman Senate, became a strategic crossroads along the Via Domitia as well as a flourishing port. It exported oil, linen, wood, hemp, the cheeses and meat from the Cévennes so much appreciated by the Romans, and later on sigillated earthenware. Most of the river shipping business, however, was centred on the Italian, Iberian and then Gallic wine trade. During this period the city expanded dramatically and was embellished with magnificent buildings.

A capital city – In 27 BC Narbonne gave its name to the Roman province created by Augustus. After the sack of Rome in 410 by the Visigoths, Narbonne became their capital. Later, it fell to the Saracens; in 759 Pépin the Short recaptured it and Charlemagne created the duchy of Gothie with Narbonne as the capital. From the 14C, the change in course of the Aude, the havoc wrought by the Hundred Years War and plague, and the departure of the Jews caused Narbonne to decline.

PALAIS DES ARCHEVÊQUES★

2hr The façade of the Archishops' Palace overlooks the lively **place de l'Hôtel-de-Ville**, in the heart of the city, where a section of the Roman Via Domitia was

Palais des Archevêques and Cathédrale St-Just

M. H. Caranague/MICHELIN

discovered. It has three square towers: framing the Passage de l'Ancre, the Tour de la Madeleine (the oldest) and Tour St-Martial; and farther to the left the Donjon Gilles-Aycelin. Between the last two, Viollet-le-Duc built the present Hôtel de Ville (town hall) in a neo-Gothic style. The Archishops' Palace is an example of religious, military and civil architecture bearing the imprint of centuries, from the 12C to the 19C Hôtel de Ville.

Donjon Gilles-Aycelin★

Open Jul-Sep 10am-6pm; Oct-Jun 9am-noon, 2-6pm. Closed 1 Jan and 25 Dec. 2.20€. 04 68 90 30 65. Entrance on the left inside the town hall. This fortified tower with its rusticated walls stands on the remains of the Gallo-Roman rampart which once protected the heart of the old town. It represented the archbishops' power as opposed to that of the viscounts, who occupied a building on the other side of place de l'Hôtel-de-Ville. From the sentinel path on the platform (162 steps), the **panorama**★ stretches over Narbonne and the cathedral, the surrounding plain and away across La Clape summit, the Corbières and the coastal lagoons as far as the Pyrenees on the horizon.

Walk through the town hall to the main courtyard of the Palais Neuf.

Palais Neuf (New Palace)

The New Palace complex surrounds the Cour d'Honneur and comprises the façade over the courtyard of the town hall, the Gilles-Aycelin keep, the St-Martial tower, the synods building and the north and south wings.

Salle des Consuls

Enter via the Cour d'honneur. Located on the ground floor of the synods building, the room is supported on part of the old Roman fortified city wall.

Leave the Palais Neuf via the door on the north side of the courtyard and enter the Palais Vieux via the door opposite, on the other side of passage de l'Ancre.

Hôtel de Ville

©Julien Leblay/Fotolia.com

Palais Vieux (Old Palace)

The Old Palace consists of two main buildings flanking the Madeleine tower. To the east, a square staircase tower divides a Romanesque façade pierced by arcades (5). Other monuments stand around Madeleine courtyard: the square Carolingian bell-tower of the church of St-Théodard (6), the apse of the Annonciade Chapel overlooked to the north by the imposing cathedral chevet, and the 14C **Tinal** (the canons' old storeroom), which has recently been restored.

Come out onto passage de l'Ancre and walk to the right.

Passage de l'Ancre

This almost fortified street with its impressive walls separates the old and new palaces and leads from place de l'Hôtel-de-Ville (between the St-Martial and Madeleine towers) to the cloisters.

Enter the Salle au Pilier via a door to the left of the stairs leading to the cathedral cloisters.

Salle au Pilier

Open Jul-Sep 10am-6pm; Oct-Jun 9am–noon, 2–6pm. Closed last 3 weeks in Jan, 1 May, 1 and 11 Nov, 25 Dec. No charge. 04 68 90 30 65. This 14C room houses the Palais shop.

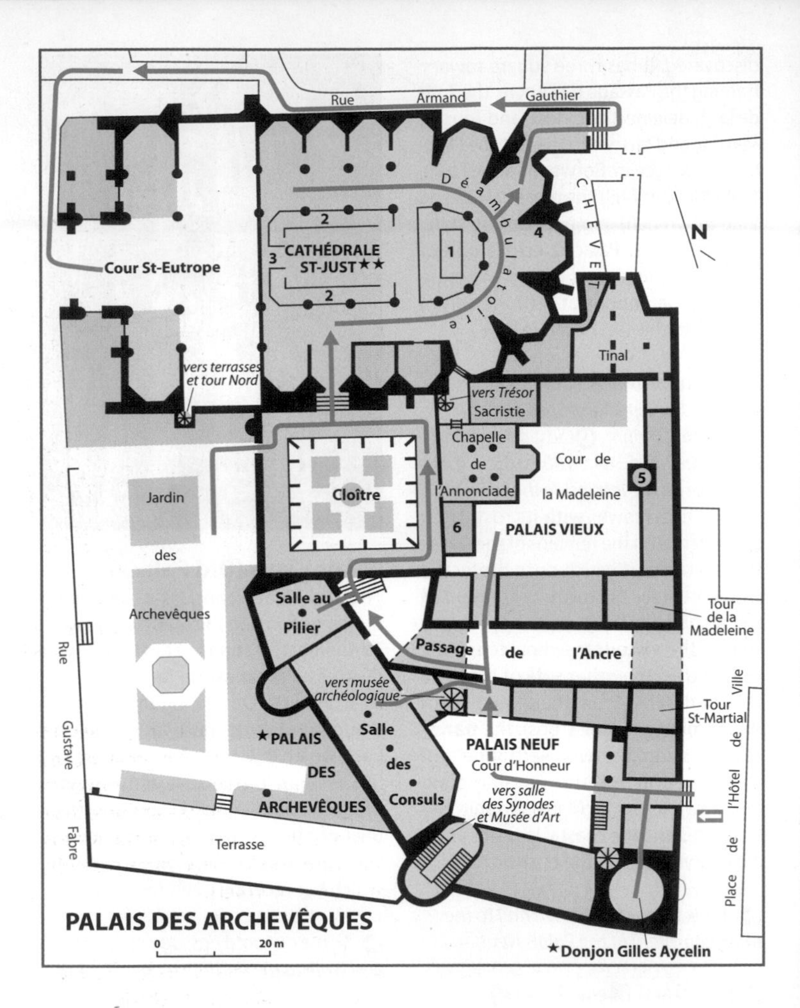

CATHÉDRALE ST-JUST-ET-ST-PASTEUR★★

It is possible to enter the cathedral via passage de l'Ancre and through the cloisters.

The first stone was laid on 3 April 1272 and by 1332, the radiating chancel had been completed in the same style as the great cathedrals of northern France. Building the nave and the transept would have involved reaching the ancient rampart which still served in troubled medieval times, so this was postponed. Today, the edifice consists of the chancel flanked by cloisters on the south side.

Cloisters

The cloisters (14C) are at the foot of the south side of the cathedral. The west gallery gives access to the archbishops' gardens. From the 18C **Jardin des Archevêques**, there is a fine view of the flying buttresses, the south tower of the cathedral and the synods building.

Inside, the strikingly well-proportioned chancel was the only part to be completed. The height of its vaulting (41m/134ft) is exceeded only by that in the cathedrals of Amiens (42m/137ft) and Beauvais (48m/157ft).

The chancel houses numerous works of art (*see diagram*). Located opposite the high altar with baldaquin (1) is the **organ case** (3) flanked by fine 18C **choir**

Cloister, Cathédrale St-Just

©Claudio Giovanni Colombo/Bigstockphoto.com

stalls (2). The Lady Chapel dedicated to Ste-Marie-de-Bethléem has regained its large Gothic **altarpiece★** (4), discovered in 1981 under a coat of stucco.

Treasury

Open Jul-Sep 11am-6pm (Sun 2–6pm); Oct-Jun 2–6pm. 2.20€. (Museum /Monuments Pass 7.50€) 04 68 90 30 65.

The treasury includes illuminated manuscripts and, together with other church plate, a fine gilt chalice (1561). The most remarkable exhibit is a late-15C Flemish tapestry depicting the **Creation★★**, woven in silk and gold thread.

Leave the cathedral via a door located in the second radiating chapel from the left.

Exterior

Note in particular the chevet with its High Gothic lancets, the great arches surmounted by merlons with arrow slits overlooking the terraces of the amulatory, the flying buttresses, the turrets and the powerful defensive buttresses, and the lofty towers.

TOWN WALK

Start from place de l'Hôtel-de-Ville and follow pedestrianised rue Droite.

The Via Domitia

The Via Domitia is the oldest of the Roman roads built in Gaul. It was named after the Consul of the Roman province of Gallia Narbonensis, Domitius Ahenoarus, who had it built in 118-117 BC at the time the province was founded.

Following an ancient route once used by the Ligurians and Iberians, the Via Domitia ran from Beaucaire (Gard) to Le Perthus (Pyrénées-Orientales), forming a communications route between Rome and Spain. Beyond the Rhône, the Via Domitia led into the Via Aurelia. Spanned by ridges and punctuated along its length by milestones marking every Roman mile (1 481.5m) and staging posts, the Via Domitia linked Beaucaire (Ugernum), Nîmes (Nemausus), Béziers (Julia Baeterrae), Narbonne (Naro Martius) and Perpignan (Ruscino).

Originally intended for military use, to enable Roman legions to reach the furthest outposts of the empire, Roman roads also aided the transportation of commercial goods and, of course, the spread of new ideas.

Place Bistan

Remnants of a 1C temple on the site of the Antique forum and Capitol.

Turn right onto Rue Girard then left onto Rue Michelet.

Église St-Sébastien

This 15C church with 17C extensions, was built, according to legend, on the site of the saint's birthplace.

Return to Place Bistan and, from the SW corner, follow Rue Rouget-de-l'Isle.

The itinerary takes you past the **Horreum**, a Roman warehouse.

Turn right onto Rue du Lieut.-Col.-Deymes and right again onto Rue Armand-Gauthier which leads to place Salengro.

La Poudrière

Situated behind the Jardin des Vicomtes, this 18C powder magazine houses temporary exhibitions.

Return to Place Salengro; right on Rue Chenneier and left on Rue du Lion-d'Or to the embankment; turn left.

Banks of the Roine

The Roine canal links the Sallèles-d'Aude junction canal to Port-la-Nouvelle.

Roman painting of Apollo, Archaeological Museum

A. Thuillier/MICHELIN

Covered market in Narbonne

©fanou111/Fotolia.com

When you reach the end of Promenade des Barques, take Pont de la Lierté across the Robine canal. Note the fine metal-framed covered market. Follow the south bank to Pont des Marchands and return to Place de l'Hôtel-de-Ville.

Pont des Marchands★

This picturesque bridge, a pedestrianised street lined with colourful shops overlooking the canal, follows the old Roman road (Via Domitia).

ADDITIONAL SIGHTS

Archaeological Museum★★

Palais Neuf. Open Apr-Sep 9.30am-12.15pm, 2-6pm; Oct-Mar daily except Mon 10am-noon, 2-5pm. 5.20€(Museum Pass 7.50€). 04 68 90 30 54.

Narbonne undoubtedly possesses one of the finest collections of **Roman paintings**★★ in France.

Museum of Art and History★

As for the Archaeological Museum. Same building as the Salle des Synodes, on the second floor.

This museum occupies the old episcopal apartments where Louis XIII stayed during the siege of Perpignan in 1642.

Lapidary Museum★

As for the Archaeological Museum.

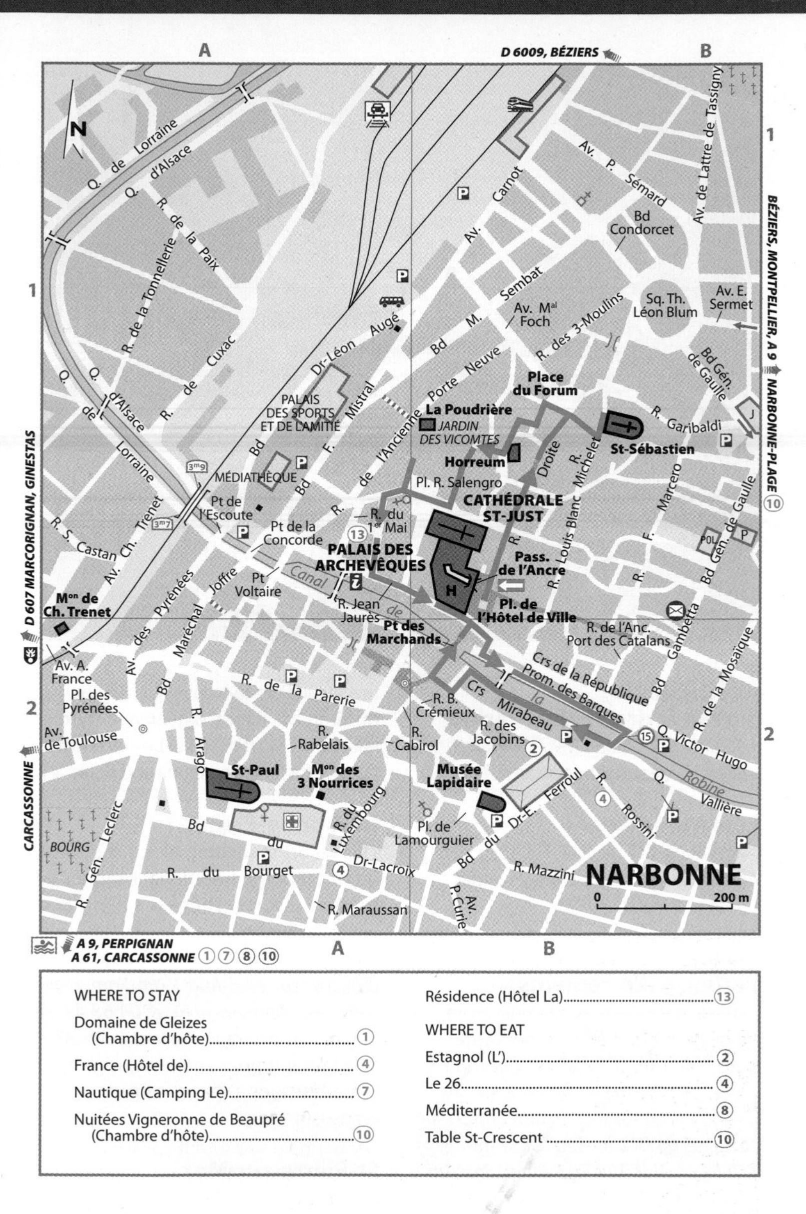

This is in the deconsecrated 13C church of Notre-Dame-de-la-Mourguié. The magnificent exterior has projecting buttresses and a crenellated chevet.

Basilique St-Paul

Open daily except Sun afternoon.

This basilica was built on the site of a 4/5C necropolis near the tomb of the city's first archbishop. The **chancel★**, begun in 1224, is notable for the height of its supporting structure and vaults.

Maison des Trois-Nourrices

In the street situated on the east side of the basilica.

This 16C house owes its unusual name ("House of the Three Wet-Nurses") to the generous curves of the caryatids supporting the lintel of a magnificent Renaissance window.

Pont des Marchands

L Campion/MICHELIN

EXCURSIONS

Sigean African Safari Park★

17km/10.5mi S along N 9. See Description under Réserve africaine de SIGEAN.

Fontfroide Aey★★

14km/8.5mi SW along N 113, then left onto D 613. See description under Abbaye de FONTFROIDE.

Amphoralis-Musée des Potiers gallo-romains★

11km/6.5mi to Sallèdes-d'Aude. From there, take D 1626 NE and follow the signs to "Musée des Potiers." The road runs alongside the junction canal linking the Canal du Midi and Canal de La Roine. Jul-Sep 10am–noon, 3-7pm; Apr-Jun Tue-Fri 2–6pm, Sat-Sun 10am–noon, 2–6pm. Closed 1 Jan, 1 May, 25 Dec. 4€. 04 68 46 89 48.

The central section of the modern museum building houses an exhibition on the craft of making amphorae, which was both varied and prolific.

Canal de la Robine

Dug at the end of the 18C through the former riverbed of the Robine, it is supplied with water from the Lampy reservoir (*see MONTAGNE NOIRE*) and reaches the sea at Port-la-Nouvelle after flowing through the Bages, Sigean and Ayrolle lakes and skirting **Ste-Lucie island**, famous for its varied fauna and flora.

Narbonne-Plage

This resort stretching along the coast is typical of the traditional Languedoc seaside resorts. There is sailing and water-skiing here.

Have fun with water at **Aquajet** park (*open early Jul-Aug 11am-7pm; May-Jun noon-6pm. 10€. 04 68 44 31 61*), which offers three water chutes, a swimming pool and aquatic games. From Narbonne-Plage, carry on to St-Pierre-sur-Mer.

St-Pierre-sur-Mer

Family seaside resort. The chasm of l'Oeil-Doux to the north is a curious natural phenomenon. It is 100m/328ft wide and contains a salt water lake 70m/229ft deep into which the sea surges.

Gruissan

See GRUISSAN.

Cimetière marin

See GRUISSAN excursions.

ADDRESSES

STAY

Hôtel de France – *6 r. Rossini. ℘04 68 32 09 75. www.hotelnarbonne.com. 15 rms. 7€.* A hotel in a late-19C building located on a quiet street downtown. The rooms are rather plain; those on the back promise a good night's sleep.

Chambre d'hôte Nuitées Vigneronne de Beaupré– *Rte d'Armissan. ℘04 68 65 85 57 – www.domaine-de-beaupre.fr – 4 rms.* Wine buffs will delight in this small B&B close to the centre of Narbonne.

Camping le Nautique – *4km/2.5mi S of Narbonne – ℘04 68 90 48 19 – www.campinglanautique.com – reservations advised – 390 places.* A large site with direct access to the Pages lagoon. Mobile homes also for hire.

Chambre d'hôte Domaine deGleizes – *℘04 68 32 94 48 – www domaine-de-gleizes.com – 4 rms.* Between vineyards and meadows, a place of calm and fresh air.

Hotel la Résidence – *6 r. du 1er-Mai. ℘04 68 32 19 41. www.hotel residence.fr. Closed 15 Jan–15 Feb. 26 rms 8.50€.* A fine hotel in a renovated 19C building.

EAT

L'Estagnol - *5 bis Cours Mirabeau. ℘04 68 65 09 27. Closed 16–24 Nov, Sun and Mon eve.* This lively brasserie situated near Les Halles, popular with the locals, specialises in traditional cuisine.

Le 26 – *8 bd Dr Lacroix – ℘04 68 4146 69. Closed Sun eve and Mon.* The chef loves to cook things slowly, filling the restaurant with the appetising aromas of cooking.

Méditerranée - *11210 Port-la-Nouvelle – ℘04 68 48 03 08 – www.hotel mediterranee.com.* Well placed along the promenade, facing the beach. Dishes centre around the sea.

Table St-Crescent – *Rte de Perpignan, au Palais du vin – ℘04 68 41 37 37 – www.la-table-saint-crescent.com. Closed Sat lunch, Sun eve and Mon.* Located at the edge of the town in a former oratory transformed into a temple of wine; inventive cuisine and superb wines from the region.

SHOPPING

Accent d'Oc – *56 R. Droite. ℘04 68 32 24 13. www.accentdoc.fr. Tue-Sun 10am-12.30pm, 2.30-7pm ; summer daily exc Mon am, 10am–1pm, 3–7pm Closed 1 May.* Numerous products prepared according to recipes from long ago: fruit jams and vegetables preserved with spices; oils and vinegars infused with herbs, olive paste etc.

Chocolaterie des Corières – *42 R. du Pont-des-Marchands. ℘04 68 32 06 93. Tue–Fri 9am–noon, 2–7pm. Closed 1st week in Feb and Oct.* Nearly 80 different types of chocolates are made in-house at this renowned confectionary.

CANALS

Autorail touristique du Minervois: Between Narbonne and Bize-Minervois; Jul-Sept: weekends and holidays, departure from quai de la rue Paul-Vieu in Narbonne at 2pm; return journey starts at 7pm; 9.50€, ℘04 68 27 05 94. The timetable allows for a visit of Amphoralis and the L'Oulio olive-oil co-operative in Bize-Minervois.

Petit train des Lagunes: From Narbonne to Port-la-Nouvelle; Jul-mid Sep daily except Sun; ℘04 68 48 16 56 or ℘04 68 48 00 51 (Port-la-Nouvelle tourist office).

Coche d'eau: From Narbonne to Port-la-Nouvelle; Jul-mid Sep: daily except Sunday, boats leave from Pont des Marchands at 9.30am and 6pm; bookings essential. ℘04 68 90 63 98.

CANAL HOUSEBOAT

Nicols – *Port du Somail - Allée de la Glacière - 11120 Le Somail - ℘04 68 46 00 97.* Rental of houseboats accommodating 2-12 people. *Reservation centre: Rte. du Puy-St-Bonnet, 49300 Cholet, ℘02 41 56 46 56. www.nicols.com*

Connoisseur – Houseboat cruises on the Canal du Midi from Trèes *(℘04 68 78 73 75)* and on the Canal de la Robine from Narbonne *(Reservation centre: ℘04 68 94 09 75 – www.connoisseurafloat.com).*

Olargues

and Monts de l'Espinouse

This village with its steep streets occupies a promontory encircled by the River Jaur. The village skyline is dominated by a tower, the vestige of an 11C feudal fortress that was converted into a bell-tower in the 15C. There is a fine overall view from the ridge, on the way in from St-Pons-de-Thomières.

- **Info:** Ave. de la Gare, 34390 Olargues, ℘04 67 97 71 26. www.olargues.org.
- **Location:** 19km/12mi NE of St Pons de Thomières by the D908 and 68km/42.5mi, NW of Béziers by the N12 then the D908.
- **Parking:** Beside the Mairie.
- **Don't Miss:** The view from the Col de l'Ourtigas and the panorama from Mt Caroux.
- **Timing:** Allow one hour for Olargues and one day for the Monts de l'Espinouse.

OLD TOWN WALK

Start from place de la Mairie. Enter the old town through the Porte Neuve (*to the left at the bottom of the square*).

From the terrace beside the bell-tower, there is a pleasant **view** of the Jaur and the 13C humpback bridge which spans it, the Espinouse mountains, and Mont Caroux to the north-east.

From rue de la Place, take the covered stairway of the Commanderie on the right; it leads to another street just below the bell-tower. The **Musée d'Olargues** is located halfway along (*open mid-Jun-mid-Sep daily except Mon 3-6pm. ℘04 67 97 71 26*). It contains

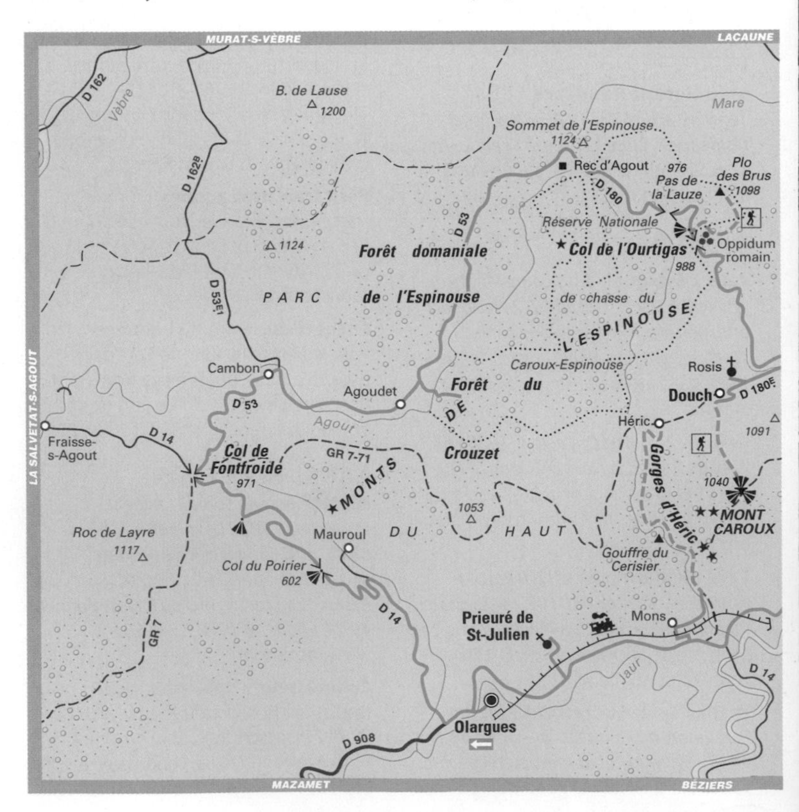

displays on traditional crafts and agricultural practices, most of which have now disappeared in the wake of modern technology.

On the way out of Olargues to the west is the **Cebenna** (*open Jul-Aug daily except Sun 9am-7pm; rest of the year daily except Sat-Sun 9am-noon, 2-6pm; closed 25 Dec–1 Jan and public holidays; kaleidoscope: 2.50€ (children under 7: no charge; 7–15 year olds: 1.50€); 04 67 97 88 00; www.cebenna.org*), a multimedia centre offering a reference library, lectures and activities.

The Jaur by the village of Olargues

J. Malburet/MICHELIN

DRIVING TOUR

Monts de l'Espinouse★

80km/50mi round tour – allow 6hr including the walk to the Caroux viewing tale. Take D 908 out of Olargues and head W towards St-Pons then turn right onto D 14 to Fraisse-sur-Agout and La Salvetat. It is possible to do this tour taking Lamalou-les-Bains as a starting point.

The pass road leading to the Col de Fontfroide along the western slopes of the

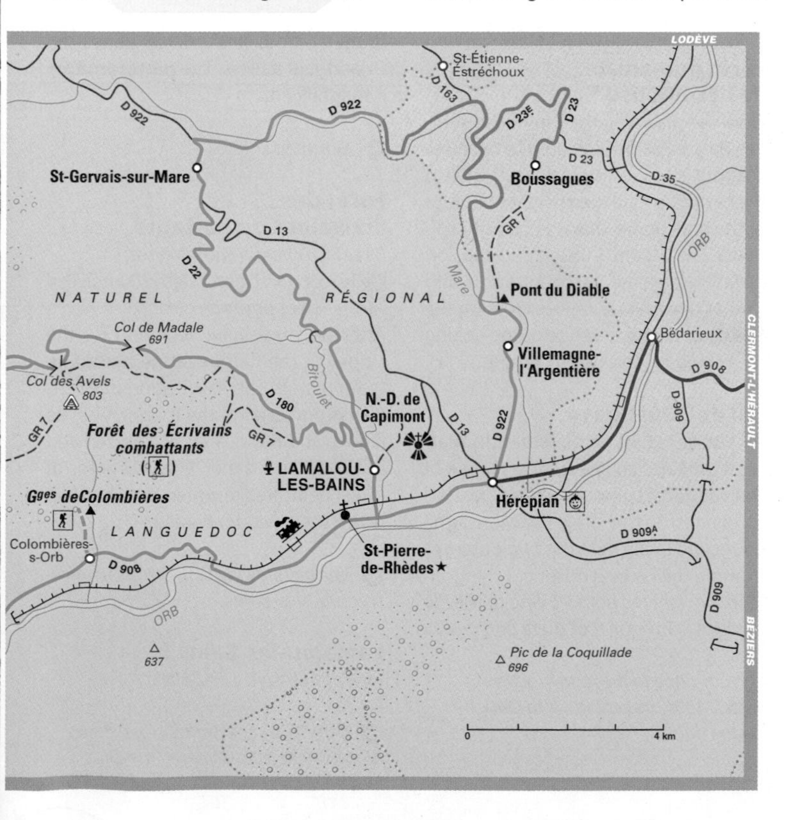

Espinouse mountains starts in a Mediterranean setting of vines, olive trees, holm-oaks and chestnut trees. At higher altitudes, the Mediterranean vegetation gives way to moorland.
From the Col du Poirier, the view extends over the mountains in the Somail to the left beyond the Coustorgues gully. There is an even wider view to the south towards the Jaur valley *(viewpoint)*.

Col de Fontfroide

Alt 971m/3 156ft.
The Col de Fontfroide is a mountain pass set in an impressively wild spot. It marks the watershed between the Mediterranean and Atlantic sides of the range.

Turn right onto D 53 to Camon.

The road runs along the banks of the Agout, through the village of Camon which gets quite lively in summer, and continues through rugged, lonely, mountainous scenery.

Forêt domaniale de l'Espinouse

From the road near the Espinouse summit, the roof of the Espinouse farm or **Rec d'Agout** is visible farther down the hill to the right. The road then reaches the foot of the bare dome-shaped crest of Espinouse (alt 1 124m/3 653ft) and runs on down through rugged countryside with ravines to each side, before crossing the **Pas de la Lauze**, a slender ridge linking the Espinouse and Caroux ranges.

Col de l'Ourtigas★

Alt 988m/3 211ft. An observation platform provides an interesting **view**★ of the rugged Espinouse range gashed by ravines. To the left is the Montagne d'Aret and to the right the two outcrops forming the Fourcat d'Héric.
To the right is a path leading to the Plo des Brus (45min on foot there and ack).

Continue to the road junction with D 180E branching off to Douch on the right.

On the right side of the road, **Église de Rosis**, a rustic church with a stone bell-tower, stands out.

Douch

The character of this village, which is typical of the Caroux region, is fairly well preserved. The narrow streets are flanked by stone houses roofed with stone slabs *(lauzes)*.

Leave the car in Douch and follow the path to the left up through the fields. Take the left fork 50m/55yd further on.

Tale d'orientation du Mont Caroux

2hr on foot there and ack.
The path climbs through clumps of broom, then a beech forest. To the left, at the top of the hill, is the highest point on Mont Caroux itself (alt 1 091m/3 546ft). The path then runs across a vast plateau to a viewing tale *(tale d'orientation)*, with the Plo de la Maurelle to the right. The rugged Caroux peak towers above the Or and Jaur valleys. The **panorama**★★ is magnificent.

Return to D 180.

Forêt des Écrivains Combattants

By car via chemin Paul-Prévost.
On foot via a flight of steps 200m/220yd further on opposite an old inn.
After the catastrophic floods in 1930, the slopes of the Caroux range had to be reafforested. The Association des Écrivains Combattants, the Touring Club de France and the villages of Combes and Rosis replanted the 78ha/193 acres of forest dedicated to writers who had laid down their lives for France.

The picturesque D 180 leads to Lamalou-les-Bains.

Lamalou-les-Bains

See LAMALOU-LES-BAINS.

Drive W out of Lamalou-les-Bains along D 908 to Colomières-sur-Or; leave the car on the left, just beyond the bridge, and follow the path along the gorge.

Gorges de Colomières

30min on foot there and back.

The footpath is fitted in places with metal ladders and handrails to allow walkers to get past difficult passages. The more adventurous will follow a 13km/8mi loop (about 5hr 30min) waymarked with blue triangles.

The path follows the stream which cascades down from one pool to the next. The section upstream from the gorge is renowned for the rock climbing opportunities it offers. The short itinerary stops by a small dam.

In Mons-la-Trivalle, travel NE along D 14E; leave the car at the entrance to the gorge. A footpath runs along the gorge to the hamlet of Héric.

Gorges d'Héric★★

See LAMALOU-LES-BAINS.

Turn right off D 908 onto D 14E20 passing beneath the railway line.

Prieuré de St-Julien

This 12C priory is surrounded by vineyards, wooded hills and cypresses.

Return to D 908 and Olargues.

Pézenas★★

Hérault

This little town, once called "Piscenae," is built in a fertile plain covered in vineyards. Pézenas prides itself on its past, reflected in its interesting little streets and its mansions unchanged since the 17C.

- **Population:** 8 511
- **Michelin Map:** 339: F-8.
- **Info:** Pl. des Etats-de-Languedoc, 34120 Pézenas, 04 67 98 36 40. www.pezenas-tourisme.fr. Guided tour of the town; Discovery tours (1hr30min) Jul-Aug daily except Sun, 5pm. 5€. Self-guided tour with brochure: 2€. Inquire at tourist office or at www.vpah.culture.fr
- **Location:** 50km/30mi SW of Montpellier. Place du 14-Juillet is the town's main square.
- **Parking:** Try the large lot near Promenade du Pré-St-Jean if you're headed downtown; for sights south of Cours Jean-Jaurès, use the car park at Place Boy-Lapointe.
- **Timing:** The walking tour of Old Pézenas could take a good part of a day, including visiting the museum. and meandering through the shops.

A BIT OF HISTORY

A wool market – A fortified town at the time of the Romans, Pézenas was even then an important trading centre for woollen cloth. After it became part of the royal estate in 1261, its trade fairs took place three times a year.

The "Versailles" of the Languedoc – For the first time, in 1456, the States General of Languedoc met at Pézenas. The town later became the residence of the governors of Languedoc: the Montmorencys, then the Contis. Armand de Bouron, Prince de Conti, transformed Pézenas into the "Versailles," or royal court, of the Languedoc and surrounded himself with a court of aristocrats, artists and writers. Each session of the States General was celebrated with lavish entertainments.

Molière at Pézenas – During one of these celebrations, Molière, attracted by the town's reputation, came to Pézenas with his Illustrious Theatre in 1650.

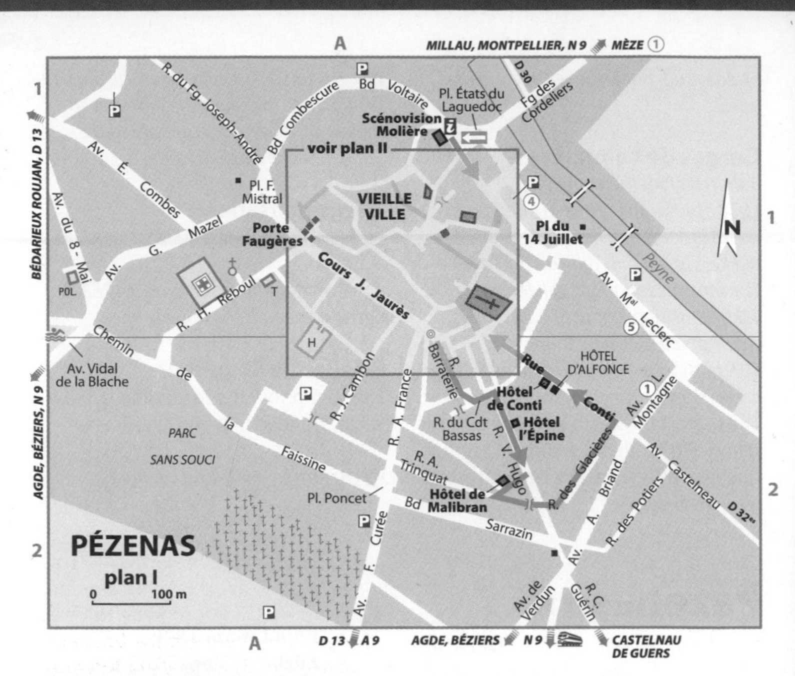

In 1653, having been permitted to put on a performance for Conti himself, he was given the title of "Actor to His Supreme Highness the Prince of Conti." A statue of Molière, by Injalert (1845-1933) stands in a small garden situated on place du 14 -Juillet.

OLD PÉZENAS WALK★★

Old mansions, or *hôtels*, with elegant balconies and ornate doorways, and workshops, now occupied by craftsmen and artists, follow one after the other along streets with evocative names: rue de la Foire, rue Triperie-Vieille, rue Fromagerie-Vieille (Fair, Old Tripe Shop, Old Cheese Shop).

Place Gambetta

A. de Valroger/MICHELIN

Leave from place du 14-Juillet.

Hôtel de Lacoste★

This early-16C mansion has a very fine staircase and galleries with Gothic arches.

Place Gambetta

This square , once known as "Place-au-led" ("village square"), has retained its medieval structure. On the left is Gély's old barbershop (*which now houses the tourist information office*) where Molière liked to go. On the right, stands the **Consular House**; its 18C façade with pediment and wrought-iron work conceals the main building, which dates from 1552. The States General of Languedoc often met here; a particularly memorable session was held in 1632, at which the rebellion of Henry II of Montmorency against the king was hatched.
At the far end of the square, there is rue **Triperie-Vieille**, once lined with market stalls. Farther down, at no 11, in a courtyard at the end of a vaulted passageway, is a fine early 17C stairwell.

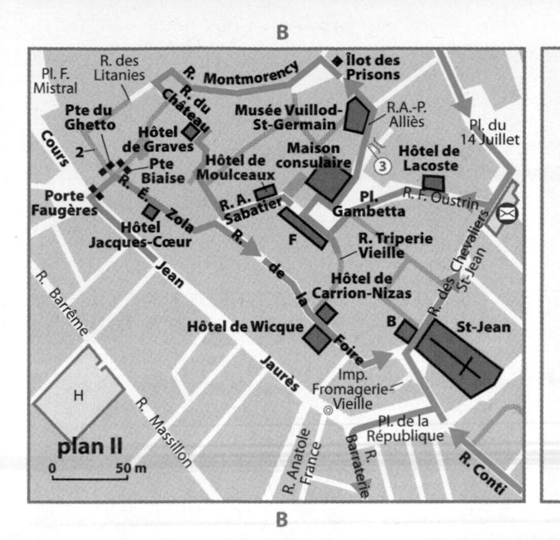

WHERE TO STAY
M. Gener (Chambre d'hôte)....... ①
Molière (Hôtel Le)....... ④

WHERE TO EAT
Entre Pots (L')....... ①
Pomme d'Amour (La)....... ③
Pré Saint-Jean (Le)....... ⑤

STREETS INDEX
Juiverie (R. de la)....... 2

Commanderie de St-Jean-de-Jérusalem....... B
Hôtel Flottes-de-Sébasan....... F

At the corner of Place Gambetta and Rue Alfred Saatier stands the **Hôtel Flottes de Séasan** with a wide 16C façade and a Renaissance (1511) corner niche which houses a 19C statue of St Roch. A plaque records that Queen Anne of Austria slept in the mansion in 1660.

Take rue A.-P.-Alliès on the right.

The **Hôtel de Saint-Germain** (*no 3*) is home to the Musée Vulliod-St-Germain.

Take rue Béranger on the left (17C house) which leads onto rue de Montmorency.

Rue de Montmorency

On the right stand the watchtowers of the **ilôt des prisons**. On the way back up the street, note on the left a 17C faïence **Pietà**, and on the right the gateway from the curtain walls of the old castle demolished on Cardinal Richelieu's orders, after the rebellion of Henry II of Montmorency.

Rue du Château

The beautiful ogee doorway of the **Hôtel de Graves** dates from the 16C.

Rue Alfred-Saatier

At no 12 the **Maison des Pauvres** (almshouse) possesses a fine staircase and 18C wrought-iron work.

Rue Émile-Zola

At no 7 the **Hôtel Jacques Cœur** features a façade adorned with culs-de-lampe in the shape of little figures. At the end of this street the **Porte du Ghetto** opens ontor**ue de la Juiverie**, two names which indicate the past role of this district.

On the left, **Porte Faugères**, which leads onto cours Jean-Jaurès, was once part of the old 14C ramparts.

Walk across cours Jean-Jaurès and take rue Reoul opposite.

Rue Henri-Reoul

The former Rue des Capucins was built in the 17C, when Pézenas started to expand beyond the medieval town walls.

At no 13, the façade of the Hôtel de Montmorency, once the residence of the governor of Languedoc, has a very fine 17C door with a pediment flanked with scrolls.

Farther down, the **Hôtel Paulhan de Guers** (now a hospital) also features an interesting 17C doorway.

Return to cours Jean-Jaurès.

Cours Jean-Jaurès

Cours Jean-Jaurès was constructed by Henry II of Montmorency. At the time it was called Le Quay, and it supplanted rue de la Foire as the town's main centre of activity. Aristocratic mansions were built facing south, the back of the house

Market in Pézenas

A. Cassaigne/MICHELIN

opening onto rue de la Foire. These mansions can be entered through vaulted passageways leading into courtyards with attractive open staircases. The most interesting buildings are at no 18, the **Hôtel de Landes de Saint-Palais** and, on the other side of the road, no 33, the **Hôtel de Latudes**.

Retrace your steps to rue du Château and turn right onto Rue de la Foire.

Rue de la Foire

Once known as rue Droite, this street was the setting for fairs and processions. At no 16, there is a carved lintel representing some charming child musicians. Note the elegant Renaissance façade of the **Hôtel de Wicque** surmounting an art gallery. Opposite stands the **Hôtel de Carrion-Nizas** with a 17C doorway.

Collégiale St-Jean

This church, designed by Avignon architect Jean-Baptiste Franque, was built in the 18C on the site of an old Templars' church which collapsed in 1733.

Commanderie de St-Jean-de-Jérusalem

The commandery features two well-preserved early 17C façades with their mullioned windows. A corner turret is supported by a masonry buttress.

Follow rue Kléer to place de la République to the right of the collegiate church.

This is where this tour leaves the old town centre to carry on into the faubourg ("suur") which grew up in the 17C and 18C around rue Conti.

From the square, take rue Barraterie (5th on the right at the end of the square) and turn left onto rue du Commandant-Bassas.

On the right, a porch leads through to the narrow rue du Jeu-de-Paume. This is believed to be the site of the theatre where Molière performed. No 3 has a fine diamond-fret door.

Turn right onto rue Victor-Hugo.

At no 11 is the fine façade of the **Hôtel l'Epine** (18C).

Hôtel de Maliran★

This mansion's magnificent 18C façade is embellished with fine windows surmounted by masks representing smiling women, whereas the balconies are supported by garlands of leaves. The door leads straight to an interior 17C staircase supported by two tiers of superimposed columns.

At the end of rue Alcide-Trinquat, walk down a flight of steps, cross rue Victor-Hugo and follow rue des Glacières opposite. Turn left onto rue Conti.

Rue Conti

Many private mansions were built along this street, which, in the 17C, was also full of inns and shops. Carry on past the **Hostellerie du Griffon d'Or** (no 36).

Hôtel d'Alfonce★

No 32 rue Conti. Open Jun-mid-Sep daily except Sun 10am–noon, 2–6pm; rest of the year by request. 2€. 04 67 98 10 38.

This fine 17C building, one of the best preserved in Pézenas, was used by Molière from November 1655 to Ferbu ary 1656. In the entrance courtyard is a pretty interior terrace adorned with balustrades. On the right, there is a fine 15C spiral staircase.

At no 30, the **Hôtel de Conti** features a façade, renovated in the 18C, with Louis XV balconies and wrought-iron window sills.

Return to St John's collegiate church via place de la République and turn right onto rue des Chevaliers-St-Jean, which leads back to place du 14-Juillet.

EXCURSION

Abbaye de Valmagne★

14km/9mi NE along N 9, N 113 to Montagnac then left on D 5.

Open mid-Jun-Sep 10am–noon, 2.30pm-6pm; early Oct-mid Jun 2-6pm. Closed Tue from mid-Dec-mid-Feb, 1 Jan and 25 Dec. 6.50€. 04 67 78 47 32. www.valmagne.com.

The great rose-coloured abbey of Valmagne, set in splendid isolation amid a clump of pine trees, rises serenely above the surrounding sea of Languedoc vineyards.

This Cistercian abbey was begun in the mid-13C and completed in the 14C. The abbey church, with its architecture and soaring nave, is an example of a classic Gothic style, as far removed from the traditions of Languedoc as it is from those of the Cistercians.

The **cloisters**, reuilt in the 14C, are charming with their golden-coloured stonework. The 12C **chapter-house** contains a delightful **fountain**★★.

ADDRESSES

STAY

Chambre d'hôte M. Gener – *34 av. Pierre-Sirven, 34530 Montagnac. 04 67 24 03 21 – 4 rms.* The rooms of this constabulary building dating from 1750 have been set up in the old stables. In the peace and quiet of a large shady courtyard, some of them have retained their loosebox separations. Breakfast is served on a terrace upstairs.

Le Molière – *pl. du 14-juillet. 04 67 98 14 00. www.hotel-le-moliere.com. 21 rms – – 9€.* Sculptures ornament the façade of his ravishing hotel located in the centre of town. Comfortable, air-conditioned rooms renovated in the southern style. Frescoes evoking the works of Molière decorate the patio-salon.

EAT

La Pomme d'Amour – *2 bis r. Alert-Paul-Allies. 04 67 98 08 40. Closed Jan, Fe, Mon evening and Tues. Reservation recommended Jul and Aug.* This 18C house near the Office de Tourisme shelters a small, intimate dining room with beams overhead. In summer the street becomes a pedestrian zone and the terrace in the shade of neighbouring houses comes into its own. Sunny southern fare.

Le Pré Saint-Jean – *18 av. du Mar.-Leclerc - 04 67 98 15 31. Closed Thu eve, Sun eve and Mon.* Choose from modern regional cuisine and a good selection of local wines.

L'Entre Pots – *8 av. Louis-Montagne – 04 67 90 00 00. Closed Sun, Mon lunch and Wed lunch.* Fresh regional produce, served in a beautiful and intimate interior; pleasing enclosed terrace.

Parc Naturel Régional du Haut-Languedoc

Info: Pl. du Foirail, 34220. ☎04 67 97 38 22. www. parc-haut-languedoc.fr

Location: 51km/32mi NW of Béziers via the N112; 19km/12mi SW of Olargues on the D908.

Timing: Allow one hour.

SAINT-PONS-DE-THOMIÉRES

This pretty mountain town in the upper Jaur valley, near the river's source, grew up around a Benedictine abbey founded in 936 by Count Raymond Pons of Toulouse. The town is a good base for exploring the region.

PARK

Maison du tourisme du Parc. Tourist information, works on local plant life, accommodation, park discovery trails, practical guides to the park.

St-Pons is now the administrative centre for the Haut Languedoc Regional Nature Park; founded in 1973 to preserve the natural wealth of the region, the park comprises the Caroux-Espinouse massif, the Sidore, part of the Montagne Noire and the Lacaune mountains. It injected new life into these breathtakingly beautiful, but isolated regions, which are too remote for any economically stimulating industrial development to be viable.

Source of the River Jaur

Access via the right river bank. The crenellated tower of the Comte de Pons, which formed part of the fortifications of the former bishopric, can be seen from the ridge over the Jaur. The River Jaur springs up at the foot of a rock then flows peacefully on.

Ancienne cathédrale

The old cathedral dates from the 12C, with modifications in the 15C, 16C and 18C. The north side retains some fortified features: two of the original four crenellated corner towers and a row of arrow slits above the windows. The richly sculpted doorway presents something of a puzzle in the shape of seven niches and four unidentified figures above the archivolt.

Musée de Préhistoire régionale

Open mid-Jun-mid-Sep 10am–noon, 3–6pm; rest of year daily except Mon 3-6pm (Wed 10am-noon, 3-6pm). 3.50€. ☎04 67 97 22 61.

The museum contains objects discovered on archaeological digs in caves in the region (particularly that at Camprafaud).

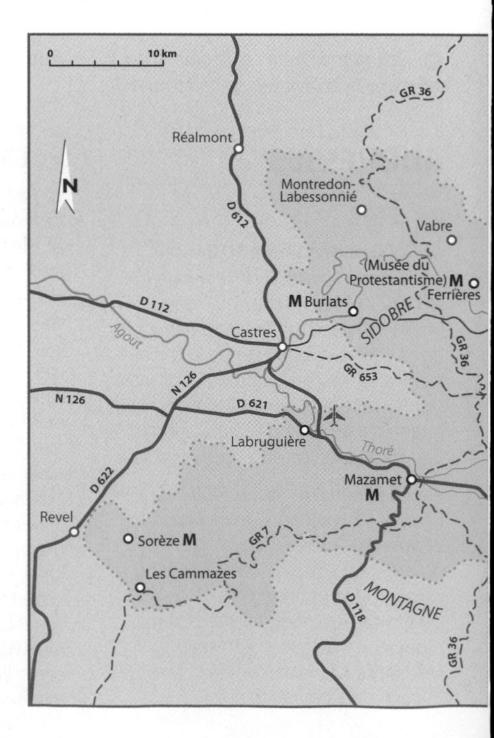

Beech forest in the Parc naturel régional du Haut-Languedoc

Grotte de la Devèze★

5km/3mi W along N112, beneath Courniou station.

Open Jul-Aug, guided tour 10am–6pm; Apr-Jun and Sep 2–5pm; rest of year Sun 2–5pm. Closed Jan. 7€ (children 4€; under 7: no charge). *04 67 97 03 24. www.cornioulesgrottes.com.*

This cave was discovered in 1886 when a tunnel was being drilled through Devèze mountain to carry the Bédarieux-Castres railway line.

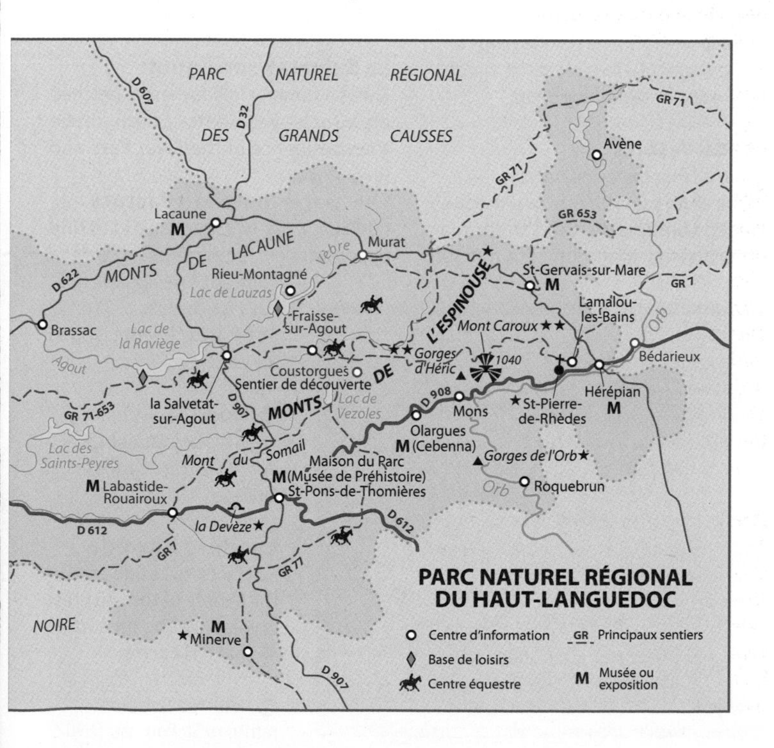

A waymarked path (*yellow markings*) starting near the entrance to the cave leads (*1hr 15min*) to seven *capitelles*, drystone shepherd huts.

DRIVING TOUR

1 LE SOMAIL

76km/47mi round tour – allow 2hr.

The Somail is the most fertile part of the Espinouse uplands. It is an area of rolling hills covered with chestnut or beech groves and carpeted with heather that takes on russet tones in the autumn.

Leave St-Pons via D 907, the Salvetat-sur-Agout road.

The road winds picturesquely uphill, providing some fine views of St-Pons and the Jaur valley before reaching the Col de Caaretou.

Beyond the pass, turn right onto D 169 that crosses the Somail plateau. A narrow road to the right signposted Saut de Vésoles leads to the shores of a lake set in the middle of woodland (parking area).

Lac de Vésoles

15min on foot there and back.

The Bureau, which flows through rugged countryside, used to form an impressive waterfall with a 200m/650ft drop over gigantic granite boulders before joining the Jaur.

Return to D 169 and head back to Fraisse-sur-Agout.

The road crosses superb heather-clad moorland and the Col de la Bane (alt 1 003m/3 260ft).

Prat d'Alaric

Jul-Aug: guided tour (2hr) Wed only from 10.30am. Departs from tourist office of Monts de l'Espinouse in Fraisse-sur-Agout. 04 67 97 53 81.

This typical Espinouse farmstead has been renovated by the Haut-Languedoc regional park authority and is now used as a visitor centre (*maison du pays*).

The peaceful village of **Fraisse-sur-Agout** is famous for its angling. It gets its name from its tall ash trees.

From the village, either head for the Col de Fontfroide and the tour through the Espinouse uplands or continue to La Salvetat.

La Salvetat-sur-Agout

This is a summer holiday resort perched on a rocky promontory high above the confluence of the River Vère and River Agout.

The **water-bottling factory** (*mid Jun-mid Sep guided tours (1hr) by appointment Tue, Wed and Fri 2pm and 3pm. Closed public holidays. No charge. 04 67 97 64 44)* at La Salvetat is open for visits.

From La Salvetat, there is a road running right round the Lac de la Raviège.

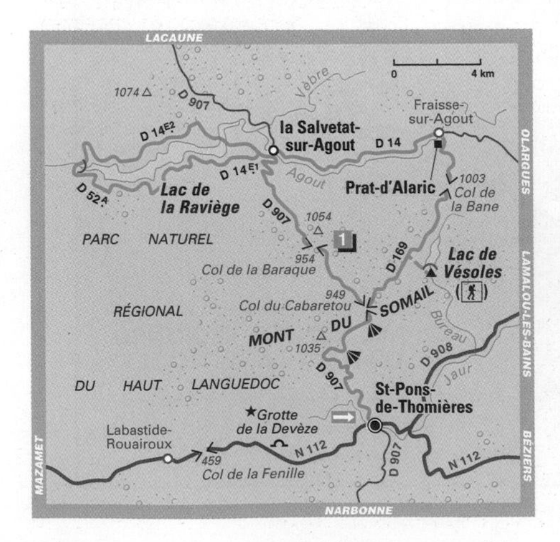

Lac de la Raviège

Not far from La Salvetat on the shores of this vast reservoir covering an area of 450ha/1 112 acres.

From La Salvetat, return to St-Pons via D 907.

Réserve Africaine de Sigean★

This safari park (nearly 300ha/740 acres) owes much of its unique character to the wild landscape of coastal Languedoc, with its *garrigues* dotted with lagoons, and to the fact that for each species large areas have been set aside, which resemble their original native environment as closely as possible.

Location: 18 km/11m S of Narbonne and 54 km/34m N of Perpignan by the N9. After Sigean follow signs – the Reserve is 7km/4m NW

Don't Miss: The Tibetan bears

Timing: Allow half a day.

Kids: A fascinating visit for children.

PARK TOUR

Visit by Car

Please observe the safety instructions displayed at the entrance. Open Apr-Sep 9am–6.30pm; rest of the year: 9am-4pm. 24€ (children 4–14 years 19€). 04 68 48 20 20. www.reserveafricainesigean.fr.

The route for visitors in cars goes through four areas, reserved for free ranging animals: **African bush** (ostriches, giraffes, impalas, **Tibetan bear park, lion park** and **African savannah** (white rhinoceros, zebras, ostriches etc).

Visit on Foot

3hr. Start from the central car parks, inside the safari park.

Walking round the safari park, visitors will come across the fauna of various continents – Tibetan bears, dromedaries, antelopes, zebras, cheetahs, alligators – and, near the lagoon of L'Oeil de Ca, bird life such as pink flamingoes, cranes, ducks, white storks, sacred ibis, macaws, swans and pelicans.

ADDRESSES

STAY

Domaine de la Pierre Chaude – *Les Campets, 11490 Portel-des-Corières. 6 km W of Réserve Africaine, towards Duran by D 611 A. 04 68 48 89 79. www.lapierrechaude.com. Closed Jan and Feb – 4 rms, 2 self-catering options.* This former *chai* (18C), nestled in a hamlet amid vines and garrique, was renovated by a student of the famed architect Gaudí. Ravishing guestrooms and lovely Andalusian-style patio shaded by fig trees.

Chambre d'hôte la Milhauque – *11440 Peyriac-de-Mer - 2km/1.25mi NW of Peyriac-sur-Mer. 04 68 41 69 76*. A restored sheepfold, tastefully restored, offers three rooms in a superb setting out in the *garrigue* and amid vineyards. *Bourride d'anguille* is a speciality dish.

One of the safari park's lions

A. Thuillier/MICHELIN

The abiding impression of the lands around Carcassonne is of never-ending vineyards, for this is the land of Corbières, Minervois, Fitou and the delightful bubbly known as Blanquette de Limoux. In recent times, it has become the focus of attention dwelling on the history of a persecuted religious sect known as the Cathars; indeed, 'Le Pay Cathare' and the numerous 'Routes du Pay Cathare' are actively, and rightly, promoted by the local tourist offices.

Highlights

1 An early evening stroll around the streets of **Carcassonne** (p206)
2 Make a visit to the mountain **Chateau de Peyrepertuse** (p233)
3 Indulge in a little wine-tasting in **Corbières** (p212)
4 Check out the seasonal cultural events in lovely **Minerve** (p226)
5 If only for the bubbly, visit charming **Limoux** (p219)

Carcassonne: the bastide

The lower town – La Ville Basse – is built around the bastide of St Louis, built in 1260 to the customary chequerboard pattern of these fortified settlements. There are over 300 in the south of France, and as well as meeting defensive strategies, they served to garrison and control the changing and feckless populations of the Middle Ages. Today, St Louis is consumed by the sprawl of modern Carcassonne, a bright, bustling place and one of the most-visited cities in the whole of Languedoc-Roussillon.

Stick in the ribs food

The extreme western part of Aude is consumed by the Pays du Lauragais, which centres of the town of Castelnaudary, arguably the cassoulet kingdom of the world. Like all French "classics", cassoulet has a legion of "genuine" interpretations. This stick-in-the-ribs concoction, widely available, is the very antithesis of junk food: this is mother's cooking, an icon of the simple life, a dish of white haricot beans, Toulouse sausage, preserved duck and belly pork.

The first "champagne"

Blanquette de Limoux, a sparkling white wine, was "invented" long before champagne. The first reference to blanquette – the Occitan word for "white" – appears in papers written by Benedictine monks in 1531 at the abbey of Sainte-Hilaire. They write of the production and distribution of Saint-Hilaire's blanquette in cork-stoppered flasks.

Local folklore asserts that Dom Pérignon invented sparkling white wine while serving in the abbey, before leaving for the Champagne region and popularising the drink.

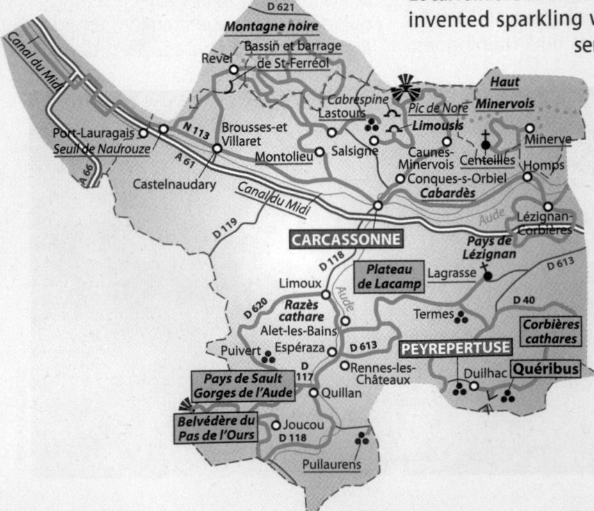

Statue of a Cathar cavalier in Avignonet-Lauragais

M.-H. Carcanague/MICHELIN

The Cathar story

The "country of the Cathars", le Pays Cathare, is widespread and spans more than one *département*, from Toulouse in the west to Carcassonne and Béziers in the east, and as far north as the town of Albi in Tarn.

Catharism (see *INTRODUCTION*) was a religious movement originating around the middle of the 10C, branded heretical by the Roman Catholic Church. It existed throughout much of Western Europe, but its home was in Languedoc and its surrounding areas in southern France. Cathar society was divided into two general categories, the **Perfecti** (Perfects) and the **Credentes** (Believers). The Perfecti were the core of the movement, though the actual number of Perfecti in Cathar society was always relatively small. Catharism was above all a popular religion and included a sizeable portion of the population of Languedoc, counting among them many noble families and courts.

Catharism was a break-away religion from the Catholic church of Rome, and its success and popularity aroused the Papacy's anger. The result was a crusade with a deadly mission, to exterminate the Cathars and all their believers. The army of crusaders, known as the *ost* was vast and powerful. Their most ignoble and inglorious moment came in 1209, as they lay siege to the city of **Béziers**. Folly on the part of some inhabitants led to soldiers of the Crusade entering the city, wreaking havoc. But, faced with hesitation on the part of some crusaders to commit the horrific acts being performed in the name of the church, Arnaud-Amaury, abbot of Cîteaux, is reported to have instructed "Kill them all! God will know his own."

It is not known how many Cathars and their followers died. Some put the estimate at well over a million. And though the sect is believed to have been exterminated, there is evidence that it still exists today.

View of four Cathar castles known as the Châteaux de Lastours

E. Larribère/MICHELIN

Carcassonne ★★★

A visit to fortified Carcassonne, a UNESCO World Heritage site, is a return to the Middle Ages. On Bastille Day (14 July) a dramatic fireworks display makes the dramatic citadel seem to go up in flames. The romantic old town contrasts sharply with the commercial Ville Basse (lower town), a *bastide* town, where Carcassonne shows off its role as the centre of the Aude *département's* wine-growing industry.

- **Population:** 43 950.
- **Michelin Map:** 344: F-3.
- **Info:** 28 rue de Verdun, 11000 Carcassonne, ✆04 68 10 24 30. www.carcassonne-tourisme.com. 20min guided tour of the ramparts by miniature railway – May-Sep, departs Pte Narbonnaise: 10am-noon, 2-6pm. 7€ (children: 3€). ✆04 68 24 45 70.
- **Location:** 96km/60mi SE of Toulouse, 60km/37.5mi W of Narbonne.
- **Don't Miss:** The "Cité", Basilique St-Nazaire.

A BIT OF HISTORY

Carcassonne commands the main communication route between the Mediterranean and Toulouse. For 400 years, Carcassonne remained the capital of a county, then of a viscountcy under the suzerainty of the counts of Toulouse. After the annexation of Roussillon under the Treaty of the Pyrenees, Carcassonne's military importance dwindled to almost nil, as some 200km/125mi separated it from the new border, guarded by Perpignan. Carcassonne was abandoned and left to decay until the Romantic movement brought the Middle Ages back into fashion.

Prosper Mérimée, appointed general inspector of Historical Monuments, celebrated the ruins in his travel memoir, *Notes d'un voyage dans le Midi de la France – 1835*. Local archaeologist Jean-Pierre Cros-Mayrevieille was passionately committed to the restoration of his native town. After visiting Carcassonne, **Viollet-le-Duc** returned to Paris with such an enthusiastic report that the Commission of Historical Monuments agreed to undertake the restoration of the Cité in 1844.

LA CITÉ★★★ WALK

The "Cité" of Carcassonne on the Aude's east bank is the largest fortress in Europe. It consists of a fortified nucleus, the Château Comtal, and a double curtain wall: the outer ramparts, with 14 towers, separated from the inner ramparts (24 towers) by the outer bailey, or lists *(lices)*. A resident population of 139 and school and post office saves Carcassonne from becoming a ghost town.

Aerial view of Carcassonne

P. Blot/MICHELIN

Leave the car in one of the car parks outside the walls in front of the gateway to the east, Porte Narbonnaise.
2hr Tour of the ramparts aboard a **tourist train** *(open May-Sep tours (25min, leaving from the Porte Narbonnaise) with explanation of the defence system 10am-noon, 2-6pm; 7€ (children 3€) 04 68 24 45 70) or a* **horse-drawn carriage** *(open Apr to Nov: discovery of the ramparts in a caleche (20min), with historical commentary. 7€ (children 4€). Route de la Cavayère, Montlegun, Carcassonne. 04 68 71 54 57 – www.carcassonne-caleches.com.*

Porte Narbonnaise

On either side of the gateway to the original fortified town are two massive Narbonne towers, and between them, a 13C statue of the Virgin Mary. Inside, the 13C rooms restored by Viollet-le-Duc house **temporary exhibitions** of modern art.

Rue Cros-Mayrevieille

This street leads directly to the castle, although you might prefer to get there by wandering the narrow winding streets of the medieval town, with its many crafts and souvenir shops.

Château Comtal

Apr-Sep 10am-6.30pm; Oct-Mar 9.30am-5pm. Closed 1 Jan, 1 May, 1 and 11 Nov, 25 Dec. 7.50€, no charge 1st Sunday in the month from Nov-Mar. 04 68 11 70 72. www.monum.fr.

The castle was originally the palace of the viscounts built in the 12C by Bernard Aton Trencavel. It became a citadel after Carcassonne was made part of the royal estate in 1226. Since the reign of St Louis IX, it has been defended by a large semicircular barbican and formidable moat.

The tour begins on the first floor, now an archaeological museum (**Musée lapidaire**). This museum exhibits archaeological remains from the fortified town and local region, including a 12C marble lavabo from the abbey of Lagrasse, late 15C stone **calvary**★ from Villanière and the recumbent figure of a knight killed in battle. A collection of prints shows the fortified town as it was before Viollet-le-Duc's restoration.

Cour d'honneur – The buildings surrounding the large main courtyard have been restored.

The building to the south has an interesting façade reflecting its three periods of construction: Romanesque, Gothic and Renaissance.

Cour du Midi – The tallest of the fortress' watchtowers, the Tour de Guet, affords a view of up to 30km/19mi away.

Leave the castle and follow rue de la Porte d'Aude on the left.

Porte d'Aude

A fortified path, the Montée d'Aude, weaves from the church of St-Gimer up to this heavily defended gateway. The west and north sections of the outer bailey are called the **"lices basses"**. The **Tour de l'Inquisition** was the seat of the Inquisitor's court, and its central pillar with chains and cell bear witness to the tortures inflicted upon heretics. The Bishop's **Tour carrée de l'Évêque** was appointed much more comfortably.

Return towards the Porte d'Aude and continue along the Lices Basses.

The itinerary takes you past the **Tour de la Justice**. The Trencavels, protectors of the Cathars, sought refuge here with the count of Toulouse during the Albigensian Crusade. This circular tower has windows whose tilting wooden shutters enabled those inside to see (and drop things on) attackers.

Walk beneath the drawbridge by the Porte Narbonnaise and continue SE.

The "lices hautes"

The wide gap between the inner and outer ramparts, edged with moats, was used for weapons practice and jousting. Beyond Porte Narbonnaise, note the three-storey Tour de la Vade on the outer curtain wall to the left. This fortified tower kept watch over all of the

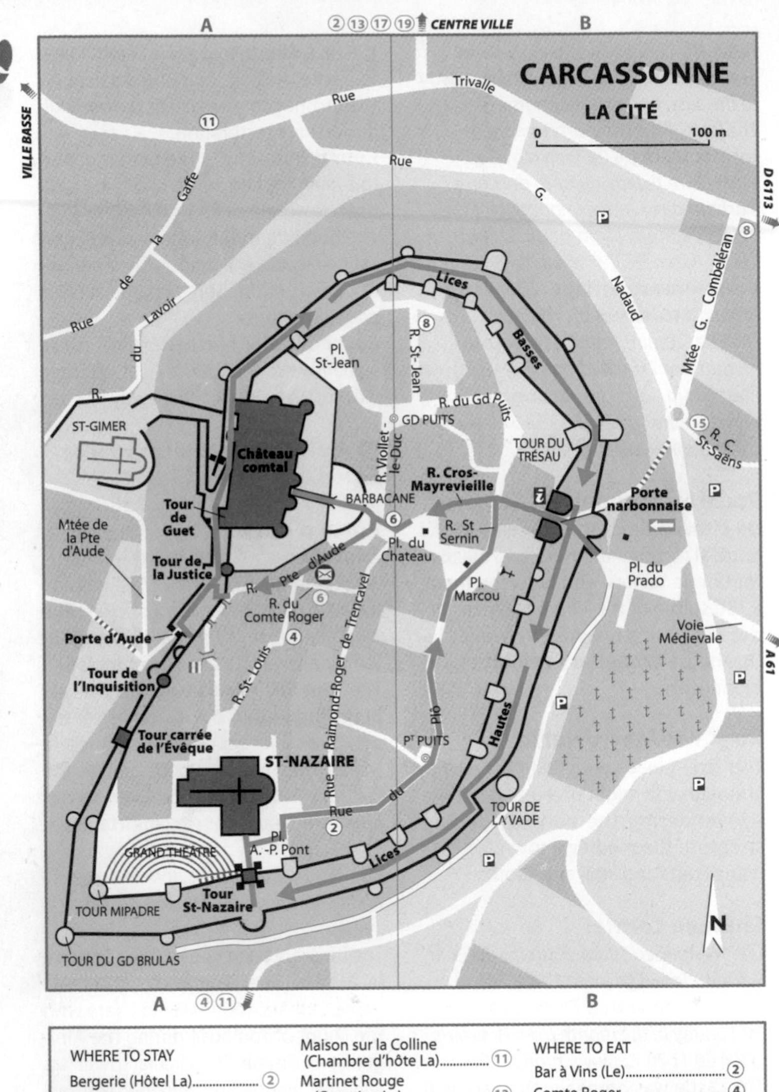

WHERE TO STAY		WHERE TO EAT
Bergerie (Hôtel La) ... ②	Maison sur la Colline (Chambre d'hôte La) ... ⑪	Bar à Vins (Le) ... ②
Château (Auberge du) ... ④	Martinet Rouge (Camping Le) ... ⑬	Comte Roger ... ④
Donjon et les Remparts (Hôtel) ... ⑥	Montmorency (Hôtel) ... ⑮	Dame Carcas (Auberge de) ... ⑥
Espace Cité (Hôtel) ... ⑧	Olivette (Chambre d'hôte L') ... ⑰	Marquière (La) ... ⑧
	St-Martin (Hostellerie) ... ⑲	Tête de l'Art (La) ... ⑪

eastern ramparts. Carry on to the Tour du Grand Brulas, on the corner opposite the Tour Mipadre.

Tour St-Nazaire

This tower's postern was only accessible by ladders. A well and an oven are still in evidence on the first floor. At the top of the tower is a viewing table.

Enter the Cité through the Porte St-Nazaire

Basilique St-Nazaire★

All that remains of the original church is the Romanesque nave. The basilica's **stained-glass windows★★** (13C-14C) are considered the most impressive in the south of France. Remarkable

statues★★ adorn the pillars around the chancel walls, and one of the most eye-catching bishops' tombs is that of Pierre de Roquefort (14C).

Return to the Porte Narbonnaise via rue du Plô.

ADDITIONAL SIGHTS

Musée des Beaux-Arts

1 rue de Verdun. Entrance: sq Gambetta. Open mid Jun-mid Sep 10am-6pm; mid Sep-mid Jun daily except Sun (other than 1st Sun in month) 10am-noon, 2-6pm. Closed public holidays. No charge. 04 68 77 73 70.

On display are 17C and 18C paintings of French, Flemish and Dutch masters, and faïence from Moustiers, Marseille and elsewhere. Works of Carcassonne painter Jacques Gamelin (1738-1803) add local interest. Note Chardin's *Les Apprêts d'un déjeuner*. Works by Courbet and other artists from the French Academy represent 19C painting.

Maison des Mémoires Joë-Bousquet

53 rue de Verdun. Open daily except Sun, Mon and Public holidays 9am-noon, 2-6pm. No charge. 04 68 72 50 83.

Paralysed during World War II, Joë Bousquet lived in this house from 1918 to 1950 and never left his closed-shutter first floor bedroom. Here he wrote his poetry and letters and received the famous writers and artists of his time – André Gide, Paul Valéry, Aragon, Michaux, Paul Éluard and Max Ernst. He founded the Carcassonne Group with two local writers and published articles in the literary magazine *Cahiers du Sud*.

DRIVING TOUR

1 CABARDÈS REGION★

Round trip from Carcassonne. Local map see la Montagne Noire. Leave Carcassonne along N 113 towards Castelnaudary. After Pezens, turn right onto D 629.

Montolieu★

This village in the Cabardès region is devoted to the world of books, with 20 or so bookshops, craft workshops (bookbinder's, copyist's, engraver's) and a **Conservatoire des Arts et Métiers du livre** dedicated to book design and production. *(open Apr-Dec 10am-noon, 2-6pm (Sun 2-6pm); Jan-Mar 2-5pm. Closed 1 Jan, 1 May and 25 Dec. 1.50€. 04 68 24 80 04).*

A small road (D 64) S of the village leads to Villelongue Abbey.

Ancienne Abbaye de Villelongue

Open Easter-Oct daily except Mon (other than Jul-Aug) 10am-noon, 2-6.30pm (Sat 6pm). 4€. Closed Nov-Apr. 04 68 76 92 58. www.abbaye-de-villelongue.com.

This old abbey church was built to a Cistercian design and was rebuilt in the late 13C and early 14C. It's interesting for its refectory with ribbed vaulting, the south gallery of the cloisters and its chapter-house.

D 164 on the right leads to Saissac.

Saissac

This village high over the Vernassonne ravine is shadowed by the ruins of a 14C castle. The largest tower in the old curtain wall affords a beautiful panorama of the site and houses **Musée des Vieux Métiers** *(temporarily closed). 04 68 24 47 80)* on the history and traditional crafts of Saissac.

Drive E along D 103.

Brousses-et-Villaret

An 18C **paper mill** manufactures paper the traditional way and its **Gutenberg Museum** *(open Jul-Aug guided tours (1hr) on the hour from 11am to 6pm; Sep 11am, 2.30pm, 3.30pm, 4.30pm and 5.30pm; Oct-Jun Mon-Fri 11am and 3.30pm, weekends and school holidays 11am, 2.30pm, 3.30pm, 4.30pm and 5.30pm. closed 1 Jan and 25 Dec. 6€. 04 68 26 67 43)* relates the history of printing techniques.

Continue on D 103 to D 118 and turn right. Beyond Cuxac-Cabardès, turn right onto D 73, follow D 9.

Mas-Cabardès

The ruins of a fortified castle tower over this village and its picturesque narrow streets. Near the **church** belfry topped by a 15C octagonal tower of Romanesque appearance, look for a 16C stone cross carved with a shuttle, emblem of weavers who worked in the Orbiel valley.

Drive S along D 101.

Châteaux de Lastours★

Departure from the village centre, at the "Accueil Village". Open Jul-Aug 9am-8pm; Apr-Jun 9am-6pm; Sep 10am-6pm; Oct 10am-5pm; Nov-Mar Sat-Sun and school holidays 10am-5pm. Closed Jan and 25 Dec. 4€. 04 68 77 56 02.

The ruins of four castles stand out in this rugged rocky landscape between the Orbiel and Grésillou valleys. The **Cabaret**, Tour Régine, Fleur d'Espine and Quertinheux castles comprised the Cabaret fortress in the 12C. Cathar refugees sought protection at Cabaret, which resisted every attack. For an exquisite **view** of the Châteaux de Lastours ruins, drive up to the viewpoint on the opposite side of Grésillou valley.

Follow D 701 to Salsigne.

Salsigne

Mining has given a livelihood to this area long before Roman and Saracen invaders extracted iron, copper, lead and silver here. After gold was discovered in 1892, mining concessions grew up at Salsigne, Lastours and Villanière. 92t of gold, 240t of silver and 30 000t of copper has been extracted since 1924.

From Salsigne, follow the signs to the Grotte de Limousis.

Grotte de Limousis

Open Jul-Aug guided tours (departing every 45min) 10.15am-6pm; Mar-Oct 2.30pm, 3.30pm, 4.30pm and 5.30pm (Apr-Jun and Sep also at 10.30am and 11.30am); Nov Sun and public holidays 2.30pm, 3.30pm and 4.30pm. Closed rest of year. 8€ (children 4€). 04 68 77 50 26.

Discovered in 1811, this cave is set in an arid, bare limestone countryside of vines and olive trees. The cave's chambers extend for 663m/2 179ft with curiously shaped concretions alternating with mirrors of limpid water. An enormous **chandelier★** of white aragonite crystals is the main feature of the cave.

Return on D 511 to D 111 and there, follow the signs to Villeneuve-Minervois. Go through the village, which earns a living mainly from wine-growing, and take D 112 towards Cabrespine.

Gorges de la Clamoux

These gorges show the striking contrast between the two slopes of Montagne Noire. The road traverses the floor of the valley and its orchards and vineyards as far as Cabrespine.

Take the small road on the left which climbs steeply to the Gouffre de Cabrespine.

Gouffre de Cabrespine

Open Jul-Aug guided tours (45min) 10am-6.30pm; Apr-Jun and Sep-Oct 10.30am, 11.30am, 2.30pm, 3.30pm, 4.30pm and 5.30pm; Nov-mid Dec and mid Feb-Mar 2pm-5.30pm. Closed rest of year. 8€ (children 4€). 04 68 26 14 22.

The upper part of this gigantic chasm is a huge network of subterranean galleries drained by the River Clamoux. The "Salle des Éboulis" (chamber of fallen earth) is 250m/820ft high. Follow the balconied walkway through stalactites and stalagmites, dazzling curtains of aragonite crystals, the "Salles Rouges" (red galleries) and the "Salle aux Cristaux" (crystal gallery).

Return to D 112. The road reaches Cabrespine, overlooked by Roc de l'Aigle, then winds up hairpin bends between chestnut groves. At Pradelles-Cabardès, take D 87 to the right towards the Pic de Nore.

Pic de Nore★

Montagne Noire's highest point, the Pic de Nore (*1 211m/3 973ft*), towers over the undulating heath-covered countryside. The **panorama★** stretches from the Lacaune, Espinouse and Corbières mountains, to Canigou, the Carlit massif and Midi de Bigorre.

Return to Pradelles-Cabardès and turn left onto D 89 towards Castans then right onto D 620 towards Caunes-Minervois.

Lespinassière

Built on an isolated peak inside a mountain cirque, Lespinassière has a towering castle with an impressive 15C square tower.

Gorges de l'Argent-Double

The River Argent-Double, which springs up near Col de la Salette, flows through a deep and sinuous gorge.

Caunes-Minervois

The village is known for its grey and white-veined red marble quarried nearby. In the 18C, this marble was used to decorate the Grand Trianon in Versailles, the Palais Garnier in Paris and the St-Sernin Basilica in Toulouse.

Two fine mansions dominate the town hall square: Hôtel Sicard (14C) and **Hôtel d'Alibert** (16C). The **abbey church** (*open Jul-Aug 10am-7pm; Apr-Jun, Sep-Oct 10am-noon, 2-6pm; Nov-Mar 10am-noon, 2-5pm; closed 1 Jan, 24, 25, 30 and 31 Dec. 4.50€. 04 68 78 09 44*) of the former Benedictine abbey has retained its 11C Romanesque east end.

Drive SW along D 620. Beyond Villegly, turn right onto D 35.

Conques-sur-Orbiel

This pretty village has traces of its earlier fortifications, including the 16C south gateway and the church belfry-porch.

ADDRESSES

STAY

Camping Le Martinet Rouge – *11390 Brousses-et-Villaret 04 68 26 51 98 – open 24 May-6 Sep – reservations advised for Jul-Aug – 35 places.* In a fabulous setting in the Montagne Noire. Swimming pool.

Hôtel Espace Cité – *132 r. Trivalle – 04 68 25 24 24 – infos@hotelespacecite.com – 48rms.* Modern hotel at the foot of the citadel, with bright and functional rooms, warm welcome, and breakfast buffet.

Hôtel Montmorency – *2 r. Camille -St-Saens 04 68 11 96 70 – www.hotelduchateau.net – – reservation advised in summer –20rms – 7€.* Close to La Cité. Very smart rooms, well furnished, but simple.

Chambre d'hôte L'Olivette – *R. Pierre-Duhem, 11160 Cabrespine 04 68 26 19 25 – 3rms.* Charming simplicity; located not far from the gouffre de Cabrespine. Table d'Hôte by arrangement.

Auberge du Château – *Château de Cavanac, 11570 Cavanac 04 68 79 61 04 – www.chateau-de-cavanac.fr – closed Jan-Feb and 2 wks in Nov – 24rms – 12€ – rest* . Beautiful rooms with view over vineyard; fine restaurant serving own wines.

Chambre d'hôte La Maison sur la Colline – *Lieu-dit Ste-Croix – 04 68 47 57 94 – closed 1 Dec-15 Feb – reservation recommended in summer – 5rms.* This restored farm has a spectacular hillside view of the Cité from its garden. Rooms are spacious and colourful. Breakfast by the pool in summer.

Hôtel La Bergerie – *Allée Pech-Marie, 11600 Aragon 04 68 26 10 65 – www.labergeriearagon.com – – 8rms – 10€ – rest.* . In a lovely village; rooms have views over vineyard. Cuisine and wines of the region.

⊜⊜⊜⊜ **Hôtel Le Donjon and les Remparts** – *2 r. du Comte-Roger ℘04 68 11 23 00 – www.bestwestern.com – P – 62 rms.* This hotel combining old stonework and renovated decor occupies part of a 15C orphanage at the heart of the Cité. Rustic style or modern rooms, and a brasserie.

EAT

⊜ **Le Bar à Vins** – *6 r. du Plo. ℘04 68 47 38 38 – closed Nov-Feb.* In the heart of the medieval Cité, this wine bar's shady garden has a view of the St-Nazaire basilica. Tapas and fast food.

⊜⊜ **La Tête de l'Art** – *37 bis r. Trivalle ℘04 68 47 36 36 – closed Sun in winter – reservation recommended at weekends.* This restaurant specialising in pork dishes, also exhibits works of modern painting and sculpture.

⊜⊜ **Auberge de Dame Carcas** – *3 pl. du Château ℘04 68 71 23 23 – closed Jan, noon and Wed.* This popular establishment in the medieval Cité has a generous menu and dining rooms on four levels.

⊜⊜ **La Marquière** – *13 r. St-Jean ℘04 68 71 52 00 – closed Wed and Thu.* Roughcast building near northern ramparts. Serves traditional cuisine.

⊜⊜⊜ **Comte Roger** – *14 r. St-Louis ℘04 68 11 93 40 – www.comteroger.com – closed Sun and Mon.* Your stroll through La Cité may well lead you to this sheltered spot.

EVENTS

Spectacles médiévaux "Carcassonne, terre d'histoire" – *Aug*: Medieval festival.
Tournois de chevalerie – *Aug*: Jousting tournament.

Les Corbières★★

Corbières is best known for its ruined castles and its wine, and a massif landscape showered with luminous Mediterranean light. The spiny sweet-smelling *garrigue* covers much of the countryside.

- **Info:** ℘04 68 45 69 40. www.corbières-sauvages.com.
- **Location:** Bounded on the S by the N117 between Perpignan and Quillan, on the W by the D118 between Quillan and Carcassonne, to the N by the A61 between Carcassonne and Narbonne, and to the E by the A9 linking Perpignan.
- **Don't Miss:** The chateaux de Peyrepertuse, *Quéribus and Puilaurens*
- **Kids:** Cathar castles and Cucugnan's "Pocket" Theatre de poche.

A BIT OF HISTORY

Vines have overgrown the area east of the Orbieu and around Limoux, the region producing sparkling white *blanquette*. The **Corbières** has recently been awarded the *Appellation d'Origine Contrôlée* for its fruity, full-bodied wines (mainly red, some white and rosé) with bouquets evocative of local flora.

The region's widely differing soil types produce a variety of grapes – Carignan, Cinsaut and Grenache, making any *dégustation* tour a real voyage of discovery. The red wines of neighbouring **Fitou**, also an *Appellation d'Origine Contrôlée*, are dark and robust with a hint of spiciness.

Many local villages have their own wine cooperatives (*cave coopérative*) and encourage customers to taste their wares, but private producers often require reservations, which makes having a wine guide listing telephone numbers quite useful.

DRIVING TOURS

CATHAR CASTLES★★

1 ROUND-TRIP FROM DUILHAC-SOUS-PEYREPERTUSE

117km/73mi – allow an overnight stopover.

Magnificent castles and castle ruins, including the "Five Sons of Carcassonne," dot the Corbières landscape. These vertiginous feudal fortresses sheltered Cathars fleeing from the Inquisition.

Duilhac-sous-Peyrepertuse
Leaving the upper town to the north, note the village fountain fed by a bursting spring.

Château de Peyrepertuse★★★
See Château de PEYREPERTUSE.

Return to Duilhac; drive to Cucugnan.

Cucugnan
This pretty village is well known from the tale of *Le Sermon du curé de Cucugnan* adapted into French by Alphonse Daudet in the second half of the 19C. The tiny Achille-Mir theatre on place du Platane hosts a virtual theatre performance on the theme of this tale. (*open Jul-Aug 10am-8.30pm; Nov-Dec 10am-6pm; Feb 10am-6.30pm; Mar 10am-7pm; Apr-Jun and Sep 10am-8pm; Oct 10am-7.30pm. closed in Jan (except school holidays), 1 Jan and 25 Dec. 5€ (ticket combined with the château de Quéribus); children 6-15 years, 3€. 04 68 45 03 69).*

Continue along D 14.

Padern
20min on foot round-trip.
Be careful; the ruins are dangerous in places. To reach the castle, follow the yellow-marked "sentier cathare."
The Château de Padern, owned by the abbots of Lagrasse until 1579, was completely rebuilt in the 17C. You can see the remains of a round tower, leading to the upper part of the keep (now in ruins) and fine views of the village and the River Verdouble.

Cucugnan and its vineyards
E. Larribére/MICHELIN

At end of D 14, turn left onto D 611.

Tuchan
This town is a production centre for Fitou wines (AOC). The picturesque D 39 winds through the Tuchan valley.

East of Tuchan, a surfaced path going through vineyards branches off D 39 to the left and leads to Aguilar Castle.

Château d'Aguilar
10min on foot from the parking area. Enter the enclosure from the SW.
On the orders of the king of France the Château d'Aguilar fortress was reinforced in the 13C, with a hexagonal curtain wall flanked by six reinforced round towers. The wall and a Romanesque chapel remain intact.

Return to Tuchan and turn right onto D 611 to Durban.

Durban-Corbières
The castle overlooking the village includes a crenellated rectangular two-storey building with 13C twin bays and 16C mullioned windows, as well as remains of curtain walls and towers.

Drive W out of Durban along D 40.

Villerouge-Termenès

At the heart of the medieval village stands the (12C-14C) **castle** flanked by four towers which was owned by the bishops of Narbonne and in 1321 witnessed the burning at the stake of the last Cathar Parfait, Guilhem Bélibaste. Audio-visual exhibits describe Bélibaste's life and works and the daily life of medieval Villerouge and its inhabitants.

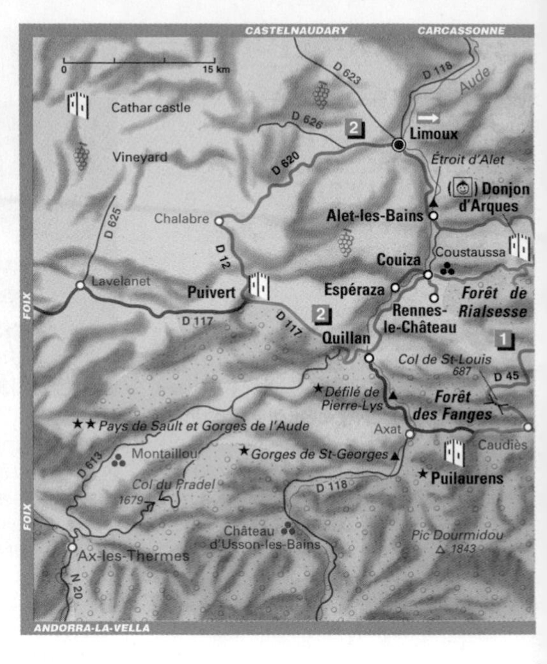

Enjoy views of the village and its surroundings from the sentry walk. Every summer Villerouge re-enacts medieval banquets and various activities evocative of life in medieval Languedoc (*Open Jul-Aug 10am-7.30pm; Apr-Jun and Sep-mid Oct 10am-1pm, 2-6pm; mid-Oct-Mar Sat-Sun, public holidays and school holidays 10am-5pm. Closed Jan. 6€. 04 68 70 09 11).*

Follow D 613 SW of Villerouge to Col de Bedos then turn right onto D 40.

Col de Bedos

Bedos Pass is located on D 40, a **ridge road**★ winding through wooded ravines. From the dip formed by the lower gorge of the Sou, see the ruins of the Château de Termes.

Château de Termes

Open Jul-Aug 9.30am-7.30pm; Apr-Jun and Sep-Oct 10am-6pm; Mar and Nov-Dec Sat-Sun, public and school holidays, 10am-5pm. Closed Jan-Feb. 3.50€. 04 68 70 09 20. www.chateau-termes.com. Leave the car at the foot of the hill, beyond the bridge. 30min on foot round-trip; follow a steep track up then climb a succession of tiers that mark the curtain walls.

The castle held by Cathar Raymond de Termes succumbed to Simon de Montfort after a four month siege (August to November 1210) during the first stage of the Albigensian Crusade. The site on the promontory defended by the natural trench of the Sou valley (Terminet gorge) is more interesting than the fortress ruins, offering good views of the **Terminet gorge** from near the northwest postern (*dangerous slopes*) and top of the rock.

Return to Col de Bedos and turn right onto D 613.

Laroque-de-Fâ

The village watered by the Sou occupies a picturesque site on a fortified spur.

Beyond Mouthoumet, as you reach Orbieu bridge, turn left onto D 212 and drive past the ruins of Auriac Castle.
In Soulatgé, turn right onto D 14 to Cubières. Turn left onto D 45 just before Bugarach.

Pic de Bugarach

The rugged Bugarach summit (*alt 1 230m/4 030ft*) is visible from the virtually deserted valleys surrounding it. The ascent to the Col du Linas, winding

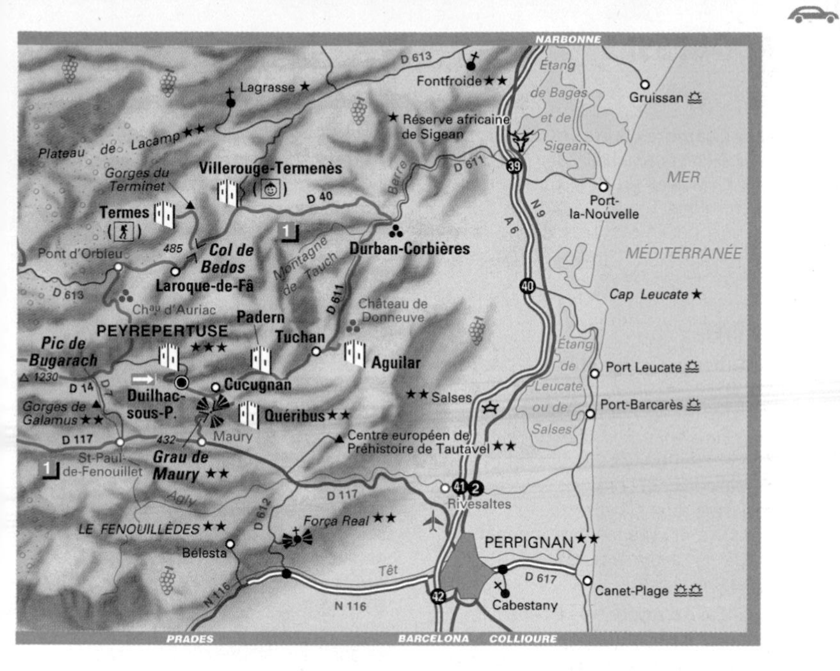

through the upper Agly valley, is particularly impressive.

Turn left onto D 46 before St-Louis, it leads to D 9 heading for Caudiès-de-Fenouillèdes.

Forêt domaniale des Fanges

This forest massif covers 1 184ha/2 924 acres and shelters exceptional Aude firs. The **Col de St-Louis** (*alt 687m/2 253ft*) is a good departure point for ramblers (rocky, often very uneven ground).

Drive on to Caudiès and turn right onto D 117 to Lapradelle.

From Lapradelle, take the small road S (D 22) and then the uphill road to the right 800m/875yd beyond Puilaurens.

Château de Puilaurens★

Open Jul-Aug 9am-8pm; Apr-Jun and Sep 10am-6pm; Oct 10am-5pm; Feb, Mar and early Nov Sat-Sun and school holidays 10am-5pm. 3.50€. 04 68 20 65 26. Leave the car and continue on foot; 30min round-trip. Closed in bad weather.

The castle high above the upper Aude Valley, with its crenellated curtain wall, four towers and projecting battlements, is impregnable from the north and remains more or less intact.

Rejoin D 117 and turn right to Maury then left onto D 19.

Grau de Maury★★

From this little pass, the southern gateway to the Corbières, is a fine panorama of mountain chains and the jagged ridge overlooking the dip formed by the Fenouillèdes to the south.

A steep narrow road to the right leads up from the Grau de Maury to the ruined fortress of Quéribus.

Château de Quéribus★★

See Château de QUÉRIBUS.

Head back to Cucugnan and turn left onto D 14 to return to Duilhac.

2 RAZÈS REGION

120km/75mi round-trip from Limoux.
See LIMOUX: Driving Tours.

ADDRESSES

STAY

Chambre d'hôte Les Ginestous – *11330 Palairac – 12km/7.5mi N of Tuchan on D 39 ℘04 68 45 01 24 – closed 1 Nov-Easter – 4rms.* This little house by the village fountain offers rustic style rooms, a sunny breakfast terrace and regional cuisine.

EAT

Auberge du Vigneron – *2 R. Achille-Mir, 11350 Cucugnan ℘04 68 45 03 00 – closed 13 Nov-28 Feb, Mon noon in Jul-Aug; Sun evening and Mon.* This village house offers guests the delights of simple cooking, Corbières wine and cosy little rooms. The restaurant occupies an old wine shop, opening onto a fine summer terrace with mountain views.

Cave d'Agnès – *29 R Gilbert-Salamo, 11510 Fitou ℘04 68 45 75 91 – closed 16 Nov-14 Mar, Thu noon and Wed – reservations required.* This resoundingly popular restaurant occupies an old barn at the top of the village. The food is fit for a king and the setting is authentic.

Le Merle Bleu – *Pl. de l'Église, 11350 Paziols ℘04 68 45 02 48 – reservations required.* Tucked at the top of the village, this little restaurant serving Mediterranean family cuisine offers a good view of the Château d'Aguilar from the terrace. Claude Nougaro's poem about the restaurant can be read on the menu.

CATHAR SITES

Centre d'Études Cathares – *Maison des Mémoires, 53 r. de Verdun, BP 197, 11004 Carcassonne Cedex ℘04 68 47 24 66 – www.cathares.org.* Research and information centre on Cathar history; open to the public.

Carte intersites – This card gives reductions on visits to 16 Cathar sites: the châteaux of Lastours, Arques, Quéribus, Puilaurens, Termes, Villerouge-Termenès, Saissac, Peyrepertuse, Usson, the Château comtal de Carcassonne, the abbeys of Caunes-Minervois, Saint-Papoul, Saint-Hilaire, Lagrasse, Fontfroide and the Musée du Quercorb in Puivert. It also gives free admission for one child. It is on sale at all the sites for 4€.

"Pays Cathare" – This is a trademark acquired by the Conseil Général de l'Aude. The logo guarantees the authenticity and the "extra" quality of the certified food products, hotels and restaurants.

Lagrasse

On the shores of the River Orbieu, the town owes its existence to its majestic abbey. An outpost of the Carolingian civilisation near Frankish Catalonia, the abbey's fortifications were added in the 14C and its embellishments added in the 18C. See the 11C humpback bridge and covered market.

- **Info:** 6 bd. de la Promenade, 11220 Lagrasse ℘04 68 43 11 56. www.lagrasse.com.
- **Location:** 42km/26.25mi SW of Narbonne. The D 212 from Fabrézan offers a sweeping view of the fortified town's bridges, ramparts, historical houses and abbey.
- **Don't Miss:** A walk along the Orbieu River.

MEDIEVAL CITY WALK

Enter the walled town via Porte du Consulat and follow the street of the same name before turning left onto Rue Paul-Vergnes. The old medieval city developed around the monastery. Stroll the narrow streets lined with medieval houses where craftsmen have set up workshops.

Église Saint-Michel

This Gothic church is flanked by nine side chapels. Note the keystones decorated with the guilds' symbols.

Lagrasse church bell-tower
D. Pazery/MICHELIN

Retrace your steps and turn left onto rue de l'Église; cross place de la Bouquerie; follow rue des Mazels.

Place de la Halle

The 14C covered market has 10 stone pillars supporting a timber framework. Medieval façades, some half-timbered, surround the square (note the 14C **Maison Maynard**). See the 16C Maison Sibra in Rue Foy, then follow Rue des Deux-Ponts to **Pont Vieux**, for access to the abbey.

ABBAYE SAINTE-MARIE-D'ORBIEU

45min Open Jul-Sep 10am-6pm; Apr-Jun and Oct 10.30am-11.30am, 2-5pm; Feb-Mar and Nov-mid Dec 10-11.30am, 2-6pm. 3.50€. 04 68 43 15 99.

The **abbot's chapel★** contains rare late-14C ceramic paving and traces of mural paintings. The Palais Vieux includes the oldest parts of the abbey. A lapidary museum displays fragments from the original cloisters. The lower level contains cellars, store rooms and bakery. The **Cloisters** were built in 1760 on the site of the visible remains of the 1280 cloisters. The 13C abbey church was built on the foundations of a Carolingian church. The 40m/131ft bell-tower built in 1537 affords an attractive view from the top.

EXCURSION

Plateau de Lacamp★★

27km/17mi SW along D 23 and D 212.

Between Caunette-sur-Lauquet and Lairière, the Louviéro Pass on D 40 gives access to the "forest track" of the western Corbières. The Plateau de Lacamp, with an average altitude of 700m/2 300ft, forms a breakwater towards the Orbieu. The track runs along the southern edge of the causse for about 3km/2mi, with sweeping **views** of the Orbieu valley, the Bugarach and Canigou peaks, St-Barthélemy, the threshold of the Lauragais and the Montagne Noire.

ADDRESSES

STAY

Hôtel Fargo – *11220 St-Pierre-des-Champs – 04 68 43 12 78 – www.lafargo.fr – closed 16 Nov-26 Mar – P – 6 rms – 6€ – restaurant .* This former catalan forge in a magnificent wooded park along the riverbank, is renovated with Colonial style furnishings. Warm welcome.

Chambre d'hôte La Bastide de Donos – *11200 Thézan-des-Corbières 04 68 43 32 11 – www.chateaudonos.com – 4 rms and 2 suites.* Offers superb view of the chateau and the old washing place. On site wine tasting. Access to private lake for swimming and boating.

EAT

Hostellerie des Corbières – *9 Ave. de la Promenade – 04 68 43 15 22 – closed 1 Dec-1Feb and Tues except July-Aug – 6 rms – 6€ – restaurant .* This pleasant small house in the heart of town has renovated, well-equipped rooms. The dining room terrace embraces a landscape of vines, olive trees and *garriques.* Traditional cuisine.

Lézignan-Corbières

Halfway between Carcassonne and the sea, Lézignan-Corbières relies on wine-growing and the Corbières wine trade. Promenades lined with plane trees, tiny squares and alleyways surround the church of St-Félix.

Info: 9 pl. de la République, 11200 Lézignan-Corbières, ℘04 68 27 05 42.

Location: 42km/26.25 mi SW of Narbonne and 51km/32mi SW of Carcassonne via 61. A exit n° 25, follow the D 611 to Fabrezan, then the D 212.

Don't Miss: A stroll by the River Orbieu and the Ste-Marie d'Orbieu Abbey

Kids: Education tours organised by the Musée de la Vigne et du Vin de Lézignan.

VISIT

Musée de la Vigne et du Vin

Open 9am-7pm. 5.50€. ℘04 68 27 07 57.

This vine and wine museum in an old vineyard has a saddle room, stables, winepress and displays of traditional cooper's tools. Also displayed are vats for treading grapes, swing-ploughs, pruning shears, grafting knives, back-baskets, wooden tubs, branding irons and the like.

DRIVING TOUR

Lézignan Region

49km/30mi round tour; about 1hr

From Lézignan drive along D 24 to Ornaisons then turn right onto D 123.

Gasparets

Espace Octaviana houses the **Musée de la Faune** (*open 9.30am-noon, 2-6pm. Closed Mon (Oct-May), 1 Jan, 25 Dec. 5€ (children 2€). ℘04 68 27 57 02)*, displaying preserved birds of prey, golden pheasant, capercaillie and crested eagle and more common species, as well as the Pyrenean brown bear and wild boars.

D 61, D 161 and D 611 via Boutenac and Ferrals lead to Fabrezan.

Fabrezan

In this picturesque village overlooks the stony Orbieu Valley. The **Musée in** the town hall (*open daily except Sat-Sun and public holidays 9am-noon, 2-6pm. No charge. ℘04 68 27 81 44)*, celebrates local inventor **Charles-Cros**.

Take D 212, then D 111 on the left towards Moux. Before the village, turn right towards Lézignan. At Conilhac, take D 165 on the left.

The road climbs a hill to the **Montbrun-des-Corbières** vineyard spread out below. Continue towards Escales, with a brief stop at the Romanesque chapel of **Notre-Dame-de-Colombier**.

D 127 and D 611 lead back to Lézignan.

ADDRESSES

STAY

Chambre d'hôte M. and Mme Tenenbaum – *5 Ave. du Minervois, 11700 Azillé ℘04 68 91 56 90 – www.pierreetclaudine.com– closed 1-15 Nov – 4 rm.* Enjoy the charming welcome, swimming pool, terraced garden and rooms furnished in a variety of styles in this 1835 family residence.

EAT

Le Tournedos – *Pl. de Lattre-de-Tassigny, 11200 Lézignan-Corbières – ℘04 68 27 11 51 – closed 24 Jan-7 Feb, 26-Sep-12 Oct, Sun evening and Mon.* This family-run house with Provençal style decor serves generous portions and has a few basic rooms available.

⊜⊜ **Auberge du Domaine des Noyers** – *11700 Montbrun-des-Corbières ℘04 68 43 94 01 – www.domainelesnoyers.fr – closed 1 Nov-Easter – reservations required evenings.* Monsieur is a wine-grower and madame does the cuisine, serving up delicious farm chicken, garden vegetables or cassoulet cooked over an open fire, complemented by house wine (vin maison). Some rooms available. Swimming pool.

Limoux

Limoux is the production centre of sparkling blanquette, made from the Mauzac, Chenin and Chardonnay grapes using the *méthode champenoise*. The town's skyline features the Gothic spire of St Martin's Church and its lively narrow streets are still partly enclosed within a 14C fortified wall.

- **Info:** Prom. du Tivoli, 11303 Limoux, ℘04 68 31 11 82.
- **Location:** 26km/16mi S of Carcassonne and 28km/17.5mi N Quillan via D 118.
- **Don't Miss:** A tasting of blanquette de Limoux, and Limoux's carnival (January to April) with streets full of costumed dancers and musicians.
- **Kids:** The Arques dungeon, and nautical activities. Musée des Dinosaurs.

SIGHTS

Musée Petiet

Prom. du Tivoli. Open Jul-Aug 9am-12.30pm, 4-7pm; Sep-Jun 9am-noon, 2pm-6pm, weekends 10am-noon, 2pm-5pm. Closed 1 Jan, 1 May and 25 Dec. ⊜3€. ℘04 68 31 85 03.

This museum in the former workshop of the Petiet family, displays local paintings such as *The Ironers* by Marie Petiet (1854-93), battle scenes from the 1870 Franco-Prussian War by Étienne Dujardin-Beaumetz, and works by Henri Lebasque (*Reading*) and Achille Laugé (*Notre-Dame de Paris*).

Carnival in Limoux

M.-H. Carcanague/MICHELIN

Musée du Piano

Pl. de 22 Septembre. Open mid Jun-Sep daily except Tue 10am-noon and 2pm-7pm (Jul-Aug 6pm); rest of year on demand. ℘04 68 31 85 03. ⊜2.50€.

An interesting exhibit of French pianos from late 18C to today, presenting the evolution of the instrument.

DRIVING TOUR

St-Polycarpe

8km/5mi SE along D 129.

The **fortified church** here was part of a Benedictine abbey which was dissolved in 1771. On display are the 14C head reliquary (bare head) of St Polycarp, St Benedict and of the Holy Thorn, as well as 8C fabrics. The walls and vault feature the restored remains of 14C frescoes.

Razès Region

120km/75mi round tour from Limoux – allow one day – local map see Les CORBIÈRES. Leave Limoux south along D 118.

Castles along this route had quite efficient defenses during the Albigensian Crusade. The Aude valley cuts across a fold in the Corbières mountain massif, before narrowing into the **Étroit d'Alet** gorge.

Alet-les-Bains

Surrounded by 12C ramparts Alet's **old town** has many interesting house on **place de la République**. Picturesque narrow streets branch off from the square to the city gates: Porte Calvière and Porte Cadène.

Not far from D 118 are the **ruins** of the 11C Romanesque abbey church, raised to the status of cathedral from 1318.

Turn left off D 118 onto D 70 then right onto a minor road towards Arques.

Donjon d'Arques

From Arques, 500m/550yd along D 613. Open Jul-Aug 9.30am-7.30pm; Apr-Jun and Sep 10am-6pm; Mar and Oct-Nov 10.30am-12.30pm. 5€ (children 2€). 04 68 69 82 87. www.chateau-arques.fr.

Used as living quarters since the late 13C, this keep of beautiful gold-coloured sandstone has three rooms open to the public. Maison Déodat Roché presents an audio-visual exhibition on the Cathar doctrine.

Slightly farther on to the left, a forest track leads through the Rialsesse Forest.

Couiza

This town curiously devoted to shoemaking is home to the mid-16C château of the dukes of Joyeuse, now a hotel with a Renaissance courtyard.

Rennes-le-Château

Rennes-le-Château stands on a plateau over the Aude valley. Rumour still abounds about the fortune of the enigmatic Father Béranger Saunière, parish priest from 1885 to his death in 1917. How from 1891 onwards was he able to fund the complete restoration of his ruined church, build a sumptuous mansion (the Villa Bétania), a bizarre, semi-fortified library-tower (the Tour Magdala) and a tropical greenhouse, and lead a life fit for a prince? The abbot must have been discovered some hidden treasure – of the Knights Templar, the Cathars, or treasure brought back from the Holy City by the Visigoths.

The **Espace Bérenger Saunière** includes a local history **museum** displaying the Visigothic pillar said to have contained Father Saunière's treasure, and the **Domaine de l'abbé Saunière**, with the priest's garden, private chapel, Villa Bétania and the Magdala tower. (*open early May to mid-Sep: 10.30am-6pm; Mar and Apr, and mid-Sep to end Oct, : 11.30am-1pm, 2-5pm (Mar-Apr 6pm); Nov-mid Jan weekends and school holidays 11am-1pm, 2-5pm. closed mid Jan-Feb. 4.50€. 04 04 68 74 72 68 - www.rennes-le-chateau.fr*).

Rennes-le-Chateau is one of the settings used in Kate Mosse's book *Sepulchre*.

Return to Couiza and follow D 118 towards Quillan.

Espéraza

This small town on the banks of the Aude was an important hat-making centre, whose past is commemorated in the **Musée de la Chapellerie** (*open Jul-Aug 10am-7pm; Feb-Jun and Sep 10.30am-12.30pm, 1.30-6pm; Nov-Dec 1.30-5.30pm (Sun and school holidays 10.30am-12.30pm, 1.30-5.30pm. Closed Jan, 25 Dec. 04 68 74 00 75 – www.museedelachapellerie.fr). No charge)*.

Organised like a factory, the museum shows the stages of making of a felt hat and displays various headdress. The **Musée des Dinosaures** reconstructs a local 19C dinosaur dig and displays bone fragments, semi-fossilised eggs and the skeleton of an enormous sauropod. (*open Jul and Aug: 10am-7pm, last admission 45min before closing; Feb-Jun and Sep-Oct 10.30am-12.30pm, 1.30-5.30pm; Nov-Jan 1.30-5.30pm (school holidays 10.30am-12.30pm, 1.30-5.30pm. closed 1 Jan, 25 Dec. 7€ (children 6-12 years 5€). 04 68 74 26 88; www.dinosauria.org.*

Magdala tower, domaine de l'abbe Saunière, Rennes-le-Château

© Jean-Paul Garcin/Photononstop/Tips Images

Conspiracies of Rennes-le-Château

As you move south from Carcassonne into the beautiful but complex folds of the mountains that were the Cathar stronghold, so you delve deeper into a world of mystery. Until recent times, the tiny and largely obscure village of Rennes-le-Château was virtually unknown. But then rumours started to surface, originating in the mid-1950s, concerning a local 19C priest. Father Bérenger Saunière arrived in the village in 1885, and acquired large sums of money during his tenure by selling masses and receiving donations. This was not uncommon, but the source of the wealth became a topic of conversation, and stories circulating within the village ranged from the priest having found hidden treasure to espionage for the Germans during World War I. During the 1950s, these rumours, in true entrepreneurial fashion, were given wide local circulation by a local man who opened a restaurant in Saunière's former estate (L'Hotel de la Tour), and hoped to use the stories to attract business.

From then on Rennes-le-Château became the centre of conspiracy theories claiming that Saunière had discovered hidden treasure and/or secrets about the history of the Church that could threaten the foundations of Catholicism. Suddenly, the area became the focus of increasingly outlandish claims involving the Knights Templar, the Priory of Sion, the Rex Deus, the Holy Grail, the treasures of the Temple of Solomon, the Ark of the Covenant, ley lines and sacred geometry alignments. Saunière's story, true or false, found its way into contemporary novels, notably *Sepulchre*, by Kate Mosse, who had previously penned a novel set in the times of the Cathars, *Labyrinth*.

Devil supporting the stoup in Rennes-le-Château church

D. Pazery/MICHELIN

This is all grist to the mill of speculation. Is there treasure here? Or is it wishful thinking?

Quillan

See QUILLAN.

Follow D 117 W to Puivert.

Puivert

The **Musée du Quercorb** on local history, traditions and livelihoods displays casts of medieval musical instruments which once ornamented the castle.(*open Jul-Aug 10am-7pm; Apr-mid Jul and Sep 10am-12.30pm, 2-6pm; Oct 2-5pm. closed Nov-Mar. 4€ (children 6-15 years 1.60€). 04 68 20 80 98). www.quercorb.com/musee.*

All that remains of **Puivert Castle** dating from before the siege of 1210, are sections of wall to the west. Of the partly destroyed 14C castle, a keep and a tower-gate decorated with the Bruyères lion are still standing. Visit the keep, chapel and "Minstrels" room evoking Puivert court life during the age of the troubadours.(*open May-Nov 9am-7pm; Dec-May daily except Sat 10am-5pm. 5€. 04 68 20 81 52. www.chateau-de-puivert.com.*

Canal du Midi★

Today's tourists enjoying the calm and beauty of the Canal du Midi have little idea of the phenomenal natural obstacles to building this canal which links the Atlantic to the Mediterranean.

- **Michelin Map:** 343: H-4 to I-4, J-5 to K-5, 334: a-1 to k-3 and 339: A-9 to F-9.
- **Info:** www.canalmidi.com, or www.canaldumidi.fr.
- **Location:** Between Naurouze and Béziers.
- **Don't Miss:** The cité de Carcassonne; the treasure of the church of Quarante; the three Malpas tunnels and Fonséranes locks.
- **Kids:** the Aiguille locks; the oppidum of Ensérune; a family cruise on the canal.

A BIT OF HISTORY

Even the Romans envisioned a canal linking the Atlantic to the Mediterranean, yet by the time of François I, Henri IV and Richelieu, nothing had been achieved. Finally **Pierre-Paul Riquet**, Baron of Bonrepos (1604-80) began the project at his own expense, spending 5 million livres, burdening himself with debts and sacrificing his daughters' dowries to do it. He died exhausted in 1680, six months before the Canal du Midi opened. **Riquet's** descendants regained their rights to a share of the canal profits, and in 1897 sold the canal to the State. Since then it has been administered as a public enterprise.

A. Thuillier/MICHELIN

Heritage and future projects – Riquet's 240km/150mi-long canal begins at Toulouse at the Port de l'Emouchure and runs into the Thau lagoon, through 91 locks. Today only pleasure-craft cruise this scenic waterway, and several companies rent houseboats or offer river cruises.

Eight locks at Foriserone

J. Maluret/MICHELIN

Canal architecture – Along the canal's banks are buildings erected to house engineers, workers and lock-keepers; buildings for technical and administrative tasks, as well as inns and mills. Canal du Midi lock-keeper's houses are rectangular, with one or two rooms on the ground floor. The façade's plaque indicates the distance to the nearest lock upstream and downstream.

Ports – Ports usually have a stone pier and an inn, and in the past there were stables for the draught-horses, a wash-house, chapel and sometimes an ice house, as at Somail. Ports like Castelnaudary and Port St-Sauveur in Toulouse have dry docks for repairing boats.

Vegetation – The canal is lined with great trees which provide shade and beauty but also limit the evaporation of canal water. Most are fast-growing species like plane trees, poplars and maritime pines. At points like Naurouze, landscaping is extensive.

DRIVING TOUR

1 TOULOUSE TO THE SEUIL DE NAUROUZE

45km/28mi along N 113; allow a few extra miles for detours – aout 2hr.

This itinerary crosses a fertile agricultural region of fine brick-built houses, castles and Toulouse Gothic style churches. (*see ST-FÉLIX-LAURAGAIS: Dyer's woad country*). A waymarked cycle path runs along the canal.

Écluse d'Ayguesvives

This picturesque lock in the centre of a hamlet faces an 1831 mill. The village of **Ayguesvives** is only 1.5km/0.9mi south. Note the brick-built Gothic church and monumental brick gateway leading to the castle.

N 113 crosses the canal. In Avignonet-Lauragais, take D 80 towards Baraigne.

Aire de Port Lauragais

The rest area along the A 61 motorway between Villefranche-de-Lauragais and Castelnaudary at Port Lauragais is on the Canal du Midi, and contains shops and cafeteria. A harbourmaster's office welcomes passing boats.

Return to Avignonet; continue east on N 113, then turn off to Montferrand.

Montferrand

This hilltop village was the site of a Cathar fortress that fell in 1211; All that remains is the fortified gate. Note the 16C belfry-wall of the deconsecrated church.

Go back to N 113 and cross via D 218.

THE PRACTICAL CANAL

WHEN TO CRUISE ALONG THE CANAL – March to November is the best time. During July and August boats for hire are difficult to find, lock traffic is intense, and prices are higher. May and June brighten the canal banks with irises and various water plants. September and October bring settled weather, mild temperatures and the countryside wears a beautiful russet mantle. Locks operate between June and August from 9am-12.30pm and 1.30-7.30pm. Some operate automatically, others manually (average time: 15min).

Hiring a boat – No licence is needed; instruction is usually provided by the boat-hire company just before departure. Maximum speed allowed: 6kph/3.7mph. Boats can be hired for a week or a weekend, for a one-way journey or for a return trip. For summer cruising, book well in advance. Bikes are very useful to have on board for shore excursions (some boat-hire companies also hire bikes). For addresses of boat-hire companies, consult the *Planning Your Trip* section at the beginning of the guide.

Béziers Croisières, Port Neuf *34545 Béziers Cedex* *℘04 67 49 08 23*, offer cruises between Béziers and Poilhès; timetable, prices and bookings by phone.

Croisières du Midi (Luc Lines) *35 quai des Tonneliers, BP 2, 11200 Homps, ℘04 68 91 33 00, 10€ (children 5.50€)* offer 2h trips aboard traditional *gabares*, starting from Homps, from April to late October. Bookings essential.

Boat trips – Several companies organise 2 to 6hr trips along the Canal du Midi, with or without lunch.

Obelisque de Riquet

Leave the car in the parking area near the monument.

The obelisk, built in 1825 by Riquet's descendants, stands in an enclosure formed by the "stones of Naurouze," between the Naurouze Pass (N 113) and the canal.

Walk to the Seuil de Naurouze.

2 HARNESSED WATER

114km/70mi from the Prise d'Alzeau to the Seuil de Naurouze – allow 5hr.

This itinerary follows the water-supply system of the Canal du Midi.

Seuil de Naurouze to Carcassonne

50km/31mi along N 113 – allow 1hr

From the watershed ridge, N 113 runs along the north bank of the canal all the way to Carcassonne.

Seuil de Naurouze★

Walk the shady path round the octagonal reservoir built 1669-1673 amidst an arboretum of Aleppo pines, nettle trees, sycamores, North-African cedars and wild cherry trees. The tour goes from the pumping station to the Canal du Midi and the Ocean lock (1671).

Return to the parking area along an alleyway lined with plane trees.

Castelnaudary

The town famous for its thick *cassoulet* stew makes an excellent stop-over for anyone cruising the Canal du Midi. The Grand Bassin offers plenty of mooring space. The restored 17C Moulin de Cugarel testifies to Castelnaudary's once important flour-milling activity.

Carcassonne

See CARCASSONNE.

3 CARCASSONNE TO BÉZIERS

120km/75mi; allow a few extra miles for detours – half a day.

Between Carcassonne and Béziers, the Canal du Midi snakes along the River Aude. D 610 follows the canal as far as Homps. Just beyond Homps, turn right onto D 124 skirting the towpath.

Canal du Midi

M.-H. Carcanague/MICHELIN

Leave the car in Rouia and walk along the towpath towards Ventenac (2.5km/1.5mi there and back).

Pont-canal de Répudre

This is the first canal-bridge built in France by Riquet in 1676. The castle overlooking Venténac-en-Minervois offers a fine view of the canal and surrounding plain.

Drive N along D 26.

Ginestas

This village set among vineyards has a **church** with a 17C gilded wood altarpiece and a 15C naïve polychrome statue of St Anne.

Drive E for 2km/1.2mi to Le Somail.

Le Somail★

This peaceful hamlet has preserved its humpback bridge and inn dating from 1773. The **Musée de la Chapellerie** contains hats and head-dresses from around the world, dating from 1885. (*open 10am-noon 2-6/7pm. 3.20€. 04 68 46 19 26).*

From Le Somail, drive N to join D 5.

The road to Béziers follows the canal part of the way. Alternatively, make a detour via the hilltop village of Quarante to the north.

In Capestang, take D 37 S to Nissan-lez-Ensérune. From there, the Oppidum d'Ensérune is signposted.

Oppidum d'Ensérune★★

See Oppidum d'ENSÉRUNE.

Nearby, the canal goes through the Malpas tunnel.

Continue to Colomiers, turn E onto D 162E then left onto N 9 and follow signposts to Écluses de Fonséranes.

Écluses de Fonséranes★

A sequence of eight locks makes up a 312m/338yd-long "staircase" enabling river craft to negotiate a drop of 25m/81ft. Today locks have been replaced by a single lock, lying parallel to the original system.

Pont-canal de l'Or

Access via the towpath downstream from the locks.

Since 1857, a canal-bridge carrying the Canal du Midi over the Or, provides an alternative to the somewhat daunting stretch of river.

Béziers★

See BÉZIERS.

ADDRESSES

STAY

Chambre d'hôte Bernard Fouissac – *La Bastide-Vieille – 34310 Capestang – 13km/8mi W of Béziers on the Rte. de Castres by D 39 – 04 67 93 46 23 – closed 1 Nov-1 Mar – 3 rms – meals* . Large, comfortable guest rooms in this 12C *bastide* among the vines. Relax in the lovely library/salon and enjoy meals in old bakery.

Chambre d'hôte Le Liet – *11610 Pennautier – 5km/3.1mi NW of Carcassonne y N 113 then D 203 – 04 68 11 19 19 – closed Nov-Feb – 6 rms and 4 self-catering cottages.* This 19C château in a wooded park has rooms and suites overlooking an unspoilt landscape. Magnificent breakfast-room.

Chambre d'hôte Abbaye de Villelongue – *11170 St-Martin-le-Vieil – 5km/3.1mi NE of St-Martin-le-Vieil by D 64 – 04 68 76 92 58 – closed late Oct – 4 rms.* Tranquility at this 12C Cistercian abbey but the comfort is anything but monk-like: lovely antiques, private bathrooms, luxurious beds. Windows open onto a ravishing cloister and its pretty garden where breakfast is served in fine weather.

Minerve★

Minerve occupies a picturesque site★★ on a promontory with views of rugged gorges.

- **Population:** 112
- **Michelin Map:** 339: B-8.
- **Info:** 9 R. des Martyrs. 04 68 91 81 43. www.minerve-tourisme.com
- **Location:** 32km/20mi NW of Narbonne via the D 607.
- **Don't Miss:** The two natural bridges sculpted by the Cesse; the château de Minerve's octagonal tower.
- **Kids:** Le musée Hurepel.

A BIT OF HISTORY

In the MIddle Ages a proud fortress that stood atop this spur witnessed one of the most dramatic events in the Albigensian Crusade. In 1210, Simon de Montfort, at the head of 7 000 men, laid seige to Minerve's proud fortress. After five weeks of siege, the townspeople, having run out of water, were forced to capitulate. They were given the choice of converting or being slaughtered. The 180 "Parfaits" who refused to surrender are commemorated by J L Séverac on place de la Mairie.

WALKING TOUR

Allow 1hr 30min. Take D 147 SW of the village. The Grand Pont is the setting of many summer cultural events.

Ponts naturels★

The road affords views of natural bridges. These were formed at the beginning of the Quartenary Era when the Cesse abandoned two meanders it once formed before flowing into the Briant, to attack the limestone cliff. As it forced its way through the many cracks in the wall, gradually enlarging them as it passed, two tunnels were formed. The first, the 250m/820ft long **Grand Pont**, ends in an opening 30m/100ft high. Upstream, the Cesse flows through the **Petit Pont**, about 15m/50ft high. Climb up to the narrow rue des Martyrs, lined with craft workshops like Maison des Templiers.

Église St-Étienne

This small Romanesque church has an 11C oven-vaulted apse and 12C nave. Its high altar table inscription tells that it was consecrated by St Rustique, Bishop of Narbonne, in 456. Look for the 5C-9C graffiti.

Walk on towards the tower standing N of the village.

This 13C octagonal tower known as "**La Candela**" and sections of the curtain

A. Thuillier/MICHELIN

wall overlooking the Briant valley are all that remains of the fortress dismantled in 1636 on order of Louis XIII.

Go back down rue des Martyrs and turn left into a narrow alley leading down to the ramparts. Parts of Minerve's 12C double curtain wall, including the pointed archway of the southern postern, still remain. Follow the path to the left along the lower edge of the village.

Puits St-Rustique

This well supplied water to the townspeople during the siege of 1210. Simon de Montfort destroyed it with a powerful catapult from across the river, forcing Minerve to capitulate.

Vallée du Briant

A narrow path skirts the village along the steep narrow Briant Valley, to emerge under the ruined "Candela."

MUSEUMS

Museum

Open Mar-mid Nov 10am-12.30pm, 1.30-6pm. Closed rest of year. 1.70€ (children 1€). 04 68 91 22 92.

This museum covers prehistory and archaeology up to the Roman and Visigoth invasions, and features a mould of Upper Paleolithic human footprints discovered in the **Grotte d'Aldène** (*see The Haut Minervois below*) dating from the Aurignacian period 15 000 years ago).

Musée Hurepel

Open Jul-Aug 10am-1pm, 2-7pm; Apr-Jun and Sep-Oct 10.30am-12.30pm, 2-6pm. 3€. 04 68 91 12 26.

Learn about the main episodes in the Albigensian Crusade through these dioramas.

DRIVING TOUR

HAUT-MINERVOIS★

35km/22mi round tour. Take D 10E1 W towards Fauzan. The road follows narrow, steep-sided meanders of the Cesse.

Canyon de la Cesse

In the early Quaternary Era, the Cesse hollowed out a canyon, enlarged existing caves and made new ones. Upstream of Minerve, the valley narrows and the river flows for 20km/12mi underground, emerging to ground level in heavy winter storms.

Turn left onto the road to Cesseras which leads down to the plain and vineyards. Go through Cesseras and turn right onto D 168 to Siran. After 2km/1mi, turn right again.

Chapelle de St-Germain
This Romanesque chapel has an apse with interesting decorations.

Return to D 168 and carry on to Siran.

Stop the car beyond the bridge over a track and take the footpath up to the top of the hill to discover an interesting **dolmen** of the covered-alleyway type, called **Mourel des Fades** ("fairies' dolmen").

Chapelle de Centeille★
N of Siran. Open Sun 3-5pm. 04 68 91 50 07.
Surrounded by cypress trees, holm-oaks and vines, this 13C chapel looks onto a panorama of vineyards, La Livinière and its basilica and the distant Pyrenees. Inside are beautiful 14C and early 15C **frescoes** and a transept with a 3C Roman mosaic. Around the chapel are drystone huts known as capitelles.

Return to Siran and, after the water tower, take a small road on the left which skirts the St-Martin peak and rejoins D 182 to the N, overlooking the Cesse gorge. Turn right towards Minerve. Just after the hamlet of Fauzan, take a small road to the left.

After 1.5km/1mi enjoy a view of the Cesse gorge and the **caves** pepping the cliff face. In one of these caves – **Aldène** – Paleolithic human footprints were discovered (*see Musée de Minerve above*). A small path leads to the **Grotte de Fauzan** where traces of prehistoric footprints were found.

Return to Minerve along the Cesse canyon.

La Montagne Noire★

The Montagne Noire or Black Mountain forms the south-western tip of the Massif Central and is separated from the Agout massif (Sidobre and the Lacaune and Espinouse ranges) by the furrow formed by the Thoré.

- **Michelin Map:** 338: E, F, G, H-10 and 344: E-2 to F-2.
- **Info:** Office du tourisme de Revel Saint-Ferréol Montagne Noire, Pl Phillippe-VI-de-Valois-Beffroi, 31250 Revel 05 34 66 67 68 – *www.revel-lauragais.com* .
- **Location**: La Montagne Noire comprises the extreme SW of the central Massif central.
- **Don't Miss:** Saint-Ferréol basin and the Abbey-école of Sorrèze.
- **Kids:** Sylvea à Revel; Explorarôme à Montégut-Lauragais.

GEOGRAPHY
The mountain's densely forested northern slope rises sharply over the Thoré and culminates in the Pic de Nore. Its more Mediterranean southern slope drops gently down to the Lauragais and Minervois plains. The rainy northern slopes shelter oak, beech, fir, spruce forests, and the rugged southern slopes are scattered with *garrigue*, gorse, sweet chestnut trees, vines and olive trees. The Montagne Noire's greatest wealth lies in its abundant reserves of water and its beautiful countryside. Only a meagre income can be made by raising stock or growing crops here, but the Salsigne gold mines still operate and marble is mined at Caunes-Minervois.

WALKS
A **forest road** marked on the IGN 2344 Ouest map stretches from the Prise

St-Ferréol reservoir

A. Thuillier/MICHELIN

d'eau d'Alzeau to the Bassin du Lampy (15km/9.3mi). The **GR 7** long-distance footpath traverses woodland, skirting the Rigole de la Montagne from the Bassin du Lampy to the Cammazes dam (11km/6.8mi). Use the IGN 2244 Est and 2344 Ouest maps for this section.
The **GR 653** long-distance footpath, the "Pierre-Paul Riquet" variation of GR 7, starts from the Bassin de St-Ferréol, links with the Rigole de la Plaine in Revel, skirtings it as far as the Poste des Thommasses (9km/5.6mi) before running on to the Seuil de Naurouze (another 24km/15mi). Use the IGN 2344 Ouest, 2244 Est and 2244 Ouest maps for this itinerary.

DRIVING TOURS

1 THE CABARDÈS REGION★

Round tour from Carcassonne–
See CARCASSONNE.

2 HARNESSED WATER★

From the Prise d'Alzeau to the Seuil de Naurouze. 114km/71mi – allow 5hr

This itinerary follows the water-supply system of the Canal du Midi devised in the 17C by Pierre-Paul Riquet and improved upon over the centuries.

From St-Denis, follow D 353 towards Lacombe then a forest road on the right.

Prise d'Alzeau

A monument commemorating Pierre-Paul Riquet, designer and builder of the Canal du Midi, retraces the various stages of canal construction.

Turn back and continue to Lacombe. Turn left towards Lampy along forest roads.

Forêt domaniale de la Montagne noire

This 3 650ha/9 000-acre forest of beech and fir trees includes the Ramondes and Hautaniboul forests. The road crosses the Alzeau in a lovely woodland setting at La Galaube.

Bassin du Lampy

This reservoir on the Lampy was built between 1776 to 1780 to supply the Canal du Midi. It flows into the Montagne Noire channel where a pleasant footpath runs for 23km/14.5mi to the village of Les Cammazes. Magnificent beech groves and shady paths make the Bassin du Lampy a popular place for a stroll.

Follow D 4 towards Saissac then turn right onto D 629. Just before Les Cammazes, turn right onto a road leading to the dam.

Cammazes Dam

The 90ha/220-acre reservoir retained by this 70m/230ft-high arch dam feeds the Canal du Midi, supplies 116 towns

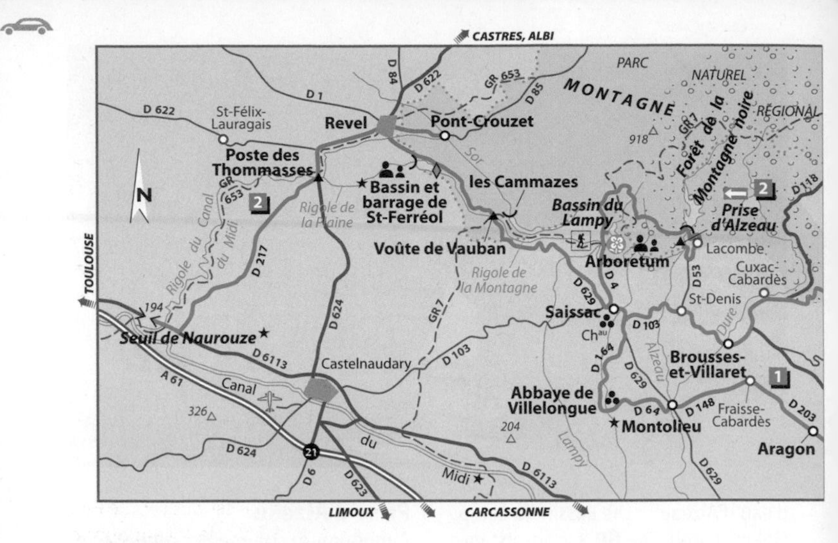

and villages with drinking water and irrigates the entire Lauragais plain east of Toulouse. Footpaths lead down to the edge of the Sor.

Return to D 629 and turn right.

The road continues alongside the Rigole de la Montagne.

Voûte de Vauban

Outside Cammazes, the Rigole de la Montagne runs through the Voûte de Vauban, a 122m/133yd-long tunnel.

Bassin and barrage de St-Ferréol★

The reservoir on the Atlantic side of the Montagne Noire stretches for 67ha/166 acres between wooded hillsides. The magnificent lake is ideal for sailing and swimming, and its shores pleasant for strolling. The **dam's construction** between 1667 and 1672 employed 1 000 men, women and children.

The English-style **park** has winding paths through forest of cedar, maritime pines and sequoias.

Revel

On the edge of the Montagne Noire and the Lauragais region, Revel's economy is based on cabinet-making, marquetry, bronze work, gold-plating and lacquer work. This bastide has a geometric street layout around a main square surrounded by covered arcades or *garlandes*. The 14C **covered market** features its original timber roof and belfry, renovated in the 19C.

Sylvea, 13 r Jean-Moulin, is a museum providing an overview of the wood trade, and the traditional skills of cartwrights, clog-makers, carpenters, joiners, coopers and violin-makers. Games and play space for children.*(guided tours available (1hr30min) Apr-Sep 9am-noon, 2pm-6pm (weekends and public holidays 2pm-6pm); Oct-Mar daily except Sun and public holidays 9am-noon, 2-6pm. closed 1 Jan, 1 May, 25 Dec. 4€ (under 15, no charge) 05 61 27 65 50. www.sylvea.com).*

Follow D 85 E to Pont-Crouzet.

Pont-Crouzet

The Rigole de la Plaine starts here. This canal collects water from the Sor and takes it to the Poste des Thommasses.

Return to Revel and follow D 622 S then D 624 towards Castelnaudary.

Poste des Thommasses

This catches the water of the Laudot from St-Ferréol and that of the Sor, diverted from Pont-Crouzet via the Rigole de la Plaine. This water is then sent onto the Seuil de Naurouze.

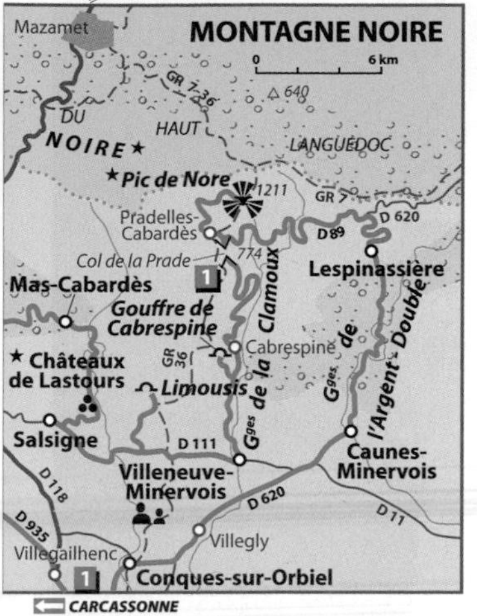

Turn right onto D 217 to the Seuil de Naurouze.

Seuil de Naurouze★

See Canal du MIDI.

3 ROUND TOUR FROM REVEL

Leave Revel SE along D 629 then turn left onto D 44 running through the picturesque Sor gorge. See map below.

Durfort

At the edge of the Sor valley, Durfort has always been a centre of copper-smithing. Coppersmiths continue this industry today, working with the last tilt-hammer (15C) still in operation to produce copper objects. The **copper museum** (*open Jun-Sep 30min guided tour daily except Tue, 3-7pm. 2€. 05 63 74 22 77*) is in an old coppersmith house.

Continue to Pont-Crouzet (see above) and turn right onto D 85 to Sorèze.

Sorèze

Sorèze is one of the centres for the Parc Naturel Régional du Haut Languedoc. This village developed in the 8C around the abbey, now in ruins except for its majestic 13C octagonal **bell-tower**. The abbey's famous **college**★ founded in the 17C by Benedictine monks became a royal military school during the reign of Louis XVI but was eventually bought back by the Dominicans in 1854. The college closed down in 1991.

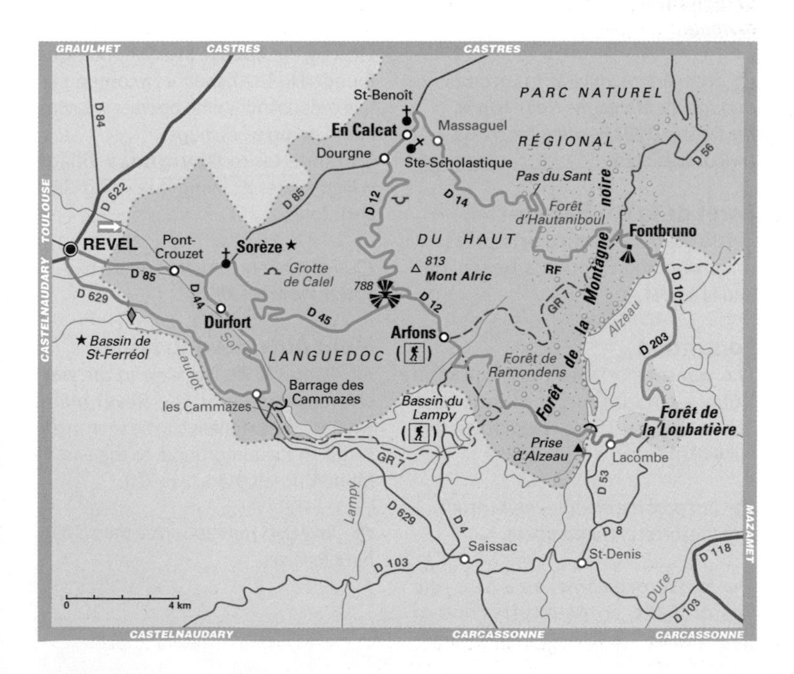

13C octagonal bell-tower in Sorèze

As you leave Sorrèze, turn right onto D 45 then bear right again onto D 12.

Arfons

Arfons is a peaceful mountain village with slate-roofed houses. On the corner of a house in the main street is a 14C stone statue of the Virgin Mary.

Surrounded by forests, Arfons is the point of departure for a number of delightful walks (*GR 7 waymarked footpath*).

From Arfons, drive SE to Lacombe through the Montagne Noire Forest, then rejoin D 203 heading N across La Loubatière Forest.

Forêt de la Loubatière

D 203 makes a particularly pleasant drive, winding through a beech, oak and fir forest.

Fontbruno

The war memorial to the Montagne Noire resistance forces stands here above a crypt. There is an attractive view of the plain.

Just past the monument, turn left into the forest of Hautaniboul.

The forest road comes to a pass, the **Pas du Sant**, at the intersection of three roads.

Take D 14 to the left, and after Massaguel turn left again onto D 85 to St-Ferréol.

En Calcat

Two Benedictine abbeys were established here by Father Romain Banquet on his personal estate. The **Monastère de St-Benoît**, for men only, was consecrated in 1896 and is still an active community. Monks here create and produce pottery, stained glass and zithers. Closeby, the **Abbaye Ste-Scholastique** founded in 1890, shelters a contemplative order of nuns who operate weaving and binding workshops.

Continue on to **Dourgne**, a village which makes its living quarrying slate and stone.

Take D 12 to the left to return to Sorèze via Mont Alric.

Mont Alric viewing table

Alt 788m/2 585ft. The view to the west stretches as far as the Revel plain, whereas the Pyrenees can be seen in the south. In the foreground, to the east, is Mont Alric (alt 813m/2 667ft).

Take D 45 right to Sorèze then D 85 back to Revel.

Château de Peyrepertuse ★★★

The craggy outline of the ruined fortress of Peyrepertuse only properly comes into view when seen from the outskirts of Rouffiac, to the north. One of the "five sons of Carcassonne," it sits on a crest in the Corbières, standing boldly atop its rocky base. The château is one of the finest examples of a medieval fortress in the Corbières.

- **Info:** Office du tourisme de Cucugnan, Chemin de Padern – 11350. ℘04 68 4569 40. www.corbieres-sauvages.com
- **Location:** Get there from Duilhac: 3.5km/2mi up a steep, narrow road. Visitors should have a good head for heights and take great care while exploring the castle, particularly if there is a strong wind. During the summer, be sure to bring drinking water, sunhats and suncream.
- **Parking:** at ticket office.
- **Don't Miss:** The view over the site and the surrounding valley from the outcrop just east of the castle.

A BIT OF HISTORY

In the 11C-12C, the castle was associated with the counts of Barcelona and Narbonne and during the Albigensian Crusade, it was handed peacefully over to the French.

VISIT

From the car park, follow a path along the north face, leading up to the castle entrance (30min on foot there and back). Allow 2hr Open Jun-Sep 8.30am–8pm; Apr, May and Oct 9am–7pm, Nov–Mar 10am–7pm. Closed Jan. No visits during stormy weather. Sturdy footwear advised. 5€. ℘06 71 58 63 36. www.chateau-peyrepertuse.com.

The layout of the chateau is complex, and barely discernible from below. From the main entrance you go left or right, turning into walled alleyways, castle rooms, ramparts, or clambering up and down steps to explore the numerous rooms. It is quite a haul on a warm day from the ticket office to the highest point of the chateau; take refreshments.

Château de Peyrepertuse

D. Pazery/MICHELIN

Quillan

Plateau and river gorges

This town is a major tourist centre for the upper Aude valley and one of the best points of departure for forays into the forests of the Pyrenean foothills. Rugby has enjoyed a passionate following locally since the period between the two World Wars, the hat-making industry's swansong. Modern local industry includes laminates (Formica), luxury and garden furniture, trousers and shoes.

- **Info:** Maison des Pyrénées cathares, pays d'accueil touristique d'Axat – Rd-pt du Pont-d'Aliès, 11140 Axat. ℘04 68 20 59 61. www.pays-axat.org.
- **Location:** 28 km/17.5m S of Limoux by the D118 and 76 km/47.5m W of Perpignan by the N9 then the D117.
- **Don't Miss:** the Belvédère du Pas de l'Ours.

TOWN

On the esplanade in front of the station there is a quaint little monument to Abbot Armand(see Défilé de Pierre-Lys below). On the east bank of the Aude stand the ruins, sadly being left to fall into disrepair, of a 13C fortress with a square ground plan – most unusual in this region.

DRIVING TOUR

Sault plateau and river gorges★★

144km/90mi round tour – allow one day. This trip includes a large stretch of the **Route du Sapin de l'Aude**, a drive through woodland where there are conifers over 50m/160ft tall.

Leave Quillan W along D 117 and turn left onto D 613 which runs across the Sault plateau. Beyond Espèze, watch out for a crossroads marked with a cross and turn right onto D 29 towards Bélesta. Take the left turn past the forest lodge, drive along the forest road to a left bend and park the car by the Langarail drinking troughs.

Langarail pastures★

45min on foot there and back.

As its name suggests, this is a rural site. Follow the stony track until the bumpy stretch from which there is a **view** to the north, beyond the Bélesta Forest as far as the foothills of the chain towards the Lauragais.

Get back onto the forest road and continue W.

Pas de l'Ours★

The road runs along a rocky cliff above the Gorges de la Frau.

At Col de la Gargante, take the steep road to the left which is signposted "belvédère à 600m."

Belvédère du Pas de l'Ours★★

15min on foot there and back.

From the look-out point, there is a magnificent view of the Gorges de la Frau; 700m/2 296ft lower down are the Montségur outcrop and the Tabe mountain; beyond these, and much higher up, the white patches of the Trimouns quarry can be seen.

Beyond Col de la Gargante, follow the road to Comus and turn right.

Gorges de la Frau★

1hr 30min on foot there and back.

Park the car at the entrance to a wide forest track climbing a tributary valley. The path runs along the base of yellow-tinged limestone cliffs. After a 45min walk, turn back at the point where the valley makes a sharp bend.

Return to Comus and take the road to the right towards Camurac.

Camurac ski area
Alt 1 400-1 800m/4 593-5 906ft.
Camurac is a family resort equipped with 16 Alpine ski runs suitable for all levels of proficiency, a country-skiing loop and a marked track for snowshoeing.

The road climbs up to Col des Sept Frères. Turn left onto D 613 then right onto D 20 to Niort de Sault; turn left.

Drive down the **Rebenty gorge**, passing beneath the impressive overhangs of the **Défilé d'Able** and through the **Défilé de Joucou**, where the road follows a series of tunnels and overhangs, to reach **Joucou**, a sheltered village gathered around an old abbey.

Turn back. After driving through a couple of tunnels, turn left onto D 29 which runs through Rodome, Aunat and Bessède-de-Sault before joining D 118. Turn left towards Axat.

This pretty stretch of road runs along the edge of the Sault plateau.

Grottes de l'Aguzou

Potholing outings by appointment (3 days in advance); departure at 9am. 1 day (7hrs): 50€; ½ day (2hrs): 30€. Take plimsolls, light walking boots or shoes and a cold meal. 04 68 20 45 38. www.grotte-aguzou.com.
This complex network of caves was discovered in 1965. On the tour, visitors can see a large number of crystals and some wonderful examples of aragonite.

River Aude runs through the gorges
A. Thuillier/MICHELIN

Gorges de St-Georges★

This river gorge, cutting straight down through bare rock, is the narrowest in the upper Aude Valley.
In the **Aude gorge**, a reach of some 10km/6mi, the river surges along between high cliffs thickly covered with plant life.

Drive on to Axat, a white-water sports resort, left onto D 177 to Quillan.

Défilé de Pierre-Lys★

This is an impressive stretch of road between the ravine's sheer cliff walls, to which the odd bush clings tenaciously. The final tunnel is known as the **Trou du Curé** ("priest's hole") in memory of Abbot Félix Armand (1742-1823), parish priest of St-Martin-Lys, who had the passage cut through the rock with pickaxes.

ADDRESSES

SPORT IN THE AUDE VALLEY

The Aude, from the Gorges de St-Georges to the Gorges Pierre-Lysis, is an idyllic setting for the practice of fresh-water sports.

Maison des Pyrénées cathares, Pays d'Accueil touristique d'Axat – *Rd-pt du Pont d'Aliès. 11140 Axat. 04 68 20 59 61. In season: 10am-1pm, 3-7pm; rest of the year: Mon-Fri, 9am-noon, 1.30-5.30pm. Closed Oct-Apr.* A wide variety of tourist brochures available for the taking.

Centre de séjour Sports et Nature – *La Forge – 04 68 20 23 79. www.quillan.fr.* In addition to the practise of freshwater and other sports, this centre proposes rock climbing, walking, cave exploration and archery.

Sud Rafting – *Rd-pt du Pont d'Aliès, 11140 Axat. . 04 68 20 53 73. Winter: 9am-noon, 2-6pm and summer: 9am–8pm. Closed Nov.* Outdoors, sports-based holidays. Freshwater and mountain adventures.

The Cote Vermeille, the undiscovered Spanish facet of France, has inspired some of the world's leading artists, and led to its own style of painting. Here the waves dash against rocky shores where craggy mountains do battle against the sea, and steeply sloping vineyards cling to the slopes. The area has been settled since prehistoric times, but the principal town of Perpignan seems to have been founded in the 10C

Highlights

1. Visit the sheltered village of **Banyuls-sur-Mer** (p240)
2. Take a walk around the artists' paradise that is **Collioure** (p245)
3. Enjoy the town walk in ancient **Perpignan** (p252)
4. Discover prehistoric tales in **Tautavel** (p260)
5. Relax and enjoy the local **wines** (pp240, 249, 256, 260)

Canet-Plage

©Iain Frazer/Bigstockphoto.com

Along the coast

This lovely stretch of coastline has a host of enchanting border villages, where the influence of Spain prevails. Castle ruins dot the landscape, and peaceful villages are found at every turn. This is the best of two worlds: a springboard for exploring the Mediterranean, yet mere minutes' drive from the Spanish Costa Brava.

The Côte Vermeille, the last stretch of French coast before Spain where the Pyrenees finally tumble down to the sea, extends from Argelès-sur-Mer, a wonderful halt for families, to the pastel-coloured border village of Cerbère, a charming and relatively quiet seaside hideaway in the valley of Cervera. The towns and villages of Collioure, Port-Vendres and Banyuls-sur-Mer run along a 20km/12mi stretch of beaches, with numerous small bays, streams and coves, and with excellent walking trails.

This is Catalonia

Neither France nor Spain, this is Catalonia, a region with a unique cultural identity of which the locals are inordinately and rightly proud. Spanish business hours are the norm here, with late lunches and prolonged dinners.

In spite of its relatively compact size, the region is widely diverse, and embraces the lovely village of Coilloure, much loved by artists as the birthplace of Fauvism, which evolved from Henri Matisse's brightly coloured paintings of the village.

Collioure is also famous for its three-day 15 August celebration, which attracts twice its population in visitors, who come to see the town's bodégas and fireworks.

What's in a word?

Le Castillet with the Catalan flag, Perpignan

L. Campion/MICHELIN

French is the official language in the south-eastern part of France known as Catalonia. But here, **Catalan**, in its Northern Catalan variety, is estimated to be spoken by a quarter of the population, and understood by a higher percentage. Catalan (see *INTRODUCTION*) is a Romance language, and the official language of Andorra.

After the Treaty of the Pyrenees, public usage of the Catalan language was forbidden by a royal decree by Louis XIV of France on 2 April 1700, which prohibited the use of Catalan language in present-day Northern Catalonia in all official documents under the threat of them being invalidated. Elsewhere, prior to the French Revolution of 1789, French kings did not hold a strong view on the language spoken by their subjects. But, in sweeping away the old provinces, *parlements* and laws, the Revolution brought about a unified system of administration. At first, the revolutionaries declared liberty of language for all citizens of the Republic, a policy that was subsequently abandoned in favour of the imposition of a common language, which was to do away with the numerous other languages of France.

Then in the 1950s, after centuries of prohibition, it was agreed that the Catalan language could be given for one hour per week in secondary schools. In the 1970s, the Arrels Association and La Bressola network of private schools started to offer complete bilingual French/Catalan classes from nursery up to secondary education.

In December 2007, the General Council of Pyrénées-Orientales finally proclaimed Catalan as one of the languages of the département, alongside French and Occitan language, with the aim of further promoting its use in public life and education.

Street signs in French and Catalan in Perpignan

©Sylvain Grandadam/Photolibrary

Argelès-Plage ☼☼☼

Argelès-Plage, with its beautiful sandy beaches, is the camping capital of Europe, with tens of thousands of holidaymakers descending on 60 parks contained within a 5km/3mi radius. Argelès-Plage is the "Kid" resort par excellence with 5km/3mi of supervised golden sand beaches (June to September) and a 2km/1.2mi-long seafront promenade with umbrella pine trees and aloe, mimosa, olive and oleander.

Info: Pl. de l'Europe, 66700 ☎04 68 81 15 85. www.argelessurmer.com.

Location: 28km/17.5mi S of Perpignan. A bus shuttle service operates from Jun-Sep between Argelès-sur-Mer (the town) and Argelès-Plage.

CHÂTEAU DE VALMY

Call for opening hours ☎04 68 81 25 70. www.chateau-valmy.com.

In the grounds of the Château de Valmy are a discovery trail and falconry featuring **eagles**, kites, vultures and other birds of prey.

EXCURSION

Argelès-sur-Mer

2.5km/1.5mi W along D 618.

In heart of the old town, the **Casa de les Albères** *4 Pl des Castellans (temporarily closed ☎04 68 81 42 74)* is a Catalan museum of folk art and traditions such as wine making, manufacturing barrels, espadrilles (rope-soled sandals) and wooden toys.

DRIVING TOUR

3 AT THE FOOT OF MONTS ALBÈRES

32km/20mi – allow 3hr – see Le BOULOU. Drive W of Argelès-Plage along D 2 to Sorède. On reaching the village centre, turn left onto "Vallée des tortues" and drive 2km/1.2mi to the parking area.

Sorède

This village is a centre for the breeding and study of tortoises.

Vallée des tortues

Open Apr 10am–2pm; May 10am-3pm; Jun-Aug 9am-4pm; Sep 10am-4pm; Oct-mid-Nov 11am-1pm. 9€ (children 3-10 7€). ☎04 68 95 50 50. www.lavalleedestortues.com.

The 2ha/5-acre park houses some 25 species of land and water tortoise from around the world.

Return to Sorède and continue left along D 2 to Laroque-des-Albères, then follow D 11 to Villelongue-dels-Monts. In the village, take Cami del Vilar to the priory 2km/1.2mi away.

Prieuré Santa Maria del Vilar

Open Apr-Oct 3-6pm (Jul-Aug 6.30pm); Nov-Mar 2.30-5.30pm. 4€; children 2€. ☎04 68 89 64 61.

The 11C priory is shaded by olive trees, holm oaks and cypresses.

Return to Villelongue-dels-Monts, turn left onto D 61A then right onto D 618 to Génis-des-Fontaines.

Saint-Génis-des-Fontaines

The decorations in the parish church and cloisters, namely the remarkable white-marble sculpted lintel dating from 1020, show the importance of this former Benedictine abbey.

Continue E along D 618.

Saint-André

Leave the car in the shaded square to the right of the village high street. Reach the church by walking through an archway.

This 12C church's exterior has pre-Romanesque fishbone features, a marble lintel and foiled altar table.

Argelès-sur-Mer

A. Thuillier/MICHELIN

Wind up your visit at the **Maison trans-frontalière d'art roman** (*open mid Jun-mid Sep daily except Mon 10-12pm; 2.30-7pm; mid Mar-mid Jun and mid Sep-mid Nov daily except Sun and Mon 10am-noon, 3-6pm. Closed mid Nov-mid Mar. 2€. 04 68 89 04 85. www.saint-andre66.fr/musee.htm).*

ADDRESSES

STAY

Camping Pujol – *04 68 81 00 25 – open Jun-Sep – reservations required – 249 pitches.* This shady camp site with jacuzzi, health club, evening dances and children's entertainment has pitches on the site of a sailing base.

Grand Hôtel du Lido – *Bd de la Mer. 04 68 81 10 32 – closed 1 Oct-27 Apr – 66 rms. 10€.* Direct access to the beach, swimming pool and shady garden. This hotel's spacious rooms have living areas and balconies overlooking the pool.

EAT

Salamandre – *3 rte de Laroque – 66690 Sorède – 9km/6mi W of Argelès-Plage on D 2 – 04 68 89 26 67 – closed 15 Jan-13 Mar, 5-20 Nov, Tues lunchtime 15 Jul-15 Sep, Sun evening and Mon.* This simple village restaurant features tempting regional dishes.

L'Amadeus – *Av. des Platanes. 04 68 81 12 38 – www.lamadeus.com – closed Dec-12 Feb, Tues, Wed and Thu in Feb-Mar and Mon except Jul-Aug.* This restaurant not far from the Argelès tourist office has a light and airy dining room, a terrace and nicely phrased menu. Terrace and patio. Well cooked regional cuisine.

SHOPPING

Marché artisanal – *Parking des Platanes – daily 5pm-midnight.* Local crafts.

SPORT AND LEISURE

Antares Sub – *Quai Marco-Polo – 04 68 81 46 30 / 06 14 98 31 37 – www.antares-sub.com – Jul-Aug daily 8am-noon, 2pm-8pm; Sep-Jun daily 8am-noon, 2pm-6pm.* The oldest scuba diving school in Argelès offers courses from levels 1-4, from beginning to advanced, including exploring wrecks.

ON THE TOWN

Carnaval Café – *14 av. des Mimosas – 04 68 81 02 06 – Apr-Sep daily 5pm-2am.* This bar-restaurant has a patio and terrace overlooking the pinewoods, and music from Latino to techno. After a few tapas or a main meal, the owners will offer you a Chupito, a very fruity liqueur.

Pub Flowers – *Av. du Gén.-de-Gaulle. 04 68 95 79 96 – Jun-Aug daily 8.30am-2am; Sep-May: Tues-Sun 4pm-2am – closed Nov.* In summer this bar with large terrace and good selection of cocktails and beers hosts African and South American music groups. Wild evenings assured.

Banyuls-sur-Mer

Set on a promontory, Banyuls is France's most southerly seaside resort, known for its lovely bay, yacht harbour, vineyards and sea-water therapy centre. Sheltered from the *tramontane*'s harsh north-westerly gusts, tropical flora like carob, eucalyptus and palms thrive along this Mediterranean coast all the way to the Riviera.

Info: Av. de la République, 66650 Banyuls-sur-Mer. 04 68 88 31 58. www.banyuls-sur-mer.com.
Location: 38km/23.75mi S of Perpignan on the N114.
Don't Miss: The view from Cap Réderis.

THE RESORT

The main beach is sheltered by a cove and two islands, Île Petite and Île Grosse. The Côte Vermeille's coastal waters are deep, clear and teeming with fish.

SIGHTS

Aquarium du Lab. Arago

Open Jul-Aug 9am-1pm, 2-9pm; Sep-Jun 9am-noon, 2-6.30pm. 4.60€ (children 6-12 2.30€). 04 68 88 73 39. www.obs-banyuls.fr.

This **Aquarium** displays Mediterranean fauna in a recreated environment.

Réserve Marine Naturelle de Banyuls-Cerbère

Created in 1974 to protect marine species endangered by intensive fishing, tourism activities and waste water pollution this conservation area covers 650ha/1 606 acres and 6.5km/4mi of rocky Languedoc-Roussillon coastline.

Écrin bleu: Underwater Trail

Part of the Banyuls-Cerbère Marine Nature Reserve. Open Jul-Aug noon-6pm. Equipment rental from noon to 5pm. Meeting point on the Peyrefite beach and information area on the yachting harbour. No charge. 04 68 88 56 87.

Observe red mullets, bass, rainbow wrasse, and on a lucky day, dolphins, loggerhead turtles and spotted sea horses. This 250m/273yd supervised underwater trail has five observation stations (at depths up to 5m/16ft) marked by buoys. Underwater information plaques guide you along.

Banyuls Wine

The famous **Banyuls wine** complements the best of tables, served as an apéritif, with dessert, or foie gras and strongly flavoured cheeses and game. Several cellars (**caves**) welcome the public, including two on the vertiginous Route des Crêtes. At the **Grande Cave** (*open Apr-Oct guided tours (1hr)*

Côte Vermeille and vineyards of Banyuls

A. Cassaigne/MICHELIN

10am-7.30pm; Nov-Mar daily except Sun 10am-1pm, 2.30-6.30pm. Closed 1 Jan and 25 Dec; no charge. 04 68 98 36 92. www.banyuls.com) see a video on the history of Banyuls and enjoy a guided tour of the oak barrel storage rooms, wines maturing in the sun and cellars containing antique casks.

The **Cellier des Templiers-cave du Mas Reig** *(Jul-Aug guided tours (45min) 10am-7.30pm; No charge; 04 68 98 36 70)* dates from the days of the (13C) Knights Templar, whose feudal castle and sub-commandery (Mas Reig) are next door *(closed to the public).*

MÉTAIRIE MAILLOL

5km/3mi SW. Open May-Sep 10am-noon, 4-7pm; Oct-Apr 10am-noon, 2-5pm. Closed public holidays. 3.50€. 04 68 88 57 11.

Aristide Maillol (1861-1944) was born in Banyuls. At 20 he "went up" to Paris to learn painting and became interested pottery and tapestry. After the age of 40 he gained renown for his sculptures of nude figures, remarkable for their grace and power. Maillol enjoyed his little country retreat, which now as the Musée Maillol, displays many of his sculptures, terracotta, paintings and drawings.

Le Boulou

This spa resort at the foot of the Albères mountains makes an ideal base for exploring the Roussillon. On the fringe of an exotic cork-oak wood, Le Boulou has two cork-making factories.

- **Population:** 4 858
- **Michelin Map:** 344: I 6-7.
- **Info:** 1 r. du Château, 66160 Le Boulou. 04 68 87 50 95. www.ot-leboulou.fr. Guided tours (*1hr 30min*) leave at 3pm on Thu from the tourist office (*4.50€*).
- **Location:** 27km/17mi S of Perpignan by D 900.
- **Don't Miss:** Céret Museum of Modern Art, the panorama from Fort de Bellegarde and Pic des Trois Termes.

VISIT

The town's medieval past is reflected in remnants of its 14C curtain wall and early 15C chapel of St-Antoine.

Église Notre-Dame d'El Voló

Open 9am-noon. 04 68 87 51 00.

Of the original 12C Romanesque church, the white-marble **portal** by the Master of Cabestany has survived. A beautiful Baroque altarpiece adorns the high altar and in the nave, a 15C predella depicts St John the Baptist and St John the Evangelist.

DRIVING TOURS

1 MONTS ALBÈRES

49km/30mi round tour – half a day.

The Albères mountain range is the last outcrop of crystalline rocks on the eastern flank of the Pyrenees. Its highest peak, Pic Neulos, towers 1 256m/4 120ft above sea level.

Leave Le Boulou W on D 115.

Céret★

See CÉRET

Leave Céret heading SW on D 13F towards Fontfrède.

This pleasant road climbs through chestnut groves, offering many pretty views. Turn right off the Las Illas road at the Col de la Brousse (alt 860m/2 820ft) into a very winding road to the **Col de Fontfrède** (June 1940-June 1944 stele). You'll find a fountain and picnic area at the pass.

Return to the Col de la Brousse and turn right towards Las Illas.

L. Campion/MICHELIN

Wise Man Bearing a Gift – Fresco in the Chapelle St-Martin-de-Fenollar

The road winds through dense vegetation, terraced gardens and scattered farmhouses, with the music of tinkling goat bells at every turn. The Case Nove mas (farmhouse) and the Mas Liansou are traditional Albères dwellings. After Las Illas, the road follows the river, clinging to the rock face and affording excellent views of the river gorge.

Maureillas-Las-Illas

In this holiday village amidst cork-oak groves and orchards, cork-cutters have created a cork museum, **Musée du Liège** (*open mid-Jun to mid-Sep 10.30am-noon/3.30-7pm, mid-Sep–mid-Jun daily except Tue 2-5pm; closed 1 Jan, 1 May, 1 Nov, 25 Dec. 3€, children 1€. 04 68 83 15 41*). Learn about cork and see astonishing cork sculptures and magnificent oak casks showcasing local handicrafts.

Chapelle St-Martin-de-Fenollar

Open mid Jun-mid Sep 10.30am-noon, 3.30-7pm; mid Sep-mid Jun daily except Tue 2-5pm. Closed 1 Jan, 1 May, 1 Nov, 25 Dec. 3€. 04 68 87 73 82.

This modest 9C chapel founded by Benedictines from Arles-sur-Tech contains interesting 12C **mural paintings★**.

N 9 leads back to Le Boulou.

2 THE ROME VALLEY

53km/33mi from Le Boulou to Pic des Trois Termes – allow half a day.

From Boulou guided tours of the Rome valley are organised by the Association pour le patrimoine de la vallée de la Rome (local heritage association). Information and reservations: Mairie du Boulou 04 68 87 51 58 and Le Boulou tourist office. 04 68 87 50 95.

The **Vallée de la Rome** is an essential communication route between France and Spain, traversed for two millennia since the Via Domitia's construction in c. 120 BC. Leave the "Catalane" motorway to discover awesome megalithic, Gallo-Roman and medieval sites in a superb landscape.

Leave Le Boulou on N 9 S towards Le Perthus.

Chapelle St-Martin-de-Fenollar

See above.

Go back to N 9.

Les Cluses

These hamlets on either side of the narrow gorge (*clusa* in Latin) between the Via Domitia and the Rome Valley contain 3C-4C Roman remains: the **Château des Maures** or "Castell d els Moros" and **Fort de la Cluse Haute**. Next to the fort, the **church of St-Nazaire** is a pre-Romanesque construction with three naves (late 10C-early 11C) and traces of frescoes attributed to the Master of Fenollar. (*open 9am-noon, 1.30-5pm. closed Sun, book in advance at town hall 04 68 87 77 20*).

Le Perthus

Since prehistory, Le Perthus has seen the comings and goings of nomadic hordes, armies, refugees and now tourists. The original hamlet became a town in the late 19C.

From the centre of Le Perthus, turn left towards the Fort de Bellegarde.

Fort de Bellegarde

Open Jun-Sep 10.30am-6.30pm 3€ (children 2€). 04 68 83 60 15.

This powerful fortress overlooking Le Perthus from 420m/1 380ft above sea level, was rebuilt by Saint Hilaire, and then by Vauban between 1679 and 1688.

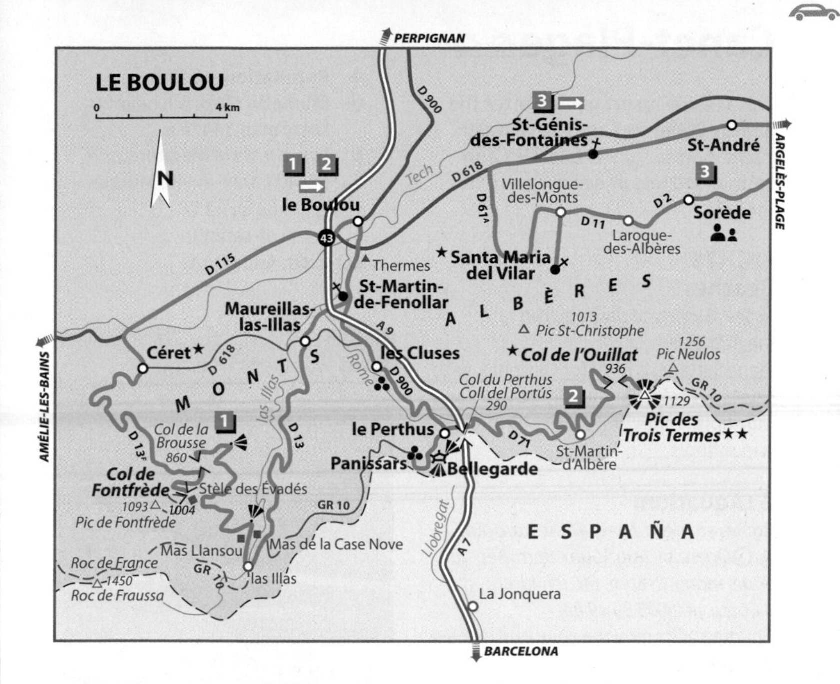

The terrace offers a vast **panorama**★★ of the Canigou and Fontfrède peaks, the Rome valley, Le Perthus, the Panissars archaeological site and in Spain, the Rio Llobregat valley and the town of La Jonquera.

Site Archéologique de Panissars

During the Roman occupation, the Panissars Pass, the "Summum Pyrenaeum," was the main Pyrenees route. In 1984, foundations of a huge Roman monument were discovered and thought to be the remains of the Trophy of Pompey, erected to celebrate Pompey's 71 BC victory in Spain against Sertorius.

Turn back and, N of Le Perthus, turn right onto D 71 to the Col de l'Ouillat.

This road passes by groves of chestnut trees and the magnificent oaks of St-Martin-de-l'Albères, with views of the Canigou and the southern Albères slopes and St-Christophe summit. *From a right-hand bend catch a view of Trois Termes Peak.*

Col de l'Ouillat★

Alt 936m/3 070ft.

A cool stopping place with a viewing terrace on the edge of the Laroque-des-Albères Forest. The road winds through beeches and pines to the rocky outcrop of Trois Termes.

Pic des Trois Termes★★

Alt 1 129m/3 703ft.

Enjoy a **panorama** of the Albères mountains, Roussillon plain and coastal lagoons, the Confluent and Vallespir valleys, and the Spanish Costa Brava.

Turn back.

The unsurfaced road between the Pic des Trois Termes and Sorède is accessible only by four-wheel-drive.

3 FOOT OF MONTS ALBÈRES

32km/20mi round tour from St-Genis-des-Fontaines.

See ST-GENIS-DES-FONTAINES.

Canet-Plage

This seaside resort named after the nearby Étang de Canet has a busy yacht marina, sports facilities and casino, and lots of nearby activities for kids.

- **Population:** 10 182.
- **Michelin Map:** Michelin Local map 344: J-6.
- **Info:** Pl. de la Méditerranée, 66140 Canet-en-Roussillon. 04 68 86 72 00. www.ot-canet.fr.
- **Kids:** Aquarium.

SIGHTS

Beaches

See 'Getting to the beach' in the Addresses.

Plage Sardinal is ideal for camping, with seven shady family-friendly beaches and minigolf, volleyball and sailing clubs and schools.

Aquarium

Boulevard de la Jetée, at the harbour. Open Jul-Aug 10am-8pm; Sep-Jun: 10am-noon, 2-6pm. 6€ (children: 3.50€). 04 68 80 49 64.

Children will enjoy the colourful display of local and tropical species.

Étang de Canet

W of Canet-Plage along D 81 towards St-Cyprien. Accessible by car (parking area), on foot or by bus. Possibility of guided tours. 04 68 80 89 78.

Canet lagoon is a protected natural environment with 300 bird species. Fishermen's huts of plaited reeds cluster around the lagoon's banks and a footpath weaves through the lagoon's flora and fauna.

Canet lagoon and Canigou Mountain

A. Thuillier/MICHELIN

EXCURSION

St-Cyprien

9km/5.6mi S.

This small elegant residential town with palm-tree-lined streets has preserved its historic Catalan village.

Collections de St-Cyprien

4 rue Émile-Zola, near the town hall. Open Jul-Aug 10am-noon, 3-7pm; Sep-Jun daily except Tue 10am-noon, 2-6pm. Closed 1 Jan, 1 May, 11 Nov, 24-25 and 31 Dec. 6€. 04 68 21 06 96. www.collectionsdesaintcyprien.com.

This museum contains works of local painter François Desnoyers (1894-1972), which trace his artistic development, as well as his personal collection of works by Gleizes, Picasso, Pierre Ambroggiani etc.

St-Cyprien-Plage

The seaside resort has a residential district, harbour and 3km/1.8mi of sandy beaches. Its lively marina is the second-largest in Mediterranean France.

ADDRESSES

STAY

Hôtel La Lagune – *66750 St-Cyprien – 9km/6mi S of Canet on D 81A – 04 68 21 24 24 – www.hotel-lalagune.com – closed 1 Oct-7 May – P – 49rms.* Two swimming pools and beach makes this holiday hotel between land and sea a real pleasure, even though rooms are plain and functional.

EAT

Le Don Quichotte – *22 av. de Catalogne - 04 68 80 35 17 – closed 10 Jan-9 Feb, Tue noon, Wed noon in Jul-Aug, Mon-Tue (except evenings in Jul-Aug).* The vibrant salmon pink dining room of this restaurant serves up classical cuisine.

RECREATION

Getting to the beach – *tram and train operates in Jul-Aug from Canet – ℘04 68 61 01 13.*

Club nautique Canet-Perpignan – *Zone technique – Le Port – ℘04 68 73 33 95 – daily 9am-noon, 2-6pm – closed 20 Dec-24 jan.* Sailing club.

Aqualand – *Av. des Champs de Neptune, Les Capellans 66750 St-Cyprien – ℘04 68 21 49 49 – mid-Jun to mid-Sep – south of Les Capellans.* Aquapark.

Club Omnipêche Plaisance – *Quai Rimbaud, 66750 St-Cyprien – ℘06 09 54 78 12 – Jun-Sep.* Halfday fishing trips and fishing lessons.

Aéro Service Littoral – *Rte de Ste-Marie – 66440 Torreilles – ℘04 68 28 13 73 – www.ulm-torreilles.com – daily 8am-12.30pm, 2pm-7pm – first flight 30P.* ULM and motorized hang-gliding courses.

Collioure★★

This colourful little fortress town on the Côte Vermeille attracts huge crowds of tourists. Its lovely setting amidst the Albères foothills has been immortalised on canvas by painters like Derain, Braque, Othon, Friesz, Matisse, Picasso and Foujita. Its many attractions include a fortified church, royal castle, seaside promenade, brightly coloured Catalan boats, old streets with flower-bedecked balconies, outdoor cafés and inviting boutiques.

- **Population:** 2 763.
- **Michelin Map:** 344: J-7, See La CÔTE VERMEILLE.
- **Info:** Collioure Tourism Office Pl du 18 Juin. ℘04 68 82 15 47. www.collioure.com.
- **Location:** 31km/19.3mi S of Perpignan via the N114 then D114.
- **Don't Miss:** Boramar beach; anchovy tastings; the Old Port; Museum of Modern Art.
- **Kids:** a diving orientation or boat ride with CIP.

A BIT OF HISTORY

When Catalan naval forces ruled the Mediterranean as far as the Levant, medieval Collioure was the trading port for Roussillon. In 1463 Louis XI's invading troops marked the beginning of a turbulent period in which the castle was built on the rocky spur separating the port into two coves. After the Peace Treaty of the Pyrenees, the enclosed town was razed to the ground in 1670 and the lower town became the main town.

SIGHTS

Walk to the old port or "Port d'Amont" via quai de l'Amirauté on the banks of the "Ravin du Douy."

Chemin du Fauvisme

A marked route through the streets of Collioure passes 20 stages celebrating city views painted by Henri Matisse

Anchovies From Collioure

Collioure anchovies feature in many Catalan dishes. *Anchoïade* is an anchovie paste mashed with olive oil, garlic and basil – delicious spread on French toast as an accompaniment to apéritifs. Collioure anchovies have been preserved in the same way for generations. The gutted fish pickle in vats of brine from May to August, then are rinsed, removed of their backbones and left to drain. Finally they are packaged into glass jars or tins filled with oil. Local **Collioure** producers have added tubes of anchovy paste and olives stuffed with anchovies to their product lines.

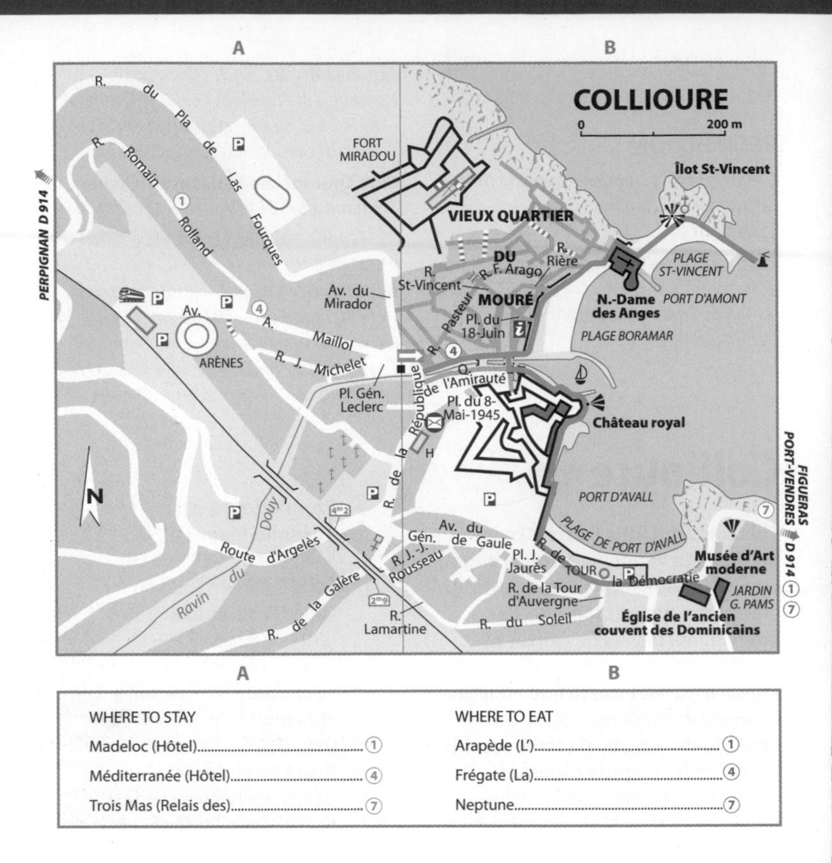

and André Derain. (*Guided tours are also available, contact the tourist office for details: ✆04 68 98 07 16*).

Église Notre-Dame-des-Anges

Built between 1684 and 1691 this church's distinctive bell-tower was once the lighthouse for the old port.

Inside are nine ornately carved and gilded **altarpieces**★ including the 1698 high altar work of Catalan artist Joseph Sunyer. An immense three-storey triptych completely hides the apse. The sacristy houses a beautiful Louis XIII vestment cupboard, 15C paintings, a 16C reliquary and 17C Madonna.

Ancien îlot St-Vincent

The former island is connected to the church by two beaches. Behind the little chapel, a panorama takes in the Côte Vermeille and a sea wall leads to the lighthouse.

Go back.

Old district of Mouré

Enjoy pleasant strolls through the steep flower-filled back streets of this old district near the church.

Cross the Douy, at the end of the marina.

The path along the quayside skirts the Château Royal's impressive walls. From the western car park, towards the Douy, is an excellent **view** of the town and port with the Albères mountains towering over the sea.

Continue to the Port d'Avall beach called the "Faubourg."

Admire the colourful boats along the way and stop under the shady palms to watch a lively game of boules.

Bell tower of Église Notre-Dame-des-Anges and Château Royal

L. Campion/MICHELIN

Église de l'ancien couvent des Dominicains

This old church now houses the local wine co-operative.

Château Royal

Open Jul-Aug 10am-7pm, Jun and Sep 10am-6pm; Oct-May 9am-5pm. Closed 1 Jan, 1 May, 15-16 Aug, 25 & 31 Dec. 4€ (children under 12 free). 04 68 82 06 43. www.cg66.fr

This imposing castle built on a Roman site juts into the sea between the Port d'Amont and the Port d'Avall. It was the summer residence of Majorcan kings from 1276 to 1344 until it was taken over by the kings of Aragón. Tour the underground passages and main courtyard, parade ground, 16C prison, 13C chapel, Queen's bedchamber and upper rooms and ramparts. The 17C barracks house exhibitions on grape vines, cork, Sorède whips, *espadrilles* (rope-soled sandals) and Catalan boats.

ADDRESSES

STAY

Hôtel Méditerranée – *Av. Aristide-Maillol. 04 68 82 08 60 – www.mediterranee-hotel.com – closed Dec-Apr – 23rms – 10€.* Retro building; rooms with balconies. Garden; solarium.

Hôtel Madeloc – *R. Romain-Rolland. 04 68 82 07 56 – www.madeloc.com – closed 3 Nov-14 Mar – P - 27rms – 11€.* Rooms furnished in rattan; some with terraces. Garden.

Relais des Trois Mas – *Rte Port-Vendres. 04 68 82 05 07 – www.relaisdestroismas.com – closed 30 Nov-7 Feb – P – 23rms – 18€.* Lovely rooms; garden, swimming pool, jacuzzi.

EAT

La Frégate – *24 quai Camille-Pelletan. 04 68 82 06 05 – www.fregatecollioure.com.* Coastal cuisine, of course; some rooms.

L'Arapède – *Rte de Port-Vendres. 04 68 98 09 59 – www.arapede.com.* Decorated with aerial photos of Collioure; terrace, regional cuisine.

Neptune – *Rte de Port-Vendres. 04 68 82 02 27.* Seafood dishes, and regional specialties; unhindered view of the Old Port from the terraces.

Côte Vermeille ★★

The resorts along this rocky stretch of coast, tucked into little bays, were once small maritime fortresses. The "vermilion" coast is named after the local landscape, whose colour is enhanced by the clear light of this region. Explore the Côte Vermeille via the Route des crêtes (N 114) mountain road, and Route du littoral, the coast road, via Collioure and Port-Vendres *(heavy summer traffic)*.

- **Michelin Map:** Michelin Local map 344: J-7 to K-8.
- **Info:** Office du Tourisme de Collioure, Pl du 18 Juin, 04 68 82 15 47 www.collioure.com
- **Location:** 30km/18.75mi SW of Perpignan by D 914. Argelès Plage is the gateway to the Vermeille Coast.
- **Don't Miss:** The picturesque port of Collioure and the Spanish ambience of Cerbère.
- **Kids:** Swimming off the beaches along the coast!

DRIVING TOURS

1 THE MOUNTAIN ROAD

37km/23mi from Argelès-Plage to Cerbère – about 2hr 30min.

Argelès-Plage

See ARGELÈS-PLAGE.

Beyond Argelès and the stretch of beach to the north, the coast becomes much more dramatic as the (N 114) climbs into the Albères foothills and cuts across rocky headlands lapped by the Mediterranean.

At the roundabout just before Collioure, take D 86 left. The road heads uphill, through the Collioure vineyards.

Turn left again at the first intersection, onto a downhill road.

Notre-Dame-de-Consolation

This hermitage is well known throughout Roussillon. Its chapel contains votive offerings from sailors.

Turn back to D 86 and turn left (note: this stretch of mountain road has no safety barriers or other protection).

Cork-oaks appear between patches of exposed black rock schist.

Cap Réderis

©Franck Guiziou/Hemis/Photoshot

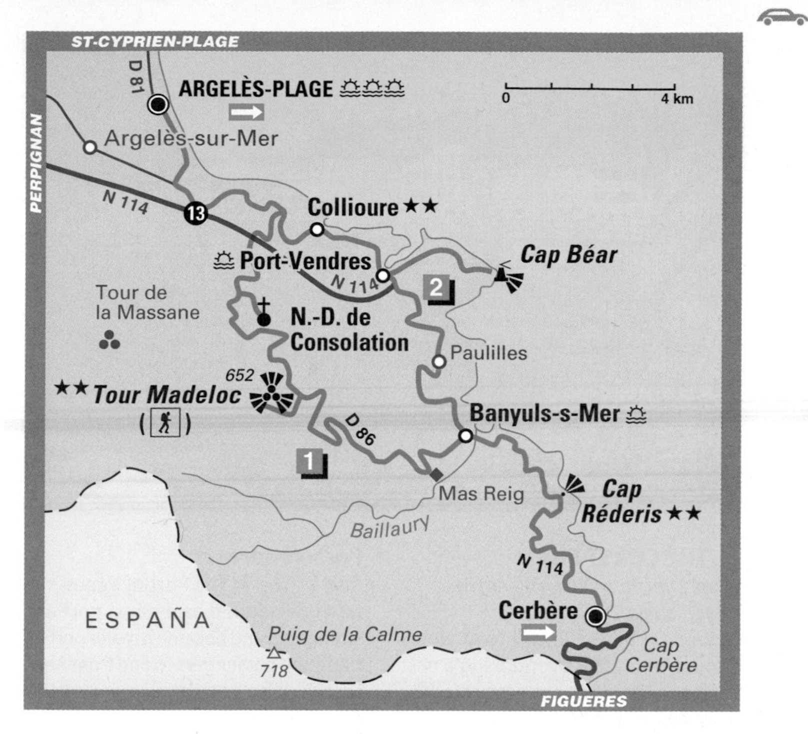

Follow the signs for the "Circuit du vignoble" wine route through the vineyards towards Banyuls.

This spectacular mountain road leads to a viewing table and ruins of an 1885 barracks.

Take the steep, narrow track to the right leading up to Tour Madeloc (Note: extreme caution required: gradient of 1:4, with tight hairpin bends and no space for passing).

The road passes two more fortified constructions before reaching a small level plateau.

Tour Madeloc

Alt 652m/2 138ft. 15min on foot round-trip.

This old round signal tower was part of a network of lookout posts during the reign of the kings of Aragón and Mallorca. Tour de la Massane surveyed the Roussillon plain and Tour Madeloc kept watch out to sea. Enjoy a splendid **panorama**★★ of the Albères mountains, the Vermeille and Roussillon coasts. The track back down to D 86 gives breathtaking **views**★ of the sea and Banyuls.

Turn right onto D 86.

The road leads to Banyuls, passing the Mas Reig underground wine cellar situated in the oldest vineyard in the Banyuls area, as well as the modern cellar in which wines from the Cave des Templiers are aged.

Banyuls

See BANYULS-SUR-MER.

Cap Réderis★★

See below.

Cerbère

This charming seaside resort is the last French town before Spain and the Costa Brava. Set in a little cove with a pebble beach, it has white houses, outdoor cafés and narrow pedestrian streets. The international railway from Paris to Barcelona stops here.

Port-Vendres

A. Thuillier/MICHELIN

2 THE COAST ROAD

33km/21mi from Cerbère to Argelès-Plage – about 2hr.

Beyond Cerbère, the cliff road winds through vineyards overlooking a vast seascape. Beaches are separated by sharp promontories.

Cap Réderis★★

Where the road edges the cliff, you'll have a magnificent **panorama** of the Languedoc and Catalonia coasts as far south as the Cabo de Creus. Farther along you'll see the bay of Banyuls, spectacular at high tide. The road drops down towards Banyuls, with views of the town and its palms and pebble beach.

Banyuls

See BANYULS-SUR-MER.

Leaving Banyuls, the road passes a seaside spa for heliotherapy. Tour Madeloc looms in the distance and before Port-Vendres is an excellent view of the port.

Turn right towards Cap Béar then, after the Hôtel des Tamarins, cross the railway line and drive round to the south of the bay.

Cap Béar

The narrow cliff road climbs steeply in tight bends. From the lighthouse on the headland, you can see down the coast from Cap Leucate to Cabo de Creus.

Port-Vendres

Also known as the Port of Venus, this town developed as a naval port and stronghold and became a major port for trade and passengers to and from Algeria. Now it is a popular pleasure boating centre, and has the most active fishing fleet on the Roussillon coast.

Collioure★★

See COLLIOURE.

The road leaves the foothills of the Albères before reaching Argelès.

ADDRESSES

STAY

Ermitage Notre Dame de Consolation – *66190 Collioure – 04 68 82 17 66 – closed 11 Nov-31 Mar – P – 12 rms.* This pilgrimage site in an oasis of greenery has fresh and colourful rooms, some in old monks' cells. Visit the chapel and enjoy the picnic area.

EAT

Ferme-auberge Les Clos de Paulilles – *66660 Port-Vendres – 3km/2mi N of Banyuls on N 114 – 04 68 98 07 58.* Terrace restaurant in a vineyard serves good country cooking.

Elne★

Set among apricot and peach orchards by the coast, Elne was named after the Empress Helen, Constantine's mother, and Iberians knew it as "Illiberis." At the end of the Roman Empire, it was the true capital of the Roussillon area and is a major stopping point on the road to Spain. The superb cathedral cloisters testify to Elne's former splendour.

- **Population:** 6 410.
- **Michelin Map:** Michelin Local map 344: I-7.
- **Info:** Office du tourisme d'Elne, Pl. Sant-Jordi ☎04 68 22 05 07. www.ot-elne.fr
- **Location:** 14km/8.75mi S of Perpignan on the N114.
- **Don't Miss:** Adam and Eve column in the Cathédrale Ste-Eulalie-et-Ste-Julie
- **Kids:** Cathedral; Tropique du Papillon.

CATHÉDRALE STE-EULALIE-ET-STE-JULIE *1hr*

Building of the cathedral began in the 11C. The ribbed vaulting of the six chapels in the south aisle, built from the 14C to the mid-15C, reflects the three stages in the evolution of Gothic architecture.

Cloisters★★

To enter the cloisters, walk round the chevet to the left. Open Jun-Sep 9.30am-6.45pm; Apr-May 9.30am-5.45pm; Oct 9.30am-12.15pm, 2pm-5.45pm; Nov-Mar 9.30am-11.45am, 2-4.45pm. Closed 1 Jan, 1 May, 25 Dec. 5€ (children 2€). ☎04 68 22 70 90. The south cloisters were built in the 12C; the other three date from the 13C and 14C. The superb **capitals** on the twin columns are decorated with imaginary animals, biblical and evangelical figures, and plants, but the most remarkable work is Capital 12, depicting Adam and Eve, in the Romanesque south gallery.

Musée d'Archéologie

Entrance up the staircase at the end of the east cloisters. The archaeological museum in the old chapel of St-Laurent exhibits 15C to 17C earthenware, Attic ceramics (4C BC) and sigillated ceramic ware from Illiberis (Elne under Roman rule) and reconstructions of Véraza culture huts of wood and reeds.

Musée d'Histoire

Entrance via the west cloisters. The history museum contains archives, literature and town seals, along with statues of the Virgin Mary, the Vierge des Tres Portalets (13C) and the Vierge du Portail de Perpignan (14C).

SIGHTS

Musée Terrus

Open Jun-Sep 9.30am-7pm; Apr-May 9.30am-6pm; Oct 9.30am-12.30pm, 2-6pm; Nov-Mar 9.30am-noon, 2-5pm. Closed 1 Jan, 1 May, 25 Dec. 2.50€ (children 1.20€) ticket combined with the Elne cloister). ☎04 68 22 88 88. This museum named after Étienne Terrus (1857-1922) displays works by him and other artists whose company he kept, such as Luce, Maillol and G de Monfreid.

Le Tropique du Papillon

Entrance via avenue Paul-Reig, at the intersection with the Argelès-Perpignan road (N 114). Open Jun-Aug 10am-7pm; mid Apr-May and Sep 10am-12.30pm, 2.30-6pm. 6€. ☎04 68 37 83 77. www.tropique-du-papillon.com. Night and day, butterflies and moths flutter freely around this tropical hothouse; there is a nursery and an educational area.

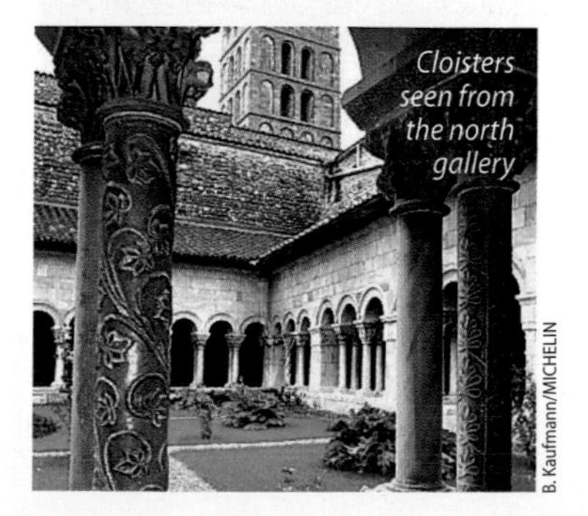
Cloisters seen from the north gallery

B. Kaufmann/MICHELIN

Perpignan★★

Perpignan, once the capital city of the counts of Roussillon and the kings of Majorca, is an outlying post of Catalan civilisation north of the Pyrenees, and a lively commercial city, with shaded walks lined with pavement cafés. The economy is largely based on tourism, wine and olive oil, and the production of cork, wool and leather.

- **Info:** Palais des Congrès, pl. A.-Lanoux, 66000 Perpignan. ℘04 68 66 30 30. www.perpignantourisme.com. Guided tour of the town: Inquire at the tourist office or at www.vpah.culture.fr.
- **Location:** The A 9 (exit 42) and the N 9 both lead to Perpignan; access to the downtown area by Boulevard Edmond Michelet (west), Avenue des Baléares *(south)* or Pont Arago *(north, over the Têt River)*.
- **Parking:** Leave your car in the lots near the Promenade des Platanes.
- **Don't Miss:** Le Castillet, symbol of Perpignan.
- **Timing:** Take the town walk first, to get the lay of the land; save time for the Palace of the Kings of Majorca; visit the Additional Sights if your time allows. The Excursion to the Rousillon Plain will require a day.
- **Kids:** Palais des Rois de Majorque.

A BIT OF HISTORY

During the 13C, the city profited from the great upsurge in trade between the south of France, and the Levant stimulated by the crusades. In 1276, Perpignan became the capital of Roussillon as part of the kingdom of Majorca.

The second Catalan city – After the kingdom of Majorca had ceased to be in 1344, Roussillon and Cerdagne were integrated into the princedom of Catalonia which, in the 14C and 15C, constituted a kind of autonomous federation in the heart of the State of Aragón. Catalan "Corts" sat at Barcelona, but delegated a "Deputation" to Perpignan. Between the two slopes of the Pyrenees, a commercial, cultural and linguistic community came into being.

French or Spanish? – In 1463, Louis XI helped King John II of Aragón to defeat the Catalans and took possession of Perpignan and Roussillon. However, hostilities with France broke out once more and French armies besieged the city. The people of Perpignan put up fierce resistance and surrendered only when ordered to do so by the king of Aragón, who gave the city the title of "Fidelissima" (most faithful).

Palais des Rois de Majorque
H. Champollion/MICHELIN

In 1493, Charles VIII gave the province of Roussillon back to the to the Spanish. Later however, Cardinal Richelieu seized the opportunity offered by a Catalan rebellion against Spain, forming an alliance with rebels and, in 1641, Louis XIII became count of Barcelona.

The final siege of Perpignan – As a Spanish garrison was holding Perpignan, the city was laid to siege. Louis XIII arrived with the elite of the French army and Perpignan finally surrendered on 9 September 1642.

The Treaty of the Pyrenees ratified the reunification of Roussillon with the

Wrought-iron campanille of Cathédrale St-Jean and the Castillet with the Catalan flag

©Bertrand Rieger/Hemis/Photoshot

French crown, and Perpignan became French once and for all.

TOWN WALK

Le Castillet★

This monument, an emblem of Perpignan dominates place de la Victoire. Its two towers are crowned with exceptionally tall crenellations and machicolations.

Promenade des Platanes

This wide avenue is lined with plane trees and adorned with fountains. Palm trees grow along the side avenues.

La Miranda

This is a small public park behind the church of St-Jacques. It is given over to the plant life of the *garrigue* and shrubs which are either native or have been introduced to the region.

Église St-Jacques

Open daily except Mon 11am–5pm.

At the west end of the nave, a vast chapel added in the 18C was reserved for the brotherhood of La Sanch ("of the precious Blood"). From 1416, this penitents' brotherhood, performed a solemn procession on Maundy Thursday (now Good Friday), carrying its *misteris* to the singing of hymns.

Place de la Loge

This square and the pedestrianised rue de la Loge, paved in pink marble, form the lively centre of town life. Here, in summer, the *sardana* is danced several times a week.

Loge de Mer★

This fine Gothic building, dating from 1397 and refurbished and extended in the 16C, once housed a commercial tribunal in charge of ruling on claims relating to maritime trade.

Hôtel de Ville★

Patio: daily except Sat–Sun and public holidays 8am–6pm (Fri 8am–5pm).

In the arcaded courtyard stands a bronze by Maillol: *The Mediterranean*. On the façade of the building, three bronze arms, which are said to symbolise the "hands" or estates of the population required to elect the five consuls, were in fact originally designed to hold torches.

Palais de la Députation

During the reign of the kings of Aragón this 15C palace was the seat of the permanent commission or *députation* representing the Catalan "Corts."

Place Arago

This lively, pleasant square, adorned with palm trees and magnolias and bordered with cafés, attracts crowds of people. In the centre stands the statue of the famous physician, astronomer and politician François Arago (1786-1853).

Return to the Palais de la Députation.

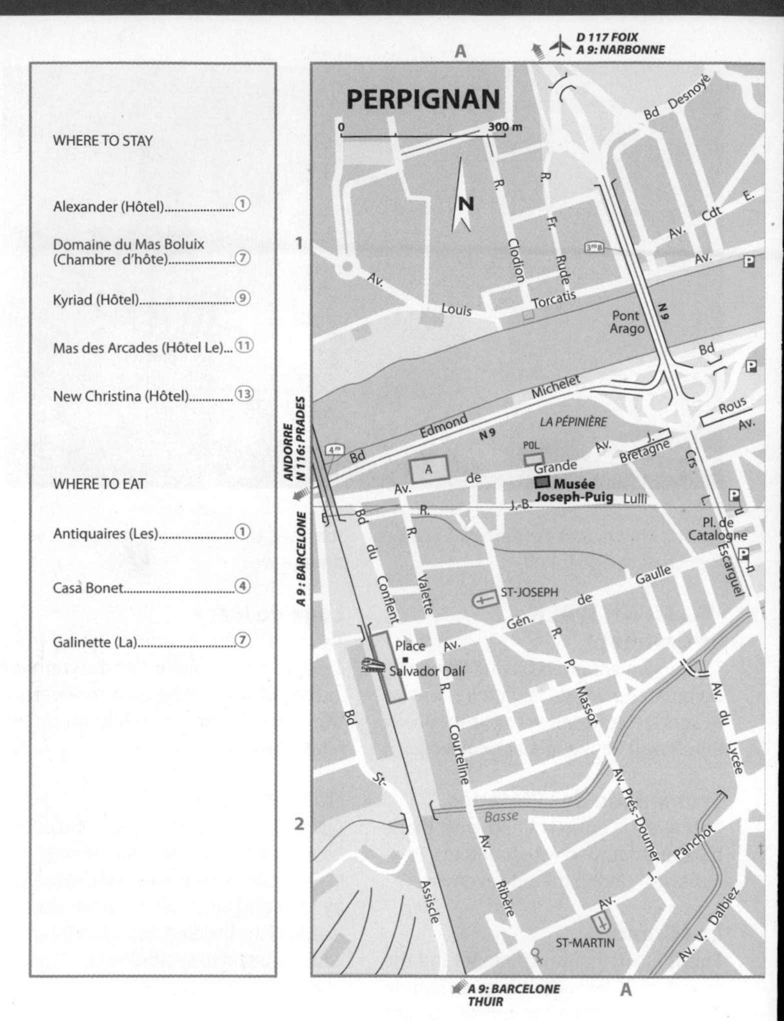

Opposite the Palais de la Députation, take a little detour down the small rue des Fabriques d'En Nabot, The **Maison Julia★** at no 2 is one of the few well-preserved *hôtels* of Perpignan, possessing a patio with 14C Gothic arcades.

Return to Le Castillet.

ADDITIONAL SIGHTS

Palais des Rois de Majorque★

Open Jun-Sep 10am–6pm (last admission 45min before closing); Oct-May 9am–5pm. Closed 1 Jan, 1 May, 1 Nov, 25 Dec. 4€ (under 12 no charge). 04 68 34 48 29.

When the kings of Majorca came to the throne in 1276, they built their palace on the hill of Puig del Rey.

A vaulted slope leads across the red-brick ramparts to a pleasant Mediterranean garden. Pass beneath a tower to the west, the **tour de l'Homage**, to get to the square-shaped main courtyard. This is open on the east and west sides with two storeys of arcades.

On the first floor of the south wing, the **great hall of Majorca** has a chimney-piece with three fireplaces. Beyond it, the Queen's suite has a superb ceiling painted with the Catalan colours (green and red). The most splendid part of the building is the **chapel-keep** of Ste-Croix rising above the east wing. It comprises two

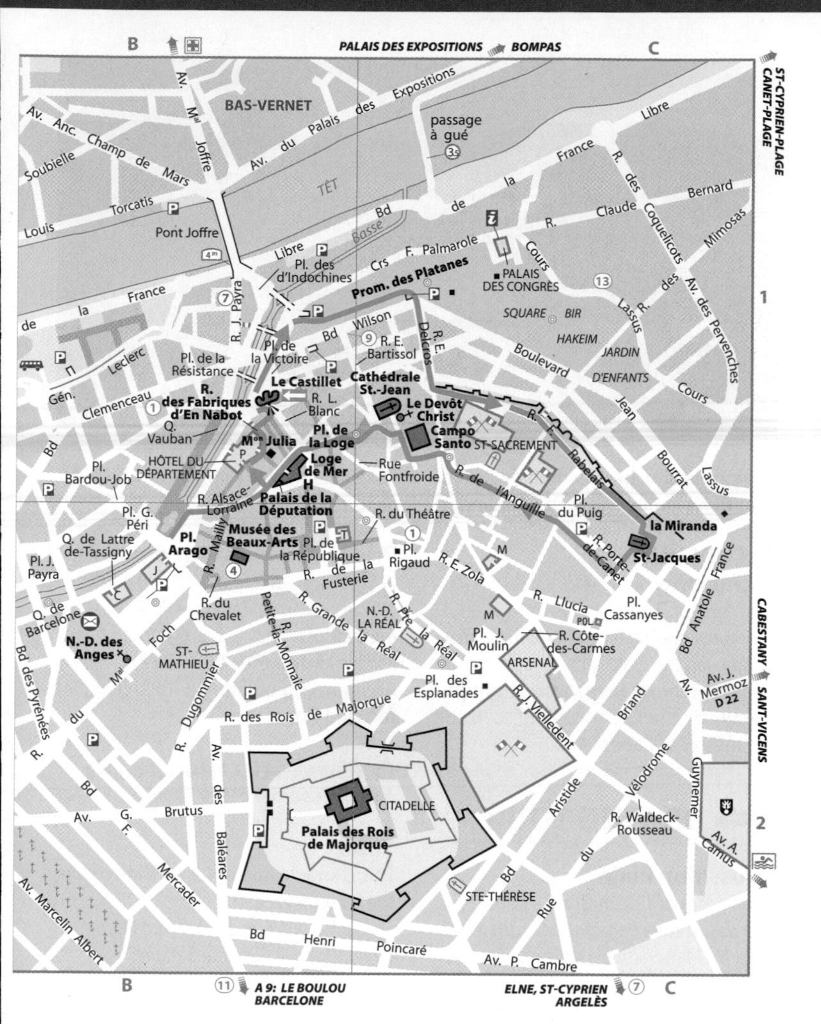

sanctuaries built one above the other in the 14C by Jaime II of Majorca.

Cathédrale St-Jean★

The main church was begun in 1324 by Sancho, second king of Majorca, but was not consecrated until 1509.

The oblong façade of the basilica is constructed from courses of pebbles alternating with bricks. It is flanked on the right by a square tower with a fine 18C wrought-iron campanile housing a 15C bell.

Campo Santo

Open Apr-Sep daily except Mon noon-7pm; Oct-Mar daily except Mon 11am-5.30pm. Closed 1 Jan, 25 Dec. No charge 04 68 66 30 30. www.perpignantourisme.com.

Situated south of the cathedral, the Campo Santo is a vast square graveyard which exhibits great architectural unity with its pointed funeral alcoves and marble recesses, set into walls adorned with pebbles and courses of brick.

Musée Numismatique Joseph-Puig★

42 Ave. de Grande-Bretagne.

Open Wed and Sat 9.30-6pm, Tue, Thu and Fri on demand. 4€. 04 68 66 24 86.

Part of the Villa "Les Tilleuls" (1907) has been converted into a museum, at the donor's request, to display the numis-

Castelnou

J. Malburet/MICHELIN

matic collection bequeathed by Joseph Puig to his native city of Perpignan.

EXCURSION

Cabestany

5km/3mi on D 22 to the SE.

Inside the church of **Notre-Dame-des-Anges**, on the wall of the chapel on the right is a famous Romanesque **tympanum**★. by the 12C travelling sculptor, the master of Cabestany.

DRIVING TOUR

Roussillon Plain

Round tour of 128km/80mi – allow one day. Leave Perpignan S, turn left onto N 114 then take a little road on the right towards Villeneuve-de-la-Raho.

Mas Palégry

Situated among vineyards, Mas Palégry is the setting for an **Aviation museum**. (*visit by arrangement. 5€. 06 18 92 64 14. www.musee-aviation.com*).

Follow D 612 towards Thuir and turn right to Ponteilla.

Jardin Exotique de Ponteilla

Open daily Jul-Aug 2-6.30pm; Apr-May and Sep Wed and weekends 2-6.30pm. Closed rest of year. 5€. 04 68 53 22 44.

A signposted botanical trail.

Turn back, cross D 612 and drive on to Trouillas, turn right onto D 37 to Villemolaque and continue along D 40 towards Passa.

Prieuré du Monastir del Camp

guided tours (45min) daily, except Thu 3pm, 4pm and 5pm (Jul-Aug additional tour at 6pm). Closed 1 Jan, 25 Dec. 4€. 04 68 38 80 71.

An imposing building with an elegant fortified front.

Drive along D 2 to Fourques then turn right onto D 615 to Thuir.

Thuir

This is known mainly for its wine cellars, the **caves Byrrh**.

(*Jul-Aug guided tour (45min) daily, 10am-11.45am, 2-6.45pm; Apr-Jun and Sep-Oct 9-11.45am, 2.30-5.45pm; Nov-Mar daily except Mon 10.45am,2.30pm and 4pm. 2€. 04 68 53 05 42. www.byrrh.com*).

Take D 48 W.

The road climbs the slopes of the Aspre. Suddenly the medieval village of Castelnou comes into sight with Mont Canigou rising in the background, making a wonderful **view**★.

Castelnou

Open Jul-Aug 10am-7pm; Apr-Jun 11-6pm; Sep-Dec and Feb-Mar 11am-5pm. Closed Jan. 4.50€. 04 68 53 22 91.

Fortified village with paved streets at the foot of the chateau.

ADDRESSES

STAY

Hôtel Alexander – *15 Bd. Clemenceau. 04 68 35 41 41. www.hotel-alexander.fr. 25rms – 7.50€ meals*. This little downtown hotel has balconied, air-conditioned guestrooms on three levels (with elevator). Enthusiastic welcome.

Chambre d'hôte Domaine du Mas Boluix – *Chemin du Pou de les Colobres. 5km/3mi S of Perpignan towards Argelès. 04 68 08 17 70. www.domaine-de-boluix.com – 7rms.* Removed from the bustle of Perpignan, this nicely restored 18C *mas* is a peaceful place in the middle of Cabestany grapevines. Each guest room is named after a local artist.

Hôtel New Christina – *51 cours Lassus. 04 68 35 12 21 – www.hotel-newchristina.com – 25rms – 10€ – meals*. A small modern hotel, close to the centre of the city; swimming pool on the roof.

Hôtel Kyriad – *8 bd. Wilson. 04 68 59 25 94 – www.kyriad.fr – 38rms – 9€.* Recently renovated hotel; functional room furnishings; intergral courtyard with fountain.

EAT

Casa Bonet – *2 R. du Chevalet. 04 68 34 19 45.* This Catalan *casa* in the pedestrian area of town houses a restaurant offering a buffet, tapas and a dozen different brochettes.

La Galinette – *23 R. Jean-Payra. 04 68 35 00 90. Closed 26 Jul–16 Aug, 23 Dec–4 Jan, Sun and Mon.* Contemporary furnishings, beautifully set tables: a refined decor in which to sample southern-style dishes created with market-fresh ingredients.

Les Antiquaires – *Pl. Desprès. 04 68 34 06 58 – closed Sun evening and Mon.* This lovely family restaurant is decorated with antique china; the chef serves a traditional and well-prepared cuisine.

TAKING A BREAK

Espi – *43 bis quai Vauban. 04 68 35 19 91. Winter: daily 7.30am–7.30pm; summer: 7.30am–12.30am.* Immense store where each type of product (sweets, pastries, etc) features specialities original to the house, such as honey ice-cream or roasted pine-nuts. Tearoom with terrace; speedy service at lunchtime.

RECREATION

Centre Équestre de Loisirs du Barcarès – *Chemin de l'Hourtou, 66420 Le Barcarès. 04 68 80 98 26. Daily 10am–noon, 2pm–8.30pm. 12€ per hour.* Tours on horseback, by the hour or the day, round Salses lake by the sea. 2-5 day excursions around the Cathar castles or along the Roussillon wine route.

SHOPPING

Markets – Fruit and vegetable markets are held daily except Mon on the place de la République and every morning place Cassanyes. Flea market Av. du Palais-des-Expositions Sun morning. Organic market place Rigaud Wed and Sat morning.

Shopping streets – Clothes shops can be found in the pedestrianised city centre (Rue Mailly). The avenue du Gén.-de-Gaulle, in a lively part of town, is full of shops. The rue de l'Adjudant-Pilote-Paratilla, also called la rue des Olives by locals, is known for its two grocery shops and delicatessen.

Au Paradis des Desserts – *13 Ave. du Gén.-de-Gaulle. 04 68 34 89 69. Tue-Sun 8am–12.10pm, 4–7.30pm. Closed public holiday afternoons and 3 wks in Aug.* Here a talented patissier devotes himself to the creation of a wide range of truly individualised taste sensations.

IN THE EVENING

A number of bars in the old part of the city have live music in the evenings, such as O'Shannons Irish pub, le Corto Maltese and le Tio Pepe or le Mediator.

Port-Barcarés

Aude

The urban planners of this resort developed this site to satisfy tourists, providing for easy access to swimming and other outdoor activities and building self-catering accommodation, family camps and conventional hotel facilities. Residential areas have been grouped together, saving the seafront from overbearing blocks of buildings that would stifle the horizon.

- **Population:** 3 514.
- **Michelin Map:** 344: J-6.
- **Info:** Pl. de la République, 66420 Port-Barcarès, 04 68 86 16 56. www.portbarcares.com.
- **Location:** 25km/15.5mi N of Perpignan and 50km/31m SW of Narbonne by the A9.
- **Parking:** Along the beaches or near the Tourist Office.
- **Kids:** Aqualand.
- **Timing:** Allow 30 minutes for sightseeing.

VISIT

The Lydia

This ship, which was deliberately run aground in 1967, is the main attraction of the new Roussillon shoreline (disco and casino). Just by the *Lydia*, along an esplanade by the sea, the **Allée des Arts** (*signposted*) hosts a small display of contemporary sculpture including the "Soleillonautes," totem poles sculpted from the trunks of trees from Gabon.

Aqualand

In Port-Leucate. Open Jul-Aug 10am-7pm (Jun 6pm). 16€ (children 16€) 04 68 40 99 98.www.aqualand.fr.
This seaside leisure park (water chutes, swimming pool) is particularly suitable for young children.

The marina

The new harbour complex of **Port-Leucate** and **Port-Barcarès** constitutes the largest marina on the French Mediterranean coast.

WALKING TOUR

Cap Leucate★

2hr via a footpath running along the cliffs. Start from the Sémaphore du cap, at Leucate-Plage (10km/6mi N of Port-Barcarès along D 627).
From the look-out point by the signal station on the cape, there is a **view**★ from Languedoc to the Albères mountains.

The Lydia

L. Campion/MICHELIN

Fort des Salses

L. Campion/MICHELIN

Fort de Salses★★

Rising above the surrounding vineyards, this half-buried fortress is surprisingly big. The colour of the brickwork, bronzed by the sun, blends harmoniously with the golden sheen of the stonework, mainly of pink sandstone. Built in the 15C, on a site with a source of spring water, the fort is a unique example of the medieval military architecture of Spain, adapted by Vauban in 1691 to the needs of the military of the time. The Treaty of the Pyrenees of 1659, however, redrew the border with Spain, and Salses then lost its strategic importance.

- **Info:** 04 68 38 60 13. www.salses.monuments-nationaux.fr.
- **Location:** 16km/10mi N of Perpignan by the N 9 (direction Sigean).

A BIT OF HISTORY

Hannibal's passage – In 218 BC, Hannibal made plans to cross Gaul and invade Italy. Rome immediately sent emissaries, to ask the Gauls to resist the Carthaginians' advance. The Gauls declined and Hannibal was allowed through as "a guest."

When the Romans, who remembered the episode with bitterness, occupied Gaul, they built a camp at Salses.

A Spanish fortress – After Roussillon had been restored to Spain in 1493, Ferdinand of Aragón had this fortress built. Designed to house a garrison of 1 500 men, it could also withstand attack by newly evolving artillery. French troops reconquered Roussillon during the mid-17C and seized Salses.

VISIT

1hr Jun-Sep 9.30am–7pm (last departure 1hr before closing); Oct-May 10am-12.15pm, 2–5pm. Closed 1 Jan, 1 May, 1 and 11 Nov, 25 Dec. 6.50€ (under 18: no charge), no charge 1st Sunday in the month (Nov-Mar).

The fortress illustrates the significant transition from that of medieval castle (with a keep and round towers framing long curtain walls) to a modern fortress. With walls from 6–10m/20–33ft thick, the construction has three wholly independent parts running from east to west. The various levels are connected by a labyrinth of passages with a zigzagging complex network of internal underground defences.

The fortress today houses rotating exhibitions of contemporary art.

Tautavel

©Gg/Photoshot

Tautavel

This little village in the Corbières, on the banks of the Verdouble, has become a major centre of prehistory due to the discovery in the area of objects which have proved to be of vital significance in the study of the origins of human life.

Info: Ave. Jean-Badia 66720. 04 68 29 44 29. www.tautavel.com

Location: 33 km/20m NW of Perpignan by the N9, then the D117 and 76km/47.5m S of Narbonne by the A9. Exit at Perpignan Nord.

Don't Miss: Le Centre Européen de Préhistoire.

Timing: Allow 2 hours.

VILLAGE

Located below a rocky escarpment, Tautavel is a pretty village of some 800 inhabitants, located in a wine growing area in the Catalan, the Corbières, between the sea and the mountains, at the bottom of the foothills of the high Pyrenees. In spite of its prehistoric notoriety, the village is equally renowned, in rather different circles, for the quality of its wine which uses grenache, syrah and carignane grapes. The remains of the village's castle are nearby, and while Tautavel is close to the mountain areas occupied by the Cathars, the village and surrounding area seem to have escaped the attention of the Crusading army.

Centre Européen de Préhistoire★★

Route de Vingrau. Open daily except for Christmas and New Year. 7€ (combined ticket with the Musée Préhistoire Européenne). 04 68 29 07 76.www.tautavel.com.

The **European Centre of Prehistory** is devoted to the evolution of man and his environment (based on the significant discoveries made in the Caune de l'Arago and surrounding area).

Musée de la Préhistoire Européenne – Préhistorama

Inside the Palais des Congrès, rue Anatole-France. Open daily except for Christmas and New Year. 7€. No charge "Printemps des Musées." 04 68 29 07 76.

Five "virtual theatres" offer visitors 3D illustrations of the daily life of Europe's first inhabitants.

Tautavel man

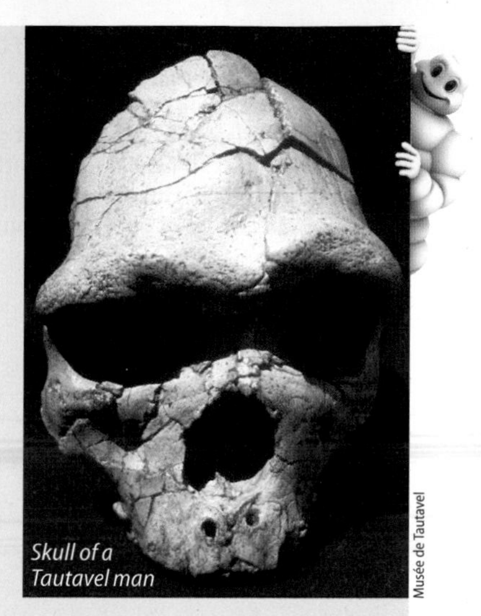
Skull of a Tautavel man

Musée de Tautavel

Tautavel man is the name of an extinct hominid that lived about 300 000–450 000 years ago. The being is named after fossils found in an ancient karst cave on the site known as Caune de l'Arago, very close to the village of Tautavel. Although excavations had been going on for some years, the skull of this early ancestor of man was found there only in 1971. It has a flat and receding forehead and a well-developed arch of the eyebrows; the face is big and has rectangular eye sockets.

The fossils that were found consist of over 80 fragments; the skull belonged to a man in his twenties, about 1.65m/5.4ft in height and weighing around 45-55kg/99-121lb. His bones are certainly more sturdy than those of modern-day humans. Other remains are two mandibles, belonging to a woman in her fifties, and to a man, about 20-25 years old. The evidence suggests that at this stage of human development the use of fire was yet to be discovered.

The evidence also points towards Tautavel man being a cannibal, or at least one who preferred to scavenge for food, rather than hunt. The bones of rhinoceros, horses, wild sheep and goats, musk ox, deer, and reindeer have all been found in the cave, and these accumulations of bones and stone implements point to some 40 different stratified periods of occupation of the Arago cave. There is an on-going debate among academics to determine whether this hominid is directly related to the Neanderthal. It has been proposed to classify them as *Homo erectus Tautavelensis*. These are without doubt the oldest human remains ever discovered in Europe. Excavations in the cave continue.

Diorama in Centre Européen de Préhistoire

Musée de Tautavel

There is about the long valley north of Canigou a certain mellow softness, almost like the downy skin of the peaches and apricots that grow here in abundance. The whole setting is gentle; pleasing. The local economy is founded on tourism, and much of that geared to exploring the mountains, which provide dazzling walking potential at all standards. The absence of heavy industry makes this among the most attractive of places, set against a stupendous backdrop of high mountains.

Highlights

1. A market day visit to the town of **Prades** (pp266, 282)
2. Spend a relaxing morning followed by lunch in **Villefrance de Conflent** (p290)
3. Take a stroll around relaxing **Vernet-les-Bains** (p289)
4. Ride the **Yellow Train** (p269)
5. Visit the solar furnace in **Mont-Louis** (p281)

Canigou

The huge mound that is the mountain of Canigou, a summit revered equally by Catalonians from both sides of the French-Spain border and a key icon of Catalan unity, overshadows the trim orchard-lands of Roussillon. Topped with patches of snow until late June, Canigou rises above a skirt of trees and rocks that, from a distance, give the landscape the slightly shabby but nonetheless appealing appearance of a badly stubbled beard. On Midsummer Eve, observing an ancient tradition, locals climb to the 2 784m/9 134ft summit and build a bonfire from which torches are lit and the "sacred flame" carried down the mountain to the adjacent Pyrenean villages. From the south-west, where the Cady rises, the melancholic clank of cow bells hangs in the air, rising from steep-sided valleys; to the north lies the course of the Têt, turbulent meltwater that scours deep pools and cascades among long-smoothed rocks, as it flows eastwards across the Roussillon subsidence plain, the Plaine Roussillonnaise, to the sea.

Pablo Casals

Prades was chosen by the world-renowned cellist Pablo Casals (1876-1973) as his exiled home, one that while not in his homeland of Spain nevertheless remained in his beloved Catalonia. Not surprisingly, many of the surrounding villages and their fine buildings are embraced in an annual Pablo Casals Festival from mid-July to mid-August, which the maestro founded in 1950.

©Corbis

Detail of mural painging depicting the conquest of Majorca by James I in 1229, Museo de Catalunya, Barcelona

Roussillon

The old province of Roussillon is an historical and cultural region, comprising what is now the southern French *département* of Pyrénées-Orientales. Roussillon encompassed an area made up of the eastern extremity of the French Pyrenees and the Mediterranean coastal lowlands adjoining them to the east. Its capital was Perpignan.

The area near Perpignan, known as Ruscino, was settled by people with Iberian affinities. In pre-Roman times, the area was under the control of Gallic peoples. Just over 2 000 years ago, Ruscino was conquered by the Romans, then the Visigoths (around AD 462) and the Arabs (in about AD 720). By the AD 750s, the Carolingian kings were in charge.

In AD 865, Septimania, part of the future Languedoc to the north and Frankish Catalonia to the south, gave rise to hereditary countships in the area, most of which were held by relatives of the contemporary counts of Barcelona, who acquired rights to Roussillon in 1172. Roussillon thus became part of Aragon, which the counts of Barcelona had also acquired. There was a great flowering of monasticism in Roussillon from the 10C, resulting in the area's wealth of Romanesque architecture.

Commerce benefited from the integration of Roussillon with neighbouring Catalonia to the south. In the 13C, Roussillon formed the core of the kingdom of Majorca, an amalgamation formed by James I of Aragon and Majorca. During the Thirty Years' War, France occupied Spain's lands north of the Pyrenees. The town of Perpignan fell to the French in 1642, and in 1659 Spain formally ceded the province to France by the Treaty of the Pyrenees. Roussillon became part of France.

Le Canigou★★★

Towering above the Roussillon orchards, Canigou mountain is revered by Catalonians from France and Spain, who still light the first of their Midsummer Eve bonfires on its summit. The best season for climbing is autumn, with mild temperatures and perfect visibility. Patches of snow cover northern slopes in Spring and early summer. Mid-summer brings heat and crowds.

Michelin Map: 344: F-7.
Location: 69km/43mi W of Perpignan by N 116/D 27.

A BIT OF HISTORY

A geographer's mistake recorded Canigou as the highest peak in the Pyrenees for quite some time. Ever since the first ascent, reputedly by King Peter of Aragon in 1285, Catalonian sportsmen have vied to conquer this peak: by bicycle in 1901, on skis and on board a Gladiator 10 CC automobile in 1903, and by horseback in 1907. Vernet-les-Bains and Prats-de-Mollo are linked only by forest roads.

DRIVING TOURS

CANIGOU MOUNTAIN ROADS★★★

1 FROM VERNET-LES-BAINS VIA MARIAILLES

12km/7.5mi – 45min by car and 10hr on foot for the return trip. Experienced hikers only. From Vernet-les-Bains (See VERNET-LES-BAINS) take D 116 to the Col de Jou via Casteil and park the car at the pass. Follow the GR 10 footpath via Mariailles, to the refuge at the summit. Continue to the Canigou peak along the Haute Randonnée Pyrénéenne.

Pic du Canigou★★★

Alt 2 784m/9 131ft.

On the Canigou summit are a cross and remains of a stone hut used in the 18C and 19C for scientific observations. Listen for the tinkling of bells from grazing animals in the Cady valley below. The viewing table offers a **panorama** of the Roussillon plain, Mediterranean coast and Costa Brava in Catalonia. Sometimes you can see Canigou all the way from Marseille's church of Notre-Dame-de-la-Garde, 253km/157mi as the crow flies.

2 FROM VERNET-LES-BAINS VIA THE CHALET-HÔTEL DES CORTALETS

23km/14.5mi – about 1hr 30min by car and 3hr 30min on foot there and back.

The track starting from Fillols is closed on the way up from 1 to 6pm and on the way down from 8am to 3pm. The old Cortalets road built for the Club Alpin in 1899 is a picturesque but rough moun-

Canigou viewed from Taurinya

M.-H. Carcanague/MICHELIN

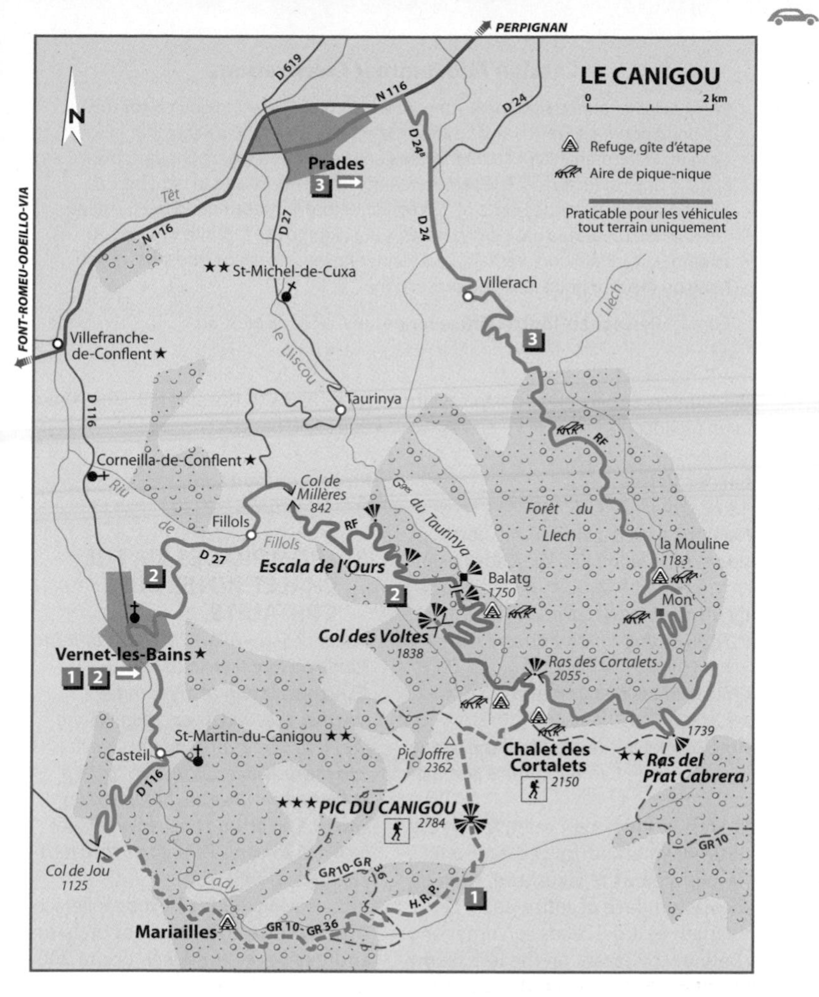

tain road, accessible only in July and August, in dry weather, in a four-wheel drive or Jeep. Jeep and Land-Rovers excursions are organised from **Vernet-les-Bains** *(Garage Villacèque, ☎04 68 05 51 14. Taxi de la gare, ☎04 68 05 62 28. Tourisme Excursions, ☎04 68 05 54 39. Consult the municipal Tourist Office for other possibilities. ☎04 68 05 55 35.) or from* **Corneilla-de-Conflent** *(Cullell – ☎04 68 05 64 61. Mid-Jun to end Sep: departures by four-wheel drive at 8am and 11am. 16€ there and back). Beware of the road's poor condition, and a very narrow 21% gradient (protected by a parapet) and 31 harrowing hairpin bends. Start your tour from Vernet-les-Bains (**See VERNET-LES-BAINS**) and take D 27 in the direction of Prades. After Fillols, turn right.*

After leaving Vernet-les-Bains, beyond Col de Millères, alt 842m/2 762ft, the road corkscrews along the rocky crest between the Fillols and Taurinya valleys, with views of Prades and St-Michel-de-Cuxa. You'll wind through larch trees and rocky outcrops to a stunning view of the Cerdagne and Fenouillèdes regions.

Escala de l'Ours

This vertiginous cliff road is the trip's most spectacular. It cuts a narrow tunnel through the rock itself, over the Taurinya gorges far below, with viewpoints along the way. Arolla pines thin out beyond the Baltag forest hut, and

Catalan Midsummer Celebrations

Every summer on the feast of St John, or Midsummer Day, Canigou celebrates the bond between French and Spanish Catalans. On 24 June a flame is lit in the Castillet at Perpignan and carried to the Canigou summit where Catalans from Spain gather to receive it. The same evening, the flame is used to light fires all over Catalonia and other parts of Perpignan before it is returned to the Castillet. Celebrations continue until dawn, when people go to the foothills of Canigou to gather St John's wort, vervain, and walnut flowers, to shape into crosses and hang on their for good luck and protection.

Contact **Perpignan Tourist Office for details**: *04 68 66 30 30.*

the countryside becomes a pastoral with open meadows.

Col des Voltes

Alt 1 838m/6 029ft.

From the pass is a view of the northern slopes of Canigou and the Cady basin.

At the Ras dels Cortalets (alt 2 055m/6 740ft; picnic area), turn right.

Chalet-hôtel des Cortalets

Alt 2 150m/7 050ft.

Hotel-chalet at the mouth of the cirque formed by the Canigou, Joffre and Barbet peaks.

West of the hotel-chalet, follow the path waymarked by red and white flashes along the lakeshore, then up the eastern face of Joffre peak. Leave the path as it descends to Vernet and continue the ascent on the left, below the ridge. A zigzag path between the rocks leads to the summit (3hr 30min there and back).

Pic du Canigou

© Jean-Paul Garcin/Photononstop/Tips Images

Pic du Canigou★★★

See 1 above.

3 FROM PRADES VIA THE CHALET-HÔTEL DES CORTALETS

20km/12.5mi – allow 2hr by car and 3hr 30min on foot there and back.

Accessible only in dry summer weather, the road is very rough along the Llech gorge; a 10km/6mi stretch cuts into the rock face. Excursions by Jeep or four-wheel drive are organised from Prades. This driving tour leaves Prades on N 116, towards Perpignan, then turn right onto D 24B.

After leaving Prades, beyond Villerach, D 24 traverses the Conflent orchards and overlooks the Llech gorge 200-300m/700-1 000ft below, before pushing up to the La Mouline forest hut *(alt 1 183m/3 880ft; picnic area).*

Ras del Prat Cabrera★★

Alt 1 739m/5 704ft.

This delightful rest stop overlooking the La Lentilla valley offers a panorama of the Roussillon plain, Albères mountains and the Mediterranean. The road opens out in the upper cirque of the Llech Valley with stupendous **views**★★★ of the Corbières southern border and the Galamus gorge.

Follow the "Balcon du Canigou" road W to the Chalet des Cortalets (see 2 above) and then on to the **Pic du Canigou**★★★ *(see 1 above).*

Le Capcir★ and around

The Capcir plateau is northern Catalonia's highest region at 1 500m/4 920ft. Its pine-forested mountains spangled with lakes have ski runs and walking and horse-riding trails, offering chance encounters with izards and moufflons. The Capcir has the largest Nordic skiing in the Pyrenees. The La Matte forest has beautiful Scots firs over 20m/65ft high. Admire them from D 118 and D 52, between Formiguères and Les Angles.

- **Michelin Map:** 344: D-7.
- **Info:** Maison du Capcir, 66210 Matemale ☎04 68 04 49 86.
- **Location:** 80km/50mi miles W of Perpignan, between Quillan and Mont-Louis.

A BIT OF HISTORY

In territorial fights over Catalonia, **France and Spain** divided the Capcir and Cerdagne between them for long periods of time. In the Middle Ages the Catalan administration governed the Capcir and although it was annexed to Roussillon in the 17C, its Catalan traditions still thrive today.

SKI AREAS

Espace Nordique du Capcir

This wide forested area of 20 000ha/49 422 acres, has cross-country skiing trails, sled-dog runs and footpaths around Les Angles, Puyvalador, Formiguères, La Quillane and Matemale.

Les Angles✻

Alt 1 600-2 400m/5 260-7 874ft. ☎04 68 04 32 76. www.les-angles.com.

The skiing areas on Le Roc d'Aude and Le Mont Claret have 40km/25mi of downhill runs for skiers of all levels. La Matte, Calvet, La Llose and Le Galbe offer 102km/63mi of cross-country skiing, dogsledding and hiking trails. Extreme sports include ice surfing, diving under frozen lakes, skiing propelled by horse, kite or sail, and major competitions involving these sports.

Formiguères

Alt 1 700–2 100 m/5 577–6 890ft. ☎04 68 04 47 35. www.station-formigueres.com.

The Formiguères resort has 18 downhill slopes for all levels, with two chair-lifts and six drag-lifts. Espace Nordique du Capcir has cross-country trails.

Puyvalador

Alt 1 700-2 400m/5 577-7 874ft.

Puyvalador means "mountain sentinel" in Catalan. This winter sports resort village overlooking the Aude gorge and Lake Puyvalador, has 16 downhill slopes traversing a pine forest. Local guides organise off-trail skiing and snowshoeing.

LAKES

Lac des Bouillouses★

14km/8.7mi NW of Mont-Louis (see MONT-LOUIS) along the Quillan road (D 118). 300m/328yd beyond the bridge spanning the River Têt, turn left onto D 60. Park and take the shuttle up to the lake. In winter, road access is only with cross-country skis or snowshoes. Access road is closed in Jul and Aug at the "Plade Barrès" locality from 7am-7pm. Access on foot, by the Font-Romeu / Pyrénées 2000 and Formiguères chair-lifts or road shuttle service. Information: Jul and Aug. ☎04 68 04 24 61.

After 8km/5mi, the road begins to climb up to the lower terrace of the Bouillouses plateau. Along with the immense Lac de Bouillouses, Bouillouses' plateau has 20 small glacial lakes and pools. A walking trail to Pic Carlit starts from the lake *(14km/9mi; allow 3hr).*

Lac de Matemale

This 240ha/593-acre reservoir amidst a beautiful forest offers water sports, walking, riding and fishing facilities.

Lac de Puyvalador

This smaller reservoir is ideal for windsurfing or taking it easy on a pedalo.

Lac des Bouillouses

E. Larribère/MICHELIN

DRIVING TOUR

Mont-Louis to Puyvalador

26km/16mi – allow half a day. Start at **Mont-Louis★** *(see MONT-LOUIS) and leave heading N on D 118.*

The gently climbing road offers an attractive citadel view with the Cambras d'Azé mountains in the foreground.

La Llagonne

This crossroads village of Haut-Conflent *(alt 1 680m/5 511ft)* is named after the Catalan word for lagoon. The fortified church of St-Vincent contains an outstanding wooden Romanesque-Byzantine Christ.

From the Col de la Quillane, the pass which marks the watershed and the mouth of the Capcir, take D 32F to the left.

Les Angles

©Laurent Giraudou/Hemis/Photoshot

Les Angles★

This Pyrenean resort overlooking the Capcir plateau grew up in 1964 around an old village which preserved its bell-tower.

Parc Animalier des Angles

Open Jul-Aug 9am-6pm; rest of year 9am-5pm. 9€ (children 7€). 04 68 04 17 20. www.faune-pyreneenne.com.

At the southern end of the village of Les Angles, take the road to the Pla del Mir and its zoological park, to see Pyrenees wildlife (moufflons, wild boars, ibexes, brown bears etc) in their mountain habitat.

Formiguères

04 68 04 47 35.
www.station-formigueres.com

A road through La Matte forest leads to this winter sports resort (18 ski slopes for all levels) and its special church with Romanesque Christ.

Take D 32B to the left to "Grotte de Fontrabiouse."

Grotte de Fontrabiouse

Jul-Aug Guided tours (1hr) 10am-7pm; Sep-Jun 10am-noon, 2-5pm. Closed mid-Nov-mid-Dec. 7€ (children 4.50€). 04 68 30 95 55. www.fontrabiouse.fr.

This cave discovered in 1962 during an onyx quarry excavation has a guided tour (disabled accessible) through amazing clusters of "organ pipes," frozen falls, "jellyfish" and "flowers" of aragonite.

La Cerdagne★

The half-French, half-Spanish Cerdagne region in the eastern Pyrenees lies in the upper valley of the Sègre, between St-Martin gorge (alt 1 000m/3 300ft) and La Perche Pass (alt 1 579m/5 179ft). This peaceful sunlit valley framed by majestic mountains is a rural idyll of fields, pastures and streams lined with alders and willows. To the north the granite massif of Le Carlit towers at 2 921m/9 581ft and to the south lies the Puigmal range (alt 2 910m/9 545ft) with its forests and ravines.

- **Michelin Map:** 344: C-7/D-8.
- **Info:** Porté-Puymorens. ℘04 68 04 82 41. www.porte-puymorens.net
- **Location:** SW of Perpignan, 1hr from Spanish border.
- **Don't Miss:** The panorama from col Puymorens and col de l'Ombrée.
- **Kids:** The solar furnace at Odeillo and the Cerdagne Museum at Ste-Léocadie.

TRAIN JAUNE

The **Train Jaune** "the Canary" (*℘08 92 35 35 35*) painted in Catalonia's yellow and red, has been running between Villfranche-de-Conflent and Latour-de-Carol (62km/38.5mi) since 1910. The Mont-Louis to Olette run crosses the Giscard Bridge and Séjourné Viaduct.

SKI AREAS

Espace Cambre d'Aze

Alt 1 600-2 400m/5 249-7874ft.

The resorts of Eyne and St-Pierre-del-Forçats comprise 27 Alpine ski runs for all levels of skiers.

Err-Puigmal 2600

Alt 1 850-2 520m/6 070-8 268ft.

18 Alpine runs and 10km/6mi of cross-country trails on Mont Puigmal.

Porté-Puymorens

Alt 1 615-2 500 m/5 298-8 202ft.

In March the Grand Prix Porté-Puymorens is held at this ski resort with 16 downhill slopes, 25km/15mi of cross-country trails, snowboarding and ski-biking.

DRIVING TOURS

1 VALLÉE DU CAROL★★

27km/16.5mi – allow 1hr.

After leaving gentle slopes of the Ariège's upper valley, the road descends deeper into the valley.

Col de Puymorens★

Alt 1 920m/6 300ft.

The pass lies on the Atlantic-Mediterranean watershed between the Ariège and the Sègre. The road crosses a bridge

Train Jaune running near La Tour de Carol-Enveigt

Col du Puymorens

©gRaNdLeMuRieN/Fotolia.com

and leads down into the Carol valley, with views of Porté-Puymorens and the glacial threshold beneath the Tour Cerdane's ruins. Beyond Porté, the road traverses a narrow ravine, the Défilé de la Faou, before squeezing between sheer valley walls on the way to Enveitg. Before Bourg-Madame, look for the Grand Hôtel de Fort-Romeu on the left, with the Spanish enclave of Llivia in the foreground. To the right, on the Spanish side, see Puigcerdà on the hilltop.

Bourg-Madame

In 1815 the duke of Angoulême named this village on the River Rahur to honour his wife Madame Royale.

2 ROUTE DE LA SOULANE★

36km/22.5mi – allow 2hr. Start at Bourg-Madame; leave north on N 20.

Ur

Note the church's Lombardy banding surmounted by a cogged frieze, and the altarpiece by Sunyer.

At Ur, turn right onto D 618 and at Villeneuve-des-Escaldes take D 10 to the left.

Dorres

The **church's** north side altar Our Lady of Sorrows typifies the Catalans' penchant for dressing up their statues. The south chapel has an impressive Black Madonna *(contact the town hall ✆04 68 04 60 69).*

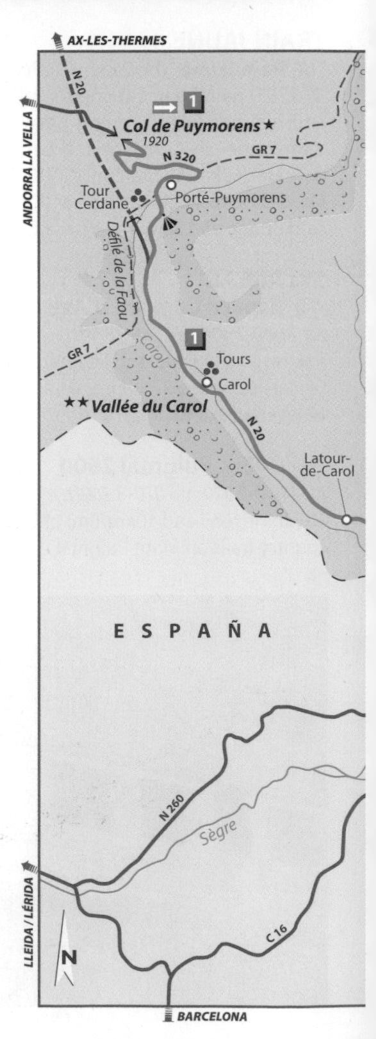

The path from the hôtel Marty in Dorres leads to a **sulphur spring** *used for open-air thermalism. Open 8.30am-8pm (Jul and Aug 8am-9pm). 3.50€. 04 68 04 66 87. 30min round-trip on foot.*

Go back to D 618.

Angoustrine

The Romanesque **church** offers guided tours (*mid-Jul to end Aug: daily except Sat-Sun 10am-noon; 04 68 30 22 89*).

Chaos de Targasonne

This gigantic heap of contorted granite boulders dates from the Quaternary Era. A short distance (2km/1.2mi) away, view the border mountains from Canigou to Puigmal and the jagged Sierra del Cadi.

Odeillo

Near the village stands the huge solar furnace inaugurated in 1969 (*open Jul-Aug 10am-7.30pm; Sep-Jun 10am-12.30; 2pm-6pm. closed 1 Jan and 25 Dec. 6€ (children 8-18 years 3.50€. 04 68 30 77 86)*. This valley's

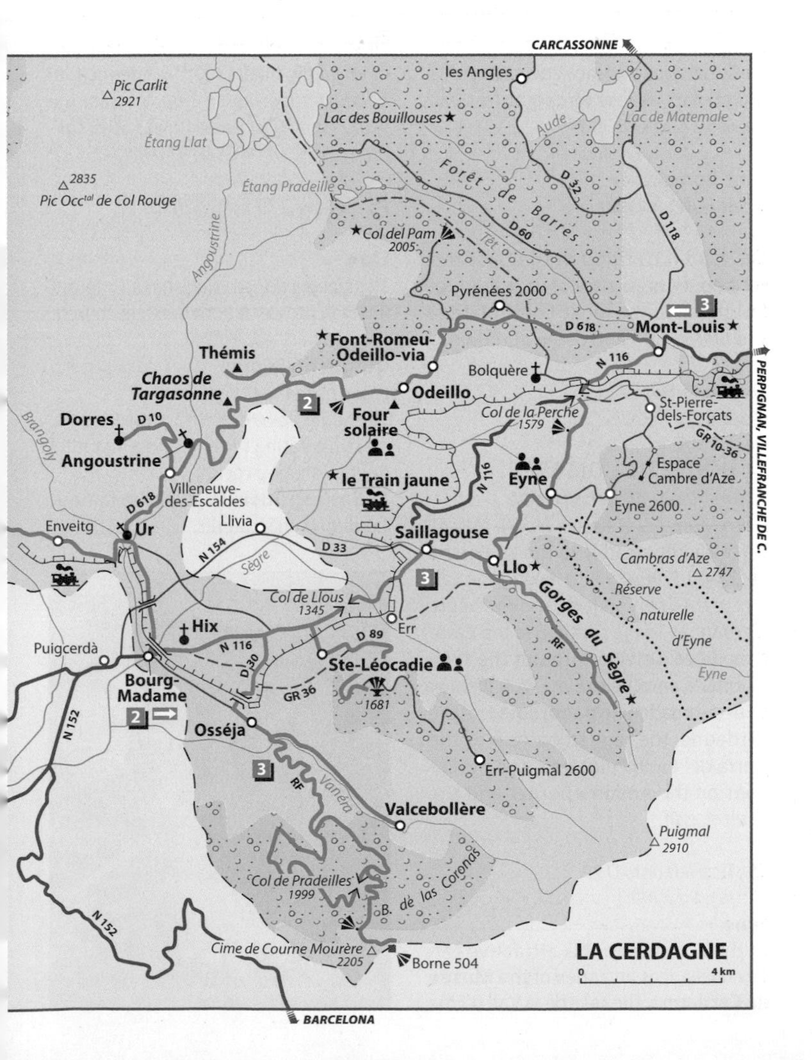

Solar furnace at Odeillo

A. Thuillier/MICHELIN

sunny slopes are reflected in the enormous parabolic surface covered with 9 130 mirrors, whose temperatures can exceed 3 500°C/6 300°F.

Font-Romeu★★
See FONT-ROMEU.

The road runs through the pine forest above the picturesque village of **Bolquère** to the Mont-Louis plateau and Aude valley and Conflent region.

Mont-Louis★
See MONT-LOUIS.

3 ROUTE DE L'OMBRÉE

112km/70mi – allow half a day.

From Mont-Louis (*see MONT-LOUIS*), N 116 climbs steadily to the La Perche Pass (*alt 1 579m/5 179ft*) linking the valleys of the Têt (Conflent) and the Sègre (Cerdagne). To the south rises the Cambras d'Azé. Driving through the high moorland enroute to Eyne, you'll enjoy an ever-broadening **panorama**★ of the Cerdagne: the ragged outline of the Sierra del Cadi, Puigcerdà, the mountains on the Andorra border and the Carlit massif.

Turn left onto D 29.

Eyne
At the entrance to this attractive terraced village is an annex of the **Musée de Cerdagne**, the casa de la Vall d'Eina all about water, and a botanical garden of endemic plants (*open school holidays 10am-noon, 2-6pm; rest of the year 2-5pm; closed Nov. 3.50€, children 1.50€. 04 68 04 97 05*).

Follow D 33 S towards Llo.

Llo★
This steeply sloped village has an interesting watchtower & Romanesque church.

Gorges du Sègre★
Leave from the church in Llo.
The Sègre flows down from the Puigmal massif, creating torrents and a beautiful needle-shaped rock.
At **Saillagouse**, look for the famous Cerdagne charcuterie.

Llo

©A.J. Cassaigne/Photononstop/Photolibrary

Continue along N 116 towards Puigcerdà.

Ste-Léocadie

Cal Mateau farm houses the **Musée de Cerdagne** *(temporarily closed. 04 68 04 08 05) (annex in Eyne, see above).* This fine 17C-18C building houses exhibitions on shepherds, horse-breeding and traditional flask-making.

Turn left onto D 89 leading to the Puigmal ski resort; at the edge of the forest, take the surfaced forest road to the right just after a hairpin bend.

Table d'Orientation de Ste-Léocadie

Alt 1 681m/5 513ft.

The viewing table here offers a **panorama**★ of the Cerdagne, the Carol valley and Fontfrède summit.

Go back to D 89 and turn right. The mountain road leads up the Err Valley. Go back to N 116, turn left and a little further on left again (D 30).

Routes forestières d'Osséja★

Just above Osséja, leave the Valcebollère road to follow the route forestière to the edge of one of the Pyrenees largest forests. Take the right fork to boundary post 504 (Courne Mourère summit, 2 205m/7 232ft above sea level). Enjoy **views**★ of the Cerdagne, the mountains on the Andorra border and Catalonia sierras.

Go back down to Osséja via the other branch of the fork in the road (completing a loop) and turn left onto N 116.

Hix

Off season, guided tours by request at the Bourg-Madame tourist office. 04 68 04 55 35.

Hix was the residence of the counts of Cerdagne and the commercial capital of the region until the 12C. The little Romanesque **church** contains an early 16C altarpiece dedicated to St Martin. a 13C seated Madonna and Romanesque Christ.

ADDRESSES

STAY

HILLTOP HIDEAWAY

Hotel Marty – *66760 Dorres. 04 68 30 07 52 – closed 25 Oct-20 Dec – – 21 rms. 9€.* This popular family-run guest house has a large dining room serving hearty regional meals; a terrace, and some rooms with verandas.

EAT

FAMILY STYLE

La Brasserie de la Vielle Maison Cerdagne – *66800 Saillagouse – 04 68 04 72 08.* At the Hôtel Planes, an old coaching stop in Saillagouse village, enjoy a range of family cuisine.

SPA BREAK

Les Bains de Llo – *Rte des Gorges de Llo, 66800 Llo. 04 68 04 74 55 – www.lesbainsdello.com – daily 10am-7.30pm/8pm. Closed 19-30 May and 6 Nov-19 Dec. 8.50€ (children 7€).* Bathe in sulphurous springs at 35° and 37°C/95°-99°F. Snack bar with fresh-squeezed fruit juice, pancakes and waffles.

LOOKING FOR A THRILL...

Compagnie des Guides des Pyrénées Catalanes – *Av. Serrat-de-l'Ours – 66210 Bolquère – 06 86 18 28 12 Early Jul- end Aug.* All-level courses and guided excursions: rock climbing, mountain biking, rambling, white-water sports, via ferrata.

...OR JUST A QUIET TIME?

Guide de Pêche Marc Ribot – *16 av. des Lupins, 66210 Bolquère. 04 68 30 30 93 or 06 89 99 22 64 – www.alamouche.com – closed early Nov-early Mar.* Explore the region with a course in fly-fishing.

Céret★

Amélie-les-Bains and around

Céret in the Vallespir region is the lively hub of Catalan tradition in the northern Pyrenees, with bullfights and *sardana* dancing. This major fruit-growing area is becoming a popular arts and crafts centre.

- **Population:** 7 500.
- **Michelin Map:** 344: H-8 also see Le BOULOU.
- **Info:** 1 av G-Clemenceau ℘04 68 87 00 53. www.ot-ceret.fr; Amélie-les-Bains Tourism Office, 22 av de Vallespir ℘04 68 39 01 98. www.amelie-les-bains.com
- **Location:** 3km/20.65mi SW of Perpignan.
- **Don't Miss:** La Féria and Folklore Festival in July.

SIGHTS

Old Céret

Majestic plane trees shade strollers between place de la République and place de la Liberté. Remnants of the original ramparts include the Porte de France in place de la République and the Porte d'Espagne in place Pablo-Picasso. The wrought iron and stainless steel monument to Picasso – *Sardane de la Paix* (1973) is based on a Picasso drawing, and the town's First World War Memorial is by Aristide Maillol.

Old Bridge★ (Vieux pont)

The 14C "Devil's Leap" bridge spans the Tech in a single 45m/150ft arch, 22m/72ft above the river. Enjoy lovely views of the Canigou massif and the Albères range. Walk downstream to the sawmill for a good view of the bridge.

Musée d'Art Moderne★★

8 bd Mar--Joffre. Open mid-Jun-Sep 10am-7pm; Oct-mid-Jun 10am-6pm. Closed 1 Jan, 1 May, 1 Nov, 25 Dec. 5.50€ (children under 12 free). ℘04 68 87 27 76. www.musee-ceret.com.

This modern building off boulevard Maréchal-Joffre was designed by Barcelona architect Jaime Freixa. Its spacious galleries let in the beautiful Mediterranean light to enhance the displayed works. The museum features ceramics by Picasso, works from the Céret period (1909-50) and contemporary works from 1960 to 1970.

EXCURSIONS

Amélie-les-Bains

℘04 68 39 01 98. www.amelie-les-bains.com.

Mediterranean flora like mimosas, oleanders, palm trees and agaves, reflects the mild climate and abundance of sun-

Vieux pont, Céret

Amélie-les-Bains

©Claudio Giovanni Colombo/Bigstockphoto.com

shine in the town named after the wife of Louis-Philippe. Queen Marie-Amélie made France's **southernmost spa town** fashionable in the 19C. The sulphur-rich spa waters here are renowned for treating rheumatic complaints and respiratory diseases.

The **Gorges du Mondony** (*30min round-trip on foot; from the Roman baths walk past the Hôtel des Gorges to the terrace overlooking the gorge; follow the cliff path and the galleries clinging to the rock face)* are a cool, pleasant place for a walk.

Palalda★

3km/2mi from the centre of Amélie.

The medieval river town of Palalda is a fine example of a Catalan village. The tiny sloping streets below the mairie are a delight to explore. The little square is particularly pretty, with its **church of St-Martin**, museum and town hall.

The **Palalda Museum** (*open May-Sep Tue-Fri 10am-noon, 2-6.30pm, Mon, Sat and public holidays 2-6.30pm; mid Feb-Apr and Oct-mid Dec Tue-Fri 10am-noon, 2-5.30pm, Mon, Sat and public holidfays 2.30-5.30pm. 2.50€. 04 68 39 34 90)* is divided into two sections:

Museum of Folk Arts and Traditions – In addition to antique tools used in trades now obsolete or mechanised, this museum features a reconstruction of an early-20C kitchen, wherein local dishes like *cargolade* (grilled snails with *aïoli* – garlic mayonnaise) were enjoyed.

Roussillon Postal Museum – This reconstruction of a late 19C post office presents the history of the local postal service and the Roussillon lighthouse system (*tours à feu*), a code using smoke signals to alert the region to the threat of enemy invasion.

Vallée du Mondony★

6km/3.5mi as far as Mas Pagris. (passing places over the last 2km/1.2mi).

The road to Montalba climbs the rocky spur of Fort-les-Bains and skirts the clifftops overlooking the Mondony gorge. It then crosses a series of stepped terraces, in full view of the jagged Roc St-Sauveur and the deserted valley below. Leaving the Montalba aerial tower to the left, it carries on through the granite gorge to valley of Mas Pagris, a good base for walks in the upper Terme valley.

ADDRESSES

STAY

Ensoleillade La Rive – *R. J. Coste. 04 68 39 06 20 – P – 14 rms.* Simple family hospitality by the Tech River, and airy rooms with rustic furnishings; some with cooking facilities.

Le Rousillon – *Av. Beau-Soleil. 04 68 39 34 39 – closed 28 Nov-20 Mar –*

- 30 rms - 7€ - meals . Situated on the way into town, this accommodation offers bright and spacious rooms. A fine 19C building adjacent houses the rest of the hotel.

EAT

Carré d'As - *Q4 av. du Dr Bouix. 04 68 39 20 00 - casino.ameliemoliflor.com - closed 15-28 Feb, 1-28 Mar, Mon and Tue except public holidays.* Local specialities in the restaurant, and pasta and pizzas in the brasserie.

SHOPPING

Marché aux légumes - *Pl. de la République - daily 7am-noon.* Fruit and vegetables.

Les Caves du Roussillon - *10 r. des Thermes. 04 68 39 00 29 - daily 9am-12.30pm, 4pm-7.30pm.* Tastings of local vintages include Banyuls, Collioure and Rivesaltes, and for purchase, over 300 Roussillon wines and some hundred Banyuls.

BARS CAFÉS

La Rosquilla Fondante Séguéla (Pâtisserie Pérez-Aubert) - *12 r. des Thermes. 04 68 39 00 16 - daily except Wed 8am-12.30pm, 3pm-7pm and holidays - closed 3 weeks Jul and 2 weeks Feb.* In 1810 pastrycook Robert Séguéla created the ***rousquille***, a lemon-flavoured iced biscuit, here. This speciality is now the hit of this tea room featuring dozens of teas and homemade ice cream and chocolates.

ON THE TOWN

Bar le Chateau - *Rte d'Arles-sur-Tech - 04 68 39 31 71 - Thu and Sat 9pm-1am, Sun 3pm-7pm - closed Oct-May.* A charming nightspot where seasoned dancers show off traditional musettes, tangos and waltzes.

Grand Café de Paris - *19 av. du Vallespir - 04 68 39 00 04 - daily 5.30am-2am - closed 2 weeks in Jan.* Large café-brasserie with reasonably price meals and dancing old favourites in the back room.

SPORTS AND LEISURE

Golf - Compact - *Parc des Sports - 04 68 39 37 66 - daily - closed 15 Dec-15 Feb, 15 Aug and 1 Nov. 1 7-hole course.*

Le Fenouillèdes★★

The Fenouillèdes region between the southern Corbières and the Conflent evokes the aromatic plant known as fennel. The region links the furrow hollowed out between the Col Campérié and the more populated Estagel area (including the Maury vineyards and "Côtes du Roussillon") and a rugged mountain range that becomes quite arid between Sournia and Prades.

- **Info:** Office du tourisme de St-Paul-de-Fenouillet, 26 bd de l'Agly 04 68 59 07 57. www.st-paul66.com
- **Location:** Estagel, 24km/15mi W of Perpignan on the D117, is the gateway to **Fenouillèdes**
- **Don't Miss:** Roman aqueduct bridge of Ansignan.

DRIVING TOUR

Round-Trip from St-Paul-de-Fenouillet

60km/37mi - about 4hr.

St-Paul-de-Fenouillet

This town is on the east bank of the Agly near its confluence with the Boulzane.

Clue de la Fou

Strong winds blow through this valley gouged out by the Agly. Cross the river and follow D 619 as it bends around the Fenouillèdes furrow and its vineyards. See the ruined Quéribus castle on its rocky pinnacle and Canigou peak in the distance. The road skirts the still-used Roman aqueduct at **Ansignan** before reaching Sournia via Pézilla-de-Conflent.

Turn right onto D 7 towards St-Prats-de-Sournia.

The road offers a fine view of the Corbières and the Mediterranean Sea through the Agly valley.

Beyond Le Vivier, turn left onto D 9 towards Caudiès.

Notre-Dame-de-Laval
Previously a **hermitage**, this Gothic church on an olive-lined esplanade contains a 15C statue of Mary and Joseph. The road climbs to **Fenouillet** with delightful views of the hermitage of Notre-Dame-de-Laval and the Bugarach summit, before reaching **Caudiès-de-Fenouillèdes**, the gateway to the Fenouillèdes.

Continue N along D 9 to Col de St-Louis then turn right onto D 46 and right again onto D 45.

Pic de Bugarach
See Les CORBIÈRES.

Turn right onto D 14.

Cubières
A rest area near the old mill has picnic tables on the shady banks of the Agly.

Turn right onto D 10 which runs alongside the Cubières stream then the River Agly.

Gorges de Galamus★★
The spectacular rock-carved road and the hermitage clinging to the hillside create a fantasy world bathed in Catalan sunlight. The steep narrow gorge offers glimpses of the mountain stream foaming below.

Ermitage St-Antoine-de-Galamus
Leave the car in the car park at the hermitage before the tunnel. 30min on foot round-trip.
The path runs down from the hermitage terrace (view of Canigou). The hermitage building conceals the

Hermitage of St-Antoine in the Galamus gorge
D. Hée/MICHELIN

chapel in the dim depths of a natural cave. The D 7 follows a sinuous course through vineyards enroute to St-Paul-de-Fenouillet.

ADDRESSES

STAY

Domaine de Coussères – *66220 Prugnanes – 5 km NW of St-Paul-de-Fenouillet by D 117 and D 20. ✆04 68 59 23 55 – Closed 1 Nov-15 Mar – 6rms.* Perched on a butte amid the vines, this superb *bastide* dominates a majestic landscape of mountains and *garrigues*. Large, tastefully decorated rooms, and a warm welcome in the dining room. Lovely garden, swimming pool and several terraces add to the charm.

EAT

Le Relais des Corbières – *10 Ave. Jean-Moulin, 66220 St-Paul-de-Fenouillet. ✆04 68 59 23 89 – www.relais.corbieres.com – closed 2-28 Jan, Sun evening and Mon except Jul-Aug and public holidays.* Enjoy a warm welcome and simple honest fare in a dining room with rustic decor or terrace.

Font-Romeu✻✻

see La CERDAGNE

Font-Romeu is a health resort on the sunny side of the French Cerdagne, higher than any other mountain village. It is protected from northerly winds and offers a superb valley panorama. Its impressive sports facilities (swimming pool, ice rink and stables) attract international athletes for altitude training programmes here.

Info: Office du tourisme de Font-Romeu-Odeillo-Via 38 av Emmanuel-Brousse-66120. ☎04 68 30 68 30. www.font-romeu.com.

Location: 89km(55.3mi) west of Perpignan and 9km(6mi) west of Mont-Louis via the D618.

Don't Miss: The panorama from the Calvary.

FONT-ROMEU / PYRÉNÉES 2000 SKI AREAS✻✻

Accessible by road or by gondola from the centre of Font-Romeu (2.5km/1.5mi via the route des pistes leading off from the calvary).

Snow-making equipment covers 85% of the area, and 40 downhill slopes accommodate skiers of all levels. The Pyrénées 2000 resort specialises in ski techniques for people with physical disabilities. The area also has a vast cross-country trail network and in February Pyrénées 2000 hosts the Transpyrénéenne cross-country race. Font-Romeu's **Centre Européen d'Entraînement Canin en Altitude** offers dog-sledding instruction year-round.

LA FONTAINE DU PÈLERIN

This hermitage bears witness to the famous Catalan pilgrimage that gave Font-Romeu its name (*fontaine du Pèlerin* or "pilgrim's fountain").

Ermitage★

The hermitage is known for its statue of the Blessed Virgin Mary called the "Vierge de l'Invention." The **chapel**★ dates from the 17C and 18C.

Its magnificent **altarpiece**★★ by Joseph Sunyer dates from 1707. The staircase to the left of the high altar leads to the **camaril**★★★, the Virgin Mary's small "reception room," Sunyer's masterpiece. (*open Jul-Aug 10am-noon, 3-6pm; for guided tours contact the tourist office. ☎04 68 30 68 30).*

Calvary

Alt 1 857m/6 035ft.

Some 300m/325yd from the hermitage on the road to Mont-Louis, turn right onto a path lined with stations of the cross. The calvary affords a **pano rama**★★ over Cerdagne and surrounding mountains.

Cross-country skiing in Font-Romeu

EXCURSIONS

Col del Pam★

From the calvary, drive to the ski slopes then continue on foot.

15min round-trip. Alt 2 005m/6 516ft.

The observation platform over the Têt Valley affords a **view** of the Carlit range, Bouillouses plateau, Capcir and Canigou summit.

Llivia

9km/5.6mi S along D 33E.

This is Spanish enclave on French territory (*see La CERDAGNE*) with picturesque lanes and the remains of a medieval castle and old towers.

Musee municipal

Closed for renovations. Contact for opening dates (00-34-972) 89 60 11.

This local museum houses the famous **Pharmacie de Llivia**★ (Llivia chemist's shop), one of the oldest in Europe, with ceramic jars and 17C and 18C objects commonly found in apothecary shops.

Angelic musician in the Ermitage chapel

A. Thuillier/MICHELIN

The **fortified church** contains Catalan wrought-iron decorations and a beautiful 1750 altarpiece.

Ille-sur-Têt

This little town in the Roussillon plain between the Têt and the Boulès is an important fruit and vegetable market. In 1834 Prosper Mérimée set his famous short story *The Venus from Ille* in Ille-sur-Têt.

- **Info:** Sq. de la Poste, 66130 Ille-sur-Têt. 04 68 84 02 62. www.ille-sur-tet.com.
- **Locatiom:** On the N116, 26km/16.25mi W of Perpignan and 21km/13mi E of Prades.
- **Don't Miss:** The Hospici d'Illa sculptures and fairy landscapes of Orgues d'Ille.

WALKING TOUR

Note the imposing Baroque façade of the **Église St-Étienne-del-Pradaguet**, a medieval sculpture **"Les Enamourats,"** on the corner of Rue des Carmes and Rue Deljat, and a magnificent 15C sculpted **Gothic cross** on Place del Ram.

Église des Carmes, a 17C Carmelite church, houses paintings from the studio of the Guerras, a family of Baroque artists from Perpignan.

Open Easter holidays and Jul-Aug: guided tours Mon, Wed, Fri 3.30-6pm and rest of year on request at the Hospici d'Illa, 10 R. de l'Hôpital, 66130 Ille-sur-Têt, 04 68 84 83 96.

SIGHTS

Hospici d'Illa

Open mid Jun-Sep 10am-noon, 2-7pm (Sat-Sun and public holidays 2-7pm); Feb-Mar and Oct-Nov daily except Tue, Sat, Sun and public hoidays 2-6pm; Apr-Jun daily except Tue 2-6pm. Closed, 1 May. 3.50€ (children under 12 free). 04 68 84 83 96.

The former Hospice St-Jacques (16C and 18C main building) houses Romanesque and Baroque paintings, sculpture

"Organ Pipes" of Ille-sur-Têt

A. Thuillier/MICHELIN

and gold and silver plate and runs Catalan cooking workshops. The museum organises visits to Baroque Catalan churches at Espira-de-Conflent, Joch and Finestret, among others.

Les Orgues d'Ille-sur-Têt★

North of Ille-sur-Têt; 15min on foot. *Open Jul-Aug 9.30am-8pm; Apr-Jun and Sep 10am-6.30pm; Feb-Mar 10am-12.30pm and 2-5.30pm; Oct 10am-12.30pm, 2-6pm; Nov-Jan 2-5pm; 3.50€ (children under 10 free). 04 68 84 13 13. www.ille-sur-tet.com.*

The D 21 passes the river and bends into a valley filled with amazing earth pillars (*cheminées de fées* or "fairies' chimneys") known as the "Organ Pipes." Towards Montalba, look for deep ochre formations to the left of the road. About 1km/0.6mi higher, a **look-out point** encompasses the Organ Pipes and Ille-sur-Têt.

DRIVING TOUR

Les Aspres★

56km/35mi from Ille-sur-Têt to Amélie-les-Bains – allow 3hrs.

In this rugged sparsely inhabited region, nothing breaks the complete stillness. The beautiful Mediterranean landscape is covered by olive groves and cork oaks.

Leave Ille-sur-Têt S on D 2, then turn right onto D 16 to Bouleternère.

D 618 (*turn left in Bouleternère*) leaves the orchards in the Têt Valley for the garrigues (scrubland) along the Boulès gorge.

After 7.5km/4.5mi turn right to Serrabone.

Prieuré de Serrabone★★

See Prieuré de SERRABONE.

Col Fourtou

Alt 646m/2 100ft.

Look back from the pass to Bugarach (1 230m/3 998ft), the highest Corbières peak, and ahead to Franco-Spanish border and Vallespir mountains and Pilon de Belmatx.

Prunet-et-Belpuig

The **Chapelle de la Trinité** (*open daily except Tue 9am-6pm)* has a door with scrolled hinges. Inside is a 12C Christ and Baroque altarpiece depicting the Holy Trinity.

Château

30min walk (there and back) from the Chapelle de la Trinité.

These brooding castle ruins on a rocky spur overlook Mont Canigou, the Albères, the Roussillon and Languedoc coasts and the Corbières (Bugarach). After the Xatard Pass the road drops down to Amélie, passing the villages of St-Marsal and Taulis and skirting the upper Ample valley.

Mont-Louis★

Mont-Louis was originally a fortified town founded in 1679 by Vauban to defend the new borders laid down in the Treaty of the Pyrenees. Mont-Louis became an excellent border stronghold. A statue in the church square of this austere fortress town pays tribute to General Dagobert, who drove the Spaniards out of the Cerdagne in 1793, during the dark hours of the invasion of Roussillon.

- **Population:** 284.
- **Michelin Map:** 344: D-7.
- **Info:** Syndicat d'initiative de Mont-Louis, 3 r Lt-Pruneta, 66210. 04 68 04 21 97. www.mont-louis.net
- **Location:** 36km/22.5mi SW of Prades via the N 116, and 9km/5.6mi E of Font-Romeu-Odeillo-Via via the D 618.
- **Don't Miss:** The citadelle and Forçats artesian wells; lakeshore walks by lac des Bouillouses.
- **Kids:** Solar furnace (Four solaire).

VISIT

The fortified town

guided tours (30min) daily except Sun Jul-mid Sep at 10am, 11am, 2pm, 3pm and 4pm; rest of year 11am and 2pm. Closed mid Dec-mid Jan. 4.50€ (children 1.50€). 04 68 04 21 97.

This consists of a citadel and a lower town, built entirely within the ramparts. The citadel has a square layout, with cut-off corners extended by bastions. Three demilunes protect the curtain walls. As the town, named after Louis XIV, the reigning monarch during its construction, was never besieged, the ramparts, the main gatehouse (Porte de France), the bastions and the watchtowers have remained intact.

Note the **Puits des Forçats**, an 18C well designed to supply the garrison with water in the event of a siege.

Four solaire (Solar Furnace)

Jul-Aug guided tours (45min) every 30 min, 10am-11.30, 2pm-6pm; Mar-Jun and Sep-Oct 10am, 11am, 2pm, 3pm, 4pm, 5pm (mid Jun-Mid Sep also at 6pm); Nov-Feb 10am, 11am, 2pm, 3p, 4pm. Closed 1 Jan, 25 Dec. 6€ (children 7-17 4€). 04 68 04 14 89. www.four-solaire.com.

The solar furnace was installed in 1953. The concentrating panel refurbished in 1980, consists of 860 parabolic mirrors and the heliostat of 546 flat mirrors. The structure focuses the sun's rays into its centre where temperatures reach up to 3 000-3 500°C/5 400-6 300°F. Since July 1993 it has been used for commercial rather than research purposes.

EXCURSIONS

Planès

6.5km/4mi S on the road to Cabanasse and St-Pierre-dels-Forçats. Leave the car in front of the Mairie-École in Planès and take the path on the right to the church.

A small cemetery around the church offers a beautiful **view** of the Carlit massif. The tiny **church**★ has a curious ground plan in the shape of a sort of five-pointed star, the "rays" of which are formed by alternately pointed or blunted semicircular chapels. The central dome rests on three semi-domes. The origins of this monument have given rise to intense speculation over the years, as its structure was extremely rare in the medieval western world. Local tradition attributes it to the Saracens, hence the church was known locally as *la mesquita* or mosque. It is probably a Romanesque building inspired by the symbol of the Holy Trinity.

Lac des Bouillouses★

See Le CAPCIR.

Le Capcir★

see Le CAPCIR.

Prades

Lying at the foot of Mont Canigou, in the midst of orchards, Prades became home to the cellist Pablo Casals (1876-1973) from 1950. The great concerts of the Pablo Casals Festival take place in the abbey of St-Michel-de-Cuxa and other fine churches in the area.

- **Population:** 6 221.
- **Michelin Map:** 344: F-7.
- **Info:** 44 r. des Marchands, 66500 Prades. 04 68 05 41 02. www.prades-tourisme.com.
- **Location:** 45km/28m W of Perpignan by the N116.
- **Don't Miss:** Musée Pablo Casals.
- **Timing:** Allow one hour.

VISIT

Église St-Pierre

The church (*open Jul-Sep Mon-Fri 10am-noon, 3.30-6pm*), rebuilt in the 17C, has nonetheless conserved its typical southern French Romanesque bell-tower. In the chancel, the Baroque **alterpiece** (1696-99) by the Catalan sculptor Joseph Sunyer includes over 100 carved figures and narrates in six sculpted scenes the life of the Apostle Peter, whose statue occupies the centre of the composition.
The **treasury** contains many reliquaries from the abbey of St-Michel-de-Cuxa (*guided tours Mon, Tue, Thu, Fri 2.30pm. 2.60€ (children 1.80€. 04 68 05 23 58)*.

Musée Pablo Casals

33 r. de l'Hospice. Open Jul-Sep Tue-Fri 9am-1pm, 2-5pm, Sat 9am-1pm; Oct-Jun Tue 10am-1pm, 4-7pm, Wed 10am-7pm, Fri 3-7pm, Sat 10am-1pm. Closed 25 Dec-7 Jan. No charge. 04 68 96 28 55.
This museum is dedicated to the world-famous Spanish violoncellist by his adopted city: recordings, concert clothes, letters, photographs, instruments all help to evoke the personality of the artist and illustrate his outstanding career.

EXCURSIONS

Abbaye de Saint-Michel de Cuxa★★

3km/2mi S. guided tour (45min) May-Sep daily 9.30-11.50am, 2-5pm (Sun and religious holidays 2-6pm); Oct-Apr daily 9.30-11.50am, 2-5pm (Sun and religious holidays 2-5pm). 4€. 04 68 96 15 35.
The elegant crenellated tower of the abbey, founded under the protection of the counts of Cerdagne-Conflent, rises from one of the valleys at the foot of Mont Canigou.
The present church, was consecrated in 974 and in the 11C, Abbot Oliba enlarged the chancel of the abbey church.
After a long period of decline, the abbey of St-Michel was abandoned, then sold during the Revolution. Its works of art

A Cellist's Happy Whim

In 1939, **Pablo Casals** fled the Franco regime in his native country, choosing to live in exile in Prades and thus not abandoning his beloved Catalonia altogether.
For 10 years this world-famous cellist, a committed pacifist, refused to play in public as a sign of protest. He relented at last in 1950, founding a festival which he dedicated to Bach, firmly stipulating, however, that the festival should take place in his adopted home town. Since then, Prades has become a major venue for chamber music. Every year, between 25 July and 15 August, some of the world's leading chamber musicians convene here to teach 150 outstandingly talented music students. Twenty-five concerts are given at the abbey of St-Michel-de-Cuxa, the church of St-Pierre in Prades and some of the other particularly beautiful churches in the region.

disappeared and the cloister galleries were dismantled.
From 1952, considerable work has been undertaken in Cuxa: the abbey church has been restored and some of the cloister galleries have been reinstated.

Cloisters★

These consist of arches and capitals found in Prades or in private ownership and recovered. These have been used to reconstruct almost half of the cloisters which now form a harmonious whole over which towers the lofty massive church.

Abbey church

The church is entered through a doorway reconstructed from a single archway, the remains of a gallery put up in the 12C at the far end of the nave. The nave is one of the very rare surviving examples of pre-Romanesque art in France.

Mosset

12km/7.5mi NW along D 619 and D 14.
The **Tour des Parfums** (*open Jul-Aug 10am-noon, 3-7pm; school holidays daily except Mon 3-6pm; rest of year weekends 3-6pm. Closed Jan and public holidays (except Jul-Aug). 3€ (children under 12 free) 04 68 05 38 32. www.mosset.fr*) houses an interactive exhibition about fragrances and organises themed walks, visits and workshops connected with the sense of smell.

Prats-de-Mollo★

Prats-de-Mollo lies in the broad upper Tech valley overlooked by the close-cropped slopes of the Costabonne massif and Mont Canigou. It combines the character of a walled fortress town designed by Vauban with the charm of a lively Catalan mountain town.
A picturesque Fête de l'Ours (bear festival) takes place in February.

- **Population:** 1 241.
- **Michelin Map:** Michelin Local map 344: F-8.
- **Info:** Pl. du Foiral, 66230 Prats-de-Mollo-la-Preste, 04 68 39 70 83. www.pratsdemollolapreste.com.
- **Location:** 63 km/39.5m SW of Perpignan by the A9 then the D115.
- **Timing:** Allow two hours for the town.
- **Kids:** Fort Lagarde.

TOWN WALK

Enter the town through Porte de France and follow the shopping street of the same name.

Opposite place d'Armes, climb the steps up rue de la Croix-de-Mission, overlooked by a Cross and Instruments of the Passion.

Church

A Romanesque church, of which only the crenellated bell-tower remains, predated the present building which has a Gothic structure, despite dating from the 17C.

Follow the south side of the church and take a fortified rampart walk round the chevet. Leave the precinct and walk uphill for about 100m/110yd towards Fort Lagarde. Turn round for a good view of the roof and upper sections of the church.

Fort Lagarde

Open Jul-Aug 11am-7pm; Apr-Jun and Sep-Oct 2-6pm. Possibility of guided tours and tours with a story

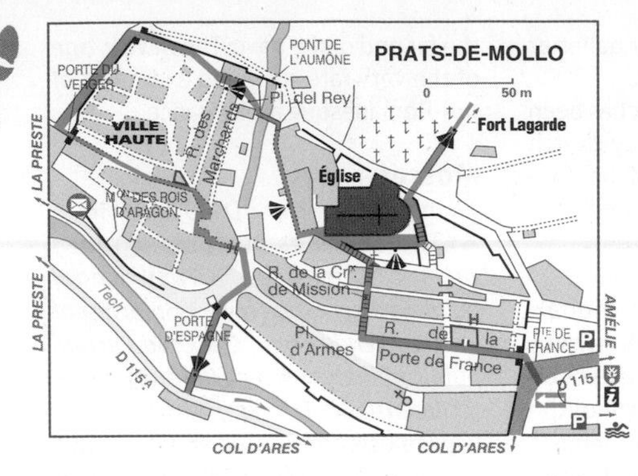

The street leads to a crossroads, overlooked by a house in the shape of a ship's prow; some people think this was once a palace of the kings of Aragón, and others think that it once housed the trade union of the weavers' guild. An alleyway leads downhill to the exit from the upper town. Go through Porte d'Espagne onto the footbridge over the Tech, from where there is a good view of the south side of the town.

of the site (inquire for information).
3.50€ (children under 12 no charge).
04 68 39 70 83.
The fortress was built in 1692 on a rocky spur overlooking the town, and at the centre of the site there are now the remains of the old castle. Take the steps up the side of the curtain wall to get to the fort.

Return to the church and take the street to the right.

In sight of the almshouse, go down the steps on the left and follow the street as it runs along below the almshouse gardens. Cross the torrent over the fortified bridge, just downstream of the old humpback bridge of La Guilhème, to get to the upper town.

(Ville haute or Ville d'Amoun)★

Place del Rey, where an old house once belonging to the military Engineers stands, used to be the site of one of the residences of the counts of Besalù, who, in the 12C, reigned over one of the pieces of land which formed part of the patchwork of Catalan territory. Where rue des Marchands leads off to the left, take a carved stairway up to the right.

Continue along the curtain wall. Leave the town through a modern gateway, and return to it through the next one round (a gatehouse), the "Porte du Verger."

EXCURSION

La Preste

8km/5mi NW along D 115A.

The spa town of La Preste has five springs (temperature 44°C/111°F) recommended for the cure of infections of the colon. Napoléon III had this road up to the spa built. He had intended to follow a course of hydrotherapy at the spa, but the war of 1870 intervened and he was forced to abandon the idea.

ADDRESSES

STAY / EAT

Hotel Bellevue – *Pl. du Forail. 04 68 39 72 48. www.lebellevue.fr.st. Closed Tue and Wed from 30 Oct–30 Mar and Tue, 30 Nov–15 Feb. 17rms. 7.50€ Restaurant* . Spa guests and tourists alike are attentively looked after in this family-run guesthouse whose young owner cooks the Catalan dishes served in the restaurant. Fresh, well-kept rooms with wood furniture. Terrace to the front and small garden at the back.

AT THE FORT

Guided tours of the fort with a military theme: costumed horsemen give demonstrations of 18C French military training. *Mid Jul-mid Aug daily except Sat show at 2.30 and 4.30; early to mid-Jul and 23–27 Aug: daily except Sat show at 2.30pm. 8€ (children: 5€). 04 68 39 70 83.*

Abbaye de Saint-Martin-du-Canigou★★

This abbey perched in its eagle's eyrie 1 055m/3 460ft above sea level is one of the prime sights to be seen in the area around Vernet-les-Bains. Guifred, Count of Cerdagne, great-grandson of Wilfred le Velu, founder of the Catalonian dynasty, chose Mont Canigou, a solitary place venerated by his people, to found a Benedictine monastery in 1001.

- **Info:** Office de tourisme de Prades – 4 r. des Marchands, 66500. 04 68 05 41 02. www.prades-tourisme.com
- **Location:** 14km/8.75mi S of Prades by N 116. The abbey can be reached from Vernet-les-Bains. Alternatively, park the car in Casteil and continue on foot.
- **Don't Miss:** The view of the abbey from the woods above.
- **Timing:** Allow two hours.

VISIT

guided tours (1hr) Jun–Sep 10am, 11am, noon, 2pm, 3pm, 4pm, 5pm (Sun and public holidays 10am, 12.30pm, 2pm, 3pm, 4pm, 5pm); Oct–May daily except Tues 10am, 11am, 2pm, 3pm, 4pm (Sun and public holidays 10am, 12.30pm, 2pm, 3pm, 4pm). Closed Jan. 5€ (children under 12 free, 12-18 3.50€). 04 68 05 50 03. http://stmartinducanigou.org.

Cloisters – At the beginning of the 20C, all that remained of the cloisters were three galleries with somewhat crude semicircular arcades. Restoration work included rebuilding a south gallery overlooking the ravine, using the marble capitals from an upper storey which was no longer extant.

Churches – The lower church (10C), dedicated to "Notre-Dame-sous-Terre" in accordance with an old Christian tradition, forms the crypt of the upper church (11C). The latter, consisting of three successive naves with parallel barrel vaults, conveys an impression of great age with its rugged, simply carved capitals.

Walk to the **viewpoint** (*after reaching the abbey, take a stairway to the left (itinerary no 9) which climbs into the woods. Just past the water outlet turn right (30min on foot there and back)*) to appreciate the originality of St-Martin's site. From here, there is an impressive view of the abbey. Its **site**★★ dominating the Casteil and Vernet valleys is most striking.

Abbaye de St-Martin-du-Canigou

Prieuré de Serrabone★★

The steep, winding road up to Serrabone in the rather bleak part of Roussillon known as Les Aspres, does not at any stage give so much as a glimpse of the splendid Romanesque priory which lies at the end of it.

Location: 41km/25.5mi W of Perpigan by the N116. After Ille sut Têt, turn left on the D618.

Don't Miss: The pink marble tribune in the church.

Timing: Allow 45 minutes.

VISIT

Entrance to the church is through the south gallery. Open 10am–6pm (last admission 30min before closing). Closed 1 Jan, 1 May, 1 Nov, 25 Dec. 3€ (children: 2€). 04 68 84 09 30. www.cg66.fr.

The exterior of the priory has an impressive, if somewhat forbidding, appearance with its rugged architectural style and dark schist stonework. The priory was founded in 1082, on the site of a pre-existing that church was enlarged and reconsecrated in 1151. Once a prosperous and flourishing priory, it saw the first signs of decline towards the end of the 13C.

South gallery★ – 12C. Overlooking the ravine, the gallery was used as a covered walkway by Augustinian canons. It is imbued with serenity and harmony, and decorated with capitals reflecting oriental themes, typical of the romantic sculptors of Roussillon.

Church – The nave dates from the 11C; the chancel, transept and the north side aisle are 12C. The church contains a pink-marble **tribune★★** with impressively rich ornamentation.

The most remarkable feature is the delicate ornamentation of three archivolts – an ornamental moulding or band following the curve of the underside of an arch.

ADDRESSES

SHOPPING

Relais de Serrabone – *66130 Boule-d'Amont. 04 68 84 26 24. At the foot of the road which leads to the priory. Jul-Aug, daily 11am-7pm; Apr-Jun and Sep-Oct, daily exc Tue.* Run by local producers, this shop presents a mouthwatering selection of honeys, aromatic herbs, charcuterie, preserved ducks and other tasty treats.

Tribune of the priory

H. Champollion/MICHELIN

Village of Tech near Arles-sur-Tech

J. Malburet/MICHELIN

Le Vallespir★

The Vallespir is the region in the eastern Pyrenees occupied by the Tech Valley. Lying upstream of Amélie-les-Bains, this area with its pastoral, highland charm has a most varied attractive appearance. It is, moreover, an area of geographical interest in that it comprises the most southern communities on French territory.

- **Location:** 27km/17m of Perpignam, Le Boulou marks the entrance to Vallespir where the D115 runs along the Tech to Prats de Mollo.
- **Don't Miss:** The mysterious "Sainte Tombe" of the abbey; the walk in the Gorges of the Feu and the view from Can Damoun.
- **Timing:** Allow a day for the circuit of the valley.

DRIVING TOUR

Vallée du Tech

Starting in Amélie-les-Bains – 120km/75mi – allow 6hr.

Arles-sur-Tech

Arles grew up around an abbey built on the banks of the Tech in around 900, of which the church and cloisters have survived.

Inside the **abbey church** *(access from the main square (S of D 115) via a flight of stairs. Open Jul-Aug daily 9am–7pm (Sun 2–5pm); Sep-Jun 9am-noon, 2-6pm (Apr-Jun and Sep-Oct) Sun 2-5pm). Closed 1 May, 1 and 11 Nov, 25 Dec and 1 Jan. 3.50€; 04 68 83 90 66)* to the left of the main door, just before entering the church, note a 4C white-marble sarcophagus behind a wrought-iron grille. This is the **Sainte Tombe** ("holy tomb") from which several hundred litres of pure clear water seep every year. To date, no scientific explanation has been found for this phenomenon. A door at the far end of the north aisle leads to the Gothic **cloisters** (13C).

Leave Arles S along D 115. The road crosses the river. Park the car near the footpath off to the right which leads to the pretty gorge of the River Fou.

Gorges de la Fou★★

Open Jul-Aug 9.30am-6.30pm; Apr-Jun and Sep 10am-6pm; Oct-Nov 10am-5pm. Closed Dec–Mar and in heavy rain. 6€. (children 5-12 years 3€). 04 68 39 16 21. 1hr 30min there and back on foot (just under a mile along footbridges).

The crevice cut by the river is less than 1m/3ft wide in some places, despite being over 200m/656ft deep. Stretches where cataracts can be seen thundering down from one deep pool to the next alternate with calmer, more open reaches.

Return to D 115 and, after 3km/1.9mi, turn left onto D 3.

The road is well laid out on the "shady" slopes of the Vallespir, covered in luxuriant vegetation (maples, chestnuts) and watered by numerous streams.

St-Laurent-de-Cerdans

This is the most populated village of the southern Vallespir region, which specialises in the production of espadrilles and the weaving of traditional Catalan fabrics. A **museum** (*open Jul-Aug 10am-noon, 2pm-6pm (Sat and Sun, 10am-noon, 3pm-5pm); Sep-Jun daily except Sat-Sun 10am-noon and 3pm-5pm. 2€. 04 68 39 55 75)* is devoted to this activity.

Coustouges

This small mountain village stands close to the Franco-Spanish border, on the site of an ancient Roman sentry post (reflected in its name). It is home to an interesting 12C fortified **church**.

Can Damoun

Panoramic **site★** sweeping across wild remote valleys. From Notre-Dame-du-Pardon oratory there is a fine view of Rosas Bay on the Costa Brava.

Turn back to La Forge-del-Mitg and bear left onto D 64 then turn left to Serralongue.

Serralongue

Walk up to the church. A nettle tree grows on the esplanade; the wood of this tree was once used for making the famous whips known as perpignans.

Turn back; take the scenic road, D 64, to the left then D 115 left to Le Tech.

Baillanouse ravine

The original road, swept away by the catastrophic floods of October 1940, was rebuilt higher up. On the left, a cavity in the side of Puig Cabrès is still visible, from which a huge landslide (6-7 million m^3/212-247 million cu ft) broke away, blocking the valley to a height of 40m/131ft.

Prats-de-Mollo★

See PRATS-DE-MOLLO.

On the way up to the Cop d'Ares, **Mir tower**, one of the highest watchtowers in Roussillon, can be seen immediately to the south. Farther on, **Cabrens towers** come into view rising above the wooded valleys converging towards Serralongue. Soon afterwards, the chapel of Notre-Dame-de-Coral appears on the left.

Col d'Ares★

Alt 1 513m/4 964ft.

Situated on the border, this pass is the gateway to Spain (Ripoll, Vich, Barcelona).

Turn back and drive to Le Tech then turn left onto D 44.

On the left stands a strange pyramid-shaped mountain topped by Cos tower (alt 1 116m/3 661ft).

Montferrer

There's a church with a delightful bell-tower; to the left are the ruins of a castle.

Carry on along D 44.

In a bend to the left, at the highest point along the road (899m/2 922ft), the panorama sweeps across the Canigou peak, the Albères mountains, Roussillon and the Mediterranean.

The road soon runs across the River Fou (good view), past the former **Corsavy** watchtower then through the village of the same name (ruins of the old parish church). D 43 runs down into the pleasant Riuferrer valley.

Vernet-les-Bains ★

Vernet's setting★, at the foot of the wooded lower slopes of Mont Canigou, on which the bell-tower of St-Martin can be seen, is one of the most refreshing in the eastern Pyrenees. The roar of the Cady torrent in the background lends an unexpectedly mountainous note to this Mediterranean setting.

Info: 2 Rue de la Chapelle, 66820 Vernet-Les-Bains, ☎04 68 05 55 35. www.ot-vernet-les-bains.fr.

Location: 171km/105mi W of Perpignan and 12km/7.5mi S of Prades by thw N116, then the D116 to Villefranche de Conflent.

Don't Miss: The view from the belvedere on the Col de Mantet.

Timing: Allow 2 hours to visit to Vernet and surroundings.

VISIT

Old town centre

From place de la République, take rue J.-Mercader, lined with little houses bright with flowers, up to the top of the hill on which the church stands.

Rudyard Kipling was inordinately fond of this place, visiting Vernet in 1910, 1911 and 1914, and writing to the French Alpine Club: "I came here in search of nothing more than a little sunshine. But I found Canigou...a magician among mountains...and I watch him with wonder and delight." Kipling also wrote a light-hearted short story – *Why snow falls at Vernet* – which pokes fun of the English habit of always talking about the weather.

Musée de Géologie

Open early Apr-Sep Tue-Sat 10am-noon, 2-6pm, Sun 2-6pm. 3€. ☎04 68 05 77 97.

Exhibits are presented by a dedicated collector: ammonites and marine fossils, including a fossilised fish, with its scales and fins still intact, going back 120 million years.

EXCURSIONS

Abbaye de St-Martin-du-Canigou★★

3km/2mi S as far as Casteil.

See ST-MARTIN-DU-CANIGOU.

Col de Mantet★

20km/12.5mi SW – allow 1hr.

The cliff road is very steep and narrow (overtaking very difficult) upstream of Py.

After leaving Vernet to the west, from Sahorre on, the road (D 27) climbs the Rotja valley, first amid apple trees then along a gorge sunk into the granite rock. Above **Py**, a pretty village 1 023m/3 356ft above sea level, the road scales steep slopes with granite outcrops bristling here and there. After 3.5km/2mi, in a wide bend in the road, a **look-out point★** gives a good view of the village with its red roofs and Mont Canigou.

The Mantet Pass opens up at an altitude of 1 761m/5 777ft, near the evergreen forest of La Ville. On the opposite slope, the strikingly austere site of **Mantet**, an almost deserted village can be seen huddled in a dip.

Vernet-les-Bains

A. Thuillier/MICHELIN

Villefranche-de-Conflent★

Villefranche-de-Conflent, founded in 1090 by Guillaume Raymond, Count of Cerdagne, occupies a remarkable site on the confluence of the Cady and the Têt, closely surrounded by rock cliffs. Villefranche was a fortified town from the start. Its fortifications were improved over the centuries and finally completed in the 17C by Vauban.

- **Info:** Pl d l'Eglise, 66500 Villefranche-de-Conflent, 04 68 96 22 96.
- **Location:** 42km/25mi E of Font-Romeu by the N116 and 8km/5mi SW of Prades.
- **Don't Miss:** Guided tour of the town – Tours are conducted by a guide-lecturer from the Rendez-Vous du Patrimoine association 04 68 96 25 64. By appointment.
- **Timing:** Allow two hours, and stay for lunch.

THE FORTIFIED TOWN★

Park the car outside the ramparts, in the car park situated by the confluence of the Têt and the Cady.

Go through the fortified wall at the Porte de France, built in Louis XVI's reign, to the left of the old gateway used by the counts.

Ramparts★

Entrance at no 32 bis, rue St-Jacques. Open Jul-Aug 10am-8pm; Jun and Sep- 10am-7pm; Apr, May and Oct 10.30am-12.30pm, 2-6pm. Rest of year 10.30-12.30pm, 2-5pm Closed Jan and 25 Dec. 4€. 04 68 96 22 96.

Rue St-Jean
©arenysam/Fotolia.com

The tour of the ramparts takes in two storeys of galleries, one above the other: the lower watch-path, dating from the construction of the fortress in the 11C, and the upper gallery, dating from the 17C.

Rue St-Jean

After returning to the Porte de France, walk through the village along rue St-Jean with its 13C and 14C houses, many of which still feature their original porches with rounded or pointed arches.

Église St-Jacques

The church, which dates from the 12C and 13C, comprises two parallel naves. Enter the church through the doorway with four columns and a cabled archivolt; the capitals are by the St-Michel-de-Cuxa School.

Porte d'Espagne

This gateway, like the Porte de France, was refurbished as a monumental entrance in 1791.

FORT LIBERIA★

Access via the staircase of a "thousand steps," via a footpath or by means of a 4-wheel-drive vehicle. Departure from within the ramparts, to the right of Porte de France. Open Jun-Sep 9am-8pm; Oct-May 10am-6pm. 6€. 04 68 96 34 01 and 04 68 05 74 29.

Watchtower with Fort Liberia in the background

H. Champollion/MICHELIN

Overlooked as it is by Mont Belloc, the town was rather too exposed to attack from any enemy encamped above it. Therefore, from 1679 when he was in charge of the project to fortify the town, Vauban planned to protect it by building a fort.

This fort, equipped with a cistern and powder magazines, clearly illustrates some of Vauban's strategic defensive designs. The "stairway of a thousand steps" (there are in fact 734) was built from pink Conflent marble to link the fort to the town by the little fortified St-Pierre bridge over the Têt.

From the fort, there are **wonderful views**★★ of the valleys below and Mont Canigou.

We recommend taking the "stairway of a thousand steps" back down into the village.

CAVES

Cova Bastera

Open Jul-Aug 11am-7pm; Jun and Sep 2-5pm. Closed rest of year. 04 68 96 23 11. www.3grottes.com

This cave, situated on the Andorra road opposite the ramparts, is at the far end of the Canalettes network. It reveals Vauban's underground fortification system and the various phases of occupation of the site, portrayed in life-size tableaux.

Grotte des Canalettes

Car park 700m/770yd S, below the Vernet road. Guided tours Jul and Aug hourly 11am-6pm. 04 68 05 20 20. www.3grottes.com.

The concretions in this cave take on an amazing variety of shapes: petrified calcite torrents and eccentrics. Some of the finest include the Table, a natural hollow *(gour)* that gradually filled up with calcite, and some dazzling white draperies.

Grotte des Grandes Canalettes

Open Jul-Aug 10am-7pm; Apr-Jun 10am–6pm; Sep-Oct 10am-5.30pm; rest of the year weekends and school holidays 2–5pm. Closed 1 Jan and 25 Dec. 04 68 96 23 20. www.3grottes.com.

This cave forms part of the same network as the Canalettes cave.

View of Montségur village in the Lasset valley

DISCOVERING MIDI-PYRÉNÉES

Nicknamed the "Pink City" for its preponderance of red-brick buildings, Toulouse, the fourth-largest conglomeration in France, is a mildly frenetic, hugely entertaining and vibrant place. Toulouse, capital of France's largest region (Midi-Pyrénées) very much has its own identity, a glorious tangle of narrow streets and squares, buildings great and small, and intimate nooks and crannies. Within sight of the Pyrenees, Toulouse is not surprisingly subject to influences from Spain, culturally, gastronomically and architecturally, although it retains and cultivates its own Occitan identity – street names, for example, are bilingual. The result is a keen, energetic and cosmopolitan setting made all the more spontaneous by the third-largest student population (over 100 000 of them) in France.

Highlights

1. Boat trip on the **Garonne** (p311)
2. Take a coffee in facing the **Capitole** and then wander the streets (p301)
3. Spend an afternoon in the **Fondation Bemberg** (p306)
4. Young and old should visit the **Cité de l'espace** (p308)
5. Afternoon tea aboard **La Maison de la Violette** (p311)

Occitan flag on the Capitole

S. Sauvignier/MICHELIN

Purely for comparison

For those who assess a city by the contentment it bestows on their stomach, Toulouse will be highly prized. Almost equidistant between the Atlantic and the Mediterranean, it has the benefit of sea food from both coasts, and perhaps more so than anywhere outside Paris, offers an opportunity to compare the oysters of Hérault with those of Charente Maritime. But equally you can gorge yourself on the glorious Toulouse sausage, which usually finds its way into the legendary cassoulet, a dish over which there can be passionate disagreement as to which is the best.

Just strolling

Toulouse is built on the alluvium of the Garonne, at a point were the river bend accumulated silt over a long enough period for it to become sufficiently stable to build on.

The present-day banks of the Garonne have been developed to enable people to flâner along the quays from place Saint-Pierre to the Quai de Tournis, very much in the manner of the French. A relaxing way to work off lunch.

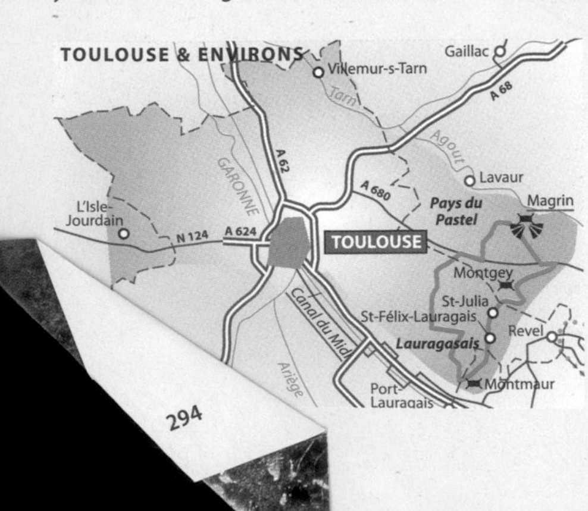

Toulouse: Heritage and Industry

Toulouse has the power of seduction, a place that captivates on first acquaintance. Yet it is anything but trivial, and within its embrace lies a fascinating history exemplified by superb Renaissance buildings, like the **Hotel d'Assézat**, emblematic of the place woad has played in the city's history, and built in 1555. Today, this grand *hotel particulière* houses the Bemberg Foundation, a supreme collection of artwork by Cézanne, Picasso, Tintoretto, Manet and others.

Bolted onto this outstanding heritage, Toulouse is very much a city of the present and the future. The city has a deep-rooted cultural identity, but accommodates this alongside its desire to be forward-looking and enterprising. The launch of the **Airbus A380**, the largest airliner in the world, has made Toulouse the European capital of aeronautics.

The **Cité de l'Espace**, on the outer ring road, is a unique concept, and the sort of inter-planetary experience wherein children can lose themselves in make believe. If it lies along the way to the stars, then the city of Toulouse rests on another pilgrims' route, that to Compostela. Indeed, the **Hotel Dieu** on the left bank of the Garonne, close by Pont Neuf, was used as a hospice for 800 years, and stood as a major site on the pilgrims' route. In the past, the building received the country's down-and-outs, beggars, vagabonds and loose women, but today it is a World Heritage Site housing the administrative centre of a teaching hospital and museum of medicine.

Culture has always been at the heart of Toulouse, and today the city has one of the most extensive and intense cultural calendars.

Cité de l'espace

Toulouse★★★

Bathed in Mediterranean light, Toulouse can take on a variety of hues depending on the time of day, ranging from scorching red to dusky pink or even violet. Once the capital of all the regions united by the Occitanian dialects *(langues d'oc)*, **Toulouse is now a famous centre of the French aeronautical construction industry, which has attracted numerous high-tech industries, as well as a lively university town.**

- **Info:** Donjon du Capitole, 38001-31080 Toulouse ℘05 61 11 02 22. www.toulouse-tourisme.com.
- **Location:** 245km/153mi SE of Bordeaux by A 62; 95km/59mi NW of Carcassonne by A 61.
- **Parking:** There is limited parking in the very centre of Toulouse, but on-street parking and multi-storey car parks close by.
- **Don't Miss:** The Old Town, Basilique St-Sernin.

A BIT OF HISTORY

From Celtic to "Capitoul" rule – The ancient settlement of the Volcae, a branch of Celtic invaders, was probably situated in Vieille-Toulouse *(9km/5mi S)*, but moved site and expanded into a large city which Rome made the intellectual centre of Gallia Narbonensis. In the 3C, it was converted to Christianity and became the third most important city in Gaul. Visigothic capital in the 5C, it then passed into the hands of the Franks. After Charlemagne, Toulouse was ruled by counts, but it was far enough removed from the seat of Frankish power to keep a large degree of autonomy. From the 9C to the 13C, under the dynasty of the counts Raimond, the court of Toulouse was one of the most gracious and magnificent in Europe. The city was administered by consuls or *capitouls*, whom the count would systematically consult concerning the defence of the city or any negotiation with neighbouring feudal lords. The administration of the *capitouls* meant that the merchants of Toulouse had the possibility of becoming members of the aristocracy (to mark their rise in station, the new-fledged noblemen would adorn their mansion with a turret). By the time the city passed under the rule of the French crown in 1271, only 12 *capitouls* remained. A Parliament, established in 1420 and reinstated in 1443, supervised law and finance.

The oldest academy in France – After the turmoil of the Albigensian conflict, Toulouse once more became a centre of artistic and literary creativity. In 1324,

PUBLIC TRANSPORT

Toulouse has an extensive public transport network: 65 bus routes and, since 1993, a metro line. Six bus routes and the metro operate at night from 10pm; the last buses on each route leave from "Matabiau SNCF" at 5 minutes past midnight; the metro runs from 5.15am to midnight from Sun to Mon; 42 min past midnight Fri and Sat departure from the terminus. Cars can be parked free of charge in the "transit car parks" and you can then take the bus or metro. A yellow ticket (1.40€ each) allows you to travel anywhere on the network for 1hr. Day round-trip tickets (2.50€), day (4.20€) and season tickets are also available. *Information: Allô Tisséo ℘05 61 41 70 70. www.tisseo.fr.*

MUSEUM PASS

Combined tickets are available for the Jacobins church and the following museums: St-Raymond, Paul-Dupuy, Georges-Labit and Augustins.
One at 6€ gives access three times; another at 9€ gives access six times. Entrance to museums is free on the 1st Sunday of each month.

Violets

The violet, originally from Parma in Italy, is thought to have been introduced to Toulouse during the 19C by French soldiers who had fought in Napoleon's Italian campaign. It was enthusiastically received by the people of Toulouse, and became the most sought-after item at florists', perfume-makers' and confectioners' (the famous sugared violets). At the beginning of the century, some 600 000 bouquets a year were being sent to the capital, Northern Europe and even Canada. Sadly, disease and mildew soon got the better of this delicate winter plant with its tiny purple flowers. However, from 1985, scientists began research into ways of saving the plant. Ten years later, they succeeded in cultivating it under glass. Nowadays, the greenhouses of Lalande, north of Toulouse, are once again fragrant with the scent of this pretty flower and Toulouse has had its emblem restored.

Every year, the *fête de la violette*, a festival in honour of this lovely bloom, is held in late February-early March.

R. Corbel/MICHELIN

seven eminent citizens desiring to preserve the *langue d'Oc* founded the "Compagnie du Gai-Savoir," one of the oldest literary societies in Europe. Every year on 3 May, the best poets were awarded the prize of a golden flower. Ronsard and Victor Hugo were honoured in this way, as was poet, playwright and revolutionary journalist Philippe-Nazaire-François Fabre (1755-94), author of the Republican calendar and the ballad *"Il pleut, il pleut, bergère,"* who immortalised his prize by changing his pen-name to **Fabre d'Églantine** (wild rose). In 1694, Louis XIV raised the society to the status of **Académie des Jeux floraux**.

The **dyer's woad boom** – In the 15C, the trade in **dyer's woad** launched the merchants of Toulouse onto the scene of international commerce, with London and Antwerp among the main outlets. Clever speculation enabled families like the Bernuys and the Assézats to lead the life of princes. Sumptuous palatial mansions were built during this period, symbolising the tremendous wealth and power of these "dyer's woad tycoons." The thriving city of Toulouse, which had been largely medieval in appearance, underwent harmonious changes influenced by Italian architectural style, in particular that of the Florentine revival. However, with the introduction of indigo into Europe and the outbreak of the Wars of Religion, the boom collapsed after 1560 and recession set in.

No head is too great – Henri de Montmorency, governor of Languedoc, "first Christian baron" and member of the most illustrious family of France, was renowned for his courage, good looks and generosity and soon became well loved in his adopted province. In 1632, he was persuaded by Gaston d'Orléans, brother of Louis XIII, to take up arms in the rebellion of the nobility against Cardinal Richelieu, a decision that was to cost him dear. Both Orléans and Montmorency were defeated at

A "Red-Brick" City

Brick, the only construction material available in any sufficient quantity in the alluvial plain of the Garonne, has long predominated in the buildings of Toulouse, lending the city its unique style and beauty. As brick is so light and mortar adheres to it easily, the master masons of Toulouse were able to construct extravagantly wide vaults spanning a single nave.

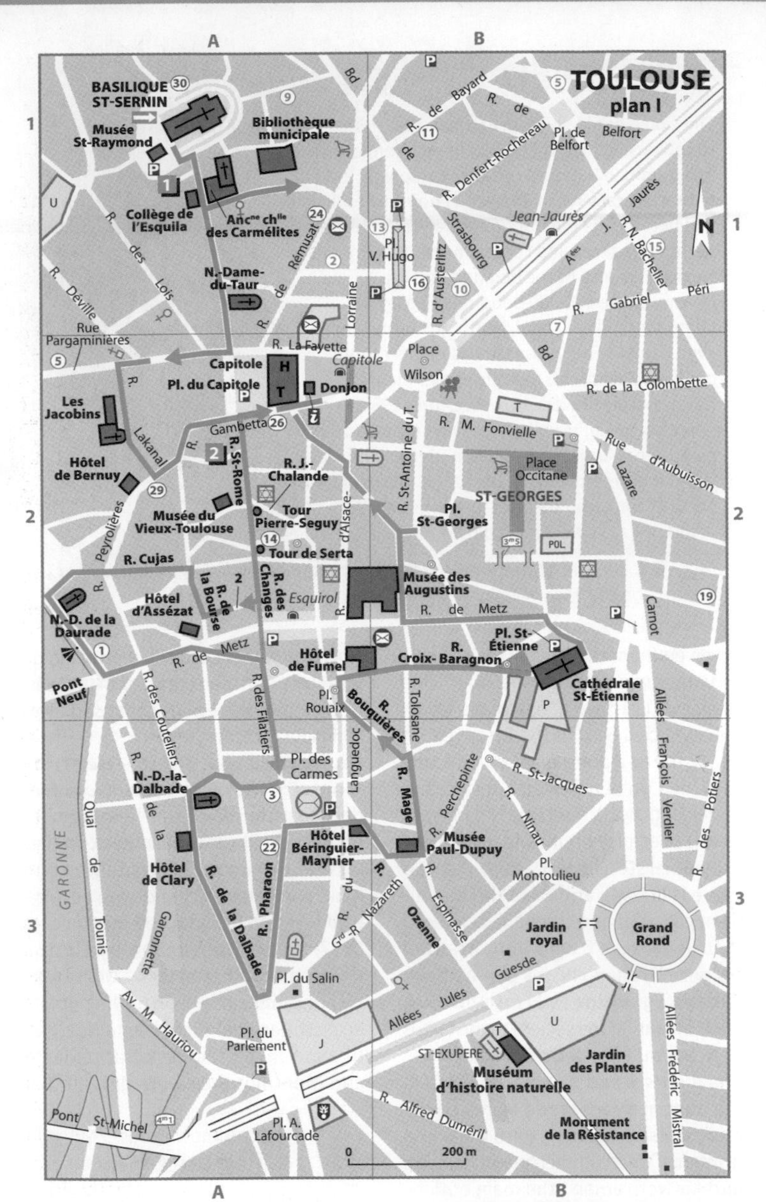

WHERE TO STAY

Albert 1er (Hôtel)........ ②
Boréal (Hôtel)........ ⑤
Castellane (Hôtel)........ ⑦
Loges de St-Sernin (Chambre d'hôte Les)........ ⑨
Ours Blanc-Centre (Hôtel de l')........ ⑩
Ours Blanc-Victor-Hugo (Hôtel de l')........ ⑬
St Claire (Hôtel)........ ⑮

WHERE TO EAT

"Beaux Arts" (Brasserie)........ ①
Carmes (Rôtisserie des)........ ③
Châteaubriand (Le)........ ⑤
Colombier........ ⑪
Faim des Haricots (La)........ ⑭
J'Go........ ⑯
Madeleine de Proust (La)........ ⑲
Mangevins (Le)........ ㉒
Michel, Marcel, Pierre et les Autres........ ㉔
Opéra (Brasserie de l')........ ㉖
Régalade (La)........ ㉙
7 Place St-Sernin........ ㉚

STREETS INDEX

Basilique Saint-Sernin

L. Cazenave/MICHELIN

Castelnaudary, where Montmorency fought valiantly, sustaining more than a dozen wounds, before being taken prisoner. He was condemned to death by the Parliament at Toulouse.

Nobody could believe that such a popular and high ranking figure would be executed, but the king, who had come in person to Toulouse with Cardinal Richelieu, turned a deaf ear to the pleas of the family, the court and the people, claiming that as king he could not afford to show favour to any particular individual. He did, however, concede that the condemned man could be beheaded inside the Capitole, instead of the market place. So, on a specially constructed scaffold in the interior courtyard, the 37-year-old duke met his death with all the dignity befitting a noble lord. When his head was shown to the crowd in front of the Capitole, there were howls of vengeance levelled at the cardinal.

Born in Toulouse – Toulouse is the birthplace of several famous French figures, including Jean-Pierre Rives, champion of the Toulouse rugby team, and Claude Nougaro, a late 20C troubadour. Those familiar with the little round tins of Lajaunie sweets (in aniseed and other flavours) will be interested to know that Lajaunie, a chemist, was also a native of Toulouse.

BASILIQUE ST-SERNIN★★★

This is the most famous and most magnificent of the great Romanesque pilgrimage churches in the south of France, and one which can also boast the largest collection of holy relics. The site was home, in the late 4C, to a basilica containing the body of St Sernin (or Saturninus). This Apostle from the Languedoc, the first bishop of Toulouse, was martyred in 250 by being tied to the legs of a bull he had refused to sacrifice to pagan gods, which dragged him down a flight of stone steps.

With the donation of numerous relics by Charlemagne, the church became a focus for pilgrims from all over Europe, and also a stopping place for pilgrims on their way to Santiago de Compostela. The present building was constructed to meet these growing needs. It was begun in c 1080 and completed in the mid-14C. General restoration was undertaken in 1860 by Viollet-le-Duc. The current programme of repair work is intended to restore the roof to its appearance prior to the work carried out in 1860. The transept arms and the nave are now covered once again by ample overhanging roofs with open galleries (mirandes) just beneath the eaves.

Exterior – St-Sernin is constructed from red brick and white stone. In the apse, begun in the late 11C, stone is much in evidence, whereas the nave is built almost all of brick, which in turn is the only material used in the belfry. The 11C **apse** is the oldest part of the building. It forms a magnificent ensemble of five chapels and four transept chapels combining with the tiered roofs of the chancel and transept, and the elegant bell-tower rising out of the whole.

The five-tier octagonal **bell-tower** stands majestically above the transept crossing. The three lower tiers are embellished with early 12C Romanesque round arches. The two upper storeys were added 150 years later; the openings, shaped like mitres, are surmounted by little decorative pediments. The spire was added in the 15C.

Interior – St-Sernin is the epitome of a major pilgrimage church. It was designed to accommodate large congregations, with room for a choir of canons and consists of a nave flanked by double side aisles, a broad transept and a chancel with an ambulatory from which five radiating chapels open off.

Chancel – Beneath the dome of the transept crossing, there is a fine table of Pyrenean marble from the old Romanesque altar signed by Bernard Gilduin and consecrated in 1096 by Pope Urban II.

Transept – The vast transept is laid out as three aisles with east-facing chapels. The capitals of the tribune gallery and the Romanesque mural paintings are worthy of attention. In the north transept, two groups of Romanesque mural paintings have been uncovered (the Resurrection and the Lamb of God presented by angels).

One of the south transept chapels is dedicated to the Virgin Mary (note the 14C statue of "Notre-Dame-la-Belle"); on the chapel's oven-vault are frescoes one above the other mingling the theme of the Virgin seated "in Majesty" (13C) with the Coronation of the Virgin.

Ambulatory and crypt (*open Jul-Aug 10am-5pm, Sun 12am-6pm; rest of year daily exc. Sun morning 10-11.30am, 2.30-5pm; closed public holidays. 2€. 05 61 21 70 18)* – Numerous altarpieces and reliquaries on display in the [a]mbulatory have led to its being known [as t]he Corps Saints, or Holy Relics, since [...]C. On the wall curving round the outside of the crypt are seven impressive late 11C **low-relief sculptures★★** in St-Béat marble from the studio of Bernard Gilduin: Christ in Majesty, with the symbols of the Evangelists, surrounded by angels and Apostles.

OLD TOWN★★★ WALK

1 St-Sernin to the Capitole

From St-Sernin follow rue du Taur, one of the favourite haunts of students, lined with many bookshops selling new and second-hand books.

Collège de l'Esquila

This opens off no 69 rue du Taur through a doorway decorated with bosses, a Renaissance work by Toulouse sculptor N Bachelier.

Turn left onto rue du Périgord.

Ancienne Chapelle des Carmelites

Open May-Sep daily except Mon 9.30am-1pm, 2-6pm; rest of the year daily except Mon 10am-1pm, 2-5pm. Closed 1 Jan, 1 May, 1 and 11 Nov, 25 Dec. 05 34 44 92 05.

The decoration of this chapel – woodwork and paintings commemorating the Carmelite order (by the Toulouse painter Despax) – is a fine example of 18C art.

Return to rue du Taur and turn left.

Église Notre-Dame-du-Taur

This church, known as St-Sernin-du-Taur until the 16C, replaced the sanctuary erected where the martyr saint was buried.

On reaching place du Capitole, turn right onto rue Romiguières then left onto rue Lakanal.

Les Jacobins★★

St Dominic, alarmed by the spread of the Albigensian heresy, founded the Order of Preachers (Dominican Order) and the first Dominican monastery was founded in Toulouse in 1216. The red-brick church is a masterpiece of the southern French Gothic, marking a

Relaxing at a café, Place du Capitole

A. Thuillier/MICHELIN

milestone in the evolution of this style (*the interior is described under Additional Sights*).

Hôtel de Bernuy (Lycée Pierre-de-Fermat)

Open Tue-Fri 10am-12.30pm, 1.30-5pm (Thu 9pm). Closed school holidays, 1 Jan, 25 Dec.

This mansion was built in two stages in the early 16C. The beautiful main doorway *(1 rue Gambetta)* blends curves and counter-curves, in typically Gothic style, with medallions. An octagonal corbelled **staircase turret★**, one of the tallest in old Toulouse, is lit through windows that neatly follow the angle where two walls meet.

Rue Gambetta leads to place du Capitole.

Place du Capitole

Along the east side of this vast square, the main meeting point for local residents, stretches the majestic façade of the Capitole building. At the centre of the square, inlaid into the paving, is an enormous bronze Occitan cross, surrounded by the signs of the zodiac, by Raymong Moretti.

Capitole★

Open Easter-end Oct 9am-7pm; rest of year 9am-5pm (first weekend of month and public holiday, 9am-7pm). Closed 1 Jan. No charge. 05 61 22 29 22.

This is the city hall of Toulouse, named after the "capitouls," or consuls, who used to run the city. The courtyard was the scene of the execution of the duke of Montmorency in 1632 (*see above*), about which there is a commemorative plaque set into the flagstones.

Enter the courtyard. The staircase, hall and various rooms, most notably the **Salle des Illustres** dedicated to the most glorious representatives of Toulouse, were decorated with appropriate grandiosity at the time of the Third Republic, by specially commissioned officially approved painters.

Cross the courtyard and walk diagonally through the gardens to get to the keep *(donjon)*, a remnant of the 16C Capitole, restored by Viollet-le-Duc. It now houses the tourist office.

2 Around the Capitole

Leave place du Capitole heading south along rue Saint-Rome.

Rue St-Rome

Pedestrian street.

This busy shopping street is part of the old *cardo maximus* (Roman road through town from north to south). At the beginning of the street (no 39) stands the interesting house of Catherine de' Medici's physician (Augier Ferrier). Pierre Séguy's fine Gothic turret is

tucked inside the courtyard of no 4 **rue Jules-Chalande**. At no 3 rue St-Rome is an elegant early 17C town house, the Hôtel de Gomère.

Rue des Changes

The square known as "Quatre Coins des Changes" is overlooked by the Sarta turret. Nos 20, 19 and 17 boast some interesting decorative features (timbering, window frames etc), whereas no 16, the 16C Hôtel d'Astorg et St-Germain, has a façade with a gallery just beneath the eaves – a local feature known as *mirandes* – and a courtyard with timber galleries and diagonally opposed spiral staircases with wooden handrails.

Turn right before reaching the place Esquirol crossroads.

Rue Malcousinat

At no 11, the 16C Hôtel de Cheverny, the attractive main building, which is Gothic-Renaissance, is flanked by an austere 15C keep.

Turn right onto rue de la Bourse.

Rue de la Bourse

Note at no 15 the Hôtel de Nupces (18C). No 20, the late-15C Hôtel Delfau, is the house of Pierre Del Fau, who hoped to become a *capitoul* but who never fulfilled his ambition.

B. Kaufmann/MICHELIN

Fondation Bemberg, Hôtel d'Assézat

The 24m/78m-high turret, pierced with five large windows, is quite remarkable.

Turn left onto rue Cujas and follow it to place de la Daurade.

Basilique Notre-Dame-de-la-Daurade

The present church, which dates from the 18C, occupies the site of a pagan temple that was converted into a church dedicated to the Virgin Mary in the 5C, and a Benedictine monastery.

Take a short stroll along **quai de la Daurade**, downstream of the Pont Neuf (16C-17C), past the fine arts academy (École des Beaux-Arts); there is a good view of the St-Cyprien district (west bank) with its two hospitals, the Hôtel-Dieu and the domed Hospice de la Grave.

rue de Metz (left); bear left again.

Hotel d'Assézat★★

This, the finest private mansion in Toulouse, was built in 1555-57 according to the plans of Nicolas Bachelier, the greatest Renaissance architect of Toulouse, for the Capitoul d'Assézat, who had made a fortune from trading in dyer's woad.

The façades of the buildings to the left of and opposite the entrance are the earliest example of the use of the Classical style in Toulouse, characterised by the three decorative orders – Doric, Ionic, Corinthian – used one above the other, creating a marvellously elegant effect. To add a bit of variety to these façades, the architect introduced rectangular windows beneath relieving arches on the ground and first floors. On the second floor, the lines are reversed, with round-arched windows beneath straight horizontal entablatures.

The sophistication of this design is matched by the elaborate decoration on the two doorways, one with twisted columns and the other adorned with scrolls and garlands. Sculpture underwent a revival in Toulouse at the time of the Renaissance, when stone began to be used again, in conjunction with brick.

On the inside of the façade facing the street, there is an elegant portico with four arcades, surmounted by a gallery. The fourth side was never completed, as Assézat, having converted to the Protestant faith, was driven into exile, a ruined man. The wall is adorned only by a covered gallery resting on graceful consoles. The mansion houses the **Bemberg Foundation**★★ (*see Museums*).

Take rue des Marchands (right), then rue des Filatiers (right), then rue des Polinaires (right) and rue H.-de-Gorsse, in which there are some attractive 16C houses. Turn left onto rue de la Dalbade.

Église Notre-Dame-la-Dalbade

The present church was built in the 16C, on the site of an earlier building, which had white walls. In 1926 the bell-tower fell in, damaging the church, which was subsequently restored, with particular attention paid to its beautiful brickwork.

Rue de la Dalbade

This street is lined with the elegant mansions of former local dignitaries. Nos 7, 11, 18 and 20 have fine 18C façades. Note no 22, the Hôtel Molinier, which boasts an extravagantly ornate, sculpted doorway (16C) of quite profane inspiration. The **Hôtel de Clary**, at no 25, has a beautiful Renaissance courtyard.

Rue Pharaon

This really pretty street has a number of interesting features: the Hôtel du Capitoul Marvejol at no 47 (charming courtyard); 18C façades at no 29; turret dating from 1478 at no 21.

Walk along rue Pharaon to place des Carmes then turn right onto rue Ozenne.

Hôtel Béringuier-Maynier (Hôtel du Vieux-Raisin)

The main building at the back of the courtyard marks the first manifestation of the Italian Renaissance in Toulouse, in the style of the châteaux of the Loire Valley (stone as well as brick work).

Behind the mansion, take rue Ozenne.

Rue Ozenne

At no 9 the Hôtel Dahus and Tournoër turret make a handsome 15C architectural group.

Take rue de la Pleau to the left.

The Hôtel Pierre-Besson houses the Musée Paul-Dupuy (*see Additional Sights*).

Rue Mage

This is one of the best-preserved streets in Toulouse, with period houses at nos 20 and 16 (Louis XIV) and no 11 (Louis XIII); the Hôtel d'Espie (no 3) is an example of French Rococo (Louis XV or Regency style).

Rue Bouquière

Note the splendid architecture of the Hôtel de Puivert (18C).

Hôtel de Fumel (Palais Consulaire)

This mansion houses the Chamber of Commerce. It features a fine 18C façade, at right angles, overlooking the garden.
From the corner of rue Tolosane, the façade and tower of the cathedral can be seen, whereas to the left the tower of Les Augustins rises from among trees. No 24 **rue Croix-Baragnon** is home to the city's Cultural Centre. No 15, "the oldest house in Toulouse," dating from the 13C, is distinguished by its gemel windows.

Place St-Étienne

In the middle of the square stands a 16C fountain – the oldest in Toulouse – known as "Le Griffoul."

Cathédrale St-Étienne★

Compared to St-Sernin, the cathedral appears curiously unharmonious in style. It was built over several centuries, from the 11C to the 17C, and combines the Gothic styles of both southern and northern France.

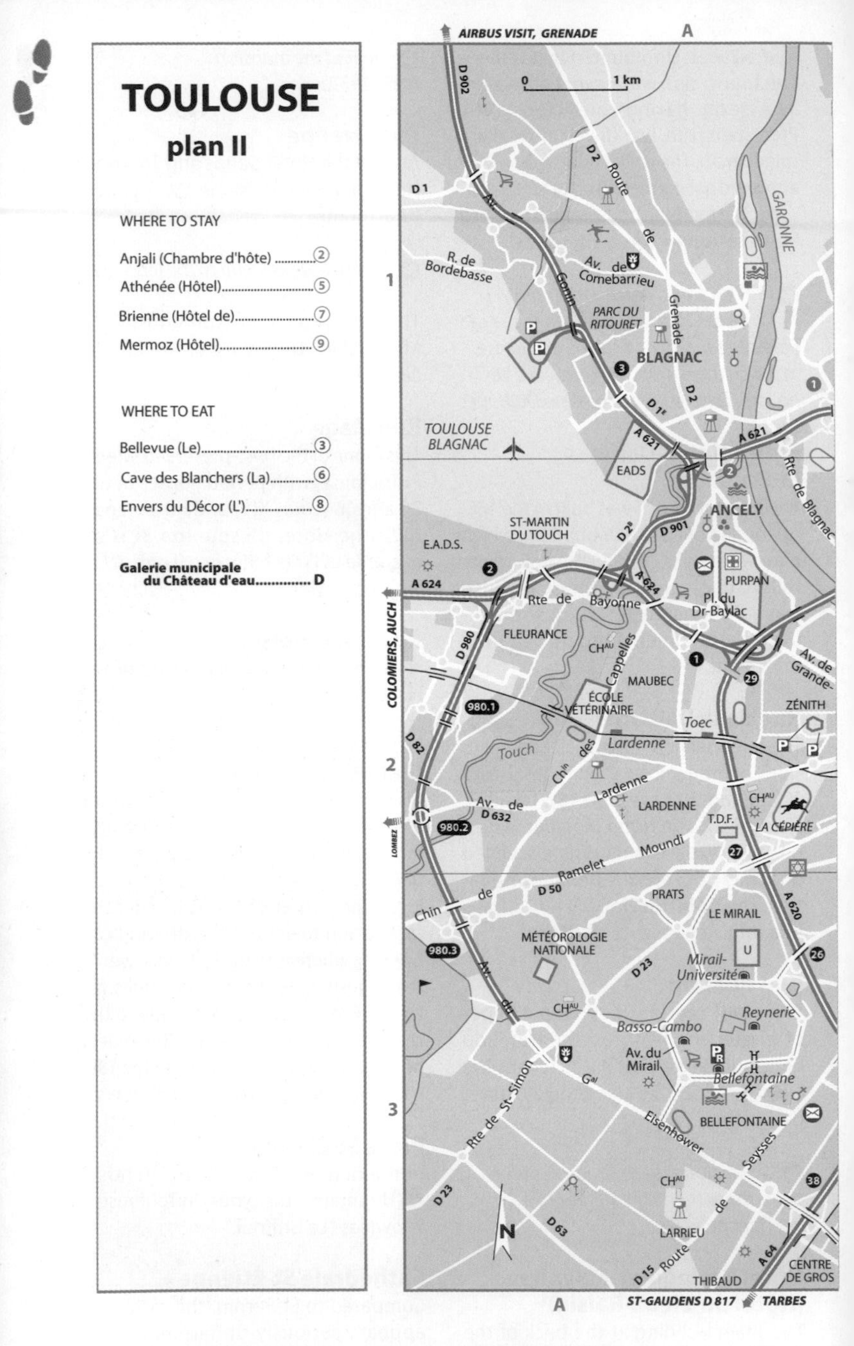

Enter through the west doorway.

The vast single nave, as wide as it is high, is the first manifestation of the southern French Gothic style and gives a good idea of the progress made in architectural techniques: St-Étienne's single vault spans 19m/62ft, and St-Sernin's Romanesque vault a mere 9m/29ft.

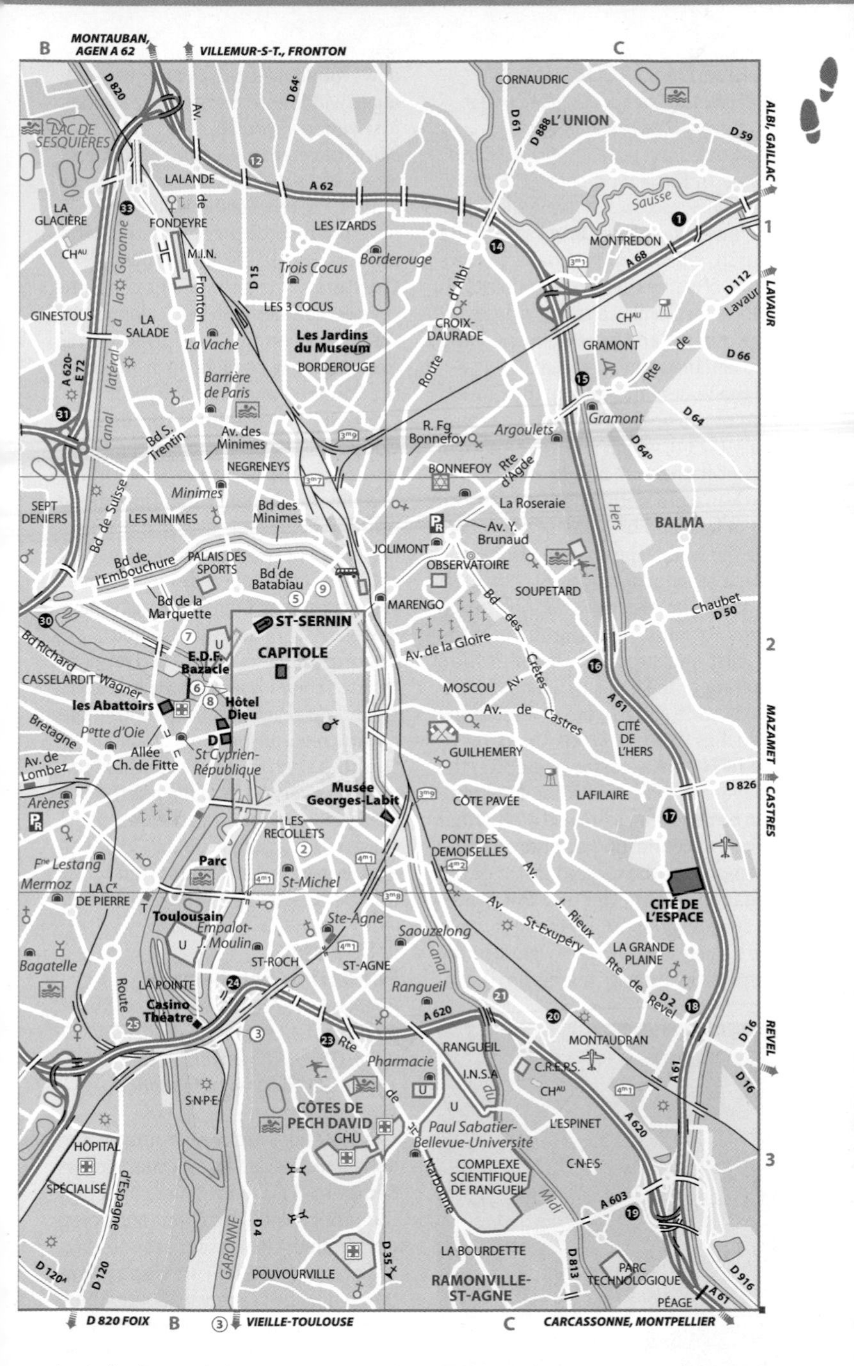

Leave by the south door and walk round the church to appreciate the robust solidity of the buttresses supporting the chancel, evidence that they were intended to support greater things...

Turn left onto rue de Metz then right onto rue des Arts and left again onto rue de la Pomme, which leads back to place du Capitole.

ÉGLISE DES JACOBINS★★

Rue Lakanal. Exterior described under 1 *above.* ♿ *Open 9am-7pm. Guided visit possible (1hr) 3€, no charge 1st Sun in the month. 05 61 22 21 92. www.jacobins.mairie-toulouse.fr.*

The awesome **main body**★★ of the church, which has two naves, is the result of successive enlargements. It reflects the Dominican Order's prestige, its prosperity and its two aims: serving God and preaching his word.

On the floor of the church, the ground plan of the original rectangular sanctuary (1234), which was covered by a timber-frame roof, is indicated by five black-marble slabs (the bases of the old pillars) and by a line of black tiles (the old walls). The church's roof vault, which reaches a height of 28m/91ft up to the keystones, is supported on seven columns. The **column**★★ at the far east end supports the entire fan vaulting of the apse; its 22 ribs, alternately wide and narrow, resemble the branches of a palm tree. Up as far as the sills of the clerestory windows, the walls are decorated with painted imitation brickwork in ochre and pink. Other stripes of contrasting colours are used to emphasise the upward thrust of the engaged colonnettes and the graceful sweep of the ribs on the roof vault. The stained-glass windows were inserted from 1923: *"grisaille"* (monotonal) windows round the apse, and brighter-coloured windows in the nave. The façade's rose windows are 14C.

Cloisters, Église des Jacobins

B. Kaufmann/MICHELIN

Since the ceremony for the seventh centenary of the death of St Thomas Aquinas in 1974, the relics of the "saintly doctor" have been on display beneath a high altar of grey marble, from Prouille.

Cloisters – The north door opens into cloisters adorned with twin colonnettes, typical of Languedoc Gothic (other examples may be found in St-Hilaire in the Corbières and Arles-sur-Tech).

Chapelle St-Antonin – This delicate Gothic chapel, on the left of the chapter-house, was built from 1337 to 1341 as a funeral chapel by friar Dominique Grima, who became bishop of Pamiers (keystone of the arch above the head of Christ of the Apocalypse). The bones were transferred from tombs in the nave into an ossuary beneath the altar.

Chapter house (c. 1300) – Two very slim facetted columns support the roof vault. The graceful apsidal chapel once more boasts colourful mural decoration.

Grand Réfectoire (*open during temporary exhibitions of modern art*) – The great refectory (north-east corner of the cloisters) is a vast room (built 1303), with a timber-frame roof supported on six transverse arches separating the bays.

MUSEUMS

Fondation Bemberg★★

Pl. d'Assézat. ♿ *Open daily except Mon 10am-12.30pm, 1.30-6pm (Thu 9pm). Closed 1 Jan and 25 Dec. 5€. 05 61 12 06 89. www.fondation-bemberg.fr.*

The Hôtel d'Assézat now houses the donation of private art collector Georges Bemberg. This impressive collection comprises painting, sculpture and objets d'art from the Renaissance to the 20C.

Old Masters (16C-18C) are displayed as they would be in a private home. There are paintings by the 18C Venetian School (vedute by Canaletto and Guardi), 15C Flemish works such as Virgin and Child from the studio of Rogier Van der Weyden and 17C Dutch painting, with Musicians by Pieter de Hooch. Displayed with the paintings are 16C objets d'art such

as a nautilus and a grisaille Limoges enamel plaque depicting Saturn.
The **Renaissance portrait gallery** includes paintings (Charles IX by François Clouet, Portrait of a Young Woman with a Ring by Ambrosius Benson and Portrait of Antoine de Bourbon by Franz Pourbus) and 16C sculpture groups. The small room adjoining this contains **bronzes** from Italy, such as a superb figure of Mars attributed to Giovanni Bologna, alongside Limoges enamels, leather-bound books and paintings by Veronese, Tintoretto and Bassano.
An open gallery overlooking the courtyard leads to the staircase up to the second floor, which is devoted to **Modern Masters** (19C-20C). The collection's highlight is the series of paintings by Bonnard, executed in a vibrant palette (Woman with a Red Cape, Le Cannet, Still Life with Lemons). The collection features other works by almost all the great names of the Modern French School from Impressionism and Pointillism to Fauvism. Artists featured include Louis Valtat, Paul Gauguin, Matisse, H-E Cross, Eugène Boudin, Claude Monet and Raoul Dufy.

Musée St-Raymond★★

Place St-Sernin. ♿ Open Jun-Aug 10am-7pm; Sep-May 10am-6pm. 3€. Free 1st Sun in month. 05 61 22 31 44.
This museum, housed in one of the buildings of the old Collège St-Raymond (13C), rebuilt in 1523 and restored by Viollet-le-Duc, was recently refurbished and now displays its collections of archaeology and antique art.

Musée des Augustins★★

Rue de Metz. ♿ Open daily except Tue 10am-6pm (Wed 9pm). Closed 1 Jan, 1 May, 25 Dec. 3€, no charge 1st Sunday in the month. 05 61 22 21 82. www.augustins.org.
This museum is housed in a former Augustinian monastery designed in the southern French Gothic style (14C and 15C); specifically the chapter-house and the great and small cloisters.
Religious painting (14C-18C) – The paintings are from the 15C, 16C and 17C (Perugino, Rubens, Murillo, Guercino, Simon Vouet, Nicolas Tournier, Murillo), and the sculptures from the 16C-17C.
Romanesque sculptures★★★ (12C) – In the western wing, built on plans by Viollet-le-Duc and punctuated by great arches, the admirable historiated or foliated capitals were mostly taken from the cloisters of St-Sernin Basilica, the monastery of Notre-Dame de la Daurade and buildings from the chapter-house of St-Étienne Cathedral.
French painting (17C-19C) – Upstairs, the *salon rouge*, which is evocative of 19C museums in its presentation (there are many paintings on the wall, some of them quite high up), is largely devoted to 19C French painting.
The salon brun is devoted to works created in Toulouse in the 17C-18C. The salon vert displays 17C-18C French paintings: Philippe de Champaigne *(Réception d'Henri d'Orléans)*, Largillière, Oudry.
After visiting the museum, return to the **cloisters**, where different gardens have been recreated as they would have existed in medieval monasteries and abbeys.

Muséum d'Histoire Naturelle★★

Located in the Jardin des Plantes (botanical gardens). Open daily except Mon 10am-6pm. Closed 1 Jan, 1 May, 25 Dec. 7€. 05 67 7384 84. www.museum.toulouse.fr.
The natural history museum has extensive collections, most notably of ornithological, prehistoric and ethnographical exhibits. Take this opportunity to discover the **Jardin des Plantes**, the **Jardin Royal** and the **Grand Rond**, well laid out gardens that make a very pleasant place for a stroll. At the southern end of allée Fréderic-Mistral, in the botanical gardens, stands the **Musée Départemental de la Résistance et de la Déportation** *(♿ open daily except weekends 9.30am-noon, 2-6pm. Closed public holidays. No charge. 05 61 14 80 40)*. An arrangement of lenses ensures that sunlight enters the crypt only on 19 August, the anniversary of the liberation of Toulouse.

Musée Paul-Dupuy★

13 rue de la Pleau. Open daily except Tue 10am-6pm (Oct-May 5pm). 3€, no charge 1st Sunday in the month. 05 61 14 65 50. www.mairie-toulouse.fr.

This museum is devoted to the applied arts from the Middle Ages to the present: metal and wood work, clock-making, weights and measures, coins, musical instruments, enamel work, gold plate, costumes and weapons.

Musée Georges-Labit★

Along the Canal du Midi, near rue du Japon. Open daily except Tue 10am-6pm (Oct-May 5pm). 3€, no charge 1st Sunday in the month. 05 61 14 65 50. www.mairie-toulouse.fr.

This museum is located in the Moorish villa in which Georges Labit (1862-99), an enthusiastic collector of anything to do with the Orient, assembled the artefacts brought back from his travels.

Les Abattoirs (Musée d'Art Moderne et Contemporain)★

76 allées Charles-de-Fitte (west bank of the Garonne). Open daily except Mon 11am-7pm. 6€, no charge 1st Sunday in the month. 05 62 48 58 00. www.lesabattoirs.org.

The brick buildings of the former slaughter houses have been turned into a museum of modern and contemporary art illustrating various post-war trends.

AEROSPACE INDUSTRY

A Bit of History

"La Ligne": During the inter-war period, Toulouse became the departure point for France's first ever scheduled airline, thanks to the efforts of industrialists such as P Latécoère, administrators such as D Daurat, and pilots such as Mermoz, Saint-Exupéry and Guillaumet.

25 Dec 1918: first trial flight from Toulouse to Barcelona.

1 Sept 1919: first airmail service between France and Morocco.

1 Jun 1925: aircraft reach Dakar. Pioneers pilot routes to and in S. America.

12 May 1930: first commercial South Atlantic crossing.

Post-war – After the Second World War and the maiden flight of the Leduc 010, prototype of high-speed aircraft on 21 April 1949, four important projects helped to boost the French aeronautical industry. Two military aircraft (Transall, Breguet Atlantic) and two civil aircraft (Caravelle, Concorde) enabled French engineers and research consultants to hone their talents as aircraft designers and to develop teamwork with their British and German counterparts.

1 May 1959: Caravelle's maiden flight on the Paris-Athens-Istanbul route.

2 Mar 1969: first test flight of "Concorde 001," the first supersonic airliner, piloted by André Turcat.

1 Jan 1970: founding of Aérospatiale, amalgamation of Nord-Aviation, Sud-Aviation and Sereb.

Airbus – A product of European ambition (initially Anglo-French, then Franco-German from 1969, and Franco-Spanish after 1987), Airbus Industrie has in 20 years become the world's second most important civil aviation manufacturer.

Aérospatiale Matra-Airbus

Colomiers, in the western suburbs of Toulouse. Visit usually by request only. 14€ plus supp. 4.50€ to see Concorde. 05 34 39 42 00. www.taxiway.fr.

This plant is the assembly site for A 330/A 340 long-distance carriers. After a bus tour, a short film, various models and explanatory panels help visitors to get a clearer idea of the Airbus programme.

Cité de l'espace★

Parc de la Plaine, along the eastern side of the ringroad. Early Jul-Aug 9.30am-7pm; rest of year 9.30am-5pm (weekends and school holidays 9.30am-6pm). 16-22€ (children 5-15 years, 12-14.50€); guided visit possible (1hr) suppl. 4€. 0 820 377 223. www.cite-espace.com.

Visible from quite a distance thanks to the rocket standing there and to a surprising contemporary sculpture which serves as the Exposition Pavilion (the work of Henri-Georges Adam – 1904-67), the Cité de l'Espace is a place for discovering, experimenting and learning about the universe.

ADDRESSES

STAY

Hotel Boréal – *20 r. Caffarelli. 05 61 62 57 21 – www.hotel-boreal.fr – res. advised – 24rms – 7€.* This red-brick hotel is ideally placed between the station and place Wilson; good prices, rooms on three floors.

Hotel Albert 1er – *8 r. Rivals. 05 61 21 17 91 – www.hotel-albert1.com – 47rms – 10€.* Ideally placed from which to explore the city on foot.

Hôtel de Brienne – *20 bd du Mar.-Leclerc. 05 61 23 60 60 – www.hoteldebrienne.com – P – 70rms – 10€.* A place most suitable for business people, but equally appropriate for those on holiday.

Hôtel de l'Ours Blanc Place Victor Hugo – *25 pl. Victor-Hugo. 05 61 23 14 55 – www.hotel-oursblanc.com – 38rms – 8€.* Opposite the market, but well soundproofed and air-conditioned; simple and very comfortable.

Hôtel Castellane – *17 r. Castellane. 05 61 62 18 82 – www.castellanehotel.com – P – 53rms – 8€.* This small hotel close to the Capitole is slightly set back from the main thoroughfare. The rooms are housed in three different buildings; some well suited to families.

Chambre d'hôte Anjali – *86 Grande rue St-Michel. 09 54 22 42 93 – www.anjali.fr – reservations essential – 3rms and 1 family room.* A lovely Toulousaine building dating from the 1870s. Most charming.

Hôtel Athénée – *13 bis r. Matabiau. 05 61 63 10 63 – www.athenee-hotel.com – P – 35rms – 10.50 €.* Just 500m from St Sernin; lovely relaxing place.

Hôtel St-Claire – *29 pl. Nicolas-Bachelier. 05 34 40 58 88 – www.stclairehotel.fr – 16rms – 9€.* Five minutes from place Wilson, a small hotel with elegant rooms, inspired by Feng Shui. Discounts at certain periods.

Hôtel de l'Ours Blanc-Centre – *2 r. Porte-Sardane. 05 61 21 25 97 – www.hotel-oursblanc.com – 44rms – 7€.* Close to the centre of the city; soundproofed and air-conditioned rooms.

Chambre d'hôte Les Loges de St-Sernin – *112 r. St-Bernard. 05 61 24 44 44. www.logessaintsernin.fr. Closed 24 Dec-2 Jan – reservations essential – 4rms.* Just a few strides from the basilica, a lovely red-brick building at the centre of Toulouse.

Hôtel Mermoz – *50 r. Matabiau 05 61 63 04 04 – www.hotelmermoz.com – 52rms – 12€.* The inner flower garden of this hotel near the city centre provides a haven of calm. Spacious rooms furnished in 1930s style.

EAT

La Faim des Haricots – *3 r. du Puits Vert. 05 61 22 49 25. www.lafaimdesharicots.fr. Closed Sun.* A mere stone's throw from the Capitole, this vegetarian restaurant gives diners a choice of varied, plentiful fixed-price menus at painless prices.

L'Envers du Décor – *22 r. desBlanchers. 05 61 23 85 33 – www.enversdudecor.info. Closed Sun.* Serves the cuisine of the southwest with an exotic touch; close to the Garonne.

La Régalade – *16 r. Gambetta. 05 61 23 20 11.* Between the Capitole and the Garonne, a small restaurant behind a red-brick façade. Traditional and regional cuisine.

Le Mangevins – *46 r. Pharaon. 05 61 52 79 16. Closed Sun.* In this local tavern where salted foie gras and beef are sold by weight, the bawdy, fun atmosphere is enhanced by ribald songs. There is no menu, but a set meal for hearty appetites.

La Madeleine de Proust – *11 r. Riquet. 05 61 63 80 88. www.madeleinedeproust.com.* Childhood memories inspire the original, carefully designed decor of this restaurant featuring yellow walls, waxed tables, antique toys, an old school desk, a time-worn cupboard. The cuisine gives the starring role to vegetables that have fallen out of common use.

Colombier – *14 r. Bayard. 05 61 62 40 05. www.restaurantlecolombier.com. Closed Sat lunch, Sun. Reservation recommended.* Opened in 1874, this is an essential stopping point for culinary pilgrims in search of authentic cassoulet. Delightful dining room with pink bricks and wall paintings. Friendly and efficient service.

⊜⊜ **Le Châteaubriand** – *42 r. Pargaminières. ℘05 61 21 50 58. www.restaurant-le-chateaubriand.com. Closed Sat lunch, and Sun*. The atmosphere in this little restaurant in old Toulouse is particularly pleasant. Cosy interior with a parquet floor, red brick walls, a huge mirror and houseplants.

⊜⊜ **Michel, Marcel, Pierre et les Autres** – *35 r. Rémusat. ℘05 61 22 47 05 – www.michelmarcelpierre.com. Closed Sun and Mon*. Conviviality guaranteed in this lovely bistro.

⊜⊜ **Brasserie de l'Opéra** – *1 pl. du Capitole. ℘05 61 21 37 03. www.brasserieopera.com. Closed Sun.* The brasserie of the Grand Hôtel de l'Opéra is the essential place to go and see and be seen. The inviting decor, leather wall seats and autographed photos of the many artists who have spent time here create a special atmosphere. Cuisine of southwest France.

⊜⊜ **Rôtisserie des Carmes** – *138 r. Polinaires. ℘05 61 53 34 88 – rotisseriedescarmes.cartesurtables.com. Closed Sun.* Next to the market, the chef serves whatever is available that day. Perfect.

⊜⊜ **J'Go** – *16 pl. Victor-Hugo. ℘05 61 23 02 03 – www.lejgo.com.* With a decor that pays homage to the region, the cuisine does the same. A diner appreciated by the locals.

⊜⊜ **La Cave des Blanchers** – *23 r. des Blanchers. ℘05 61 22 47 47. www.table online.fr. Closed Mon and Tue.* In a street lined with restaurants, the cuisine here stands out, serving regional produce with imagination.

⊜⊜ **Le Bellevue** – *1 av. des Pyrénées, 31120 Lacroix-Falgarde. ℘05 61 76 94 97 – www.restaurant-lebellevue.com. Closed Tue and Wed.* This former dance hall was in its prime in the 1940s. Now a restaurant, it is enjoying a revival of its fortunes.

⊜⊜⊜ **Brasserie "Beaux Arts"** – *1 quai Daurade. ℘05 61 21 12 12. www.brasserielesbeauxarts.com.* The atmosphere of a 1930s brasserie is recreated here with bistro-style chairs, wall seats, retro lighting, wood panelling and mirrors. The cuisine, in keeping with the decor, features seafood, sauerkraut and a few regional specialities.

TAKING A BREAK

Maison Octave – *11 allée Franklin-Roosevelt. ℘05 62 27 05 21. Daily noon–midnight.* Come to this famous ice cream parlour for a overwhelming choice of sherbets, ice cream, *vacherins*. Over 30 flavours to enjoy in the parlour or take home.

ON THE TOWN

Le Bibent – *5 pl. du Capitole. ℘05 61 23 89 03. daily 7am–1am.* Classified as an historic monument because of its Belle Époque decor, this roomy café has a superb terrace giving onto the Place du Capitole.

Au Père Louis – *45 r. des Tourneurs ℘05 61 21 33 45. Mon–Sat 8.30am–2.30pm, 5–10.30pm. Closed 1 week in Spring, Christmas–1 Jan and public holidays.* First opened in 1889 and now a registered historical building, this wine bar is a local institution. Wine is sipped around fat-bellied barrels; an appetizing choice of open-faced sandwiches is available in the evening.

Place du Capitole – The famous central square of the city is a pedestrians-only meeting place where numerous markets are held. It is surrounded by alluring terraces, notably those belonging to the Brasserie Le Bibent (magnificent panelling), Le Café des Arcades and the Brasserie de l'Opéra, all facing the Capitole.

SHOWTIME

The magazine *Toulouse Cultures* (monthly) and its *Agenda Cultures* (every 2 months) list current and upcoming events.

Cinémathèque de Toulouse – *69 r. du Taur, BP 824. ℘05 62 30 30 10 / 11. Tue–Sat 2pm–10pm, Sun 2pm–7pm.* This cinematic citadel, founded in 1950 by Raymond Borde, was overseen by Daniel Toscan du Plantier between 1996 and 2003. Numerous theme cycles and film festivals. Exhibition hall, library and bar.

SHOPPING

Markets – The Sunday morning country market held round the Eglise St-Aubin is where farmers sell their fruit, vegetables and poultry, live or butchered. Wednesday and Friday from November to March, geese, ducks and foie gras are sold place du Salin. Saturday mornings an organic farmers' market is held place du Capitole. Tuesday mornings L'Inquet, a renowned flea market, takes place around the Basilique St-Sernin. Used-book sellers gather around place St-Étienne Saturdays and place Arnaud-Bernard Thursdays (many are present at L'Inquet as well).

Shopping streets – The main shopping streets are rue d'Alsace-Lorraine, rue Croix-Baragnon, rue St-Antoine-du-T., rue Boulbonne, rue des Arts and the pedestrian sections of rue St-Rome, rue des Filatiers, rue Baronie and rue de la Pomme. There is also a shopping mall, St-Georges, in the centre of the city.

La Maison de la Violette – *Bd de Bonrepas – Canal du Midi. ✆05 61 99 01 30. www.lamaisondelaviolette.fr. Tue–Sat 10am–12.30pm, 2pm–7pm. Closed 2nd week Jan.* The celebrated Toulouse violet is the star of this shop and café on a pastel barge. The owner's enthusiasm for this noble flower is contagious.

Olivier Confiseur-Chocolatier – *20 r. Lafayette. ✆05 61 23 21 87. http://chocolatsolivier.com. Mon–Sat 9.30am–12.30pm, 1.45pm–7.15pm.* Olivier, a master chocolate maker, produces irresistible specialities, including the famous sugared violets, capitouls (almonds covered in dark chocolate), *Clémence Isaure* (Armagnac-soaked grapes covered in dark chocolate), *brindilles* (nougatine covered in chocolate praline) and *Péché du Diable*, The Devil's Sin, (dark chocolate ganache with orange peel and ginger). Heaven help us!

RECREATION

Toulouse Croisières – *Quai de la Daurade – ✆05 61 25 72 57. Jul–Sept daily at 10.30am, 3pm, 4.30pm, 6pm; Apr–Jun and Oct daily at 10.30am, 3pm, 4.30pm. 8€ (children: 5€); Jul–Aug: night cruises, 9pm, 10pm. 5€ (children: 3.50€).* Embark upon the pleasure steamer Le Capitole for a cruise along the Garonne. You'll discover the Pont Neuf, the Saint-Michel lock, the untamed banks of the Île du Grand Ramier.

Parc toulousain – Set on an island in the River Garonne, the Parc Toulousain offers four swimming pools, three outdoors and one covered; the Stadium, where the Stade Toulousain rugby team plays; the Parc des Expositions and the Palais des Congrès.

Péniche Baladine – *✆05 61 80 22 26 or 06 74 64 52 36. www.bateaux-toulousains.com. Departs quai de la Daurade. Oct–May: Wed, Sat, Sun and public holidays; Jun-Sep and school holidays: open every day.* Canal du Midi cruises *(1hr 15mins)* depart at 10.50am and 4pm, Garonne cruises *(1hr 15mins)* depart at 2.30pm, 5.30pm and 7pm. 7€. Details of night cruises on request.

Golf club de Toulouse – *31320 Vieille-Toulouse. ✆05 61 73 45 48.* 18 holes.

Golf club de Toulouse Palmola – *Rte d'Albi. A 68 exit N° 4 .31660 Buzet-sur-Tarn. ✆05 61 84 20 50. www.golfdepalmola.com. 9am–6.30pm. Closed Mar.* 18-hole golf course. Clubhouse with restaurant, tennis court and swimming pool.

CALENDAR OF EVENTS

Fête de la violette *Feb. ✆05 62 16 31 31.* Growing, selling, exhibiting… the ideal opportunity to learn all about the flower that is the city's emblem.

Printemps du rire – *Late Mar–early Apl ✆05 62 21 23 24. www.printemps-du-rire.com.* Spring comedy festival.

Piano aux Jacobins *Sept ✆05 61 22 40 05. www.pianojacobins.com.*

Le Printemps de Septembre *Late Sept, noon–7pm Mon–Fri, 11am–7pm Sat–Sun. ✆01 43 38 00 11, www.printempsde septembre.com.* Festival of photography and visual arts.

Festival Occitania *Oct – ✆05 61 11 24 87, www.ieotolosa.free.fr.* Regional culture celebrated through various media (cinema, poetry, song etc…).

Jazz sur son 31 *Oct (2nd and 3rd) weeks ✆05 34 45 05 92, www.jazz31.com.* Large jazz festival established 18 years ago.

Cinespaña – *Oct ✆05 61 12 12 20. www.cinespagnol.com.* Spanish cinema.

l'Isle-Jourdain

and Le Gimontois

Isle Jourdain was a stopover on the road to Santiago de Compostela. Bertrand de l'Isle, founder of Saint-Bertrand-de-Comminges, was born here (*See ST-BERTRAND-DE-COMMINGES***). Its lake has water sports facilities.**

- **Info:** Au bord du lac, 32600 L'Isle-Jourdain, 05 62 07 25 57; www.mairie-islejourdain.com
- **Location:** 30km/18.7mi from Toulouse.
- **Don't Miss:** Musée d'Art Campanaire.
- **Kids**: The yak and bison at the Bisonnerie de Borde Basse.

TOWN CENTRE

The main attraction in place de l'Hôtel-de-Ville are the stained-glass windows and façade sculptures on the turn-of-the-century house of Claude Auge. The 18C Collegiate Church has arresting neo-Classical architecture and painted frescoes.

Musée d'Art Campanaire★

Open mid Jun-mid Sep 10am-noon, 2.30-6.30pm; rest of year daily except Tue 10am-noon, 2.30-5.30pm. Closed Mar, 1 May, 25 Dec, 1st two weeks of Jan. 4€ (children 2€). 05 62 07 30 01.

This bell museum has over 1 000 bells from around the world.

The "foundry" exhibit explains how bells are made. There are several carillons, some which visitors may play, bells from Europe, America, the South Pacific, Asia and Africa, and **subrejougs** (harness bells from Vallée de la Save) with remarkable polychrome decorations.

19C ceremonial subrejoug from Arzidas, Gers, Musée Européen d'Art Campanaire

Jean-Claude Salles/Musée Européen d'Art Campanaire

DRIVING TOUR

Le Gimontois

Round trip of 21km/13mi – allow 2hr 30min. Leave L'Isle-Jourdain to the west on N 124.

Gimont

The main street of this *bastide* founded in 1266 runs through the old covered market place. Foie gras and bullfighting are local specialities.

Leave Gimont W on D 12, route de Saramon.

Chapelle Notre-Dame-de-Cahuzac

This 16C brick and stone chapel has a Gothic doorway and 400 marble plaques, medallions and ex-votos left by pilgrims.

Continue along D 12.

Abbaye de Planselve

Open by request at the tourist office in Gimont; only the entry hall and the pigeon houses are accessible to visitors. 2€. 05 62 67 77 87.

This 12C Cistercian abbey destroyed in 1789 is partly restored. Remains include the lay brothers' building with its ten 12C Romanesque bays and two dovecots.

Saint-Félix-Lauragais

and Dyer's Wood Country

Saint-Félix in a pretty site★ overlooking the Lauragais plain, passed into history (or legend, as some see it) when the Cathars held a council here to set up their church.

- **Population:** 1 354.
- **Michelin Map:** 343: J-4.
- **Info:** Pl. Guillaume-de-Nogaret, 31540 St-Félix-Lauragais, ✆ 05 62 18 96 99. www.revel-lauragais.com.
- **Location:** 10km/6mi W of Revel, not far from Toulouse and Canal du Midi.
- **Don't Miss:** The Château-Musée du Pastel at Magrin.
- **Timing:** Allow half a day for the driving tour.

A BIT OF HISTORY

Déodat de Séverac – Saint-Félix prides itself on being the birthplace of this composer (1873-1921) of melodies evoking the beauty of nature and the countryside. Debussy said of De Séverac's music that "it smelt good." A pupil of Vincent d'Indy and Magnard at the Schola Cantorum in Paris, Déodat de Séverac was also profoundly influenced by Debussy's work.

Dyer's Woad – Known for its medicinal properties since ancient times, and still used today for fodder, dyer's woad or *Isatis tinctoria* (*pastel* in French) is the plant traditionally used by dyers to obtain varying shades of blue dye.

Mainly grown around the Mediterranean, dyer's woad was cultivated particularly intensively in the triangle formed by Albi, Toulouse and Carcassonne. The 14C marked the beginning of an astonishing boom in woad production and trade in the Albi area. Results were so successful that the cultivation of dyer's woad gradually spread farther south until it reached the Lauragais region and eventually Toulouse merchants took control of the industry. This was the golden age of dyer's woad in the "Pays du Cocagne" which, despite a large number of cultural and economic initiatives, was only to last about 60 years. Decline was rapid, due to the Wars of Religion and the arrival on the scene of indigo.

SIGHTS

Castle

There is a pleasant walkway round this castle, built in the 13C and later extended and remodelled, which affords fine views to the east over the Montagne Noire with Revel at its foot. To the north, the belfry of St-Julia and, high up, the castle of Montgey can be seen.

Products made from dyer's woad

S. Sauvignier/MICHELIN

Belfry-wall of St-Julia
©Franck Guiziou/Hemis/Photoshot

Church
This collegiate church dates from the 14C and was rebuilt at the beginning of the 17C. To the right of the church stands the sober façade of the chapter house.

Walk
Not far from the church, a vaulted passageway leads to an area where there is a view to the west over peaceful countryside with hills and cypresses.

DRIVING TOUR

Dyer's Woad Country
80km/50mi – about 2hr.
Today the plain is given over to the cultivation of wheat, barley and rape seed, and stock raising (cattle, sheep and poultry). An offshoot of poultry rearing has been the installation of factories for food processing.

From St-Félix-Lauragais head N on D 67.

St-Julia
An old fortified "free" town, with some ramparts and a church with an unusual belfry-wall.

Drive north to the intersection with D 1, turn left towards Montégut-Lauragais, then immediately left towards Puéchoursi; after the village turn right.

Montgey
High on a hill, this village has a big **castle** (*Park and terraces: 10am–6pm. 05 63 75 75 81*), an old medieval fortress that was captured by Simon de Montfort in 1211, then renovated in the 15C and 17C. From the terrace, there is a view over the Lauragais hills.

Drive W to Aguts along D 45 then N along D 92 to Puylaurens and turn left onto D 12 to Magrin.

Magrin
This little village in the Tarn Valley is famous for its castle (12C-16C), which has housed the only museum on dyer's woad in France since 1982.
Perched on top of a hill, the Château de Magrin offers a splendid **panorama★** of the Montagne Noire and the Pyrenees.

Château de Magrin-musée du Pastel★
guided tours (1hr30min) Jul-Sep 3-6pm; mid Jan-Jun and Oct-mid Dec Sun and public holidays, 3-6pm. Closed mid-Dec to mid-Jan. 7€. 05 63 70 63 82. www.pastel-chateau-musee.com.
The dyer's woad museum contains a woad mill and drying rack and presents

the various stages involved in making blue dye from dyer's woad, including the history of the *Isatis tinctoria* plant.

Leave the Château de Magrin heading NW on D 12.

Château de Roquevidal
guided tours (45min) mid Jul-mid Sep Sun and public holidays 4-7pm. 3.50€. 05 63 41 32 32. The body of the castle is flanked by four corner towers. The main façade shows the influence of the Renaissance.

On leaving the castle, take two right turnings to join D 43.

En Olivier
This little hamlet is home to the **Musée Nostra Terra Occitana** *(currently closed; for information: 05 63 75 72 95)*, devoted to agricultural tools and machinery.

Go back to N 126 and head in the direction of Toulouse.

Loubens-Lauragais
This charming village, bright with flowers in season, is tucked up against a **château** *(open Aug Thu-Sun 2.30-6.30pm; May-Nov 12, Sun and public holidays 2.30-6.30pm. 5€. 05 61 83 12 08).* www.chateaudeloubens.com).
A tour round this follows the story of the Loubens family, which gave the French State a number of fine civil servants.

Drive S along D 11 to Caraman, then follow D 25 towards Villefranche-de-Lauragais; 8km/5mi farther on, turn left on D 2.

Vaux
This hilltop village has a Gothic church, which has retained its turreted belfry-wall (1551). The **château** *(guided visits May-Oct Sat-Sun 2.30–6pm; closed public holidays (unless weekends). 4€; 05 62 18 94 00)* is a Renaissance work

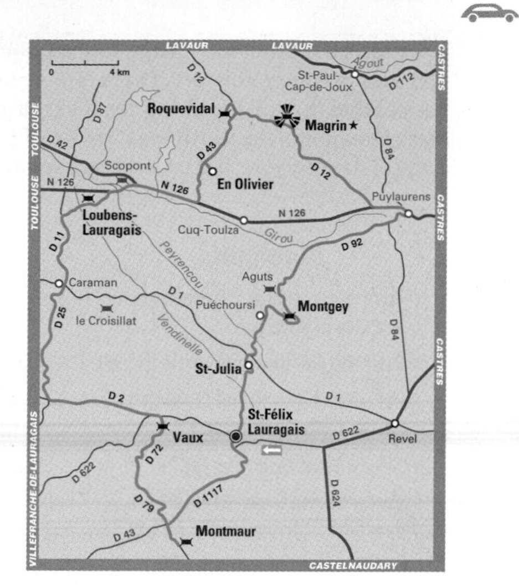

(1550-60), as illustrated by the many mullion windows.

Leave Vaux S on D 72 to Mourvilles-hautes then turn left onto D 79 to Montmaur.

Château de Montmaur
Outside only open to the public. This castle was taken time and again by Simon de Montfort, in 1211 and 1212; pillaged by Protestants in 1577; and rebuilt in the 16C-17C. The main building is square, flanked by four round towers.

Return to St-Félix-Lauragais.

Château de Loubens
Bertrand Bouret/Wikimedia Commons

Albi draws the curious; its name forever pinned onto one of the worst episodes in France's history. There is pleasure in the countryside all around, permeating the villages along the River Tarn, up the Montagne Noire (the Black Mountain), the south-western tip of the Massif Central, and a broad ridge of densely forested upland that separates Tarn from Aude to the south.

Highlights

1. Take a leisurely stroll around the old city of **Albi** (pp317, 318)
2. Visit the **Gaillac** vineyards (p335)
3. Take lunch along the Quai des Jacobins in **Castres** (p325)
4. Take a **Tarn** boat trip (p324)
5. Enjoy **Cordes-sur-Ciel** (p331)

Bastides

This part of France, the Midi-Pyrénées and parts of Languedoc-Roussillon, is 'bastide' country. Bastides are semi-fortified towns, generally dating from the 13C and 14C, born of intermittent warfare stemming from the time of the Cathar persecution. Among the best, Cordes-sur-Ciel, a tiny perched village of less than 1,000 souls, sits on a rocky outcrop, the Puech de Mordagne high above the Cérou valley of which it holds a superb view. Like so many other villages in Tarn, Cordes flourished in the years following the end of the Cathar crusades on the production of wool, leather and cloth. Raymond VII, the Count of Toulouse built a superb bastide when he constructed Castelnau de Montmirail. The village has a splendid central square with a well, surrounded by timber arcades and timber-framed houses mostly dating from the 16th and 17th centuries.

Another bastide, Castelnau-sur-Lévis, is easily missed. But the village is overlooked by the ruins of an ancient chateau with a tall and intact square watch tower. The feudal chateau was built in 1235 and commands a superb view across the surrounding countryside.

An oversight

Cordes lies along one of the routes to Compostella. Surprisingly, Cordes doesn't rank among the 'Plus Beaux Villages de France', which is somewhat immaterial as you can see for yourself what an oversight this is. Cordes is one of those mesmeric places, far removed from Paris and the major cities of France, that remind you what the 'real' France is all about.

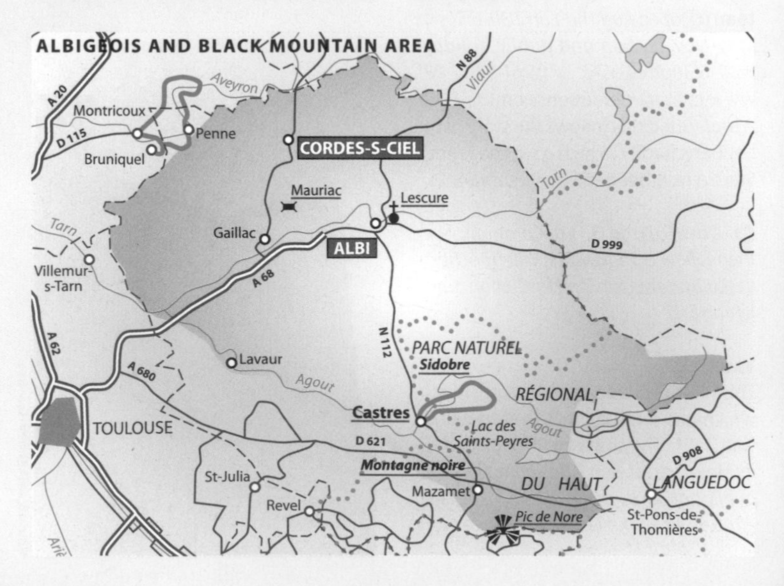

Palais de la Berbie

©jean-pierre Soulac/Fotolia.com

Albi the Red

The banks of the River Tarn have yielded clay for the manufacture of bricks for centuries. Not surprisingly, brick is arguably the favourite building material in Albi; it casts the city in shades of pastel pink or luxurious red. On some bricks you can still see fingerprints of the men who made them before they were dried in kilns. Brick is everywhere: if you sit opposite the Cathédrale de Ste-Cécile in Albi, taking a coffee to wile away the times between meals, it's difficult not to start counting bricks. This huge, fortified red-brick monolith of religious architecture must have been a hod carrier's nightmare during the 200 years of building that began in the 13th century. The oldest quarters of Albi, where brick is uniformly dominant, are Castelvieil, Rivière, Castelnau and Patus Cremat, close to the cathedral.

The history of brick begins over 10 000 years ago, the oldest known traces being found in the Near East. The first "fired" bricks appeared 5 000 years ago, in Mesopotamia.

The use of brick flourished in Tarn for practical reasons: the presence of extensive deposits of marl and clay; the need to build speedily with readily available and inexpensive materials; issues of safety – the use of brick decreased the risk of fire, and it gave more solid support, and a greater load-bearing capacity.

The influence of brick on Albi is quite stunning, bringing a warmth and vibrancy that is not experienced with other building materials. The brick introduces variations of colour according to the intensity of the light, even, at times, veering towards ochre, and generating constantly changing nuances of shade. It is especially glorious in the early hours of morning sunlight.

Pont-Vieux in foreground

©Jacques Croizer/iStockphoto.com

Albi★★★

The beautiful Renaissance mansions of Albi "la rouge" on the banks of the Tarn are showpieces of the city's mid-15C–mid-16C economic boom in the textile and dyeing industries.

- **Info**: Palais de la Berbie, pl. Ste-Cécile, 81000 Albi. 05 63 49 48 80. www.albi-tourisme.fr.
- **Location:** 76km/47.5mi NE of Toulouse. View this charming town from the 11C **Pont Vieux**, or on a stroll through its narrow winding streets. **Restored mills** now contain local tourist board offices, a museum honouring Lapérouse, a hotel and private residences. The terrace in Botany Bay square affords **views** of the Tarn, the Pont Vieux and the towering cathedral.
- **Don't Miss:** Cathédrale Ste-Cécile; Palais de la Berbie; Musée Toulouse-Lautrec.

A BIT OF HISTORY

The "Albigensian Crusade" –

The 12C-13C crusade against the followers of Catharism became known as the **Albigensian Crusade**, perhaps because Albi offered them refuge. The crusade, launched by **Pope Innocent III**, brought Occitania into the sphere of the French monarch, but it was to take an Inquisition, torture, murder and the 1244 massacre at Montségur to end the so-called heresy.

Henri de Toulouse-Lautrec

The famous artist born in Albi in 1864 was the son of Comte Alphonse de Toulouse-Lautrec Montfa and Adèle Tapié de Celeyran. Childhood accidents left Toulouse-Lautrec crippled for life. In

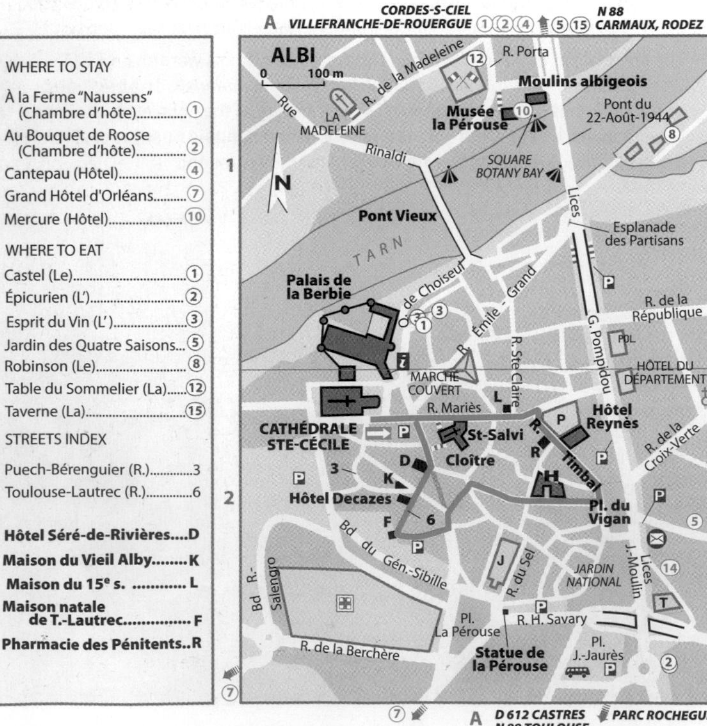

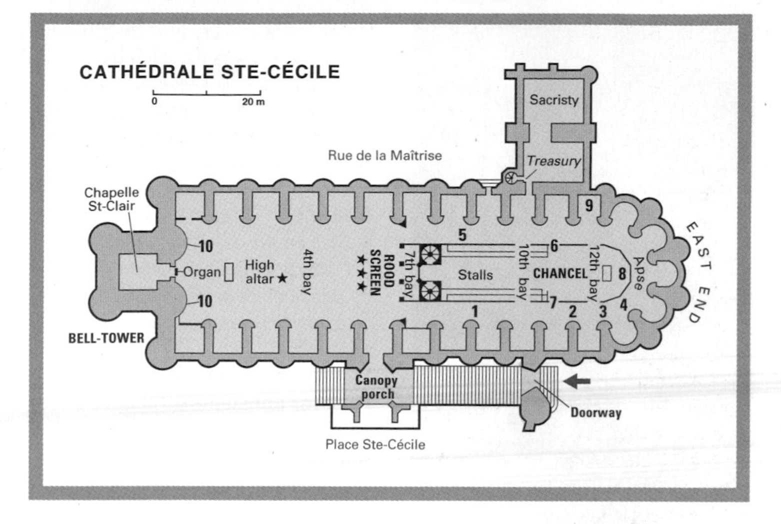

1882 he moved to Montmartre and lost himself in the seamy life of Paris bars and brothels, and portrayed them in his paintings. From 1891 his talent as a lithographer won him fame. By 1899, his alcoholism and debauchery landed him in a sanatorium in Neuilly. **Toulouse-Lautrec** left Paris in 1901, died in the family château at Malromé on 9 September of that year, and was buried in Verdelais.

CATHÉDRALE STE-CÉCILE★★★

The cathedral's massive proportions are best appreciated from the Pont du 22-Août bridge or from the cathedral square.

The Catholic Church reclaimed its authority after the Albigensian Crusade. Roman Catholic bishops became as powerful as lords. **Bernard de Combret**, bishop from 1254 to 1271, began constructing a bishops' palace in 1265, and **Bernard de Castanet** (1276-1308) began building the cathedral of Ste-Cécile, which took 200 years. Successive bishops added finishing touches.

The sheer red-brick walls were replaced in 1849 by false machicolations, a rampart walk and bell turrets.

Doorway and canopy porch★ – The main entrance through a 15C doorway winds up a grand staircase to a carved stone canopy forming the porch. This

Cathédrale Ste-Cécile and Palais de la Berbie

B. Kaufmann/MICHELIN

Last judgement in Treasury, Cathédrale Ste-Cécile

B. Kaufmann/MICHELIN

work of art was added under Louis I of Amboise (1520).

Bell-tower – The original tower was a square, keep-like structure about as high as the nave. Between 1485 and 1492, Louis I added three storeys.

Rood screen★★★ – After the church was consecrated around 1480, Louis I of Amboise built the chancel, closed off by a carved stone rood screen. The resulting interlaced motifs, pinnacles and arches typify Late Flamboyant Gothic decoration. The carved stone screen around the outside of the choir consists of ornate ogee arcading with Flamboyant tracery and the Chi-Rho Christogram. Against each of the pillars between the arches is a polychrome statue of an Old Testament figure, fine examples of the naturalism of Gothic sculpture in France.

Chancel

Open Jun-Sep 9am-6.30pm; Oct-May 9am-noon, 2-6.30pm. audioguide 2€. 05 63 43 23 43 http://perso.wanadoo.fr/paroisse.ste-cecile.albi.

Statues of Charlemagne (6) and the Emperor Constantine (7) gaze down from the entrance doorways, and other statues depict New Testament figures. The 15C stained-glass windows around the apse were restored in the 19C. The chapel of the Sainte-Croix (9) is worth a view.

The monumental **organ** built by Christophe Moucherel in 1734-6 was restored in 1981. Below the organ stands the new **high altar★**, a creation in black marble by Jean-Paul Froidevaux.

Treasury

Open Jun-Sep 9am-6.30pm; Oct-May 9am-noon, 2-6.30pm. 3€. 05 63 43 23 43.

As long ago as the 13C this chapel was designated to house the cathedral's archives and precious objects, including a 14C polychrome reliquary of St Ursula, a 13C crosier from the Limoges region, a 14C episcopal ring and Sienese polyptych.

The Last Judgement (10) – This magnificent three-tiered mural, executed in the late 15C, was stripped of its image of Christ in 1693, when the chapel of St-Clair was added to the cathedral.

Cathedral vault – Louis II of Amboise commissioned Bolognese artists to embellish the nave of the cathedral with dazzling paintings inspired by the Italian Renaissance, the Quattrocento (15C).

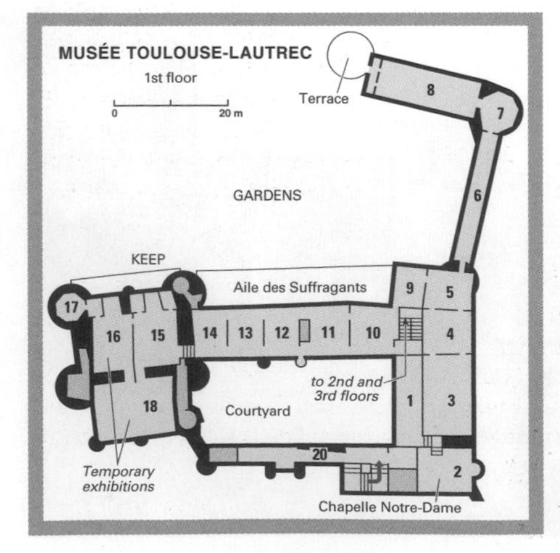

PALAIS DE LA BERBIE★

The name of Bernard de Combret's bishops' palace "Berbie" derives from bisbia or "bishopric" in local dialect. Bernard de Castenet transformed the original building with a massive keep and curtain wall. The Edict of Nantes in 1598 removed the need for this fortress, and since 1922 it has housed the Musée Toulouse-Lautrec.

Musée Toulouse-Lautrec★★

Extensive restoration until 2010-11, but you can still see all the works, though they may be in different parts of the museum.

A grand 17C staircase leads to archaeological exhibits (20) on the first floor; note the tiny, 20 000-year-old *Vénus de Courbet* discovered at Penne in the Tarn *département*.

The 13C chapel of Notre-Dame (2) has ribbed vaulting and colourful decor by the Marseille artist Antoine Lombard.

The comprehensive **Toulouse-Lautrec collection** was bequeathed to Albi by the artist's mother, the Comtesse Alphonse de Toulouse-Lautrec in 1922 and was augmented by other family members. Javal's portrait of the artist captures the dignity in Toulouse-Lautrec's gaze. Early works such as *Artilleur sellant son cheval* – a soldier saddling his horse, painted when the artist was only 16 show his early interest in animals and people. Other works evoke Toulouse-Lautrec's life in Montmartre.

OLD ALBI★★ WALK *1hr*

From place Ste-Cécile, take rue Ste-Cécile and then rue St-Clair (2nd on the right). A covered passage on the left offers glimpses of the **Saint-Salvy cloisters, a later stop on this walk**.

Hôtel Séré de Rivières

This 15C-18C mansion belonged to a family of dyer's woad merchants ennobled in the 18C. A notable member was General **Raymond Séré de Rivières** (1815-95), designer of France's border defence system after the eastern provinces fell to Prussia (1870-71).

This was indeed Paris

Room 11 of the Musée Toulouse Lautrec contains one of Toulouse-Lautrec's most famous works: *Au Salon de La Rue des Moulins*, with the pastel study and finished painting of 1894 on opposite walls. The work shows the artist's supreme skill as a draughtsman and his sensitivity as an observer of the harsh realities of life. Other works portray the world of Parisian music halls and theatres that Toulouse-Lautrec knew so well. Here are portraits of Valentin "le Désossé" ("boneless") who danced with La Goulue at the Moulin de la Galette; the singer-songwriter Aristide Briant, who sang in slang at the cabaret Le Mirliton; the café-concert artist Caudieux; Jane Avril, nicknamed "Le Mélinite," and the singer Yvette Guilbert, once passionately pursued by the artist.

Maison du vieil Alby

This restored medieval house, between pretty Croix-Blanche and Puech-Berenguier streets, hosts local craft exhibitions and has literature on Albi. Beneath the eaves of this building is a solelhièr, or woad drying room.

Rue Toulouse-Lautrec

At no 8, the **Hôtel Decazes** on the site of the 14C fortifications features a handsome courtyard with a balustraded staircase and galleries. The Maison La Pérouse, named after a seaman (1741-88) (see Musée La Pérouse), houses a **waxworks museum** and the Hôtel du Bosc, where Toulouse-Lautrec was born.

Turn left onto rue de Verdusse then right onto rue Saunal.

Note a wealthy 16C woad merchant's mansion and the fine 17C town hall on the corner of rue des Pénitents and rue de l'Hôtel-de-Ville.

Façade decoration of Pharmacie des Pénitents
A. Thuillier/MICHELIN

Rue de l'Hôtel-de-Ville leads to the restored place du Vigan with its 81 fountains and the Jardin National.

Follow rue Timbal.

Hôtel de Reynès★

Headquarters of the local chamber of commerce. This wealthy merchant family's Renaissance stone and brick mansion has a courtyard featuring busts of François I and Eleanor of Austria, and window mullions adorned with mermaids.

Pharmacie des Pénitents★ (or Maison Enjalbert)

This 16C house features timbering and crisscross-pattern brickwork typical of the Albi region. The façade's decoration is typically Renaissance.

Take rue Mariès towards the cathedral.

Note no 6 on the right, an attractive 15C timber-and-brick building.

Collégiale St-Salvi

St Salvi was a lawyer before becoming Bishop of Albi in the 6C. He brought Christianity to the region and is buried on the site of this church, which has seen a turbulent history. The church's layout and foundations date from the Carolingian period. The 11C saw the building of a church and Romanesque cloisters. Work was interrupted by the Albigensian Crusade and was resumed in the 13C, in the Gothic style.

Interior – *Enter by the north door.* All that remains of the Romanesque doorway is the archivolt, the arch mouldings and two capitals. The first four bays are Romanesque and retain their 12C capitals. Two apsidal chapels in the chancel also remain from the original construction. The chancel and the remaining bays of the nave are in the Flamboyant Gothic style. The **cloisters** were rebuilt by Vidal de Malvesi in the 13C. All that remains is the east gallery, with Romanesque historiated capitals and Gothic ones decorated with plant motifs.

BERGES DU TARN★★

Follow the Azure circuit starting from the tourist office.

The banks of the Tarn offer splendid **views**★★ of the town and the old fortifications and a peaceful stroll away from the town's bustle.

ADDITIONAL SIGHTS

Musée La Pérouse

Botany-Bay Square, entrance in rue Porta. Open Jul-Aug 9am-noon, 2-6pm (weekends 10am-noon, 2-7pm); Mar-Jun and Sep-Oct daily except Mon 9am-noon, 2-6pm; Nov-Feb daily except Mon 10am-noon, 2-5pm. Closed 1 Jan, 1 May, 1 Nov, 25 Dec. 3€. 05 63 46 01 87. www.laperouse-france.fr.

The navigational instruments, maps, charts and models ships in these handsome vaulted rooms recall the naval expeditions of Admiral Jean-François de Galaup de La Pérouse, born in the Manoir du Go outside Albi in 1741. In 1785, Lapérouse embarked upon a scientific expedition with two frigates, the *Boussole* and the *Astrolabe*, but he perished when the latter was shipwrecked off Vanikoro Island, north of the New Hebrides. An international team carried out investigations of the wreck of the *Astrolabe* in 1986.

Statue of La Pérouse
This memorial to the famous seaman graces the square named in his honour.

EXCURSIONS
Église St-Michel de Lescure★
5km/3mi NE towards Carmaux-Rodez, then right at the signpost to Lescure. Open daily except weekends 9am-noon, 1.30-5.30pm. Contact the town hall for the key. 05 63 60 76 73.
The old priory church in Lescure cemetery was built in the 11C by Benedictine monks from Gaillac Abbey. Its 12C Romanesque doorway is most interesting. Four capitals display narrative scenes, like those of the St-Sernin basilica in Toulouse and the church of St-Pierre in Moissac.

Notre-Dame-de-la-Drèche
5km/3mi N on the road to Carmaux-Rodez, then left towards Cagnac-les-Mines. Guided tours Sun 4pm; Sanctuary 8.30am-noon, 2-6pm; Museum afternoons only. No charge. 05 63 53 75 00.
This strikingly large 19C shrine built is consecrated to the "Vierge d'Or de Clermont," a mid-10C gold statue of the Virgin Mary in Majesty from the Auvergne. The interior of this octagonal rotunda contains murals designed by Bernard Bénézet and executed by Father Léon Valette.
The **musée-sacristie** contains a remarkable gold brocade altar hanging made by nuns of the Order of St Clare in Mazamet.

Castelnau-de-Lévis
7km/4.5mi W. Leave Albi on the road to Cordes-sur-Ciel, then take D 1 left.
The remains of this 13C fortress offer pleasing views of Albi, its towering cathedral and surrounding Tarn valley.

St-Juéry
6km/3.7mi E towards Millau, follow signs for "Site du Saut du Tarn".

Musée culturel du Saut du Tarn
(*open Jul-Aug guided visit at 1.30pm 4.50€; Mar-Apr Wed, Sun and public holidays 2-6pm; May-mid Nov 2-7pm. 3.50€. Closed Sat, 1 Nov. 05 63 45 91 01*), is located in a former hydroelectric power station, and **Ambialet** (20km/12.4mi E) on a peninsula formed by a meandering river.

ADDRESSES

STAY

Chambre d'hôte au Bouquet de Roose – *Jussens, 81150 Castelnau-de-Levis (5km/3mi from Albi by D 1). 05 63 45 59 75. www.chambre-hote-tarn.com – 3rms.* Within sight of the city centre, but essentially out in the countryside, offering peace and quiet.

Chambre d'hôte à la Ferme Naussens – *81150 Castanet. 05 63 55 22 56. – 5rms. Closed Dec-March.* A convivial farmer's welcome and Mediterranean-accented cuisine.

Hotel Cantepau – *9 r. Cantepau – 05 63 60 75 80 www.hotel-cantepau.accueilweb.com– closed 25 Dec-11 Jan – P – 33 rms – 15€.* Wicker furniture, subdued hues and fans give this hotel a colonial feel. Friendly welcome; generous breakfasts.

Grand Hôtel d'Orléans – *pl. Stalingrad. 05 63 54 16 56. http://hotel-orleans-albi.com.* Simple and unfussy hotel; swimming pool; traditional dishes.

Hôtel Mercure – *41 bis r. Porta – 05 63 47 66 66 – h1211-gm@accor.com – P – 56 rms.* This modern hotel in an 18C red-brick mill on the banks of the Tarn has lovely views of the river and cathedral.

EAT

La Table du Sommelier – *20 r. Porta – 05 63 46 20 10 – closed Sun and Mon.* The proprietor sets the scene with wine cases piled high in the entrance and rustic dining room with mezzanine.

This wine-focused bistro serves refined cuisine with fresh ingredients.

⊖⊖ **Le Castel** – *23 r. d'Engueysse. ☎05 63 36 94 79. Closed Sun and Mon lunch from Oct-Apr.* Designed like the inside of a cask, this inexpensive restaurant is just 200m from the cathedral.

⊖⊖ **Le Robinson** – *142 r. Édouard-Branly – ☎05 63 46 15 69. Closed Nov-Feb, Mon and Tue.* This isle of green on the banks of the Tarn is accessible from the pont Neuf. Dating from the 1920s, the old-fashioned dance hall has an exuberant charm. The food is simple and the welcome warm.

⊖⊖ **Jardin des Quatre Saisons** – *19 bd de Strasbourg. ☎05 63 60 77 76 – www.lejardindes4saisons.fr.st. Closed Sun evening and Mon.* A reliable favourite with a good selection of wines and traditional cuisine.

⊖⊖ **La Taverne** – *R. Aubijoux, 81150 Castelnau-de-Levis. ☎05 63 60 90 16 – www.tavernebesson.com. Closed Mon and Tue.* Housed in an old bakery, with two traditional brick ovens – lots of charm.

⊖⊖ **L'Épicurien** – *42 pl. Jean-Jaurès. ☎05 63 53 10 70. www.restaurantlepicurien.com. Closed Sun and Mon.* Refined but welcoming atmosphere, with a view into the kitchens. Daily menus.

⊖⊖⊖ **L'Esprit du Vin** – *11 quai Choiseul – ☎05 63 54 60 44. Closed Sun and Mon.* This old red brick outbuilding of the Berbie Palace has two cosy dining rooms serving creative cuisine.

TOUR

Guided tour of the Old Town *(1hr) – organised by the Tourist Office, mid-Jul-late Aug: Mon-Sat except public holidays at 12.15pm.* Book at the Tourist Office. 4€ (under 14: no charge).

Walks – Three themed walks depart from the Tourist Office. The Circuit Pourpre through the heart of old Albi takes in historic sites, characters and monuments. The Circuit Or focuses on Albi's growth over 2,000 years. The Circuit Azur along the banks of the Tarn, takes in the Pont Vieux and the Pont Neuf, with fine views of the town.

TAKING A BREAK

La Berbie – *17 pl. Ste-Cécile. ☎05 63 54 13 86.* This attractive tea room on place Ste-Cécile, serves teas, coffees, home-baked pastries, ice-cream sundaes and pancakes. Luncheon menu.

SHOPPING

The Old Town (especially ***rues Mariès, Ste-Cécile et Verdrusse***) offers a variety of antique shopping, boutiques and establishments selling food and drink.

L'Artisan Pastellier – *5 r. Puech-Bérenguier. ☎05 63 38 59 18. www.artisanpastellier.com – Tue-Sat 10am-noon, 2-7pm, Mon mid Jun-mid Sep and Sun in Aug 3-6.30pm. Closed 20 Jan-10 Feb, 14 Jul, 15 Aug, Sun and Mon out of season.* At this shop near the Maison du vieil Alby, Claire and her husband prepare quality artists' materials, including calligraphy inks.

Marché biologique – *Pl. F.-Pelloutier – Tue 5-7pm.* Organic produce, local crafts and books are sold here.

Markets– *Pl. Ste-Cécile.* Saturdays on place Ste-Cécile selling fruit, vegetables, garlic from Lautrec, charcuterie from Lacaune, and foie gras in season,

Patisserie J.P. Galy – *7 r. Saunal. ☎05 63 54 13 37 – Tue-Sat 9.45am-7pm – closed 1 week in Feb and 4 weeks Sep-early Oct and holidays.* Galy pastrycooks' fine pastries and regional specialities sell like hotcakes!

RECREATION

Boat trip on the Tarn – *Berges du Tarn. ☎05 63 43 59 63 – www.albi-croisieres.com – Jun-Sep 11am, 11.45am and 2-6pm departing every 40mn. 6€ (children 3-12 years 4€).* Enjoy a pleasure cruise on a traditional gabarre, a flat-bottomed barge used for transporting goods until the 19C. Leave the old harbour at the foot of the Palais de la Berbie ramparts, and float along the Tarn past the old mills and locks.

CALENDAR OF EVENTS

Free organ concerts in the cathedral – *Wed and Sun afternoons in Jul and Aug.*

Son et Lumière – *at Ambialet, Jul-Aug Thu evening 6€. ☎05 63 55 37 91.*

Carnaval – *end of February.*

Le Grand Pri Automobile – *September.*

Castres★

This busy city on the banks of the Agout makes an excellent base for excursions to the Sidobre region, the Lacaune mountains and Montagne Noire. Castres has a remarkable museum devoted to Spanish painting, particularly the works of Goya. The Castres area is the French wool-carding centre, and with textile and spinning mills, dyeing and dressing workshops, its wool industry is second only to that of Roubaix-Tourcoing.

- **Population:** 43 496.
- **Michelin Map:** 338: F-9.
- **Info:** Office du tourisme de Castres, 2 place de la République, 81100 Castres. ☎05 63 62 63 62. www.tourisme-castres.fr.
- **Location:** 40km/25mi S of Albi.
- **Don't Miss:** Le musée Goya
- **Kids:** Le planétarium-observatoire de Montredon-Labessonnié.

A BIT OF HISTORY

A self-governed city – Castres grew up on the west bank of the Agout, around a Benedictine monastery founded c810. At the end of the 9C veneration of the relics of St Vincent, one of the preachers who took the Gospel to Spain, made Castres a stopping place on the pilgrim route to Santiago de Compostela. In the 10C, the town came under the rule of the viscounts of Albi and Lautrec. In the 11C, the viscount of Albi granted Castres the right to self-government by a college of "consuls" or capitouls.

The town managed to keep out of trouble during the Cathar heresy by submitting to Simon de Montfort.

The Reformation – From 1563, the Reformation attracted numerous followers. Once the city's capitouls had renounced Roman Catholicism, Castres became one of the strongholds of Calvinism in Languedoc. It was caught up in the Wars of Religion, which the Peace Treaty of Alès, Henri IV's ascent to the throne and the promulgation of the Edict of Nantes eventually brought to an end. In the 17C, the city hosted one of the four chambers set up by the Edict of Nantes to regulate differences between Protestants and Roman Catholics. This was a prosperous period during which local magistrates and merchants built luxurious town houses and the bishopric a magnificent episcopal palace.

However, the confrontations between Protestants and Roman Catholics persisted after the revocation of the Edict

Quai des Jacobins

B. Kaufmann/MICHELIN

Purple garlic from Lautrec

Coveted by gourmets for its flavour and storage-life, the purple garlic cultivated in and around Lautrec has an annual production exceeding 4 000 tonne. On the first Friday in August, locals hold a competition of garlic sculpting, followed by a tasting of special garlic soup. Festivities culminate with locals sharing an enormous pot of *cassoulet* accompanied by *confit de canard*. Lautrec cuisine features garlic crushed into sauces, rubbed onto croutons, added to soups, vegetable dishes and stews, and in the old days, a handful of raw garlic cloves and a chunk of hearty bread was the favourite packed lunch of local labourers.

of Nantes until the French Revolution, forcing numerous Huguenots to flee into exile.

Jean Jaurès – The famous Socialist leader was born in Castres on 3 September 1859 and spent part of his childhood in Saïx, a little village on the banks of the Agout, southwest of Castres. He was a student at the lycée that now bears his name, and went on to train as a teacher at the École Normale Supérieure in Paris, after which he taught philosophy at the lycée in Albi and at the University of Toulouse. Attracted by politics, he was elected Republican Member of Parliament for the Tarn in 1885, then Socialist Member for Carmaux, where he took up the miners' cause in 1893.

At the next elections, however, Jaurès was defeated, largely because of his support for Dreyfus, victim of what was eventually proved to be a military conspiracy which led to his being falsely convicted of selling sensitive information to the Germans, an affair which provoked bitter controversy throughout France. Jaurès nonetheless became head of the United Socialist Party (SFIO) not long after its foundation in 1905. As war approached, he put his influential voice to the service of promoting peace and devoted himself to the cause of international brotherhood. He was assassinated at the Café du Croissant in Paris on 31 July 1914. War was declared two days later. In 1924, his remains were transferred to the Panthéon, Paris.

OLD CASTRES WALK *1hr 30min*

Start from the theatre.

Opposite are the superb **formal gardens** (Jardin de l'Évêché) designed by Le Nôtre in 1676. The town hall **Hôtel de Ville** occupies the **former bishops' palace** designed by Mansart and built in 1669. The massive Romanesque **Tour St-Benoît** is all that remains of the former abbey of St-Benoît.

Cathédrale St-Benoît

This cathedral dedicated to St Benoît de Nursie and designed by the architect Caillau in 1677 was built on the site of a 9C Benedictine abbey. Eustache Lagon took charge of construction of this enormous Baroque edifice in 1710.

Cross place du 8-mai-1945.

Quai des Jacobins

The Pont Neuf and quay afford attractive views of bright coloured medieval houses lining the banks of the Agout. Homes of weavers and dyers in the Middle Ages, they are built over vast stone cellars opening directly onto the water.

Place Jean-Jaurès

The early 19C houses around this square feature Classical sandstone façades. Admire Gaston Pech's statue of Jean Jaurès and the fountain inspired by that on place de la Concorde in Paris.

Cross place Jean-Jaurès; right onto rue Henri-IV; left onto rue du Consulat.

Hôtel de Nayrac★

12 rue Frédéric-Thomas.

Beautiful 1620 brick and stone mansion typical of Toulouse civil architecture.

Take rue Émile-Zola and rue Victor-Hugo.

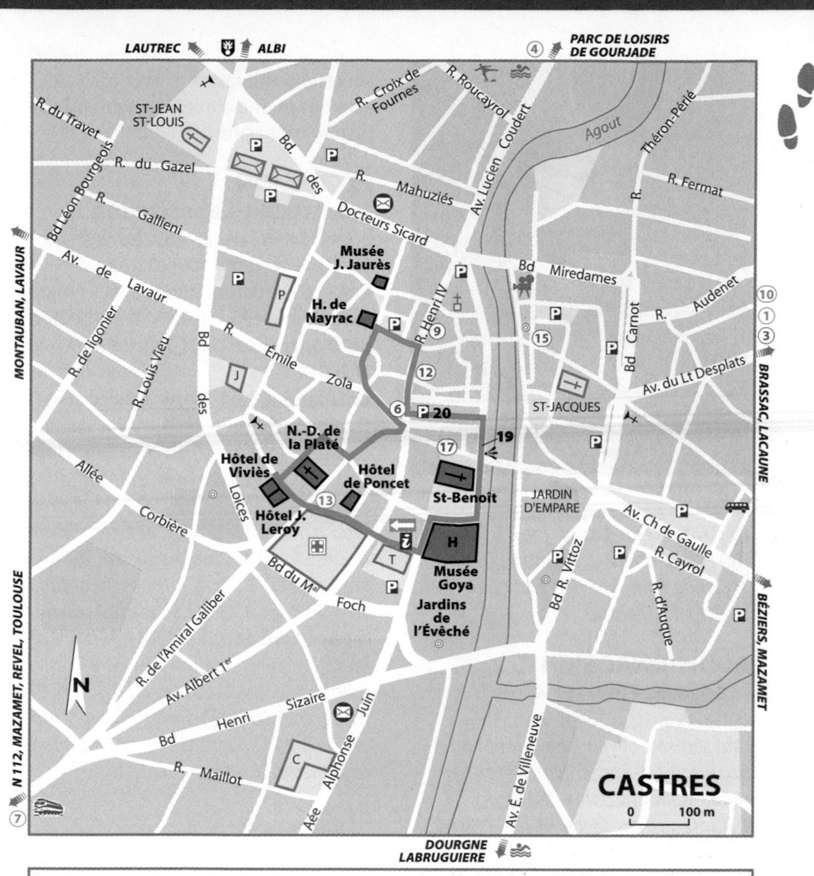

WHERE TO STAY		WHERE TO EAT	
Crémaussel (Auberge de)	1	Café de Paris	3
Castel de Burlats (Hôtel Le)	4	Europe (Brasserie de L')	6
Pasteillé (Chambre d'hôte Le)	7	Mandragore (La)	9
Plô (Camping Le)	10	Pescadou (Le)	12
Renaissance (Hôtel La)	13	Relais du Vieux Pont (Le)	15
		Victoria (Le)	17
Quai des Jacobins	**19**	**Place Jean-Jaurès**	**20**

Église Notre-Dame-de-la-Platé

This Baroque-style church was rebuilt between 1743 and 1755. Note the high altar's Assumption of the Virgin in Carrara marble, by Isidora and Antonio Baratta (Bernini School), and the fine 18C organ.

Retrace your steps and turn left onto rue de l'Hôtel-de-Ville.

At no 31, admire the doorway with its round arch on fluted columns surmounted by a carved pediment depicting pistol, sabre and cannon.

Turn left onto rue de la Platé leading to rue Chambre-de-l'Édit.

Hôtel de Viviès

No 35. This 16C building with a square corner tower houses the **Centre d'Art contemporain** (*open daily except Mon 2-7pm. closed public and Christmas school holidays. 2€. 05 63 59 30 20).*

Self-portrait with glasses (1800) by Francisco de Goya

J.-C. Ouradou/Musée Goya, Castres

Hôtel Jean-Leroy (no 31, 16C) and Hôtel de Poncet (rue Gabriel-Guy, 17C). Rue Chambre-de-l'Édit goes back to the theatre.

ADDITIONAL SIGHTS

Musée Goya★

Open Jul-Aug 10am-6pm; Apr-Jun and Sep; rest of year daily except Mon 9am-noon, 2-6pm (10am Sun and public holidays; 5pm Oct-Mar). Closed 1 Jan, 1 May, 14 Jul, 1 Nov, 25 Dec. 2.30€ (children under 18 free); no charge 1st Sunday in the month. 05 63 71 59 28. www.ville-castres.fr.

This museum in the Hôtel de Ville (*see Old Castres, above*) contains works by **Goya**★★, as well as 14C Spanish Primitives, and 17C works by Murillo, Valdès Leal and Ribera. Admire Goya's etchings *Los Desastres de la Guerra* (The Disasters of War) inspired by the Spanish War of Independence (1808–14). *Los Caprichos* (Caprices) expresses the isolation and contemplation provoked by the artist's deafness in 1792.

Centre national et musée Jean-Jaurès

Open Jul-Aug 10am-noon, 2-6pm; rest of year daily except Mon 10am-noon, 2-6pm (Oct-Mar 5pm). Closed Sun from Nov-Mar, 1 Jan, 1 May, 1 Nov, 25 Dec. 1.50€. 05 63 62 41 83. www.ville-castres.fr.

This museum devoted to the life and work of the great Socialist, as well as society in the late 19C and early 20C, also has an information centre on the history of socialism.

EXCURSION

Montredon-Labessionné

21km/13mi NE along D 89 then left 5km/3mi beyond Roquecourbe.

Camels, kangaroos and monkeys roam around in relative freedom at the **Zoo de Montredon** (*closed until end of 2009*).

The **Planétarium-Observatoire** stages shows for children, on the solar system, constellations and their associated legends. (**Planétarium**: *Jul-Aug daily except Mon 4pm (other school holidays Wed and Sun 4pm. 6.50€ (children 4.50€);* **Ateliers fusées à eau:** *Jul-Aug Wed and Fri 3.30pm (other school holidays Wed 2pm). 7.50€;* **Seasonal soirées d'observation** *Tue-Fri Jul 9.30pm; Aug 9pm. 11€-13 € (children 7€-8.50€) (other school holidays Wed and Fri 8.30pm; 9€ (children 5.50€). closed 25 Dec-1 Jan. 05 63 75 63 12; http://assoc.wanadoo.fr/planetarn).*

DRIVING TOUR

Le Sidobre★

53km/33mi round tour – allow 3hr. Leave Castres on D 622 to Brassac. Turn right at the hamlet of La Fontasse.

The Sidobre massif contained within the Parc Naturel Régional du Haut Languedoc, has fascinating granite landscapes sculpted by erosion, which make it a renowned tourist attraction.

Chaos de St-Dominique

This river of rocks in a pleasant wooded setting covers the real River Lézert for 4km/2.5mi *(rocks are slippery in rainy weather)*.

Grotte de St-Dominique

15min on foot round-trip. Not accessible to those with reduced mobility.

The cave overlooks a glade and once gave refuge to a disciple of St Dominic during the Revolution.

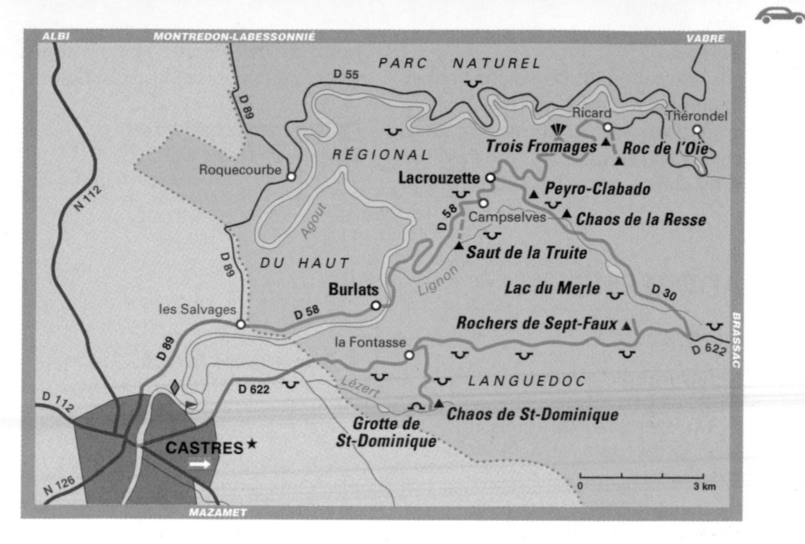

Return to D 622 and head back towards Brassac. After 5km/3mi, just past a café, turn left, then in the hamlet of Loustalou stop at the café-tabac "Au Rocher Tremblant".

Rocher de Sept-Faux

This extraordinary rocking-stone consists of two blocks poised on top of one another, weighing 900 tonne, which can be rocked by simply pressing on a wooden lever.

Return to the Brassac road and turn left towards Lacrouzette.

Lac du Merle

This fine lake surrounded by forests is fed by the waters of the Lignon.

Chaos de la Resse (or "River of Rocks")

A chaotic heap of rocks covers the River Lignon, whose roar is quite impressive.

Peyro Clabado

The Peyro Clabado rock is a 780 tonne granite boulder balanced on a tiny pedestal of rocks.

Lacrouzette

Most of the town's inhabitants earn their living from quarrying granite.

From Lacrouzette, take D 58 to Thérondel.

This splendid road offers a panorama of the Agout Valley.

Stop at the village of Ricard and take the footpath to the Trois Fromages and Roc de l'Oie.

Trois Fromages; Roc de l'Oie

45min on foot round-trip. Follow the red and white flashes marking the GR footpath through the woods.

The **Trois Fromages** ("three cheeses") rock is a single boulder fractured by erosion into three rounded fragments. Further on, the **Roc de l'Oie** resembles a goose – hence its name.

Return to D 58 and follow signposts to Lacrouzette and Burlats. About 2km/1mi beyond Lacrouzette, after the turnoff to Campselves, a little road is signposted to the left.

Saut de la Truite

Stop near the River Lignon.

Take a footpath to the right of the torrent. 10min on foot round-trip as far as the foot of the waterfall.

At this gushing waterfall the fresh green landscape becomes more arid.

Burlats
The remains of this Benedictine abbey founded in the 10C retain their Romanesque doorways, capitals and mouldings and mullioned windows. The **Pavillon d'Adélaïde was the** 12C home to Adélaïde de Toulouse and her court, whose troubadours sang of courtly love.

Return to Castres via Les Salvages and D 89.

ADDRESSES

STAY

Auberge de Crémaussel – *Lieu-dit Crémaussel, 81210 Lacrouzette. ℘05 63 50 61 33. Closed 25 Dec-Jan – 5rms.* This rural auberge has bright rooms facing onto the countryside. Regional cuisine.

Chambre d'hôte le Pasteillé – *La Ferme, 81290 Viviers-les-Montagnes. ℘05 63 72 15 64 ou 06 08 85 34 89 – 4rms.* An ancient farm in large private grounds; one room for people of reduced mobility; peaceful and welcoming.

Camping le Plô – *81260 Le Bez. ℘05 63 74 00 82. Open from mid-May-mid Sep – reservations advised– 60 pitches.* Isolated in Montagne Noire at the edge of a forest. Everything is simple, but spick and span.

Hotel le Castel de Burlats – *8 pl. du 8-Mai-1945, 81100 Burlats. ℘05 63 35 29 20 – www.lecasteldeburlats.fr.st. Closed 15-22 Feb and 25-31 Aug – P – 10rms – 10€.* This fine 14C and 16C palace in a formal French style garden has comfortable spacious rooms overlooking the hill, and a charming Renaissance style salon.

Hôtel La Renaissance – *17 r. Victor-Hugo. ℘05 63 59 30 42. www. hotelrenai sance.fr – 22rms – 8€.* 17C house in a pedestrianed area of the old town; the rooms are original and decorated in various styles.

EAT

La Mandragore – *1 r. Malpas – ℘05 63 59 51 27 – closed Sun-Mon and 19 Sep-4 Oct and 16-31 Jan.* This little restaurant in Old Castres offers reasonable, family-style traditional cuisine amidst a contemporary decor.

Le Victoria – *24 pl. du 8-Mai-1945 – ℘05 63 59 14 68 – closed Sat lunchtime and Sun.* This restaurant's three vaulted stone cellars are said to have been part of a monastery. Seasonal cuisine.

Brasserie de L'Europe – *1 pl. Jean-Jaurès. ℘05 63 59 01 44. Closed Sun.* The most popular brasserie in Castres, enjoying a lovely situation close to Agout; good choice of meat dishes, pizzas and salads.

Le Relais du Pont Vieux – *3 pl. Roger-Salengro. ℘05 63 35 56 14 – www. hotelmiredames.com.* This restaurant enjoys a certain notoriety in Castres, housing as it does the first "Resto Philo" in France, a place of debate and discussion.

Café de Paris – *8 pl. de l'Hôtel-de-Ville, 81260 Brassac - ℘05 63 74 00 31.* A lovely and simple place without pretensions, close to the 12C bridge; simple regional and traditional cuisine.

Le Pescadou – *18-20 r. des 3-Rois. ℘05 63 72 32 22.* Specialising in seafood dishes, including bouillabaisse; simple decor, and terrace in summer.

TAKING A BREAK

Signovert – *5 r. Émile-Zola – ℘05 63 59 21 77.* This pastry shop and chocolatier founded in 1928 features a local nougat, *le Granit du Sidobre*.

RECREATION

Le Coche d'eau – *R. Milhau-Ducommun – ℘05 63 62 41 76 – leaves from the city centre. Closed Nov-Apr. 4€ (children under 5 free).* For a cruise on the Agout, hop aboard the *Miredames*, a fine wooden boat inspired by the old "water coaches" once pulled by horses.

Gourjade recreation area – North of town on ave de Roquecourbe, the park has a golf course, walking paths, picnic areas, an orienteering trail, children's play areas, and a swimming pool (skating rink in winter).

Cordes-sur-Ciel ★★★

Cordes-sur-Ciel occupies a remarkable site★★ on the Puech de Mordagne rocky outcrop, overlooking the Cérou valley. On a bright day the sunlight enhances the soft pink and grey hues of the old façades. The village may owe its name to the textile and leather industry which prospered here in the 13C and 14C.

- **Population:** 996.
- **Michelin Map:** 338: D-6.
- **Info:** Office du tourisme de Cordes, Pl. Jeanne-Ramel-Cals 05 63 56 00 52. www.cordesurciel.eu
- **Location:** NW of the Tarn, 27km/16.8mi from Albi.
- **Don't Miss:** A promenade through the Upper Town.
- **Kids:** Jardin des Paradis; Musée de l'Art du Sucre.

A BIT OF HISTORY

Fortified town – In 1222, during the Albigensian Crusade, the Count of Toulouse, Raymond VII, decided to build the fortified town of Cordes in response to destruction of the stronghold of St-Marcel by Simon de Montfort's troops.

The charter of customs and privileges enjoyed by the inhabitants of Cordes included, among other things, exemption from taxes and tolls. The town-cum-fortress rapidly became a favourite haunt of heretics, and the Inquisition found rich pickings during its work here.

The end of the campaign against the Cathars ushered in a period of prosperity. In the 14C, the leather and cloth trades flourished; craftsmen wove linen and hemp cultivated on the surrounding plains, whereas the dyers on the banks of the Cérou used the **pastel** (blue dyer's woad) and saffron which grew so abundantly in the region. The beautiful houses built during this period bear witness to the wealth of the inhabitants.

Decline and revival – The quarrels among the bishops of Albi, which affected the entire region, the resistance of Cordes to the Huguenots during the Wars of Religion and two plague epidemics put an end to this golden age in the 15C. After a brief burst of life at the end of the 19C, due to the introduction of mechanical embroidery looms, Cordes, which had originally been designed to be isolated, finally fell into decline, cut off as it was from the main communication routes. Fortunately, the threatened demolition of its Gothic houses spurred the population into action and a number of measures to classify some of its buildings as historic monuments were taken

Cordes-sur-Ciel

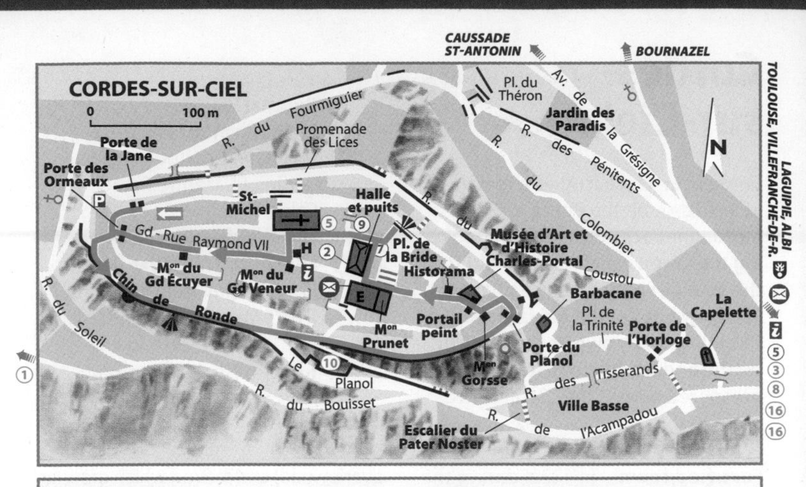

WHERE TO STAY	
Aurifat (Chambre d'hôte)	1
Cayrols (Chambre d'hôte Le)	3
Cité (Hôtel La)	5
Envolée Sauvage (Chambre d'hôte L')	8
Maison Bakea (Chambre d'hôte La)	10
Moulin de Julien (Camping)	16

WHERE TO EAT	
Arcades (Les)	2
Bouriette (Auberge de la)	5
Vieux Cordes (Hostellerie du)	9

Maison Fonpeyrouse d'Alayrac (Hôtel de ville)	**H**
Maison du Grand Fauconnier	**E**

in 1923. But those most susceptible to the charm of Cordes were the artists and craftsmen who rallied to the cause and helped to put the town back on the map. Restoration is still being carried out, preserving the original character of Cordes. In 1970 the town also became a venue for musical entertainment.

The winding, steeply sloping, stone streets are home to an ironmonger, an enameller and a sculptor of figurines, not to mention weavers, engravers, sculptors and painters, who practise their crafts in the beautiful old houses whose original appearance has been so successfully conserved.

UPPER TOWN★★

Traffic is banned in the upper town in summer. Park for a fee near the Porte de la Jane or at the bottom of Grande Rue de l'Horloge. The upper town is accessible by shuttle (every 15min in season).

Cordes' beautiful **Gothic houses**★★ (13C-14C) have richly **sculpted façades** and the largest and best-preserved line the Grand-Rue (or rue Droite). Laid out in a diamond-shape, Cordes had two curtain walls built around it in 1222. The **Porte de la Jane**, a remnant of the second curtain wall, doubled the Porte des Ormeaux. Assailants who fought their way past the Porte de la Jane were surprised to be confronted by the massive towers of this second fortified gateway, the **Porte des Ormeaux**. The southern wards (Planol haut) and those of rue du Planol offer attractive views of the surrounding countryside.

Maison Gorsse

The façade of this house features some beautiful Renaissance mullioned windows.

Portail peint

The Painted Gate is probably named after the painted Madonna which once adorned it. It houses the **Musée Charles-Portal** (*see Additional Sights*).

Grand-Rue, which is cobbled and very steep, leads to the heart of the fortified town.

The **Maison Prunet** houses the Musée de l'Art du Sucre (*see Additional Sights*).

Maison du Grand Fauconnier★

This beautiful old mansion now housing the town hall was named after its roof corbels decorated with falcons. Its remarkably elegant façade was restored in the 19C.

Covered market and well

This market place once rang to the sound of cloth merchants and today is the city's hub. Its roof is supported by 24 octagonal wooden pillars. Nearby is a **well**, 114m/372ft deep.

The shaded **Place de la Bride** offers sweeping views of the Cérou Valley to the northeast, against the slender silhouette of the Bournazel belfry to the north.

Église St-Michel

This church has its original 13C chancel and transept and a splendid 14C rose window. Enjoy the panorama from atop the watchtower.

Maison Fonpeyrouse d'Alayrac

This late-13C mansion which now houses the tourist office has an interesting inner courtyard. Two timber galleries give access to the upper storeys.

Maison du Grand Veneur★

This mansion named after the Master of the Royal Hunt, has a distinctive three-storey façade depicting hunting scenes.

Maison du Grand Écuyer

The elegant façade of this mansion is built of beautiful Salles sandstone and adorned with imaginative figures sculpted in the round.

Return to the Porte des Ormeaux.

LOWER TOWN

As suburbs sprang up around the citadel, a fourth and fifth curtain wall were built in the 14C. East of the town the clock gateway, or **Porte de l'Horloge**, is a remnant of the fourth wall. Reach it from place de Lacampadou by climbing the **Escalier du Pater Noster**, which has as many steps as the prayer has words.

La Capelette

The interior of this old chapel, built in 1511, was decorated by Yves Brayer (*see Additional sights below*).

MUSEUMS

Musée d'Art et d'Histoire Charles-Portal★

Enquire at the tourist office for opening hours and tarifs. 05 63 56 06 11.

This local history museum, located inside the Portail Peint, was named in honour of Charles Portal, keeper of public records for the Tarn *département* and great historian of Cordes.

On the ground floor are some antique grain measures, a rather unusual sarcophagus from the Merovingian necropolis (6C) in Vindrac (5km/3mi W of Cordes), the beautiful studded door from the Maison du Grand Fauconnier and the falcons (faucons) to which this house owes its name.

A room on the first floor is devoted to the architecture of Cordes. The second floor houses interesting collections of local prehistoric exhibits and some opulent Gallo-Roman furniture which belonged to the temple at Loubers.

Another room contains the *libre ferrat* or iron book, so-called because its binding incorporated an iron chain. This record book contains the town's regulations from the end of the 13C to the 17C. New consuls were sworn in on the Gospel extracts inside it.

The third floor displays objects found during excavation of the Vindrac necropolis: jewellery, buckles, a set of antefixes and earthenware from Gallo-Roman times.

Musée de l'Art du sucre

Open Jul-Aug 10.30am-12.30pm, 1.30-7pm; Mar-May and Sep-Nov daily except Mon morning and Tue 10.30am-12.30, 1.30-6pm. 3€ (children 2€). 05 63 56 02 40.

This unusual museum housed in a rose-coloured Prunet mansion contains art made entirely of sugar, paintings and miscellaneous exhibits (stamp album, Provençal market, musical instruments).

Musée d'Art moderne et contemporain Yves-Brayer

Housed in the Maison du Grand Fauconnier. Open Jun-Sep 11am-12.30pm, 2-7pm; Apr-May and Oct 11am-12.30pm, 2 6pm; Nov-Mar 2-5pm. 3.50€ (children 2€). 05 63 56 14 79.
A 15C spiral staircase leads to the **Salle Yves-Brayer** containing the painter's drawings, lithographs, etchings and watercolours. The **Salle de la Broderie cordaise** offers embroidery demonstrations on a tambour frame.
The mechanical embroidery frames, from St-Gall in Switzerland, brought Cordes prosperity in the late 19C and early 20C. The **Salle de la Fresque** contains modern and contemporary paintings, stained glass and ceramics.

EXCURSIONS

Le Cayla

11km/7mi SW on D 922 (signposted).
Musée Maurice-et-Eugénie-de-Guérin commemorates romantic writers and poets such as **Maurice de Guérin** (1810-39) and his sister **Eugénie** (1805-48).

Monestiés

15km/9mi E on D 922 towards Villefranche, then D 91 to Carmaux.
Chapelle St-Jacques
Open Jul-Aug 10am-12.30pm, 2-6.30pm; mid Mar-Jun and Sep-Oct 10am-noon, 2-6pm; Nov-mid Mar 10am-noon, 2-5pm. Closed 1 Jan and 25 Dec. 3.50€ (combined ticket with the Bajén-Vega centre: 5€). 05 63 76 41 63. www.monesties.com.
The **Mise au tombeau★★** has remarkable elegance, and presents, on three levels, the final episodes of the Passion.
The **Centre contemporain Bajén-Vega** (*open Jul-Aug 10am-12.30pm, 2-6.30pm; mid Mar-Jun, Sep-Oct 10am-noon, 2-6pm; Nov-mid Mar daily except weekends 2-5pm. Closed 1 Jan and 25 Dec. 3€ (ticket also valid for the tour of the Chapelle St-Jacques) 05 63 76 19 17. www.monesties.com)* houses paintings by Spanish political refugees Martine Vega and Francisco Bajén .

ADDRESSES

STAY

Camping Moulin de Julien – *05 63 56 11 10. Open May-Sep – reservation recommended – 130 sites.* Pitch your tent at the foot of the medieval city. This campsite has a water chute plunging into the pool, a children's play area and chalets for hire.

Chambre d'hôte le Cayrols – *Livers Cazelles. 05 63 56 22 46 .www. lecayrols.com. Closed Nov-Mar – 5rms.* This old farm, tastefully restored houses simple rooms; many leisure activities suitable for children, including swimming pool, toboggan, minigolf...

Chambre d'hôte Aurifat – *05 63 56 07 03 – www.aurifat.com. Closed mid Dec-mid-Feb – 4 rms.* The restored 13C watch tower in an enchanting spot has charming rooms, swimming pool and terraced garden.

Hôtel la Cité – *21 r. St-Michel. 05 63 56 03 53. www.thuries.fr . Closed Nov-Apr – 8rms – 9€ – meals.* Built into the ramparts of the city; rooms are decorated in the original styles.

Chambre d'hôte la Maison Bakea – *26/28 le Planol. 05 63 56 29 54. http://maisonbakea.chez-alice.fr. Closed mid-Oct-mid-Mar – 5rms.* This 13C house in the medieval city has a delightful internal courtyard, and lovely, well-furnished rooms.

Chambre d'hôte l'Envolée sauvage – *La Borie - Livers Cazelles Village. 05 63 56 88 52. www.lenvolee-sauvage.com – 4rms. Closed Oct-Mar.* The rooms of the 18C farm are decorated with good taste; cuisine is based on domestic and market produce.

EAT

Auberge de la Bouriette – *Campes – 4km/2.5mi NE of Cordes-sur-Ciel on D 922 then D 98. 05 63 56 07 32. www.cordes-sur-ciel.org. Closed 15 Dec-15 Feb.*
This working farm offering 5 B&B rooms has a dining room with a view in the old barn; simple fare using local produce; terrace and swimming pool.

⊖ **Les Arcades** – *3 pl. de la Halle - ☎05 63 56 93 96. Closed Christmas to Feb.* Eating here won't break the bank; simple rustic dishes inspired by regional produce.

⊖⊖ **Hostellerie du Vieux Cordes** – *21 r. St-Michel. ☎05 63 53 79 20. www.thuries.fr. Closed Jan.* Local cuisine served in an old monastery at the heart of the medieval city.

SHOPPING

Pâtisserie Andrieu – *Grand Rue de l'Horloge – ☎05 63 56 01 02 – 8am-8pm. Oublies (waffles) and croquants de Cordes are specialities in this shop.*

Art'Cord – *Maison de Grand Fauconnier ☎05 63 56 14 79. www.cordes-sur-ciel. org Open daily; 10.30am-12.30pm, 2.30-6pm – closed Jan.* Inside the Grand Fauconnier house, you will find displays of the work of about 20 local artists.

L'atelier du Laguiole – *26 R. Raymond-VII – ☎05 63 56 10 83 – 10am-noon, 2-6pm.* Buy famous and unique Laguiole knives made here, for your pocket, the dinner table, for professional use or as collector's items.

LEISURE ACTIVITIES

Jardin des Paradis – *☎05 63 56 29 77 – Jul-mid Sep. 6€ (children under 12 free).* Themed guided tours to study the stars or learn about aromatic plants, floral composition or jellys made from flowers.

Fêtes du Grand Fauconnier – *Around 14 July.* Journey back to medieval times to admire the costumes, the troubadours, jugglers and archers.

"Musiques sur Ciel" – *ACADOC – ☎05 63 56 00 75. www.festivalmusique surciel.com – last fortnight in July.* Chamber music festival.

Gaillac

For many years Gaillac's wealth came from riverboat traffic and trade on the Tarn. The old town has charming squares with fountains and narrow streets lined with old timber and brick houses.

Info: Abbaye St-Michel, 81600 Gaillac. ☎05 63 57 14 65. www.ville-gaillac.fr.

Location: Gaillac is a transportation crossroads linking Montauban and Albi by river, rail and road.

Don't Miss: A local wine tasting and the Château de Mauriac's "herbarium."

Kids: The Museum of Chocolate Art at Lisle-sur-Tarn.

SIGHTS

Abbatiale Saint-Michel

In the 7C, Benedictine monks founded an abbey here dedicated to St Michael. The abbey church, built between the 11C and 14C, contains a 14C polychrome statue of the Madonna and Child. Abbey buildings now house the **Maison des Vins de Gaillac** and **Musée des Arts et Traditions populaires**, about journeymen (*compagnons*), work in local vineyards, and objects of local historical interest.

Tour Pierre de Brens

This brick tower dating from the 14C and 15C has gargoyles, mullioned windows and a remarkable projecting gallery.

The Gaillac vineyards

The south bank of the Tarn grows red grapes: Gamay, Braucol, Syrah and Duras. Vineyards on the north bank grow red varieties (Duras, Braucol, Syrah, Cabernet and Merlot) and also Mauzac, Loin de l'œil and Sauvignon varieties for white wines. Gaillac wines are AOC *(Appellation d'Origine Contrôlée)* and these vineyards rank among the foremost wine producers in the southwest of France.

Parc de Foucaud

The terraced gardens above the Tarn were laid out by André Le Nôtre, the famous 17C French designer of the Versailles gardens. The château contains the **Musée des Beaux-Arts** (*open Jul-Aug daily except Tue 10am-noon, 2-6pm; rest of year Fri-Sun 10am-noon, 2-6pm. 2.50€. 05 63 57 18 25*) showing works by local painters and sculptors.

EXCURSIONS

Lisle-sur-Tarn

9km/5.5mi SW via N 88.

This town has a vast **square** with covered arcades and fountain, vestiges of its *bastide* days (1248), and 16C to 18C brick and timber houses. **Notre-Dame de la Jonquière** church has a Romanesque portal and Toulouse style bell-tower. The **Musée Raymond-Lafage** (*open mid Mar-mid Oct daily except Tue 10am-noon, 2-6pm; guided tours possible (45min); 2€; 05 63 40 45 45; www.ville-lisle-sur-tarn.fr*) presents drawings and engravings by Raymond-Lafage, the 17C Lisle draughtsman, Gallo-Roman and medieval artefacts, works of sacred art, and portraits by Victor Maziès (1836-95).

Château de Mauriac★

11km/7mi N on D 922. Turn right just before Cahuzac. guided tours May-Oct 3-6pm; Nov-Apr, Sundays and public holidays 3-6pm. 6€ (children: 4€). Enquire with M. Emmanuel Bistes 05 63 41 71 18. www.bistes.com.

This castle dating from the 14C has a beautiful façade and rooms displaying paintings by Bernard Bistes, the castle's owner. The French-style ceiling of the "Polish Room" is decorated with 360 panels depicting a fresh-looking **herbarium**★.

Castelnau-de-Montmiral

13km/8mi NW on D 964.

This picturesque village high above the Vère valley and Grésigne forest is an old bastide founded in the 13C by Raymond VII, Count of Toulouse. **Place des Arcades** is flanked by arcades topped with corbelled half-timbered houses, some dating from the 17C. In the 15C **parish church**, note the polychrome stone statue of Christ Bound (15C), Baroque altarpiece and 13C **gem-encrusted cross-reliquary**★ of the counts of Armagnac known as the Montmiral Cross.

ADDRESSES

STAY

Hôtel Verrerie – *R. de l'Égalité. 05 63 57 32 77. www.la-verrerie.com – P – 14rms – 11€.* This 19C glass-making factory has contemporary rooms; the dining room opens onto a terrace.

EAT

La Table du Sommelier – *34 Pl. Thiers. 05 63 81 20 10. Closed Sun (except in Jul and Aug) and Mon.* Warm, rustic decor attracting regulars with appetizer plates and interesting wines.

Les Sarments – *27 R. Cabrol (behind the Abbaye St-Michel). 05 63 57 62 61. www.restaurantslessarments.com. Closed 25 Apr-3 May, 19 Dec-10 Jan, 21 Feb-7 Mar, Sun evenings, Wed evenings and Mon.* This 14C-16C wine storehouse in the heart of the old town serves regional dishes, accompanied by Gaillac vintages.

La Falaise – *Rte de Cordes ,81140 Cahuzac-sur-Vère - 11km/7mi N of Gaillac by D 922. 05 63 33 96 31. www.lafalaiserestaurant.com. Closed Sun evening, Tue lunch, and Mon.* Located at the edge of the village; serves mouth-watering dishes based on local produce.

WINE SHOPPING

Maison des Vins de Gaillac – Caveau St-Michel – *Abbaye St-Michel. 05 63 57 15 40 – www.vins-gaillac.com – Jul-Aug: 10am-1pm, 2-7pm; rest of the year: 10am-noon, 2-6pm – closed Christmas, 1 Jan, 1 May and 1 Nov.* This wine centre on the River Tarn sells products from 82 different vineyards and 3 cooperatives producing Gaillac wine. Tastings, presentation of the vineyards and sales.

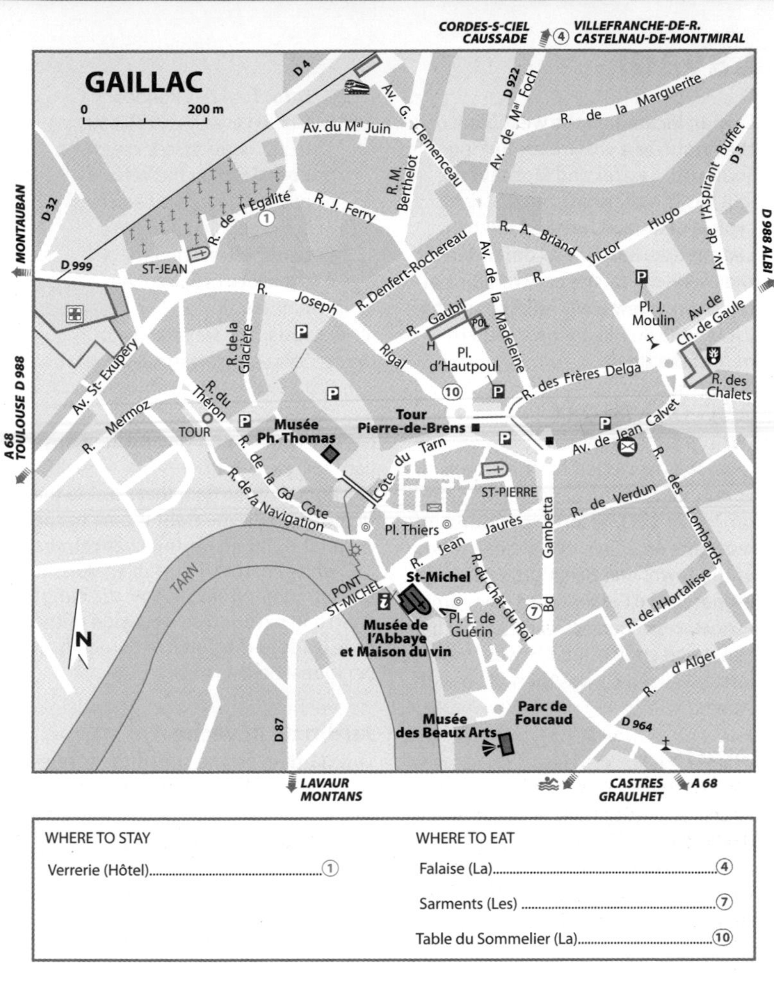

Cave de Labastide-de-Lévis – *B.P. 12 – 81150 Marssac-sur-Tarn. ☎05 63 53 73 73 – www.cave-labastide.com – mid Jun-mid Sept, daily except Sun: 9am-12.30pm, 2pm-7pm; rest of the year: 9am-noon, 2pm-6pm – closed Sun and public holidays.* This wine co-operative represents about 15per cent of Gaillac vineyards and 50per cent of its production is classified AOC, including the famous Gaillac "perlé." A tour covers every stage of wine production. Free tastings.

Domaine du Moulin – *Chemin de Bastié. ☎05 63 57 20 52. Mon-Sat 9am-noon, 2pm-7pm, Sun by appointment.* This estate has been voted best red Gaillac in the barrel for the last 8 years at the Gaillac and Paris wine competition. The Hirissou family has tended the vines for 9 generations, and these vineyards have found favour with stars like Charles Aznavour, Johnny Halliday and Claude Chabrol. Tastings.

Château Raynal – *La Brunerie, 81600 Senouillac. ☎05 63 41 70 02 – www.ville-gaillac.fr – museum: daily guided tour by appointment – closed mid to late Aug.* Visit the small museum on farming in the Gaillac region, and sample some good local wine. Hospitable welcome from this winegrowing family.

Château de Mayragues – *81140 Castelnau-de-Montmiral. ☎05 63 33 94 08 – www.chateau-de-mayragues.com – Mon-Sat 9am-7pm; closed Sundays and Christmas.* Visit this château for its 14-16C architecture, hilly setting, its vineyards and Gaillac wines.

Lavaur

Lavaur, located on the west bank of the Agout, at a crossroads linking Toulouse, Castres and Montauban, still has the charming old districts typical of a small fortified town in Languedoc. Lavaur was defended by the castle of Plo, the only remains of which are a few walls holding up the Esplanade du Plo, in the southern part of the town.

- **Info:** Tour des Rondes, 81500 Lavaur, ℘05 63 58 02 00. www.ville-lavaur.fr.
- **Location:** On the W bank of the Agout, between Lauragais and Albigeois.
- **Don't Miss:** The Jack-o'-the-clock of Saint-Alain Cathedral.
- **Kids:** The steam train at Saint-Lieux-les-Lavaur.

A BIT OF HISTORY

During the Albigensian Crusade, the town was besieged by the troops of Simon de Montfort and surrendered on 3 May 1211, after two months of resistance organised by Guiraude, a lady of the town, and 80 knights who had espoused the Cathar cause. They were hanged, other heretics were burnt at the stake, and Lady Guiraude was thrown into a well which was then filled with stones.

SIGHTS

Cathédrale St-Alain★

The original Romanesque building destroyed in 1211, was rebuilt in 1254. At the top of a Romanesque tower the famous 1523 painted **Jack-o'-the-clock** strikes the hour and half-hour.

The cathedral's southern French Gothic style interior has an imposing single nave (13C-14C) and seven-sided apse (late 15C-early 16C).

The Romanesque door that leads to the first chapel on the right is part of the original building. In the chancel, the 11C white-marble altar-table (Moissac School) comes from Ste-Foy, the oldest church in Lavaur. The west side of the nave leads to the porch underneath an octagonal belfry.

Jardins des Martels

Jardins des Martels

Jardin de l'Évêché

This garden, on the site of the former bishops' palace, has ancient cedars and carefully tended flowerbeds, making it a pleasant place for a quiet walk.

EXCURSION

St-Lieux-les-Lavaur

10km/6mi NW on D 87 and D 631 to the left.

The Tarn tourist **steam train** (*times vary. 5.50€ (children 4.50€). ℘05 61 47 44 52; www.cftt.org*) running as far as Giroussens leaves from this charming site in the Agout valley.

Giroussens Jardins des Martels★

9km/5.6mi NW along D 87 and D 631. Open May-Aug 11am-6pm; Apr 1-6pm; Sep-Oct 1-6pm (weekends and public holidays 11am-6pm); Nov weekends and public holidays 1-6pm. 6.50€ (children 11-18 years 5€, 4-10 years 4€). Closed Dec-Mar. ℘05 63 41 61 42. www.jardinsdesmartels.com.

These English-style gardens feature water lily pools, flower beds, woodland and a mini-farm for children.

Mazamet

Situated at the foot of the Montagne Noire, Mazamet still thrives on the wool industry that brought prosperity to the area in the 18C. Specialising in the "pulled wool" technique, the town is also renowned for tawing the pelts once the wool has been removed. Today, sheepskins are mainly imported from Australia, South Africa and Argentina, wool is exported to Italy and skins to Spain, Belgium, Italy and the USA.

- **Population:** 10 300.
- **Michelin Map:** Michelin Local map 338: G-10.
- **Info:** R. des Casernes, 81200 Mazamet. ℘05 63 61 27 07. www.tourisme-mazamet.com.
- **Location:** 60km/37.5mi south of Albi.
- **Kids:** La Maison du bois et du jouet.

A BIT OF HISTORY

Hilltop village – In the 5C, the Visigoths built Hautpoul clinging to a hilltop site to protect it from would-be attackers. Nonetheless, Simon de Montfort managed to storm the stronghold in 1212 and the Wars of Religion finished off what he left standing. In the valley below, the textile industry expanded, thanks to the supply of pure water from the Arnette ideal for washing wool. With the advent of machinery, the river was harnessed to provide the necessary power to drive it. The inhabitants of Hautpoul were thus persuaded to abandon their hilltop site to found Mazamet.

Centre of the wool industry – With woad, madder and saffron produced in the neighbouring plains, the Montagne Noire specialising in sheep rearing, and the Arnette and Thoré providing water, Mazamet became a major 18C wool industry centre. In 1851, the company of Houlès Père et Fils et Cormouls imported sheepskins from Buenos Aires and stripped them of their wool, opening up an industry for "pulled wool." Learn about this along two marked trails *"Mazamet au fil de la laine"* from the tourist office or public park.

VISIT

Maison Fuzier

R. de Casernes, 81200 Mazamet. Open Jun-Aug 3-6pm; Sep-May daily except Mon, Tue and public holidays 2.30-5.30pm. Closed Jan, 1 May, 24, 25 and 31 Dec. 3€. ℘05 63 61 56 56. www.maison-memoires.com.

The Maison Fuzier houses the tourist office and a **Maison des Mémoires de Mazamet**, with an exhibition on types of local burial procedure dating back to earliest times.

EXCURSIONS

Hautpoul

4km/2.5mi S along D 54 then the first road on the right.

This hamlet directly above the **Gorges de l'Arnette** was the birthplace of Mazamet and offers an attractive **view**★ of Mazamet and the Thoré Valley.

Adults and children will appreciate the **Maison du Bois et du Jouet**, a craft centre (*open Jul-Aug 11am-7pm; Jun and Sep daily except Mon 2-6pm; Feb-May and Oct-Dec Wed, Sat-Sun and public holidays 2-6pm (school holidays daily except Mon). closed 1 Jan, 25 Dec. 5€ (4-14 years 3€). ℘05 63 61 42 70. www.hautpoul.org).*

Lac des Montagnès

6km/3.7mi S along D 118.

Set against a backdrop of hills and woodland, this beautiful reservoir is popular with anglers, swimmers and walkers.

ADDRESSES

STAY / EAT

Hotel Mets et Plaisirs – *7 ave. A.-Rouvière – ℘05 63 61 56 93 – www.metsetplaisirs.com.* This old family mansion opposite the post office serves traditional country fare. It also has 11 rooms of accommodation, simply furnished.

Ariège is one of the original 83 *départements* created on 4 March 1790, from the counties of Foix and Couserans. Foix, the administrative centre, is an agreeable medieval town with a fortress balanced on a hill above the town. Pamiers has a large commercial centre, while Mirepoix, in complete contrast, revolves around its delightful central square. Saint-Girons has one of the best markets in this part of France, and is a predominantly agricultural centre.

Highlights

1 A visit to the ruins of **Montségur** (pp348, 352)

2 The arcades and half-timbered houses of **Mirepoix** (p351)

3 Travel back in time at the **Grotte du Mas-d'Azil** (p350)

4 Ride a subterranean river at **Labouiche** (p348)

5 Go animal spotting in the **Orlu valley** (p342)

Half-timbered houses

The region of Ariège is particularly well-endowed with fine examples of half-timbered houses (*colombages*), notably in Mirepoix. Also known as *maison à pans de bois*, the houses consist of a framework (*ossature*) made from wood, and the in-filling, the *colombage*, which forms the walls and has the functions of filling and strengthening. This technique, well-known through Britian also, dates from Roman times, and has been in use in France from the Middle Ages until the 19C.

More frontiers than one

The Ariège enjoys a number of frontiers, some more evident than others. Obviously, it forms a frontier with Spain and Andorra, but less clearly it is the dividing line between Gascony to the west and Languedoc to the east. This particular distinction was rather more evident during the time of the Cathars, who thrived on the Languedoc side. The Couserans, in western Ariège, is arguably the least inhabited region, but it has two beautiful rivers, the Salat and the Lez. With their numerous tributaries, they have fashioned valleys since before man. These delightful valleys – Biros, Bethmale, Riberot and others – offer some of the finest walking in the Pyrenees, set against the majestic Mont Valier (2 855m/9 369ft), once thought to be the highest summit of the range. At the opposite end of the scale, Ariège has a clutch of caves, all with outstanding prehistoric artwork and artefacts. This is nowhere better exemplified that in the upper Arriège valley, around Tarascon-sur-Ariège, a major crossroads since the arrival of man, at the dawn of time.

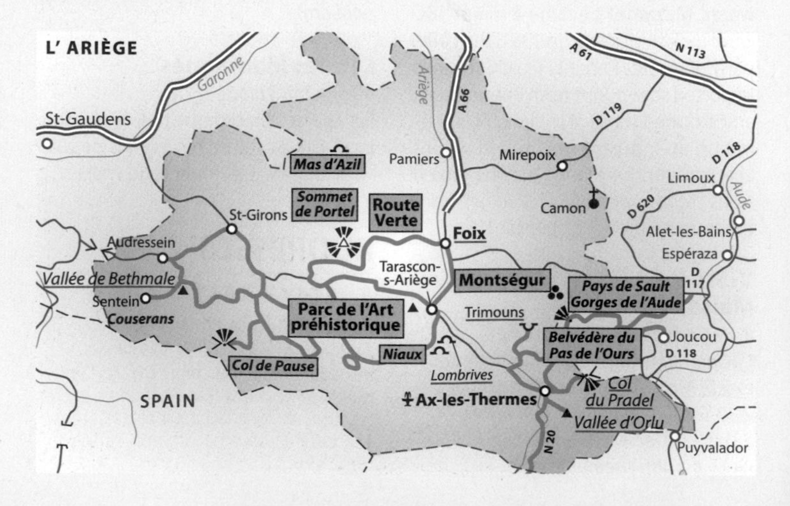

Grotte du Mas-d'Azil
A. Thuillier/MICHELIN

Cave dwellings

Ariège is a hugely fascinating destination for anyone interested in prehistory, having, as it does, the largest concentration of caves (*grottes*) in France. That at **Mas d'Azil** yielded important discoveries that led to the identification of the so-called Azilian Age, a period about 10 000 years ago. Large quantities of tools and other artefacts were found there. The **grotte de Lombrives** is the largest cave in Europe, while the **grotte de Niaux** is especially renowned for its cave paintings of bison, horse and ibex. The **grotte de Bedeilhac** is generally thought to be a splendid and typical example of a large Pyrenean cave: prehistoric drawings, paintings and clay mouldings of bison, horse, reindeer and ibex were first discovered here in 1906.

The **grotte de la Vache**, at Alliat, lower down the valley, is the smallest of the caves open to the public. It was clearly a well-used site of encampments, with, in consequence, thousands of man-made artefacts being discovered there.

Much of the story of these magnificent caves is told in the **Parc de la Préhistoire** at Tarascon, which features reproductions of sanctuaries and paintings from other caves in the Pyrenees that are inaccessible or closed to the public. The drawings in the Salon Noir in the Niaux cave are reproduced in their entirety. Outside there are examples of the types of shelters constructed by Magdalenien people, and the site also offers demonstrations of flint knapping and fire making.

Between Foix and the Bastide de Sérou, the subterranean river at **Labouiche** is the longest underground river in Europe. First explored in 1905, it is now possible to enjoy boat trips through high and low-vaulted galleries decorated with stalagmites, stalactites and crashing waterfalls.

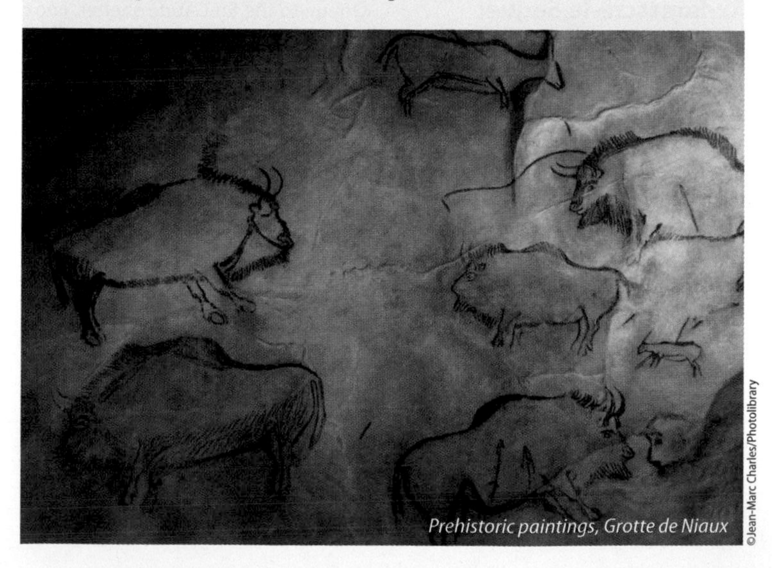
Prehistoric paintings, Grotte de Niaux

Ax-les-Thermes

and the Donézan

The valley spa and winter sports town of Ax, at the confluence of the Oriège and Lauze rivers, really bustles, summer or winter.

Location: 128km/80mi S of Toulouse.
Kids: Maison des Loups.

THE SPA

Eighty mineral springs, at temperatures ranging from 18-78°C/64-172°F, supply three pump rooms: the Couloubret, the Modèle and the Teich. The main afflictions treated here are rheumatism, respiratory disorders and some skin problems. The focal point of the resort is the Promenade du Couloubret.

Bassin des Ladres

On place du Breilh, a jet of steam marks the site of this hot water basin which is filled in the morning and can be used as a public wash-house. St Louis had it built for soldiers returning from the Crusades suffering from leprosy – hence its name "Lepers' Basin." The hospital of St-Louis (1846), easily recognised by its bellcote, is a typical example of 19C "spa town" architecture.

SKI AREAS

Ax-Bonascre-le-Saquet

Alt 1 400-2 400m/4 600-7 870ft.

The ski area has 75km/44mi of forested Alpine ski runs for all levels of skiers, and grass skiing in summer!

The **gondola** goes to the Saquet plateau (*open at varying times throughout the year; check locally for current information. 6.50€ round-trip. 05 61 64 20 06. www.vallees-ax.com).*

Ascou-Pailhères

Alt 1 500-2 030m/4 921-6 660ft.

This family resort offers 15 Alpine ski runs for all levels.

Le Chioula

Alt 1 240-1 650m/4 068-5 413ft.

There are 65km/40.6mi of cross-country trails and 6km/3.6mi of free trails for those learning cross-country techniques. Lodging adjacent to the trails.

Mijanès-Donézan

Alt 1 530-2 000m/5 019-6 561ft.

The "Québec of Ariège" on the Donézan plateau offers 10 downhill slopes and 25km/15.6mi of cross-country trails. This family resort caters to children with play groups and sledding.

WALKS

Réserve Nationale d'Orlu

8.5km/5mi to the starting point of the footpath. Leave Ax on the road to Andorra and turn off towards Orlu just before the bridge over the Oriège; stay on the north bank of the river. This walk (3hr round-trip) is suitable for all walking enthusiasts.

The road skirts the **Orlu valley**★ and reservoir shore, with Orgeix manor house reflected in the waters of the dam. Take the road on the left before the old Orlu ironworks. Leave the car in Pont de Caralp carpark and walk along the track closed to motorised vehicles.

The path climbs the west bank of the Oriège to the En Gaudu shelter. Look for marmots and izards in early morning and late afternoon. Farther up (a 2hr round-trip), the path crosses a stream and from Pas de Balussière continues along the east bank of the Oriège.

Farther up (an additional 2hr round-trip), the path crosses a stream, then, from Pas de Balussière, it continues along the east bank of the Oriège. Farther up still, the **Étang de Beys** comes into view.

Signal de Chioula★

45min on foot round-trip.

Leave Ax on D 613 N, following the Ariège Valley in a series of hairpin bends.

At the Chioula Pass, a wide footpath leads to the beacon (alt 1 507m/4 898ft; 45min round-trip), and a view of the peaks framing the upper Ariège valley.

Trimouns quarry

A. Thuillier/MICHELIN

EXCURSIONS

Maison des Loups

8.5km/5.3mi. Leave Ax on the road to Andorra and turn towards Orlu just before the bridge on the Oriège; drive to the end of the valley as far as Les Forges. Open Jul-Aug 10am-7pm; Apr-Jun 10am-5.30pm; Sep-Oct daily except Mon and Tue 11am-5pm. Closed Nov-Mar. 6.50€ (children 4-12 years 4€). 05 61 64 02 66. www.maisondesloups.com.
Observation platforms scattered across a magnificent woodland site, with mountain streams rushing through it, offer an opportunity to see different species of wolves roaming around in vast enclosures and being fed. Kids will enjoy the donkeys, goats, lambs and baby pigs.

Plateau de Bonascre★

8km/5mi. Leave Ax on N 20 to Tarascon and turn off left onto D 820.
The road climbs steeply in hairpin bends, with views of the three river valleys which converge on Ax. On the Bonascre plateau at the top is the ski resort of **Ax-Bonascre-le-Saquet**, and a gondola leading to the **Plateau du Saquet** (alt 2 030m/6 598ft).

Col du Pradel★

30km/18.5mi. Leave Ax to the E on the road to Quillan. 3.5km/2mi out of town, turn left onto D 22.
The narrow pass road is closed from 15 November to 14 May.
The distinctive **Dent d'Orlu** (alt 2 222m/7 222ft) can be seen to the south-east. The road corkscrews up the pass (alt 1 680m/5 460ft) around tight hairpin bends with views of the mountains.

DRIVING TOURS

THE DONÉZAN

66km/41mi round-trip – allow half a day. Leave Ax-les-Thermes E along D 613 towards Le Chioula and, 3.5km/2.5mi farther on, turn right onto D 25 towards Ascou-Pailhères.
The road runs through the **Donézan** region, set in a hollowed-out basin in the granite plateaux of the Quérigut. It is one of the wildest areas of the Pyrenees, with villages at altitudes of 1 200m/3 936ft.

In Mijanès, turn left onto a minor road leading to Usson.

Usson-les-Bains

The imposing castle ruins stand guard over the confluence of La Bruyante and the Aude.

THE CLIMB TO TRIMOUNS★★

39km/24mi round-trip – allow 3hr.

Leave Ax-les-Thermes NW along N 20 towards Tarascon.

Luzenac

This village has been famed since the late 19C for its French chalk quarried at the **Carrière de Trimouns**★. Find tourist information at 6 rue de la Mairie.

The Izard

About 40 years ago, the izard, a variety of wild goat found in the Pyrenees, had been all but killed off by hunters' bullets. Nowadays it is a protected species. There are over 1 000 in the Orlu valley, which has been designated a nature reserve since 1981. The izard is found between 1 600-2 500m/5 250-8 200ft above sea level, but it does venture below 900m/2 950ft. It is gradually taking over those areas which have been abandoned by man. The izard's coat changes colour depending on the season: it is red-gold in the summer and dark brown with patches of white in the winter, when it also becomes much thicker to combat the cold. The animals are not that timid and can be observed quite easily, especially during spring or autumn. The summer heat and winter cold force them to take refuge in the undergrowth. Izards are perfectly suited to their environment and can climb up and down even quite steep slopes with impressive agility.

Leave Luzenac across the bridge spanning the Ariège and follow D 2 towards Caussou.

Unac

Note the pretty Romanesque church towering above the valley.

Continue along D 2, the "Route des Corniches," with aerial views of the Ariège valley, then turn left towards Lordat.

Château de Lordat

This ruined castle on a limestone outcrop served as a Cathar refuge after the seige of Montésgur.

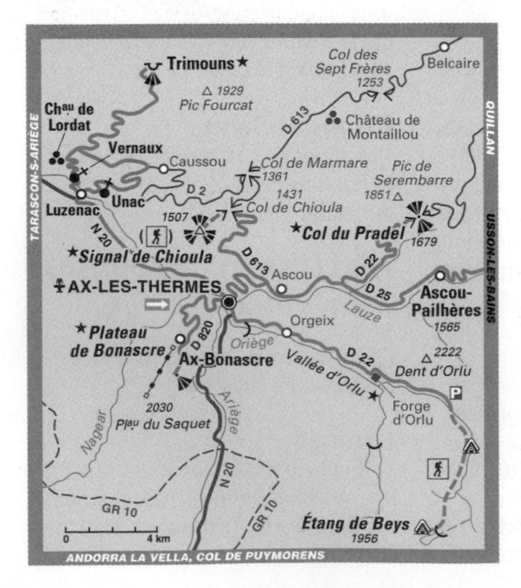

Return to the Route des Corniches crossroads and go straight on towards Trimouns.

Carrière de Trimouns★

guided tours according to weather conditions (1hr in autocar) mid May-mid Oct daily except Sat-Sun 10am, 11am, 2pm, 3pm and 4pm. Closed mid-Oct-mid-May. 7€ (children under 12 2.50€). 05 61 64 68 06.

The chalk quarry at Trimouns is one of the largest in the world. The huge white seam of French chalk itself is impressive, as is the **panorama**★★ of the upper Ariège mountains.

Return to Lordat, then onto Luzenac via Vernaux.

Vernaux

Below the village, the road runs past an isolated Romanesque church.

Take N 20 back to Ax-les-Thermes.

Foix★

Route Verte & Crouzette★★, Cathars, Plantaurel Hills

Foix, ruggedly set★ against a skyline of jagged peaks and three castle towers, overlooks the Plantaurel hills. Its old narrow streets radiate from Rue de Labistour and Rue des Marchands, starkly contrasting with the 19C administrative area fanning out from the Allées de la Villote and the Champ de Mars.

- **Info:** 29 R. Delcassé, 09000 Foix, 05 61 65 12 12. www.ot-foix.fr.
- **Location:** 88km/55mi S of Toulouse. The old town's centre and fountain is at the corner of rue de Labistour and des Marchands.
- **Kids:** The Reptile Farm, and Labouiche river; Les Forges de Pyrène.

A BIT OF HISTORY

Once part of the Duchy of Aquitaine, the Foix region became a county in the 11C. Under the 1229 Treaty of Paris, the count of Foix was forced to become a vassal to the king of France. In 1290 the Foix family inherited Béarn and settled there rather than submit to royal authority. In 1607 King Henri IV inherited the county and it was annexed to the crown.

The waters of the Ariège contain gold dust. Between the Middle Ages and late 19C, *orpailleurs* panned for gold in the sandy river beds. Nuggets weighing 15g/5oz were found between Varilhes and Pamiers. Pyrenean iron ore, highly reputed for its richness, was first extracted long ago. In 1833, seventy-four "Catalan" iron foundries were still supplied by the mine at Le Rancié, which closed in 1931.

SIGHTS

Château

Open Jul-Aug 9.45am-6.30pm; Jun and Sep 9.45am-noon, 2-6pm; May 10.30am-noon, 2-6pm (weekends and public holidays 9.45am-noon); Apr and Oct 10.30am-noon, 2-5.30pm; Feb-Mar and Nov-Dec 10.30am-noon, 2-6pm; Jan weekends 10.30-noon; 2-6pm. Closed Tue outside school holidays, and public holidays from Nov-Mar. 4.50€. 05 34 09 83 83. www.sesta.fr.

The Pont de Vernajoul bridge over the River Arget has a great view of the 10C castle. Simon de Montfort did not attack this sturdy stronghold during the Albigensian Crusade in 1211-17. But in 1272, when the Count of Foix ignored the sovereignty of the King of France, Philip the Bold's troops sacked the town and the count surrendered. In the 16C, Henri IV used the castle as a prison and it remained a place of internment until 1864. Today it houses a museum and offers a **panorama**★ of Foix, the Ariège Valley, and the Pain de Sucre ("sugar loaf") in Montgaillard.

The **Musée Départemental de l'Ariège** houses collections of military and hunting weapons that recall the castle's original function.

Église St-Volusien

Guided tours Jul-Aug 11am-12.30pm, 4-6pm; rest of the year; daily except Sun afternoon 11am-12.30pm, 4-6pm. No charge.

This fine Gothic church has a 14C nave, an early 15C chancel and a Renaissance altar of polychrome stone. Opposite the church (*no 1 Rue de la Préfecture*) see the elegant mansion decorated with caryatids.

DRIVING TOURS

1 ROUTE VERTE AND ROUTE DE LA CROUZETTE★★

Round-trip 93km/58mi – allow 5hrs. Head W from Foix along D 17. The road is usually blocked by snow from mid-December to mid-June between the Col des Marrous and the Col de la Crouzette. It may also be blocked at the Col des Caougnous.

Pont du Diable

A. Thuillier/MICHELIN

Route Verte★★

The "green road" climbs up the **Arget** (or Barguillère) **valley** through woodland and becomes steeper after La Mouline. In Burret, it parts company with the Arget and the landscape becomes pastoral.

Col des Marrous

Alt 990m/3 218ft.

From the pass, extensive views to the south overlook the Arget valley and Arize Forest.

The road climbs through a beech forest into fine views of the Plantaurel area and La Bastide-de-Sérou. Beyond the Col de Jouels, the road clings to the upper slopes of the wooded Caplong cirque, with panoramic views of countryside. In the background is the truncated pyramid of Mont Valier (*alt 2 838m/9 223ft*). **Col de Péguère** (*alt 1 375m/4 469ft*) offers an uninterrupted panorama.

Tour Laffon

15min on foot round-trip.

Follow the path to the right behind the hut.

Magnificent **vista**★ of the central and Ariège Pyrenees, from Pic de Fontfrède (1 617m/5 255ft) to Pic de Cagire (1 912m/6 214ft) beyond the Col de Portet d'Aspet.

Route de la Crouzette★★

This hilltop road skirts the bracken-covered crests of the Arize range and overlooks the forested cirques to the north and gently hollowed out Massat valley to the south.

Sommet de Portel★★

15min on foot round-trip.

Alt 1 485m/4 826ft. Leave the car in a wide bend on the road, at a mountain pass 3.5km/2mi beyond the Col de Péguère.

Climb the grassy bank to the northwest, to the foundations of an old beacon. Enjoy the **panorama** of the peaks in the upper Couserans region. From this summit, the old track drops down to the Coulat spring in just a few minutes, ideal for a picnic or a stroll. Beyond the Col de la Crouzette, during the steep descent to Massat via Biert and then D 618 to the left, is a view of the upper Couserans region and peaks below the Col de Pause, Aulus and the Garbet Valley.

Massat

This small local capital boasts a gabled church flanked by an elegant 15C octagonal tower 58m/190ft high. On the top, the muzzles of decorative cannon project through diamond-shaped apertures.

Continue along D 618.

East of Massat the upper Arac basin widens with attractive views of the Massat countryside. Farther on, the majestic Mont Valier range looms into sight and the road climbs to the Col des Caougnous. Before this pass, the gap formed by the Col de Port offers views of the jagged summit of Pic des Trois Seigneurs. The road winds through hamlets with impressive views of Mont Valier before entering a moorland of ferns and broom.

Col de Port

Alt 1 250m/4 100ft.

This pass marks a natural boundary between the "green" Pyrenees on the Atlantic watershed and the "sunny" Pyrenees towards the Mediterranean. The road traverses the Saurat valley's fertile land exposed to sunshine, and beyond Saurat is the Montorgueil tower and two enormous rocks named Soudour and Calamès.

Grotte de Bédeilhac and Tarascon-sur-Ariège

See TARASCON-SUR-ARIÈGE.

Leave Tarascon N on the road to Mercus-Garrabet, along the east bank of the Ariège.

Beyond the Pic de Soudour (alt 1 070m/3 478ft) look out for the Romanesque church of **Mercus-Garrabet** on a rocky outcrop in the middle of its graveyard.

Pont du Diable

Keep following the road along the east bank of the Ariège. Leave the car just beyond the level crossing.

This fortified bridge spanning the Ariège once struck terror into the hearts of local people. It was rebuilt over a dozen times as, legend has it, all the work done each day collapsed during the night – hence the bridge's name (*diable* = "devil"). Observe the system of fortification on the side of the west bank (door and lower chamber). Beyond the turn-off to Lavelanet, the **Pain de Sucre** ("sugar loaf") looms into view with the village of **Montgaillard** below.

Drive into the village and follow signs for "Les Forges de Pyrène."

Les Forges de Pyrène★

Open Jul-Aug 10am-7pm; Jun and Sep 10am-12.30pm, 1.30-6pm (Sun and public holidays 6.30pm); Apr-May and Oct-Nov 1.30-6pm (Sun and public holidays 10am-12.30pm, 1.30-6.30pm; end Mar-early Apr Sun and public holidays 10.30am-12.30pm,1.30-6pm; mid Feb-mid Mar and Christmas holidays 1.30-6pm. Closed mid-Jan-early Feb, mid-Nov–mid-Dec, 25 Dec. 7.50€ (children 8-11 years 4€, 12–18year 6€) 05 34 09 30 60. www.sesta.fr.

This open-air museum covering 5ha/12 acres celebrates 120 traditional crafts and trades, from the dairywoman with her dog team to the wax maker's candles. Workshops show smithies, bakers, sculptors and their like demonstrating their skills.

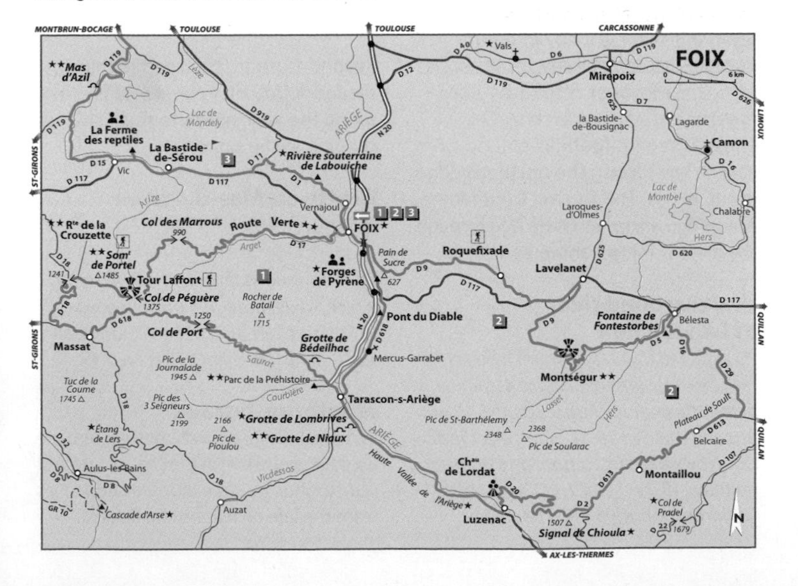

2 THE CATHARS

It was among the mountains around Foix that the Cathars, far from all easy means of communication, and therefore relatively safe, made their stronghold. The village of **Roquefixade**, a 13C bastide, is dominated by the castle on the cliff above, albeit one that is surprisingly easy to miss on a misty day. The present castle at Roquefixade, built to protect the lands of the Count of Foix, post-dates the Cathar episode, although the site did serve as a place of refuge for them during the crusade.

But it is **Montségur** that has become the symbol of the Cathar resistance, and the last place to hold out. In March 1244, the Cathars finally surrendered their stronghold, and more than 220 of them were burned alive en masse when they refused to renounce their faith. This castle, too, post-dates the Cathar period, but remains an imposing edifice perched high above a charming village.

Montaillou acquired sudden notoriety with the publication of a book – *Montaillou, village occitan de 1294 à 1324* – based on the records of the bishop of Pamiers at the time of the Inquisition. The **Château de Lordat**, now in ruins, served as a refuge for Cathars following the siege of Montségur.

3 PLANTAUREL HILLS

58km/36mi from Foix to Montbrun-Bocage – allow half a day. Leave Foix N along the west bank of the River Ariège to Vernajoul and turn left onto D 1.

These Pyrenees foothills extend from east to west along the northern edge of the range. The Touyre, Douctouyre, Ariège and Arize rivers have dug through the hills, forming transverse valleys.

Underground river of Labouiche★

guided tours (1hr15min) by boat for 12 people (last departure 45min before closing) Jul-Aug 9.30am-5.15pm; Apr-Jun and Sep 10-11.15am, 2-5.15pm; Oct-Nov weekends, school and public holidays 10-11.15am, 2-6.30pm. 8€ (children 6€). 05 61 65 04 11.

The **subterranean gallery** hollowed out by the Labouiche underground river was first explored in 1905. The boat trip runs 70m/230ft below ground level through high and low-vaulted galleries, with two changes of craft. Enjoy stalactites and stalagmites and the vision of a beautiful underground waterfall.

Continue along D 1, turn left onto D 11 and left again onto D 117.

La Bastide-de-Sérou

The church in the old part of town contains a 15C carved-wood crucifix from the Rhine region and a late 15C Pietà.

Continue along D 117 then turn right onto D 49 to Brouzenac.

La Ferme des reptiles

guided tours mid Jun-mid Sep 10am-noon, 2pm–7pm; Feb-mid Jun and mid Sep-mid Nov Sun, public and school holidays 2-6pm. Closed mid Nov-Jan. 7€ (children 5€). 05 61 65 82 13. www.lafermedesreptiles.com.

Hands-on guided tour of this zoo showcases reptiles from common grass snakes to powerful pythons, and iguanas and tortoises.

Return to D 117 and turn right then right again onto D 15.

Beyond Durban, the road follows the shaded Arize valley towards Mas-d'Azil. Along the way, note the small chapels clinging to the slopes.

Grotte du Mas-d'Azil★★

See Grotte du MAS-D'AZIL.

Continue alongside the River Arize, which flows through a narrow gorge, to Sabarat; left on D 628 to Daumazan-sur-Arize. In the village, left on D 19.

Montbrun-bocage

The small village **church** contains remarkable 16C **murals**★; in the chancel, note St Christopher, the Tree of Jesse and scenes from the Life of St John the Baptist.

ADDRESSES

STAY

Chambre d'hôte M. and Mme Savignol – *Chemin du Rec, 09000 St-Paul-de-Jarrat – 7km/4mi SE of Foix on N 20 then D 117. 05 61 65 14 26. Closed Oct-May – 3rms.* This spacious modern house designed by its architect owner offers every comfort. A large terrace overlooks the swimming pool and flower garden.

Lons – *6 Pl. G.-Dutilh – 05 61 65 52 44. Closed 21 Dec-5 Jan – 38rms – 7€.* In the old town dominated by the château, this historic establishment features simple, practical rooms. High ceilings, cornices and mouldings lend charm to the restaurant overlooking the Arlège. .

Auberge les Myrtilles – *At Col des Marrous – 19km/11.8mi W of Foix by D 17. 05 61 65 16 46. Closed 3 Nov-3 Mar, Tues from Sep-May, Wed from Mar-May and Mon. – P – 7rms – 6€.* Like a mountain chalet, this little inn is worth the climb to the pass. Regional fare is served in the terrace garden or in the cheery dining room. Modest rooms with pine furniture.

EAT

Au Grilladou – *7 R. La Faurie. 05 61 64 00 74. www.augrilladou.com. Closed Wed evening, Sat lunchtime and Sun from end Sep-late Jun.* This little restaurant on a pedestrian street at the foot of the château offers pizzas, salads and grilled dishes at very reasonable prices. Simple décor, efficient service and warm welcome.

Ferme-auberge le Plantié – *09000 Vernajoul – 5km/3mi NW of Foix on D 1 (towards Grotte de Labouiche). 05 61 65 41 96. Closed Sun evening – reservations required.* This farm inn surrounded by fields and woodland, offers a respite from Foix's hustle and bustle. Homegrown *foie gras* and poultry feature on the menu in the rustic dining room. Produce is for sale.

Le Phœbus – *3 Cours Irénée-Cros. 05 61 65 10 42. www.ariege.com/lephoebus. Closed 18 Jul-18 Aug, Sat lunchtime and Mon.* The owner offers a menu printed entirely in Braille for sight-impaired visitors. Comfortable dining room overlooks the Arège; traditional cuisine prepared with care.

Ferme-auberge de Mailhac – *Mailhac, 09000 Loubières. 05 61 05 29 51 – reservations required.* Exposed beams and stonework, antique furniture, peasants' tools: this 18C country farm has been beautifully restored. Family cuisine with traditional flair, served on the terrace in fine weather.

Ferme-auberge de Caussou – *09000 Cos – 2.5km/1.5mi au NW of Foix on D 117. 05 61 65 34 42 – www.ariege.com/fermedecaussou– closed 15 Dec-15 Mar – reservations required.* This cattle and sheep farm dates from the end of the 18C. The large dining room has stone and half-timbered walls and offers beef specialities such as ***blanquette au "millas."*** First floor rooms offer a view of the garden and valley.

SHOPPING

Azema Bigou – *Camp Redon, 09300 Lesparrou – 05 61 01 11 09 – Daily except weekends 10am-noon, 2-5pm.* This family-run business which has been making traditional horn combs since 1820, is the only such surviving entreprise in Europe. Tour the workshop and visit the shop.

SPORT

Centre équestre de Cantegril – *7km/4.2mi W of Foix on D 117 – 09000 St-Martin-de-Caralp. 05 61 65 15 43 http://perso-wanadoo.fr/cantegril-equitation-open summer 9am-9pm, winter 9am-7.30pm – closed Mon except during school holidays – 17€, per hour's ride (beginners or advanced).* This family-oriented centre offers introductory breaks or courses for perfecting techniques such as acrobatic riding, dressage, jumps and riding excursions. More sporty types may like to try out horse-ball and take part in competitions.

Grotte du Mas-d'Azil★★

This cave is one of the most interesting natural sights in the Ariège. It is also a famous prehistoric milestone in the scientific world as it is here that the Azilian culture was studied and defined.

Michelin Map: 343: G-6.
Info: 17 av. de la Gare, 09290 Le Mas-d'Azil ☎05 61 69 99 90. www.tourisme-arize-leze.com
Visit: Jul and Aug: guided tours (45min) 10am-6pm; Jun and Sep: 10am-noon, 2-6pm; Apr and May: 2-6pm, Sun, public holidays and Easter school holidays 10am-noon, 2-6pm; Mar, Oct and Nov: Sun and public holidays 2-6pm. Closed Mon (except Jul-Aug, school holidays and public holidays). 6.10€ (children: 3.10€), ticket combined with the museum. ☎05 61 69 97 71.
Location: North of Ariège, Mas-d'Azil is also a village 23km/14mi northwest of Saint-Girons and 34km/21mi northwest of Foix.
Don't Miss: The 'fawn with birds' carving at the Musée de la Préhistoire,
Kids: The Affabuloscope – www.affabuloscope.fr.

A BIT OF HISTORY

In 1887, as a result of methodical excavations, Édouard Piette discovered a new layer of evidence of human habitation dating from between the end of the Magdalenian (30 000 BC) period and the beginning of the Neolithic – this was the Azilian period (9 500 BC). Research continued under Abbé Breuil and Joseph Mandement, and others such as Boule and Cartailhac. The items excavated are exhibited in the cave and the town of Mas-d'Azil.

THE CAVE

The cave, hollowed out by the Arize underneath the Plantaurel mountain range, is 420m/1 378ft long with an average width of 50m/160ft. Upstream, the entrance forms a magnificent archway (65m/213ft high), whereas downstream, a flattened opening (8m/25ft or so) pierces a sheer rock 140m/460ft high. The path follows this passageway alongside a torrent, whose waters are gradually eroding the limestone walls, then under a majestic vault, shored up in the centre by a huge pillar of rock.

The four floors of excavated galleries run for 2km/1mi through limestone which is sufficiently homogeneous to prevent infiltration and propagation of moisture. The tour includes the **Salle du Temple**, a Protestant place of refuge, the intermediate floor of which was destroyed under Richelieu after the fruitless siege of 1625. Display cases contain exhibits dating from the Magdalenian (scrapers, chisels, needles, a moulding of the famous neighing horse head) and Azilian periods (harpoons made from antlers – the reindeer moved northwards as the climate became warmer – arrowheads, coloured pebbles and miniaturised tools).

The Salle Mandement contains the remains of animals (mainly mammoth and bear), coated in rubble and doubtless reduced to a heap of bones by subterranean flooding (the Arize, which was 10 times the volume that it is today, made the water level reach the roof).

The **Musée de la Préhistoire** *(☎05 61 69 97 22; www.sesta.fr)* contains the famous Magdalenian carving of a fawn with birds (*Faon aux oiseaux*).

In the nearby town of Castelnau-Durban is **Asinerie de Feillet "Asinus"** *(Le Feillet; visit by appointment; ☎05 61 96 38 93; www.asinus.fr)*, a donkey-breeding operation, which uses the animal's milk to make cosmetic products and fine soap.

Mirepoix

In the 13C, many Cathars settled in the town of Mirepoix, including the seigneur, Pierre Roger de Mirepoix who played an important role in the defence of Montségur during the 1243 siege. However, in 1209 Simon de Montfort had handed the city over to one of his lieutenants, Guy de Lévis. Shortly thereafter, Mirepoix was devastated by a flood from the waters of Lake Puivert. Jean, the son of Guy de Lévis, rebuilt the town in a safer place, at the confluence of the River Hers and River Countirou, and built the bastide we see today.

- **Population:** 3 060.
- **Michelin Map:** 343: J-6.
- **Info:** Pl. du Mar.-Leclerc, 09500 Mirepoix 05 61 68 83 76. www.tourisme-mirepoix.com.
- **Location:** 22km/13.75mi E of Pamiers.
- **Kids:** La fête médiévale in July and the international Marionette festival in August.

TOWN

All roads lead into the focal point of the place Principale, with its lovely arcades sheltering cafés and shops, and half-timbered houses supported on pillars.

Place Principale★★ (Place Mar.-Leclerc)

The main square is a pleasant place with public gardens, old-world shops and cafés surrounded by late 13C-15C houses. Note the **Maison des Consuls** decorated with carved heads.

Cathedral St-Maurice

The cathedral surmounted by an elegant Gothic spire, was begun in 1343 and only completed in 1865. Enter through the north door. The early 16C nave is the widest (31.60m/104ft) of any built for a French Gothic church. It is flanked with chapels set between the interior buttresses, following Gothic tradition in the south of France.

EXCURSIONS

Camon

8km/5mi SE, on D 625, then D 7.

The little village of Camon with its imposing **abbey** (*contact the tourist office. 05 61 68 88 26)* is set against the Ariège hills. Visit the fortifications, then enter the village through the Porte de l'Horloge to see the conventual buildings renovated by Philippe de Lévis, Bishop of Mirepoix, in the 16C. There are the remains of the old cloisters and the oratory decorated with 14C mural paintings.

Pamiers

21km/13mi E along D 922.

Pamiers is situated on the east bank of the River Ariège, on the edge of a fertile plain well protected from floods. Since it became a bishopric in 1295, it has been home to four monastic communities. The **Cathédrale St-Antonin**, in place du Mercadel, has a handsome bell-tower in the Toulouse style, resting on a fortified base. All that remains of the original 12C church is the doorway.

The church of **Notre-Dame-du-Camp** (*open daily except Sat-Sun 9-11.30am, 3-6pm)*, in Rue du Camp, features a monumental brick façade with crenellations and two towers, and a single 17C nave inside. Pamiers has several interesting **old towers**: the Clocher des Cordeliers (*Rue des Cordeliers*), similar to the tower of this name in Toulouse; the Tour de la Monnaie (*near Rimbaud School*); the square Tour du Carmel (*Place Eugène-Soula*), originally a keep built by Count Roger-Bernard III of Foix in 1285; the tower of the Couvent des Augustins (*near the hospital*); and the brick and stone Porte de Nerviau (*near the town hall*).

The **Promenade du Castella** is a walkway which follows the line of the old castle, the foundations of which are still visible between the Porte de Nerviau and the Pont-Neuf. At the top of the hill is a bust of the composer **Gabriel Fauré**, born in Pamiers in 1845.

Montségur★★

The holocaust of the Cathar religion is poignantly recalled by Montségur, which became the setting for the final days of the Albigensian Crusade, an episode that brought about the political downfall of Languedoc at the hands of the Capetian dynasty. High up on this rocky peak (alt 1 216m/3 989ft) stand the ruins of a castle.

- **Michelin Map:** 343: I-7 12km/7.5mi S of Lavelanet.
- **Info:** Montségur 09300; 05 61 03 03 0. www.montsegur.fr.
- **Parking:** You'll find a parking lot along the D 9 from which to begin the climb.
- **Location:** 12km/7.5mi S of Lavelanet and 33km/20.6mi SW of Foix.
- **Don't Miss:** The fortress view over the surrounding mountains.
- **Timing:** Walking up to the château and back takes about an hour and a half.

A BIT OF HISTORY

Explore the ruins of the castle at Montségur built over an old fortress in 1204. At one time it was occupied by 100 men under the command of Pierre-Roger de Mirepoix, and beyond its ramparts lived a community of Cathar refugees with their bishop, deacons and *parfaits*. In 1242 a band of Montségur men massacred members of the Inquisition at Avignonet, and this lead to the seige of the fortress in July, 1243 by Roman Catholic armies said to have numbered 10 000 men. An unprecedented truce was eventually agreed, allowing a 15 day period of peace.

Montségur was to become the property of the king, soldiers would be permitted to depart, ordinary men and women would go unharmed, as would any Cathar who recanted; those who did not would die. On 16 March, over 200 Cathars were pushed roughly from the castle and into a compound of fencing and posts; a pyre was lit beneath them, and they were said to have experienced the fires of Hell.

CHÂTEAU★

Leave the car in the car park along D 9. 1hr 30min there and back along a steep rocky footpath along the sheer face of the crag. Open May-Aug 9am-7.30pm; Apr and Sep-Oct 9.30am-6pm; Mar 10am-5pm; Nov 10am-5.30pm; Feb 10.30am-4pm; Dec 10am-4.30pm. Guided tours (1hr) available. Closed Jan, 25 Dec. 50min guided tour 3.70€, unaccompanied visit 4€ (children 2.10 €) combined ticket with Musée Archéologique. 05 61 01 10 27 or 05 61 01 06 94. www.montsegur.fr.

The castle **site**★★ on cliffs over 305m/1 000ft high offers a remarkable panorama over the Plantaurel, the deep Aude valley. Around the inner courtyard of the pentagon-shaped fortress, various buildings (living quarters, annexes) back onto the ramparts. The remains of the "Cathar village" at the foot of the rock in the Lasset Valley are being excavated.

VILAGE

The village lies at the foot of the rock in the Lasset valley. An **archaeological museum** (*opening times vary; 05 61 01 10 27*) in the town hall (*mairie*) contains information on Cathar philosophy and displays objects from the excavations. Furniture from the 13C and tools have enabled experts to trace occupation of the Montségur crag back to Neolithic times.

EXCURSION

Intermittent fountain of Fontestorbes

11.5km/7mi NE along D 9 then D 5.

Fontestorbes spring, which emerges from a rock cave in the Hers valley, is the resurgence of water that has soaked into the chalky soil of part of Sault plateau.

Saint-Girons

Le Couserans, Upper Salat and Garbet valleys★

Situated at the confluence of three rivers, St-Girons soon became an important market town and the main administrative centre of the Couserans region, known locally as "18 valleys" country. This region, just north of the "axial zone" or backbone of the Pyrenees, was closely linked with the neighbouring district of Le Comminges in medieval times.

- **Population:** 6 552.
- **Michelin Map:** 343: E-7.
- **Info:** Pl. Alphonse-Sentein, 09200 St-Girons ✆05 61 96 26 60. www.ville-st-girons.fr.
- **Location:** 28km/17.5mi S of Junction 20 of the A64 Toulouse to Bayonne Autoroute.
- **Don't Miss:** Le Col de Pause ; La Cascade d'Arse.
- **Timing:** Allow one and a half days to see the whole area.

DRIVING TOURS

LE COUSERANS

1 BIROS AND BETHMALE VALLEYS

Round trip from St-Girons. 78km/48mi – about 4hr. Leave St-Girons SW along D 618 towards Luchon.

The picturesque road follows the River Lez through a wide sunny valley dotted with attractive villages.

Audressein

This is a pleasant little village at the junction of the River Bouigane and River Lez.

The route follows the Lez Valley upstream.

Castillon-en-Couserans

This little village on the east bank of the Lez is built at the foot of a wooded hill. The 12C **Chapelle-St-Pierre**, in Parc du Calvaire, was fortified in the 16C.

Les Bordes

At the entrance to the village, next to a roadside cross, there is a scenic view of the oldest bridge in the Couserans area and the Romanesque church in Ourjout.

This marks the beginning of the Biros Valley.

Vallée de Biros

Climbing up the valley of the River Lez, the road passes a number of tributary valleys on the south side, at the far end of which are glimpses of the mountains along the border.

Sentein

This village makes a good base camp for mountain climbing.

Walking enthusiasts and nature lovers could continue to the end of the valley, the road ending at Eylie.

Turn around and go back down the valley to Les Bordes. Turn right on D 17.

Vallée de Bethmale★

The valley is wide open, its hilly slopes dappled with barns and tightly clustered villages.

The village of Bethmale used to be known for the imposing bearing of its population and their distinctive dress – the traditional men's jackets, for example, were made of raw wool with multicoloured facings – a fact which continues to intrigue ethnologists and experts in folklore, for similar garments are a part of ceremonial peasant costume in the Balkans.

Ayet

The church, built on a raised site, contains examples of 18C "primitive" woodwork.

About 5km/3mi farther on, park by the roadside near a sharp bend to the left and walk into Bethmale Forest.

Lac de Bethmale

15min on foot round trip. The lake sits in an attractive setting surrounded by beech trees.

The road climbs through a cirque of pastureland to Col de la Core, which looks back down over Bethmale valley. The road goes back down past orchards and barns to the junction of the River Salat and River Garbet near Oust, the geographic centre of the Upper Salat region.

Seix

The village is overlooked by a 16C château.

Vic

The **church** here is typical of those in the Ariège *département*, with a wall-belfry and Romanesque triple apse.

To return to St-Girons, turn left onto D 3 towards the Gorges de Ribaouto. Alternatively, you could continue your journey through the Upper Salat and Garbet valleys.

UPPER SALAT AND GARBET VALLEYS★

2 Round tour from Seix

78km/48mi – allow 1 day. From Seix, drive S along D 3 which follows the Upper Salat upstream as far as Salau, quite close to the Spanish border. For 10km/6mi beyond Seix, the road runs alongside the river; at the entrance to Couflens, branch off towards Col de Pause and Port d'Aula. The surface of this very steep, narrow road is poor and badly rutted over the final 3km/1.8mi (generally obstructed by snow from October to May).

The little road climbs above the impressive, forested Vallée d'Angouls. Off to the south, through the gap carved out by the Salat, the summits of the valley's last cirque can be seen above Salau; the highest is Mont Rouch (alt 2 858m/ 9 377ft). The route continues beyond the strikingly situated village of Faup, perched on a rocky ledge, to the pass.

Col de Pause★★

Alt 1 527m/5 010ft.

The road above the pass, on the right-hand slope beneath Pic de Fonta, offers a different **view** of Mont Valier on the far side of the Vallée d'Estours breach. The chasms gashing the east face of the summit and the ridges of its northern foothills are clearly visible.

Beyond Col de Pause, the steep and narrow road to Port d'Aula is in very poor condition. Return to Pont de la Taule and turn right on D 8.

The road follows **Vallée d'Ustou**, climbs for a few miles, and then drops down again in a series of sharp bends to Aulus-les-Bains. There are fine views during the descent.

Guzet

This peaceful winter resort, with its chalets dotted among fir trees, stands in very picturesque surroundings in the Upper Ustou valley.

Aulus-les-Bains

The sulphur, calcium and magnesium-containing mineral waters which rumble through Aulus are used to treat metabolic disorders. Aulus is a convenient starting point for excursions into the three upper valleys of the Garbet (the Fouillet, the Arse and the Upper Garbet), all of which abound in waterfalls and small lakes.

Continue SE up Vallée du Garbet. After 1km/0.6mi, park the car and take the signposted GR 10 path, on the right (5km/3mi on foot).

Cascade d'Arse
A. Thuillier/MICHELIN

Cascade d'Arse★

After crossing the river and winding south, GR 10 leads to the foot of these superb falls which plunge 110m/360ft in three separate stages.

Return to Aulus and take D 32 N down the Garbet Valley.

Vallée du Garbet★

This is one of those most regularly formed and best exposed valleys in the Upper Couserans. It was once known locally as *Terra Santa* (The Holy Land) on account of the large number of chapels and wayside shrines.

At the far end of the valley, the road goes through Oust then Seix.

Tarascon-sur-Ariège

Upper Ariège valley★ and Route du Port de Lers

Tarascon lies in an accessible, sheltered site in the centre of the Ariège valley floor. The surrounding chalk cliffs carved out by the river's passage, and the tributary River Vicdessos add to the charm of the site. The town is a major centre in the Pyrenees for speleological experts (mainly engaged in studies of the Neolithic period). It is also of interest to amateur enthusiasts, seeking to unravel the mysteries in the many caves that pepper the slopes at this confluence of river valleys, called Sabarthès in the Middle Ages.

Info: Ave Paul-Joucia, 09400 Tarascon-sur-Ariège, ✆05 61 05 94 94. www.pays-du-montcalm.com. Bureau d'Auzat, Rue des Pyrénées. ✆05 61 64 87 53

Location: 15km/9.5mi S of Foix on the N20.

PREHISTORY

With its 12 decorated caves and its splendid park devoted to prehistoric art, the Ariège *département* can rightly claim to be one of the main centres of Prehistory in France.

Parc de la Préhistoire★★

1km/0.6mi N. Drive along N 20 towards Foix then follow the signposts (parking area). Open Jul-Aug 10am–8pm; Apr-Jun 10am-6pm (Sat-Sun and public holidays 10am-7pm); Sep-Oct daily except Mon, 10am-6pm (Sat-Sun and public holidays, 10am-7pm). Closed Nov-Mar. 9.40€ (children 5-12 years 5.80€, 13-18 years 7€). 05 61 05 10 10. www.sesta.fr.

This museum of prehistoric art, located in a beautiful mountain setting at Lacombe on the road to Banat *(NW of Tarascon)*, is devoted to cave wall paintings. A resolutely contemporary building beside a lake houses the **Grand Atelier**, where visitors wearing infrared helmets go round an initiatory exhibition in semi-darkness. In the entrance corridor, drops of water falling on steel cylinders evoke the passage of time, while the history of art since its origins unfolds on screens on the walls. A reconstruction of the Dune des Pas gallery from the Clastres network at Niaux *(some sections not open to the public)* shows the poignant imprint of children's feet in the ground made thousands of years ago. From the same part of the subterranean network, the skilfully executed sketches of a weasel and a horse have been reproduced on a neighbouring wall. The next part of the visit is a short film on methods of excavation and dating used by archaeologists with an overview of cave wall art from all over the world. It illustrates the path taken by prehistoric artists as they searched for the right place to adorn with their images of animals.

The exhibition also covers themes such as painted symbols, carved weapons and jewellery, other carvings and techniques used by artists of the Magdalenian period. At the end of the exhibition there is a life-size reproduction of the Salon Noir at Niaux, its walls decorated with paintings of horses, ibex and bison and carved symbols.

Grotte de Niaux★★

5km/3mi S. Turn right off N 20 onto D 8. *See p358.*

Grotte de la Vache

8km/5mi S. Carry on along D 8 and turn right towards Alliat. guided visits daily except Sun: Jul-Aug 10am-6pm; May-Jun, Sep and school holidays 2.30pm and 4pm. 8€ (children over 5 years 5€). 05 61 05 95 06. www.grotte-de-la-vache.org.

This cave was occupied at the end of the Magdalenian period and consists of two galleries, one of which is called Monique, explored up until 1967.

Grotte de Bédeilhac

6km/3.7mi NW along D 618. guided visits (1h 30mn): Jul-Aug 10am–6pm; May-Jun, Sep and school holidays 2.30pm and 4pm; low season Sun 3pm. 9€ (children over 5 years 5€). 05 61 05 95 06. www.grotte-de-bedeilhac.org.

This cave has a huge entrance (36m/118ft wide by 25m/82ft high), large enough to allow a plane to take off and land during a film that was once shot here.

Grotte de Lombrives★

3km/1.9mi S. *See below.*

DRIVING TOURS

UPPER ARIÈGE VALLEY★

From Tarascon-sur-Ariège towards the Col de Puymorens – 54km/33.6mi – allow half a day.

The Ariège rises on the Andorra border, in the Font-Nègre cirque, and flows into the Garonne just south of Toulouse, having covered 170km/106m. In its upper reaches, the river flows along a glacial channel which widens out and changes direction at Ax. The traces of the old glacier are much in evidence around Tarascon. The Ariège then flows through the Labarre ravine, cutting across the limestone Plantaurel range to reach the Pamiers plain, laid down by the river's own alluvial deposits, where it finally leaves the Pyrenees.

Leave Tarascon along N 20 towards Ax-les-Thermes.

Grotte de Lombrives★

guided tours (1hr30min) on a tourist train: Jul-Aug 10am-7pm; Jun and Sep weekends and public holidays

10am, 10.45am and 2–5.30pm every 45 mins; May 2-5.30 pm every 45 mins; rest of year weekends 2pm and 3.30pm. tariffs vary according to circuit. 06 61 05 98 40/05 70 74 32 80. www.grotte-lombrives.fr.

These vast caves, south of Tarascon and just north of Ussat-les-Bains, have certainly been used as a shelter for many centuries. While the first people to enter the cave may have been seeking protection from wild animals or bad weather, later the cave become a hideout for bandits, or a place of refuge for those fleeing religious persecution. Today, visitors can take the short tour *(1hr 30min)* of the upper and lower galleries, and admire some of the spectacular formations, or one of the longer tours *(3hr or 5hr)* which are more adventurous and include views of an underground lake and many remarkable formations.

Beyond the dip in which the village of Les Cabannes lies, where the River Aston flows into the Ariège, the road enters the Sabarthès region. The steep valley sides, riddled with caves, make up the Val d'Ariège at this point – once a glacial valley, as its deep, symmetrical cross-section suggests.

From Les Cabannes, the narrow D 522 on the right leads to the Plateau de Beille.

Plateau de Beille ski area

Alt 1 800-2 000m/5 905-6 561ft.

This is one of the loveliest places for cross-country skiing in the Pyrenees, with beautiful views over the mountain range and the peaks of Andorra. The high altitude guarantees snow cover from December to May, on 65km/40mi of groomed trails. There is also a dog sled run and a snowshoe trail.

Continue along N 20.

The contrast between the slope facing the sun, covered with fields of crops and farmhouses, and the slope in the shade, clad in forests, is particularly striking along the next stretch of road. On the closer outcrops to the right of the road the Ermitage de St-Pierre can be seen, against the towering backdrop of the Pic de St-Barthélemy (alt 2 438m/7 999ft). On the way to Ax-les-Thermes, the road crosses the River Ariège to run along the south-west bank. On the other side of the river, the lovely Romanesque bell-tower of the church at Unac can be seen (*see AX-LES-THERMES driving tours map*).

Ax-les-Thermes

See AX-LES-THERMES.

Continue along N 20 towards Puymorens and Andorra.

The road runs alongside some of the bridges – remarkable engineering feats – of the trans-Pyrenean railway line, one of the highest in Europe.

Mérens-les-Vals

The village was rebuilt along the roadside after the fire that destroyed Mérens-d'en-Haut in 1811 in an arson attack by the "Miquelets" (Spanish mercenaries feared since the 16C), during the Franco-Spanish Napoleonic War.

Beyond Mérens and the Mérens gorge, the road runs upstream along the upper valley of the Ariège in between magnificent forests. On the left is the peak called "Dent d'Orlu."

Centrale de Mérens

Alt 1 100m/3 575ft.

This automated power plant is the middle stage of the hydroelectric project of the same name, made possible by the raising of the level of Lake Lanoux. This reservoir, fed by redirecting the tributary waters of the River Segre (and so also the River Ebro) in Spain into the Garonne Valley, is the object of an agreement between the French and Spanish governments, to compensate Spain for the loss of water. There is a viewing table to help you identify the mountain peaks at the far end of the valley.

L'Hospitalet

Alt 1 436m/4 667ft.

This is the first village in the Ariège valley. As the road climbs towards it, the landscape becomes bleaker and more rugged; keep careful watch for the troops of wild horses that frequently follow this route.

Beyond L'Hospitalet, one can either continue up to the **Col de Puymorens** (alt 1 920m/6 300ft) and drive through the Cerdagne region into Spanish Catalonia or follow N 22 towards Pas de la Casa and Andorra (*see ANDORRA*).

ROUTE DU PORT DE LERS

87km/54mi round trip – allow 3hr. Leave Tarascon-sur-Ariège towards Ax-les-Thermes and turn immediately right onto D 8 towards Alliat.

The Port de Lers road reveals the marked contrast between the wooded, coppiced landscape of the Atlantic watershed and the harsher, more rugged countryside towards the Mediterranean.

Grotte de Niaux★★

Take a road uphill just after leaving the village of Niaux. Guided tours by reservation only. Closed 1 Jan and 25 Dec. 9.40€.

The path to follow for the visit is long and over rough ground, wear sturdy shoes or boots in rainy weather; reservations strongly recommended. 05 61 05 88 37 or 05 61 05 10 10.

This cave in the Vicdessos valley is famous for its remarkably well-preserved prehistoric wall drawings.

On entering the cave's vast entrance porch, 678m/2 224ft above sea level, the extent of the glacial erosion that occurred many thousands of years ago in the massif of the Cap de la Lesse, where the cave is situated, becomes immediately clear.

The Cave★★ consists of vast, high chambers and long passageways leading, 775m/850yd from the entrance, to a kind of natural rotunda known as the **"Salon Noir"** ("Black Chamber").

Niaux – On the edge of the village, the **musée pyrénéen de Niaux** (*open Jul-Aug 9am-8pm; rest of year 10am–noon, 2–7pm; 8€. 05 61 05 88 36; www.musee-pyreneen-de-niaux.com*) is devoted to traditional popular crafts of the region. High on a rocky promontory, stand the ruins of the 14C Château de Miglos. The route continues to Junac, where the monument to the dead of the First World War was sculpted by Bourdelle. At Laramade the valley opens out to the left as it is joined by the Siguer valley. The Port de Siguer (alt 2 396m/7 860ft) is a pass that was frequently involved in the exchanges between France, Andorra and Spain.

The road follows the deep, rugged **vallée du Vicdessos** where the extended pasturelands play host to flocks of sheep and herds of cattle, with little sign of human habitation. To the right the villages of Orus and Illier perch on the steep mountainside.

Vicdessos

This mountain village is built on a site carved out by glacial action below the hanging Suc valley.

Take D 18 to the right up to Port de Lers.

Port de Lers

Alt 1 517m/4 980ft. As you climb, look back for a good view of the Goulier Valley. The road runs alongside a rushing stream, past several waterfalls. It is here

The Puymorens Tunnel

Since 20 October 1994, a tunnel has enabled traffic to avoid the trip across the Puymorens Pass itself, which tends to be a difficult journey in the winter. The building of the Puymorens tunnel, 4 820m/almost 3mi in length, was welcomed by local residents, although it was less well received by ecologists. The tunnel was a physical realisation of the economic and cultural opening up of the Ariège region to Catalonia. The improved communications between France and Spain are expected to be greatly helped by a road which is planned to link Toulouse and Barcelona. This highway between Toulouse and the Spanish border is due for completion in 2010.

Drystone Huts

The countryside around Auzat and Vicdessos is dotted with numerous drystone shepherd's huts – known as orris – with corbelled roof vaults covered with tufts of a particular species of local grass which keeps the water out. These huts were used by shepherds during the summer grazing season. Two footpaths have recently been marked out to enable visitors to explore the area and its huts, some of which date from the 13C. The first path leaves from Pradières and for much of its length follows the GR 10 long-distance footpath, going past the huts at La Caudière and Journosque and running above Lake Izourt and the Arties Valley. The second leaves from the Carla huts, which have just been restored, and leads past several more huts and the lakes of Roumazet and Soucarrane. Further details are available from the local tourist office (rue des Pyrénées, Auzat,. ✆05 61 64 87 53).

that the difference between the Atlantic and the Mediterranean vegetation can most clearly be seen.

Lers-Trois Seigneurs ski area

Alt 1 275-1 600m/4 183-5 250ft. Some 35km/21mi of cross-country trails go around the lake, at the foot of the Pic de Montbéas.

Étang de Lers★

This superb, solitary lake at the foot of the Pic de Montbéas is set in mountain scenery carved out long ago by glacier action. The road carries on round the Cirque de Lers, where horses, sheep and herds of cattle, complete with tinkling cowbells, share the pastures.

Peyre Auselère

This is the first hamlet in the sparsely inhabited Courtignou valley. Leave the car in the village for a short break at the side of the pleasant waterfalls of the Courtignou.

After Mouréou the landscape becomes less austere, then the road runs across narrow valleys cut through schist.

Massat

See FOIX: Excursions.

Drive E along D 618.

Col de Port

See FOIX: Excursions.

D 618 leads back to Tarascon-sur-Ariège.

ADDRESSES

STAY

Parc – *09400 Ussat. 2km/1mi SE of Tarascon-sur-Ariège on D 123. ✆05 61 02 20 20. Closed 3 Jan-6 Feb and 1 Nov-18 Dec. 49 rm. 6.50€ Restaurant.* This recently built hotel stands opposite a lovely wooded park. Rooms are sober and functional. There are thermal baths on the first floor, a covered pool and terrace solarium on the roof.

SPICE OF LIFE

Hypocras – *1 R. Croix-de-Quié. ✆05 61 05 60 38. www.hypocras.com. Tue–Sat 3–7pm. Closed holidays.* Hypocras is a spiced medieval aperitif. The original recipe has just been rediscovered and is a well-kept secret. Gaston Fébus, the 14C Sun Prince, is said to have been particularly fond of this beverage.

THE LITTLE IN AT NIAUX

La Petite Auberge de Niaux – *✆05 61 05 79 79. www.ariege.com/aubergedeniaux. Closed 3 weeks in Mar and 3 weeks in Nov. Reservation recommended.* Occupying a stone house, this likeable restaurant has a smart dining room with exposed beams, wooden chairs and coloured tablecloths.

WORKSHOP VISIT

Filature Jean-Jacques Laffont – *09400 Niaux. ✆05 61 01 43 43. Jul-Aug: workshop visits daily except Mon and Sat-Sun 3pm. – Closed Feb holidays, Sun and Mon off season.* See the wool weavers at work.

LE COMMINGES *and Haut-Garonne*

The region of Comminges, historically and ecclesiastically a province of the ancient kingdom of Gascony, lies at the centre of the Pyrenees, halfway between the Atlantic and the Mediterranean. It was at one time attached to the Couserans area and Val d'Aran. Geographically, Comminges extends from the heights of the Upper Garonne basin to the mild alluvial plains irrigated by the river after it emerges from the mountains. The southern limits include the peaks of the Maladetta massif (Pic d'Aneto, at 3 404m/11 164ft, is the highest peak in the Pyrenees). The northern flatlands stretch as far as Muret, 19km/12mi from Toulouse, taking in grandiose landscapes, a renowned spa (Bagnères-de-Luchon) and a famous artistic and spiritual centre (St-Bertrand-de-Comminges).

Geography

Granite and marble – The Luchon sector of the Pyrenees, still scoured by a number of glaciers, forms an east-west barrier of granite crests, all of them over 3 000m/ 9 800ft high. Within this massif lie the valleys of the Oô (Spijoles, Gourgs Blancs, Perdiguère) and the Lys (Crabioules, Maupas). Port de Vénasque, the most marked depression, is still almost 2 500m above sea level.

Limestone foothills north of the Marignac basin, on the east bank of the Garonne, culminate in Pic de Cagire (alt 1 912m/6 272ft), which rises from the forest to form a striking landmark in front of the snow-covered crests in the distance. The forest, mainly beech, continues eastwards as far as Massif d'Arbas (Pic de Paloumère – alt 1 608m/5 276ft), which is honeycombed with subterranean cavities and frequently used as a training ground for speleologists.

The lower part of Gascony, for years ignored by sightseers and tourists, has revealed evidence, during the past century, of an important colonisation in Paleolithic times (Aurignac, Save and Seygouade Gorges, near Montmaurin), as well as the remains of Gallo-Roman villas (Montmaurin). It was here in the 5C, before the first barbarian invasions, that the golden era of large estates, furnished with marble from the quarries of St-Béat, drew to a close in Aquitaine.

Pyrenean Garonne – In Vallée d'Aran, on the Spanish side of the frontier, the word *garona* is used for several different mountain streams. The largest, Río Garona de Ruda, rises near Monte Saboredo (alt 2 830m/9 285ft), south of Puerto de la Bonaigua (Bonaigua Pass). Several tributaries flow into the river, notably Río Garona de Jueu, which appears in the middle of a forest as a spring gushing from rock fissures in a fan of cataracts 30m/100ft high. According to the speleologist Norbert Casteret, who made a study of the north face of the Maladetta in 1931, the waters are a resurgence of melted ice from glaciers higher up the massif.

The Garonne reaches France at Pont du Roi. At this point, it is no more than a typical high mountain stream, with a steeply sloping bed and a variable flow, shrunken in winter and swollen in May and June. In the Comminges region, the Garonne is broadened by the Pique, the River Ourse and River Aure. At Montréjeau, flowing into a regular channel lying along the foot of the range from La Barthe-de-Neste to Boussens, it curves suddenly eastwards to cross St-Gaudens plain. The Boussens *cluse* marks the Garonne's final exit from the Pyrenees.

A Bit of History

A creation of the Romans – In the year 76 BC, the Roman Triumvir, Pompey, on his way to a campaign in Spain, annexed the upper valley of the Garonne and incorporated it in the Roman province of Transalpine Gaul. On his return four years later, he founded the town of Lugdunum Convenarum (today St-Bertrand-de-Comminges) attracting a population of convenae (people of all origins) largely drawn from the ranks of brigands, mountain dwellers and shepherds. The town prospered and grew rapidly. In the more remote valleys of the Pyrenees, local devotion to pagan deities was intense. These cults managed to survive for many years alongside both Celtic and Imperial divinities, dying out only gradually under the influence of Christianity. Most of the mountain churches in the Luchon area – especially in the Oueil and Larboust valleys – have stonework built into their walls which once formed part of the fabric of pagan temples.

Comté de Comminges – Comminges, which at first formed part of the Duchy of Aquitaine, was joined to Couserans in the 10C to create a fief under the suzerainty of the Comtes de Toulouse and reverted to France in 1454. However, the treaty of Corbeil, concluded between St Louis of France and Iago (James) I of Spain in 1258, reserved the claim of Aragón to the Vallée d'Aran, which today still forms part of Spanish Catalonia.

Failing agreement on the delineation of a new *département* to be called the Central Pyrenees, the Comminges district was incorporated into the Haute-Garonne *département* in 1790.

DRIVING TOURS★

1 ROUNDTRIP FROM ARREAU

52km/32mi – 4hr.

Arreau

See La BIGORRE. Leave E via D 112.

Jézeau

The village **church** houses a fine carved, gilded and painted wood Renaissance **reredos**. The wooden vault in the single nave displays paintings of the Last Judgement.

Go back to D 618 SE of Arreau.

The road climbs up Louron River valley, past scattered villages, some partly abandoned.

Vielle-Louron

Don't miss the Église St-Mercurial, one of the most beautiful painted churches in the Vallée du Louron.

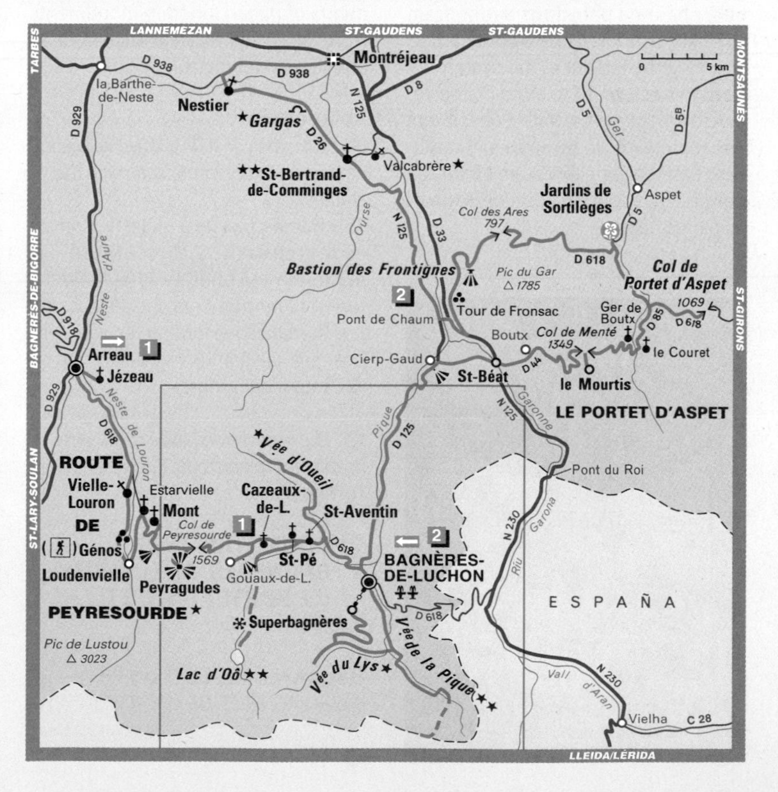

Génos

15min round trip on foot. At the top of the hill, just before the entrance sign, take the road leading up to the church.
Ancient castle ruins overlook a recreational lake and fine **view** of the valley and mountains.

Drive onto Loudenvielle on the other side of the lake.

Loudenvielle

L'Arixo offers an insight into life, traditions and religious art in the Louron valley (*open Jul-Aug daily except Tue 10am-noon, 2.30-6.30pm; call for other hours. 4.50€. 05 62 99 95 94 or 05 62 99 68 02/97 70).*

Follow D 25 running along the opposite shore of Génos Lake and drive to Estarvielle via Armenteule.

Mont

The Romanesque church with square belfry has fine **paintings** dating from 1574 and attributed to Melchior Rodigis adorning the interior of the church. Beyond the turn-off to Mont is a belvedere overlooking the Vallée de Louron. The road leads up through a magnificent Balestas pine forest, and through Col de Peyresourde, at an altitude of 1 569m/5 148ft.

Fresco in the church at Cazeaux-de-Larboust

A. Thuillier/MICHELIN

Peyragudes

This ski resort is a merger of the Peyresourde and Les Agudes ski resorts. The hilltop offers a **panorama** of the jagged Néouvielle massif. Take D 618 and the cliff road to Gouaux-de-Larboust for the **views**★★ over the Vallée d'Oô and the slate roofs of Oô village.

Ski area

Alt 1 600-2 400m/5 249-7 864ft.
17 ski lifts.
Here are 38 ski runs for skiers of all levels, and the ski pass is valid in the other Haute-Garonne resorts; ski tracks totalling 15km/9mi. The January Peyragudes Rider's Cup snowboarding competition is a popular event.

Cazeaux-de-Larboust

The church is decorated with 15C **murals**.

Chapelle St-Pé (St-Pierre-de-la-Moraine)

The chapel buttresses incorporate fragments of pagan funerary monuments. Here are many traces of ancient Celtic and Roman religions.

St-Aventin

Leave the car 100m/110yd before the beginning of the ramp leading to the church.
This hamlet boasts a majestic Romanesque **church** with sculpted 12C **Madonna and Child**★ and Gallo-Roman funerary monuments. Inside, note the pre-Romanesque font carved with symbolic animals (lambs, fish, doves) and the 12C mural paintings.

The tree-shaded road continues its descent towards the Bagnères-de-Luchon basin.

2 ROUNDTRIP FROM BAGNÈRES-DE-LUCHON (LE PORTET D'ASPET)

94km/58mi – 3hr

Bagnères-de-Luchon‡‡

See BAGNÈRES-DE-LUCHON.

Leave Luchon N via D 125.

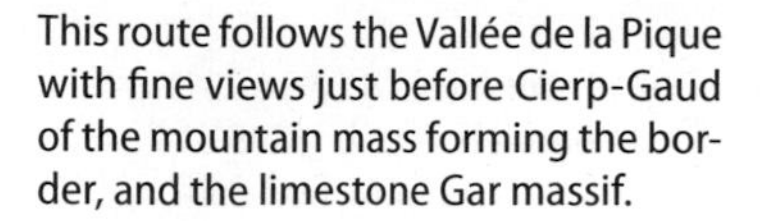
This route follows the Vallée de la Pique with fine views just before Cierp-Gaud of the mountain mass forming the border, and the limestone Gar massif.

St-Béat

The former stronghold of St-Béat commanded the site where Val d'Aran opens out into Gascony. The 12C keep, used as a clock tower, and a few crenellated ramparts are all that remains of the 14C-15C citadel.

The local white and grey marble which has made Béat famous since Roman times (*see MONTMAURIN*)became fountains and statues in the gardens of Versailles.

Le Mourtis

This quiet convivial winter sports resort has chalets and apartments graced by an ancient forest of lichen-covered firs. Descending the eastern slope of Menté Pass, the road passes through the Upper Ger valley scattered with villages and churches with triple-spired belfry-walls.

Col de Portet d'Aspet

Alt 1 069m/3 507ft.

Enjoy a lovely mountain panorama encompassing Mont Valier (*alt 2 838m/ 9 311ft*).

Turn back and continue the itinerary along D 618.

The route follows the Vallée du Ger through a spectacular wooded gorge.

Turn right onto D 5 towards Sengouagnet.

Jardins des Sortilèges

Open 10am-noon, 3-6pm: Jul-Aug daily except Mon; Jun and Sep Sat-Sun only. unaccompanied visit 4€, guided visit 6€. 05 61 88 59 51. www.jardins.terran.fr.

These seven gardens are devoted to the secrets of many common plants.

Turn back then right onto D 618 again.

From Col des Ares (alt 797m/2 615ft), the road descends through the pretty Frontignes countryside.

Bastion des Frontignes

The hairpin bend before the village of Antichan offers a fine **view** of the Luchon massif and its glaciers. *Viewing table.* Skirting Pic du Gar, the route affords views of the Garonne River valley, Bagnères-de-Luchon and the ruins of the **Tour de Fronsac**, remains of an ancient fortress of the Comtes of Comminges.

At Pont de Chaum (Chaum bridge) turn right on N 125.

St-Bertrand-de-Comminges★★

See St-BERTRAND-DE-COMMINGES.

Follow D 26.

Grottes préhistoriques de Gargas

Open Jan-Jun, and Sep-Dec 10am-noon, 2-5pm; Jul-Aug 10am-noon, 2-6pm. 7€ (children 4€). Closed 1 Jan. 05 62 39 72 39. www.gargas.org. Reservations advised at all times.

These two-storey caves contain 200 mysterious prehistoric handprints, and paintings, carvings of animals and fine concretions.

Nestier

The **calvary** on Mont Arès is remarkable, as are the 12 stone chapels built in 1854 by the vicar of Nestier. An outdoor theatre stages various shows.

Drive N along D 75 to St-Laurent-de-Neste and turn right onto D 938.

Montréjeau

This former *bastide* (stronghold) founded in 1272, offers several vantage points: place de Verdun (covered market and public gardens), place Valentin-Abeille (central fountain, arcading and fine timber-framed house at no 21), boulevard de Lassus (cliff road).

Bagnères-de-Luchon ♨♨

and local valleys

Bagnères-de-Luchon or Luchon as it is more commonly known, is a lively spa lying in a beautiful setting half way along the scenic Route des Pyrénées, appreciated for the restorative virtues of the fine climate as well as the waters. It is the busiest and most fashionable cure resort in the region, and also a tourist and winter sports centre with a wide choice of ski runs, climbs and excursions. In the winter, the town serves as a base for skiers attracted by the slopes at Superbagnères, the resort's high-altitude annex, and slopes around other resorts such as Peyragude and Le Mourtis.

- **Info:** Allées d'Étigny, 31110 Bagnères-de-L. 05 61 79 21 21. www.luchon.com.
- **Location:** In the far south of the Haute-Garonne.
- **Don't Miss:** Lac d'Oô and Vallée de la Pique.

A BIT OF HISTORY

Baths of Ilixo – In Gallo-Roman times, the Vallée d'One (the land of the Onesii) was already famous for its healing waters. Ilixo, the centre's divine custodian, presided over the magnificent baths which were second only to those in Naples, according to an inscription in Latin on the wall of the bath house. Excavations have revealed traces of enormous pools lined with marble, and systems for circulating warm air and steam. A Roman road linked the baths to Lugdunum Convenarum (St-Bertrand-de-Comminges).

The Great Intendant – In 1759, Baron d'Étigny, who lived at Auch, visited Luchon for the first time. The baron, who was Intendant (Royal Steward) of

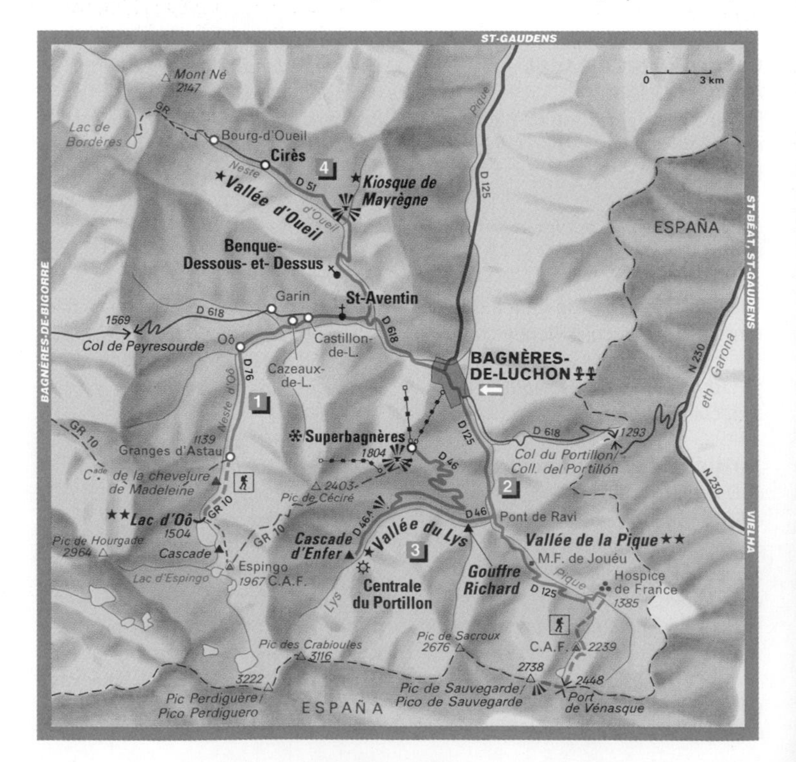

Gascony, Béarn and Navarre, was so impressed with the spa that he determined to restore it to its former glory. By 1762, a carriage road linked Luchon to Montréjeau in the north. The splendid avenue – which today bears the nobleman's name – was officially inaugurated, and planted with rows of lime trees which had to be guarded by soldiers as the inhabitants were hostile to such innovations. D'Étigny then replaced the original common pool with nine double troughs made of wood, each with a removable cover which had a hole for the bathers' heads.

This was a substantial improvement, though those taking the waters still had to undress in the open air, screened only by a board fence. D'Étigny was also the first person to think of appointing a regular doctor to a thermal spa.

The next step was to advertise the town. D'Étigny persuaded the governor of the province, Maréchal Duc de Richelieu, to take a cure. The duke, enchanted by the Roman ruins, was delighted. He extolled the merits of the spa back at the palace in Versailles and returned for a second cure. From then on, the town's success was assured. Even the premature death of Baron d'Étigny, in 1767, did not halt Luchon's development.

THE SPA

Life in Luchon centres on **allées d'Étigny**, the main avenue leading to the baths. The mansion at no 18, built in the 18C, was where the Duc de Richelieu resided. It now houses the tourist office and local museum.

Cures – Water from some 80 springs is piped from Superbagnères mountain to the spa. Combining the effects of sulphur and radioactivity to treat respiratory disorders, the Luchon cures have long been favoured by famous singers, actors, lawyers and preachers. More recently, there has been increasing success in treating rheumatic complaints and physiotherapy, by combining alluvial mud steeped in colonies of algae and bacteria giving off sulphur, found only in extremely hot water, with sulphurous emanations in a specially fitted-out grotto or **Radio-Vaporarium**, where the temperature is 38-42°C/98-109°F. The Radio-Vaporarium is located in Luchon's most luxurious spa treatment centre.

Lac d'Oô

A. Thuillier/MICHELIN

Musée du Pays de Luchon

Open 9am-noon, 2-6pm. Closed public holidays. 2€. (children 6-15 years 1€). 05 61 79 29 87.

This local history and folk museum features Iron Age artefacts, statues and votive altars from the Gallo-Roman period, as well as weavers' looms, shepherds' crooks, farming tools and religious items, mementoes of famous Pyrenees climbers, and photographs of the town and its thermal cures.

DRIVING TOURS

THE VALLEYS

1 Lac d'Oô★★

Leave Luchon via D 618, the road to Col de Peyresourde. At Castillon, fork left onto the Vallée d'Oô road (D 76), which skirts the base of the huge moraine sheltering the villages of Cazeaux and Garin.

2hr 30min round trip walk along the footpath marked GR 10.

Alt 1 504m/4 934ft.

The lake lies in a magnificent setting with the torrent from Lac d'Espingo, in the background, cascading down a

Mountains near Luchon in summer

spectacular 275m/902ft. The lake (covering 38ha/94 acres; maximum depth 67m/220ft) fuels the Oô hydroelectric power station.

2 VALLÉE DE LA PIQUE★★

Leave Luchon via D 125.

The road follows the Vallée de la Pique upstream, rising through meadows and beech forests. Cross the river and turn left onto the D 125 leading to the Maison Forestière de Jouéu of the University of Toulouse, a botanical laboratory.

Park the car and continue on foot.

Set amid forests, waterfalls and high pastureland typical of the Pyrenees, the Hospice de France, at 1 385m/4 544ft, makes an excellent base for ramblers. Hearty walkers can get a closer view of the highest point in the Pyrenees by leaving the Hospice in early morning on the mule track to **Port de Vénasque** (*alt 2 448m/8 032ft*). From the foothills on the Spanish side of the pass (*4hr 30min round trip*) or from Pic de Sauvegarde, which rises to 2 738m/8 983ft (*6hr round trip*), is a superb panorama of the Maladetta massif.

3 VALLÉE DU LYS★

32km/20mi S from Luchon to Superbagnères – allow 2hr 30min. Leave Luchon S along D 125 then turn right onto D 46. Park the car 2km/1.2mi beyond the second Pont de Ravi.

This valley's name *Bat de Lys* comes from *bat*, Gascon for *valley*.

Gouffre Richard

The base of an electricity pylon (*left*), offers a good view of a waterfall plummeting down into a rocky cauldron. After the turnoff to Superbagnères on the left, the road veers southwards, revealing a **panorama**★ of the highest peaks encompassing the cirque.

Park in the (free) car park of Les Délices du Lys restaurant.

Centrale du Portillon (Portillon Power Station)

The hydroelectric station is powered by water falling from 1 419m/4 656ft, a drop considered sensational when the station opened in 1941.

Cascade d'Enfer (Hell's Waterfall)

This is the last leap of the Enfer stream.

Return to D 46 and take the turnoff to Superbagnères on the left. The road runs through beech woods.

Luchon-Superbagnères ski area

Alt 1 440m/4 723ft-2 260m/7 413ft. This ski complex has 14 lifts, 24 downhill slopes for all levels and snow-making equipment.

Superbagnères★

The Superbagnères alpine ski centre can be reached from Bagnères-de-Luchon by cableway. The impressive Grand Hôtel built in 1922 and now owned by Club Méditerranée affords a **view**★★ of the Pyrenees and the Maladetta massif glaciers beyond.

4 VALLÉE D'OUEIL★

15km/9mi NW from Luchon to Cirès – 30min. Leave Luchon by D 618.

After several sharp bends, turn right on D 51. About 2km/1mi along, a track (*left*) leads to **Benque-Dessous-et-Dessus**, whose church in the upper village contains 15C murals. The lower **Vallée d'Oueil**★ has pretty pastures and clustered villages.

Kiosque de Mayrègne★

Free access to the viewing table on the café terrace.

The **panorama** encompasses the peaks along the Spanish border, from the sombre Vénasque massif, to the glacier-coated peaks of the Portillon d'Oô, and beyond, the highest peak in the Pyrenees, the Pic d'Aneto.

Cirès

The houses in this tiny picturesque hamlet have pointed roofs with lofts for storing the abundant hay.

ADDRESSES

STAY

⊖ **Hôtel des Deux Nations** – *5 r. Victor-Hugo. ℘05 61 79 01 71. www.hotel-des2nations.com – 28rms.* This hotel which has been operated by the same family since 1917, offers clean simple accommodation and a restaurant with an attractive flowering terrace.

⊖ **Chambre d'hôte Le Poujastou** – *R. du Sabotier, 31110 Juzet-de-Luchon. ℘05 61 94 32 88 – www.lepoujastou.com – closed Nov. – 5rms.* Facing due south towards the Luchonnais peaks, this 18C establishment is the village café, and also provides contemporary rooms painted in ochre hues.

⊖ **La Petite Auberge** – *15 r. Lamartine. ℘05 61 79 02 88. Closed late Oct-26 Dec – P – 30rms.* A hotel since the 1960s, this historic residence is situated mid-way between the Baths and the cable car for Superbagnères. Pleasant terrace.

⊖⊖ **Hôtel Rencluse** – *St-Mamet, 31110 Bagnères-de-Luchon. ℘05 61 79 02 81 – www.hotel-larencluse.com. Closed 5 Mar-30 Apr and 7 Oct-2 Feb – P – 24rms.* This friendly country family home has airy and comfortable rooms (those in the annex are quietest). Simple classic cuisine in a pleasant rustic setting.

EAT

⊖⊖ **Le Clos du Silène** – *19 cours des Quinconces. ℘05 61 79 12 00. Closed 17 Nov-10 Dec, Tue noon and Mon except public and school holidays.* Across from the spa centre, this new elegant restaurant has made a name for itself with its refined cuisine and excellent desserts.

⊖⊖ **Ferme d'Espiau** – *31110 Billière – 9km/5.4km outside Bagnères-de-Luchon. ℘05 61 79 69 69. Closed Mon-Wed except school holidays.* This mountain farm has a shaded terrace with a splendid view over the Peyresourde region. Enjoy hearty dishes and grilled meats in the pretty, country-style dining room.

SPORT AND RECREATION

Domaine skiable de Luchon-Superbagnères – *Alt. 1 440-2 260 m.* 14 lifts. This vast sunny ski area benefits from 28 runs and several snow cannons. The lower Coumes section has easy slopes for beginners. The Lac sector's intermediate runs traverse the forest, and thrill-seekers will love the black runs of the Arbesquens.

Golf club de Luchon – *Rte de Montauban, 31110 Montauban-de-Luchon. ℘05 61 79 03 27 – 9am-6pm – closed Nov-Mar.* Founded in 1909, this 9-hole course is the region's oldest. Fine mountain backdrop, clubhouse with restaurant and tearoom.

Rafting, Canoeing and kayaking centre – *31110 Antignac. ℘05 61 79 19 20 – www.antignac-rafting.com.* This watersports centre offers a variety of activities including canoeing, kayaking and air-boats, plus a host of other activities.

Montmaurin

Nestled in the Gascony hills, Montmaurin offers fine views of the Pyrenees and the archaeological attraction of the remains of a Gallo-Roman villa outside the village *(1km/0.6mi SE).*

- **Population:** 213.
- **Michelin Map:** 343: B-5.
- **Location:** Montmaurin is 10km/6.25mi S of Boulogne-sur-Gesse.
- **Don't Miss:** The Gallo-Roman Villa.

VISIT

Villa gallo-romaine

May-Aug 9.30am-noon, 2pm-6pm; rest of year daily except Monday 9.30am-noon, 2pm-5pm. Closed 1 Jan, 1 May, 11 Nov and 25 Dec. 05 61 88 74 73. 5€ (children under 17 free). http://montmaurin.monuments-nationaux.fr.

The descendants of a certain Nepotius inherited a territory near Montmaurin extending over about 7 000ha/17 300 acres. The original *villa rustica* built on this land in the 1C AD concentrated the agricultural and rural dependencies around the big house, much like large farms do today. In the 4C this residence was replaced by a marble mansion. This *villa urbana* was adorned with gardens, colonnades and statues of nymphs. Thermal baths and a system of hot air circulating beneath the tiled floors assured comfort, however inclement the weather. The mansion comprised 200 rooms arranged around a row of three separate courtyards graced with peristyles and pergolas. Summer apartments set on tiered terraces completed complex.

Museum

Ground floor of the town hall (Mairie). Open May-Aug 9.30-noon, 2pm-6pm; rest of year daily except Mon. 9.30am-noon, 2pm-5pm. Closed 1 Jan, 1 May, 11 Nov, 25 Dec. 05 61 88 17 18.

This museum is devoted to local prehistoric finds and the archaeologists who discovered them, and the local Gallo-Roman civilisation.

Viewing Table

800m/880yd N of the village.

The viewing table offers a **panorama**★★ extending from the Pyrenees in the Ariège département to Pic du Midi de Bigorre and Pic de Ger. Through the gap carved by the Garonne see the Maladetta massif and glaciated sections of the Luchon heights on the frontier.

DRIVING TOUR

Gorges de la Save

Follow the Save valley downstream for 1km/0.6mi, then cross the river.

Château de Lespugue

The ruins crown a rocky spur above Save gorge. Reach them on foot by descending through an oak grove and climbing through the woods on the opposite slope of the valley.

Return to the car and continue down to the river. Just before the bridge, turn left on D 9.

Gorges de la Save

Carving a deep channel through limestone folds of the Lesser Pyrenees, the Save torrent has hollowed out caves beneath the rock. Excavated between 1912 and 1922 by the Comte and Comtesse de Saint-Périer, several of these yielded finds from the Magdalenian (late Palaeolithic) and Azilian (transitional Paleolithic-Neolithic) periods. Notable is the statuette the **Vénus de Lespugue**, whose original is in the Musée des Antiquités Nationales in St-Germain-en-Laye.

La Hillère

On the way out of the gorge, archaeological digs have revealed a sanctuary including temples, baths, fountain and market, built during the 4C on the spot where the River Save resurfaces.

Return to Montmaurin.

St-Bertrand-de-Comminges★★

Haute-Garonne

- **Population:** 240.
- **Michelin Map:** 343: B-6 .
- **Info:** Les Olivétains – Parvis de la cathédrale. 05 61 95 44 44.
- **Location:** St.Bertrand is 10km/6mi S of Junction 17 of the A64 Toulouse to Bayonne Autoroute.
- **Don't Miss:** The Cloisters and the woodcarvings in the Cathedral.
- **Timing:** Allow half a day.

St-Bertrand is one of the most picturesque villages in the foothills of the Pyrenees, perched on an isolated hilltop at the entrance to the upper valley of the River Garonne. It is encircled by ancient ramparts and dominated by an imposing cathedral; the belfry-porch of this sanctuary, crowned by a defensive wooden gallery, is a landmark visible for miles around. Apart from its remarkable site★★, St-Bertrand is noted for the artistic and architectural treasure it contains, and for the charm of its steep, narrow streets crowded with medieval houses and artisans' workshops. In summer, in conjunction with nearby Valcabrère and St-Gaudens, the village holds a music festival. Today St-Bertrand-de-Comminges, formerly a stopping place on the pilgrims' route to Santiago de Compostela, remains one of the most impressive sights on any journey through the Pyrenees.

A BIT OF HISTORY

Memories of Herod – The town that preceded St-Bertrand enjoyed a distinguished Roman past as **Lugdunum Convenarum**, capital of the tribe of Convenae in the 1C BC; it is thought to have had between 5 and 10 000 inhabitants. The Jewish historian Flavius Josephus asserts that it was the place of exile of Herod, the Tetrarch of Galilee, and his wife Herodias, responsible for the decapitation of John the Baptist, four years after the death of Christ.

Ongoing **excavations** have unearthed two Roman bathhouses, the remains of a theatre, a temple probably consecrated to Rome and to Augustus, a 5C Christian basilica and a market place on one side of a large square flanked by porticoes.

Two Bertrands – The Roman colonial capital was eventually sacked by the Barbarians. Subsequently rebuilt on the hill only and enclosed within a wall, it was totally destroyed for a second time by the Burgundians in the 6C. For nearly

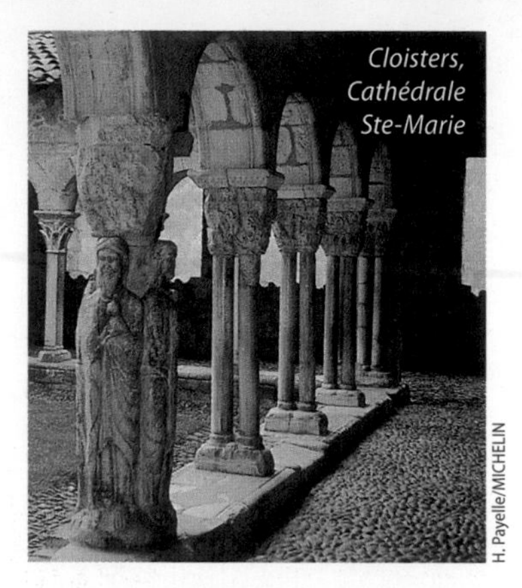
Cloisters, Cathédrale Ste-Marie

H. Payelle/MICHELIN

500 years after that the town stood empty and fell into decay.
Around 1120 the Bishop of Comminges, Bertrand de L'Îsle-Jourdain, appreciating the site of the old acropolis, had the ruins cleared and built a cathedral. To serve it he appointed a chapter of canons. The effects of the future St Bertrand's actions were felt almost immediately; the faithful flocked to the town that grew up around the church, and pilgrims broke their journey here. The town adopted the name of the man who had brought it back to life.
By the end of the 13C the cathedral founded by St Bertrand was no longer large enough for its congregation. A namesake, Bertrand de Got, who was himself destined to become Clement V, the first Avignon Pope, continued the bishop's work; the enlargement of the church was completed by his successors in 1352.

CATHÉDRALE STE-MARIE★

2hr Jun-Sep 9am-7pm (Sun 2-7pm); Feb-Apr and Oct 10am-noon, 2-6pm (Sun 2-6pm); May 9am-6pm (Sun 2–6pm); Nov-Jan 10am-noon, 2-5pm (Sun 2-5pm). Guided tours available by appointment (cloisters, terraces and treasury). Charge for Cloisters, Treasury etc.. 4€. 05 61 89 04 91.

The Romanesque part of the cathedral comprises the west front crowned with an 18C belfry, the porch and the three western bays; the rest is Gothic. The tympanum (west door) is carved with an effigy of Bishop St Bertrand and an Adoration of the Magi.

Cloisters★★

The pervading sense of spiritual peace and retreat from the world distilled by the architectural setting is enhanced by the temporal poetry of the splendid mountain landscape visible through the arcades of the south gallery, open to the outside world.
One gallery is Romanesque (12C), the other three are Gothic; the gallery adjoining the church was altered in the 15C and 16C – it houses several sarcophagi. The capitals in the cloisters are exceptional for their carvings showing biblical scenes, foliage and scrolls. Note the celebrated pillar portraying the Evangelists Matthew, Mark, Luke and John (**1**), with its capital representing the signs of the zodiac for each of the seasons.

Trésor★

The treasury is located above the northern gallery (*access from inside the church*). The upper level chapel and the former chapter rooms contain 16C Tournai tapestries, episcopal ornaments, a mitre, two liturgical copes (the needlework on these vestments represents the Virgin Mary and the Passion), and the shaft of St Bertrand's crook, fashioned from the tusk of a narwhal whale. The copes, exquisitely embroidered in *broderie anglaise*, were the gift of Bertrand de Got on the occasion of the translation of Bishop St Bertrand's relics (1309).

Canons' Chancel

The chancel boasts the superb **woodwork**★★ commissioned from sculptors in Toulouse by Bishop Jean de Mauléon and inaugurated by him in 1535.
The carvings include the rood screen, the choir screen, the high altar reredos – unfortunately disfigured by painting – a bishop's throne surmounted by a three-tiered pyramidal dome, and 66

stalls, 38 of them with tall backs and canopies. Piety, wit, satire – even lechery – are given free reign in the little world created by the craftsmen, the general theme of which is the Redemption.

St Bertrand's Tomb

The tomb is a 15C stone-built tabernacle in the form of a shrine, covered in paintings depicting the miracles of St Bertrand; it supports an altar.

Lady Chapel

The chapel, a 16C addition on the northern side of the church, contains the marble tomb of Hugues de Chatillon, who completed the building in the 14C. The lierne and tierceron vaulting signify the end of the Gothic period.

Nave and narthex

Space for the congregation on the outer side of the rood screen is somewhat limited but this is compensated for in the richness of the furnishings: a 16C **organ**★ (recitals are given in season); a 16C pulpit; the former parish altar, which dates from 1621. The altar frontispiece is made of Cordoba leather.

EXCURSIONS

Valcabrère★

2km/1mi N.

The 11C-12C **Basilique St-Just**★(*open Jun-Sep 9am-7pm; Apr and Oct 10am-noon and 2-6pm; May 9am-noon, 2-7pm;*

Basilique St-Just

Jacass/MICHELIN

2–6pm, Nov-Mar weekends and winter school hols 2–5pm. 2€ 05 61 95 49 06 or 05 61 88 31 31) stands isolated in the middle of fields.

The Romanesque basilica is one of the concert venues of the Comminges Music Festival.

St-Gaudens

17km/10mi NE via D 26, D 33 and D 8.

The **Musée de St-Gaudens et du Comminges** (*open May-Aug daily 10am-noon, 2-6pm; guided tour (30min) available; closed Sun, Mon, 8 and 21 May. 3€. 05 61 89 05 42)* focuses on local history, folklore and customs, porcelain, religious art, and has an important mineral collection.

ADDRESSES

STAY

Hôtel l'Oppidum – *R. de la Poste. 05 61 88 33 50. Closed 15 Nov-15 Dec, Sun evening and Mon off-season. 15 rms. 7€ Restaurant*. This establishment is very nicely situated at the foot of the Sainte-Marie cathedral. The rather confined rooms are reasonably well fitted-out; many come with new bathrooms. One room also has a terrace.

EAT

Chez Simone – *R. du Musée. 05 61 94 91 05. Closed Toussaint and Christmas school holidays, and evenings off-season* – A couple of streets from the cathedral, Simone offers simple family fare. The rustic dining room features wooden beams, chequered oilcloths and decorative copper vessels, while outside there is a terrace beneath the lime trees.

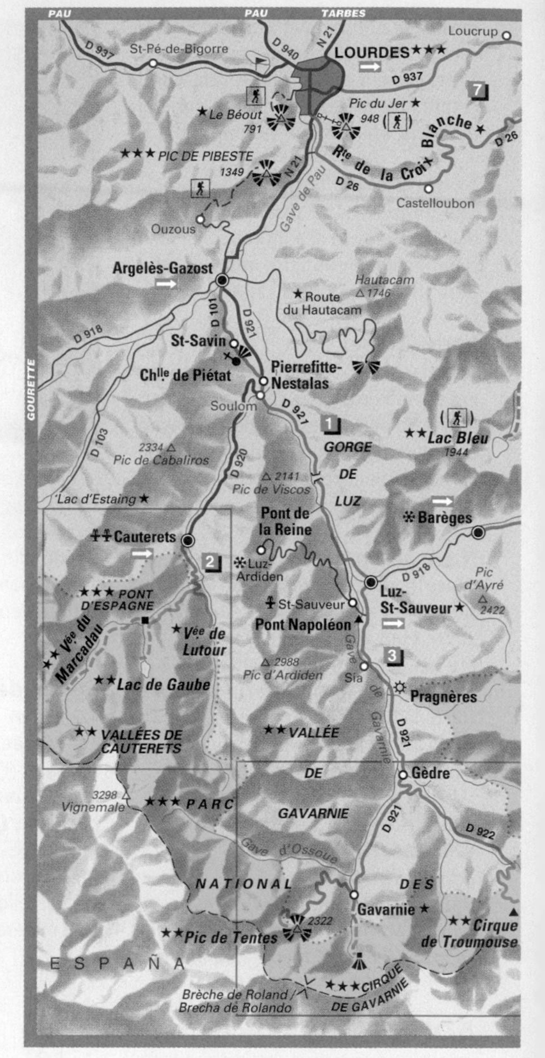

Bigorre, together with the Pays des Quatre Vallées, forms part of the attractive central Pyrenees with the tallest summits in the region, including Vignemale (3 289m/10 817ft), Pic Long (3 192m/10 469ft) and Balaïtous (3 146m/10 322ft). Visitors' favourites are Gavarnie, Cauterets and Pont d'Espagne.

Geography

Wild and craggy landscapes and foaming mountain streams compliment these landscapes within the Parc national des Pyrénées. The few border *ports* (small passes) linking this region with Spain are almost as high as the summits and can only be accessed by local mountain people and their mules. The Bielsa Tunnel, opened in 1976 at the head of Vallée d'Aure, facilitates summer traffic between Gascony and Aragon in Spain. Bigorre's busiest areas are in the prosperous basins of Lourdes and Bagnères and on the Tarbes plain.

A Bit of History

Comté de Bigorre – In 1097 Count Bernard II instituted local laws confirming the two-way relationship between the people and their overlord. The Salic Law, which prevented women succeeding to the French Crown in the north, did not apply in the Pyrenean States. This enabled formidable women like the 13C Countess Petronilla to rule the region. She had five husbands in 13 years, and daughters by each one of them, which made questions of succession extremely complicated. Bigorre was united with the French Crown in 1607.

Lavedan – The mountainous part of the Bigorre region, from south of Lourdes to the Spanish border, was known as the Seven Valleys of the Lavedan. In the 10C,

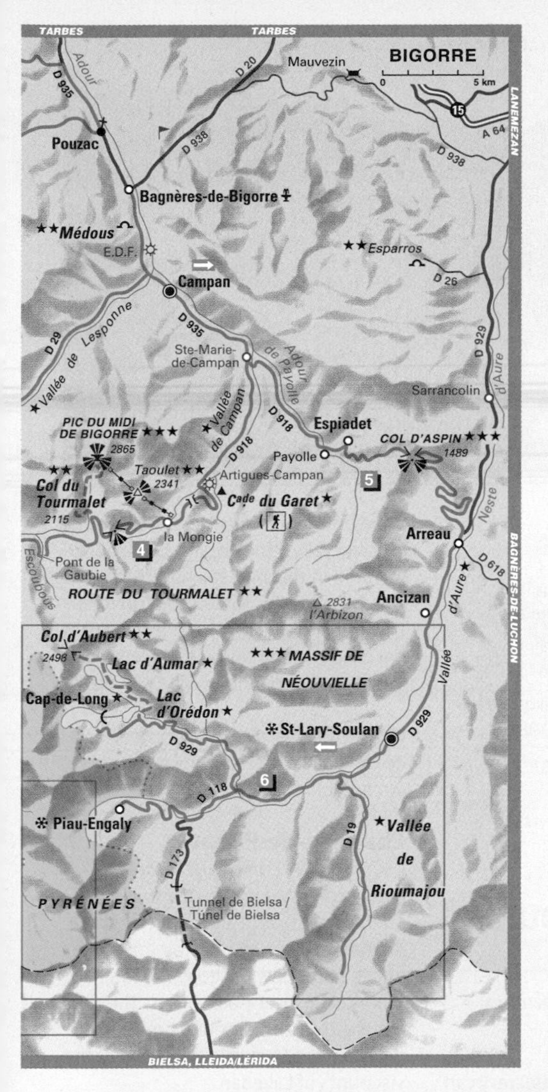

it was administered by viscounts, who were direct vassals of the Comtes de Bigorre. The largest valley, known then as the Vallée de Barèges, lies in the middle (Luz). Four other valleys – Azun, Estrem de Salles, Bats-Surguère and St-Savin (Cauterets) – were on the western side of the Gave de Pau.

The remaining two, less important, were on the east – Davant-Aygue and Castelloubon (Vallée du Néez). On his accession, the Comte de Bigorre would visit each valley to swear an oath to the Lavedan people to respect their customs. They would swear loyalty to him in return. As a precaution, hostages taken from the most prosperous families in the community were detained in the château in Lourdes until the safe return of the Earl.

Fighting spirit – The mountain dwellers of Bigorre, who are characteristically small, dark and wiry, are a robust people, who used to boast of being "always kings in our own country".

Men from the Vallée de Barèges helped to storm the castle in Lourdes and drive the English out of Castelnau-d'Azun in 1407. Warriors from Bigorre were just as ruthless with their own countrymen; in the 15C, a king's officer whose zeal had exasperated the inhabitants was thrown over a cliff.

Colbert provoked several revolts by trying to apply the salt tax in the region – where the population, in any case, obtained their salt from Béarn or Spain. One of the local gentry, Audijos, enrolled 7 000 men from Bigorre under his banner and defied the king's commissioners for 12 years.

Religious Bigorre – When Bernard I placed his fief under the protection of Notre-Dame du Puy-en-Velay (south-east of Clermont-Ferrand) in 1062, he could not have foreseen that, eight centuries later, the fame of a sanctuary in Bigorre would far outshine that of his patroness.

Today, millions of faithful from all over the world have been to visit Lourdes. Other abbeys have also played an important role in defining the spiritual identity of the region of Bigorre: St-Pé-de-Bigorre, St-Savin and St-Orens *(south-east of Condom).*

View from the summit, Pic du Midi de Bigorre

M.-H. Carcanague/MICHELIN

Highlights

1 Visit **Pont d'Espagne** (p395), and breath the mountain air.
2 Drive the road above Gavarnie to the **Col du Boucharo** (p400)
3 Take a walk up to the **Cirque de Gavarnie** (pp395, 397, 398)
4 Enjoy market day in **Argelès-Gazost** (p378)
5 See eagles fly in **Beaucens** (p378)

DRIVING TOURS

1 GORGE DE LUZ

18km/11mi. From Argelès-Gazost to Luz-St-Sauveur– allow 1hr.

At Pierrefitte-Nestalas, the itinerary can be extended to explore valleys around Cauterets – Pont d'Espagne, Lac de Gaube and Marcadau.

Argelès-Gazost

See ARGELÈS-GAZOST.

Drive S out of Argelès along D 101.

St-Savin

This village, which makes an interesting stop enroute to Cauterets or Luz, was once a popular Bigorre religious centre. Its **church** belonged to a Benedictine abbey, and its abbots were overlords of St-Savin Valley. The 11C and 12C building, fortified in the 14C, still has its internal watch-path, and a lantern-belfry crowns the 14C tower. The organ loft (16C) is decorated with masks whose eyes and mouths moved as the organ played.

Beyond the village, Chapelle-de-Piétat, perched on its rock, comes into view.

Chapelle-de-Piétat

Cars can be parked just before the bend in the road skirting the spur.
The sanctuary is in a very poetic **site**★. A small terrace shaded by lime trees offers a fine view of St-Savin Church set among chestnut trees. Across the river are the reddish ruins of Beaucens Castle, once the favourite residence of the viscounts of Lavedan.

Pierrefitte-Nestalas

The **Aquarium Tropical du Haut-Lavedan** (*open 9.30am-noon, 2-6.30pm daily except Mon. 8.50€ (children 5.50€). 05 62 92 79 56)* shows off a collection of tropical marine fauna from all over the world, including a live coral reef.
Beyond Pierrefitte is the awe-inspiring Luz gorge, with its dark walls of vertical shale and tumbling waterfalls. Before the mid-18C, the only direct way to Luz was via a precarious mule track called

Les Échelles de Barèges, the Barèges Stepladders. **Pont de la Reine** marks the end of the enclosed section. Beyond the bridge is Pays Toy (Luz basin) with villages nestled among the trees. The Néouvielle massif foothills appear to the left of Pic de Bergons. Then the route finally reaches Luz or, on the west bank of the river, St-Sauveur.

Luz-St-Sauveur★

See LUZ-ST-SAUVEUR.

2 VALLÉES DE CAUTERETS★★

See Parc National de Pyrénées.

Cauterets is a stepping stone to a fabulous region of superb high mountains and lakes beyond the locale known as Pont d'Espagne. You'll get wet taking a picture of the ancient bridge, but there is so much white and turbulent water here that a gentle spray will seem like gossamer. All the way up from the main valley, you are accompanied by the most dazzling displays of waterfalls and cascades.

3 VALLÉE DE GAVARNIE★★

See Parc National de Pyrénées.

The great central river of the Vallée de Gavarnie is borne from the mountain snows and the Grande Cascade, a torrent of turbulent turquoise bullying its way northwards through the steep-sided valley.

4 ROUTE DU TOURMALET★★

From Barèges to Bagnères-de-Bigorre. 48km/30mi – about 3hr. Col du Tourmalet gets blocked by snow Nov-Jun.

Impressive mountain road on the slopes near Barèges.

Barèges❄

This ski resort at the highest altitude of 1 250m/4 100ft was the cradle of the Pyrenean ski school. Today it is linked with three ski areas: Le Tourmalet, La Mongie and Super-Barèges. The road crosses the desolate Vallon d'Escoubous, where the stream winds through stony pastures. After Pont de la Gaubie, look for the craggy, glacier-flanked pyramid of Pic de Néouvielle. Before long, bold rocky crests appears to the south and to the north, a view of Pic du Midi de Bigorre.

Col du Tourmalet★★

Alt 2 115m/6 937ft.

From the pass, enjoy the **panorama** of rugged mountain summits and the distant Ardiden range. The old road from the pass takes ramblers to the summit of Pic du Midi (700m/2 297ft) in 2hr 30min. Return by cable car.

Pic du Midi de Bigorre★★★

Arrival: level 4. Alt 2 865m/9 400ft.

The summit of Pic du Midi de Bigorre can be reached only by cable-car, from

Observatory, Pic du Midi de Bigorre

La Mongie (see La BIGORRE) or along waymarked footpaths (warm clothing, sunglasses and suncream are recommended). Departure from la Mongie: Open Jun-Sep: 9am-7pm; Oct-May 10am-5.30pm. Closed Nov. 30€ (children under 12 years 21€). 0825 002 877. www.picdumidi.com. Visits are discouraged in the case of pregnant women, small children and those with cardiac conditions.

This familiar mountain landmark for the Gascons offers easy access and outstanding views. A glassed-in gallery and several terraces offer the most impressive **panorama**★★★ in the Pyrenees. As the 19C climber and explorer **Henry Russell** (1834-1909) said, there are mornings here "which must make the Saints long to be on Earth!"

The University of Toulouse Pic du Midi **Observatory and Institute of World Physics** founded in 1878 is one of the most important high-altitude scientific research centres in the world. Its interactive **Vaisseau des étoiles** museum offers a fascinating view of Earth from outer space and insight into mysteries of our universe.

La Mongie*

This high-altitude (1 800m/5 900ft) winter sports resort has downhill runs, cross-country ski trails and guided ascents, with ski slopes above Barèges. A gondola lift links the resort to **Le Taoulet**★★ (alt 2 341m/7 681ft) and splendid **views**★★ of the Néouvielle, Arbizon massifs and the Vallée de Campan★.

Cascade du Garet★

Park by the Hôtel des Pyrénées in Artigues. Walk through the hamlet and cross a small bridge upstream from the power station.

A footpath traverses the valley of the Garet tributary and a fir wood. Steps cut into the rock lead to a great view of the falls. The road descends into the **Vallée de Campan**★, with lush green meadows and Flemish-style houses and barns. After Ste-Marie-de-Campan, the D 935 north drops into the Vallée de l'Adour, with glimpses of the Pic du Midi de Bigorre.

Campan

The small town includes a 16C covered market, 18C fountain and 16C church.

Grotte de Médous★★

See BAGNÈRES-DE-BIGORRE.

Beyond Médous, D 935 continues to Bagnères.

Bagnères-de-Bigorre

See BAGNÈRES-DE-BIGORRE.

Espiadet

This hamlet is at the foot of the Campan marble quarry, whose famous red and white-veined green stone made the columns of the Grand Trianon in Versailles, and Garnier's Parisian Opera

Transhumance at Col d'Aspin

M.-H. Carcanague/MICHELIN

House. Beyond Espiadet, the road rises to Col d'Aspin, with glimpses of the Arbizon massif.

Col d'Aspin★★★

Alt 1 489m/4 884ft.

The Col d'Aspin offers a **panorama** of mountain masses, snowy peaks and distant forests. Beyond the pass, the narrow road drops steeply in hairpin bends, with thrilling views of the Arbizon massif and the Arreau basin.

Arreau

This pleasant town of slate-roofed houses was once the capital of the Four Valleys Region. Note the 16C corbelled **Maison du Lys and the halles** (covered market) with basket-handled arches forming the ground floor of the town hall. The chapel features a Romanesque doorway with marble columns and storiated capitals. The D 929 follows the River Neste d'Aure upstream along a wide and pleasant valley.

Ancizan

A group of 16C houses recalls the former prosperity of this small town, which boasted 1 000 weavers producing *cadis*, the coarse, thick cloth of undyed wool. The **Musée de la Vallée d'Aure** provides an insight into the life of the 19C valley's inhabitants *(♿ open Jul and Aug: 10am-noon, 2-7pm; Sep-Jun: Wed, Fri and Sat-Sun 10am-noon, 2-6pm; 5€; children under 15: 3€; closed early Nov to Dec school holidays; ☎05 62 39 97 75)*. Beyond Ancizan, the valley floor is studded with hillocks, remnants of the glacial moraine. Before Guchan, the road traverses the River Neste d'Aure with fine views of the mountain horizon.

6 MASSIF DE NÉOUVIELLE ★★★

See Parc National de Pyrénées.

A rich and fecund landscape punctuated by rugged and inspiring mountain summits and countless lakes awaits your visit to Néouvielle. Shuttle bus operates in summer months in some areas.

7 ROUTE DE LA CROIX BLANCHE★

See LOURDES.

The route fashions a journey through the foothills of the Pyrenees, heading south from Lourdes.

ADDRESSES

STAY

Chambre d'hôte Maison Buret – *67 Le Cap-de-la-Vielle, 65200 Montgaillard - 5km/3mi N of Pouzac on D 935. ☎05 62 91 54 29. Closed 1 week early Jun and 1 week end Oct - 3 rms.* Built in 1791, this fine farmhouse boasting a large fireplace in the dining room still exudes its traditional character. Note the sculpted staircase, pigeon-loft, stables, and small Folk Museum housed here. Warm welcome and good value.

Hostellerie du Val d'Aure – *Rte de St-Lary-Soulan, 65240 Cadéac - 3km/2mi S of Arreau on D 929. ☎05 62 98 60 63. Closed 27 Sep-19 May, Sat-Sun, Feb school holidays and Christmas - P - 23 rms.* What could be more relaxing than a few leisurely lengths of the pool in full view of the mountains. Rooms are classic in decor and dining room with terrace overlooks the garden.

Hôtel Catala – *65710 Beaudéan - 4.5km/3mi S of Bagnères-de-Bigorre on D 935. ☎05 62 91 75 20. Closed 3-31 Jan, Sun evenings and Mon – P – 22rms.* This hotel in a quiet spot in a small village has original frescoes adorning the doors of some rooms, and a view of the church from the terrace.

EAT

Ferme-auberge La Couriole – *65380 Layrisse - 4.5km/3mi Nw of Loucrup on D 937, D 407 then a B-road. ☎05 62 45 42 25 - closed 2-15 Jan and Sun evening to Thu evening - reservations required.* The stunning view from this farmhouse inn takes in the majestic summits of Midi de Bigorre, Montaigu and Vignemale. On the menu: garbure, magrets aux pêches and home-made pastries.

Argelès-Gazost

Argelès-Gazost, nestled in a mountain valley with a mild climate, became a residential spa town and resort in the 19C. Isolated by the gorges of the upper Bigorre to the north and the high valleys of Cauterets and Luz to the south, the Argelès basin contains many attractive villages and picturesque sanctuaries.

Location: 13km/8mi S of Lourdes.

UPPER TOWN

The oldest and busiest district stands above the fast-flowing Gave de Pau and its thermal cure resort. The drama of this **panorama** is heightened by the jagged teeth of the Viscos and the peaks of the distant Néouvielle massif. Enjoy fine valley and mountain views from the Terrace des Étrangers (Foreigners' Terrace) off place de la République.

Parc animalier des Pyrénées "La Colline aux marmottes"

Situated at the entrance of the town, coming from Lourdes along N 21.

In an hour you can discover nine Pyrenean species, including izard, ibex, bear and marmot. Three exhibition rooms display mounted wildlife from Europe, Africa, America's Far North; from wild boar to antelope and impala.

WALK

Pic de Pibeste★★★

4.5km/2.5mi N via N 21 and D 102 (left) as far as Ouzous. Car park near the church. Allow at least 4hr 30min round trip on foot. It is essential to have sturdy shoes or boots, warm clothing and a supply of food.

Despite its relatively modest height (alt 1 349m/4 426ft), the Pibeste Peak offers one of the finest views in the central Pyrenees. The footpath rises gently to the panorama over Ouzous, then climbs in hairpin bends, getting tougher and steeper. From the summit you can see southwards towards Pic du Midi de Bigorre, the Luz and Cauterets mountains, and several distant peaks over 3 000m/9 850ft high.

EXCURSIONS

Beaucens, Donjon des Aigles

6.5km/4mi SE. Take D 100 and then D 13 as far as Beaucens.There is a car park at the foot of the castle. Open for visits Apr-Sep 10am-noon. Flying demonstrations at 3.30pm, 5pm (Aug 3pm, 4.30pm and 6pm). 10€ (children 6€). 05 62 97 19 59. www.donjon-des-aigles.com.

The **Beaucens ruins** provide an atmospheric setting for showing off indigenous birds of prey: vultures, eagles, falcons, kites, buzzards, and owls and condors from the Andes, African vultures, and American eagles.

Route du Hautacam★

20km/12mi E. Leave Argelès via D 100, which crosses the Azun and climbs, after Ayros, the eastern slope of the Argelès basin.

Artalens

Beyond the village, the road crosses a small valley, where the remains of five old watermills, prominent throughout the Bigorre district in the 19C, flank a stream. After Artalens, the road offers **views**★ of the Vignemale beyond Vallée de Cauterets, and Balaïtous towering over the mountains surrounding Vallée d'Arrens.

Hautacam-ski area

Alt 1 500-1 800m/4 900-5 900ft.

This picturesque winter sports resort in a forest conservation is a hang-glider's paradise, and offers 11 lifts and 18 downhill slopes for all levels. Some 15km/7mi of cross-country trails offer beautiful views of the Argelès valley and the Pyrenees.

Arrens-Marsous

12km/7.5mi SW. D 918, which follows the picturesque Azun valley, leads to Arrens-Marsous on the edge of the Parc National des Pyrénées.

Monument des Géodésiens (Surveyors' Monument)

Outside Argelès-Gazost is a tower shaped like a geodetic instrument, which was built in 1925 on the hundredth anniversary of the first ascent of the Balaïtous crest, by a team of military surveyors.

Nestled in the valley, **Arrens-Marsous** is both a holiday resort and a centre for high-altitude rambles to the Balaïtous massif.

ADDRESSES

STAY

Camping Les Trois Vallées – *Sortie Nord. ℘05 62 90 35 47. Open 10 March-Oct– reservation recommended – 380 sites.* This campsite has a water sports complex, shops and a captivating flower display.

Chambre d'hôte Mme Vermeil – *3 r. du Château, 65400 Arcizans-Avant – 5km/3mi S of Argelès on D 101 then D 13 – ℘05 62 97 55 96 – 3rms.* This fine 19C residence typical of the Bigorre region has a splendid view of the valley, and rooms panelled and furnished in pine. The mountaineer owner is happy to advise walkers.

Chambre d'hôte M. and Mme Domec – *65400 Gez – 2.5km/1.5mi NW of Argelès on D 918 then a B-road. ℘05 62 97 28 61. Closed Oct-Apr – 5rms.* This old typical Pyrenees stone barn has been converted into functional guestrooms with mountain views, gardens and a barbecue.

Chambre d'hôte Eth Béryè Petit – *15 rte de Vielle, 65400 Beaucens – 8.5km/5mi SE of Argelès on D 100 and a B-road. ℘05 62 97 90 02 – www.berye petit.com – Closed 15 Dec-15 Jan – 3rms.* This fine 1790 family mansion with splendid views over the valley has been artistically restored.

Hôtel Picors – *Rte d'Aubisque, 65400 Aucun – 10km/6mi W on the rte du col d'Aubisque road. ℘05 62 97 40 90 – P – 48 rms.* Impressive facade, fine views of the Pyrenees and the added attractions of sauna, tennis, minigolf and indoor pool.

Chambre d'hôte Le Belvédère – *6 r. de l'Église, 65400 Salles-Argelès – 4km/2.4mi N of Argelès on D 102. ℘05 62 97 23 68. Closed Nov – 4rms.* The view from this traditional regional style manoir extends over the valley to the Pyrenees. Savour breakfast under the arbour in the park.

EAT

Lac d'Estaing – *Au Lac, 65400 Estaing. ℘05 62 97 06 25. Closed 16 Oct-30 Apr.* This small unpretentious inn serving classic cuisine has an enchanting setting with spellbinding lake and mountain views.

Auberge de l'Arrioutou – *Rte du Hautacam, 65400 Beaucens – 14.5km/9mi SE of Argelès on D 100. ℘05 62 97 11 32. Open during school holidays and public holidays.* 1 350m/4 428ft above sea level, these old stables converted into a restaurant feature a terrace with cartwheel tables, and afternoon pancakes with home-made jam.

La Châtaigneraie – *65400 Salles-Argelès – 4km/2.4mi N of Argelès on D 102. ℘05 62 97 17 84. Closed Jan and Mon. Reservation required.* In the warm atmosphere of this nicely restored grange, old furnishings glow in the candlelight. Summer offers the shade of the pergola, and winter the aroma of charcuterie grilling on the fireplace.

RECREATION

Les Gaves Sauvages – *2 av. des Pyrénées. ℘05 62 97 06 06 or 06 13 79 09 58 – July-Sep 9am-1pm, 3-7pm – Rest of the year by reservation.* Both beginners and experienced will appreciate the services of a licensed guide for exploring the waterways by canoe, kayak or raft.

Le Lac-Vert – *Village – 65400 Agos-Vidalos 6km/3.6mi SW of Argelès on N21. ℘05 62 97 99 99 – open from mid Jun-mid Sep: daily 10am-6pm.* This old quarry has been converted into a water sports park (*base de loisirs*) with pedalos, rafting, fishing, swimming pools, picnic areas and a bar.

Bagnères-de-Bigorre

This picturesque spa lies in attractive pastureland, north of the Vallée de Campan, on the west bank of the River Adour. The waters of the cure centre, which are rich in calcium and sulphur salts, are drawn from 13 bores. These are used in the treatment of respiratory, rheumatic and psychosomatic disorders. Bagnères-de-Bigorre is also a nucleus around which much Pyrenees folklore is centred, and was the home of a well-known 19C literary society, specialising in works inspired by the mountains. A choral society, known as the Chanteurs Montagnards, which travelled to London, Rome, Jerusalem and Moscow in the mid-1800s, still survives.

- **Info:** 3 allée Tournefort, 65200 Bagnères. ℘05 62 95 50 71. www.bagneresde-bigorre-lamongie.com.
- **Location:** 22km/14mi S of Tarbes.

SIGHTS

Parc thermal de Salut★

45min round trip on foot.

A gateway at the end of avenue Nogués *(south of the town plan)* marks the entrance to this 100ha/247 acre park, offering pleasant walks under fine, shady trees. The central avenue crosses the park and skirts the garden leading to the former Établissement thermal de Salut – the old spa centre.

Old Town

Among the attractions of this area (bordered to the east by the busiest part of the town, allées des Coustous) are **St Vincent's**, a 16C church with a belfry-wall pierced by three rows of arcades, **Tour des Jacobins**, a tower which is all that remains of a 15C monastery destroyed during the Revolution, and the **cloister ruins** on the corner of rue St-Jean and rue des Thermes. The charming **half-timbered house** at the junction of rue du Vieux-Moulin and rue Victor-Hugo dates from the 15C.

Musée Salies

guided tour Open Jun-Oct Wed-Fri 10am-noon, 2-6pm, weekends 3-6pm (Jul-Aug 7pm). 4€. ℘05 62 91 07 26. www.museesbagneres.fr.

This museum displays ceramics and paintings by Joos van Cleve, Chasseriau, Jongkind, Picabia and others.

Pastureland around Bagnères-de-Bigorre

J. Bouraly/MICHELIN

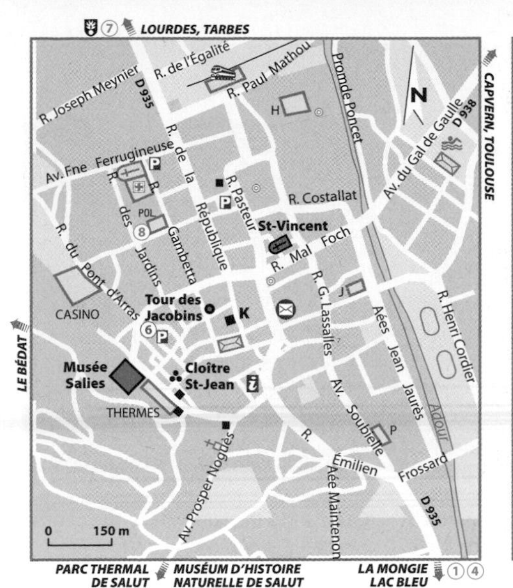

BAGNÈRES-DE-BIGORRE

WHERE TO STAY

Catala (Hôtel) .... ①
Hostellerie d'Asté .... ④
Maison Burret (Chambre d'hôte) .... ⑦
Petites Vosges (Chambre d'hôte Les) .... ⑧

WHERE TO EAT

Auberge Gourmande (L') .... ③

Maison à colombages .... K

Muséum d'Histoire naturelle de Salut

Open May-Oct daily except Mon and Tue 3-6pm; Nov-Apr Sun and Wed 3-6pm. 4€. 05 62 91 12 05 or 05 62 91 07 26 (winter months).
Displays of beautiful marble in colors you'd never dream of, from France, Europe and the Middle East.

Musée du Vieux Moulin

Open daily except Sat-Sun and Mon 10am-noon, 2-6pm. Closed Oct and public holidays. 2€. 05 62 91 07 33.
The old watermill is now a museum on crafts and folk traditions of the Bigorre mountain region.

EXCURSIONS

Gouffre d'Esparros★★

29km/18mi E along D84 and D26. Jun-Sep and school holidays guided tours (1hr) 10am-noon, 1.30pm-6pm (Jul-Aug: booking advised); rest of year weekends and public holidays 10am-noon, 2-5pm, Wed 2-5pm. Closed Nov to mid-Dec, 1 Jan, 25 Dec. 7€ (children 6-16 years 5€). 05 62 39 11 80. www.gouffre-esparros.com. Access is limited and bookings are recommended. Admire exceptionally fine aragonite formations like snow crystals and the **Salle du Lac gallery**.

Grotte de Médous★★

2.5km/1.5mi S by D935. guided tours only (1hr) Jul-Aug 9am-noon, 2pm-6pm; Apr-Jun and Sep-Oct 9-11.30am, 2-5pm. Closed mid Oct-Mar. 7.50€ (children: 4€). 05 62 91 78 46. www.grottes-medous.com.
In 1948 three speleologists from Bagnères-de-Bigorre, exploring a gallery which did not penetrate very far into the rock, discovered a blow-hole which suggested the existence of a substantial cavern close by. The site, not far from Bagnères, was near a resurgent spring watering the pools in the grounds of Médous Château. The cavers gouged a larger hole in the rock wall, squeezed through an opening not much bigger than a cat flap and found themselves in a series of galleries full of marvellous rock formations.
The 1km/0.6mi route twists through an enchanted land of stalactites, stalagmites and broad petrified flows of calcite (carbonate of lime) which have hardened over the ages into fantastic forms evoking waterfalls, hanging draperies, a magnificent church organ etc; the chambers have subsequently been given suitably fanciful names. After the Gallery of Marvels, the Hindu Temple, the Cervin Halls and the Great Organ Chamber, the visit includes a boat

Lac Bleu

A. Thuillier/MICHELIN

trip along a short subterranean stretch of the River Adour: the caverns have been hollowed out over the millennia by waters siphoned off from the main river through a tunnel near Campan, only emerging into the open-air again in the grounds of Médous Château.

Lac Bleu★★

Alt 1 944m/6 378ft.
Leave Bagnères S along D 935 and, beyond Baudéan, 1km/0.6mi before Campan, turn right onto D 29.
Walk through the Lesponne valley, starting from Bagnères-de-Bigorre. Allow 4hr there and back.

The road runs along the charming **Vallée de Lesponne**★, which offers views of Pic du Midi de Bigorre and Pic de Montaigu, especially attractive in spring and autumn when they are snow-capped. The Chiroulet inns, near the top of the valley, are the starting point of the walk to **Lac Bleu**, a lake-reservoir in a splendidly isolated spot.

WALK

Le Bédat★

1hr 30min round trip on foot.

At the junction of three by-roads, a path to the left leads to the Fontaine des Fées (Fairy Fountain) and a statue of the Bédat Virgin. Behind the statue, another path follows the crest to the lookout point (alt 881m/2 890ft), encompassing the Baronnies and Lannemezan plateau (*east*) and across the Vallée de Campan to the summits of the Central Pyrenees (*south*).

ADDRESSES

STAY

Chambre d'hôte Maison Burret – *Le Cap-de-la-Vielle - 65200 Montgaillard. 05 62 91 54 29. www.maisonburret.com. Closed Nov-Jan and 10 days in May – 2rms and 1 suite.* A lovely Bigourdan farmhouse dating from 18C.

Hostellerie d'Asté – *Rte de Campan. 05 62 91 74 27. www.hotel-aste.com. Closed 12 Nov-12 Dec – P – 21rms.* Guests may wish to try a little fishing in the river running at the bottom of the hotel's large garden, or enjoy a game of tennis. A friendly welcome, with small but well presented rooms, some of which have balconies.

Chambre d'hôte Les Petites Vosges – *17 bd Carnot. 05 62 91 55 30 - www.lespetitesvosges.com – 4rms.* A cost little place near the casino.

Hôtel Catala – *12 r. Larrey. 65710 Beaudéan. 05 62 91 75 20 – P – 24rms.* A peaceful setting in a small village; smart, functional rooms.

EAT

L'Auberge Gourmande – *1 bd Lyperon. 05 62 95 52 01. Closed Mon, Tue and Sun even out of season.* Opposite the casino, a family restaurant serving local cuisine.

Lourdes★

The town of Lourdes on the banks of the Pau torrent, is famous the world over as a religious pilgrimage centre. The great ceremonies, which take place from Easter to All Saints' Day, with processions of believers and invalids buoyed by faith and hope, lend the town its surreal atmosphere.

- **Population:** 15 100.
- **Michelin Map:** 342: L-4.
- **Info:** 1 av. Monseigneur Théas, 65100 Lourdes. ℘05 62 42 78 78. www.lourdes-france.com.
- **Location:** served by the Tarbes-Lourdes-Pyrénées airport 10km/6.25mi away, the TGV Atlantique train and by the Toulouse-Bayonne A64 autoroute.
- **Don't Miss:** The Lourdes wax museum.
- **Kids:** The Aquarium, Musée du Petit Lourdes and auquarium.

PILGRIMAGE

A few figures – Pilgrimages are mainly held at Easter and during Holy Week, attracting over 6 million visitors a year, three-quarters of whom are French and 80 000 sick or handicapped. Considered to be the most important place of pilgrimage in the western hemisphere, among French towns, Lourdes is second only to Paris in providing tourist accommodation (350 hotels, 40 000 beds). The town has 600 shops, 80percent of them selling religious items.

Some 700 special trains and 400 planes service Lourdes every year (via the Tarbes-Ossun-Lourdes International Airport). The TGV Atlantique (high-speed train) has been coming here since 1993. A ring road links D 940 and D 937 (Pau-Lourdes) and N 21 (Tarbes-Argelès-Gazost), diverting traffic from the town centre.

Bernadette Soubirous (1844-79) – The Soubirous family was poor and the parents, millers, brought up their four children with difficulty. Bernadette, the eldest, was born in Lourdes but spent her first few months with a wet-nurse at Bartrès, not far from Lourdes. In early 1858, when she was 14, she was living with her parents in their single room and attending a school for poor children run by the Sisters of Charity. At weekends, preparing for her First Communion, she went to parish Catechism classes.

On Thursday 11 February, a school holiday, Bernadette was gathering wood on the river bank near a local landmark known as Massabielle Rock, accompanied by one of her sisters and a neigh-

THE PRACTICAL PILGRIM

Tourist train – A small train runs from late Mar-early Nov; departures from place Mgr-Laurence every 20min between 9am-noon and 1.30-6.30pm; 8-11pm. ♿ Accessible to persons of impaired mobility. 5.50€ (children: 2.70€). **Discounts** – The "Visa pour Lourdes" pass allows you to visit all the main city sites by train for 29.50€ (children 6-12 15€; *2nd child free with two paying adults). ℘06 11 40 25 16. www.lourdesvisites.com.*

Pilgrimage – Before 5am, only the path to the Calvary is open (Les Lacets entrance). At 9am, pilgrims group on the Esplanade du Rosaire to celebrate the Queen of Heaven (Easter to 31 October). Then the grotto opens. Thousands of votive candles flicker along the path and in front of the entrance and pilgrims seeking miracle cures immerse themselves in blue marble pools. At 4.30pm, the Holy Eucharist is borne from the Chapelle de l'Adoration to the Esplanade du Rosaire and the blessing of the sick begins.

bour. It was then, in a grotto hollowed out from the rock, that she saw for the first time the vision of the Immaculate Conception; the beautiful Lady was to appear to her 18 times in total.

Massabielle Grotto – Although Massabielle Rock was not easily accessible at the time, a crowd of believers and unbelievers alike began to form around its cave, and increased daily as news of Bernadette's vision spread. During the ninth apparition Bernadette began to scrabble with her fingers in the earth floor of the cave and suddenly a spring, never before suspected, gushed forth and continued to flow in front of the startled spectators.

In 1862 the Church decided that a sanctuary should be built around the grotto. The first procession was organised in 1864 during which a statue dedicated to Our Lady of Lourdes, and lodged within the cave where the apparitions occurred, was officially blessed.

In 1866, Bernadette entered the St-Gildard convent belonging to the Sisters of Charity Order. She died in April 1879, was beatified in 1925 and canonised in 1933.

World's largest pilgrimage – The earliest visits, at first at parish and then diocesan level, were expanded in 1873 into a national event organised by the Fathers of the Assumption in Paris. A year later, a second event included arrangements for 14 invalids to be treated at Lourdes. From then on, attention to the sick and the lame became a priority.

Since the celebration of Bernadette's centenary in 1958 and the Vatican II Council, planning of organised pilgrimages has taken a new turn. All the great traditional events, such as the Holy Sacrament Procession and the Torchlight Procession, have been retained but there have been new initiatives concerning meetings, the reception of pilgrims etc. The grotto has been relieved of certain "accessories" and the Basilique du Rosaire, renowned for its organ and acoustics, now welcomes secular concerts and musical events.

Grotte miraculeuse

S. Sauvignier/MICHELIN

THE VICINITY OF THE GROTTO

The two avenues leading to Esplanade du Rosaire are used for important church rites and processions. A large statue of the crowned Virgin Mary stands at the entrance to the plaza.

Sanctuaries and places of prayer – The neo-Byzantine **Basilique du Rosaire**, consecrated and blessed in 1889, occupies the lower level, between two curving ramps embracing the wide circular esplanade and leading upwards. The basilica (2 000m²/2 392sq yd) can accommodate a congregation of 2 000. Mosaics in the side chapels represent the Mysteries of the Rosary.

Between this building and the Upper Basilica lies the crypt, reserved in the daytime for silent prayer. Bernadette was present when the **crypt** was consecrated on 19 May 1866. The neo-Gothic **Basilique Supérieure**, slender and white, was dedicated to the Immaculate Conception and consecrated in 1871. The interior comprises a single nave divided into five bays of equal size. Twenty-one altars and numerous votive offerings decorate the walls. The vaulting in the side chapels carries inscriptions quoting the words Bernadette heard from the Virgin Mary.

Below the Upper Basilica, beside the river, is **La Grotte miraculeuse**, the cave where the visions appeared; a Virgin Mary in Carrara marble marks the spot.

Basilique du Rosaire

©Serge Villa/Dreamstime.com

Two bridges span the river to give access to the north bank meadow where the **Espace Ste-Bernadette** has been built. The church in this complex, echoing the shape of the esplanade's open circle, was consecrated in 1988. It is large enough to accommodate 7 000 worshippers. The Assembly of French Bishops meets here each year in plenary session. Larger still is the colossal **Basilique Souterraine de St-Pie X**, the underground basilica consecrated on 25 March 1958 to solemnise the official centenary of the apparitions. The huge oval hall built beneath the esplanade, on the side of the southern avenue, can hold up to 20 000 pilgrims – more than the entire population of Lourdes. It is one of the largest churches in the world, measuring 201m×81m/660ft×266ft at its widest point and covering an area of 12 000m²/14 350sq yd. Pre-stressed concrete supports the low vaulting, with no need for intermediate columns.

The **Chemin du Calvaire** (Road to Calvary) starts beside the grotto and winds up through the trees past 14 Stations of the Cross in bronze statuary. It ends at the Cross of Calvary. Nearby are the grottoes of St Madeleine and Our Lady of Sorrows (Notre-Dame-des-Douleurs), in the natural cavern on the flank of Mont des Espélugues.

Pavillon Notre-Dame

On the ground floor of this building is the **Musée Sainte Bernadette** (*Apr-Oct: 9am-11.45am, 2-5.45pm; Nov-Mar: school holidays 10am-noon, 2.30-5pm. No charge. ☎ 05 62 42 78 78)* containing mementoes of the young saint, together with pictorial material on the site of the 18 apparitions and on the history of the pilgrimages.

The basement houses the **Musée d'Art sacré du Gemmail** (*Mid-Apr to end Oct 9am-noon, 2-7pm. No charge.*) (Gemmail is a technique which involves the juxtaposition and superposition of coloured glass fragments illuminated from the interior by artificial light, to produce a form of stained-glass window without the lead armatures). The museum compares this contemporary expression of sacred art with more traditional examples in the same material throughout the ages.

A gallery annex opens on alternate (*odd*) years to display the work of the winner of the biennial festival and competition devoted to religious art in this medium. The laureate is authorised to use the title Painter of Light.

COMMEMORATIVE SITES

Cachot

15 rue des Petits-Fossés.
Open Mar-Oct 9am-noon, 2-7pm; rest of year 9.30am-noon, 2-5.30pm.
05 62 94 51 30.

At the time of the apparitions, the Soubirous family were living in a state of penury in an unused prison.

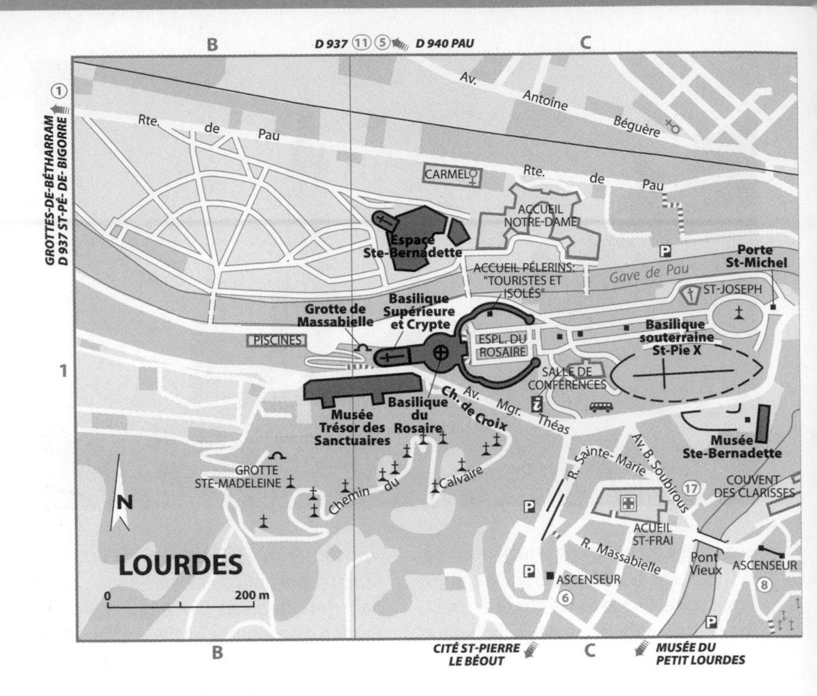

Hospice Sainte-Bernadette

Beneath the colonnade, follow the signs marked Visite Chapelle Open Mar-Oct 9.30/10am-noon, 3-6pm. No charge. 05 62 42 42 42.
Bernadette attended classes at this hospital run by the Sisters of Charity before being admitted as a boarder from 1860-1866. See personal souvenirs of the saint, and her communicant's cape, Catechism, Holy Bible and prayer stool.

Moulin de Boly: Maison Natale de Bernadette

12 rue Bernadette-Soubirous. Open 9/10am-noon, 2/3pm-5pm/7pm. No charge. 05 62 42 78 78.
The old mill where Bernadette was born on 7 January 1844 contains an exhibit on the Soubirous family.

Église du Sacré-Cœur

This parish church was built in 1867 and Marie-Bernard (Bernadette) Soubirous was baptised at this font.

Bartrès

3km/1.8mi N. As a baby Bernadette was entrusted to the wet-nurse Marie Aravant-Lagües in this village. **Maison Lagües displays** mementoes of Bernadette's return visits. (*Open early Apr to mid-Oct: daily except Sun 8.30am-noon, 2-6pm. No charge. 05 62 42 02 03.).*

SIGHTS

Château Fort★

Access via the Saracens' Staircase (131 steps) or the castle ramp from rue du Bourg, past the small Basque cemetery. Open mid Jul-mid Aug 9am-6.30pm; Apr-mid Jul and mid Aug-Sep 9am-noon, 1.30-6.30pm; Oct-Mar 9am-noon, 2-6pm (Fri 5pm). Closed 1 Jan, 1 and 11 Nov, 25 Dec. 5€ (children 6-18 tears 2.50€). 05 62 42 37 37. www.lourdes-visite.fr.
The fortress guarding the gateway to the Central Pyrenees, a fine example of medieval military architecture, became the state prison in the 17C and 18C. The Pointe du Cavalier (Rider's Bluff) panorama covers the valley of the Pau torrent and Pyrenean chain.
The **Pyrenean Folk Museum**★ exhibits local costumes, musical instruments, fine ceramics, a Béarnaise kitchen, *sur-jougs* (harness bells on wooden frames)

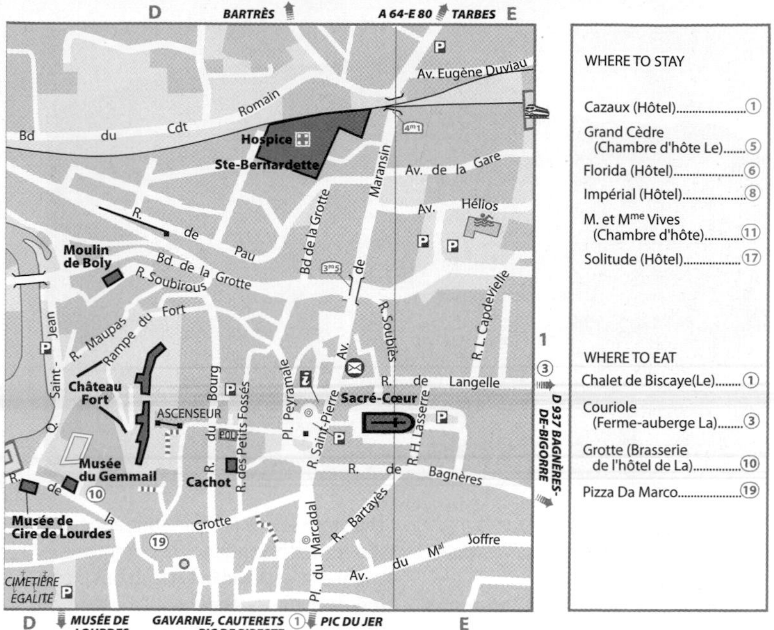

and displays on paleontology and prehistory.

Musée de Cire de Lourdes★

Open mid Jul-Aug 9am-6.30pm (Sun 10am); Apr-mid Jul and Sep-Oct 9am-noon, 1.45-6.30pm (Sun 10am-noon, 1.45-6.30pm). Closed Nov-Mar. 6.50€ (children under 12 years 3.20€). 05 62 94 33 74. www.museedecirelourdes.com.

This museum traces the life of Bernadette Soubirous. Its terrace overlooks the château, Pau torrent and sanctuaries.

Musée du Petit Lourdes

Open Apr-Oct 9am-noon, 1.30-7pm. 5.50€ (children 6-12 years 2.70€) 05 62 94 24 36.

This open-air reconstruction of Lourdes in the year 1858.

Musée du Gemmail

Open Easter-Oct 9am-noon, 2-7pm (Sun2-7pm). No charge. 04 47 61 01 19. www.gemmail.com.

This museum contains copies of artworks signed by Rembrandt, Manet, Van Gogh, Vuillard, Degas and Picasso.

Musée de Lourdes

Open Apr-Oct 9am-noon, 1.30-7pm. 5.50€ (children 6-12 years 2.70€). 05 62 94 28 00.

Reconstruction of the town centre around 1858 with artisans' workshops (shoemaker, cabinetmaker and basketmaker) and a pastoral shepherd's hut.

Aquarium

At the entrance to the town, on the Tarbes road. Open Jul-Aug noon-7pm; Apr-mid Jul and mid Aug-Oct 10am-noon, 2-6pm; May-Jun daily except Mon 10am-noon, 2-6pm. Closed Nov-Mar. 9€ (children 2-16 years 7€). 05 62 42 01 00. www.aquarium-lourdes.com.

This aquarium devoted to Pyrenean fish features a hands-on pool.

EXCURSIONS

Tarbes

19km/12mi NE of Lourdes by N 21.

Tarbes has been the capital of Bigorre since the 9C. Tarbes is also an important trading centre and the traditional home of fairs and markets, as well as the second-largest university centre in the Midi-Pyrénées region after Toulouse.

View to the Pic du Pibeste

© Charly Loumena/Fotolia.com

Pic du Jer★

59 av. Francis-Lagardère; the mountain summit is SE of Lourdes

A **funicular railway** offers a **panorama** of the Central Pyrenees (*open Jul-Aug 9am-8pm; Mar-Jun and Sep-Nov 9.30am-6pm. 9€ return (children 6-14 years 6.50€) one way. 05 62 94 00 41)* rising to 948m/3 110ft.

Le Béout★

Alt 791m/2 595ft. S of Lourdes.

Take the footpath from the Cité-Secours-St-Pierre rescue centre.

The **view** of Lourdes, Pic du Jer, Pic de Montaigu, the Argelès valley and Bat-Surguère and Castelloubon valleys is splendid. Continue along the ridge to the far end to admire the Pic du Midi de Bigorre, Lac de Lourdes, Pic Long in the Néouvielle massif, the Marboré Cylinder and Monte Perdido.

Pic de Pibeste★★★

Take N 21 from Lourdes to parallel the Gave de Pau. After 9km/5.5mi take D 102 to Ouzous, starting point for ascents of Pic de Pibeste.

See ARGELÈS-GAZOST.

St-Pé-de-Bigorre

Leave Lourdes by D 937. Before reaching St-Pé, cross the river then follow the road through Lourdes Forest and rejoin D 937 before St-Pé-de-Bigorre.

This small town's Romanesque abbey on the route to Santiago de Compostela, was the largest and finest religious monument in the Pyrenees until the Wars of Religion and 1661 earthquake.

DRIVING TOUR

7 ROUTE DE LA CROIX BLANCHE★

Round tour from Lourdes. 48km/30mi

local map see La BIGORRE. Leave Lourdes via D 937. It is a steep winding road through Pyrenean foothills. Turn right on D 935 to Bagnères-de-Bigorre.

Pouzac

The 16C church contains an impressive 17C sculpted altarpiece by Élie Corau from Bagnères and Jean Ferrère from Asté. Jean Catau painted the late 17C wooden vaulting.

Continue along D 26.

This road through valleys cooled with oak, birch and chestnut links the Ardour valley with Gave de Pau. The road climbs between the Oussouet and Castelloubon valleys, offering views of Pic de Montaigu and Pic du Midi de Bigorre, the lava flow of the Adour and the lowlands, and Balaïtous Massif.

Return to Lourdes via N 21.

ADDRESSES

STAY

Hôtel Cazaux – *2 chemin Rochers. 05 62 94 22 65. Closed end Oct-Easter – 20rms.* This small hotel near the market offers scrupulously kept rooms, a friendly welcome and reasonable prices.

Chambre d'hôte M. and Mme Vives – *28 rte de Bartrès – 65100 Loubajac – 6km/4mi NW of Lourdes on D 940 towards Pau. 05 62 94 44 17. www.anousta.com closed 11 Nov until Feb holidays – 6rms.* Enjoy a stunning backdrop of the Pyrenees and farm atmosphere. (Sheep, chickens and ducks are raised and consumed here). Four rooms with beams and sloping ceilings, and two others with a terrace. Fine garden and children's play area.

Chambre d'hôte Le Grand Cèdre – *6 r. du Barry, 65270 St-Pé-de-Bigorre. 05 62 41 82 04. www.grandcedre.com – 4 rms.* This lovely 17C manor features 4 rooms decorated in art deco, Louis XV, Henri II, Louis-Philippe. Dining room, music room and superb park with a vegetable garden.

Hôtel Florida – *3 r. Carrières-Peyramale. 05 62 94 51 15. www.ifrance.com/hotels-lourdes. Closed Nov-mid Mar. – P – 115rms – 6€. rest.* Well sound proofed rooms, some specially for families

Hôtel Solitude – *3 passage St-Louis. 05 62 42 71 71. www.hotelsolitude.com. Closed 6 Nov-31 Mar – 293rms.* This imposing modern hotel on the banks of the Pau has a small rooftop swimming pool. The rotunda dining room has a terrace overlooking the river. Rooms are comfortable. Ask for one on the riverside.

Hôtel Impérial – *3 av. du Paradis. 05 62 94 06 30. www.mercurelourdes.com. Closed 16 Dec-31 Jan – 93rms.* This 1935 hotel renovated in its original art deco style, is near the cave. Rooms are furnished in soothing mahogany tones and the classic style dining and drawing rooms open onto a small garden.

EAT

Pizza da Marco – *47 r. de la Grotte. 05 62 94 03 59. Closed Sun and Mon.* A pleasant place for crispy pizza and efficient service.

Brasserie de l'hôtel de la Grotte – *66 r. de la Grotte. 05 62 42 39 34. www.hoteldelagrotte.com – 1 Apr-31 Oct.* A dining room, veranda and terrace, and menu to suit all budgets. Extravagant diners can decamp to the more formal adjacent restaurant.

Le Chalet de Biscaye – *26 rte du Lac. 05 62 94 12 26. Closed Mon evening, and Tue.* A family restaurant with a tasty traditional cuisine. Shady terrace and warm dining room.

LEISURE ACTIVITIES

Sarl La Truite des Pyrénées – *65400 Lau-Balagnas. 05 62 97 02 05. Apr-Sep 9am-noon, 3pm-7pm; Oct-Mar daily except Sun 9am-noon, 3pm-6pm; closed 1st & 11th Nov.* Everything you need to know about trout fishing (equipment and instruction available) and a shop and exhibition on fish-farming.

Sports Nature – *3 imp. la Pradette, 65270 St-Pé-de-Bigorre. 05 62 41 81 48. www.sport-nature.org – early Apr-15 Sep: open 24hrs a day; winter: every day 8.30am-5.30pm.* Outdoor activity center with camping and *gite* accommodation.

Lourdes Forest – *Leave town on D 937; just before St-Pé, cross the river to the left then turn right onto the forest road.* The forest of maples, oaks and beeches has picnic facilities and attracts joggers.

Lac de Lourdes – *Leave town W along D 940 and turn left onto the path leading to the edge of the lake via l'Embarcadère restaurant.* This deep glacial lake offers water sports facilities (unsupervised bathing), fishing and golf (Lourdes 18-hole golf course to the south). A footpath around the lake offers fine views of the Pyrenean foothills.

Voie Verte des Gaves – This is a 17km/10.6mi-long cycle track between Lourdes and Soulom to the west. *Information from Association française de développement des Véloroutes et Voies Vertes – Délégation Grand Sud-Ouest – 5 av F.-Collignon, 31200 Toulouse. 05 34 30 05 59 – www.af3v.org.*

Parc National des Pyrénées★★★

The Pyrénées National Park was created in 1967 with the aim of preserving the beauty of the natural environment. The park varies in width from 1km/0.6mi to 15km/9mi, at an altitude between 1 000m/3 250ft and 3 298m/10 820ft (Vignemale). Including the Néouvielle Nature Reserve, the park covers an area of 45 700ha/176sq mi.
The Parc National des Pyrénées and its peripheral area attract thousands of tourists every year. In winter, the mountains are a kingdom where skiers reign – children and adults, beginners and experts alike. In summer, both experienced and occasional walkers take to the mountain trails. Although the park can be toured by car, the countryside is better appreciated on foot.

- **Michelin Map:** 342: K-5.
- **Location:** The park extends for more than 100km/60mi along the French border region from Vallée d'Aspe in the west to Vallée d'Aure in the east. Seven Maisons du Parc and several other seasonal outposts offer maps, brochures and tourist information (*see Addresses*).

GEOLOGY

The park itself is surrounded by a peripheral area of 206 000ha/795sq mi, including 86 municipalities in the Hautes-Pyrénées and Pyrénées-Atlantiques *départements*. The development programme in this area has concentrated on revitalising the pastoral economy of the mountain villages and improving tourist facilities.

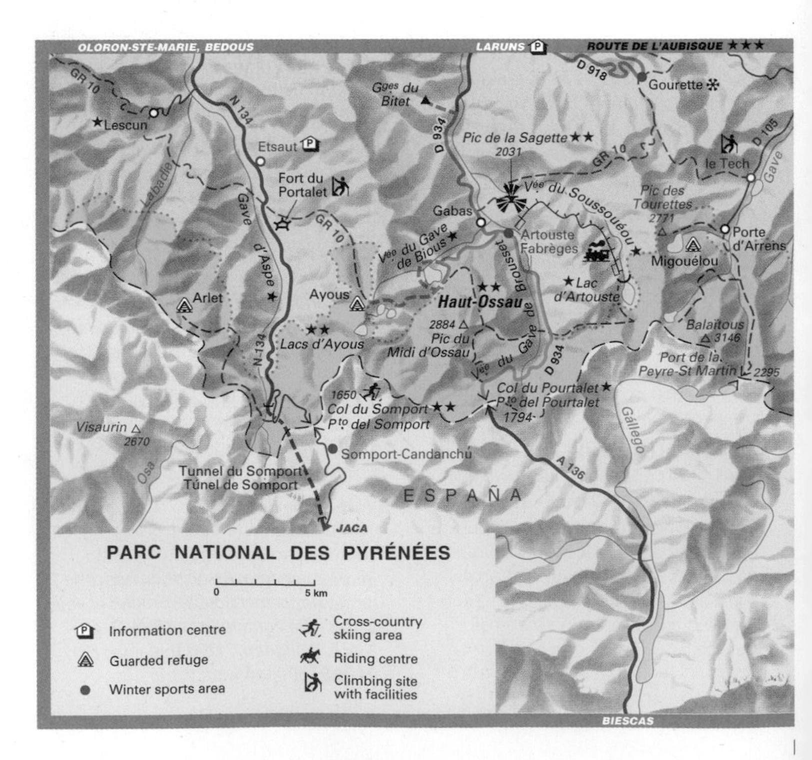

The park provides shelter for 4 000 izards, a local species of chamois, particularly in the valleys of Ossau and Cauterets, where they can be easily spotted, as well as more than 200 colonies of marmots. It is now very rare to catch sight of one of the few remaining brown bears, but it is not unusual to see vultures, royal eagles or huge bearded vultures in flight in a region still frequented by wood grouse, ptarmigan and Pyrenean muskrats.

DRIVING TOURS

2 VALLÉES DES CAUTERETS★★

Zoom map on p394.
For walks in the region, see pp398-399.

The town of Cauterets is a traditional base for holidaymakers, providing access to the neighbouring valleys of Cambasque, Jéret, Gaube and Lutour, with their foaming mountain streams right in the heart of the Parc National des Pyrénées.

Cauterets

Population: 1 107. Tourism office, 1 Pl du Mar-Foch, 05 62 92 50 50. www.cauterets.com. **Shuttle** – *This bus runs every 10min between Cauterets (Lys gondola station, beginning at 9am) and the Courbet gondola, and another shuttle connects the Cauterets bus terminal with the Pont d'Espagne. Schedule at the tourist office.* **Skiers' special** – *Ski passes are available at the cable-car departure points and many hotels.*

Set amid high wooded mountains where the Gave de Cauterets meets the Gave de Cambasque, Cauterets is one of the main spas in the Pyrenees. The town is also a bustling summer resort, a popular excursion and mountaineering centre (Vignemale) and a booming winter sports resort.

Enjoy a beautiful forest walk, following the **Sentier des Cascades**★ from Cauterets (*5hr round-trip*) or from the car park by Pont de la Raillère (bridge), near the Griffons spa centre *(4hr round-trip; shuttle service between Gare des Oeufs car park and La Raillère).*

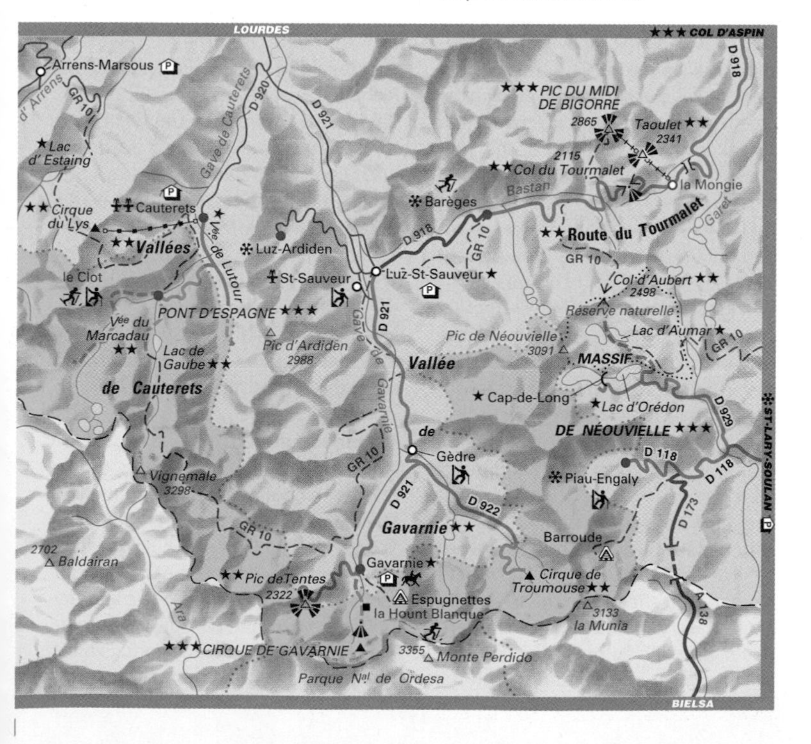

Birth and development of the resort – There is no known documentation on Cauterets before the 10C, although a 4C thermal pool was discovered in Pauze. In the 10C, Raymond, Earl of Bigorre, bequeathed the Vallée de Cauterets to St-Savin Abbey, on condition that the abbot build a church to St-Martin Abbey and "always maintain buildings here for the use of thermal cures." It was not until the 11C that the abbot of St-Savin took effective control of the valley and carried out the prescribed tasks. Cauterets-Dessus was built on the slopes of Pic des Bains near Pauze.

By the 14C, the village was bursting at the seams, so the monks gave permission to found Cauterets-Debat, and transfer the church, houses and baths to the present site on the plateau, overlooking the stream. This is where the town stands today.

The hot springs still remain the property of a group of surrounding municipalities, left over from the very old communal organisation of the Vallée de St-Savin (see **La BIGORRE** 1). Despite the discovery of the Raillère spring in the 17C, there was a dearth of activity. The opening of the Pierrefitte-Cauterets road in 1763 marked a major turning point in the prosperity of the resort, which reached a peak in the second half of the 19C. Construction of prestigious hotels and urbanisation of the left bank began in 1860. The inauguration of two electrified rail links in 1897-98 (*now closed*) increased the number of visitors.

Taking the waters became less popular in the 20C and the large 19C hotels have now been converted into apartments. Nevertheless, some thermal establishments have been revived including Thermes de César, which are open all year round, and offer skiers additional relaxation.

The sulphurous waters of the 10 springs which bubble out at temperatures between 36°C/97°F and 53°C/127°F have been proved effective in the treatment of respiratory and rheumatic disorders. Other specialised prescriptions also exist however, in accordance with the local saying, *A Cautarès, tout que garech* (At Cauterets, you can be cured of anything).

Famous visitors – The beneficial effects of the waters drew famous visitors. In the 16C, Marguerite de Navarre wrote a part of her *Héptaméron* while being treated for rheumatism. In 1765, a small building was constructed for Maréchal de Richelieu on the Raillère spring. During the Empire and Restoration, there was a new influx of celebrities. The most memorable visits were those of Queen Hortense de Beauharnais, the petulant Duchesse de Berry, George Sand, Vigny, Châteaubriand and Victor Hugo, who all found the setting appropriate for a few chapters in the novels of their whirlwind lives.

The Spa – The thermal district is characterised by its narrow streets and high houses clustered on the right bank of the river, at the foot of Thermes de César, modelled on the thermal baths of Antiquity (triangular pediment and marble columns). Note, opposite the church, the lovely façade adorned with wrought-iron balconies and grey-marble window frames. There are other noteworthy façades along rue de la Raillère and rue Richelieu.

Early 20C town – On the left bank, boulevard Latapie-Flurin is bordered with luxury hotels built during Cauterets' heyday. Hôtel Continental and Hôtel d'Angleterre, founded by Alphonse Meillon (one of the gentlemen innkeepers synonymous with the popularity of the Pyrenees at the time), have impressive neo-Classical façades, lavishly decorated with cornices, pillars, caryatids and wrought-iron balconies.

Esplanade des Œufs

Named after the Œufs spring, this is lined with boutiques built from metallic structures left over from the 1889 Paris World Fair. The Gare des Œufs provides a bus shuttle service to the Griffons spa centre. The astonishing wood construction which formed part of the Norwegian pavilion at the 1889 World Exhibition is now the **railway station**.

USEFUL ADDRESSES

Parc National des Pyrénées – *59 rte de Pau, 65000 Tarbes ☏05 62 44 36 60. www.parc-pyrenees.com.*

Maisons du Parc – These visitor centres provide information on the flora and fauna in the park, hiking in the mountains and present exhibits on topics such as the Pyrenean bear and the history of mountain exploration. Maison du Parc **(Vallée d'Aure)** – *65170 St-Lary-Soulan – ☏05 62 39 40 91*; Maison du Parc **(Vallée de Luz-Gavarnie)** – *65120 Luz-St-Sauveur – ☏05 62 92 38 38;* Maison du Parc **(Vallée de Luz-Gavarnie)** – *65120 Gavarnie – ☏05 62 92 42 48*; Maison du Parc **(Vallée de Cauterets)**, *65110 Cauterets – ☏05 62 92 52 56*; Maison du Parc **(Vallée d'Azun)** – *65400 Arrens-Marsous – ☏ 05 62 97 43 13*; Maison du Parc **(Vallée d'Ossau)** – *64440 Laruns. ☏05 59 05 41 59*; Maison du Parc **(Vallée d'Aspe)** – *64880 Etsaut. ☏05 59 34 88 30.* Information points in summer: **Réserve Naturelle du Néouvielle** (Vallée d'Aure) and **Pont d'Espagne** (Vallée du Cauterets).

Leisure and Recreation

Activities in the Parc National des Pyrénées – There are more than 350km/210mi of marked footpaths in the park. The GR 10, sentier de grande randonnée, crosses the park in several places.

Hunting, picking flowers, lighting campfires, and bringing in dogs are all prohibited. However, fishing in the rapid streams and the park's 250 lakes is subject to ordinary regulations on the sport.

Ski area

Alt 1 450-1 630m/4 757-5 348ft. The ski fields in Cauterets are divided into two parts. Cirque du Lys is the largest and has a constant snowfall from December through to May, with a wide variety of runs (25 in all) suitable for both beginners and experienced skiers. It has a chair-lift, a gondola lift and about 15 drag lifts. Weather permitting, it is possible to ski down to Cambasque (where the lift makes an intermediate halt).

At Pont d'Espagne, four ski-lifts, including the Gaube chair-lift, offer skiers the possibility of practising downhill skiing in a relaxed atmosphere away from the crowds, in the very heart of the Parc National des Pyrénées, or of taking advantage of the 36km/22mi of cross-country skiing trails divided into five loops in the Vallée du Marcadau.

Maison du Parc Nationale des Pyrénées Cauterets

Open Jun–Sep 9.30am-noon, 3-7pm; rest of year closed weekends and holidays. Closed 15 Oct–20 Nov, 1 Jan,

Lac d'Ilheou, Cirque du Lys

Pont d'Espagne

1 and 8 May, 25 Dec. No charge ☎05 62 92 52 56. www.parc-pyrenees.com. This information centre at the town's entrance covers the natural environment of the Parc national des Pyrénées, including its fauna, flora, geology and human story.

Cirque du Lys★★

Access via the **Lys gondola lift** (*open Jul-Aug and Dec-Apr 9am-11.30am, 1.45-5.15pm. closed rest of year. 7.50€ round-trip (chair-lift and cable-car for the crêtes du Lys: 9.50€).* *☎05 69 92 50 27)* and the **Grand Barbat chair-lift** (*open Jul-Aug and Dec-Apr 9am-5pm. closed rest of year ☎05 62 92 50 50).*

As you cross the Cambasque plateau, a superb **panorama** from Crête du Lys (2 303m/7 577ft) overlooks the spectacular Pic du Midi de Bigorre, Vignemale and Balaïtous (*viewing table*). You can take a mountain bike to ride back to Cauterets from the Grand Barbat chair-lift station.

It takes 1hr on foot to get to Ilhéou Lake (or Blue Lake) via the GR 10 rambling path.

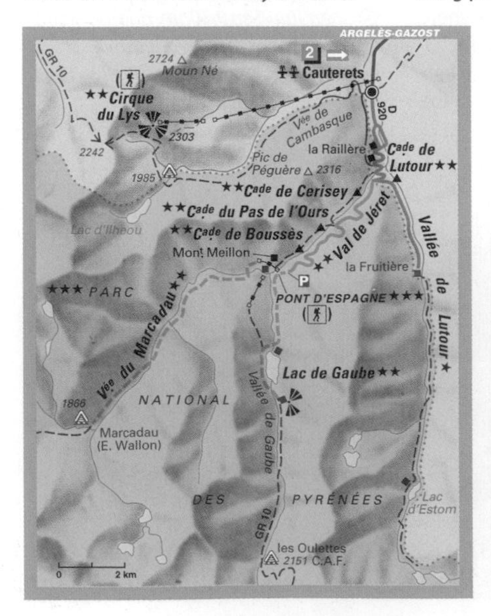

Val de Jéret★★

8km/5mi – about 2hr.
Leave Cauterets by D 920, on the west bank behind the casino. After La Raillère cure centre (right), park in the official car park beyond Pont de Benquès (bridge).

Another alternative is to follow **Chemin des Cascades**★ on foot from Cauterets (*5hr round-trip*) or from the car park by Pont de la Raillère (bridge), near the Griffons spa centre *(4hr round-trip; shuttle service between the Gare des Oeufs car park and La Raillère)*. It is a beautiful forest walk, providing a closer view of the waterfalls, which are at their most attractive when the flowers are in bloom.

Cascade de Lutour★★

A footbridge spans the pool below the last four waterfalls of Gave de Lutour.

The road continues up the valley; narrow, steep, heavily wooded, boulder-strewn and cooled by waterfalls.

Cascades de Cerisey, Pas de l'Ours and Boussès★★

These three attractive waterfalls are all very different. Above the Boussès waterfall, the river divides around Sarah Bernhardt's Island *(parking in the glade)*.

Pont d'Espagne★★★

Park in the Puntas car park (3€ per hour-6€ per day; no charge after 9pm), and take the Puntas ***cable shuttle*** *(15min – open Jun and Sep enquire at tourist office. Closed Oct–early Dec. 2.60€ round-trip. 05 62 92 50 50) as far as Plateau du Clot (activity centre with cross-country ski trails and rambling paths) or go by foot to the bridge.*

This bridge is named after an ancient mule track which once lead to Spain. The magnificent site marks the confluence of the Gave de Gaube and Gave de Marcadau, and several footbridges and viewpoints offer breathtaking scenes of foaming cascades. A path to the Pont d'Espagne from the Puntas parking area meanders through firs and pines, and meadows dotted with mountain flowers stretch across the landscape. Ideal for winter cross-country skiing.

Monument Meillon

15min round trip on foot.

Behind Pont d'Espagne Hotel, take a stony footpath on the right. Further on, the path branches off (right) to the monument.

Through the fir trees, glimpse the Vignemale massif and the main falls at Pont d'Espagne, the starting point of several walks.

The walks to Lac de Gaube (4hr) and into Marcadau (full day) are especially rewarding.

3 VALLÉE DE GAVARNIE★★

Zoom map on p396. 20km/12mi itinerary from Luz-St-Sauveur – 3hr 30min Zoom map p 396. For walks in the region, see pp398-399.

The Vallée de Gavarnie and the Cirque de Gavarnie have been UNESCO World Heritage sites since 1997. The forbidding landscape provoked the Baroness Dudevant (George Sand) to write: "From Luz to Gavarnie is primeval chaos; it is hell itself." Victor Hugo described the track through the Chaos de Coumély as "a black and hideous path." The Pragnères, Gèdre and Gavarnie basins were gouged by Quaternary Age glaciers. Their melting waters created narrows, the most typical of which is St-Sauveur Gorge. Temporary dwellings perch on the ledges; torrents cascade from the tributary valleys.

Luz-St-Sauveur★

30km/18.75mi south of Lourdes, in a picturesque mountain setting. Population: 1 098. Pl du 8 Mai 65120 Luz-Saint-Sauveur, 05 62 92 81 60, www.luz.org.

Luz – Capital of a small mountain canton, Luz was a fashionable 18C and 19C summer resort and today is a busy a tourist centre. Luz's **fortified church★** was built in the 12C and fortified in the 14C. It has a watch-path, crenellated wall and two square towers. There is a small museum of religious art in the Chapelle Notre-Dame-de-la-Pitié and a museum of ethnography in the Arsenal tower.

St-Sauveur – The town's single street is named after the Duchesse de Berry

Fortified Church

A. Thuillier/MICHELIN

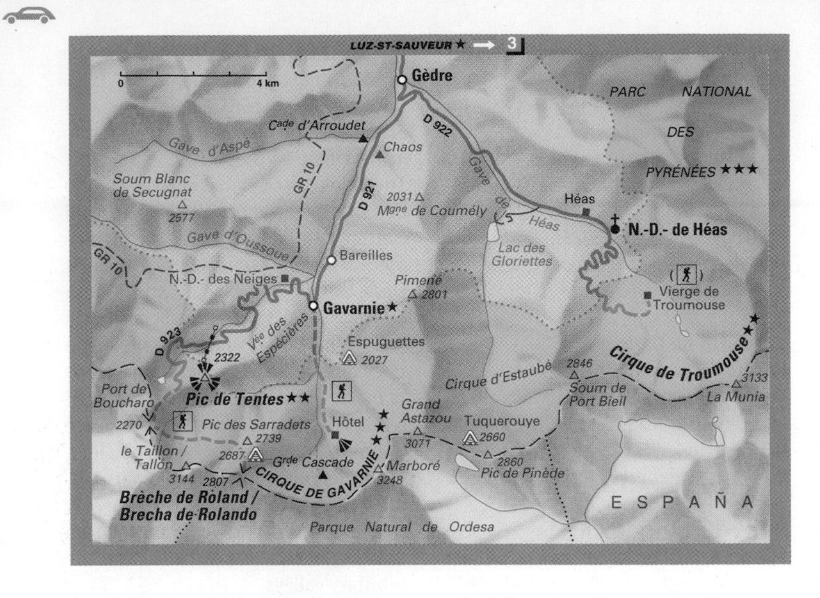

at one end, and Empress Eugénie on the other.

Luz Ardiden – Luz Ardiden's setting (alt 1 680m/5 527ft - 2 450m/8 060ft) still remains unspoilt. The ski area is serviced by 19 lifts. The Aulian and Bédéret slopes offer 32 runs for all levels. Skiers can slalom around moguls, and schuss or monoski in Snowboard Space. There is off-piste skiing in the adjacent valley of Bernazaou. The Ticket-Toy ski pass includes the neighbouring Barèges and Gavarnie-Gèdre resorts.

Leave the town via D 921.

Pont Napoléon

Avoid the 3pm jam of excursion coaches near the Pont Napoléon.

This arched bridge, ordered by Napoleon III in 1860, spans the gorge channelled by the Pau Torrent. The road carved from the bed-rock, twists through another gorge and passes through the hamlet of Sia. The bridge is a favourite for bungey jumping.

Gèdre

This village at the confluence of the Héas and Gavarnie torrents makes a charming halt enroute to Cirque de Gavarnie, and is base for driving tours to the Troumouse and Estaubé cirques.

Follow the toll road to the Cirque de Troumouse (15km/9mi), usually obstructed by snow from December to April.

Héas

The **chapel** is the site of regular pilgrimages. Most of the original building was swept away in an avalanche in 1915 and rebuilt 10 years later, but the north aisle and statues, paintings, the 1643 bell, a stoup and 18C processional Cross still remain.

Cirque de Troumouse★★

This amphitheatre is best viewed from a rocky spur, in the centre of which stands the Vierge de Troumouse *(45min round trip walk)*. The amphitheatre can accommodate three million spectators. Carpeted in meadow grass and flowers, it is enclosed by a rampart of mountains 10km/6mi around. The highest peak is Pic de la Munia and below it are twinned rock pinnacles "the Two Sisters."

Return to Gèdre and continue along D 921.

The scenery gets wild with the spectacular Cascade d'Arroudet dashing down into the hanging valley of the Aspé Torrent. The road crosses the rock-strewn

The Pyrenean Bear

In France, the only place to find the European brown bear (*Ursus arctos*) is the central Pyrenees mountains, in particular on rocky slopes and in beech and fir forests which overlook the Aspe and Ossau valleys at an altitude of 1 500-1 700m/4 921-5 577ft. This once carnivorous plantigrade animal now varies its diet according to the season, eating tubers, fruit, insects, acorns but also small mammals and sometimes sheep. Unfortunately, the extension of the road network as well as of forestry work and tourism combined with the bear's slow reproduction cycle (females have a cub every two years), have led to the regression of the species. Its numbers have dwindled from 40 twenty years ago to a mere six or seven.

In order to save this endangered species, a five-year charter was signed in 1994; its aim was to include the safeguard of bears in a wider nature-protection programme. Thus, hunting is banned in an area of 7 000ha/17 300 acres during the autumn period when bears stock up for their long hibernation period.

In addition, a programme of reintroduction of bears in the area was launched: in June 1996, two females from Slovenia – Melba and Ziva – were released in the central Pyrenees followed in 1997 by a male called Pyros, also from Slovenia. More were introduced in 2006. Melba had three cubs in 1997. Unfortunately she was shot by a hunter in early 1998. It is believed that one of the three cubs survived and is somewhere between France and Spain. Ziva, on the other hand, is bringing up two cubs. The total bear population of the Pyrenees mountains is therefore estimated to be around 20.

Chaos de Coumély and begins the final ascent towards Gavarnie. Beyond the Fausse Brèche and Pic des Sarradets the snow-covered ledges of the amphitheatre come into view, with the summits of Le Casque, La Tour and Pic du Marboré. The road follows the hamlet of Bareilles and then, on the Turon de Holle, the monumental statue of Notre-Dame-des-Neiges.

Gavarnie

From the village, you can reach the Cirque de Gavarnie astride a donkey or a horse. Find them near the parking area closest to the main street). 05 62 92 49 10. www.gavarnie.com.

Since 1864 Gavarnie has provided various mounts for the trek to the Cirque. In summer this small town is packed with day-trippers. Once they've gone and the mules, donkeys and ponies return to their pastures, Gavarnie becomes a base for mountaineers.

Gavarnie, the highest village in the Pyrenees, is very crowded in the summer. Park outside the town, and walk into town. (*cont. p400*)

Cirque de Troumouse

Lac de Gaube

© Pierre Jean Durieu/Dreamstime.com

Walks in the Pyrenees

Vallées des Cauterets *Map pp391, 394*

Lac de Gaube★★ – *1hr 30min round trip by GR 10 rambling path, downstream from Pont d'Espagne. The* **Gaube chair-lift** *(open Jul-Aug 9.15am-5.45pm; May-Jun and Sep 9.45am-5.30pm. Closed Oct-mid Dec. 6.50€ Round-trip (7€ for Puntas gondola and Gaube chair-lift). 05 62 92 52 19) from Plateau de Clots can be taken most of the way, followed by a 15min walk to a bar-café by the lake.* At the top of the chair-lift, nature information panels describe forest flora and fauna and the izard, a local species of chamois. Its austere yet beautiful site provides a view of the Vignemale massif and glaciers. A footpath along the river's west bank looks onto Pique Longue du Vignemale, 3 298m/10 820ft, one of the highest peaks in the Pyrenees.

Vallée du Marcadau★★ – *6.5km/4mi; 6hr round trip on foot from the Pont d'Espagne parking area.* Once a favourite route for crossing into Spain, this path has grass-covered shoulders and meandering mountain streams, alternating with glacial thresholds and twisted mountain pines. The Wallon refuge stands at an altitude of 1 866m/6 122ft, and beyond it is a cirque of pastureland scattered with lakes. Marcadau means market place, which this once was.

Vallée de Lutour★ – *6km/3.6mi. Take the Pont d'Espagne road as far as a series of hairpin bends. Just before the Le Bois thermal establishment, turn sharply left onto the narrow steep forest road to La Fruitière.* The track offers glimpses of the upper Lutour falls, then emerges into peaceful pastureland.

Vallée de Gavarnie *Map pp391, 396*

Cirque de Gavarnie★★★ – *2hr on foot there and back.* At the end of the village, take the unsurfaced path then follow the true left bank of the *gave* (mountain stream). Cross over an old stone bridge and walk up through the woods, with the river now to your right. The last part of the walk climbs through mixed vegetation to the first rocky folds marking the approach of the Cirque itself. Then the Cirque de Gavarnie comes into view. Gazing at its majesty of sheer walls and tiered snow platforms, Victor Hugo exclaimed: "It is

both a mountain and a rampart; it is the most mysterious of structures by the most mysterious of architects; it is Nature's Colosseum – it is Gavarnie!"

The mounted Driving Tours end at the Hôtel du Cirque but it is possible to continue, on foot (*1hr there and back*), to the Grande Cascade. This impressive waterfall is fed by melt-water from the frozen lake on Monte Perdido on the Spanish side of the frontier. The cascade drops 422m/1 385ft into the void.

Brèche de Roland (Roland's Gap) – *4hr on foot there and back – for experienced mountain walkers only: beware of the névés from September to early July. Follow the marked path starting E of Port de Boucharo.* The path follows the Haute Route des Pyrénées and fords a waterfall at the foot of the Taillon glacier. From the pass admire the Grande Cascade of the Cirque de Gavarnie. Beyond the Sarradets refuge, the climb to the gap is long and more difficult due to snow and *névés*. The breach named after the gallant 8C knight Rolland offers a **view** of Monte Perdido and the barren Spanish side.

Massif de Néouvielle

Map pp391, 401

Camping at Col Aubert, Massif de Néouvielle

©gRaNdLeMuRieN/Fotolia.com

The Massif de Néouvielle is the ideal area for family walks as well as for more demanding walks in the mountains. There are numerous marked itineraries and appropriate topoguides are on sale in local shops or in the **Maison du Parc** in Saint-Lary-Soulan (*05 62 39 40 91*); information is available from the **Bureau des Guides** in Saint-Lary-Soulan (*05 62 40 02 58 or 05 62 39 41 97*).

Col (or hourquette) d'Aubert★★ – *3hr on foot to the pass. From the Lac d'Aubert parking area, follow the marked path that skirts the lake by the NE. Alt 2 498m/8 196ft.* This pass links the depression cradling the Aubert and Aumar lakes with the desolate Escoubous coomb on the slopes towards Barèges. There is a remarkable **view**★★ of the tiered lakes at the foot of Pic de Néouvielle.

Lac d'Aubert and Lac d'Aumar

A. Thuiller/MICHELIN

Grand Cascade, Cirque de Gavarnie
M.-H. Carcanague/MICHELIN

The 14C **church** on the old pilgrims' route to Port de Boucharo contains a polychrome statue of St James of Compostela, two statuettes of Compostela pilgrims, and a Virgin Mary holding a pilgrim's water flask.

Col du Boucharo★★ and Pic de Tentes★★

In the summer months you can drive from Gavarnie up to the Col bu Boucharo. Parking is limited at the col, which is the frontier with Spain. 11km/7mi, by the Port de Boucharo road. Leaving Gavarnie in the direction of Luz (north), turn left just before the bridge. The road skirts the statue of Notre-Dame-des-Neiges at the mouth of the Vallée d'Ossoue, then enters the Vallée des Espécières. When you reach Col de Tentes, leave the car at the saddle and walk to the rounded summit of Pic de Tentes (alt 2 322m/ 7 618ft), to the NE.

The summit offers a **panorama**★★★ of peaks surrounding the Cirque de Gavarnie, including Le Taillon and Pic du Marboré, gashed by the Grande Cascade glacier. More distant still rises Le Petit Vignemale and, shouldering the Ossoue glacier, Vignemale itself, so beloved of Henry Russell, who built a cave on the mountain in which he entertained guests. To the north-east the Néouvielle massif stands in front of Pic du Midi de Bigorre.

6 MASSIF DE NÉOUVIELLE★★★

St-Lary-Soulon to the Lakes

70km/43mi round tour – allow 5hr. The best access to the massif is through the Bielsa tunnel; stop at the information centre in St-Lary-Soulon first, for maps and brochures. Zoom map opposite. For walks, see pp398-399.

The **lake road** *is closed to traffic in July and August (9.30am-6.30pm; shuttle service operates from Lake Orédon Jul-mid-Sep: departures every 30min 9.30am-6pm; 2.50€ one-way; 05 62 39 62 63). Take the driving tour in the early summer, as soon as the road (closed October to early summer) and the path to Col d'Aubert are free of snow; the waterfalls and the lakes are at their best when water is most abundant.*

Office du tourisme d'Aragnouet Piau-Engaly, Bât. Le Pôle 65170 Aragnouet 05 62 39 61 69. www.piau-engaly.com.

This granite mountain mass attracts a great number of sightseers and walkers because of its hundred or so lakes and the clear air around it. The massif offers many examples of glacial relief, culminating in the 3 192m/10 465ft-high Pic Long.

Since 1850 tributaries of the Neste d'Aure (Aure Torrent) originating in the Néouvielle have helped regulate the flow of rivers from the hills of Gascony; these waters are used today in the production of hydro-electric power.

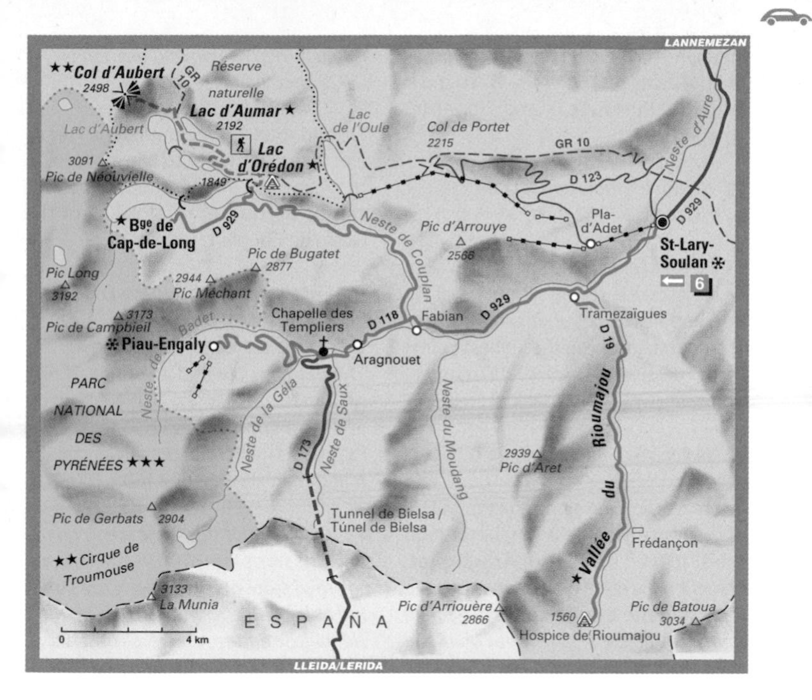

St-Lary-Soulan✻

This small **winter sports resort** has developed since 1950 along the western slopes of the Vallée d'Aure.

Access to the ski slopes above the town at Pla d'Adet and Espiaude (alt 830-2 450m/2 723-8 038ft; 48 skilifts) is either via a gondola lift or by road.

Leave St-Lary SW along D 929.

Beyond St-Lary, the valley narrows to a gorge. Up on the left is the village of Tramezaïgues. From Tramezaïgues take D 19, a road that is only partly surfaced. Beyond Fredançon, the last 4km/2mi of the road are so narrow that traffic is one-way only.

Vallée du Rioumajou★

This is a densely wooded valley with numerous waterfalls. Not far from the

Massif de Néouvielle

M.-H. Carcanague/MICHELIN

Spanish frontier the former Rioumajou hospice (alt 1 560m/5 117ft), now a mountain refuge, stands in a fine amphitheatre.

Return to Tramezaïgues and turn left on D 929.

As the road follows the line of the Vallée de la Neste d'Aure, the silhouette of Pic de Campbieil comes gradually into view. The mountain, one of the highest points in the massif at 3 173m/10 407ft, is recognisable by its twin-peaked crest.

Beyond Fabian turn left on D 118.

The road, climbing alongside the waters of the Neste de la Géla, passes through the scattered hamlets of **Aragnouet**. Below, on the right, the belfry-wall of the 12C **Chapelle des Templiers** (*open mid-Jul-Aug every day except Mon and Tue 3-6pm; low season: by request at the town hall. 05 62 39 62 63*) appears.

Leave the route leading to the Bielsa tunnel on the left.

Piau*

At an altitude of 1 850m/6 000ft, the highest ski resort in the French Pyrenees is a stone's throw from the nature reserves of the Parc National des Pyrénées and the Parque Nacional de Ordesa y Monte Perdido in Spain.

Pic du Midi d'Ossau
A. Thuillier/MICHELIN

Return to Fabian and turn left on D 929 heading N.

The old road, carved out by the French electricity authority to allow access to the Cap-de-Long site (*see below*), climbs up through the valley of the Neste de Couplan.

Continue to Lake Cap-de-Long.

Barrage de Cap-de-Long★

The dam has created a volume of 67.5 million m^3/89.7 million cu yd of water and is an important component of the Pragnères hydro-electric power station. It lies at an altitude of 2 160m/7 087ft.

Retrace your steps. The scenic Route des Lacs starts from the Orédon fork and the road stops at the Orédon Lake parking area. A path continues through the Néouvielle nature reserve, a conservation area for the local fauna and flora.

Lac d'Orédon★

Alt 1 849m/6 066ft. The chalet-hotel makes this spot a good base-camp for mountain expeditions.
Leave the car in the **car park** *(1/2h: no charge; 3hr: 2€; 8hr: 4€; over 8hr: 5€.).*

Continue on foot along the Sentier des Laquettes (1hr 30min) or take the shuttle to Lac d'Aubert.

From here, continue the excursion on foot: walk back a short distance and take the trail marked GR 10, which skirts Lake Aumar.

Lac d'Aumar★

Alt 2 192m/7 192ft. At the northern end of the lake the summit of Pic de Néouvielle (alt 3 091m/10 142ft), bordered by a small glacier, comes into view.

Haut Ossau★★

This area offers three itineraries: **Vallée du gave de Bious**★, **Vallée du Soussouéou**★, and **Vallée du gave de Brousset** (*see The Green Guide French Atlantic Coast*).

ADDRESSES

STAY

REFUGES DU PARC

In the park, there are refuge huts, some of which have wardens present (these are open only from mid-June to September) and others which are classified as *"non gardés,"* (usually there is room for about 10 people). Walkers passing through may use them. In the *refuges gardés,* you may either prepare your own food or eat meals prepared by the warden. In the summer months, places in these refuges (usually 30 to 40) are in great demand. Advance reservations are imperative. The list with telephone numbers is available from the Parc National des Pyrénées. There are five refuges managed by the Park:

Refuge de Barroude
(2 370m/7 773ft), in the **Aure valley**, accommodates 35, *℘05 62 39 61 10.*

Refuge des Espuguettes
(2 077m/6 812ft), in the **Luz valley**, accommodates 60, *℘05 62 92 40 63.*

Refuge de Migouélou
(2 290m/7 511ft), in the **Azun valley**, accommodates 35, *℘05 62 97 44 92.*

Refuge d'Ayous
(1 960m/6 429ft), in the **Ossau valley**, accommodates 50, *℘05 59 05 37 00.*

Refuge d'Arlet
(1 990m/6 527ft), in the **Aspe valley**, accommodates 40, *℘05 59 36 00 99.*

Refuges managed by the Club Alpin – Most of the refuges that are not part of the park services are managed by the Club Alpin Français – *Service du Patrimoine bâti, 24 Ave.de Laumière, 75019 Paris. ℘01 53 72 87 55.*

CAMPING

Camping is prohibited in the national park, but bivouacking is tolerated (overnight or in case of bad weather, it is permissible to set up a tent, on the condition that you are more than a 1hr walk from a road used by motor vehicles). Tourist offices and syndicats d'initiative can provide you with a list of campsites near the park.

CAUTERETS

Chambre d'hôte les Ruisseaux – *Rte de Pierrefitte – 7km/4.2mi N of Cauterets, rte de Pierrefitte. ℘05 62 92 28 02. – 4 rms.* This bed and breakfast is in a house built in the 1920-30s and now owned by an English couple. The spacious rooms are newly furnished and immpeccable kept.

Hôtel du Lion d'Or – *12 r. Richelieu. ℘05 62 92 52 87 – www.hotel-lion-dor.net. Closed 30 Sep-20 Dec – 22 rms – 10€.* A nice family hotel only 100m/110yd from the Lys cable-car, with cosy rooms and wrought iron balconies. The flower adorned patio makes a pleasant place to relax.

Chambre d'hôte Grange St-Jean – *Rte de Lourdes, quartier Calypso. ℘05 62 92 58 58. Closed 2 weeks in May and 2 weeks in Nov – 3 rms.* This converted barn B&B with blue and yellow façade has rooms are decorated on a mountain theme and a garden facing a meadow.

EAT

CAUTERETS

L'Aragon – *R. de Belfort. ℘05 62 92 54 94 – Sun-Thu 7.30am-2am; Fri-Sat 7.30am-3am.* This lively snack bar with cosy wood fire serves salads, cold cuts, soups and omlettes.

TAKING A BREAK

Aux Délices – *Pl. Georges-Clemenceau. ℘05 62 92 07 08 – www.berlingots.com – daily 9am-12.30pm, 2.30pm-7.30pm – closed Nov.* Visitors can help to make *berlingots,* a local Cauterets sweet, at this shop which has been hand-making them for three generations.

SPA TREATMENT

Thermes de César – *Av. du Dr-Domer. ℘05 62 92 51 60/14 20. www.thermesdes-cauterets.com* This spa in the town centre offers treatments including water-jet therapy, mud packs, water massage and pool therapy.

LE GERS

Characterised by charming bastide villages and with the rippling heights of the Pyrenees to the south, Le Gers was created (in 1790, following the Revolution) from parts of the former provinces of Guyenne and Gascony. The economy is largely agricultural, with particular emphasis on local gastronomic specialities like Armagnac brandy, Côtes de Gascogne wines, Floc de Gascogne (a regional aperitif with AOC status since 1990), foie gras and wild mushrooms. The local language is a dialect of Occitan, but is not widely spoken. Perhaps the most famous son of Le Gers is a fictional character, d'Artagnan, who makes his first appearance as the fourth musketeer in the novel, The Three Musketeers (Les Trois Mousquetaires), by Alexandre Dumas Senior. The Gers is one of the least populated and most rural areas of France, indeed of western Europe. Le Gers' most important city is Auch.

Highlights

1. Take a walking tour of **Auch** (p406)
2. Visit the bastide of **Mirande** (p414)
3. Explore the town of **Condom** (p409)
4. Visit lovely **Lavardens** (p408)
5. Acquire a taste for **Armagnac** (p412)

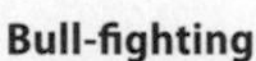

Bull-fighting

Mid-August is a period for bullfighting festivals, or "férias", in the French south and south-west. Bullfighting is banned in France but legally tolerated in those areas which can claim an unbroken local "tradition". In practice, French courts have allowed bullfighting to spread to towns in the south where no such tradition exists. But while there is considerable opposition to bullfighting, it should be remembered that in the French tradition the bull is not killed and survives to fight again, often more than once. In French bullfighting, the men (*raseteurs*) have to retrieve ribbons or rosettes (*cocarde*) tied to the horns of bulls.

Musketeer

Although centred on a fictional character, musketeers did exist and were an early type of infantry soldier equipped with a musket. They were an important part of early modern armies, particularly in Europe. In France, musketeers were created in 1622 when Louis XIII furnished a company of light cavalry (the "carabiniers") with muskets. They fought both on foot and horseback.

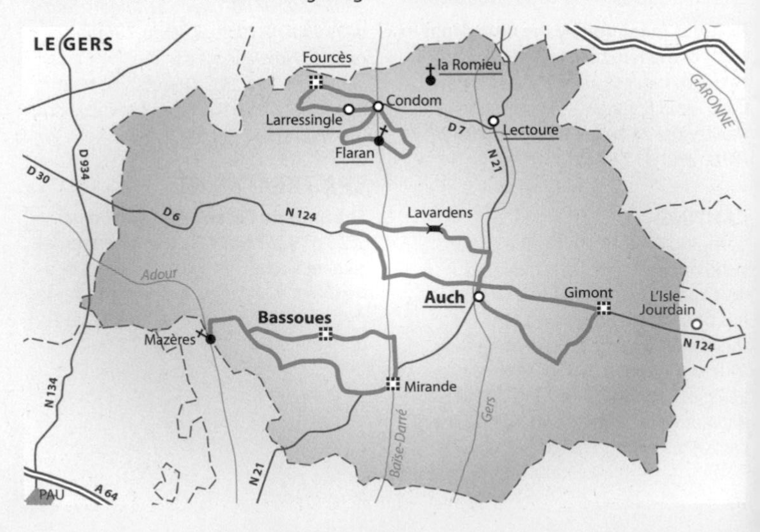

Lavardens

J. Malburet/MICHELIN

Bastides

Rapid population growth and the need to effect better control of the development, in particular, of the region of southwest France known as the 'Rouergue' – originally the homeland of a Celtic tribe (the 'Rutheni') – brought about the medieval equivalent of a rural development policy. It heralded a period of fortified town building by king and count alike that was to last for 150 years, from 1222 (Cordes-sur-Ciel) until 1372 (La Bastide d'Anjou), during which hundreds of bastides (*see INTRODUCTION*), or 'new towns' were built; some put the number as high as 700, although a figure of half that is the generally accepted number. As well as meeting defensive strategies, they served to colonise the wilder parts of southern France, and to garrison and control the changing and feckless populations of the Middle Ages.

In spite of their number, and many common characteristics, the bastides retain individuality and are fascinating settlements to visit. They were invariably built on a hilltop, or some other easily defensible position, and had a fortified perimeter. Most usual of all, they were built to a rectangular grid layout, with narrow alleys (*carreyous*) for access to backs of houses and their gardens, and a narrow separating gap (*andrones*) between houses to limit the spread of fire and enable rain and waste water disposal. Typically, bastides were built around a market square, often with a covered section (*les halles*) or covered arcades (*cornières*) built out of the ground floor of the houses surrounding the square. The bastides were also an attempt by landowners to generate taxes on trade rather than on production. Farmers who moved to bastides ceased to be vassals of the local lord, and effectively became free men. Bastides were a force in the decline of feudalism.

Cornières – covered arcades in Montréal

Auch★

The Heart of Gascony and East of Auch

An important crossroads since Roman times on the busy trade route linking Toulouse to the Atlantic – before traffic was diverted along the River Garonne – Auch was revived in the 18C by the administrator Étigny and embellished during the Second Empire. The bustling street life and busy Saturday markets underline its position as administrative capital of Gascony. The main streets converge on place de la Libération.
The Episcopal district stands apart above the River Gers.

> **Location:** 76km/47.5mi W of Toulouse.

OLD TOWN

Escalier monumental

The 232 steps of this monumental staircase link place Salinis, the square next to the cathedral which overlooks the Gers Valley, with the quays below. The statue of d'Artagnan, dating from 1931, is halfway down. Climbing back up the steps, gives you a fine view of the 14C **Tour d'Armagnac** (the 40m/130ft-high watchtower of the municipal prison) and the abutments and double-course flying buttresses around the cathedral.

Cathédrale Ste-Marie★★

Closed at lunchtime (except mid Jul-Aug). Audio tour of the gallery and windows available. 2€, identity document retained as guarantee.
Construction of the cathedral of Ste-Marie began in 1489 and was completed two centuries later. The solid 16C and 17C **façade** presents a balanced relationship between pilasters, columns, cornices, balustrades and niches. The quadripartite vaulting, dating from the mid-17C, lends a stylistic unity to the interior, done in the French Gothic style. Treasures are the early-16C *Christ Entombed in the* Chapel of the Holy Sepulchre, and the 16C stone altarpiece of the St Catherine's Chapel.

Stained-glass windows★★ – Eighteen works by the Gascon painter Arnaud de Moles embellish the early-16C ambulatory chapels windows, noted for their rich colours, large panes and expressive figures linking the Old and New Testaments and the pagan world.

Choir Stalls★★★ (*open mid Jul-Aug 8.30am-6pm; Apr-mid Jul and Sep-Oct 8.30am-noon, 2-6pm; Nov-Mar 9.30am-*

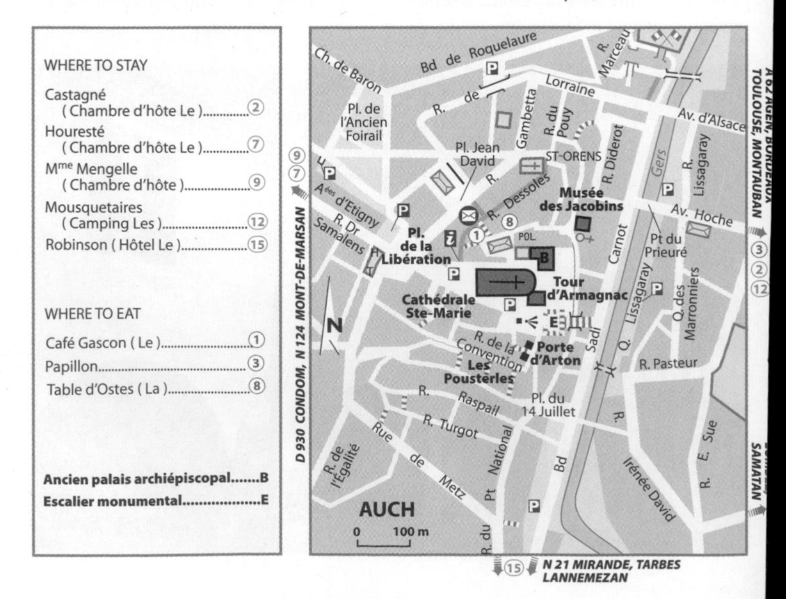

noon, 2-5pm. ⊜2€) – Auch woodcarvers took 50 years (c 1500-52) to complete the 113 stalls decorated with over 1 500 exquisitely carved oak figures drawn from the Bible, secular history, myths and legends. The splendid tones of the great organ (1694), constructed by Jean de Joyeuse, ring forth from May to September during **concerts**.

Place de la République leads to place de la Libération.

Place de la Libération

This is the centre of action in the upper town.

Turn right onto rue Salleneuve (stone steps).

The **Musée des Jacobins** displaying Gallo-Roman archaeology and South American colonial art is housed in the former Couvent des Jacobins *(open Apr-Oct 10am-noon, 2-6pm; Feb-Mar and Nov-Dec 2-5pm. closed 1 and 11 Nov, 25 Dec. ⊜3€. 05 62 05 74 79).*

At the southwest corner of the cathedral take rue d'Espagne. Turn left onto rue de la Convention.

Les Pousterles

Pousterles is the medieval term used to designate posterns set in the walls of the fortified upper town. **Porte d'Arton** was the main entrance to the town. Before joining place Salinis, Rue Fabre-d'Églantine skirts the walls of the lycée, founded as a Jesuit college in 1545.

A. Thuillier/MICHELIN

Stained-glass, Cathedral Ste-Marie

EXCURSIONS

Pavie

5km/3mi S via N 21.

Originally a Gallo-Roman villa, Pavie became a *bastide* in 1281. Rue d'Étigny and rue de la Guérite contain beautiful examples of old half-timbered houses. The 13C church, restored in the 19C, has kept its 14C square belfry. A Gothic bridge with three arches spans the River Gers.

d'Artagnan, the Real Musketeer

A. Thuillier/MICHELIN

The town statue honouring d'Artagnan portrays him as the famous musketeer immortalised by novelist Alexandre Dumas in *The Three Musketeers*. The real-life character, Charles de Batz (born c. 1615), borrowed the name d'Artagnan from the Montesquiou family on his mother's side before joining the French Guards (d'Artagnan was more suitable for court use).

As a young soldier, he was already favoured by Cardinal Mazarin (1602-61), Richelieu's successor, and divided his time between battle campaigns, diplomatic missions and bawdy back street life. Louis XIV entrusted him with the arrest of Finance Minister Jules Fouquet, who had grown extremely rich at the State's expense. D'Artagnan, a Captain-Lieutenant in the 1st Company of the King's Musketeers, died a hero's death at the siege of Maastricht in 1673.

DRIVING TOURS

HEART OF GASCONY

Half-day round-trip (72km/45mi). Leave Auch on N 21 (N); 8km/5mi then left on D 272. Passing right of Roquelaure, take D 148 along the ridge. Continue beyond Mérens on D 518 to Lavardens. The road runs through an undulating landscape with **view★** *of Lavardens.*

Lavardens

This picturesque village with narrow streets is noted for its imposing castle, attractive church belfry. and visible remains of ancient ramparts and towers. The original **castle** *(open Jul-Aug 10am-7pm; Apr-Jun and Sep-Oct 10.30am-12.30pm, 2-6pm; Feb-Mar and Nov-Dec 10.30am-12.30pm, 2-5pm; closed Jan: 5€; 05 62 58 10 61; www.chateau lavardens.com)* was razed in the 15C. The 17C structure standing today, pierced with mullion and transom windows, has a façade flanked with square towers.

Continue along D 103 West.

Jegun

This village stands on a rocky spur within the ground-plan of a bastide. Highlights are the old market, fine half-timbered old houses and the 13C collegiate church of Ste-Candide.

Vic-Fézensac

This town holds busy markets and *féria*, traditional festivals with bullfighting.

Leave Vic-Fézensac heading SE via N 124 towards Auch. At St-Jean-Poutge turn right on D 939 towards L'Isle-de-Noé.

After about 4km/2mi, before turning left on D 374, note the unusual **Gallo-Roman pier** with a niche.

Biran

This small *castelnau* is built on a spur; a single road links the fortified gateway to the remains of the keep. The **church** Notre-Dame-de-Pitié shelters a monumental carved stone altarpiece, carved with scenes including the Pietà.

Continue along D 374 and rejoin N 124 to return to Auch.

Other local *bastides* of interest include Fleurance, St-Clar, Cologne and Beaumont-de-Lomagne.

EAST OF AUCH

Round-trip of 57km/35mi – allow half a day. Leave Auch heading E via N 124 and follow signs to Château de St-Cricq.

Château de St-Cricq

The 16C château is now the town's reception and conference centre.

Continue along N 124 towards Toulouse.

After 7.5km/4.5mi look for the long south façade of the **Château de Marsan** (18C-19C), owned by the Montesquiou family.

Gimont

See Toulouse and Environs.

Leave Gimont heading SW via D 12 and continue for 12km/7mi to Boulaur.

Boulaur

This village over the Gimone valley has a 12C monastery now inhabited by Cistercian monks.

The twisting D 626 leads to Castelnau-Barbarens.

Castelnau-Barbarens

The houses of this 12C village radiate in concentric arcs from the church-topped hill.

Drive towards Auch.

On the plateau, D 626 offers a fine **panorama★** of the Pyrenees. The route crosses **Pessan**, an old *sauveté* (a rural township founded by a monastery as a sanctuary for fugitives), which developed around an abbey, founded in the 9C.

ADDRESSES

STAY

Chambre d'hôte le Houresté – *32360 Jégun – 3km/1.8mi W of Jégun on D 103 rte de Vic-Fézensac. ☎05 62 64 51 96 – 4rms.* This 19C house on a working farm offers small but well appointed guestrooms in a mini-chalet and old dovecot. Flower gardens, orchard and barnyard animals add to the charm.

Chambre d'hôte le Castagné – *Rte de Toulouse. ☎05 62 63 32 56 / 06 07 97 40 37. www.domainelecastagne.com – 4 rms.* Quite a leisure spot with swimming, minigolf, fishing, pedalos, perfect for kids.

Chambre d'hôte Mme Mengelle – *Au village, 32360 Jégun. ☎05 62 64 55 03. Closed Nov-Mar – 5rms.* Lovely B&B decorated with tapestries, antique furniture and wallpaper in muted colours.

Camping les Mousquetaires – *32390 Mirepoix. ☎05 62 64 33 66. www.chaletsmousquetaires.com – reservations essential; 11 chalets.* Comprising a group of chalets only; breakfast included.

Hôtel Le Robinson – *Rte de Tarbes. ☎05 62 05 02 83. www.hotelrobinson.net. Closed Christmas period – P – 23rms – 6.50€.* 1960s hotel set back from the road; some rooms have balconies.

EAT

La Table d'Ostes – *7 r. Lamartine. ☎05 62 05 55 62. www.table-oste restaurant.com. Closed 2-9 Mar, 30 Jun-6 Jul, 21-28 Sep, 21-31 Dec, Sun and Wed – reservations required.* In the old town, this rustic restaurant across from the covered market and cathedral, is a pleasant venue serving quality regional cuisine.

Le Café Gascon – *5 r. Lamartine. ☎05 62 61 88 08. Closed Sun, and Mon-Tue evenings.* This small restaurant serves authentic local fare freshly prepared for your order. The speciality café gascon is prepared at table.

Papillon – *Le Petit Guilhem, RN 21 - 32810 Montaux-les-Crénaux. ☎05 62 65 51 29. www.restaurant-lepapillon.com.* Offers a substantial and varied menu, a regional taster menu, and Gascon specialties; pleasurable dining experience.

Condom

Wine country, Vallée de l'Ossé, Vallée d'Auzoue

Condom is the main town in the Armagnac region, an area with many attractive rural churches and manor houses. The old mansions of Condom itself give the town a typically Gascon appearance. Its economic activities – selling grain and Armagnac, flour-milling and the timber industry – are also the traditional activities of the region. The River Baïse, stretching alongside the old quays, was channelled long ago to transport brandy to Bordeaux.

- **Population:** 7 158.
- **Michelin Map:** 336: E-6.
- **Info:** Office du Tourisme de la Ténarèze, Pl Bossuet, 32100 Condom ☎05 62 28 00 80 www.tourisme-tenareze.com.
- **Location:** 45km/28mi N of d'Auch.
- **Don't Miss:** La cathédrale Saint-Pierre, Fourcès, Larresingle.
- **Kids:** La Halte du pé lerin Museum and la Cité des machines du Moyen Age in Larresingle.

TOWN CENTRE WALK

1hr 30min.
Start from place St-Pierre.

Cathédrale St-Pierre★

The belfry rises majestically above the cathedral, one of the last in the Gers region built (1507-31) in the Gothic style

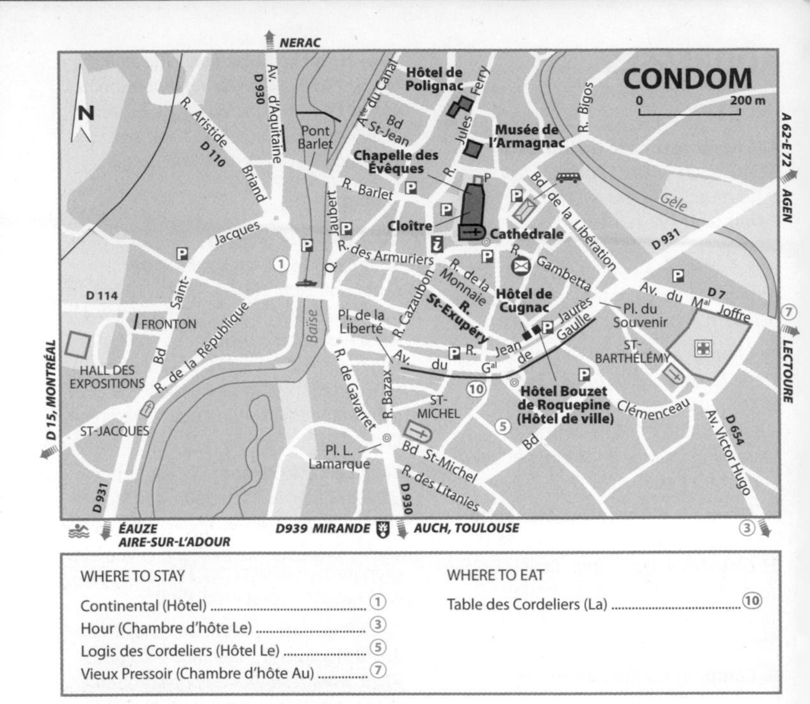

Cloisters, Cathédrale St-Pierre

A. Thuillier/MICHELIN

of South-West France. The Flamboyant Gothic south door still has 24 small statues in the niches of the archivolt. The nave is illuminated by windows with Flamboyant tracery, and the **cloisters**★ feature attractive keystones on the polychrome vaulting.

Chapelle des Évêques

Open daily except weekends 9am-noon, 2-4pm.

The chapel built in Gothic style has a Renaissance doorway surmounted by a baldaquin window.

Walk along rue Lannelongue to rue Jules-Ferry.

On the right stand the former bishop's stables, now the Musée de l'Armagnac.

Musée de l'Armagnac

2 r Jules-Ferry. Open Apr-Oct daily except Tue 10am-noon, 3-6pm: Nov-Mar daily except Mon and Tue 2-5pm. Closed 1 Jan, 1 May, 25 Dec. 2.20€. 05 62 28 47 17. www.condom.org.

This museum contains rare vine-growers' tools and machinery – an 18t press and a grape-crushing roller, cooper's tools and bottle samples produced by Gascon gentlemen-glassmakers and various stills.

Hôtel de Polignac, Hôtel de Cugnac – Maison Ryst-Dupeyron (*open guided visits (1hr) 10am-noon, 2-5pm (Jul-Aug 6pm). closed 1 Jan, 25 Dec. No charge. 05 62 28 08 08*), *18C cellars – and* **Hôtel de Riberot** *(fine 18C mansions).*

EXCURSIONS

La Romieu★

11km/6.6mi E on D 931 and D 41.

The entrance to the late-12C to early-13C **collegiate church★** is through the cloisters, with their interesting (though damaged) decorative motifs and through a doorway beneath a machicolated arch. The octagonal **eastern tower** stands apart. 14C murals may still be seen in the sacristy – 16 angels adorn the vaulting. A spiral staircase (153 steps) leads up to the platform which provides good views of the rooftops of the village, the belfry-tower and the cloisters.

Lectoure★

21km/13mi E along D 7.

The capital of the Lomagne region occupies a remarkable **site★** on a promontory overlooking the Gers valley. The resort's appeal is enhanced by the Lac des Trois Vallées (3km/1.9mi SE) offering a choice of outdoor activities. Not to be missed are the **cathedral** remodelled several times but still representative of the regional Gothic style and the **Musée gallo-romain★** housed in the cellars of the former 17C bishops' palace; the museum contains interesting archaeological collections including a group of 20 taurobolia, pagan altars discovered in 1540 beneath the cathedral adorned with bulls' or rams' heads.

The ancient rue Fontélie lined with ochre-coloured houses, runs down to the 13C Fontaine Diane enclosed by a 15C wrought-iron railing.

DRIVING TOURS

VALLÉE DE L'OSSÉ AND VALLÉE D'AUZOUE

Round trip 40km/25mi W of Condom – allow half a day. Leave Condom via D 15 towards Montréal.

Larressingle★

The walls of this 13C fortified village surround a ruined three-storey keep, a Romanesque church and a few restored houses. The **Cité des machines du Moyen-Âge** reconstructs a 13C siege

Entrance to the fortified village of Larressingle

A. Thuillier/MICHELIN

camp with machines like the trebuchet which fired cannon balls weighing over 100kg/220lb at a target 220m/240yd away.

Montréal

One of the earliest to be built in Gascony (1256), this *bastide* over the River Auzoue valley has a fortified Gothic church and a main square bordered by houses with arcades. The **Musée archéologique** exhibits pottery, iron objects, and Merovingian buckles found at Séviac. *(♿ open Jul-Aug 10am-12.30pm, 2-7pm; Mar-Jun and Sep-Nov 10am-12.30, 2-6pm; Dec-Feb 10am-12.30pm, 2-5.30pm; closed Sun, Mon, public holidays except 14 Jul and 15 Aug; free admission: 05 62 29 42 85).*

Follow signs W of Montréal to reach Séviac.

Séviac, Gallo-Roman villa

Open Jul-Aug 10am-7pm; Mar-Jun, Sep-Nov 10am-noon, 2-6pm. Closed Dec-Feb.. 4€. 05 62 29 48 57. www.seviac-villa.fr.st.

Archaeological excavations here reveal the foundations of a fabulous 4C Gallo-Roman villa with pool and baths richly decorated with coloured marble and ornate mosaics, and vestiges of paleo-Christian and Merovingian buildings, indicating permanent occupation from the 2C to the 7C.

Armagnac

Armagnac is always served after a meal, at room temperature, in special glasses which allow the elixir to be warmed with the palms to release the bouquet. Three main grades are determined by age: the 3-star or 3-crown Armagnac spends at least 18 months in a cask; the VO (Very Old) and VSOP (Very Superior Old Pale) a minimum of four and a half years and the XO, Hors d'âge, Napoléon and Extra must be over five and a half years old.

D 29, N out of Montréal, follows the course of the River Auzoue.

Fourcès★

A small bridge across the Auzoue, bordered by a 15C and 16C castle, leads to this picturesque *bastide* founded by the English in the 13C. The unusual village with its circular ground plan still has half-timbered houses with stone or wood arcades, around a large shaded main square with a stone cross in the centre.

Return to Condom via D 114.

WINE COUNTRY

Round trip 50km/31mi – allow half a day. Leave Condom via D 931 SW.

This tour, best in autumn when vines are golden brown, encompasses Armagnac's wine country and châteaux where visitors can taste and buy.

Mouchan

The village's Romanesque **church** dates back to the 10C.

Go to Cassaigne Château via D 208.

Château de Cassaigne

guided visits: mid Jun-mid Sep 9am-12pm; 2pm-7pm; rest of year daily except Mon 9am-12pm; 2pm-6pm. Closed Dec 25, 1 Jan. No charge. 05 62 28 04 02. www.chateaudecassaigne.com.

This 13C castle was the country residence of the bishops of Condom. Visit cellars where Armagnac is aged in oak barrels, the 16C kitchen filled with tin and copper kitchen utensils, earthenware and solid wood furniture and enjoy an Armagnac tasting session.

Take D 229 towards Lagardère, then turn right after 4.5km/3mi.

Château du Busca-Maniban

Apr-Oct: guided tours (45min) daily except Sun and public holidays 2-6pm (last admission 5pm). 6€. 05 62 28 40 38. www.buscamaniban.com.

This two-storey castle features a remarkably majestic hall, monumental staircase, Italian Room with fine furniture and 15C chapel. From the terrace you can gaze across to the Pyrenees.

Return to Cassaigne.

On the way down, vine-covered hillsides overlook the Mansecôme Castle ruins.

At Cassaigne, turn right on D 142.

Abbaye de Flaran★

Open Jul-Aug- 9.30am-7pm; rest of year 9.30am-12.30pm, 2-6pm. Closed 1 Jan, 2 weeks in Jan, 1 May and 25 Dec. 4€ (no charge 1st Sunday in the month Nov-Mar). 05 62 28 50 19 19. www.gers-gascogne.com.

The abbey on the outskirts of Valence-sur-Baïse was founded in 1151 as the Cistercian Order expanded throughout Gascony. It is now a **cultural centre** hosting concerts, exhibitions and seminars.

The abbey's façade contains a lovely rose window. The 18C **living quarters** of the Prior have the charm of a small Gascon château. The **abbey church** built between 1180 and 1210 comprises a nave surmounted by broken-barrel vaulting. Of the four original cloister galleries, only that on the west side (early 14C) remains today. The **monastic buildings** extend from the northern arm of the transept. The **armarium** or library is entered via the **chapter-house** containing columns of beautiful Pyrenees marble. The **monks' common room** and **storeroom** contain an exhibition on the Santiago de Compostela pilgrimage with maps, sculptures, and pilgrims' funerary crosses. A stone staircase leads to the **monks' dormitory, which was** converted into separate cells in the 17C. Enjoy the French formal **garden** and garden of medicinal and aromatic plants.

Valence-sur-Baïse

This *bastide* resulted from a 1274 feudal contract giving equal rights to the Abbot of Flaran and Comte Géraud V d'Armagnac. At the confluence of the River Baïse and River Auzoue, the town square contains a 14C church.

Leave Valence via D 232 N to visit the ruins of Château de Tauzia on a small road to the left.

Château de Tauzia

This modest 13C fortress with two side towers is now in ruins.

Go back to D 142 via Maignaut-Tauzia. Turn left on D 42 to St-Puy.

Château Monluc

guided tours (1hr): Jun-Sep daily except Mon 10am-noon, 3-7pm (Sun and public holidays 3-7pm); rest of year daily except Sun and Mon 10am-noon, 3-7pm. Closed Jan, 1 May and 25 Dec. No charge. 05 62 28 94 00. www. monluc.fr.

For centuries France and England fought over the medieval fortress of St-Puy, once owned by the illustrious Maréchal Blaïse de Monluc. Château Monluc originated **pousse-rapière** (rapier thrust), a precious liqueur made by soaking fruit in Armagnac. Tour the vaulted cellars to learn how the drink is made.

Follow D 654 towards Condom then turn right onto D 232 to St-Orens.

St-Orens

St-Orens is a fortified village perched on a hill. A ramparts gateway leads to the promontory and castle.

Return to Condom via D 654.

ADDRESSES

STAY

Hôtel Continental – *20 r. du Mar.-Foch. 05 62 68 37 00. www.lecontinental.net. Closed 23 Dec-17 Jan – 25rms – 10€. Restaurant.* Early 20C hotel, close to la Baïse, completely renovated, modern rooms, soundproofing and air conditioning.

Chambre d'hôte au Vieux Pressoir – *St-Fort, 32100 Caussens. 05 62 68 21 32. Closed Feb holidays. Reservations necessary – 4rms.* Large 17C building with lovely view over the countryside; meals are based on local produce.

Chambre d'hôte le Hour – *32100 Béraut. 05 62 68 48 33 ou 06 85 63 96 03. www.le-hour.com – 5rms.* The rooms are decorated with an astute collection of old things; swimming pool and games for children.

Hôtel Le Logis des Cordeliers – *R. de la Paix. 05 62 28 03 68. www.logisdescordeliers.com. Closed 2 Jan-7 Feb – P – 21rms – 8€.* Located in a quiet part of the town centre; some rooms have balconies overlooking the swimming pool; these are the best.

EAT

La Table des Cordeliers – *1 r. des Cordeliers. 05 62 68 43 82. www.latabledescordeliers.fr. Closed 15 Jan-5 Feb; Mon (except evenings from Jul-Sep); Wed lunch in summer, and Sun evenings.* Close to the Logis des Cordeliers (see above), the restaurant occupies a 14C chapel. A lovely place to eat in summer, under majestic Gothic arches, illuminated by stained glass windows. Cuisine is based on what is available at the market; menu changes daily.

Mirande

local bastides and castelnaux

The lively town of Mirande is one of France's most characteristic south-western *bastides*, founded in 1281 by the Abbé de Berdoues Bernard VII, Comte d'Astarac, and Eustache de Beaumarchés. The village retains its chessboard symmetry, at the centre of which is a covered market "place à couverts."

- **Population:** 3 691.
- **Michelin Map:** 336: E-8.
- **Info:** R. de l'Évêché, 32300 Mirande. 05 62 66 68 10. www.ot-mirande.com.
- **Location:** 25km/15.6mi SW of Auch, on the N 21 to Tarbes.

TOWN

Stroll through the **place d'Astarac** and **rue de l'Évêché** to see period half-timbered houses. The turreted belfry of early-15C **Église Sainte-Marie** sanctuary provided shelter to *bastide* defenders. Its tower is pierced by openwork Gothic bays. The **Musée des Beaux-Arts**★ *(13 ru de l'Évêché. 05 62 66 68 10. www.gers-gasgogne.com; open daily except Sun and public holidays 10am-noon, 2-6pm. 2€)*, founded by Joseph Delort, contains antique ceramics, 17C-19C glazed earthenware and porcelain from such renowned centres as Moustiers, Samadet, Dax and Nevers, plus 15C–19C paintings.

DRIVING TOURS

BASTIDES AND CASTELNAUX★

93km/58mi – allow 1 day. Leave Mirande via N 21 NE towards Auch. After 3km/1.8mi turn left on D 939.

This itinerary follows a triangle formed by D 943 to the north, D 3 and the Vallée du Bouès to the west, and N 21 to the east. It visits *bastides* and *castelnaux*, well-planned villages and towns built by seigneurs around their châteaux or strongholds. The route crosses **L'Isle-de-Noé** village and its 18C château.

Take D 943 on the right.

Barran

This *bastide* on the site of an earlier ecclesiastical settlement has a church, fortified gateway and covered market.

Return to L'Isle-de-Noé; continue West.

Montesquiou

This *castelnau* rises on a spur high above the Vallée de l'Osse. A gateway on the main street is all that remains of the 13C outer wall. Close by is a picturesque row of half-timbered houses.

Bassoues

The 14C **keep**★ *(open Jul and Aug 10am-7pm;rest of year daily except Tue 10am-noon, 2-6pm. closed 15 Dec-15 Feb. 4€. 05 62 70 97 34; www.bassoues.net)* is a magnificent example of military architecture, and its rooms contain exhibitions tracing the evolu tion of Gascon villages.

The top-floor platform, where round watchtowers rise between the terrace and the top of the buttresses, offers a good **view**★ to the north-east.

The village **church** was remodelled in the 16C and 19C and contains a fine 15C stone pulpit. D 946 now descends, via a 12km/7mi **crest route**★, to the Rivière Basse depression, with views through the Adour gap to the Pyrenees.

Beaumarchés

This royal *bastide* was founded in 1288 as the result of a *contrat de paréage*, requiring that a lesser noble hands over part of his revenue to a greater noble in return for protection. The Gothic church has a striking massive appearance and 15C porch. A frieze of carved male and female heads runs around the upper gallery.

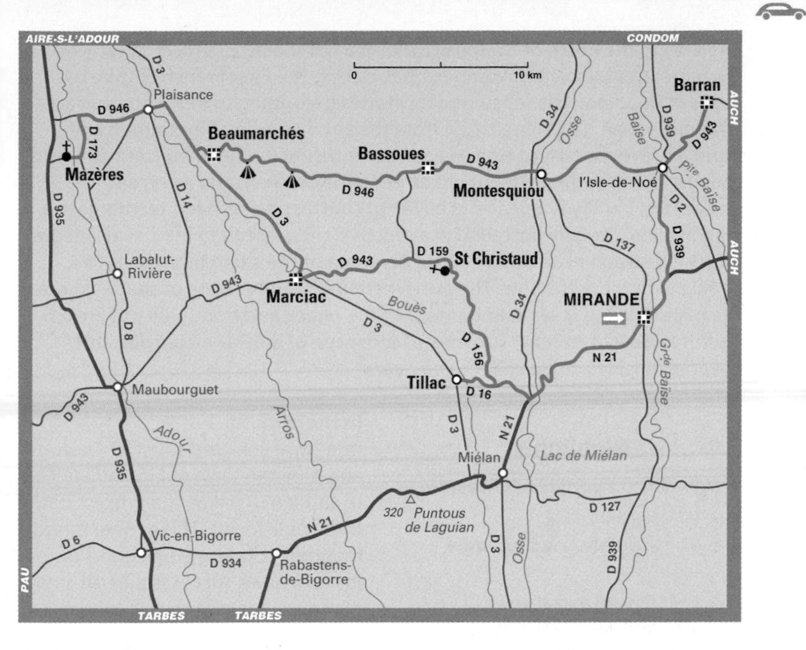

Drive to Plaisance, turn left onto D 946 to Préhac-sur-Adour then left again onto D 173.

Mazères

Note the Romanesque **church** with gable belfry flanked by buttresses. The chancel retains its Romanesque capitals and a special marble reliquary (1342) for pilgrims.

Return to Beaumarchés and continue along D 3, which runs alongside the artificial lake at Marciac.

Marciac

This *bastide* dates from the late 13C. A tall stone steeple crowns the belfry of the 14C **Église Notre-Dame**.

Les Territoires du Jazz

Pl. du Chevalier-d'Antras ℘05 62 08 26 60. www.marciactourisme.com. Open Jun-Aug 9.30am-12.30, 2.30-6.30pm. Closed 1 May, 24 Dec. 5€ (children under 18 3€).

Swing to the rhythm of Dixieland, blues and ragtime at this museum celebrating the history of jazz. The first two weeks of August the town hosts a convivial, high-quality jazz festival drawing an eclectic crowd of enthusiasts and well-known performers.

Head E towards Auch, following the picturesque D 943 above the River Bouès valley. At the top of the climb turn onto D 159, a crest road with fine views of the Pyrenees. Northwards (left) are glimpses of the impressive keep rising above Bassoues. Turn right onto D 156 to St-Christaud. Here the road crosses the Via Tolosane, the ancient route followed by Provence pilgrims on their way to Santiago de Compostela.

St-Christaud

The village **church** facing the distant Pyrenees features square windows, between buttresses, set in a diamond shape.

9km/5mi further on, turn right onto D 16.

Tillac

This small *castelnau* has picturesque half-timbered houses and a fortified tower with a 14C **church**.

Return to Mirande along D 16 and N 21.

The area to the north of Toulouse forms part of the *département* of Tarn-et-Garonne, created on 4 November 1808, during the First French Empire by order of Napoleon I; it subsumed territories belonging to neighbouring areas, with more than half being taken from the Lot (including Montauban and Moissac), over one-third from Haute-Garonne (including Castelsarrasin), and the rest from the department of Lot-et-Garonne, Gers, and Aveyron.
The area generally is a peaceful haven of contrasting scenery, teeming with wild life and liberally dotted with attractive and appealing medieval villages. There is a strong historical heritage here, but at the same time the area's profile with tourists is low. The overwhelming feeling is one of space, where the pace of living is set at andante, and the peace and tranquillity of French countryside is at its most sublime, a landscape of limestone gorges, tree-covered hillsides, deep valleys and rivers.

Highlights

1. Explore the **gorges de l'Aveyron** (pp417, 427)
2. Visit the chateau in **Bruniquel** (p418)
3. Walk around the old town of **Montauban** (p421)
4. Check out the Romanesque art in **Moissac** (p419)
5. Make time to see **Saint Antonin-noble-val** (p425)

A gem

The Abbaye de Saint-Pierre in Moissac is a gem among French religious architecture. Founded in 506, it is a masterpiece of church-building and one of the most beautiful extant buildings dating from the Middle Ages.

In the pink

In a light-hearted joust at Toulouse and Albi, the town of Montauban likes to think of itself as the pinkest of the three pink towns. This ancient bastide, founded in 1144 by the Counts of Toulouse was so successful as an urban planning concept that it gave rise to the wider development of bastide settlements throughout the south of France. Normally, at the centre of a bastide is a square, except that in the case of Montauban to describe the irregular-shaped Place Nationale as a square you have to be very poor at drawing squares. Of course, that does nothing to detract from the delightful centre with its unique double-cloistered arcades beneath which merchants plied their trade, town proclamations were announced, and more than one hapless soul was hanged.

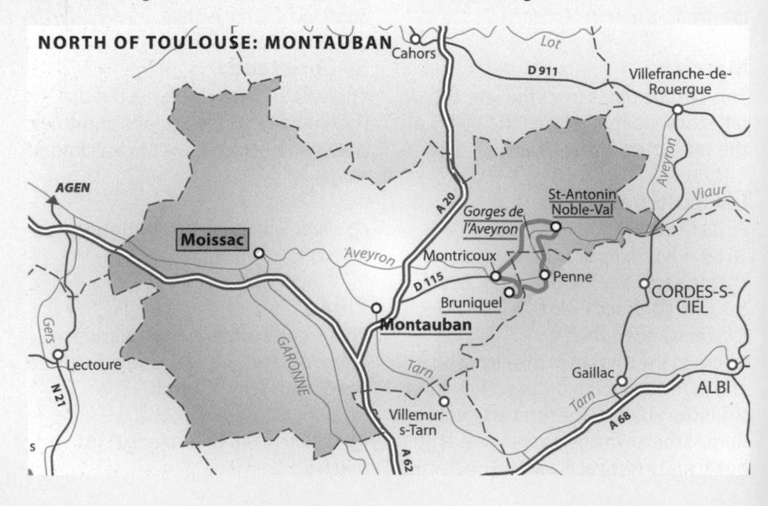

Montauban by the River Tarn

©nougaro/Fotolia.com

Along the Aveyron Gorge

The Aveyron River rises east of Rodez and extends westwards to Montauban, where it joins the Tarn, which in turn joins the Garonne and so through to the Atlantic at Bordeaux.

The section from north of Najac to Bruniquel, known as the '**Gorges de l'Aveyron**', is outstandingly attractive. The scenery is dramatic and there are many lovely riverside villages to visit. The village of Bruniquel, for example, is classified as one of the 'most beautiful villages of France', and its setting high up on the cliffs above the Aveyron is both dramatic and impressive. A medieval château dominates the surrounding area, perched on a precipitous rockface.

Because of its riverside location, overlooked by the cliffs of the Aveyron Gorge, **St Antonin-noble-val** has become a centre for all manner of sporting activity. The rushing white water sparkles in the sunshine, enticing to canoeists to brave its rapids, and for whom the views of the gorge take on a new perspective.

Rock-climbing on the **Roc d'Anglars** tempts the bold, while the chance to hire a mountain bike and explore the many trails and tracks should not be dismissed.

St Antonin's Sunday market is renowned. The picturesque narrow streets and market square bustle with the produce of farmers, artisans and wine growers. The fruit and vegetables on the stalls change with the season, and there is always a good selection of bread, meat, charcuterie, herbs and spices.

Château de Bruniquel

©Yvann K/Fotolia.com

Bruniquel★

With the bold outline of its castle rising like a crown above the town, Bruniquel lies in a picturesque setting★ at the mouth of the great gorges that the Aveyron has cut through the limestone of the Causse de Limogne.

- **Population:** 587.
- **Michelin Map:** 337: F-7.
- **Info:** Prom. du Ravelin, 82800 Bruniquel. 05 63 67 29 84.
- **Location:** This town is on a magical site at the mouth of the Aveyron gorge.
- **Don't Miss:** The old town and painted murals in the Maison Payrol.

A BIT OF HISTORY

According to Gregory of Tours (bishop, theologian and historian 538-594), Bruniquel has its origins in the founding of a fortress on this site by Brunhilda, daughter of the king of the Visigoths and wife of Sigebert, King of Austrasia. The memory of this princess is perpetuated by the castle tower that bears her name. The bitter rivalry between her and her sister-in-law Fredegund caused war to break out between Austrasia and Neustria in the 6C. The brutality of Brunhilda's own death is legendary; she was bound by her hair, an arm and a leg to the tail of an unbroken horse and smashed to pieces.

OLD TOWN★

Stroll past the ruined fortifications and town gateways, along narrow streets lined with pantile roofed houses. Especially pretty are rue du Mazel, rue Droite-de-Trauc and rue Droite-de-la-Peyre.

Château

Open Jul-Aug 10am-7pm; Mar-Jun and Sep-mid Nov 10am-6pm. Guided tours. 3.50€. 05 63 67 27 67. http://bruniquel.org.

Although the castle's foundations probably date from the 6C, most of it was built from the 12C to 18C. The barbican, which defended the approaches to the castle from the side of the village, stands on the esplanade in front of the main buildings. Inside, the decor of the 12C-13C Knights' Hall features colonnettes with capitals. Stairs lead to the first floor where the guard-room boasts a beautiful 17C chimney-piece. In the seigneurial wing of the castle, a Renaissance loggia overlooks the sheer cliff, in which numerous rock shelters have been hollowed out, giving an open **view★** of the bend in the river below.

Maison Payrol

Open Apr-Sep 10am-6pm (Jul-Aug 7pm); Mar and Oct weekends 10am-5pm. Closed Nov-Mar. 3€. 05 63 67 26 42. http://bruniquel.org.

This town house owned by the influential Payrols family was built between the 13C and 17C. The 13C **murals★** and imposing Renaissance ceiling are outstanding.

ADDRESSES

STAY

Chambre d'hôte Les Brunis – *4965 rte deMontricoux, 82800 Nègrepelisse – 7km/4mi W of Bruniquel on D 115 then D 958. 05 63 67 24 08 www.chambres-aveyron.com – 5rms.* Behind the renovated façade of this 19C farmhouse is a a lovely swimming pool and green oasis for breakfasting in the shade of the paulownia. Rustic decor and table d'hôte meals.

EAT

Terrassier – *Au bourg, 82800 Vaissac. 05 63 30 94 60 - www.chezterrassier. com - Closed 1-15 Jan, 19-25 Nov, Fri evening, Sun evening.* A lovely auberge perfectly placed for trips along the Quercy and the Albigeois. Also has 18rms of accommodation.

Moissac★★

The town of Moissac lies clustered around the ancient abbey of St-Pierre (a site of major interest for lovers of Romanesque art), in a fresh and pretty setting on the north bank of the Tarn and either side of the Garonne branch canal. A jazz festival brings life to the town in July and classical music concerts are given throughout July and August. The surrounding hillsides are covered with orchards and vineyards which produce the reputed Chasselas grape variety (a white grape).

- **Population:** 12 300.
- **Michelin Map:** Michelin Local map 337: C-7.
- **Info:** Pl. Durand-de-Bredon, 82200 Moissac, ℘05 63 04 01 85. www.moissac.fr.
- **Location:** 72km/45mi NW of Toulouse. To get to the abbey by car, follow the signs and big orange arrows pointing the way.
- **Don't Miss:** Tasting the famed Chasselas grape.

A BIT OF HISTORY

The golden age of the abbey – It was during the 11C and 12C that Moissac Abbey was at its most influential. Probably founded in the 7C by a Benedictine monk from the Norman abbey of St-Wandrille, the young abbey of Moissac did not escape from the pillage and destruction wrought by Arabs, Norsemen and Hungarians.

It was struggling to right itself again when, in 1047, an event occurred which was to change its destiny. On his way through Quercy, St Odilon, the famous and influential abbot of Cluny, who had just laid down the rules at the monastery at Carennac, affiliated the abbey of Moissac to that of Cluny. This marked the beginning of a period of prosperity. With the support of Cluny, Moissac Abbey set up priories throughout the region, extending its influence as far as Catalonia.

A series of misfortunes – The Hundred Years War, during which Moissac was occupied twice by the English, and then the Wars of Religion dealt the abbey some fearsome blows. It was secularised in 1628 and then suppressed altogether during the Revolution. In 1793, during the Reign of Terror, the archives were dispersed, the art treasures pillaged and numerous sculptures disfigured. In the mid 19C, it narrowly escaped complete destruction when there was question of demolishing the monastery buildings and cloisters to make way for the railway line from Bordeaux to Sète. The intervention of the Beaux-Arts commission saved it from ruin.

Cloisters, Abbaye de Moissac

L. Cazenave/MICHELIN

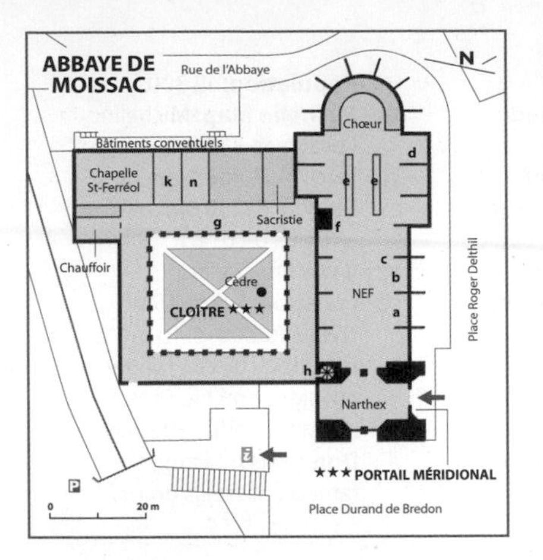

ABBEY★★ *1hr*

Église St-Pierre★

All that remains of the original 11C abbey church is the belfry porch, fortified c 1180 with a watch-path, crenellated parapet, loopholes and machicolated gallery. The nave is partly Romanesque and partly 15C French Gothic.

The majestic tympanum above this **South portal** ★★★ doorway, executed c 1130, is one of the finest Romanesque sculptures in France. The nave contains an Our Lady of Pity from 1476 (**a**), a Flight into Egypt from the late 15C (**b**), a magnificent Romanesque **Crucifix**★ (12C) (**c**) and an Entombment (**d**) from 1485. The chancel is enclosed by a 16C carved stone screen and the choir stalls (**e**) date from the 17C. In an alcove beneath the organ is a white Pyrenean marble Merovingian sarcophagus (**f**).

Cloisters★★★

Entrance through the tourist office. Open Jul-Aug 9am-7pm; Apr-Jun and Sep-Oct 9am-noon, 2-6pm (Sat-Sun and public holidays 10am-noon, 2-6pm); Nov-Mar 10am-noon, 2-5pm (Sat-Sun and public holidays 2-5pm). Closed 1 Jan and 25 Dec. 5€, ticket combined with the Musée Marguerite-Vidal and Centre d'art roman 05 63 04 01 85.

These late 11C cloisters have delicate arcades in harmonious tones of white, pink, green and grey marble, and sculpted decoration featuring animal, botanical, geometric and historiated motifs. A staircase in the south-west corner (**h**) leads to the first floor of the narthex and roof views of the cloisters, town and Tarn Valley beyond.

The conventual buildings include the calefactory, St-Ferréol Chapel containing some 12C capitals, a room (**k**) illustrating Moissac's influence on sculpture in the Quercy region, and another (**n**) housing religious art and liturgical vestments.

ADDITIONAL SIGHT

Musée Marguerite-Vidal

Open daily except Sun morning and Mon: Jul-Aug 10am-1pm, 3-7pm; Apr-Jun and Sep 10an-noon, 2-6pm; Oct-Mar 10am-noon, 2-5pm. Closed 1 Jan, 1 May, 25 Dec. 5€, ticket combined with the cloister. 05 63 04 03 08. www.moissac.fr.

The museum housed in the original abbot's lodgings celebrates the abbey's importance during the Middle Ages and its influence throughout the South-West France. The 17C stairwell displays religious items of historical interest. Collections show regional history and traditions with ceramics, furniture, Moissac headdresses, reconstructed 19C kitchen from the Bas Quercy region, and local craftwork and costumes.

EXCURSIONS

Boudou

7km/4.5mi west of Moissac. Leave by the D 813 in the direction of Agen.

From a promontory, to the south of the church there is a fine **panorama**★ of the Garonne valley. The river passes below a range of low hills covered with vines.

Castelsagrat

18km/11mi north of Moissac.

Picturesque *bastide* with arcaded square, old well, houses roofed with round tiles. The façade of the 14C church conceals a fine Gothic nave at the heart of which is a large and unexpected gilt-wood altarpiece. The village is quiet and full of charm.

ADDRESSES

STAY

Chambre d'hôte Ferme de la Marquise – *Brassac, 82190 Bourg-de-Visa – 16km/10mi NW of Moissac on D 7. ℘05 63 94 25 16 – www.fermelamarquise.com – 4rms – meal*. This venerable working farm offers a glimpse of rural life in Quercy. Guest rooms feature handsome exposed beams and meals prepared with farm produce, are a credit to the cooking of southwest France.

Chambre d'hôte Le Platane – *Coques-Lunel – 82130 Lafrançaise – 10km/6mi E of Moissac on D 927, D 2 and D 68 – ℘05 63 65 92 18 – www.leplatane.fr.tt – 4rms – meals*. This brick mansion, with its stables and dovecote, has been restored with comfort in mind. Relax by the pool or enquire about going horse-riding.

EAT

Le Chapon Fin – 3 *Pl. des Récollets. ℘05 63 04 04 22. www.lechaponfin-moissac.com. Closed 10 Nov-7 Dec, Mon between Nov-Easter.* This establishment on the market square pampers its customers. The dining room in contemporary pastels serves classic cuisine. In season, try the delicious chasselas doré de Moissac grapes. A few renovated bedrooms.

SHOPPING

Jacques Laporte – *6 R. du Marché. ℘05 63 04 03 05 – daily except Mon 8am-12.30pm, 2.30-7.30pm (Sun 8am-1pm) – closed 2 wks at end of Jan and 2 wks in Jul.* The cakes and other sweet treats sold in this pastry shop-chocolatier-ice cream parlour have a fine local reputation. The house speciality is the grain doré de Moissac, a delectable filled chocolate.

"La rue des Arts" – *9 R. Jean-Moura. ℘05 63 04 21 46 – daily from 9am.* At this appealing shop handicrafts are in the spotlight. Antique frames, paintings, ceramics and porcelain are restored here; glass is blown and lace tatted as one watches. Artisans share their enthusiasm and knowledge with interested visitors.

RECREATION

France Fluviale – *Quai Charles-de-Gaulle. ℘05 63 04 09 89 – www.bourgone-fluviale.com – Mar-Oct daily 9am-noon, 2pm-7pm; Nov-Feb daily except weekends 9am-12.30pm, 2-5.30pm.* Leisurely barge trips on the Canal des Deux-Mers and on the Tarn allow day sailors to discover the Moissac canal bridge and other attractions.

Montauban★

On the boundary between the hillsides of Bas Quercy and the rich alluvial plains of the Garonne and the Tarn, the old bastide of Montauban, built with a geometric street layout, is an important crossroads and a good point of departure for excursions into the Aveyron gorges. It is an active market town, selling fruit and vegetables from market gardens from all over the region. The almost exclusive use of pink brick lends the buildings here a distinctive character, found in most of the towns in Bas Quercy and the Toulouse area.

- **Population:** 53 200.
- **Michelin Map:** Michelin Local map 337: E-7.
- **Info:** 4 R. du Collège (pedestrian access Pl. Prax), 82000 Montauban, ℘05 63 63 60 60. www.montauban-tourisme.com
- **Location:** Administrative headquarters of the Tarn-et-Garonne departement, Montauban is served by the A 20.
- **Don't Miss:** The Musée Ingres ; La place Nationale in Old Montauban.

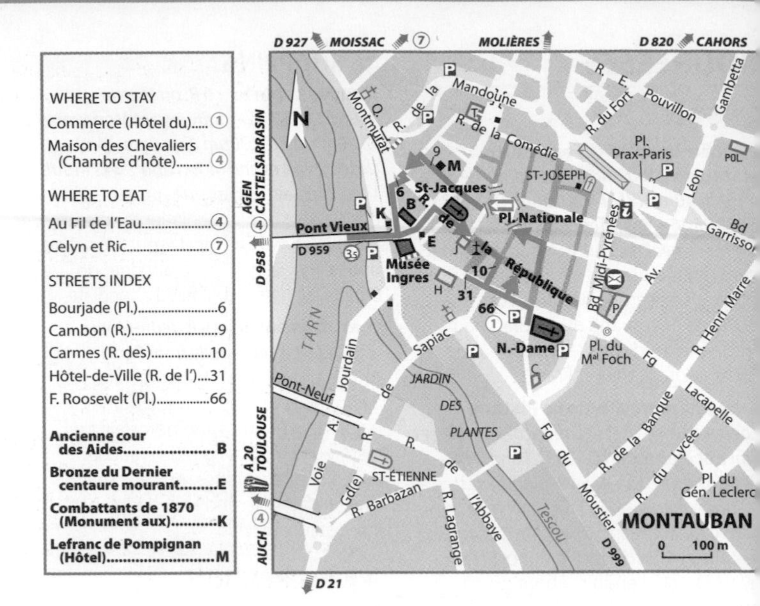

A BIT OF HISTORY

A powerful stronghold – In the 8C, there were already several communities on the site of the modern suburb of Moustier, on a hillside overlooking the Tescou. A Benedictine monastery was later established, around which a village called Montauriol grew up. The present town was founded in the 12C. Fed up with being exploited by the Abbot of Montauriol and the neighbouring feudal lords, the town's inhabitants sought protection from their overlord, the Count of Toulouse, who founded a bastide in 1144 on a plateau overlooking the east bank of the Tarn to which he accorded a liberal town charter. The inhabitants of Montauriol flocked there, contributing to its rapid expansion. Its name, *Mons albanus*, later became Montauban.

A Citadel of Protestantism – By 1561, most of the town was Reformist; the two town consuls were Calvinists and encouraged the inhabitants to pillage churches and convents, while the Catholic reaction failed to check the surge for reform. By the time of the Peace Treaty of St-Germain in 1570, Montauban was a safe refuge for Protestants. Henri of Navarre reinforced its fortifications, and it was on this site that the general meeting of all the reformed churches in France was held on three occasions.

The accession of Louis XIII heralded "Catholic reconquest." In 1621, Montauban was besieged by an army of 20 000 men, under the direct command of the king and his favourite, De Luynes. The townspeople resisted, repelling three assaults. Success was short-lived, and when La Rochelle fell in 1628, Montauban, the last bastion of Protestantism saw Louis XIII's army marching on it once more. This time, the town acquiesced peacefully and recognised the king and Cardinal Richelieu.

Famous Local Artists – Born in 1780 **Jean Auguste Dominique Ingres**, son of a minor painter and craftsman attended the studio of the Toulouse painter Roques. He spent nearly 2 years in Italy before opening a studio and founding a school in Paris. **Ingres** achieved a purity of line verging on technical perfection, while imbuing his works with personality and sensuality. Ingres won considerable recognition and glory before his death at the age of 87, when a major part of his work was bequeathed to his home town (see *Musée Ingres*).

Also born in Montauban, **Antoine Bourdelle** (1861-1929) owes much to his master, Rodin. His busts and sculpted groups combine strong energetic poses with simplicity of line and noble sentiment

OLD TOWN★ WALK

Restorations have made the historic centre a pleasure to stroll through. At the heart of the town is **Place Nationale★**, the starting point for this walk. Every morning the square comes to life with a busy, colourful market. The arcades were rebuilt in brick in the 17C to replace the wooden *couverts* destroyed by fires in 1614 and 1649. The pink-brick houses surrounding this beautiful square have high façades divided into bays by pilasters. On the corner of rue Malcousinat is a drapers' measure on the first pillar.

Head west towards Rue Cambon.

Rue Cambon

Hôtel Lefranc de Pompignan boasts a handsome brick **doorway★**.

In the courtyard of no 12 is an elegant wooden gallery supported by a stone colonnade.

Turn left at the end of the street, then left again.

Place Léon-Bourjade

The brasserie terrace offers a good view of the **Pont-Vieux** spanning the Tarn.

Continue to the River Tarn.

Pont-Vieux

Built in the 14C by architects Étienne de Ferrières and Mathieu de Verdun, the 205m/672ft long Pont-Vieux spans the Tarn in seven arches resting on piers protected by cutwaters. Like the Pont Valentré in Cahors, it was also fortified.

Ancienne Cour des Aides

This beautiful 17C building which once housed the Court of Excise Taxes contains two museums (*see Museums*).

Église St-Jacques

The tower façade of this fortified church dedicated to St James still bears traces of cannonballs fired during the 1621 siege. The **belfry** resting on a machicolated square tower dates from the late 13C. It is built of brick on an octagonal plan with three rows of windows. The nave was renovated in the 15C and rib vaulting was added in the 18C.

Continue along Rue de la République alongside Église St-Jacques as far as Rue des Carmes and turn right.

Rue des Carmes

At no 24, the **Hôtel Mila de Cabarieu** features an interesting red-brick portico with surbased arcades.

Turn right on rue de l'Hôtel-de-Ville.

Rue de l'Hôtel de Ville

Note the late 18C Hôtel Sermet-Deymie with an entrance doorway flanked by four Ionic columns.

Beneath the arcades on place Nationale

Retrace your steps; follow Rue du Dr-Lacaze.

Cathédrale Notre-Dame-de-l'Assomption

The cathedral is a classical building of vast proportions. The façade, framed by two square towers, has an imposing peristyle supporting colossal statues of the four Evangelists. In the north arm of the transept is a famous painting by Ingres, the **Vow of Louis XIII**.

Place Franklin-Roosevelt

Next to the building with caryatids, the Passage du Vieux-Palais linking two Renaissance courtyards leads to **Rue de la République**, emerging at no 25. At no 23 there is an attractive courtyard with multi-storey arcades.

Return to Place Nationale via Rue de la Résistance and Rue Michelet (left).

MUSEUMS AND CHÂTEAU

Musée Ingres★

19 r. de l'Hôtel-de-Ville. Open Jul-Aug daily 10am-6pm; rest of the year: daily except Mon 10am-noon, 2-6pm. Closed Sun morning from Nov-Mar, 1 Jan, 1 May, 14 Jul, 1 Nov, 25 Dec. 6€; no charge 1st Sunday in the month. 05 63 22 12 91.

The museum is housed in what used to be the bishops' palace, built in 1664 on the site of two castles. The first castle, called the "Château-bas," was built in the 12C by the Count of Toulouse. Demolished in 1229, it was replaced a century later by another fortress, built on the orders of the Black Prince, of which a few rooms still remain. The current palace was bought by the municipality when the diocese was suppressed at the time of the Revolution and converted to a museum in 1843. It is an imposing, sober pink-brick edifice.

The works of Ingres are the museum's main attraction. His admirable canvas *Jesus among the Doctors* was completed when he was 82. There are numerous sketches, academic studies, **portraits** – of Gilbert, Madame Gonse, Belvèze – and *Ossian's Dream*, executed in 1812 for Napoleon's bedchamber in Rome. A glass display contains the master's paintbox and famous violin, and 4 000 of his **drawings** in rotation.

Other museum highlights are works by primitive schools and **paintings from the 14C to 18C**, 15C Italian works, 17C Flemish paintings (Jordaens, Van Dyck), Dutch and Spanish (José de Ribera) schools and the sculptures of **Bourdelle**. In the surviving part of the 14C castle, vaulted rooms display **regional archaeology, local history, applied arts** and temporary exhibitions.

Opposite the Musée Ingres stands the admirable bronze **The Last of the Centaurs Dies**★ by Bourdelle (1914) and on quai de Montmurat, the 1870 War Memorial showing Bourdelle's architectural capacities.

Musée du Terroir

Ground floor, 2 pl. Antoine-Bourdelle. Open Tue-Sat 10am-noon, 2pm-6pm. 2.50€ (children free). 05 63 66 46 34.

On the ground floor of this regional folk museum, the local society "Escolo Carsinol" presents a display on daily life in Bas Quercy. Most traditional crafts are represented by tools, instruments and model figures. One room reconstructs the inside of a 19C peasant home.

Musée d'Histoire Naturelle

First floor, 2 pl. Antoine-Bourdelle. Open daily except Mon 10am-noon, 2-6pm (Sun 2-6pm). Closed public holidays. 2.50€, no charge 1st Sunday in the month. 05 63 22 13 85.

Several rooms contain a variety of zoological exhibits and a huge ornithologi cal collection including exotic parrots, humming birds and birds of Paradise.

Château de Reyniès

Leave Montauban travelling S on D 21 towards Villemur-sur-Tarn. Guided tours of the exterior only: Jul-Sep daily except Wed 10am-6pm. 2€. 05 63 64 04 02.

Built in 1289 then destroyed during the Wars of Religion after the Latour family converted to Protestantism.

Saint-Antonin-Noble-Val★

and Aveyron gorges

The town's houses, with virtually flat roofs covered in half-cylindrical tiles faded by the sun, are built in gentle tiers on the north bank of the river.

- **Population:** 1 797.
- **Michelin Map:** 337: G-7.
- **Info:** Place de la Mairie, 82140 St-Antonin-Noble-Val, ℘05 63 30 63 47. www.saint-antonin-noble-val.com.
- **Location:** 24km/15mi W of Caussade D926 then the D5 and 31km/19.5mi NW of Cordes sur Ciel on the D600 then the D115.
- **Parking:** Place des Tilleuls in the direction of Caylus.
- **Don't Miss:** The Ancien Hôtel de Ville and the Musée Marcel-Lenoir à Montricoux.

A BIT OF HISTORY

So delightful was the setting of the Gallo-Roman settlement, forerunner of the present town, that it was given the name "glorious valley" (noble val). An oratory founded by Saint Antonin, who came to convert this part of the Rouergue, was replaced in the 8C by an abbey.The viscount of Saint Antonin, Ramon Jordan, born in 1150, ranks among the most gifted troubadours of his age.

TOWN WALK

The town developed rapidly during the Middle Ages, due to trade in cloth, fur and leather, as can be seen by the 13C, 14C and 15C houses which were once the residences of wealthy merchants.

Ancien hôtel de ville★

This mansion was built in 1125 for a rich, newly ennobled townsman, Pons de Granholet, and is one of the oldest examples of civil architecture in France. In the 14C, it was the consuls' residence. Viollet-le-Duc restored it in the 19C, adding a square belfry crowned by a machicolated loggia in the Tuscan style, based on a project he presented in 1845.

The façade is composed of two storeys. The gallery of colonnettes on the first storey is decorated with two pillars bearing statues of King Solomon and Adam and Eve.

The building now houses a **museum** (*open Jul-Aug daily except Tue 10am-1pm and 3-6pm; rest of the year book 2/3 days in advance. 2.50€. ℘05 63 68 23 52)* accessed through the arcaded ground floor. The museum contains prehistoric collections and is particularly rich in material from the Magdalenian Period. One room covers local traditions and folklore.

S. Sauvignier/MICHELIN

Pillar of Adam and Eve, Ancien Hôtel de Ville

Rue Guilhem Peyre

This street leads off from beneath the belfry of the old town hall. It used to be the grand route taken by all processions. On the right there is what used to be the Royal Barracks, known as the "English Barracks," and in a bend in the road a splendid 13C-16C mansion.

Walk down the street towards Place de Payrols then turn right.

St-Antonin-Nobel-Val
J. Boyer/MICHELIN

Rue des Grandes Boucheries

The Maison du Roy, now a restaurant, situated on the corner of rue de l'Église, has five large pointed arches looking in at ground-floor level, and the same number of twin windows on the first floor, with youthful faces adorning the capitals.

Walk up Rue de l'Église towards the new town hall.

Ancien Couvent des Génovéfains

Built in 1751, this convent of the Order of St Genevieve is now home to the town hall and the tourist office.

Walk to Place de la Halle via Rue Saint-Angel and Place du Buoc.

Croix de la Halle

In front of the solid pillars of the covered market, there is a strange lollipop-shaped 14C **Cross**, carved on both sides. This rare piece of work would once have stood at the entrance to or in the middle of the town graveyard.

Rue de la Pélisserie

There are 13C-14C houses redolent of the former wealth of master tanners and furriers all along this street.

Turn left onto Rue des Banhs.

Rue Rive-Valat

A little canal spanned by bridges flows along this street; it is one of many tributaries of the River Bonnière which were dug during the Middle Ages to provide a main drainage system and water for the tanneries. These have open top floors, which are used to store and dry skins.

Rue Rive-Valat leads back to Place de la Halle via Rue Droite.

Rue Droite

Two houses stand out because of their interesting carved keystones: the late-15C **Maison de l'Amour** (House of Love) where a man and woman are depicted chastely touching lips, and the **Maison du Repentir** (House of Repentance) where, in contrast, two faces are shown turned away from one another. About halfway along the street, there is a beautiful double-corbelled façade, decorated with half-timbering interspersed with slightly golden porous limestone and wooden mullions.

Walk left to Place des Capucins then along Rue du Pont-des-Vierges.

Rue du Pont-des-Vierges

Close to place du Bessarel, an old walnut-oil press can be visited (*apply to the museum*).

Château de Penne

DRIVING TOUR

GORGES DE L'AVEYRON★

Round trip of 49km/30mi – allow 3hrs. Leave St-Antonin S, crossing the bridge over the Aveyron and turning right onto D 115 which runs alongside the river.

After 2.5km/1.5mi turn left onto a steeply climbing, narrow road up to the top of the cliffs (*signposted "corniche"*). This picturesque **scenic route**★★ leads through the hamlet of Viel-Four with its pantiled roofs. As the road drops back towards the river, the picturesque hamlet of **Brousses** comes into sight.

At Cazals, cross the river and turn left.

The road (D 173) begins to climb again immediately, heading through farming country, giving good views of the Aveyron's meanders and the valley floor covered with peach and apple orchards and fields divided by rows of poplar trees.

Cross back to the south bank of the Aveyron.

Penne

This old village, overlooked by its castle ruins, occupies the most remarkable **site**★, perched on the tip of a bulbous rocky outcrop rising sheer from the south bank of the Aveyron and somewhat precariously overhanging the river on one of the prettiest reaches of its course.

Park the car by the side of the road (D 9), at the entrance to the village.

From the belfry, a pretty little street lined with old houses leads up to the castle, then down to Peyrière gate on the opposite side of the village. The 17C plague cross marks the beginning of the steep footpath that leads up the rockface to the **castle** ruins.
From the tip of the promontory, there is a good **view**★ of the towers and jagged walls of the castle, the village of Penne and the Aveyron Valley.

Leave Penne S on D 9.

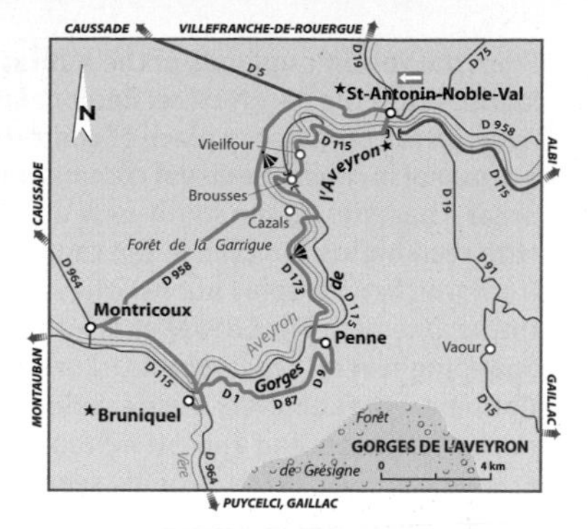

There are some excellent **views**★ of the village. The road scales the edge of the plateau before crossing a region of sparse vegetation and then dropping into the valley once more.

D 1E on the left leads to Bruniquel.

Bruniquel★

See BRUNIQUEL.

Cross the Aveyron and follow the road along the north bank to Montricoux.

Montricoux

Montricoux is built on terraces above the north bank of the Aveyron where it broadens out into a wide plain. The town's old curtain walls are still standing. Place Marcel-Lenoir and some of the streets contain picturesque medieval half-timbered houses with over-hanging upper floors (13C-16C). Inside the château at Montricoux is the **Musée Marcel-Lenoir**★ (*open early May-Sep 10am-6pm; guided visit possible (45 mins). 5€. 05 63 67 26 48; www.marcel-lenoir.com*), an exhibition of most of the work of painter Marcel Lenoir, born in 1872 in Montauban.

Take D 958 back to St-Antonin.

This road runs through the forest of La Garrigue, giving glimpses of the Aveyron below and to the right. The final stretch before St-Antonin is once again a spectacular cliff road overlooking the river.

From the volcanic uplands of the Aubrac in the north-west to the undulating landscape of the Parc Naturel Régional des Grands Causses in the south, Aveyron is a hummocky place of contrasts and many stories. In the west lie a group of fortified medieval communities designed for defence, law and order – bastides. In the south-east the towns and villages have strong links with the Knights Templar. In the centre, lies the great cathedral city of Rodez from which roads splay out like the spokes of a wheel leading to all parts of the *département*. The Lot valley is lush and green and sparsely populated. Spanning several *départements* – Lozère, Cantal, Aveyron, Lot and Lot-et-Garonne – the Lot offers a wide variety of attractions, landscapes from ruined fortresses and ancient hilltop villages, to peaceful winding rivers and dramatic gorges. Often wrongly seen as an extension of the Dordogne, the Lot very much has its own identity.

Highlights

1. Enjoy a visit to **Conques** (p431)
2. Invest in the excellent **Laguiole cutlery** (pp429, 436)
3. Tour the Aveyron **bastide towns** like Najac (p441) and Villefranche-de-Rouergue (p448).
4. Try the regional lunchtime specialty **aligot** (p430)
5. Explore the covered passage ways of **Entraygues** (p434)

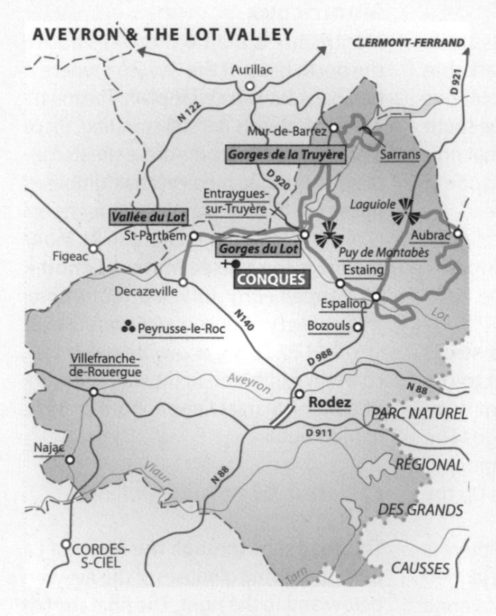

A taste of the region

One of the specialist dishes of the region is **aligot**, a delicious and stringy mash of melted Tomme cheese, preferably made from the milk of Aubrac cows, blended with potatoes and often with garlic. The dish was originally made from bread by monks travelling the pilgrims' way to Santiago de Compostella, but potatoes replaced bread after they were introduced into mainstream cooking in France. Equally mouth-watering, other than for vegetarians, is the steak that comes from Aubrac cattle.

Accompanied by a simple salad or *frites*, and a glass of Marcillac wine, there is nothing more satisfying at lunchtime.

Marcillac is in the northwest of Aveyron, and enjoys a micro-climate that favours wine production. On the lighter side of things, *galette des rois* is a popular French cake that is usually eaten to celebrate Epiphany (6th January), the day when the Three Kings are said to have visited the baby Jesus. Customarily, a "fève" – a small china figurine – is baked into the cake.

The one who finds it is crowned king or queen, and chooses his or her partner from among the assembled guests.

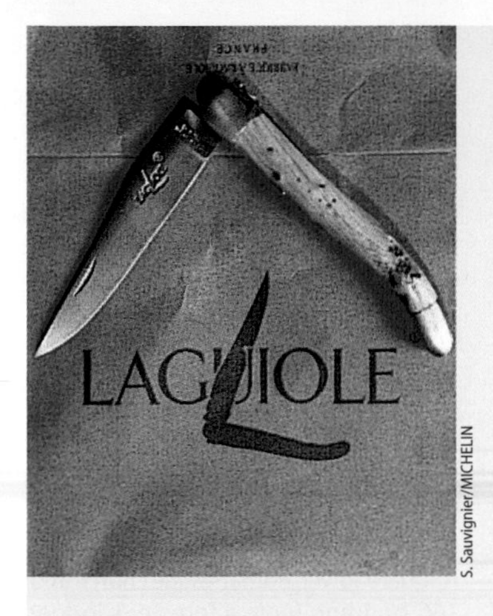

S. Sauvignier/MICHELIN

A cut above the rest

There is in Aveyron one hallmark above all else known throughout France, that of **Laguiole** (pronounced la-yol or laïole, and in some parts of France with a hard 'g' – Lag-iol). No discerning sommelier would be without a Laguiole *tire-buchon*, almost as if using one makes the wine taste so much better.

Laguiole is one of the liveliest small communities in the Massif Central. In winter, the rippling Roussillon heights of the adjacent Aubrac mountains are popular with skiers, snowboarders and snow-shoers; in summer, husbands drag along their wives in order to explain what all the knifely fuss is about, and why they must have one – that, and the production of Aubrac cattle (symbolised by a huge bronze bull in the Place du Foirail).

The Aubrac cattle have been around for hundreds of years, the Laguiole knife only since 1829, when it was invented by a local man, Pierre-Jean Calmels. This simple implement became the peasants' general purpose tool, and a sign of recognition for those who migrated to Paris. Napoleon III granted permission to mark each knife with a symbolic bee, while a nose for a good marketing ploy has seen to it that each knife or corkscrew carries further symbolic designs.

If imitation is the sincerest form of flattery, then the makers of Laguiole implements have much to be proud of, but whether that is the case is another matter. The industry virtually collapsed in the 1950s, but was revived with a vengeance thirty years later. Now almost the whole of the main street in Laguiole is devoted to knives, forks, corkscrews and a comprehensive range of instruments of uncertain intent.

S. Sauvignier/MICHELIN

Aubrac★

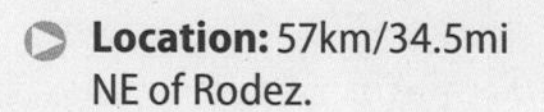

Location: 57km/34.5mi NE of Rodez.

Situated at 1 300m/4 225ft above sea level, Aubrac is a small holiday resort that offers plenty of sunshine and fresh air during the summer months, but is also popular for winter sports. Parisians with roots in the Auvergne return here to enjoy local treats such as aligot, a potato dish made with lashings of local Tomme cheese. After a few days of good cooking and fresh air, they depart homewards sufficiently revitalised to cope with city life again.

Aligot – a speciality from Aubrac

S. Sauvignier/MICHELIN

RESORT

Aubrac is also the name of the most southerly of the volcanic uplands of the Auvergne. It is a region of ponderous, rolling hills, with vast stretches of countryside covered in pastureland on which herds of cattle, named after the region, graze during the summer (Fête de la Transhumance in late May). While travelling through the area, keep an eye out for the drailles, trails occasionally lined with low drystone walls along which animals are herded from one seasonal pasture to another.

In winter, cross-country skiers arrive at the resorts of the Espace Nordique des Monts d'Aubrac, set up in 1985 (Aubrac, Bonnecombe, Brameloup, Lacalm, Laguiole, Nasbinals, St-Urcize).

A square tower, Romanesque church and 16C building (now a forester's lodge) are all that remain of the estate of the Brothers Hospitaller of Aubrac, monastic knights who, from the 12C to the 17C, escorted pilgrims to Rocamadour or Santiago de Compostela.

DRIVING TOUR

WESTERN AUBRAC DRIVING TOUR

Round-trip of 117km/73mi leaving from Aubrac – allow 4hr. Take D 533 S to Boralde de St-Chély Valley. Turn left onto D 19 to Bonnefon. From Bonnefon; D629 left, then right.

The road twists uphill with beautiful views of the Lot Valley and Sévérac plateau. Just past a forester's lodge, it enters the beech wood forest of Aubrac.

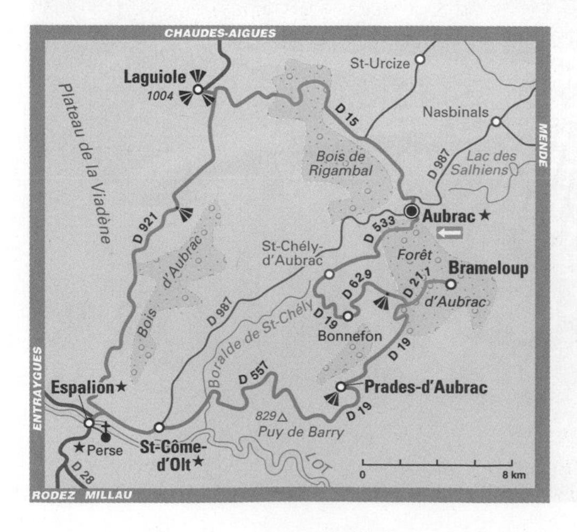

Brameloup

This small winter sports resort, named after the Occitan word loba for mountain, has many wide forest trails.

Turn back and take D 19 to the left.

Prades-d'Aubrac
Note the octagonal bell tower on this village's 16C church. The road descends towards the Lot with views over the Rouergue plateaux of moorlands, meadows, fields of crops, groves of chestnuts, and luscious orchards.

St-Côme-d'Olt★
The houses of this small fortified town have spread beyond the limits of the old curtain wall, with 15C and 16C houses lining its narrow streets. The village church features a Flamboyant style (16C) spiral bell-tower and Renaissance style sculpted and panelled door.

Espalion★
See LOT VALLEY. Leave Espalion on D 921 N. The road climbs towards Laguiole providing views of the Aubrac mountains and the Viadène plateau.

Laguiole
See LAGUIOLE.

Take D 15 from the entrance to Laguiole.

East of Laguiole, this road, one of the highest in the Aubrac region crosses pastureland and beech woods, offering views of the Viadène and Rouergue plateaux and the Margeride.

Conques★★★

This peaceful little village beautifully set★ on the steep slopes of the Ouche gorge has a splendid Romanesque church and remains of an abbey which still offers shelter to pilgrims en route to Santiago de Compostela.

- **Population:** 302.
- **Michelin Map:** Michelin Local map 338: G-3.
- **Info:** Office de tourisme de Conques – R. du Chanoine-Benazech, 12320 Conques. ✆05 65 72 85 00. www.conques.fr.
- **Location:** 39km/24mi N of Rodez.
- **Don't Miss:** Spectacular view looking down on Conques from the site du Bancarel. The treasury of the Sainte-Foy Abbey and the Tympanan du portail occidental.

A BIT OF HISTORY
St Faith
The Sainte-Foy Abbey became famous only after it acquired (in a very dubious manner) the relics of a 13-year-old Christian girl martyred around 303 AD in Agen – St Faith (known to the French as Sainte Foy). In the 9C, the legend goes, a monk from Conques went to Agen where St Faith's relics were guarded, with the intent of stealing them. After 10 years, he managed to win the confidence of the community and was placed in charge of guarding the relics, whereupon he promptly stole them and took them back with him to Conques. Once there, the saint doubled the number of miracles performed, called the "japes and jests of St Faith."

Pilgrimages
Construction of the present church began in the 11C. Its architecture is similar to Santiago de Compostela, St-Sernin in Toulouse, St-Martin in Tours and St-Martial in Limoges. Between Le Puy and Moissac, Conques was a stopover in the guide book for pilgrims on their way to Santiago de Compostela, and this pilgrim traffic brought about Conques' Golden Age between the 11C to the 13C.
The monastery was eventually converted into a collegiate church of canons, but in 1561 was reduced to ruins by the Protestants. The church was on the point of complete collapse when the writer Pros-

Abbatiale Ste-Foy

Jacass/MICHELIN

per Mérimée gave such a heart-rending account of its plight that he saved it.

VILLAGE★

The steep little streets are lined with lovely old houses in red stone which harmonises with their limestone roof slabs (*lauzes*). Above the church of Ste-Foy, the village is spread out on the hillside along rue Charlemagne, the path once climbed by the pilgrims on their way to the abbey. From this street, a rocky path leads to a hillock topped by the chapel of St-Roch and a calvary. From here there is a beautiful view of Conques clustered around the abbey church. Above the church, more streets lead to the remains of old fortifications.

At the war memorial, turn left towards place du Château.

In the square stands the fine Château d'Humières (15C-16C) with its carved consoles. Farther on is one of the three remaining 12C gates, the Porte de Vinzelle. From the cemetery, a corner of which is occupied by the funerary chapel of the abbots of Conques, there is a pretty view of the Ouche.

ABBATIALE STE-FOY★★

Allow half a day. This magnificent Romanesque abbey church was built between the mid-11C and 12C.

Tympanum above the west door★★★

The originality and dimensions of the tympanum make it a masterpiece of 12C Romanesque sculpture. Its elaborate detailed carved images and inscriptions – with angels, knights, devils, leviathans, saints and images of Christ, Hell and Paradise must have made quite a strong impression on pilgrims making their way to Santiago de Compostela.

Interior

The church's inside makes a striking impression because of its enormous height (22m/72ft) and simplicity of line, verging on the austere. As in other pilgrimage churches, the chancel is wide and surrounded by an ambulatory to allow the faithful to see the relics of St Faith, once displayed there.

The sacristy walls show traces of 15C frescoes depicting the martyrdom of St Faith. The ornate 12C railings in front of the choir replaced a screen said to have been made from the fetters of prisoners released by St Faith. Above the passage connecting the galleries is a beautiful sculpture group of the Annunciation. Note the contemporary stained-glass windows, the work of Pierre Soulages from Aveyron.

Cloisters

In 1975, the ground plan was reconstructed with paving stones. All that remains of the cloisters are arcades opening onto what was the refectory and a beautiful serpentine marble basin, once part of the monks' lavabo.

Trésor de Conques★★★ (Treasury)

Open Apr-Sep 9.30am-12.30pm, 2-6.30pm; rest of year 10am-noon, 2-6pm. 6€. 05 65 72 85 00.

The treasury of the abbey of Conques houses the most comprehensive collection of silver and gold plate which display the evolution of church plate in France from the 9C to the 16C. A particularly interesting set of reliquaries was produced by a goldsmithing workshop set up in the abbey in the 11C. Listed below, in chronological order, are the most important exhibits.

9C – Reliquary of Pepin, gold leaves embossed on a wooden core – thought to be a gift from Pepin, this exhibit is inlaid with numerous precious stones, including an antique intaglio depicting the god Apollo.

10C – Reliquary statue of St Faith **(Statue-reliquaire de Sainte Foy)**, the main piece in the collection, gold and silver gilt plating on a wooden core. Over the years the statue has had numerous precious stones added to it, as well as the 14C monstrance through which the relic can be seen (in the middle of her chest, just behind the head of the little figure in her lap). This unique piece of craftsmanship is also adorned with cameos and antique intaglios. The figure of the saint is holding tiny tubes designed to take flowers between her fingers.

11C – Portable alabaster altar, known as the *autel de Sainte Foy*, featuring embossed silver and enamel work; reliquary thought to be of Pope Pascal II, in silver on a wooden core, reworked several times; the *A de Charlemagne*, in gold-plated silver on a wooden core. Tradition has it that the Emperor, wishing to assign all the abbeys in Gaul with a letter of the alphabet according to their order of importance, awarded Conques the letter "A."

12C – St Faith's reliquary chest – this leather chest decorated with 31 enamel medallions still contains the remains of the saint; portable altar of the Abbot Bégon, consisting of a red porphyry plate in an engraved, niello silver mounting; reliquary known as the Lanterne de Bégon III or "St Vincent" reliquary, silver on a wooden core; five-and six-sided silver, gilt and enamel reliquaries, made in the 12C with much older fragments.

13C – Arm reliquary thought to be of St George, in silver on a wooden core, the hand making a sign of blessing; embossed and gold-plated silver triptych; Virgin and Child, in silver on a wooden core – this type of reliquary statue was very popular during the reign of St Louis.

14C – Head-reliquaries of St Liberate and St Marse, silver and painted canvas – small silver shrine of St Faith.

16C – Gilt gospel bookbinding; processional cross, made from embossed silver leaf on a wooden core with a relic of the true cross beneath the figure of Christ.

Trésor II (Musée Joseph-Fau)

Entrance through the tourist office.

This old house, located opposite the pilgrims' fountain, contains 17C furniture, statues, neo-Gothic reliquaries and Felletin tapestries from the abbey (*ground and first floors*). The basement contains a lapidary museum with a beautiful collection of Romanesque capitals and abaci, which are remains of the old cloisters.

VISIT

Centre européen d'Art et de Civilisation médiévale

Open daily except Sat-Sun 9am-noon, 2pm-6pm. Closed public holidays. No charge. 05 65 71 24 00. www.conques.com.

This new complex is a cultural reference centre for the historical period from 476 to 1453. Its unique documentary collection inspires a cultural programme of seminars, national heritage classes, presentations and concerts aimed at researchers, the general public and those interested in medieval civilisation.

EXCURSION

Château de Pruines

15km/9.3mi SE via D 901 to St-Cyprien-sur-Dourdou, then D 502. Open Jul-Aug 10am-7pm; Jun and Sep daily except Tue 2-7pm; Oct-Nov weekends and public holidays 2-6pm. Closed Dec-May. Guided tours possible (1hr). 05 65 72 91 64.

This pink-sandstone 17C manor houses an unusual **collection of ceramics★**.

ADDRESSES

COUNTRY CHARM

Ferme-auberge Domaine des Costes Rouges – *Combret – 12330 Nauviale – 13km/8mi S of Conques on D 901 then B-road. 05 65 72 83 85. www.domaine-descostes-rouges.fr – reservations required.* A rustic inn run by a friendly couple who prepare a selection of old traditional local favourites: saucisse à l'huile, canards à la broche flambés au capucin, home-baked pastries, accom[panied by locally produced wines. Three guest rooms in a house in the village. Swimming pool.

Auberge St-Jacques – *Au bourg 05 65 72 86 36. www.aubergestjacques.fr. Closed 2 Jan-2 Feb – 13rms – 8€.* This house is several centuries old, but the rustic style rooms are quite comfortable. Traditional local cuisine served in the dining room or ground floor brasserie.

Entraygues-sur-Truyère★

and Gorges de la Truyère

This small town founded in the 13C by the Count of Rodez at the confluence of the Lot and Truyère rivers, has hillsides covered with meadows, fruit trees and vines producing excellent wine. It is now a sports and leisure resort attracting canoeists and walkers. There is a good view of the village from the Condat viewpoint.

- **Population:** 1 182.
- **Michelin Map:** Michelin Local map 338: H-3.
- **Info:** Office du tourisme d'Entraygues-sur-Truyère, Pl. de la Republique, 05 65 44 56 10. www.tourisme-entraygues.com.
- **Don't Miss:** The old town with its Gothic bridge and covered passageways.
- **Kids:** A fairytale visit to the Valon château.

SIGHTS

Gothic bridge★

One-way traffic in summer.

The bridge across the Truyère dates from the end of the 13C.

Old town

To see the covered passageways known as "*cantous*" and houses with overhanging upper storeys, start from the place Albert-Castanié or place de la Croix and walk down Rue Droite. On the right is a fine 16C entrance with a knocker placed above the door so that riders did not have to dismount. Turn left on Rue du Collège and follow **Rue Basse★**, Entraygues' best preserved street. Continue along the water's edge (quai des Gabares) to a fine view of the castle dating from the 13C (*not open to the public*).

EXCURSIONS

Puy de Montabès★

11km/6.8mi NE along D 34 then right on D 652. 15min on foot round-trip.

Superb **panoramic view★** over the mountains of Cantal, Aubrac and Rouergue (and the cathedral in Rodez in clear weather).

Entraygues-sur-Truyére

©Hervé Lenain/Photoshot

DRIVING TOUR

Gorges de la Truyère★

80km/50mi round-trip – allow 3hr.

Leave Entraygues heading N along D 34.

The River Truyère flows through narrow sinuous gorges which are some of the finest natural sights in central France. Hydroelectric dams have not spoiled the character of the gorges. Roads traverse the valley with fine viewpoints over the river and its gorges.

Barrage de Cambeyrac

The 14.5m/47ft-high Cambeyrac dam is the last Truyère valley hydroelectric installation before the river flows into the Lot. Farther upstream is the Lardit hydroelectric power station.

In the hamlet of Banhars, turn left onto D 34. Beyond the bridge over the Selves, continue right along D 34.

The road winds through the Selves valley before reaching the Volonzac plateau.

In Volonzac, turn right onto a narrow road leading to Bez-Bedène.

Bez-Bedène

This typical Rouergue-style village occupies a harsh, isolated setting and consists of a few houses strung out along a rocky ridge enclosed within a meander of the Selves. Of note are the small 12C church with a bellcote, and the 14C bridge.

Continue along the same road to the crossroads with D 34, into which you turn right towards St-Amans-des-Cots. D 97 leads to the Maury dam.

Barrage de Maury

The Maury dam reservoir covering 166ha/410 acres lies in a varied, colourful landscape.

Drive back to St-Amans-des-Cots along D 97.

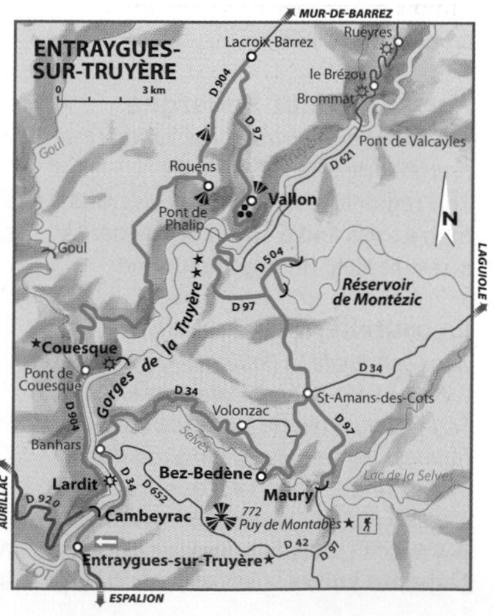

Réservoir de Montézic
The Montézic reservoir with a surface area of 245ha/605 acres is formed by two dams on the Plane rivulet.

Return to D 97; cross the Phalip suspension bridge over Couesque reservoir.

The road skirts the ruined castle of **Vallon**, and the hamlet offers a view over the Truyère gorges.

Follow D 904 S.

The road winds to **Rouens** and downhill from its church is a scenic view of Couesque reservoir and Phalip bridge. The road continues to the valley floor, with views of the Truyère gorges, Couesque dam and its reservoir.

Before the Couesque bridge on the Goul, take a road to the left which leads to the Couesque plant and dam.

Couesque dam★
The reservoir of this dam stretches as far as the confluence of the Bromme and the Truyère, where the tail-race from the Brommat underground plant emerges. As the road travels south, the valley gradually offers a landscape of meadows, vineyards and orchards. Ahead, the **Lardit hydroelectric power station** uses water from the Selves and the Selvet.

Laguiole

Laguiole (pronounced Laïole) is famous for its elegant pocket knives with distinctive handles made of horn, wood, and more rarely, ivory. Laguiole is also a winter sports resort and produces an excellent Tomme cheese from cows' milk.

- **Info:** Pl. de la Mairie, 12210 Laguiole. 05 65 44 35 94. www.laguiole-online.com.
- **Location:** On an Aubrac hillside, this peaceful town lies 24km(15mi) N of Espalion
- **Don't Miss:** Visiting a Laguiole knife factory.
- **Kids:** Le grenier de Capou at Soulages-Bonneval – interactive!

RESORT

Ski area
The Laguiole ski area above 1 000m/3 281ft part of the **Espace nordique des monts d'Aubrac**, is a favourite with cross-country skiers.

Musée du Haut-Rouergue
Currently being restructured; contact the tourist office. 05 65 44 35 94.
This regional museum contains craftsmen's tools and a *buron* or cowherd's hut, inhabited during the summer.

La coutellerie de Laguiole
Zone artisanale La Poujade. Open Jul -Aug 9am-noon, 2-7pm; Jan-Jun and Sep-Dec daily except Sun and public holidays 9am-noon, 2-7pm. Workshops open 11am-2.30pm, 3.45-7pm. 3.50€. 05 65 51 23 47. www.layole.com.
Watch craftsmen making famous Laguiole knives – collector's items – before your eyes. First manufactured in 1829, the Laguiole knife evolved as an all-purpose tool with a corkscrew and a pointed implement known as a "hoof-pick." Production was revived in the 1980s, and is now knife making is the town's leading industry. Knife making workshops line the main street, and the official trademark "Laguiole Origine Garantie" has been adopted for quality control.

EXCURSION

Château du Bousquet
5km/3mi SW. Open school holidays. 05 65 48 41 13.
Austere 14C castle built of volcanic basalt.

Lot Valley★★

The River Lot begins its long journey across in the sparsely populated Lozère in Languedoc, before flowing through Cantal in the south of the Auvergne to continue west through Aveyron and Lot to finish in Lot-et-Garonne in historic Aquitaine. In the process traversing the most agreeable landscapes of southern France.

Don't Miss: The portal of the Persea Romanesque church in Espalion, and the Gorges du Lot.

Kids: Château de Calmont d'Olt.

REGION

The region is one of charming towns and villages, including numerous bastides like Monflanquin and Villeneuve-sur-Lot. The region also has its share of 'most beautiful' villages, not least the exquisite Conques, Najac and St Cirq Lapopie.

The Lot Valley's spas enjoy renewed popularity today, not just for their curative powers, but for restoring a sense of well-being.

CHÂTEAU

Château de Calmont-d'Olt

Leave Espalion S along D 920 and follow the signs to the car park. *Open Jul-Aug 9am-7pm; May-Jun and Sep 10am-noon, 2-6pm. 5€ (children 5-12 years 3.50€). 05 65 44 15 89. www.chateau calmont.org.*

DRIVING TOURS

LOT VALLEY★★

54km/37mi – allow one day. Start at Espalion.

Espalion★

Population: 4,360.
Michelin Local map 338: I-3 . Office du tourisme d'Espalion, 2 r. St-Antoine. 05 65 44 10 63. www.ot-espalion.fr.

Espalion lies in a pleasant fertile basin crossed by the River Lot. The feudal ruins of Calmont d'Olt are above the town.

Vieux pont (*spanning the Lot*) – The most famous monument in town, the 11C bridge frames a lovely tableau of the old tanneries lining the river banks.

Vieux palais – This 16C palace was the residence of the governors of Espalion.

Église de Perse★ *(1km/0.6mi SE along avenue de la Gare)* – This 11C Romanesque church is dedicated to St Hilarian, Charlemagne's confessor, who legend says retired to Espalion and was beheaded by Moors. A south side

Tanners' houses by the old bridge on the River Lot, Espalion

Estaing by the River Lot

B. Kaufmann/MICHELIN

portal★ includes a tympanum depicting Pentecost.

Musée Joseph-Vaylet et musée du Scaphandre *(38 r Droite; open Jul-Aug Tue, Wed, Fri, Sat 10am-noon, 2-6pm, Mon, Thu 2-6pm, Sun and public holidays 10am-noon; closed rest of year; combined ticket 4€; 05 65 44 09 18)* – The museum displays traditional weaponry, furniture, glassware, religious artefacts and pottery. Adjacent is a diving **museum** honouring the three Espalion men who invented the aqualung and the depressuriser (gas regulator) in 1860.

Musée du Rouergue *(Pl.Frontin; open Jul-Aug daily 10am-noon, 2-7pm (Sat 2-7pm); closed Sep-Jun; 3€; 05 65 73 80 68; www.aveyron-culture.com)* – Former prison cells house exhibits on local life and customs and a costume collection.

Romanesque chapel, St-Pierre-de-Bessuéjouls

A. Thuillier/MICHELIN

Leave Espalion west via D 556 (av. de St-Pierre). At St-Pierre cross the bridge (left) and follow the track on the left.

St-Pierre-de-Bessuéjouls

This modest church in a rustic setting shelters an outstanding **Romanesque chapel★** beneath its bell-tower. The 11C chapel is decorated with knotwork, palmettes, Maltese crosses and historiated capitals.

Estaing★

Population: 612. Michelin Local map 338: I-3. Syndicat d'initiative d'Estaing, 24 r François-d'Estang. 05 65 44 03 22.

Old houses in Estaing huddle around the castle named after the family whose fame and fortune spanned several centuries until the 1789 Revolution. Estaing is a pleasant holiday resort and an ideal base for exploring Entraygues and Espalion.

From the Entraygues road is a picturesque view of the Lot, the old bridge and the castle high above the village. The Laguiole road affords a delightful morning view of the church chevet and the old village houses.

Château *(guided visits 1h30 mid Jun-mid Sep 9.30am-12.30pm, 2.30-7pm; rest of year daily except Sun and Mon 9am-noon, 2pm-6pm. closed 1 May. 5€ (children 3.50€). 05 65 44 72 24)* – Built between 15C-16C with a variety of materials, the castle shows a curious mix of architectural styles. Great view of the old town and River Lot from the west terrace.

Church (*opposite the chateau*) – Fine Gothic crosses enhance the front of this 15C church containing the relics of St Fleuret.

The **Gothic bridge** features a statue of François d'Estaing, Bishop of Rodez, who had the superb bell-tower built on the town's cathedral.

Maison Cayron in the old town retains its Renaissance windows and houses the town hall (*mairie*).

Leaving Estaing, the road offers an attractive view of the Lot, the old bridge and the castle.

Gorges du Lot★★

As the valley narrows into rugged gorges some 300m/1 000ft deep and 1 500m/5 000ft across at the top of the valley walls, jagged rocky silhouettes rise up from the woods covering the sides of the gorges. A few miles from Estaing is the **Golinhac dam** and farther along is the hydroelectric plant.

Entraygues-sur-Truyère★, Gorges de la Truyère★

See ENTRAYGUES-SUR-TRUYÈRE.

Follow D 107 W.

Sweeping views of Entraygues and its castle highlight this road. The widening Lot valley becomes scenic, dotted with farmhouses and terraced vineyards producing wine (VDQS Entraygues-le-Fel).

Vieillevie

Beautiful Renaissance castle, topped with protective defence walling (*visit in summer, please inquire*).

Follow D 42 towards Decazeville. A minor road to the right leads steeply up to La Vinzelle, a tiny village hanging on to the mountain slope with a wide view of the Lot Valley. Turn back to rejoin D 42 and continue towards Decazeville.

St-Parthem

The River Lot flows through the Lozère region for 480km/298mi before reaching the Garonne. Learn about it at the **Maison de la rivière Olt** (*open Jul-Aug daily except Friday 11am-1pm, 2-6pm; May-Jun and Sep daily except Fri and Sat 2-6pm; Oct Wed 2-6pm. 5.50€ (children 7-15 years 3€). 05 65 64 13 22. www.maison-riviere.com*).

Continue along D 42 to Decazeville

The site of this medieval fortress affords a fine **view**★ of the Lot valley, the Aubrac and the Causse du Comtal.

Renaissance castle at Vieillevie

Mur-de-Barrez
and the Carladez Region

This pretty little town occupying a volcanic ridge between the valleys of the Goul and the Bromme, is the ideal starting point for excursions in the surrounding countryside.

- **Population:** 837.
- **Michelin Map:** Michelin Local map 338: H-1.
- **Info:** 12 Grand-Rue, 12600 Mur-de-Barrez, ✆05 65 66 10 16. www.carladez.fr.
- **Location:** A peaceful and isolated region NE of Conque between Aveyron and Cantal.
- **Don't Miss:** The old town, the Sarrans dam and presqu'île de Laussac.
- **Kids:** Les sentiers de l'imaginaire in Carladez.

OLD TOWN

Beyond the Porte de Monaco, visitors discover narrow streets lined with fine Renaissance houses like the Maison consulaire decorated with coats of arms. Note the Porte de l'Horloge, once part of the town's fortified wall.

Château

The site of the castle ruins offers a good view of the Cantal mountains, Bromme Valley, Planèze and the Aubrac mountains. To the east are the convent of Ste-Claire, surrounded by typical houses with steeply pitched four-sided roofs.

Église

The town's Gothic style church was nearly demolished by Calvinists. Inside are some interesting capitals and a 17C altarpiece representing the murder of Thomas Becket in Canterbury Cathedral.

DRIVING TOUR

CARLADEZ REGION

35km/22mi round tour – allow 2hr. Leave Mur-de-Barrez on D 900 SE.

Gorges de la Bromme

The road follows the course of the Bromme along a deep rugged gorge. Farther on, the River Truyère comes into view. Its flow is diverted by the **Barthe dam** and forms part of the Sarrans-Brommat complex.

After negotiating several hairpin bends, turn left onto D 537, then D 98 towards the Sarrans dam; 1.5km/0.9mi before reaching the dam are fine views of the Sarrans installations.

Sarrans dam★

This dam, one of the most important hydroelectric installations in the Massif Central, is 220m/722ft long, 105m/344ft high and 75m/246ft thick at its base.

Having passed the crest of the dam, D 98 runs alongside the reservoir as far as the outskirts of the village of Laussac, which is reached along D 537.

Laussac

The village is built on a promontory which, owing to the flooding of the valley, has become a peninsula.

Rejoin D 98 and turn right.

Continue 1.5km/1mi on from the junction for a fine view of the reservoir.

Carry on along D 98 as far as a crossroads and turn right onto D 139.

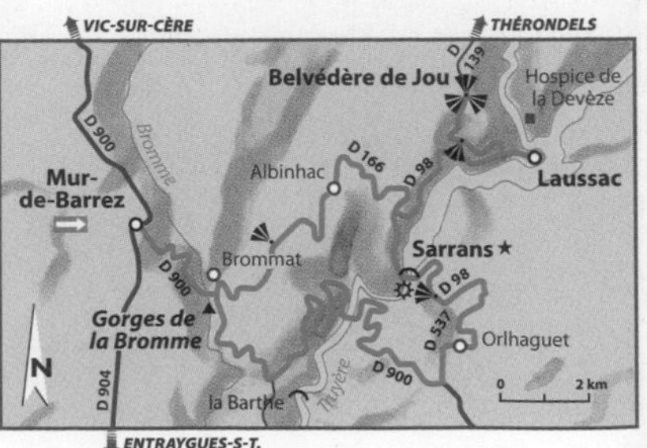

Belvédère de Jou

Beyond the hamlet of Jou, there is a panorama of Laussac peninsula, Devèze hospice and Sarrans reservoir.

Return to Laussac along D 98 to the left, and then take D 166 towards Albinhac and Brommat.

The road offers sweeping views of the Barrez countryside, and the Cantal and Aubrac hills. Note the pretty four-sided roofs, covered with limestone slabs typical of the region.

Beyond Brommat, D 900 leads back to Mur-de-Barrez.

Najac★

Stretching along a promontory enclosed in a meander of the Aveyron, on the boundary of Rouergue and Quercy, the ancient village of Najac occupies a remarkable site★★. The ruins of the fortified castle tower above the slate rooftops of the village. Two large holiday villages *(villages de vacances)* in the vicinity contribute to the lively local atmosphere.

- **Population:** 744.
- **Michelin Map:** Michelin Local map 338: D-5.
- **Info:** Pl. du Faubourg, 12270 Najac, 05 65 29 72 05.
- **Location:** Midway between Rodez and Montauban.
- **Parking:** Traffic is barred from the village in high season. Park at the western entrance to the village.

VISIT

The village

The village extends to the foot of the fortress. Place du Faubourg with its covered arcades was already the hub of activity in the 14C. Near the town hall, a fountain, carved from an enormous monolithic slab of granite dated 1344, bears the arms of Blanche de Castille, King Louis IX's (St Louis) mother.
Beyond the square, the village high street, rue du Bourguet, is lined with a few corbelled houses mainly built between the 13C and the 16C.

Turn right, leaving rue des Comtes-de-Toulouse to your left.

Along rue Médiévale, near a former fortified gate is the **Château des Gouverneurs**, once a noble residence; a little farther up towards the fortress, on the left, note the equally elegant 13C-15C **Maison du Sénéchal**.

Fortress★

Open Jul-Aug 10am-1.30pm, 2.30-7pm; Apr-May and Sep-Oct 10am-12.30pm, 3-5.30pm; Jun 10am-12.30pm, 3-6.30pm. Closed Nov-Mar. 4€. 05 65 29 71 65. www.seigneurs-du-rouergue.com.
This masterpiece of 13C military architecture guarded the Aveyron valley. Of the three original curtain walls there still remain considerable fortifications flanked by large round towers. The castle itself, built partly from pale-coloured sandstone, is protected by thick walls and is shaped like a trapezium. The most impregnable of the towers, on the south-east, was the keep.

Walk down from the castle towards rue de l'Église.

The 13C **Porte de Pique** is the only one left of the 10 original gates.

Church

This interesting Gothic building has a west front adorned with a rose window. Inside, the single nave ends with a flat chevet.

Return via rue des Comtes-de-Toulouse, lined with medieval houses.

Peyrusse-le-Roc★

Situated on the basalt plateaux separating the Aveyron and Lot valleys, Peyrusse-le-Roc offers visitors a journey back in time. The fortress had an eventful past, as can be seen from the remains of its old buildings.

Info: Le Rempart, Place des Treize-Vents , 12220 Peyrusse-le-Roc. 05 65 80 49 33.
Location: 8.5km/5mi W of Montbazens on the D87.
Don't Miss: The view from theRoc del Thaluc.

A BIT OF HISTORY

Handed over to England in 1152 after the divorce of Louis VII and Eleanor of Aquitaine, ancient Petrucia was the capital of the bailiwick until the 18C. During certain periods, it could number more than 3 000 inhabitants, and it prospered, largely due to its silver mines. These ceased to be mined, when silver arrived from America in the 18C. Having lost its raison d'être, the fortified lower town was abandoned and the present village of Peyrusse-le-Roc started to evolve on the plateau.

MEDIEVAL RUINS

1hr 30min Jul-Aug 10am-noon, 3–6pm; rest of year every day except Sun, 10am-noon. guided tours possible Jul-Aug Tue 10am-noon. Closed 1 Jan, 1 May. No charge. 05 65 80 49 33.

Walk across **place St-Georges** and through **Porte du Château**, the castle gate forming part of the medieval curtain wall, to reach **place des Treize-Vents**. In the Middle Ages, this square was the site of the castle of the lords of Peyrusse.

All that is now left of it is a room that was used as a prison, and a tower (the church bell-tower), which houses a small **archaeological museum** (*currently closed; information 05 65 80 49 33*).

Go through the Porte Neuve and the fortifications to the left of the church. The footpath on the left leads to the medieval site; beyond the graveyard, bear right (stairway).

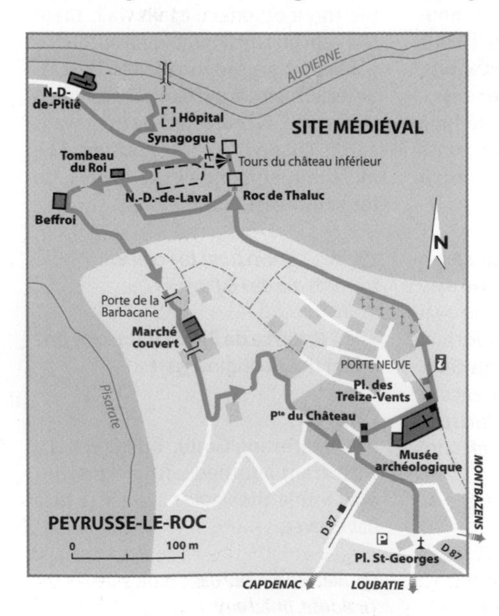

Metal steps (*particular care needed on some sections*) lead to the **Roc del Thaluc**. From this rock it is easy to understand the role played by Peyrusse as an important strategic look-out post during troubled medieval times.

Follow the footpath to the bottom.

A small chapel houses the Tombeau du Roi, a richly sculpted royal mausoleum probably dating from the

Remains of old buildings in Peyrusse-le-Roc

H. Champollion/MICHELIN

14C. Turn back then right to the **Hôpital des Anglais** (13C). This "English Hospital" still features its fine round exterior chimney.
On the way back to the village, stop by the **Beffroi** (belfry), a tall square tower, which, together with the **Porte de la Barbacane**, protected the town to the north-west.

ADDRESSES

EAT

Restaurant Savignac – *Au Bourg.* *05 65 80 43 91.* This village grocer/tobacconist/restaurant has been run by the same family for four generations. The proprietor herself whips up local dishes, including a curious omelette with apples flambéed in plum brandy.

Rodez★

Aveyron

Once the capital of the Rouergue, Rodez is situated on the borders of two very different regions, the dry Causses plateaux and the well-watered Ségala hills.

- **Population:** 23 900.
- **Michelin Map:** 338: H-4.
- **Info:** Pl. Mar. Foch, 12005 Rodez, 05 65 75 76 77. www.ot-rodez.fr.
- **Location:** 66km/41mi NW of Albi on the N88 and 63km/39.5mi SE of Figeac on the D840.
- **Parking:** Boulevard Galy near the Place Foch.
- **Don't Miss:** The Bell Tower of the Cathedral and the Musée Fenaille.
- **Timing:** Allow one full day.

A BIT OF HISTORY

Divided loyalties – In the Middle Ages, the town was shared between two masters. The bishops, who for a long time were the more powerful, occupied the Cité; the counts ruled the Bourg. These two adjacent areas were separated by tall fortifications and for many centuries the rivalry prompted endless fighting between the inhabitants. The two main squares, place de la Cité and place du Bourg, reflect the former duality. When Henri IV became king, the Comté de Rodez joined the French crown and the bishops took contol of the town.

CATHÉDRALE NOTRE-DAME★★

1hr The red-sandstone cathedral was begun in 1277 after the collapse, a year earlier, of the choir and bell-tower of the previous building.

Façade of Cathédral Notre-Dame

©Flö/Fotolia.com

Exterior – The west front overlooking place d'Armes has a forbidding, fortress-like appearance. The lower half of the wall is quite bare, with no porch and only the occasional arrow slit. This austere façade, built outside the city wall, acted as an advance bastion to defend the city. Go round the church to the left. The late-15C north door, known as the Portail de l'Évêché (bishops' doorway), opens beneath three rows of archivolts and a pointed arch. The magnificent **bell-tower★★★**, which interestingly stands apart from the cathedral, comprises six tiers *(by request at the tourist office daily except Sun 3pm (Aug 3pm, 4.45pm). 4.50€. 05 65 75 76 77)*. The third tier, built in the 16C, is decorated with large window openings with distinctive tracery; the fourth, octagonal in shape, has statues of the Apostles adorning the niches in between the window openings; the fifth is elaborately decorated.
Interior – *1hr.* The elegance of the Gothic style is apparent in the soaring elevation of the chancel with its delicate lancet windows and in the height of the great arches surmounted by a triforium which reproduces the same pattern as that of the upper windows.

OLD RODEZ WALK

The old town, which formed part of the bishops' estate, lies around the cathedral. Several interesting houses and mansions still remain. Start from the north side of the cathedral. Cross Rue Frayssinous and enter the courtyard of the bishops' palace.

Palais épiscopal

The courtyard of the bishops' palace offers the best **view** of the bell-tower of Notre-Dame.

Tour Corbières, Tour Raynalde

These two 15C towers are the vestiges of the walls and the 30 towers that once fortified the town.

Opposite the portal of the church of Sacré-Cœur, take the stairway leading to impasse Cambon.

Hôtel Delauro

This 16C and 17C mansion, once a canon's residence, now belongs to an association – the Compagnons du Devoir – who restored it.

Return to Rue Frayssinous and carry on to Place de la Cité.

Place de la Cité

At the east end stands the bronze statue of an illustrious local hero, Monseigneur Affre, Archbishop of Paris, who was killed on the barricades of Faubourg St-Antoine on 25 June 1848 whilst attempting to make peace. Take rue de Bonald then rue de l'Embergue past beautiful old houses, antique shops and craft workshops.

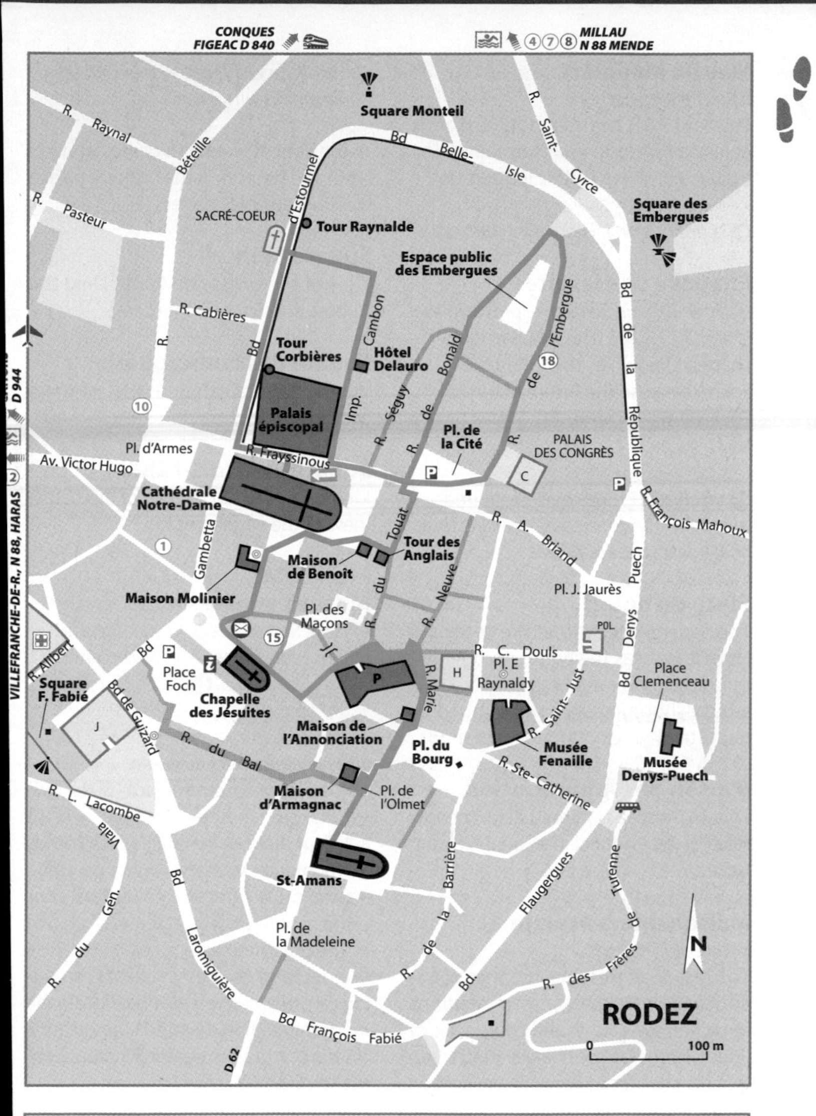

WHERE TO STAY	
Biney (Hôtel)	1
Deltour (Hôtel)	4
Ibis (Hôtel)	7
Midi (Hôtel du)	10

WHERE TO EAT	
Ady (Auberge de l')	8
Jardins d'Acropolis (Les)	12
Petit Moka (Le)	15
Taverne (La)	18

Cross place de la Cité diagonally and follow Rue du Touat, until it intersects with Rue Bosc.

Maison de Guitard dite Tour des Anglais

This 14C house (also known as the Tower of the English) features a massive fortified tower and fine gemel windows. The Guitards were rich bankers in the 14C.

Maison de Benoît

Place d'Estaing. A Gothic gallery runs along two sides of the courtyard *(private)* of this Renaissance house.

Maison Molinier

2 Rue Penavayre.
This old 15C canon's house stands behind an enclosing wall surmounted by a gallery and two Gothic loggias (15C).

Continue on r. Penavayre; turn right.

Chapelle des Jésuites

Open Jul-mid Sep 9am-1pm, 2-7pm. 05 65 73 80 68. This 17C Baroque chapel is known as the "Chapelle Foch," because the future Maréchal Foch went to school at the *lycée* next to it.

Walk along Rue Louis-Blanc and round the handsome 18C mansion that now houses the Préfecture.

Place du Bourg

This square, once the centre of the old town known as the Bourg, frequented by counts and merchants alike, is still a busy shopping area surrounded by pedestrian precincts lined with shops.

Maison de l'Annonciation

This 16C house is named after the low relief of the Annunciation on the corner turret.

Maison dite d'Armagnac

4 Place de l'Olmet.
The façade of this fine 16C mansion is adorned with charming medallions depicting the counts and countesses of Rodez. From place de l'Olmet, a 16C house that now houses a chemist's can be seen in rue d'Armagnac.

Église St-Amans

This church was built in the 12C, but the exterior was completely restored in the 18C. Inside, it has some of the original fine Romanesque capitals.

NEW TOWN WALK

From its site on a hill, Rodez offers numerous points of view of the surrounding countryside. The boulevards built on the line of the old ramparts render it possible to make a round tour of the town by car (*outside peak times*).

Leave from Place d'Armes and take Boulevard Estourmel.

To the right, the remains of the ramparts (16C) and terraces of the bishops' palace lead to Corbières tower (14C).

Square Monteil

View of the Causse de Comtal and the Aubrac and Cantal mountains.

Square des Embergues

Views to the north and west of town (*viewing table).*

Square François-Fabié

Memorial to the local poet of this name. View of the Ségala region.

MUSEUMS

Musée Fenaille★★

14 place Raynaldy. Open Tue, Thu and Fri 10am-noon, 2-6pm; Wed and Sat 1-7pm, Sun 2-6pm. Closed Mon, and 1 Jan, 1 May, 1 Nov, 25 Dec. 3€, no charge 1st Sun in month. 05 65 73 84 30. www.musee-fenaille.com.
The museum is housed partly in the oldest mansion in Rodez and partly in an adjacent modern building which blends harmoniously with its neighbour. Inside are the most extensive collections concerning the Rouergue region, each section displaying a time scale for easy reference. In order to follow the exhibition's chronological order, start on the third floor in the modern building devoted to prehistory. Note in particular the menhir-statues from the south of Aveyron.

Musée Denys-Puech

Boulevard Denys-Puech. Tue-Fri 10am-noon, 2-6pm, weekends and public holidays 2-6pm. guided visits possible. Closed 1 Jan, 1 May, 1 Nov and 25 Dec. 2.50€ (4€ combined ticket with Musée Fenaille) No charge Fri and 1st Sunday in the month. 05 65 77 89 60.www.mairie-rodez.fr.
Founded in 1910 by the sculptor **Denys Puech** (1854-1942), born in the Aveyron, this museum contains both permanent collections of 19C and 20C art and temporary exhibitions on contemporary art.

EXCURSIONS

Bozouls★

20km/12mi NE of Rodez. Population 2723. Michelin Local map 338: I-4.
Pl. de l'Hôtel-de-Ville, 12340 Bozouls. 05 65 48 50 52. www.bozouls.com.
Bozouls is distinguished from afar by its modern church (1964), south of D 20. Its sanctuary in the shape of a ship's prow houses a statue of the Virgin Mary by local sculptor Denys Puech.
Trou de Bozouls★ – The terrace next to the war memorial affords the best view of this 800m/2 600ft canyon, hollowed out of the Causse de Comtal by the River Dourdou.
From the town hall, walk round the south side of the "Trou" for the **Ancienne Église Ste-Fauste**. The church's 12C nave, with its raised, semicircular barrel vaulting, was originally roofed with heavy limestone slabs (lauzes). Under this enormous weight, the pillars sagged and the old roof was replaced by a timber-frame one in the 17C. View the Dourdou gorge from the shady terrace to the left of the church.

Montrozier

10km/6mi south of Bozouls.
Drive 3.5km/2.2mi along D 988 then turn left onto D 126.
On the banks of the Aveyron is the picturesque village of Montrozier, with an old Gothic bridge spanning the river. The 15C-16C castle *(closed to the public)* has a five-storey round keep.
The **Musée archéologique de Rouergue** *(open Jul-Aug 10am-12.30pm, 2-7pm; Jun and Sep: 2-6pm; Jan-May daily except Mon and weekends 2-6pm. Closed Oct-Apr. 3€. 05 65 70 71 45. www.aspaa.fr)* offers thematic temporary exhibitions and audio-visual presentations on the region's archaeological heritage.

ADDRESSES

STAY

Hôtel du Midi – *1 R. Béteille. 05 65 68 02 07. www.hotelmidi. com. Closed 20 Dec–6 Jan – P – 34rms. 7.50€ Restaurant.* Facing the cathedral, this hotel has simple, well-kept and well-lit rooms. Two dining rooms. Classic regional cuisine.

Biney – *R. Victoire-Massol. 05 65 68 01 24 . www.hotel-biney.com. 26rms. 15€.* This modern hotel near the centre of town is part of a building complex surrounding a quiet green park. The salon is cute and the rooms are furnished simply.

Deltour Hôtel – *Av. de la Gineste. 05 65 71 22 11. www.deltourhotel.com – P – 26rms – 7€.* A little way out of town by easily accessible. All rooms equipped with WiFi; reduced prices at weekends.

Hotel Ibis – *46 r. St-Cyrice. 05 65 76 10 30. www.ibis.com – 45rms – 7.50€.* Familiar hotel chain offering small and simple rooms at reasonable prices; some rooms have balconies. Meeting room and bar.

EAT

La Taverne – *23 R. de l'Embergue. 05 65 42 14 51. www.tavernerodez. com. Closed 1 week in May, 2 weeks in Sep, Sun and holidays.* The owner calls his restaurant "a country inn in town." The cuisine is distinctly regional, including such specialities as picaùcel, and of course l'aligot.

Le Petit Moka – *Pl. des Maçons. 05 65 75 63 34. Closed Sun and Mon.* Enjoys a lovely location in old Rodez, and offers simple cuisine – salads, croques, tarts, crepes and pancakes. Great choice of teas and coffees to enjoy on the terrace.

Auberge de l'Ady – *1 av. du Pont-de-Malakoff (near the church) in Valady (20 km/12mi N of Rodez). 05 65 72 70 24. Closed Sun evening, Tue evening and Mon; Jan.* Agreeable auberge at the heart of a pretty village, serving local and regional cuisine.

Les Jardins de l'Acropolis – *R. Athènes, in Bourran. 05 65 68 40 07. Closed 2–16 Aug, Sun eve. and Mon.* This restaurant offers two contemporary dining rooms with rosewood accoutrements. Sophisticated modern cuisine.

Villefranche-de-Rouergue★

On the border of the Rouergue and Quercy regions, the ancient bastide of Villefranche-de-Rouergue, with its rooftops clustered round the foot of the massive tower of the church of Notre-Dame, lies in the bottom of a valley surrounded by green hills, at the confluence of the Aveyron and the Alzou.

- **Info:** Prom. du Guiraudet, 12200 Villefranche-De-Rouergue, ℘05 65 45 13 18. www.villefranche.com.
- **Location:** Villefranche is on the right bank of the Aveyron at the entrance to the Gorges, 40km/25mi W of Rodez.
- **Parking:** Arriving by the D922, there is parking on the Promenade St-Jean on the riverbank. Also the Place de la Liberté and the Prom. de Languedoc.
- **Don't Miss:** Guided tour of the town – The tourist office organises a commented tour of the town (1hr) in Jul-Aug, Mon-Fri at 3pm. 4€.

A BIT OF HISTORY

Trade and prosperity – Villefranche was founded in 1099 by Raymond IV de Saint-Gilles, Count of Toulouse, on the south bank of the Aveyron.

The town enjoyed a new phase of expansion when, in 1252, Alphonse de Poitiers, brother of St Louis, decided to build a new town on the north bank of the river. This was built with the geometric layout typical of a bastide and completed in 1256. Despite the disagreement between the founder and the bishop of Rodez, who went so far as to excommunicate any newcomers, the town's population soon grew. Its situation near the Causses and the Ségala region, at the crossroads of major routes used since the days of Antiquity, made Villefranche an important trade centre during the Middle Ages. It was also a stopping place for pilgrims on their way to Santiago de Compostela. In the 15C, Charles V granted the town the right to mint money, and silver and copper mines added to the town's wealth, as it prospered in its function as seat of the Rouergue seneschalsy and capital of Haute Guyenne. The Wars of Religion halted the town's expansion.

Villefranche is now a centre of the farm-produce and metallurgy (bolts) industries.

Croisters, Ancienne Chartreuse St-Sauveur

THE BASTIDE★

With the destruction of its moats, its ramparts and its fortified gates, Villefranche has lost some of its medieval appearance, although it has kept many of the features of a bastide with its main square and its grid street plan.

Guided tours of the town are organised by the tourist office, Jul-Aug daily except Sat-Sun 3pm. 4€.

Place Notre-Dame★

This fine square, in the heart of the town and always buzzing with life on market days (*Thursdays*), is framed by houses with covered arcades, some of which have retained their mullioned windows and stone turrets. On one side of the square the tall, solid shape of the old collegiate church can be seen.

Go round the arcades (*avoiding the cars*) to take a closer look at the arches and old sculpted doorways. In front of the terrace overlooking the square to the north stands a large ironwork figure of Christ. The whole scene is reminiscent of Spain, which inspired André Malraux to shoot some scenes from his film L'Espoir (*Hope*) here.

At the corner of rue Marcellin-Fabre and the square, there is a lovely 15C half-timbered house facing the street; the central section, which is seven storeys high, houses a staircase lit through mullioned windows. This staircase can be entered through a fine **stone door** on which the lower part of the canopy is adorned with sculpted scrolls and foliage.

On rue du Sergent-Boriès, south of the square, the first **house** on the right features another fine staircase tower (late 15C), with pilasters and a carved tympanum.

Maison du Président Raynal

This has a fine 15C façade with adjoining windows, on three storeys, in the Romanesque tradition.

Maison Dardennes

Next to the Maison du Président Raynal.

At the far end of the courtyard, a Renaissance staircase tower features two galleries adorned with sculpted portraits.

Église Notre-Dame★

The construction of this church, which began with the apse in 1260, lasted for over 300 years. The belfry-porch bears witness to the rivalry between Villefranche-de-Rouergue and Rodez, with each town intending their cathedral spire to be the highest.

Chapelle des Pénitents Noirs

Bd de Haute-Guyenne. Open Jul-mid Sep 10am-noon, 2-6pm; mid Sep-end Sep and Apr-Jun Tue-Sat 2-6pm. 05 65 45 13 18. 4€.

This chapel, surmounted by a curious double turret, was built in the 17C.

Musée Urbain-Cabrol

Rue du Sénéchal. Open Jul-Aug Tue–Sat 10am-noon, 2-6pm; May-Jun and Sep Tue -Sat 2-6pm; Closed Oct-Apr, Sun, Mon and public holidays. No charge. 05 65 45 44 37.

The collections of Urbain Cabrol on archaeology, history, and the popular traditions of Villefranche and the region are on display in a Louis XV mansion.

Ancienne Chartreuse St-Sauveur★

Take D 922 towards Najac and Laguépie. Jul-mid Sep 10am-noon, 2-6pm; mid-end Sep and Apr-Jun Tue-Sat 2-6pm. Closed Oct-Easter. 4€. 05 65 45 13 18.

This charter house, founded in 1451 by Vézian-Valette, a wealthy local merchant, was built in eight years of continuous effort, which resulted in an almost perfectly consistent Gothic style. The **Chapelle des Étrangers** used to stand outside the charter house wall, and It housed pilgrims on their way to Santiago de Compostela. The **great cloisters** are some of the largest in France (66x44m/216x144ft) while the **small cloisters** are the only authentic "cloisters," in the strictly monastic sense (gallery with communal buildings opening onto it). Don't miss the 16C stained-glass windows in the **Chapter house** which depict, in the centre, the Shepherds being told of the Birth of Christ, and the founders on either side.

This small independent state has a total area of 468sqkm/180sq mi (about one and a third times the area of the Isle of Wight). Andorra lies at the heart of the Pyrenees and has remained curiously apart from its neighbours, France and Spain. Visitors are attracted by its rugged scenery and picturesque villages.

Highlights

1. Visit **Caldea** and enjoy the water sports (p451)
2. Take a stroll around **Andorra la Vella** (p452)
3. Visit the **Valira d'Orient** for relaxed walking (p453)
4. Come in winter, and try **skiing**, it's a whole new world (p451)

A Bit of History

"Charlemagne the great, my father, delivered me from the Arabs" begins the Andorran national anthem, which then continues, "I alone remain the only daughter of Charlemagne. Christian and free for 11 centuries, Christian and free I shall carry on between my two valiant guardians, my two protecting princes."

From co-principality to independent sovereignty

Until 1993, Andorra was a co-principality under a regime of dual allegiance, a legacy from the medieval feudal system. Under such a contract, two neighbouring lords would define the limits of their respective rights and authority over a territory that they held in common fief. Andorra was unusual, however, in that its two lords came to be of different nationality, but left the status of the territory as it was under feudal law, with the result that neither of them could claim possession of the land. This dual allegiance to two co-princes was established in 1278 by the Bishop of Urgell and Roger Bernard III, Count of Foix. However, while the bishops of Urgell remained co-princes, the counts of Foix passed their lordship on to France (when Henri IV, Count of Foix and Béarn, became king in 1589) and thus eventually to the President of the French Republic. On 14 March 1993 the Andorrans voted in a referendum to adopt a new democratic constitution making the principality a fully independent state. The official language of the country is Catalan. The principality has signed a treaty of cooperation with France and Spain, the first countries to officially recognise its independence. It has also become a member of the United Nations.

A taste for liberty

Andorrans pride themselves above all on seeking and fiercely defending their liberty and independence. A long-standing system of representative government and 11 centuries of peace have given them little incentive to alter the country's administration. The country is governed by a General Council, which holds its sessions at the "Casa de la Vall" and ensures the proportional representation of the various elements of the Andorran population and the seven parishes. Andorrans do not pay any direct taxes, nor do they have to do military service. They also have free postal services within their country. Most of the land is communally owned, so there are very few private landowners.

Work and play

Until recently this essentially patriarchal society traditionally made a living from stock rearing and crop cultivation. In between the high summer pastures and the hamlets you can still see the old cortals, groups of barns or farmhouses, which are gradually becoming more accessible as the tracks leading up to them are made suitable for vehicles. The mountain slopes exposed to the sun are cultivated in terraces. Tobacco, the main crop in the Sant Juliá de Lòria Valley, is grown up to an altitude of 1 600m/5 200ft. The first roads suitable for vehicles linking it with the outside world were not opened until 1913, on the Spanish side, and 1931, on the French. The population of Andorra numbered 76 900 in 2004, most of whom speak Catalan.

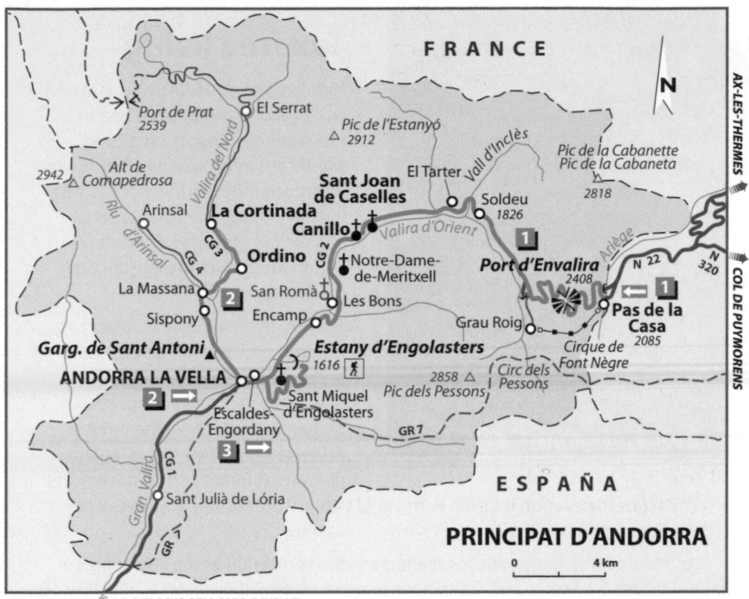

RECREATION

Soldeu El Tarter Ski Area

Alt 1 710-2 560m/5 610-8 398ft.

52 trails over 1150 hectares for skiers of all levels – 241 snow-making machines ensure permanent coverage of 14km/9mi of trails.

Pas de la Casa-Grau Roig Ski Area

Linked together, Pas de la Casa and Grau Roig accommodate over half of all skiers in Andorra, with 100km/60mi of slopes over 626 hectares for skiers and snowboarders.

Caldea

1 000m/3 250ft above sea level.

Open Aug and Easter school holidays 9am-midnight; rest of the year 9.30am-11pm. Closed 1 Jan (morning), from mid to end May, 13-17 Nov, 25 Dec. 29.50€ (3hr), 78€ (3 days), 118€ (5 days). 00 376 80 09 99.

Pas de la Casa

Tobacco plantation in Canillo
©Joris Van Ostaeyen/Bigstockphoto.com

Tax free living

High among encircling hills, isolated and in economically poor health, mountainous Andorra achieved significant affluence since World War II almost entirely through its tourist industry. Many immigrants (legal and illegal) are today drawn to the region attracted by its absence of income taxes.

Tourism, the mainstay of Andorra's tiny, but now well-to-do economy, accounts for more than 80% of GDP. Almost 12 million tourists visit annually to make the most of Andorra's duty-free status, and to enjoy its summer and winter resorts. The highest elevation is Coma Pedrosa (2 946m/9 665ft), and the lowest, the Riu Runer (840m/2 756ft).

Andorra's comparative advantage has eroded somewhat as the economies of neighbouring France and Spain have expanded, providing wider availability of goods and lower tariffs. The banking sector, with its partial "tax haven" status, also contributes substantially to the economy.

Agricultural production is limited – only 2.2% of the land is arable – and most food is imported. The principal livestock activity is sheep raising. Manufacturing output consists principally of cigarettes, cigars, and furniture. Andorra is a member of the EU Customs Union and is treated as an EU member for trade in manufactured goods (no tariffs) and as a non-EU member for agricultural products.

Nor is it just the scenery that makes you feel better. Andorra is second only to Macau in the world for life expectancy at birth: the average is 82.51 years, with males expected to live for 80.33 years, and women for 84.84. The UK by comparison ranks 36th, France 9th, Spain 23rd, and the USA 50th! The total population of Andorra (2009) is 83 888.

This gigantic futuristic water sports complex fed by the 68°C/155°F spa waters of Escaldes-Engordany was designed by French architect Jean-Michel Ruols.

ANDORRA LA VELLA

Andorra's capital 1 409m/4 620ft above the Gran Valira valley, is a bustling commercial town, but hidden away from the busy main axis you'll find traditional quiet old streets. This is the highest capital city in Europe, and also, at 3hrs driving time, the furthest from the nearest airports at Toulouse, Girona, Perpignan and Barcelona.

Casa de la Vall

Guided tours daily (30min) May-Oct 9.30am-1.30pm, 3-7pm (Sun and public holidays 10am-2pm; rest of year daily except Sun and public holidays 9.30am-1.30pm, 3-7pm. Book in advance on 00 376 82 91 29. Closed when parliament is in session. No charge.

The Casa houses Andorra's Parliament building and its Law Courts in a massive 16C stone building. Its main doorway is framed by characteristic Aragon long heavy archstones and 16C murals decorate its first floor. The council chamber guarding the national archives contains the famous "cupboard with the seven keys," each held by the seven parishes.

Port d'Envalira

DRIVING TOURS

1 VALIRA D'ORIENT VALLEY★

From Andorra la Vella towards the Puymorens Pass – 36km/22.5mi – allow 1hr 30min. The Envalira Pass can be blocked by snow, but is always reopened within 24hr. In bad weather, the Puymorens Pass road may be open only in the direction of Porté and the Cerdagne.

The road leaves the outskirts of Escaldes and climbs the steep and rugged valley, leaving behind the startling neo-Romanesque bell-tower of the Andorra radio station. After Encamp, the road veers sharply before reaching the hamlet of **Les Bons**, on a rocky spur beneath the ruins of its castle.

Canillo

This village church has the tallest bell-tower in Andorra (27m/88ft). Nearby is Andorra's national shrine, the **chapel of Our Lady of Meritxell** (*open daily except Tue 9.15am-1pm, 3-6pm; Jul-Aug possibility of guided tours. No charge. 00 376 85 12 53*).

Saint Joan de Caselles

Open Jul-Aug 9am-1pm, 3-6pm; rest of the year by request. 03 376 85 11 15 or 00 376 85 14 34.

This lone church with three-storeyed bell-tower is a fine example of Romanesque Andorran architecture. The last restoration in 1963 uncovered a Romanesque **Crucifixion**★ and a Calvary scene fresco.

Port d'Envalira★★

Alt 2 407m/7 823ft.

The highest pass in the Pyrenees, marking the watershed between the Mediterranean (Valira) and the Atlantic (Ariège) has a good road. Its **panorama** includes the Andorra mountains(2 942m/9 653ft) stretching away to Coma Pedrosa. The road descends to Pas de la Casa, offering spectacular views of the **Font-Nègre** cirque and lake.

Saint Joan de Caselles

A culture shock

Until the 1950s, Andorra's population, almost entirely Andorran-born, barely exceeded 6 000. These days only about 25% of the population - almost two-thirds of whom live in Andorra la Vella and around - are Andorran nationals. The remainder are largely Spanish, French and Portuguese.

The official language is Catalan (Català), a Romance language closely related to Provençal, but with roots in Castilian and French. Local spin has it that everyone in Andorra speaks Catalan, Spanish and French, but there are plenty of people who can't understand more than a few words of French; hardly anyone speaks English.

Andorran cuisine is mainly Catalan, with significant French and, perhaps surprisingly, Italian influences. Sauces are typically served with meat and fish. Pasta is also common. Local dishes include *cunillo* (rabbit cooked in tomato sauce), *xai* (roast lamb), *trinxat* (bacon, potatoes and cabbage) and *escudella* (a stew of chicken, sausage and meatballs).

Given the fondness of the Catalans for music, it is no surprise that Andorra has a Chamber Orchestra, and that it also stages a famous international singing contest. In 2004, Andorra participated in the Eurovision Song Contest for the first time. This attracted media attention from Catalonia, since it was the first song to be sung in Catalan.

But the single most important event in Andorran cultural life is the Escaldes-Engordany international jazz festival, which has features such international stars such as Miles Davis, Fats Domino and B.B. King.

Typical dances, such as the marratxa and the contrapàs, are especially popular at feasts, at which exuberant Andorran people tend to celebrate enthusiastically and loudly.

Church of Sant Miguel, Engolasters

A. Thuillier/MICHELIN

Pas de la Casa✻

Alt 2 091m/6 861ft. Andorra highest frontier village is a major ski resort.

Road N 22 traverses a desolate landscape as far as N 20, leading to the Puymorens Pass.

2 VALIRA DEL NORD VALLEY★

From Andorra La Vella to La Cortinada – 9km/5.5mi.

This isolated upper valley has kept the old Andorran way of life and traditions. The road climbs quickly up out of Andorra-Escaldes.

Gargantas de Sant Antoni

From a bridge across the Valira del Nord you can see the old humpback bridge used by muleteers. The Coma Pedrosa peaks loom in the distance beyond the Arinsal valley.

Go through the pleasant holiday village of La Massana to Ordino.

Ordino

Park the car in the upper village, in the square near the church.

This village's picturesque streets are worth exploring. Old Catalan forges produced attractive wrought-iron works like the the balcony of "Don Guillem's" house, the gates of the church and (1676) **Casa museu Areny-Plandolit** (*Open daily except Mon 9.30am-1.30pm, 3-6.30pm (Sun 10am-1.30pm); 6€; Closed 14 Mar, 1 May, 8 Sep, 25-26 Dec. 00 376 83 69 08).*

La Cortinada

Village highlights are its pleasant setting, a splendid house with galleries and dovecot, and the Romanesque frescoes and Baroque altarpieces in the **church of Sant Marti** (*open Jul-Aug guided tours 10am-1pm, 3-7pm; rest of the year by request. 00 376 84 41 41).*

The road continues northwards, with plans to link it with Vicdessos, via the Port de Rat (alt 2 539m/8 330ft).

3 ESTANY D'ENGOLASTERS

9km/5.5mi, then 30min round-trip on foot. Leave Escaldes E of Andorra, on the road to France, and at the outskirts of the village turn right, doubling back slightly, to follow the Engolasters mountain road.

The outstanding landmark on the Engolasters plateau is the lovely Romanesque bell-tower of **Sant Miguel**. Enjoy a walk to the dam, and lake reflections of the dark forest lining its shores.

ADDRESSES

STAY

Hôtel Cerqueda – *R. Mossen-Lluis-Pujol, Santa Coloma – 3km/2mi SW of Andorre-la-Vieille. (00-376) 82 02 35. Closed 7 Jan to 6 Feb – P – 65rms.* This friendly, peaceful family-run hotel has recently decorated bathrooms, and a swimming pool.

Hôtel Coma Bella – *Sant Julià de Lòria – 7km/4mi au SW of Andorre-la-Vieille. (00-376) 84 12 20. Closed 5-23 Nov - P – 30rms.* This hotel in the peaceful La Rabassa forest features rooms decorated with contemporary Andorran furnishings.

Font del Marge – *Baixada del Moli 49, Andorre-la-Vieille (00-376) 84 14 43 – margeandorra.ad. Closed Nov – 42 rms.* This quiet hotel with a family ambience has a restaurant featuring seafood and a rotisserie.

EAT

Don Pernil – *Av. d'Enclar 94, Santa Coloma – 3km/2mi SW of Andorre-la-Vieille – (00-376) 86 52 55. Closed Jan.* Wood-fired barbecues and regional dishes prepared by the owners attract an appreciative flow of diners.

Can Manel – *R. Mestre-Xavier-Plana 6 – Andorre-la-Vieille. (00-376) 82 23 97. Closed 1-15 Jul and Wed.* This small family-run restaurant offers regional dishes based on locally grown fare.

Borda Estevet – *Rte de La Comella 2 – Andorre-la-Vieille. (00-376) 86 40 26 – bordaestevet andorra.com.* This old stone-walled house welcomes its clients with rustic decor, local Pyrenean cooking and a wow of a dessert trolley.

ON THE TOWN

Topic – *Carretera Général, Ordino. (00-376) 73 61 02 – 8-2am.* The Hotel Coma's bar-restaurant serves drinks, tapas, salads, sandwiches, pizzas, and grilled meat and fish dishes in a futurist interior and a on the terrace.

SHOPPING

Shoppers love Andorra for its many luxury products at duty-free prices. Usual store hours are 9am-1pm and 4-8pm (9pm during holiday periods).

INDEX

D

E

F

G

H

I

J

K

L

MAPS AND PLANS

THEMATIC MAPS

TOWN PLANS

LOCATOR MAPS

MONUMENTS AND SITES

REGIONAL TOURING MAPS

MAP LEGEND

	Sight	Seaside resort	Winter sports resort	Spa
Highly recommended	★★★			
Recommended	★★			
Interesting	★			

Additional symbols

- Tourist information
- Motorway or other primary route
- Junction: complete, limited
- Pedestrian street
- Unsuitable for traffic, street subject to restrictions
- Steps – Footpath
- Train station – Auto-train station
- S.N.C.F. Coach (bus) station
- Tram
- Metro, underground
- Park-and-Ride
- Access for the disabled
- Post office
- Telephone
- Covered market
- Barracks
- Drawbridge
- Quarry
- Mine
- B F Car ferry (river or lake)
- Ferry service: cars and passengers
- Foot passengers only
- ③ Access route number common to Michelin maps and town plans
- Bert (R.)... Main shopping street
- AZ B Map co-ordinates

Selected monuments and sights

- Tour - Departure point
- Catholic church
- Protestant church, other temple
- Synagogue - Mosque
- Building
- Statue, small building
- Calvary, wayside cross
- Fountain
- Rampart - Tower - Gate
- Château, castle, historic house
- Ruins
- Dam
- Factory, power plant
- Fort
- Cave
- Troglodyte dwelling
- Prehistoric site
- Viewing table
- Viewpoint
- Other place of interest

Special symbol

Fortified town (bastide): in southwest France, a new town built in the 13-14C and typified by a geometrical layout.

Map Legend continued overleaf

Abbreviations

A	Agricultural office (Chambre d'agriculture)
C	Chamber of Commerce (Chambre de commerce)
H	Town hall (Hôtel de ville)
J	Law courts (Palais de justice)
M	Museum (Musée)
P	Local authority offices (Préfecture, sous-préfecture)
POL.	Police station (Police)
	Police station (Gendarmerie)
T	Theatre (Théâtre)
U	University (Université)

Sports and recreation

Racecourse

Skating rink

Outdoor, indoor swimming pool

Multiplex Cinema

Marina, sailing centre

Trail refuge hut

Cable cars, gondolas

Funicular, rack railway

Tourist train

Recreation area, park

Theme, amusement park

Wildlife park, zoo

Gardens, park, arboretum

Bird sanctuary, aviary

Walking tour, footpath

Of special interest to children

COMPANION PUBLICATIONS

Motorists who plan ahead will always have the appropriate maps at hand. Michelin products are complementary: for each of the sights listed in *The Green Guide*, map references are indicated which help you find your location on our maps.

To travel the roads in this region, you may use any of the following:

- the series of Local maps at a scale of 1:150 000 include useful symbols for identifying tourist attractions, town plans and an index. The diagram opposite indicates which maps you need to travel in Languedoc-Roussillon-Tarn Gorges.
- the Regional maps at a scale of 1:200 000 **nos 526, and 527** cover the main roads and secondary roads and show castles, churches and other religious edifices, scenic view points, megalithic monuments, swimming beaches on lakes and rivers, swimming pools, golf courses, race tracks, air fields, and more. And remember to travel with the latest edition of the **map of France 721**, which gives an overall view of the region, and the main access roads that connect it to the rest of France. Also available in atlas and mini-atlas formats.

Michelin is pleased to offer a route-planning service on the Internet: **www.ViaMichelin.com**. Choose the shortest route, a route without tolls, or the Michelin recommended route to your destination; you can also access information about hotels and restaurants from *The Michelin Guide*, and tourist sites from *The Green Guide*.

Bon voyage!

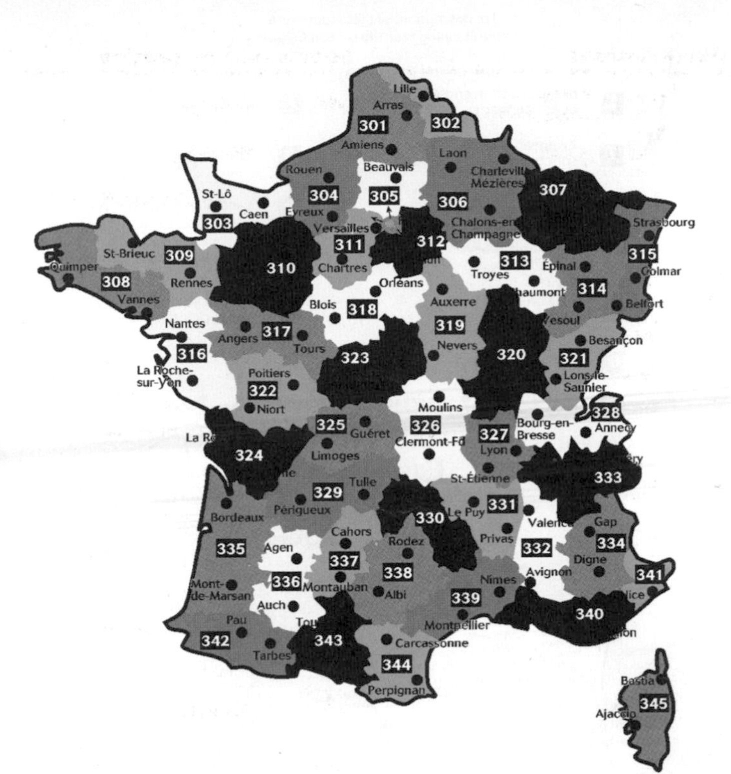

Michelin Apa Publications Ltd

A joint venture between Michelin and Langenscheidt

58 Borough High Street, London SE1 1XF, United Kingdom

ISBN 978-1-906261-84-9
Printed: November 2009
Printed and bound in Germany

REGIONAL DRIVING TOURS

For descriptions of these tours, turn to the Planning Your Trip section following

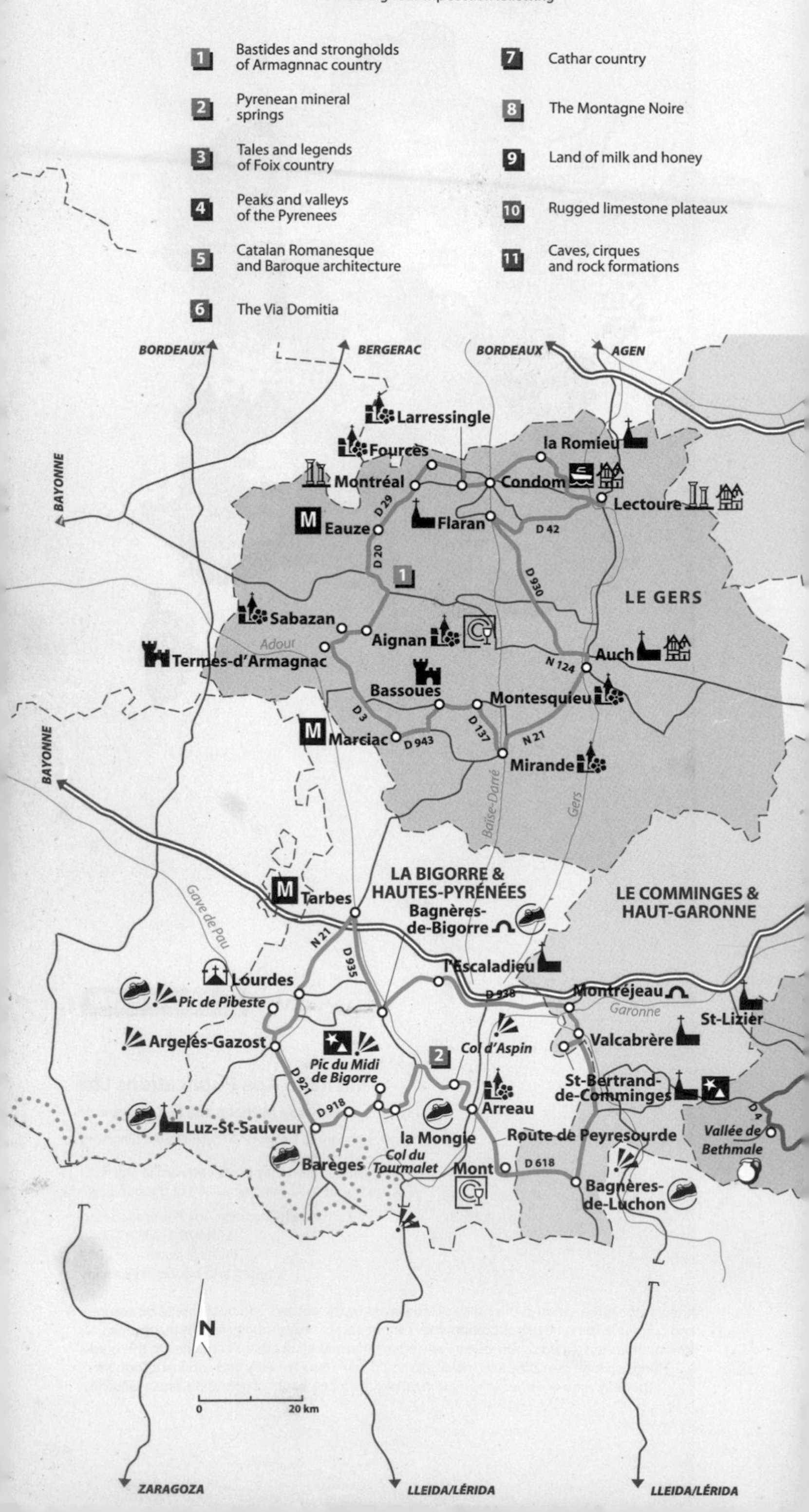